Seeing Ourselves

Classic, Contemporary, and Cross-Cultural Readings in Sociology

Canadian Edition

Edited by

John J. Macionis
Kenyon College

Nijole V. Benokraitis
University of Baltimore

Bruce Ravelli
Mount Royal College

PEARSON
Prentice
Hall

Toronto

National Library of Canada Cataloguing in Publication

Seeing ourselves: classic, contemporary, and cross-cultural readings in sociology/ edited by John J. Macionis, Nijole V. Benokraitis, Bruce Ravelli.—Canadian ed.

ISBN 0-13-039121-2

1. Sociology. I. Benokraitis, Nijole V. (Nijole Vaicaitis) II. Macionis, John J. III. Ravelli, Bruce Douglas, 1963–

HM586.S37 2004301   C2003-901700-1

ISBN 0-13-039121-2

Vice President, Editorial Director: Michael J. Young
Executive Acquisitions Editor: Jessica Mosher
Signing Representative: Gillian Swann
Senior Developmental Editor: Martina van de Velde
Marketing Manager: Judith Allen
Production Editor: Cheryl Jackson
Copy Editor: Dawn Hunter
Proofreader: Tara Tovell
Production Coordinator: Heather Bean
Page Layout: Anne MacInnis
Art Director: Julia Hall
Interior Design: Dave Mckay
Cover Design: Gillian Tsintziras
Cover Image: Tsilli Pines/Veer Inc.

3 4 5 08 07 06 05 04

Printed and bound in Canada.

To C.W. Mills, although we never met, you changed my life. And to my parents, Nello and Shirley Ravelli, who taught me more about the world from the kitchen table than I ever learned in school.

Contents

Preface

I remember reading C.W. Mills' article, "The Promise of Sociology" for the first time while teaching anthropology at a small college in British Columbia. I was surprised by the impact the article had on me and how Mills' perspective on society changed the way I viewed the social world. In fact, I was so inspired by this new perspective that the following year I left a tenured teaching position (in anthropology) and returned to school to complete my Ph.D. in sociology. For me, Mills' approach defines the very best of sociology and what it can offer those who study it—learning the ability to systematically reflect on the dynamic relationship between the individual and the social. For Mills, people exposed to what he termed the *sociological imagination* would be able to see more clearly the social landscape in which we all travel. *Seeing Ourselves,* Canadian Edition, offers students a unique opportunity to discover their sociological imagination through the exploration of sociology from personal, national, and global perspectives.

Seeing Ourselves, Canadian Edition, presents the very best of sociological thought, from the work of the discipline's pioneers to the men and women who are doing today's leading-edge research. The articles in this anthology explore Canadian and American social issues as well as the global trends influencing us all. This reader provides excellent material for a wide range of courses, including introductory sociology, social problems, cultural anthropology, social theory, social stratification, Canadian and American studies, women's studies, and marriage and the family.

THE THREE Cs: CLASSIC, CONTEMPORARY, AND CROSS-CULTURAL

Since its introduction a decade ago, the American edition of *Seeing Ourselves* has been a popular reader in the discipline. This Canadian edition offers seventy-two selections that represent a diverse cross-section of the discipline and those areas of interest to sociologists. The Canadian edition is not only the most extensive anthology currently available, it is the only one that systematically weaves together three themes into its selections. For each topic typically covered in a sociology course, three types of articles are offered: *classic, contemporary*, and *cross-cultural.*

Classic articles, 25 in all, are sociological statements of recognized importance and lasting significance. Included here are the ideas of sociology's founders and supporters—including Émile Durkheim, Karl Marx, Max Weber, Georg Simmel, as well as Margaret Mead, George Herbert Mead, and Thomas Robert Malthus. Also found in the classic sections are more recent contributions by Alfred Kinsey, Jessie Bernard, John Porter, Erving Goffman, Peter Berger, C. Wright Mills, Talcott Parsons, and Jo Freeman.

Twenty-four *contemporary* selections (16 of which are Canadian) focus on current sociological issues, controversies, and applications. These articles show sociologists at work and demonstrate the importance of investigating our social environment and the forces influencing it. Each article makes for stimulating reading and offers thought-provoking insights about ourselves and the world around us. Among the contemporary selections some of the topics covered include: the importance of social research, the defining features of Canadian sociology, the differences between Canadian and American values, adolescent girls' impressions of their bodies, Canadian children's socialization, life inside a Canadian biker gang, how advertising influences society, lesbians' use of "gaydar," female athletes' experiences with sexual harassment, the role ethnicity plays in Canadian society, how Native Canadians' identity has been defined by historical factors as well as the residential school system and treaty processes, the training of medical doctors in Canada, and how environmentalism and globalization influence our collective futures. All these articles demonstrate how the sociological imagination can be used to achieve a deeper understanding of contemporary society.

The 23 *cross-cultural* selections offer sociological insights about cultural diversity around the world. Included are well-known works such as "Body Ritual among the Nacirema" by Horace Miner, "India's Sacred Cow" by Marvin Harris, "The Amish: A Small Society" by John Hostetler, J.M. Carrier's "Homosexual Behavior in Cross-Cultural Perspective," and Elijah Anderson's "The Code of the Streets." Other articles explore issues and problems including how familiar gestures can offend people in other societies, how Japanese and U.S. business people behave according to different sets of rules, the staggering burden of African poverty, women's social standing around the world, cross-cultural patterns of mate selection, Islam's view of women, academic achievement among Southeast Asian immigrants, and the rising global population. Cross-cultural selections stimulate critical thinking about social diversity across North America as well as broaden students' understanding of, and appreciation for, other cultures.

ORGANIZATION OF THE READER

This reader parallels the chapter sequence common to many textbooks used in introductory sociology.

Instructors can easily and effectively use these articles in a host of other courses, just as teachers can assign articles in any order they wish. For each of the twenty-three general topics, a cluster of three or four articles is presented, each cluster including at least one classic, one contemporary, and one cross-cultural selection. The expansive coverage of these 72 articles ensures that instructors can choose readings well suited to their own classes, preferences and course outcomes.

The first grouping of articles describes the distinctive sociological perspective, brings to life the promise and pitfalls of sociological research, and demonstrates the discipline's application to a variety of issues. The selections that follow focus on key concepts: culture, society, socialization, social interaction, groups and organizations, deviance, and human sexuality. The focus then turns to various dimensions of social inequality, with attention to class, gender, race and ethnicity, and aging. The major social institutions are covered next, including the economy and work; politics, government, and the military; family; religion; education; and health and medicine. The final sets of articles explore dimensions of global transformation—including population growth, urbanization, the natural environment, social movements, and social change.

A NOTE ON LANGUAGE

All readings are presented in their original form but some may have been edited for length. Readers should be aware that some of the older selections—especially the *classic* selections— use male pronouns rather than more contemporary gender-neutral terminology.

TEACHING FEATURES

This reader has two features that enhance the learning of students. First, a brief introduction that precedes each selection presents the essential argument, and highlights important issues to keep in mind while completing the reading. Second, each article is followed by three or four "Critical-Thinking Questions" that develop the significance of the reading, help students evaluate their own learning, and stimulate class discussion.

INTERNET SITES

Readers are also invited to visit our sociology Web sites. At **www.pearsoned.ca/macionis/sociology.html** students will find online study material for Macionis/Gerber, Sociology, Fourth Canadian Edition.
At **www.pearsoned.ca/macionis/basics.html** students will find online study material from Macionis/Jansson/Benoit, Society: The Basics, Second Canadian Edition.

Both sites feature chapter overviews, test questions, Web destinations, and much more. Readers are also invited to provide us with feedback on the text. Please visit us at **www.seeingourselves.ca** and let us know what you think.

INSTRUCTOR'S TEST ITEM FILE

Pearson Education Canada also supports *Seeing Ourselves*, Canadian Edition, with a printed Test Item File that provides instructors with six multiple choice questions (with answers) and several essay questions for easy test creation for each of the 72 selections.

ACKNOWLEDGMENTS

I am grateful to many people for their help in preparing this reader. First, I would like to recognize the administration and faculty of Mount Royal College, who supported this endeavour through a leave granted for the 2002/2003 academic year. Without their financial and intellectual support this reader would not have been possible. Second, the efforts of the acquisition and editorial staff at Pearson Education Canada have been invaluable. In particular, Jessica Mosher, Executive Acquisitions Editor, was instrumental for supporting my belief in the need for a Canadian introductory cross-cultural reader. As well, Martina van de Velde, Senior Developmental Editor, was always quick to offer advice and thoughtful reflection at every step of the writing process. Third, I would like to thank all of my students (past, present, and future) for their enthusiasm and their desire to learn more about the world—all of you inspire me to become a better teacher and sociologist. Fourth, I would like to thank the reviewers: Gerald Booth, University of Windsor; Lesley Hulcoop, Trent University; Shelly Ungar, University of Toronto; Erica van Roosmalen, Dalhousie University; Donald Clairmont, Dalhousie University; Lorne Tepperman, University of Toronto; Nan McBlane, University College of the Cariboo; Harry Rosenbaum, University of Winnipeg; and Barry Green, University of Toronto. And last, I would like to thank my family for their confidence in me and their love, and in particular, my wife Sacha who makes each day better than the last.

I welcome all faculty and students to share their thoughts and reactions to this reader with me in whatever form they find most convenient. You can write to me at: Bruce Ravelli, Department of Behavioural Sciences, Mount Royal College, 4825 Richard Road, S.W. Calgary, Alberta T3E 6K6. You can send me an email at: **bravelli@mtroyal.ab.ca**. Also, please visit us at **www.seeingourselves.ca** and let us know what you think of the text and how we can make it better.

1

The Promise of Sociology

C. Wright Mills

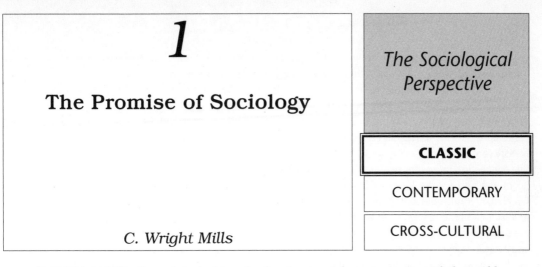

The Sociological Perspective

CLASSIC

CONTEMPORARY

CROSS-CULTURAL

To C. Wright Mills, the sociological imagination *is a special way to engage with the world. To think sociologically is to realize that what we experience as personal problems are often widely shared by others similar to ourselves. Thus, many personal problems are actually social issues. For Mills, as one of sociology's most outspoken activists, the sociological imagination encouraged collective action that would change the world.*

Nowadays men often feel that their private lives are a series of traps. They sense that within their everyday worlds, they cannot overcome their troubles, and in this feeling, they are often quite correct: What ordinary men are directly aware of and what they try to do are bounded by the private orbits in which they live; their visions and their powers are limited to the close-up scenes of job, family, neighborhood; in other milieux, they move vicariously and remain spectators. And the more aware they become, however vaguely, of ambitions and of threats which transcend their immediate locales, the more trapped they seem to feel.

Alex Colville (1920–), *To Prince Edward Island*, 1965, acrylic emulsion on masonite, 61.9 x 92.5 cm. National Gallery of Canada, Ottawa. © NGC/MBAC.

Source: From *The Sociological Imagination* by C. Wright Mills. Copyright © 1959 by Oxford University Press, Inc. Renewed 1987 by Yaraslava Mills. Used by permission of Oxford University Press, Inc.

Underlying this sense of being trapped are seemingly impersonal changes in the very structure of continent-wide societies. The facts of contemporary history are also facts about the success and the failure of individual men and women. When a society is industrialized, a peasant becomes a worker; a feudal lord is liquidated or becomes a businessman. When classes rise or fall, a man is employed or unemployed; when the rate of investment goes up or down, a man takes new heart or goes broke. When wars happen, an insurance salesman becomes a rocket launcher; a store clerk, a radar man; a wife lives alone; a child grows up without a father. Neither the life of an individual nor the history of a society can be understood without understanding both.

Yet men do not usually define the troubles they

endure in terms of historical change and institutional contradiction. The well-being they enjoy, they do not usually impute to the big ups and downs of the societies in which they live. Seldom aware of the intricate connection between the patterns of their own lives and the course of world history, ordinary men do not usually know what this connection means for the kinds of men they are becoming and for the kinds of history-making in which they might take part. They do not possess the quality of mind essential to grasp the interplay of man and society, of biography and history, of self and world. They cannot cope with their personal troubles in such ways as to control the structural transformations that usually lie behind them.

Surely it is no wonder. In what period have so many men been so totally exposed at so fast a pace to such earthquakes of change? That Americans have not known such catastrophic changes as have the men and women of other societies is due to historical facts that are now quickly becoming "merely history." The history that now affects every man is world history. Within this scene and this period, in the course of a single generation, one-sixth of mankind is transformed from all that is feudal and backward into all that is modern, advanced, and fearful. Political colonies are freed; new and less visible forms of imperialism installed. Revolutions occur; men feel the intimate grip of new kinds of authority. Totalitarian societies rise, and are smashed to bits—or succeed fabulously. After two centuries of ascendancy, capitalism is shown up as only one way to make society into an industrial apparatus. After two centuries of hope, even formal democracy is restricted to a quite small portion of mankind. Everywhere in the underdeveloped world, ancient ways of life are broken up and vague expectations become urgent demands. Everywhere in the overdeveloped world, the means of authority and of violence become total in scope and bureaucratic in form. Humanity itself now lies before us, the super-nation at either pole concentrating its most coordinated and massive efforts upon the preparation of World War III.

The very shaping of history now outpaces the ability of men to orient themselves in accordance with cherished values. And which values? Even when they do not panic, men often sense that older ways of feeling and thinking have collapsed and that newer beginnings are ambiguous to the point of moral stasis. Is it any wonder that ordinary men feel they cannot cope with the larger worlds with which they are so suddenly confronted? That they cannot understand the meaning of their epoch for their own lives? That—in defense of selfhood—they become morally insensible, trying to remain altogether private men? Is it any wonder that they come to be possessed by a sense of the trap?

It is not only information that they need—in this Age of Fact, information often dominates their attention and overwhelms their capacities to assimilate it. It is not only the skills of reason that they need—although their struggles to acquire these often exhaust their limited moral energy.

What they need, and what they feel they need, is a quality of mind that will help them to use information and to develop reason in order to achieve lucid summations of what is going on in the world and of what may be happening within themselves. It is this quality, I am going to contend, that journalists and scholars, artists and publics, scientists and editors are coming to expect of what may be called the sociological imagination.

The sociological imagination enables its possessor to understand the larger historical scene in terms of its meaning for the inner life and the external career of a variety of individuals. It enables him to take into account how individuals, in the welter of their daily experience, often become falsely conscious of their social positions. Within that welter, the framework of modern society is sought, and within that framework the psychologies of a variety of men and women are formulated. By such means the personal uneasiness of individuals is focused upon explicit troubles and the indifference of publics is transformed into involvement with public issues.

The first fruit of this imagination—and the first lesson of the social science that embodies it—is the idea that the individual can understand his own experience and gauge his own fate only by locating himself within his period, that he can know his own chances in life by becoming aware of those of all individuals in his circumstances. In many ways it is a terrible lesson; in many ways [it is] a magnificent one. We do not know the limits of man's capacities for supreme effort or willing degradation, for agony or glee, for pleasurable brutality or the sweetness of reason. But in our time we have come to know that the limits of "human nature" are frighteningly broad. We have come to know that every individual lives, from one generation to the next, in some society, that he lives out a biography, and that he lives it out within some historical sequence. By the fact of his living he contributes, however minutely, to the shaping of this society and to the course of its history, even as he is made by society and by its historical push and shove.

The sociological imagination enables us to grasp history and biography and the relations between the two within society. That is its task and its promise. To recognize this task and this promise is the mark of the classic social analyst. It is characteristic of Herbert Spencer—turgid, polysyllabic, comprehensive; of E. A. Ross—graceful, muckraking, upright; of Auguste Comte and Emile Durkheim; of the intricate and subtle Karl Mannheim. It is the quality of all that is intellectually excellent in Karl Marx; it is the clue to Thorstein Veblen's brilliant and ironic insight, to Joseph Schumpeter's many-sided constructions of reality; it is the basis of the psychological sweep of W. E. H. Lecky no less than of the profundity and clarity of Max Weber. And it is the signal of what is best in contemporary studies of man and society.

No social study that does not come back to the problems of biography, of history, and of their intersections within a society has completed its intellectual journey. Whatever the specific problems of the classic social analysts, however limited or however broad the features of social reality they have examined, those who have been imaginatively aware of the promise of their work have consistently asked three sorts of questions:

1. What is the structure of this particular society as a whole? What are its essential components, and how are they related to one another? How does it differ from other varieties of social order? Within it, what is the meaning of any particular feature for its continuance and for its change?

2. Where does this society stand in human history? What are the mechanics by which it is changing? What is its place within and its meaning for the development of humanity as a whole? How does any particular feature we are examining affect, and how is it affected by, the historical period in which it moves? And this period—what are its essential features? How does it differ from other periods? What are its characteristic ways of history-making?

3. What varieties of men and women now prevail in this society and in this period? And what varieties are coming to prevail? In what ways are they selected and formed, liberated and repressed, made sensitive and blunted? What kinds of "human nature" are revealed in the conduct and character we observe in this society in this period? And what is the meaning for "human nature" of each and every feature of the society we are examining?

Whether the point of interest is a great power state or a minor literary mood, a family, a prison, a creed—these are the kinds of questions the best social analysts have asked. They are the intellectual pivots of classic studies of man in society—and they are the questions inevitably raised by any mind possessing the sociological imagination. For that imagination is the capacity to shift from one perspective to another—from the political to the psychological; from examination of a single family to comparative assessment of the national budgets of the world; from the theological school to the military establishment; from considerations of an oil industry to studies of contemporary poetry. It is the capacity to range from the most impersonal and remote transform-ations to the most intimate features of the human self—and to see the relations between the two. [At the b]ack of its use there is always the urge to know the social and historical meaning of the individual in the society and in the period in which he has his quality and his being.

That, in brief, is why it is by means of the soci-ological imagination that men now hope to grasp what is going on in the world, and to understand what is happening in themselves as minute points of the intersections of biography and history within society. In large part, contemporary man's self-conscious view of himself as at least an outsider, if not a permanent stranger, rests upon an absorbed realization of social relativity and of the transformative power of history. The socio-logical imagination is the most fruitful form of this self-consciousness. By its use men whose mentalities have swept only a series of limited orbits often come to feel as if [they have] suddenly awakened in a house with which they had only supposed themselves to be familiar. Correctly or incorrectly, they often come to feel that they can now provide themselves with adequate summations, cohesive assessments, comprehensive orientations. Older decisions that once appeared sound now seem to them products of a mind unaccountably dense. Their capacity for astonishment is made lively again. They acquire a new way of thinking, they experience a transvaluation of values: In a word, by their reflection and by their sensibility, they realize the cultural meaning of the social sciences.

Perhaps the most fruitful distinction with which the sociological imagination works is between "the personal troubles of milieu" and "the public issues of social structure." This distinction is an essential tool of the sociological imagination and a feature of all classic work in social science.

Troubles occur within the character of the individual and within the range of his immediate relations with others; they have to do with his self and with those limited areas of social life of which he is directly and personally aware. Accordingly, the statement and the resolution of troubles properly lie within the individual as a biographical entity and within the scope of his immediate milieu—the social setting that is directly open to his personal experience and to some extent his willful activity. A trouble is a private matter: Values cherished by an individual are felt by him to be threatened.

Issues have to do with matters that transcend these local environments of the individual and the range of his inner life. They have to do with the organization of many such milieux into the institu-tions of an historical society as a whole, with the ways in which various milieux overlap and inter-penetrate to form the larger structure of social and historical life. An issue is a public matter: Some value cherished by publics is felt to be threatened. Often there is a debate about what that value really is and about what it is that really threatens it. This debate is often without focus if only because it is the very nature of an issue, unlike even widespread trouble, that it cannot very well be defined in terms of the immediate and everyday environ-ments of ordinary men. An issue, in fact, often involves a crisis in institutional arrangements, and often too it involves what Marxists call "contra-dictions" or "antagonisms."

In these terms, consider unemployment. When, in a city of 100,000, only one man is unemployed, that is his personal trouble, and for its relief we properly look to the character of the man, his skills, and his immediate opportunities. But when in a nation of 50 million employees, 15 million men are unemployed, that is an issue, and we may not hope to find its solution within the range of opportunities open to any one indi-vidual. The very structure of opportunities has collapsed. Both the correct statement of the prob-lem and the range of possible solutions require us to consider the economic and political institu-tions of the society and not merely the personal situation and character of a scatter of individuals.

Consider war. The personal problem of war, when it occurs, may be how to survive it or how to die in it with honor; how to make money out of it; how to climb into the higher safety of the military apparatus; or how to contribute to the war's termination. In short, according to one's values, to find a set of milieux and within it to survive the war or make one's death in it meaningful. But the structural issues of war have to do with its causes; with what types of men it throws up into command; with its effects upon economic and political, family and religious institutions, with the unorganized irresponsibility of a world of nation-states.

Consider marriage. Inside a marriage a man and a woman may experience personal troubles, but when the divorce rate during the first four years of marriage is 250 out of every 1,000 attempts, this is an indication of a structural issue having to do with the institutions of marriage and the family and other institutions that bear upon them.

Or consider the metropolis—the horrible, beautiful, ugly, magnificent sprawl of the great city. For many upper-class people, the personal solution to "the problem of the city" is to have an apartment with private garage under it in the heart of the city and, forty miles out, a house by Henry Hill, garden by Garrett Eckbo, on a hundred acres of private land. In these two controlled environments—with a small staff at each end and a private helicopter connection—most people could solve many of the problems of personal milieux caused by the facts of the city. But all this, however splendid, does not solve the public issues that the structural fact of the city poses. What should be done with this wonderful monstrosity? Break it up into scattered units, combining residence and work? Refurbish it as it stands? Or, after evacuation, dynamite it and build new cities according to new plans in new places? What should those plans be? And who is to decide and to accomplish whatever choice is made? These are structural issues; to confront them and to solve them requires us to consider political and economic issues that affect innumerable milieux.

Insofar as an economy is so arranged that slumps occur, the problem of unemployment becomes incapable of personal solution. Insofar as war is inherent in the nation-state system and in the uneven industrialization of the world, the ordinary individual in his restricted milieu will be powerless—with or without psychiatric aid—to solve the troubles this system or lack of system imposes upon him. Insofar as the family as an institution turns women into darling little slaves and men into their chief providers and unweaned dependents, the problem of a satisfactory marriage remains incapable of purely private solution. Insofar as the overdeveloped megalopolis and the overdeveloped automobile are built-in features of the overdeveloped society, the issues of urban living will not be solved by personal ingenuity and private wealth.

What we experience in various and specific milieux, I have noted, is often caused by structural changes. Accordingly, to understand the changes of many personal milieux, we are required to look beyond them. And the number and variety of such structural changes increase as the institutions within which we live become more embracing and more intricately connected with one another. To be aware of the idea of social structure and to use it with sensibility is to be capable of tracing such linkages among a great variety of milieux. To be able to do that is to possess the sociological imagination....

CRITICAL THINKING QUESTIONS

1. Why do people tend to think of the operation of society in personal terms?
2. What are the practical benefits of the sociological perspective? Are there liabilities?
3. What does Mills have in mind when he suggests that by developing the sociological imagination, we learn to assemble facts into social analysis?

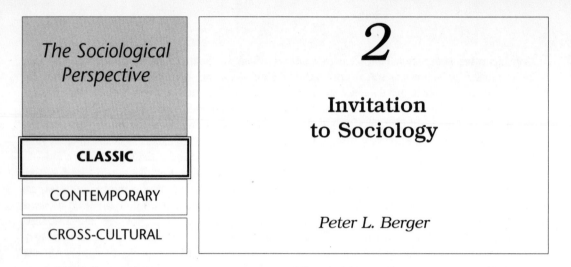

The Sociological Perspective

CLASSIC

CONTEMPORARY

CROSS-CULTURAL

2

Invitation to Sociology

Peter L. Berger

Using the sociological perspective changes how we perceive the surrounding world and ourselves. Peter Berger compares thinking sociologically with entering a new and unfamiliar society—one in which "things are no longer what they seem." This article should cause you to rethink your social world and become aware of issues you may have never before considered.

...It can be said that the first wisdom of sociology is this—things are not what they seem. This too is a deceptively simple statement. It ceases to be simple after a while. Social reality turns out to have many layers of meaning. The discovery of each new layer changes the perception of the whole.

Anthropologists use the term "culture shock" to describe the impact of a totally new culture upon a newcomer. In an extreme instance such shock will be experienced by the Western explorer who is told, halfway through dinner, that he is eating the nice old lady he had been chatting with the previous day—a shock with predictable physiological if not moral consequences. Most explorers no longer encounter cannibalism in their travels today. However, the first encounters

Source: From *Invitation to Sociology* by Peter L. Berger. Copyright © 1963 by Peter L. Berger, Bantam, Doubleday Dell Publishing Group, Inc. Reprinted with permission of Bantam, Doubleday Dell Publishing Group, Inc.

with polygamy or with puberty rites or even with the way some nations drive their automobiles can be quite a shock to an American visitor. With the shock may go not only disapproval or disgust but a sense of excitement that things can *really* be that different from what they are at home. To some extent, at least, this is the excitement of any first travel abroad. The experience of sociological discovery could be described as "culture shock" minus geographical displacement. In other words, the sociologist travels at home—with shocking results. He is unlikely to find that he is eating a nice old lady for dinner. But the discovery, for instance, that his own church has considerable money invested in the missile industry or that a few blocks from his home there are people who engage in cultic orgies may not be drastically different in emotional impact. Yet we would not want to imply that sociological discoveries are always or even usually outrageous to moral sentiment. Not at all. What they have in common with exploration in distant lands, however, is the sudden illumination of new and unsuspected facets of human existence in society. This is the excitement and, as we shall try to show later, the humanistic justification of sociology.

People who like to avoid shocking discoveries, who prefer to believe that society is just what they were taught in Sunday school, who like the safety of the rules and the maxims of what Alfred Schuetz has called the "world-taken-for-granted," should stay away from sociology. People who feel no temptation before closed doors, who have no curiosity about human beings, who are content to admire scenery without wondering about the people who live in those houses on the other side of that river, should probably also stay away from sociology. They will find it unpleasant or, at any rate, unrewarding. People who are interested in human beings only if they can change, convert, or reform them should also be warned, for they will find sociology much less useful than they hoped. And people whose interest is mainly in their own conceptual constructions will do just as well to turn to the study of little white mice. Sociology will be satisfying, in the long run, only to those who can think of nothing more entrancing than to watch men and to understand things human....

To ask sociological questions, then, presupposes that one is interested in looking some distance beyond the commonly accepted or officially defined goals of human actions. It presupposes a certain awareness that human events have different levels of meaning, some of which are hidden from the consciousness of everyday life. It may even presuppose a measure of suspicion about the way in which human events are officially interpreted by the authorities, be they political, juridical, or religious in character. If one is willing to go as far as that, it would seem evident that not all historical circumstances are equally favorable for the development of sociological perspective.

It would appear plausible, in consequence, that sociological thought would have the best chance to develop in historical circumstances marked by severe jolts to the self-conception, especially the official and authoritative and generally accepted self-conception, of a culture. It is only in such circumstances that perceptive men are likely to be motivated to think beyond the assertions of this self-conception and, as a result, question the authorities....

Sociological perspective can then be understood in terms of such phrases as "seeing through," "looking behind," very much as such phrases would be employed in common speech—"seeing through his game," "looking behind the scenes"—in other words, "being up on all the tricks."

...We could think of this in terms of a common experience of people living in large cities. One of the fascinations of a large city is the immense variety of human activities taking place behind the seemingly anonymous and endlessly undifferentiated rows of houses. A person who lives in such a city will time and again experience surprise or even shock as he discovers the strange pursuits that some men engage in quite unobtrusively in houses that, from the outside, look like all the others on a certain street. Having had this experience once or twice, one will repeatedly find oneself walking down a street, perhaps late in the evening, and wondering what may be going on under the bright lights showing through a line of drawn curtains. An ordinary family engaged in pleasant talk with guests? A scene of desperation amid illness or death? Or a scene of debauched pleasures? Perhaps a strange cult or a dangerous conspiracy? The facades of the houses cannot tell us, proclaiming nothing but an architectural conformity to the tastes of some group or class that may not even inhabit the street any longer. The social mysteries lie behind the facades. The wish to penetrate these mysteries is an analogon to sociological curiosity. In some cities that are suddenly struck by calamity this wish may be abruptly realized. Those who have experienced wartime bombings know of the sudden encounters with unsuspected (and sometimes unimaginable) fellow tenants in the air-raid shelter of one's apartment building. Or they can recollect the startling morning sight of a house hit by a bomb during the night, neatly sliced in half, the facade torn away and the previously hidden interior mercilessly revealed in the daylight. But in most cities that one may normally live in, the facades must be penetrated by one's own inquisitive intrusions. Similarly, there are historical situations in which the facades of society are violently torn apart and all but the most incurious are forced to see that there was a reality behind the facades all along. Usually this does not happen, and the facades continue to confront us with seemingly rocklike permanence. The perception of the reality behind the facades then demands a considerable intellectual effort.

A few examples of the way in which sociology "looks behind" the facades of social structures might serve to make our argument clearer. Take, for instance, the political organization of a community. If one wants to find out how a modern American city is governed, it is very easy to get the official information about this subject. The city will have a charter, operating under the laws of the state. With some advice from informed individuals, one may look up various statutes that define the constitution of the city. Thus one may find out that this particular community has a city-manager form of administration, or that party affiliations do not appear on the ballot in municipal elections, or that the city government participates in a regional water district. In similar fashion, with the help of some newspaper reading, one may find out the officially recognized political problems of the community. One may read that the city plans to annex a certain suburban area, or that there has been a change in the zoning ordinances to facilitate industrial development in another area, or even that one of the members of the city council has been accused of using his office for personal gain. All such matters still occur on the, as it were, visible, official, or public level of political life. However, it would be an exceedingly naive

person who would believe that this kind of information gives him a rounded picture of the political reality of that community. The sociologist will want to know above all the constituency of the "informal power structure" (as it has been called by Floyd Hunter, an American sociologist interested in such studies), which is a configuration of men and their power that cannot be found in any statutes, and probably cannot be read about in the newspapers. The political scientist or the legal expert might find it very interesting to compare the city charter with the constitutions of other similar communities. The sociologist will be far more concerned with discovering the way in which powerful vested interests influence or even control the actions of officials elected under the charter. These vested interests will not be found in city hall, but rather in the executive suites of corporations that may not even be located in that community, in the private mansions of a handful of powerful men, perhaps in the offices of certain labor unions, or even, in some instances, in the headquarters of criminal organizations. When the sociologist concerns himself with power, he will "look behind" the official mechanisms that are supposed to regulate power in the community. This does not necessarily mean that he will regard the official mechanisms as totally ineffective or their legal definition as totally illusionary. But at the very least he will insist that there is another level of reality to be investigated in the particular system of power. In some cases he might conclude that to look for real power in the publicly recognized places is quite delusional....

Let us take one further example. In Western countries, and especially in America, it is assumed that men and women marry because they are in love. There is a broadly based popular mythology about the character of love as a violent, irresistible emotion that strikes where it will, a mystery that is the goal of most young people and often of the not-so-young as well. As soon as one investigates, however, which people actually marry each other, one finds that the lightning-shaft of Cupid seems to be guided rather strongly within very definite channels of class, income, education, [and] racial and religious background. If one then investigates a little further into the behavior that is engaged in prior to marriage under the rather misleading euphemism of "courtship," one finds channels of interaction that are often rigid to the point of ritual. The suspicion begins to dawn on one that, most of the time, it is not so much the emotion of love that creates a certain kind of relationship, but that carefully predefined and often planned relationships eventually generate the desired emotion. In other words, when certain conditions are met or have been constructed, one allows oneself "to fall in love." The sociologist investigating our patterns of "courtship" and marriage soon discovers a complex web of motives related in many ways to the entire institutional structure within which an individual lives his life—class, career, economic ambition, aspirations of power and prestige. The miracle of love now begins to look somewhat synthetic. Again, this need not mean in any given instance that the sociologist will declare the romantic interpretation to be an illusion. But, once more, he will look beyond the immediately given and publicly approved interpretations....

We would contend, then, that there is a debunking motif inherent in sociological consciousness. The sociologist will be driven time and again, by the very logic of his discipline, to debunk the social systems he is studying. This unmasking tendency need not necessarily be due to the sociologist's temperament or inclinations. Indeed, it may happen that the sociologist, who as an individual may be of a conciliatory disposition and quite disinclined to disturb the comfortable assumptions on which he rests his own social existence, is nevertheless compelled by what he is doing to fly in the face of what those around him take for granted. In other words, we would contend that the roots of the debunking motif in sociology are not psychological but methodological. The sociological frame of reference, with its built-in procedure of looking for levels of reality other than those given in the official interpretations of society, carries with it a logical imperative to unmask the pretensions and the propaganda by which men cloak their actions with each other. This unmasking imperative is one of the characteristics of sociology particularly at home in the temper of the modern era....

CRITICAL THINKING QUESTIONS

1. How can we explain the fact that people within any society tend to take their own way of life for granted?
2. What does Berger think is the justification for studying sociology?
3. What is involved in sociological "debunking"? How are others likely to respond to sociological insights?

The Sociological Perspective

CLASSIC

CONTEMPORARY

CROSS-CULTURAL

3

Defining Features
of Canadian Sociology

Bruce Ravelli

In this brief review, Bruce Ravelli looks at some of the defining features of Canadian sociology. This article should inspire you to think about Canadian society and whether you believe it is reflected in Canadian sociology.

Canadian sociology often mirrors the nature of Canada itself: a diverse landscape where Canadians struggle to find their unique voice within a chorus dominated by Americans. In fact, some analysts suggest that Canadian sociology is a product of its experiences with, and at times its resistance to, the larger and more dominant American sociological tradition (see Brym & Saint-Pierre, 1997; Hiller, 2001; Hiller & Di Luzio, 2001). The dominance of the American sociological tradition in Canada is largely due to its longer history[1] and its sheer size.[2] However, at least four elements influence the presence of a distinctly Canadian sociology:

1. Canada's physical geography, defined by its vast and often challenging physical environment, and its regionalism, evidenced in the important role Quebec plays in Canadian sociology's intellectual development
2. Canadian sociology's focus on the political economy
3. The Canadianization movement of the 1960s and 1970s in response to the number of American faculty in our postsecondary institutions
4. The radical nature of Canadian sociology

CANADA'S GEOGRAPHY AND REGIONALISM

Canada, the world's second-largest country—in terms of total area, not population—(Countries of the World, 2002), is blessed with rich natural resources and a beautiful and diverse landscape. As we will see, these environmental factors have influenced Canadian sociology. According to Hiller (2001), Canadian sociology is not simply a culmination of the varieties of sociology practised in Canada; it is instead the product of Canadian sociologists' efforts to understand the Canadian experience. For Hiller (2001), one of Canadian sociology's defining pursuits has been the attempt to understand a changing national society. Everett Hughes asserted in 1959 that Canadian sociology should be grounded in its own societal context: as society changes, so too should its sociology (cited in Hiller, 2001). Sociology "should reflect both the unique aspects of the society's character as well as the evolution of that society" (Hiller, 2001: 262).

External and internal forces help to shape and define a Canadian sociology. The particular nature of the relationship between Canada's physical landscape and Canadian sociology is seen clearly in Brym and Saint Pierre (1997). They suggest that one defining characteristic of Canadian sociology is its survivalism (1997: 543) and propose that a core theme of Canadian sociology is the development and maintenance of a community in the face of hostile elements (e.g., geographically, socially) and outside forces (i.e., political and intellectual pressures from the United States and American sociologists). One inside force defining Canadian sociology is the role that regionalism plays in our country's development (e.g., west versus east) and, in particular, Quebec's influence. Quebec has a unique linguistic and cultural influence on Canadian society generally and on Canadian sociology specifically.

The teaching of Canadian francophone sociology began in 1943, when the Faculty of Social Sciences was established at Laval University in Quebec City. Although francophone sociology is comparatively young, it experienced explosive growth from the 1960s to the 1980s, as demonstrated by rising student enrolment and the wealth of research produced by francophone sociologists (Brym & Saint-Pierre, 1997: 544). During the 1960s, a social movement in Quebec called the Quiet Revolution saw the influence of the Catholic Church diminish, replaced by an expanded provincial bureaucracy and, ultimately, a resurgence in nationalistic sentiments (seen in the rising popularity of the separatist movement and the growing influence of the Parti Québécois and its then-leader, René Lévesque).

The Quiet Revolution not only inspired changes in Quebec society and politics, but it also influenced sociologists to focus on issues of social class and social policy (see Brym & Saint-Pierre, 1997; Hiller, 2001). In fact, some Quebec sociologists have played leadership roles in the transformation of francophone society as senior advisors and civil servants for the provincial government (Brym & Saint-Pierre, 1997: 544). This is consistent with Southcott's (1999: 459) position that francophone sociologists are more likely to see themselves as "agents of change" than are their anglophone colleagues. Again, we see that the society in which sociologists work affects their approach to the discipline. One of those approaches involves an interest in the political economy.

CANADIAN FOCUS ON THE POLITICAL ECONOMY

Wallace Clement (2001), a leading figure in Canadian sociology, believes that one of the defining elements of Canadian sociology is its interest in the political economy. The political economy encompasses politics, government, and governing, as well as the social and cultural constitution of markets, institutions, and actors (Clement, 2001: 406). For Clement, this intellectual pursuit is characterized by the attempt to uncover tensions and contradictions within society and use them as the bases for social change.

Arguably, the first Canadian sociologist to investigate Canada's political economy was Harold A. Innis in *The Fur Trade in Canada* (1970/1930) and *The Cod Fisheries* (1954/1940). In these works, Innis develops what has been termed the *staples thesis*, which contends that Canada's development was based on the exploitation of raw materials sent back to European countries to satisfy their industrial thirsts. Innis suggests that each staple (e.g., commercial: cod, fur, timber; industrial: pulp and paper, minerals) had its own characteristics that imposed a particular logic on its individual development (Clement, 2001: 407). As Canada grew and these economic developments continued, these raw materials were sent abroad, refined into more valuable commodities (e.g., furniture, automobiles), and returned to Canada at vastly inflated prices. Innis suggests that since Canada's economic position was subordinate to Britain and to the United States, Canadians were seen as "hewers of wood, drawers of water"—people who performed menial tasks. Certainly, the historical development of Canada's natural resources suggests that Canadian society has been, at least in part, defined by the realization that Canada is not one of the world's major economic or social forces. This underdog mentality was evident in the attempt by Canadian universities in the 1960s and 1970s to Canadianize our postsecondary education system.

THE CANADIANIZATION MOVEMENT

The development of Canadian anglophone sociology was influenced by American sociology as practised at the University of Chicago (see Brym & Saint-Pierre, 1997; Eichler, 2001; Hiller, 2001; Hiller & Di Luzio, 2001; Langlois, 2000; McKay, 1998).

Founded in 1892 by Albion Small, the department of sociology at the University of Chicago defined the American sociological tradition for much of the early twentieth century. The Chicago School of sociology was dominated by the symbolic-interactionist approach, focusing on social reform and collective social responsibility. The Chicago School's influence was most profound on early francophone sociology in Quebec, particularly at Canada's founding department of sociology, McGill. In fact, many influential sociologists in Canada trained at the University of Chicago (such as C. A. Dawson, Everett Hughes, Harold Innis, A. C. McCrimmon, and Roderick D. McKenzie). The Chicago School was instrumental in defining Canadian sociology, but in the 1950s and 1960s, a movement to increase the number of Canadian faculty teaching at Canadian universities began.

During the late 1960s, Connors and Curtis (1970, cited in Hiller & Di Luzio, 2001: 494) found that more than 60 percent of sociologists in Canada had received their highest degree from a foreign institution. Even in 1971, Hedley and Warburton (1973: 305, cited in Hiller & Di Luzio, 2001: 494) found that in large Canadian sociology departments (those with more than twenty faculty members), more than 50 percent of instructors were American, 20 percent were from other countries, and 30 percent were Canadian. These finding were important as they emphasized the need to hire and train more Canadian sociologists if we ever hoped to investigate and understand Canadian society.

The discipline's Canadianization movement was also prompted by the explosion in the number of university enrolments in Canada beginning in the 1950s. In 1962–63, full-time university enrolment in Canada was 132 681, while only 10 years later (1972–73) it had more than doubled to 284 897. Ten years later (1982–83) the number had reached 640 000 (Hiller & Di Luzio, 2001: 491), and at the end of 1999, the number of full-time Canadian university enrolments hovered around 580 000 (Statistics Canada, 1999). Clearly, the need for Canadian-trained sociologists to teach students about Canadian society was a pressing one. This sentiment was clearly expressed when the Association of Universities and Colleges of Canada appointed a Commission on Canadian Studies in 1972, which resulted in The Symons Report (1975).

The report called on the Canadian academic community to increase its efforts to contribute to the knowledge of their own society. The reaction to this report came in an increase in the number of Canadian society courses taught by sociologists across the country, as well as in an increased focus on publishing sociological materials for Canadian sociology students. The assertion that these measures have worked has some support in the number of part- and full-time students who are undergraduate majors in sociology: the figure rose from 13 638 in 1982–83 to 21 028 in 1996–97 (Hiller & Di Luzio, 2001: 493). These students are making a sociological analysis of their own society, and they are also learning about the comparatively radical nature of Canadian sociology.

THE RADICAL NATURE OF CANADIAN SOCIOLOGY

Brym and Saint-Pierre (1997) suggest that one of the defining features of English-Canadian sociology is its radical nature, seen in its focus on the political economy and feminist ideas and perspectives. The important distinction these authors add, however, is how little of this radicalism is seen by the public (1997: 546). Certainly, Quebec sociologists are more focused on the policy ramifications of their endeavours, but Brym and Saint-Pierre recognize that many leading English-Canadian sociologists (such as Margrit Eichler, Graham Lowe, and Susan McDaniel) are mindful of the impact their ideas have on the larger society (1997: 546). Their investigations into the political economy was instrumental in showing that Canadian sociology was not afraid to uncover the hidden power structures that influence and guide society. Canadian feminist sociologists continue this tradition by looking at how gender acts as a locus of oppression and domination.

Margrit Eichler (2001) suggests that the simultaneous emergence of the Canadianization movement and the feminist movement led to a politics of knowledge that proved helpful to both groups. By expanding university departments by adding Canadian academics during the 1960s and 1970s, the feminist movement found a new voice on university campuses. In Eichler's paper *Women Pioneers in Canadian Sociology: The Effects of a Politics of Gender and a Politics of Knowledge* (2001), she attempts to reverse the politics of erasure that she argues effectively allowed the historical contributions of female sociologists in Canada to be written out of the literature. Eichler undertakes the project by conducting interviews with ten of the leading

female sociologists born before 1930. Through the interviews, Eichler utilizes a life-history approach, allowing the women to tell their own stories about being female sociologists during a period of rapid growth within the university system in general, and sociology departments in particular, as well as in a period when feminist issues first entered the sociological discourse.

One important finding from Eichler's investigation into these women's lives is the fact that they never had problems finding jobs in academe (2001: 393). The expanding university system, as well as the emerging recognition of feminist issues, allowed these women to begin full-time careers with little effort. Although they all faced sexism in some form during their careers, they were able to initiate significant institutional change by their mere presence on campus (e.g., pay equity measures, sexual harassment policies). Their ability to be a critical social presence within the academic community was an important factor in advancing feminist issues on university campuses and in the larger society as the feminist movement gained momentum in Canada.

That impetus led to the establishment of the Royal Commission on the Status of Women in 1967 to "inquire into and report upon the status of women in Canada, and to recommend what steps might be taken by the Federal Government to ensure for women equal opportunities with men in all aspects of Canadian society" (Cross, 2000). The final report was released in 1970 with 167 recommendations and "became the blueprint for mainstream feminist activism" (Womenspace, 2002). The feminist movement inspired women to reflect differently on their social surroundings and reinforced the need to question social convention. The influence on early female sociology pioneers was equally important, as it encouraged them to critique their own intellectual foundations generally and sociology specifically. As Dorothy Smith notes about this time, "Because we were free to take up issues for women, we didn't feel committed to reproducing the discipline,…it had the effect…of really liberating the discipline in general in Canada, so that you now have an orientation where people feel absolutely comfortable in raising current issues, in addressing what's going on in Canada" (cited in Eichler, 2001: 394). The Royal Commission report opened the debate on women's positions in Canadian society and resulted in the formation of the women's caucus at the Canadian Sociology and Anthropology Association, which still exists today. The feminist movement, and sociology's role within it, is just one example of Canadian sociology's critical foundation and how Canada continues to influence the discipline today.

CONCLUSION

Canadian sociology is defined by its geography, focus on the political economy, the Canadianization movement, and its radical approach to social issues. This brief review should give you some appreciation for the flavour of Canadian sociology and how it represents a unique approach to the discipline and to our understanding of what it means to be Canadian.

CRITICAL THINKING QUESTIONS

1. Do you believe that social forces influence how academics in a given country see the world? Support your answer.
2. Provide examples of how Canadian winters influence the way Canadians think about themselves. Can similar examples be found for how Canadian summers influence our national identity?
3. In your opinion, was the Canadianization movement at universities and colleges necessary? Why or why not?

NOTES

1. The University of Chicago established the first American department of sociology in 1892 and McGill University established the first Canadian one in 1924.
2. The American postsecondary system serves more than 14 800 000 students and the Canadian system around 827 000 (NCES, 2002; Statistics Canada, 1999). In 1999 more than 2400 departments of sociology existed in the United States (ASA, 2002). Canada had around 45 university departments of sociology—including joint sociology/anthropology departments—(McMaster, 2002) and approximately 150 colleges, the majority of which offered at least introductory sociology (ACCC, 2002).

REFERENCES

ACCC (Association of Canadian Community Colleges). 2002. Membership list. [Online]: Available: **http://www.accc.ca/english/colleges/ membership_list.cfm**. Accessed October 27, 2002.

ASA (American Sociological Association). 2002. Departmental listings for 1999. [Online]. Available: **http://www.asanet.org/pubs/dod.html**. Accessed October 27, 2002.

Brym, R., and C. Saint-Pierre. 1997. Canadian sociology. *Contemporary Sociology*, 26(5): 543–46.

Clement, W. 2001. Canadian political economy's legacy for sociology. *Canadian Journal of Sociology*, 26(3): 405–20.

Connor, D. M., and E. Curtis. 1970. *Sociology and anthropology in Canada: Some characteristics of the disciplines and their current university programs*. Montreal: Canadian Sociology and Anthropology Association.

Countries of the World. 2002. Country statistics at a glance. [Online]. Available: **http://www.infoplease.com/ipa/ A0762380.html**. Accessed July 17, 2002.

Cross, P. 2000. Report of the Royal Commission on the Status of Women: Where are we after thirty years? [Online]. Available: **http://www.owjn.org/issues/equality/thirty.htm**. Accessed January 31, 2003.

Eichler, M. 2001. Women pioneers in Canadian sociology: The effects of a politics of gender and a politics of knowledge. *Canadian Journal of Sociology*, 26(3): 375–403.

Hedley, R. A., and R. T. Warburton. 1973. The role of national courses in the teaching and development of sociology: The Canadian case. *Sociological Review*, 21(2): 299–319.

Hiller, H. H. 2001. Legacy for a new millennium: Canadian sociology in the twentieth century as seen through its publications. *Canadian Journal of Sociology*, 26(3): 257–63.

Hiller, H. H., and L. Di Luzio. 2001. Text and context: Another "chapter" in the evolution of sociology in Canada. *Canadian Journal of Sociology*, 26(3): 487–512.

Innis, H. A. 1954. *The cod fisheries: The history of an international economy.* University of Toronto Press (original work published 1940).

———. 1970. *The fur trade in Canada.* Toronto: University of Toronto Press (original work published 1930).

Langlois, S. 2000. A productive decade in the tradition of Canadian sociology. *Canadian Journal of Sociology,* 25(3): 391–97.

McKay, I. 1998. Changing the subject(s) of the "History of Canadian sociology": The case of Colin McKay and Spencerian Marxism, 1890–1940." *Canadian Journal of Sociology,* 23(4): 389–426.

McMaster University. 2002. Sociology institutions—departments. [Online]. Available: **http://www.mcmaster.ca/ socscidocs/w3virtsoclib/cansoc.htm**. Retrieved October 27, 2002.

NCES (National Center for Education Statistics). 2002. Digest of education statistics, 2001—Chapter 3: Postsecondary education. [Online]. Available: **http://nces.ed.gov//pubs2002/digest2001/ch3.asp#1**. Accessed January 31, 2003.

Southcott, C. 1999. The study of regional inequality in Quebec and English Canada: A comparative analysis of perspectives. *Canadian Journal of Sociology,* 24(4): 457–84.

Statistics Canada. 1999. University enrolment, full-time and part-time, by sex. [Online]. Available: **http://www.statcan.ca/english/Pgdb/educ03a.htm**. Accessed October 27, 2002.

Womenspace. 2002. Since the Royal Commission on the Status of Women. [Online]. Available: **http:// herstory.womenspace.ca/ RCSW.html**. Retrieved October 23.

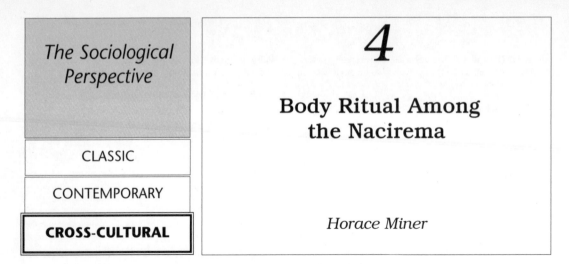

The Sociological Perspective

CLASSIC

CONTEMPORARY

CROSS-CULTURAL

4

Body Ritual Among the Nacirema

Horace Miner

Most people take their life for granted; when they think about society at all, they usually view it as both natural and good. To help us step back from our society, anthropologist Horace Miner describes the Nacirema, a peculiar people living in North America (whose lives should seem familiar). Miner's intellectual sleight of hand illustrates how the sociological perspective involves detachment, so that everyday life becomes something new and unusual.

The anthropologist has become so familiar with the diversity of ways in which different peoples behave in similar situations that he is not apt to be surprised by even the most exotic customs. In fact, if all of the logically possible combinations of behavior have not been found somewhere in the world, he is apt to suspect that they must be present in some yet undescribed tribe. This point has, in fact, been expressed with respect to clan organization by Murdock (1949: 71). In this light, the magical beliefs and practices of the Nacirema present such unusual aspects that it seems desirable to describe them as an example of the extremes to which human behavior can go.

Professor Linton first brought the ritual of the Nacirema to the attention of anthropologists twenty years ago (1936: 326), but the culture of this people is still very poorly understood. They are a North American group living in the territory between the Canadian Cree, the Yaqui and Tarahumare of Mexico, and the Carib and

Source: "Body Ritual among the Nacirema" by Horace Miner. Reproduced by permission of the *American Anthropological Association* from *American Anthropologist*, vol. 58, no. 3, June, 1956. Not for further reproduction.

Arawak of the Antilles. Little is known of their origin, although tradition states that they came from the east. According to Nacirema mythology, their nation was originated by a culture hero, Notgnihsaw, who is otherwise known for two great feats of strength—the throwing of a piece of wampum across the river Pa-To-Mac and the chopping down of a cherry tree in which the Spirit of Truth resided.

Nacirema culture is characterized by a highly developed market economy which has evolved in a rich natural habitat. While much of the people's time is devoted to economic pursuits, a large part of the fruits of these labors and a considerable portion of the day are spent in ritual activity. The focus of this activity is the human body, the appearance and health of which loom as a dominant concern in the ethos of the people. While such concern is certainly not unusual, its ceremonial aspects and associated philosophy are unique.

The fundamental belief underlying the whole system appears to be that the human body is ugly and that its natural tendency is to debility and disease. Incarcerated in such a body, man's only hope is to avert these characteristics through the use of the powerful influences of ritual and ceremony. Every household has one or more shrines devoted to this purpose. The more powerful individuals in this society have several shrines in their houses, and, in fact, the opulence of a house is often referred to in terms of the number of such ritual centers it possesses. Most houses are of wattle and daub construction, but the shrine rooms of the more wealthy are walled with stone. Poorer families imitate the rich by applying pottery plaques to their shrine walls.

While each family has at least one such shrine, the rituals associated with it are not family ceremonies but are private and secret. The rites are normally only discussed with children, and then only during the period when they are being initiated into these mysteries. I was able, however, to establish sufficient rapport with the natives to examine these shrines and to have the rituals described to me.

The focal point of the shrine is a box or chest which is built into the wall. In this chest are kept the many charms and magical potions without which no native believes he could live. These preparations are secured from a variety of specialized practitioners. The most powerful of these are the medicine men, whose assistance must be rewarded with substantial gifts. However, the medicine men do not provide the curative potions for their clients, but [they] decide what the ingredients should be and then write them down in an ancient and secret language. This writing is understood only by the medicine men and by the herbalists who, for another gift, provide the required charm.

The charm is not disposed of after it has served its purpose, but is placed in the charm-box of the household shrine. As these magical materials are specific for certain ills, and the real or imagined maladies of the people are many, the charm-box is usually full to overflowing. The magical packets are so numerous that people forget what their purposes were and fear to use them again. While the natives are very vague on this point, we can only assume that the idea in retaining all the old magical materials is that their presence in the charm-box, before which the body rituals are conducted, will in some way protect the worshipper.

Beneath the charm-box is a small font. Each day every member of the family, in succession, enters the shrine room, bows his head before the charm-box, mingles different sorts of holy water in the font, and proceeds with a brief rite of ablution. The holy waters are secured from the Water Temple of the community, where the priests conduct elaborate ceremonies to make the liquid ritually pure.

In the hierarchy of magical practitioners, and below the medicine men in prestige, are specialists whose designation is best translated "holy-mouth-men." The Nacirema have an almost pathological horror of and fascination with the mouth, the condition of which is believed to have a supernatural influence on all social relationships. Were it not for the rituals of the mouth, they believe that their teeth would fall out, their gums bleed, their jaws shrink, their friends desert them, and their lovers reject them. They also believe that a strong relationship exists between oral and moral characteristics. For example, there is a ritual ablution of the mouth for children which is supposed to improve their moral fiber.

The daily body ritual performed by everyone includes a mouth-rite. Despite the fact that these people are so punctilious about care of the mouth, this rite involves a practice which strikes the uninitiated stranger as revolting. It was reported to me that the ritual consists of inserting a small bundle of hog hairs into the mouth, along with certain magical powders, and then moving the bundle in a highly formalized series of gestures.

In addition to the private mouth-rite, the people seek out a holy-mouth-man once or twice a year. These practitioners have an impressive set of paraphernalia, consisting of a variety of augers, awls, probes, and prods. The use of these objects in the exorcism of the evils of the mouth involves almost unbelievable ritual torture of the client. The holy-mouth-man opens the client's mouth and, using the above-mentioned tools, enlarges any holes which decay may have created in the teeth. Magical materials are put into these holes. If there are no naturally occurring holes in the teeth, large sections of one or more teeth are gouged out so that the supernatural substance can be applied. In the client's view, the purpose of these ministrations is to arrest decay and to draw friends. The extremely sacred and traditional character of the rite is evident in the fact that the natives return to the holy-mouth-man year after year, despite the fact that their teeth continue to decay.

It is to be hoped that, when a thorough study of the Nacirema is made, there will be careful inquiry into the personality structure of these people. One has but to watch the gleam in the eye of a holy-mouth-man, as he jabs an awl into an exposed nerve, to suspect that a certain amount of sadism is involved. If this can be established, a very interesting pattern emerges, for most of the population shows definite masochistic tendencies. It was to these that Professor Linton referred in discussing a distinctive part of the daily body ritual which is performed only by men. This part of the rite involves scraping and lacerating the surface of the face with a sharp instrument. Special women's rites are performed only four times during each lunar month, but what they lack in frequency is made up in barbarity. As part of this ceremony, women bake their heads in small ovens for about an hour. The theoretically interesting point is that what seems to be a preponderantly masochistic people have developed sadistic specialists.

The medicine men have an imposing temple, or *latipso*, in every community of any size. The more elaborate ceremonies required to treat very sick patients can only be performed at this temple. These ceremonies involve not only the thaumaturge but a permanent group of vestal maidens who move sedately about the temple chambers in distinctive costume and headdress.

The *latipso* ceremonies are so harsh that it is phenomenal that a fair proportion of the really sick natives who enter the temple ever recover. Small children whose indoctrination is still incomplete have been known to resist attempts to take them to the temple because "that is where you go to die." Despite this fact, sick adults are not only willing but eager to undergo the protracted ritual purification, if they can afford to do so. No matter how ill the supplicant or how grave the emergency, the guardians of many temples will not admit a client if he cannot give a rich gift to the custodian. Even after one has gained admission and survived the ceremonies, the guardians will not permit the neophyte to leave until he makes still another gift.

The supplicant entering the temple is first stripped of all his or her clothes. In everyday life the Nacirema avoids exposure of his body and its natural functions. Bathing and excretory acts are performed only in the secrecy of the household shrine, where they are ritualized as part of the body-rites. Psychological shock results from the fact that body secrecy is suddenly lost upon entry into the *latipso*. A man, whose own wife has never seen him in an excretory act, suddenly finds himself naked and assisted by a vestal maiden while he performs his natural functions into a sacred vessel. This sort of ceremonial treatment is necessitated by the fact that the excreta are used by a diviner to ascertain the course and nature of the client's sickness. Female clients, on the other hand, find their naked bodies are subjected to the scrutiny, manipulation, and prodding of the medicine men.

Few supplicants in the temple are well enough to do anything but lie on their hard beds. The daily ceremonies, like the rites of the holy-mouth-men, involve discomfort and torture. With ritual precision, the vestals awaken their miserable charges each dawn and roll them about on their beds of pain while performing ablutions, in the formal movements of which the maidens are highly trained. At other times they insert magic wands in the supplicant's mouth or force him to eat substances which are supposed to be healing.

From time to time the medicine men come to their clients and jab magically treated needles into their flesh. The fact that these temple ceremonies may not cure, and may even kill, the neophyte, in no way decreases the people's faith in the medicine men.

There remains one other kind of practitioner, known as a "listener." This witch-doctor has the power to exorcise the devils that lodge in the heads of people who have been bewitched. The Nacirema believe that parents bewitch their own children. Mothers are particularly suspected of putting a curse on children while teaching them the secret body rituals. The counter-magic of the witch-doctor is unusual in its lack of ritual. The patient simply tells the "listener" all his troubles and fears, beginning with the earliest difficulties he can remember. The memory displayed by the Nacirema in these exorcism sessions is truly remarkable. It is not uncommon for the patient to bemoan the rejection he felt upon being weaned as a babe, and a few individuals even see their troubles going back to the traumatic effects of their own birth.

In conclusion, mention must be made of certain practices which have their base in native esthetics but which depend upon the pervasive aversion to the natural body and its functions. There are ritual fasts to make fat people thin and ceremonial feasts to make thin people fat. Still other rites are used to make women's breasts larger if they are small, and smaller if they are large. General dissatisfaction with breast shape is symbolized in the fact that the ideal form is virtually outside the range of human variation. A few women afflicted with almost inhuman hyper-mammary development are so idolized that they make a handsome living by simply going from village to village and permitting the natives to stare at them for a fee.

Reference has already been made to the fact that excretory functions are ritualized, routinized, and relegated to secrecy. Natural reproductive functions are similarly distorted. Intercourse is taboo as a topic and scheduled as an act. Efforts are made to avoid pregnancy by the use of magical materials or by limiting intercourse to certain phases of the moon. Conception is actually very infrequent. When pregnant, women dress so as to hide their condition. Parturition takes place in secret, without friends or relatives to assist, and the majority of women do not nurse their infants.

Our review of the ritual life of the Nacirema has certainly shown them to be a magic-ridden people. It is hard to understand how they have managed to exist so long under the burdens which they have imposed upon themselves. But even such exotic customs as these take on real meaning when they are viewed with the insight provided by Malinowski when he wrote (1948: 70):

> Looking from far and above, from our high places of safety in the developed civilization, it is easy to see all the crudity and irrelevance of magic. But without its power and guidance early man could not have mastered his practical difficulties as he has done, nor could man have advanced to the higher stages of civilization.

CRITICAL THINKING QUESTIONS

1. When did you realize (if you did) that Miner is describing the "American"—Nacirema spelled backwards? Why do we not recognize this right away?
2. Using Miner's approach, describe a baseball game, an auction, shoppers in a supermarket, or a university classroom.
3. What do we gain from being able to step back from our way of life as Miner has done here?

REFERENCES

Linton, R. 1936. *The study of man.* New York: Appleton-Century.

Malinowski, B. 1948. *Magic, science and religion.* Glencoe, Ill.: Free Press.

Murdock, G. P. 1949. *Social structure.* New York: Macmillan.

*Sociological
Research*

CLASSIC

CONTEMPORARY

CROSS-CULTURAL

5

The Case for Value-Free Sociology

Max Weber

The following is part of a lecture given in 1918 at Germany's Munich University by Max Weber, one of sociology's pioneers. Weber lived in politically turbulent times, in which the government and other organizations were demanding that university faculty teach the "right" ideas. Weber responded to these pressures by encouraging everyone to be politically involved as citizens, while maintaining that teachers and scholars should prize dispassionate analysis rather than political advocacy. This selection stimulates critical thinking about the mix of fact and value that is found in all sociological research.

Let us consider the disciplines close to me: sociology, history, economics, political science, and those types of cultural philosophy that make it their task to interpret the sciences. It is said, and I agree, that politics is out of place in the lecture-room. It does not belong there on the part of the students.... Neither does [it] belong in the lecture-room on the part of the [instructors], and when the [instructor] is scientifically concerned with politics, it belongs there least of all.

To take a practical stand is one thing, and to analyze political structures and party positions is another. When speaking in a political meeting about democracy, one does not hide one's personal standpoint; indeed, to come out clearly and take a stand is one's damned duty. The words one uses in such a meeting are not means of scientific analysis but means of canvassing votes and winning over others. They are not plowshares to loosen the soil of contemplative thought; they are swords against the enemies: Such words are weapons. It would be an outrage, however, to use words in this fashion in a lecture or in the lecture-room. If, for in stance, "democracy" is under discussion, one considers its various forms, analyzes them in the way they function, determines what results for the conditions of life the one form has as compared with the other. Then one confronts the forms of democracy with nondemocratic forms of political order and endeavors to come to a position where the student may find the point from which, in terms of his ultimate ideals, he can take a stand. But the true teacher will beware of imposing from the platform any political position upon the student, whether it is expressed or suggested. "To let the facts speak for themselves" is the most unfair way of putting over a political position to the student.

Why should we abstain from doing this? I state in advance that some highly esteemed colleagues are of the opinion that it is not possible to carry through this self-restraint and that, even if it were possible, it would be a whim to avoid declaring oneself. Now one cannot demonstrate scientifically what the duty of an academic teacher is. One can only demand of the teacher that he have the intellectual integrity to see that it is one thing to state facts, to determine mathematical or logical relations or the internal structure of cultural values, while it is another thing to answer questions of the value of culture and its individual contents and the question of how one should act in the cultural community and in political associations. These are quite heterogeneous problems. If he asks further why he should not deal with both types of problems in the lecture-room, the answer is: because the prophet and the demagogue do not belong on the academic platform.

To the prophet and the demagogue, it is said: "Go your ways out into the streets and speak openly to the world," that is, speak where criticism is possible. In the lecture-room we stand opposite our audience, and it has to remain silent. I deem it irresponsible to exploit the circumstance that for the sake of their career the students have to attend a teacher's course while there is nobody present to oppose him with criticism. The task of the teacher is to serve the students with his knowledge and scientific experience and not to imprint upon them his personal political views. It is certainly possible that the individual teacher will not entirely succeed in eliminating his personal sympathies. He is then exposed to the sharpest criticism in the forum of his own conscience. And this deficiency does not prove anything; other errors are also possible, for instance, erroneous statements of fact, and yet they prove nothing against the duty of searching for the truth. I also reject this in the very interest of science. I am ready to prove from the works of our historians that whenever the man of science introduces his personal value judgment, a full understanding of the facts ceases....

The primary task of a useful teacher is to teach his students to recognize "inconvenient" facts—I mean facts that are inconvenient for their party opinions. And for every party opinion there are facts that are extremely inconvenient, for my own opinion no less than for others. I believe the teacher accomplishes more than a mere intellectual task if he compels his audience to accustom itself to the existence of such facts. I would be so immodest as even to apply the expression "moral achievement," though perhaps this may sound too grandiose for something that should go without saying.

CRITICAL THINKING QUESTIONS

1. Why does Weber seek to set the campus apart from society as an "ivory tower"?
2. How is the classroom a distinctive setting in terms of political neutrality? If instructors cannot be entirely free from value positions, why should they strive to point out "inconvenient facts" to their students?
3. Do you see arguments *for* instructors presenting passionate advocacy of issues that are of great political and moral significance?

6

The Importance
of Social Research

Earl Babbie

How do we know what we know? Tradition, religion, laws, the media, personal experiences, and people in authority shape our everyday beliefs and behaviours. In this selection, Earl Babbie argues that social problems such as poverty could be diminished if policymakers and the general public based their responses on rigorous social science research results rather than on emotions and stereotypes.

...We can't solve our social problems until we understand how they come about, persist. Social science research offers a way to examine and understand the operation of human social affairs. It provides points of view and technical procedures that uncover things that would otherwise escape our awareness. Often, as the cliché goes, things are not what they seem; social science research can make that clear. One example illustrates this fact.

Poverty is a persistent problem in the United States, and none of its intended solutions is more controversial than *welfare*. Although the program is intended to give the poor a helping hand while they reestablish their financial viability, many complain that it has the opposite effect.

Part of the public image of welfare in action was crystallized by Susan Sheehan (1976) in her book *A Welfare Mother*, which describes the situ-

ation of a three-generation welfare family, suggesting that the welfare system trapped the poor rather than liberate[d] them. Martin Anderson (1978: 56) agreed with Sheehan's assessment and charged that the welfare system had established a caste system in America, "perhaps as much as one-tenth of this nation—a caste of people almost totally dependent on the state, with little hope or prospect of breaking free. Perhaps we should call them the Dependent Americans."

George Gilder (1990) has spoken for many who believe the poor are poor mainly because they refuse to work, saying the welfare system saps their incentive to take care of themselves. Ralph Segalman and David Marsland (1989: 6–7) support the view that welfare has become an intergenerational way of life for the poor in welfare systems around the world. Children raised in welfare families, they assert, will likely live their adult lives on welfare:

This conflict between the intent of welfare as a temporary aid (as so understood by most of the public) and welfare as a permanent right (as understood by the

Source: From *Practice of Social Research (with InfoTrac)*, 8th edition, by E. R. Babbie, copyright © 1998. Reprinted with permission of Wadsworth Publishing, a division of Thomson Learning.

welfare bureaucracy and welfare state planners) has serious implications. The welfare state nations, by and large, have given up on the concept of client rehabilitation for self-sufficiency, an intent originally supported by most welfare state proponents. What was to have been a temporary condition has become a permanent cost on the welfare state. As a result, welfare discourages productivity and self-sufficiency and establishes a new mode of approved behavior in the society—one of acceptance of dependency as the norm.

These negative views of the effects of the welfare system are widely shared by the general public, even among those basically sympathetic to the aims of the program. Greg Duncan (1984: 2–3) at the University of Michigan's Survey Research Center points out that census data would seem to confirm the impression that a hard core of the poor have become trapped in their poverty. Speaking of the percentage of the population living in poverty at any given time, he says,

Year-to-year changes in these fractions are typically less than 1 percent, and the Census survey's other measures show little change in the characteristic of the poor from one year to the next. They have shown repeatedly that the individuals who are poor are more likely to be in families headed by a woman, by someone with low education, and by blacks.

Evidence that one-eighth of the population was poor in two consecutive years, and that those poor shared similar characteristics, is consistent with an inference of absolutely no turnover in the poverty population. Moreover, the evidence seems to fit the stereotype that those families that are poor are likely to remain poor, and that there is a hard-core population of poor families for whom there is little hope of self-improvement.

Duncan continues, however, to warn that such snapshots of the population can conceal changes taking place. Specifically, an unchanging percentage of the population living in poverty does not necessarily mean the *same* families are poor from year to year. Theoretically, it could be a totally different set of families each year.

To determine the real nature of poverty and welfare, the University of Michigan undertook a "Panel Study of Income Dynamics" in which they followed the economic fate of 5,000 families

from 1969 to 1978, or ten years, the period supposedly typified by Sheehan's "welfare mother." At the beginning, the researchers found that in 1978, 8.1 percent of these families were receiving some welfare benefits and 3.5 percent depended on welfare for more than half their income. Moreover, these percentages did not differ drastically over the ten-year period (Duncan 1984: 75).

Looking beyond these surface data, however, the researchers found something you might not have expected. During the ten-year period, about one-fourth of the 5,000 families received welfare benefits at least once. However, only 8.7 percent of the families were ever dependent on welfare for more than half their income. *"Only a little over one-half of the individuals living in poverty in one year are found to be poor in the next, and considerably less than one-half of those who experience poverty remain persistently poor over many years"* (Duncan 1984: 3; emphasis original).

Only 2 percent of the families received welfare each of the ten years, and less than 1 percent were continuously dependent on welfare for the ten years. Table 6.1 summarizes these findings.

These data paint a much different picture of poverty than people commonly assume. In a summary of his findings, Duncan (1984: 4–5) says:

While nearly one-quarter of the population received income from welfare sources at least once in the decade, only about 2 percent of all the population could be characterized as dependent upon this income for extended periods of time. Many families receiving welfare benefits at any given time were in the early stages of recovering from an economic crisis caused by the death, departure, or disability of a husband, a recovery that often lifted them out of welfare when they found full-time employment, or remarried, or both. Furthermore, most of the children raised in welfare families did not themselves receive welfare benefits after they left home and formed their own households.

Many of the things social scientists study—including [the issue of welfare] you've just read about—generate deep emotions and firm convictions in most people. This makes effective

TABLE 6.1 Incidence of Short- and Long-Run Welfare Receipt and Dependence, 1969–1978

	Percent of U.S. Population:	
	Receiving Any Welfare Income	*Dependent on Welfare for More than 50% of Family Income*
Welfare in 1978	8.1%	3.5%
Welfare in 1 or more years, 1969–78	25.2	8.7
Welfare in 5 or more years, 1969–78	8.3	3.5
Welfare in all 10 years, 1969–78	2.0	0.7
"Persistent welfare" (welfare in 8 or more years), 1969–78	4.4	2.0

Source: Greg J. Duncan, *Years of Poverty, Years of Plenty: The Changing Fortunes of American Workers and Families* (Ann Arbor: University of Michigan, 1984), 75.

inquiry into the facts difficult at best; all too often, researchers manage only to confirm their initial prejudices. The special value of social science research methods is that they offer a way to address such issues with logical and observational rigor. They let us all pierce through our personal viewpoints and take a look at the world that lies beyond our own perspectives. And it is that "world beyond" that holds the solutions to the social problems we face today.

At a time of increased depression and disillusionment, we are continually tempted to turn away from confronting social problems and retreat into the concerns of our own self-interest. Social science research offers an opportunity to take on those problems and discover the experience of making a difference after all. The choice is yours; I invite you to take on the challenge....

CRITICAL THINKING QUESTIONS

1. What does Babbie mean when he says that "things are not what they seem" when we read about controversial issues such as welfare?
2. Many people believe that welfare has become an intergenerational way of life. What data does Babbie present that challenges such beliefs?

3. In the classical selection "The Case for Value-Free Sociology," Max Weber asserts that "The primary task of a useful teacher is to teach his students to recognize 'inconvenient' facts—I mean facts that are inconvenient for their party opinions." Do you think some instructors (and students) feel pressure to conform to approved points of view, whether religious or political? Should faculty and students ignore research findings that contradict such perspectives?

REFERENCES

Anderson, M. 1978. *Welfare: The political economy of welfare reform in the United States.* Stanford, Calif.: Hoover Institution Press.

Duncan, G. J., with R. D. Coe, M. E. Corcoran, M. S. Hill, S. D. Hoffman, and J. N. Morgan (eds.). 1984. *Years of poverty, years of plenty: The changing economic fortunes of American workers and families.* Ann Arbor, Mich.: Survey Research Center Institute.

Gilder, G. 1990. The nature of poverty. In *The American polity* reader, eds. A. Serow, W. Shannon, and E. Ladd, 658–63. New York: Norton.

Segalman, R., and D. Marsland. 1989. *Cradle to grave: Comparative perspectives on the state of welfare.* New York: St. Martin's Press.

Sheehan, S. 1976. *A welfare mother.* New York: Mentor.

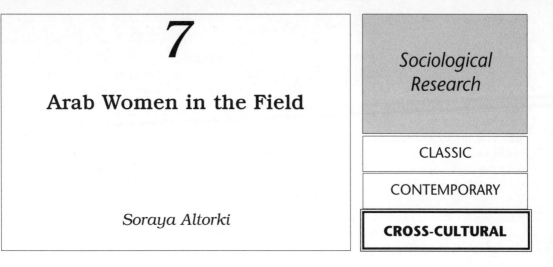

7

Arab Women in the Field

Soraya Altorki

Sociological Research

CLASSIC

CONTEMPORARY

CROSS-CULTURAL

Social scientists often rely on ethnography—*the study of people using observation or interviews—to provide detailed descriptions of groups, organizations, and communities. Such fieldwork, like other data collection methods, has both strengths and limitations. As Soraya Altorki shows, a major advantage of studying one's own culture is a familiarity with the people and the environment; however, the researcher also encounters several problems. One of Altorki's challenges, for example, was resocializing herself into her culture, having been abroad for many years. She also had to overcome the subjects' reluctance to address sensitive questions about their religious practices and family life to an "outsider."*

AT HOME IN THE FIELD

Having been socialized many years in Egypt and identifying with its people, I had regarded it, on one level, to be my home. On another level, however, I had been brought up in a Saudi Arabian family committed in great measure to that country's cultural heritage and the observance of its cultural norms, even while selectively observing certain Egyptian values and practices. Throughout my college days, I had been reminded that I could not do what my Egyptian girlfriends could do, because "our" traditions were different and for "us" such behavior was unacceptable.

Source: "At Home in the Field," by Soraya Altorki, in *Arab Women in the Field: Studying Your Own Society*, eds. Soraya Altorki and Camillia Fawzi El-Solh, pp. 51–9. New York: Syracuse University Press, 1988. Reprinted by permission.

Besides, it was not only the constraining elements of Saudi Arabian culture that molded my growing-up experiences in Egypt, but also the rich rewards that I reaped from kinship support and shared cultural knowledge. These provided for me the security of a closure that was not attainable in Egypt. Thus, Saudi Arabia was home for me on a more fundamental level.

Arriving in Jiddah [Saudi Arabia], my native city, I knew I wanted to study urban life. Although the entire northern portion of the Arabian Peninsula was virtually unknown to social scientists,…early travelers and even scholars avoided its study in favor of the nomad and the camel. Barring Hürgrouje and Burton, almost nothing was known about urban life. In retrospect, I believe that my choice to focus on urban society was partly a reaction to the stereotypical view of Saudi Arabia as a society of nomads and oil wells.

There were also social constraints to my choice. I knew that, as an unmarried woman, I could neither travel alone in the country nor wander around with the nomads. Living alone, anywhere in the country, was out of the question. Thus, for many considerations, an urban-based study seemed most appropriate, and the city of Jiddah the most convenient.

The realities of being an unmarried woman in many ways dictated my field of research, although it did not determine my choice of research topic within that field (Altorki, 1986). This essentially meant that I could work with women and that I had limited access to men. Within these bounds, my choice was absolutely free....

INSIDER/OUTSIDER

Being literally at home in Jiddah, I was spared having to worry about the problems of settling in that most anthropologists face when entering the field. Furthermore, I needed no research permit (or if I did, I never bothered to find out) and no letters of guarantee. Neither was I required to make commitments to local authorities and research institutes concerning the conduct of my work and the use and distribution of my data.

The people I studied saw me as one of themselves. Some of them had ties of kinship and friendship to my family. Others knew my family members by name. This state of affairs provided me with significant advantages. Others, working in their own society, have observed similar benefits in knowing the culture and consequently being able to select their research agenda in consonance with what is most expedient for the research task and what is most feasible within the limits of what will be allowed by the subjects under investigation (see Stephenson & Greer, 1981: 126).

However, some facets of my life concerned my informants. Why, for example, was I not a married woman with children, like all my peers? And why was I still living abroad rather than residing in Jiddah, awaiting marriage? My unmarried status at the age of twenty-two made me somewhat of an anomaly. More distressing to the older women among whom I worked was the conclusion that I was more interested in following my studies than in settling down to married life. Although the role of an educated woman had come to be accepted by the community at large and the elite in particular, the problem was in the priorities this role took over what was perceived to be the more important aspect of gender role, namely the status that marriage and motherhood bring. According to both men and women, it is these dimensions of womanhood that are primary. In fact, given the segregation of Saudi Arabian women from men, and their isolation from public life, marriage and motherhood become a woman's avenues to maturity, security, and greater prestige. Being a member of the society, I anticipated this and was well prepared to deal with its consequences.

Although women come of age with marriage, and prestige for them is attained by motherhood, my status within the community had to rest on other things: It relied greatly on my education. Lacking husband and child, I predicated my adulthood on education and depended on the community's acceptance of it as a legitimate goal for women to attain. Men and women alike respected this, although never failing to remind me of the fundamentals of my role as a woman. As one older woman put it to me: "Education is good, but women are weak. No matter how much money they have, no matter their education, they cannot manage without men. May Allah save your father and your brother. But you have to start your own family." That statement accurately reflects the dependence of women on men, a dependence that also correlates with their segregation in Saudi Arabian society. But my role as a Saudi Arabian woman, educated abroad, permitted me more flexibility and autonomy. For one thing, my interaction with men who were not my relatives was tolerated.

My long absence abroad was an additional factor leading to more mobility. While abroad, I had been immersed in a different way of life, and hence women and men alike did not expect me to conform totally to the cultural norms governing the relationship of men and women in Saudi Arabian society. My absence had a complex effect on my reentry into my own community. On the one hand, it allowed more maneuverability in my role as an unmarried woman, and, on the other hand, it made conformity especially expedient in strengthening my ties to my informants.

Repeatedly, men and women expressed their surprise and approval when my behavior showed conformity to Saudi Arabian culture. They were, for example, delighted that my many years in Egypt had not changed my accent to Egyptian. Whenever I showed observance of norms that young people my age had begun to modify, members of the older generation were astonished and particularly delighted. Those of the younger generation, however, saw such conformity as awkward and continued to remind me that times had changed: "Nobody is observing such things these days."

For example, norms of deference to older siblings necessitate that they be addressed in specific terms. To an older brother and kinsmen his age the term is *sidi*, which means "my master." My use of these terms of address was welcomed by all, barring girls of my age who by then were seeking to substitute as equivalent for the term *sidi* those of *akhuya* (my brother) and the sobriquet *abu flan* (father of). In doing this, I took my cues from young men who had obtained their college education abroad, sometimes through graduate school, and who continued to use traditional terms of reference in addressing older female siblings and other kinswomen in their age group.

It was in the same spirit that I observed some norms of modesty, particularly those related to veiling. Such practices were changing at the time of my fieldwork, so that the families I studied showed the whole spectrum of veiling practices, from those who had considerably modified its use to leave the face bare, to those who still observed the traditional practice of covering the face as well. While visiting the homes of the latter, I made sure to conform and to cover my face carefully. This gesture of respect did not go unnoticed: Women and men alike commented that my many years abroad had not made me behave like a "foreigner."

The years abroad had been spent as a student, and now I had come back as a researcher with the intention of recording a way of life that had not previously been studied. Everyone understood that role. Female education was not a novelty. Girls were sent to *faqihas* (informal traditional schools) as far back as older informants could remember; and formal girls' schools were opened by the government in 1960. By the time I went to the field, the first women's university had already opened in Jiddah. College education was thoroughly acceptable for women; indeed, it had become greatly valued.

Thus, I had no problem in defining part of my role to the subjects of my research. I wanted to study social life, family organization, rituals, beliefs, and customs, and to document how these have changed for the younger people in the study. In another way, my role was more ascribed. My return to Jiddah meant taking my place in a family and getting involved in the various ramifications of family life. It also meant belonging to a class with the task of conforming to the behavior of that class. I was aware that I could in fact not conform to that behavior, but I had little choice with regard to involvement in family life.

The ascribed aspects of my role, i.e., gender, age, and kinship, were more fundamental in people's perception of me, which may be unavoidable in doing research among one's own people. My education was important in allowing me to explore areas of social life (e.g., more access to the world of men) that other women could not undertake. Despite my research objective, known and accepted to all the families, I remained primarily a Saudi Arabian woman. As such, I was known to some as the daughter or a sister of a friend, while to others as a member of a lineage they knew from other mutual friends. These considerations were always present in my interaction with others.

While criteria centering on the individual are not without relevance in structuring relations, the world of these elite families was in the first instance structured by consanguineous and marital ties, and in the second place by friendship and business networks.

Within this world an individual—whether man or woman—is deeply embedded in the *'aila* (family). One's status is, to a considerable degree, ascribed by the status of the *'aila*. Individual achievement is an avenue to mobility, but clearly it is the achievement of men and not of women that is associated with family prestige. Recent changes in the wider society have introduced more emphasis on individuality and an increase of distance from the *'aila*. This is evidenced in neolocal residence patterns, more individual involvement in marriage choice, relative reduction of parental authority, independent career choices for men, and less observance of traditional obligations to kinsmen (Altorki, 1986).

On the whole, I experienced no problems in establishing rapport—that quality in the relationship between the ethnographer and the host community that the introductions to ethnographic monographs rarely fail to mention, but which probably involves the most enigmatic aspect of our methodological trademark: participant observation. I spoke the language, and the trademark itself had no special meaning for me, although, as I will explain, it had very special implications in my case.

In short, I found practical advantages in my particular field situation: Unencumbered by bureaucratic impediments, comfortably set up in my family's home, fluent in the vernacular, and personally known in some of the households I was to study, I could begin my research under very auspicious circumstances—or so it seemed until I realized the implications of being an indigenous anthropologist. I discovered that almost every one of the advantages had its negative side.

In a very real sense, my fieldwork experience was a process of resocialization into my own society. Although I was raised in a Saudi Arabian family, my long years of residence abroad had established considerable distance between me and my society. The advantages were that much of the culture was not so familiar that it could easily escape my notice. This problem in the collection of data has been observed by other ethnographers working under similar conditions (cf. Spradley & McCurdy, 1972; Ablon, 1977; Stephenson & Greer, 1981), but it is one that can be overcome by rigorous training. The researcher can counteract familiarity by close observation, meticulous recording of ethnographic scenes, and detailed probing to uncover the "taken-for-granted" world he or she may share with members of the community being studied.

Living at home meant that I had to assume the role expected of a family member in my position within the household group. The ordinary field situation reversed itself in my case. I became what may best be described as an observant participant. My primary duty was to participate. To observe became an incidental privilege.

My status did not afford me immunity from observing all the taboos and attending to all the obligations my culture prescribed for me—an immunity usually granted to foreign anthropologists. I had to accept severe restrictions on my movements and on my interaction with other people. For example, I had no freedom to move in public on my own, and challenging any norms of conduct would have jeopardized my relationships with the families I had decided to study. Had I not conformed, I would have risked ostracism and termination of my research. Persistently, if slowly, I achieved a precarious balance of roles that allowed me mobility and freedom to do my research as well as to be accepted and taken seriously. I became a conscious witness to my own resocialization as an Arab woman in my society and thus learned and comprehended many aspects of this role in the best possible manner.

This, perhaps, is one of the hidden advantages of being an insider. For example, veiling norms can be observed and described by an outsider, and one can also learn about the meaning of veiling by soliciting relevant information from informants. Yet the participant charged with the task of abiding by the norms experiences the constraints, to be sure, but also the rewards of these norms on a more basic level. In that sense, my resocialization generated data on an experiential level different from that to which an outsider could bear witness. This point has also been observed as a merit of indigenous research elsewhere. Aguilar, for example, summarizing the pros and cons of this kind of research, mentions that its advocates insist "that the covert culture of the insider has the heuristic value of lending psychological reality (or cultural reality) to ethnographic analyses" (1981: 16).

My status affected my research in another way. Restricted possibilities for movement outside the house and pervasive segregation of men and women in public confined the research predominantly to the world of women. These realities affected the choice of topic for investigation. I could not study market or political relations, for example. Neither could I investigate any other subject in which men, rather than women, are the dominant actors. Family organization seemed the most accessible for a female researcher, and elites became my focus. Within that, my emphasis was on how ideology and practice affect and are influenced by one another. But, as noted elsewhere, elites are the least accessible to inquiry, especially through the technique of prolonged participant observation. The families I elected to study formed closed groups, and although the observation of and participation in their daily lives was possible for me as a member of the group, even I could gain their confidence only through patient approaches along the lines of friendship.

Although generous hospitality is highly valued behavior, there remain degrees of formality that the families must always maintain vis-à-vis the whole community. Only with considerable caution can a nonmember see their lives as they live them, as opposed to how they want the rest of the community to perceive them. For example, it takes a long time, coupled with intensive interaction, before people allow a friend to move within their home free of the façade of formality exhibited to outsiders. Indeed, it took between six and eight months before I could develop the friendships that made close observation of their daily lives possible to the degree that my presence was more or less ignored. Being an insider has even more serious consequences for research. Information may be withheld when it relates to behavior that must be concealed from public knowledge. If one is outside the system, one's awareness of goings-on may not be problematical. But as a participant, the researcher constitutes a threat of exposure and judgment. Lewis (1973: 588) explains this situation very well:

> There is a growing fear that the information collected by an outsider, someone not constrained by group values and interests, will expose the group to outside manipulation and control.... The insider, on the other hand, is accountable; s/he must remain in the community and take responsibility for her/his actions. Thus, s/he is forced through self-interest to exercise discretion.

This was one of the hardest areas to overcome in doing research among one's own people. For example, family solidarity and cohesion are greatly valued. Verbally, men and women endorse the ideal of love and support between siblings; respect and obedience in filial relations; and honoring family duties of financial support to the needy and maintenance of elderly parents. In practice, the older generations approximated many of these ideals (Altorki, 1986).

But family conflict does occur, and younger generation members have begun to modify family obligations in general. Differences over inheritance constitute the most serious threat to family solidarity—a threat that mounts as the stakes become higher and people's wealth increases. The ideal remains that such differences must be kept out of the public eye and should be reconciled between family members without recourse to the courts. So important is this family ideal that information about conflict, especially that considered to be serious, was at first not revealed to me. I learned about such conflicts indirectly from domestic servants working in these homes who, by coincidence, happened to be related to women working in my family's household. On other occasions, I obtained relevant information from women with whom I had established such strong ties of friendship that we had come to be considered "sisters." This family idiom symbolized our enclosure in the same kinship group and, by implication, showed our interest in protecting that group and shielding it from public criticism.

On one point, my learning about family conflicts was fortuitous. Is it conceivable that I would have returned from the field with the belief that the ideal of family solidarity was the reality? By being an insider, and from my own kinship network, I "experienced" the fact that reality was different and that disagreement can escalate to conflicts between family members. The problem, however, was in collecting data about conflict from the other families to uncover patterns in its expression and management. What, for example, were the patterns for the expression of intrafamily conflict? How was it managed, and what are the patterns for its resolution?

In this respect, my status as an insider prevented people from divulging such information for fear of having it exposed to the wider community. Obviously, disseminating information about intrafamilial conflict to the community also implies that the disseminator, i.e., the indigenous anthropologist, has judged it negatively and is now taking an active role in censoring the behavior it bespeaks. While the question of exposure to the public can be bridged by trust and confidence in the researcher, the threat of judgment is harder to overcome. Being a participating family member implies, of course, subscribing to the cultural norms and values of the group and to the sanctions that follow a breach of valued behavior.

These considerations are different for a foreign anthropologist. As an outsider investigating family organization and interfamilial conflict,

she or he must gain the confidence of the people and be trusted not to expose family differences to the community. But outsider status does not imply shared cultural knowledge, and thus protects the outsider from applying the same moral judgments. The nonindigenous researcher is outside the system, and for this very reason people may not conceal family differences to the same degree as they would from a member of their own group. In collecting relevant data, the indigenous researcher is twice bound and must be able to overcome barriers to confidence and to potential value judgment.

Other social scientists have made similar observations. Aguilar, for example, highlights the constraints indigenous status may place on access to data (1981: 21), although, as he points out, other anthropologists claim the opposite (1981: 18). However, the Saudi Arabian case indicates that while confidence can be established, a morally neutral judgment is harder to demonstrate. An effective strategy is to be drawn into the same closure that allows sharing of such delicate information. In my case, the idiom of kinship and the ties of close friendships provided such a closure.

My general familiarity with these families had another irksome drawback. My informants presumed that I knew my own culture, and for a long time they either misinterpreted my questions as implying an unbecoming skepticism or failed to appreciate that I truly did not know what I had asked them to explain. This was especially true for knowledge of religious beliefs and rituals, which for me was a difficult area to explore. Such knowledge is essential to an adult Muslim, and any queries about it reveal a lapse in religious duties. Fed up with my questions, an older woman put it to me this way: "Are you not ashamed that you do not know how to pray at your age? What then did they teach you abroad?"

This revealed to me the cultural givens of the community and the cultural repertoire indispensable to membership in it. The best research strategy to circumvent this role was to openly admit my ignorance and to blame it all on my long absence abroad. Women and men patiently explained matters to me in a desire to resocialize me as a Muslim Arab woman. In fact, it was especially pleasing to the older women, often illiterate, to instruct me despite my higher formal education.

These considerations have been well described by Stephenson and Greer. They note that while familiarity with the culture under study can be a bonus, prior knowledge of the people studied provides no guaranteed advantage. The expectations people may have of the investigator could make it more difficult for her or him to break out of fixed patterns and thus serve to restrict the work at hand (1981: 129). The role that the community attributes to the researcher may inhibit other relationships and bias the researcher's thoughts. Moreover, the role ascribed by kinship to the indigenous anthropologist may forcefully draw that person into factionalism within the community and thereby limit the work that can be accomplished. Sometimes, such problems can be circumvented by conscious strategy. As Stephenson and Greer observe, "the researcher can mitigate the effects of already established roles by emphasizing some over others" 1981: 127)....

CRITICAL THINKING QUESTIONS

1. How did Altorki's sex and background influence her decisions about where and how to conduct her research on Arab society?
2. Field researchers must often balance the advantages and disadvantages of playing "insider" and "outsider" roles. How did being an insider both benefit and limit Altorki's research? What barriers did she have to overcome?
3. What strengths and weaknesses did Altorki have as an outsider? Is it possible for researchers who are outsiders to offer information about and valid insights into the societies they study? Explain your answer.

REFERENCES

Ablon, J. 1977. Field methods in working with middle class Americans: New issues of values, personality and reciprocity. *Human Organization*, 36(1): 69–72.

Aguilar, J. 1981. Insider research: An ethnography of a debate. In *Anthropologists at home in North America: Methods and issues in the study of one's own society*, ed. D. A. Messerschmidt. Cambridge: Cambridge University Press.

Altorki, S. 1986. *Women in Saudi Arabia: Ideology and behavior among the elite.* New York: Columbia University Press.

Lewis, D. 1973. Anthropology and colonialism. *Current Anthropology*, 14(12): 581–602.

Spradley, J. P., and D. W. McCurdy. 1972. *The cultural experience.* Chicago: Science Research Association.

Stephenson, J. B., and L. S. Greer. 1981. Ethnographers in their own cultures: Two Appalachian cases. *Human Organization*, 40(2): 123–30.

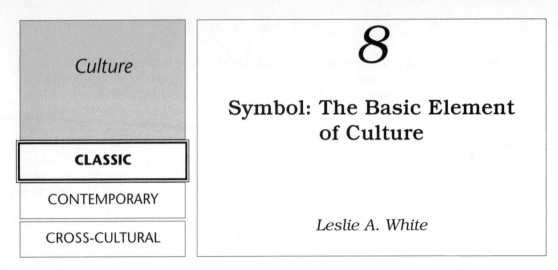

Culture	8
CLASSIC	**Symbol: The Basic Element of Culture**
CONTEMPORARY	
CROSS-CULTURAL	*Leslie A. White*

Leslie A. White, a noted anthropologist, argues in this selection that the key to human existence is the ability to use symbols. Although all animals are capable of complex behaviour, only humans depend on symbolic activity. This special power underlies our autonomy as the only creatures who live according to meanings we set for ourselves. Thus, symbols convert our animal species into humanity, in the process transforming social behaviour into true civilization.

…All human behavior originates in the use of symbols. It was the symbol which transformed our anthropoid ancestors into men and made them human. All civilizations have been generated, and are perpetuated, only by the use of symbols. It is the symbol which transforms an infant of *Homo sapiens* into a human being; deaf mutes who grow up without the use of symbols are not human beings. All human behavior consists of, or is dependent upon, the use of symbols. Human behavior is symbolic behavior; symbolic behavior is human behavior. The symbol is the universe of humanity.…

Source: From "The symbol: The origin and the basis of human behavior," in *The Science of Culture: A Study of Man and Civilization* by Leslie White. Copyright © 1949 Leslie White. Copyright renewed 1976 by Crocker National Bank. Reprinted by permission of Farrar, Straus & Giroux, LLC.

That there are numerous and impressive similarities between the behavior of man and that of ape is fairly obvious; it is quite possible that chimpanzees and gorillas in zoos have noted and appreciated them. Fairly apparent, too, are man's behavioral similarities to many other kinds of animals. Almost as obvious, but not easy to define, is a difference in behavior which distinguishes man from all other living creatures. I say "obvious" because it is quite apparent to the common man that the nonhuman animals with which he is familiar do not and cannot enter, and

participate in, the world in which he, as a human being, lives. It is impossible for a dog, horse, bird, or even an ape, to have *any* understanding of the meaning of the sign of the cross to a Christian, or of the fact that black (white among the Chinese) is the color of mourning. No chimpanzee or laboratory rat can appreciate the difference between Holy water and distilled water, or grasp the meaning of *Tuesday*, *3*, or *sin*. No animal save man can distinguish a cousin from an uncle, or a cross cousin from a parallel cousin. Only man can commit the crime of incest or adultery; only he can remember the Sabbath and keep it Holy. It is not, as we well know, that the lower animals can do these things but to a lesser degree than ourselves; they cannot perform these acts of appreciation and distinction at all. It is, as Descartes said long ago, "not only that the brutes have less Reason than man, but that they have none at all."…

A symbol may be defined as a thing the value or meaning of which is bestowed upon it by those who use it. I say "thing" because a symbol may have any kind of physical form; it may have the form of a material object, a color, a sound, an odor, a motion of an object, a taste.

The meaning, or value, of a symbol is in no instance derived from or determined by properties intrinsic in its physical form: The color appropriate to mourning may be yellow, green, or any other color; purple need not be the color of royalty; among the Manchu rulers of China it was yellow.… The meaning of symbols is derived from and determined by the organisms who use them; meaning is bestowed by human organisms upon physical things or events which thereupon become symbols. Symbols "have their signification," to use John Locke's phrase, "from the arbitrary imposition of men."

All symbols must have a physical form otherwise they could not enter our experience.… But the meaning of a symbol cannot be discovered by mere sensory examination of its physical form. One cannot tell by looking at an *x* in an algebraic equation what it stands for; one cannot ascertain with the ears alone the symbolic value of the phonetic compound *si*; one cannot tell merely by weighing a pig how much gold he will exchange for; one cannot tell from the wave length of a color whether it stands for courage or cowardice, "stop" or "go"; nor can one discover the spirit in a fetish by any amount of physical or chemical

examination. The meaning of a symbol can be grasped only by nonsensory, symbolic means.…

Thus Darwin says: "That which distinguishes man from the lower animals is not the understanding of articulate sounds, for as everyone knows, dogs understand many words and sentences."[1]…

The man differs from the dog—and all other creatures—in that *he can and does play an active role in determining what value the vocal stimulus is to have, and the dog cannot*. The dog does not and cannot play an active part in determining the value of the vocal stimulus. Whether he is to roll over or go fetch at a given stimulus, or whether the stimulus for roll over be one combination of sounds or another is a matter in which the dog has nothing whatever to "say." He plays a purely passive role and can do nothing else. He learns the meaning of a vocal command just as his salivary glands may learn to respond to the sound of a bell. But man plays an active role and thus becomes a creator: Let *x* equal three pounds of coal and it does equal three pounds of coal; let removal of the hat in a house of worship indicate respect and it becomes so. This creative faculty, that of freely, actively, and arbitrarily bestowing value upon things, is one of the most commonplace as well as *the* most important characteristic of man. Children employ it freely in their play: "Let's pretend that this rock is a wolf."…

All culture (civilization) depends upon the symbol. It was the exercise of the symbolic faculty that brought culture into existence, and it is the use of symbols that makes the perpetuation of culture possible. Without the symbol there would be no culture, and man would be merely an animal, not a human being.

Articulate speech is the most important form of symbolic expression. Remove speech from culture and what would remain? Let us see.

Without articulate speech we would have no *human* social organization. Families we might have, but this form of organization is not peculiar to man; it is not *per se*, human. But we would have no prohibitions of incest, no rules prescribing exogamy and endogamy, polygamy, monogamy.

How could marriage with a cross cousin be prescribed, marriage with a parallel cousin proscribed, without articulate speech? How could rules which prohibit plural mates possessed simultaneously but permit them if possessed one at a time, exist without speech?

Without speech we would have no political, economic, ecclesiastic, or military organization; no codes of etiquette or ethics; no laws; no science, theology, or literature; no games or music, except on an ape level. Rituals and ceremonial paraphernalia would be meaningless without articulate speech. Indeed, without articulate speech we would be all but toolless: We would have only the occasional and insignificant use of the tool such as we find today among the higher apes, for it was articulate speech that transformed the nonprogressive tool-using of the ape into the progressive, cumulative tool-using of man, the human being.

In short, without symbolic communication in some form, we would have no culture. "In the Word was the beginning" of culture—and its perpetuation also.

To be sure, with all his culture man is still an animal and strives for the same ends that all other living creatures strive for: the preservation of the individual and the perpetuation of the [species]. In concrete terms these ends are food, shelter from the elements, defense from enemies, health, and offspring. The fact that man strives for these ends just as all other animals do has, no doubt, led many to declare that there is "no fundamental difference between the behavior of man and of other creatures." But man does differ, not in *ends* but in *means*. Man's means are cultural means: Culture is simply the human animal's way of living. And, since these means, culture, are dependent upon a faculty possessed by man alone, the ability to use symbols, the difference between the behavior of man and of all other creatures is not merely great, but basic and fundamental.

The behavior of man is of two distinct kinds: symbolic and nonsymbolic. Man yawns, stretches, coughs, scratches himself, cries out in pain, shrinks with fear, "bristles" with anger, and so on. Nonsymbolic behavior of this sort is not peculiar to man; he shares it not only with the other primates but with many other animal species as well. But man communicates with his fellows with articulate speech, uses amulets, confesses sins, makes laws, observes codes of etiquette, explains his dreams, classifies his relatives in designated categories, and so on. This kind of behavior is unique; only man is capable of it; it is peculiar to man because it consists of, or is dependent upon, the use of symbols. The nonsymbolic behavior of *Homo sapiens* is the behavior of man the animal; the symbolic behavior is that of man the human being. It is the symbol which has transformed man from a mere animal to a human animal....

The infant of the species *Homo sapiens* becomes human only when and as he exercises his symbol faculty. Only through articulate speech—not necessarily vocal—can he enter the world of human beings and take part in their affairs. The questions asked earlier may be repeated now. How could a growing child know and appreciate such things as social organization, ethics, etiquette, ritual, science, religion, art, and games without symbolic communication? The answer is of course that he could know nothing of these things and have no appreciation of them at all....

Children who have been cut off from human intercourse for years by blindness and deafness but who have eventually effected communication with their fellows on a symbolic level are exceedingly illuminating. The case of Helen Keller is exceptionally instructive....

Helen Keller was rendered blind and deaf at an early age by illness. She grew up as a child without symbolic contact with anyone. Descriptions of her at the age of seven, the time at which her teacher, Miss Sullivan, came to her home, disclosed no *human* attributes of Helen's behavior at all. She was a headstrong, undisciplined, and unruly little animal.

Within a day or so after her arrival at the Keller home, Miss Sullivan taught Helen her first word, spelling it into her hand. But this word was merely a sign, not a symbol. A week later Helen knew several words but, as Miss Sullivan reports, she had "no idea how to use them or that everything has a name." Within three weeks Helen knew eighteen nouns and three verbs. But she was still on the level of signs; she still had no notion "that everything has a name."

Helen confused the word signs for "mug" and "water" because, apparently, both were associated with drinking. Miss Sullivan made a few attempts to clear up this confusion but without success. One morning, however, about a month after Miss Sullivan's arrival, the two went out to the pump in the garden. What happened then is best told in their own words:

I made Helen hold her mug under the spout while I pumped. As the cold water gushed forth, filling the mug, I spelled "w-a-t-e-r" into Helen's free hand. The word coming so close upon the sensation of cold water rushing over her hand seemed to startle her. She dropped the mug and stood as one transfixed. A new light came into her face. She spelled "water" several times. Then she dropped on the ground and asked for its name and pointed to the pump and the trellis, and suddenly turning round she asked for my name.... *In a few hours she had added thirty new words to her vocabulary.*

But these words were now more than mere signs as they are to a dog and as they had been to Helen up to then. They were *symbols*. Helen had at last grasped and turned the key that admitted her for the first time to a new universe: the world of human beings. Helen describes this marvelous experience herself:

We walked down the path to the well-house, attracted by the fragrance of the honeysuckle with which it was covered. Someone was drawing water and my teacher placed my hand under the spout. As the cool stream gushed over one hand she spelled into the other the word *water*, first slowly, then rapidly. I stood still, my whole attention fixed upon the motion of her fingers. Suddenly I felt a misty consciousness as of something forgotten—a thrill of returning thought; and *somehow the mystery of language was revealed to me.* I knew then that "w-a-t-e-r" meant the

wonderful cool something that was flowing over my hand. That living word awakened my soul, gave it light, hope, joy, set it free!

Helen was transformed on the instant by this experience. Miss Sullivan had managed to touch Helen's symbol mechanism and set it in motion. Helen, on her part, grasped the external world with this mechanism that had lain dormant and inert all these years, sealed in dark and silent isolation by eyes that could not see and ears that heard not. But now she had crossed the boundary and entered a new land. Henceforth the progress would be rapid.

"I left the well-house," Helen reports, "eager to learn. Everything had a name, and each name gave birth to a new thought. As we returned to the house every object which I touched seemed to quiver with life. That was because I saw everything with the strange new sight that had come to me."

Helen became humanized rapidly. "I see an improvement in Helen from day to day," Miss Sullivan wrote in her diary, "*almost from hour to hour*. Everything must have a name now.... She drops the signs and pantomime she used before as soon as she has words to supply their place.... We notice her face grows more expressive each day...."

A more eloquent and convincing account of the significance of symbols and of the great gulf between the human mind and that of minds without symbols could hardly be imagined.

The natural processes of biologic evolution brought into existence in man, and man alone, a new and distinctive ability: the ability to use symbols. The most important form of symbolic expression is articulate speech. Articulate speech means communication of ideas; communication means preservation—tradition—and preservation means accumulation and progress. The emergence of the faculty of symboling has resulted in the genesis of a new order of phenomena: an extra-somatic, cultural order. All civilizations are born of, and are perpetuated by, the use of symbols. A culture, or civilization, is but a particular kind of form which the biologic, life-perpetuating activities of a particular animal, man, assume.

Human behavior is symbolic behavior; if it is not symbolic, it is not human. The infant of the genus *Homo* becomes a human being only as he is introduced into and participates in that order of phenomena which is culture. And the key to this world and the means of participation in it is—the symbol.

CRITICAL THINKING QUESTIONS

1. Why does White argue that a someone who is deaf and mute and unable to communicate symbolically is not fully human? What opposing argument might be made? What position would White take in the pro-choice versus pro-life abortion controversy?
2. Because the reality we experience is based on a particular system of symbols, how do we tend to view members of other cultures? What special efforts are needed to overcome the tendency to treat people of other cultures as less worthy than we are?
3. How did gaining the capacity to use symbols transform Helen Keller? How did this ability alter her capacity for further learning?

NOTE

1. Charles Darwin, *The Descent of Man*, chap. 3, 1871.

9

Canada and the United States: A Comparative View

Seymour Martin Lipset

Culture

CLASSIC

CONTEMPORARY

CROSS-CULTURAL

Lipset suggests that Canadian and American values are fundamentally different and result from each nation's response to the American Revolution. For Lipset, this historical event continues to define each society's values along predictable and observable lines.

The 23 independent states plus the assorted colonies and autonomous commonwealths of North and South America provide a magnificent laboratory for comparative analysis, of which relatively few social scientists have taken advantage. The obvious advantage for such an analysis of common cultural and linguistic origin among twenty of those societies, the Latin-American republics and Puerto Rico, has not encouraged many systematic efforts to account for their differences. The Caribbean nations offer the diversity of being former colonies of six foreign powers and the similarity of having preponderantly Negro populations of slave descent, providing an interesting and as yet relatively untapped arena for comparative research. English-speaking Canada and the United States have long presented unused opportunities to analyse the variations in institutional arrangements in highly similar cultural contexts.

As an illustration of the value of such comparative analysis within the Americas, I would like to deal briefly with the two northernmost nations. There is little question that a comprehensive analysis of institutional patterns and groups in the United States and Canada would be enormously fruitful for sociologists. These two nations share a British legacy, frontier areas, immigrants of comparable origin from the same historic epoch, and comparable ecological conditions. Both have attained a high level of economic development and stable democratic political institutions.

Although the United States and English-speaking Canada probably resemble each other as much as any two nations on earth, the fact remains that various observers have noted a consistent pattern of differences between them.

Source: S. M. Lipset. (1964). Canada and the United States: A Comparative View. *The Canadian Review of Sociology and Anthropology*, 1, 173–185. Reprinted by permission of the Canadian Sociology and Anthropology Association.

To analyse the factors which underlie the perpetuation of small differences among nations is one of the more intriguing and difficult tasks in comparative study. What makes the Canadian more law-abiding? Why is there a much lower divorce rate in Canada? Why do fewer Canadians than Americans or Filipinos or Puerto Ricans attend universities? Why is the Canadian "quieter" in many of his behaviour traits than his American neighbour? Many of our assumptions about sources of national differences can be tested in this North American laboratory.

To a considerable extent comparative macroscopic sociology deals with polarity concepts when it seeks to compare core aspects of societies—gemeinschaft-gesellschaft, organic solidarity–mechanical solidarity, inner-directed versus other-directed, diffuseness-specificity, achievement-ascription, traditional-modern, and so forth. As I have attempted to demonstrate elsewhere, one particularly effective set of polarities for systematically classifying the central values of social systems is the pattern variables as originally set forth by Talcott Parsons.[1] Pattern variables are dichotomous categories of interaction in different structures. Those distinctions which seem particularly suitable for the analysis of Canada and the United States are achievement-ascription, universalism-particularism, self-orientation–collectivity-orientation, and equalitarianism-elitism. (The latter is not one of Parsons' distinctions, but one added here.) A society's value system may emphasize that a person in his orientation to others treats them in terms of their abilities and performances or in terms of inherited qualities (achievement-ascription); applies a general standard or responds to some personal attribute or relationship (universalism-particularism); perceives the separate needs of others or subordinates the individual's needs to the defined interests of the larger group (self-orientation–collectivity-orientation); and stresses that all persons must be respected because they are human beings or emphasizes the general superiority of those who hold elite positions (equalitarianism-elitism).[2]

The great mass of literature on these two democracies suggests the United States to be more achievement-oriented, universalistic, equalitarian, and self-oriented than Canada. Because the value differences of Canada and the United States are not great, the test of the utility of the comparative approach to the two North American societies depends upon specifying the special differences that *do* exist and identifying the historic issues and problems which sustain the near differences between them.

Though many factors in the history of these nations account for the variations between them, the following factors may be singled out: varying origins in their political systems and national identities, varying religious traditions, and varying frontier experiences. In general terms, the value orientations of Canada stem from a counter-revolutionary past, a need to differentiate itself from the United States, the influence of monarchical institutions, a dominant Anglican religious tradition, and a less individualistic and more governmentally controlled expansion of the Canadian than of the American frontier.

HOW DIFFERENT, HOW SIMILAR?

Both nations are largely urbanized, heavily industrialized, and politically stabilized. They share many of the same ecological and demographic conditions, approximately the same level of economic development, similar rates of upward and downward social mobility. To a very great extent Canada and the United States share the same values but, as Kaspar Naegele has pointed out, in Canada these values are held much more tentatively.[3] Both are new peoples and new states, but Canada's relationship to Britain has helped perpetuate in a North American nation the elements of a set of values having Old World origins and a conservative character. Thus, while equality and achievement, for example, are values emphasized in both American societies, in Canada the emphasis is somewhat less and therefore the contrast between the nations remains one of degree.

Perhaps no other value emphases are as paramount in American life as the twin values of equalitarianism and achievement. Both have been strongest in the school system where the principles of the "common school," and "equal opportunity for success" remain viable educational ideals. By contrast, in Canada education has held a more elitist and ascriptive import. These value differences are quantitatively indicated by a comparison of college enrolment figures. If we relate the number enrolled in institutions of higher learning to the size of the age cohort 20 to 24, we find that 30.2 per cent in the United States were attending universities in 1960, compared with 9.2 per cent in Canada.[4]

It has been suggested that elitist tendencies among the Canadians account for the education of a limited few at the college level. Some Canadian writers have pointed out that until very recently education in their country was designed to train an ecclesiastical and political *élite* much in the British tradition.[5] Canadian educators, unlike American, have shown resistance to the introduction into higher education of purely vocational training. Technical training has been viewed as corrupting the "aristocracy of intellect," those being educated for political and social leadership.

Status distinctions, which exist in the United States as in all nations, do not have as much legitimacy as in Canada. For example, the greater strength of elitist and ascriptive value emphases in Canada would seem to be reflected comparatively in the paternalistic organization of the family, in the reverence paid to the clergy by the laity, in the diffuse deference granted the old by the young, men by women, teachers by students, and politicians by the electorate.[6] From James Bryce to S. D. Clark, sociological observers have stressed the greater respect in Canada for political leaders than in the United States. The democratic ethos with its stress on populist values derivative from equalitarian emphases in the United States also "leads to certain impatience with legal process and, occasionally, to outright disrespect for the law."[7]

There are several indicators of the differences in Canadian and American respect for public authority. Where diffuse respect for public authority exists, we should expect to find greater reliance on informal social controls based on traditional obligations. One indicator of the relative strength of the informal normative mechanisms of social control as compared with the restrictive emphases of legal sanctions may be the extent to which a nation requires police protection. The data in Table 9.1 indicate that the ratio of police to population is more than one-third greater in the United States than in Canada. In 1961 only one police officer in Canada was killed by criminal action while on duty, compared to 37 police officers killed in the United States. By 1963, the latter figure had risen to 55 police officers in a single year while the former remained at one.[8] (The United States has about ten times the population of Canada.) The proportionately fewer lawyers in private practice in Canada (one for 1,630 people) as compared to the United States (one for 868) suggests the lesser propensity of Canadians to rely on the law even for civil matters.[9]

TABLE 9.1   Number and Rates of Police Protection in Canada and the United States

Country	Number of Police Personnel	Ratio per 100,000 Population
Canada (1961)	26,189	143.2
United States (1962)	360,000	193.8

Source: Canada: Dominion Bureau of Statistics, *Police Administration Statistics*, 1961, 18; United States: United States Department of Commerce, Bureau of the Census, *Statistical Abstracts of the United States*, 1963, 436.

The greater obedience paid to the law by Canadians may be reflected also in the rates of charges for criminal offences in the two countries. Though data on crime rates are far from amenable to accurate cross-national comparisons, both countries offer the same definition and report statistics for several major criminal offences. The data in Table 9.2 indicate that crime rates for particular offences are substantially higher in the United States than in Canada.

The greater respect for the law in Canada, as compared to the United States, may underlie the greater freedom of political dissent, and the lesser corruption.[10] In English-speaking Canada it is not at all unexpected that one writer has remarked that "Canadians are today perhaps more aware of the differences in their attitudes toward the law than anything else distinguishing them from Americans."[11]

The variation in the strength of the achievement and self-orientations in the United States and Canada may account for another political difference, the fact that "free enterprise" ideology, though accepted in Canada, has never been the source of as violent political conflicts there as in the United States. The greater respect for government and political leaders, derived in part from elitism and in part from the need dictated by special historic circumstances (see below) requiring that the central government intervene repeatedly in economic and local political matters to assure national survival, has inhibited the development of strong economic individualism as a dominant political virtue. Canada has been much more collectivity-oriented than the United States: proposals for medicare, support for large families, government intervention in the economy, and public ownership of major enterprises have encountered much less opposition north of the border than south of it. "The extreme economic individualism expressed by such slogans as 'the best government is the one that governs least' does not have such deep roots in Canada" as it has in the United States.[12] As one English writer notes:

One of the strange contradictions of Canada is that although it has never had anything resembling a Socialist Government in Ottawa, the list of its "nationalized" industries is almost as imposing as Britain's: more than half the railways; the principal airline; most of radio and television; the Atomic Energy Corporation and one of the biggest uranium producers; a big plastics industry; many of the power utilities [and telephone and telegraph]; and the entire liquor retailing business.[13]

TABLE 9.2   Adults Charged on Selected Indictable Offences, by Class of Offence, 1960, for Canada and the United States

	Canada Rate per 100,000		United States* Rate per 100,000	
	Number	Population	Number	Population
Burglary	8,267	46.4	137,800	126.7
Criminal homicide	207	1.16	7,956	7.3
Forgery and counterfeiting	1,158	6.4	25,244	23.2
Fraud and embezzlement	2,414	13.5	42,189	38.8
Theft-larceny	15,545	87.2	237,193	218.1

Source: Canada: Dominion Bureau of Statistics, *Canada Year Book*, 1962, 356; United States: United States Bureau of the Census, *Statistical Abstracts of the United States*, 1962, 152.

*The rate for the United States was computed from a total population base of 108,779,000; for Canada's rates, the population base used was 17,814,000. The weaker authority over local policing of the American federal government as compared to the Canadian makes it more difficult for the former to collect reliable crime statistics; hence the discrepancy in the proportion of the total population for whom data exist.

And as a Canadian points out, "it is interesting to note that at a time when the *laissez-faire* philosophy was prevailing in the rest of the Western World, there was no protest in Canada against government intervention and interference, not even from business circles."[14] Far from turning to McCarthyism or Goldwaterism, Canadian conservatives responded to years of political defeat by renaming their party the *Progressive* Conservatives.

The lower divorce rate in Canada, compared to that in the United States, presented in Table 9.3, may be viewed as another reflection of the strength of collectivity-orientation in the North. The semi-Establishment status of churches in Canada has lent strong support to traditional morality. It is more difficult to obtain a divorce in all the Canadian provinces than in almost all of the American states. S. D. Clark argues that "the institution of the family [in Canada] has found support in much the same set of conservative forces which have upheld the institutions of law and order."[15]

TABLE 9.3 Divorce Rates per 1,000 Marriages for Specified Years in Canada and the United States

Year	Canada	United States
1891	less than 1	60.0
1911	less than 1	93.4
1941	29.3	168.5
1951	41.0	230.4
1956	45.2	233.0
1960	53.5	257.3

Source: Canada: Dominion Bureau of Statistics, *Canada Year Book*, 1962, 209, 211; United States: United States Department of Commerce, Bureau of the Census, *Statistical Abstracts of the United States*, 1962, 52, and United Nations, Demographic Yearbook, 1960 (New York), 607. See also Lincoln Day, "Patterns of Divorce in Australia and the United States," *American Sociological Review*, XXIX, 4, 1964, 509–22, n.b. Table II.

The weakness in Canada of the sort of rugged individualism (self-orientation) and emphasis on achievement so characteristic of its neighbour to the south may be reflected also in the reluctance of Canadians to be over-optimistic, assertive, or experimentally inclined. Alistair Horne points out that Canadian caution manifests itself in several ways: "one is that Canadians take out more insurance per capita than any other race in the world. Another is that they buy considerably less on hire-purchase [installment plan] than the Americans…. The average Canadian is also cautious about his savings, favoring Government bonds and savings banks. Whereas over the years the American big investor has tended to take a risk on the future of Canada and invest heavily in more speculative Canadian enterprises, the wealthy Canadian cautiously puts his money into Standard Oil of New Jersey."[16] It has been more difficult for the Horatio Alger model of success to take hold in Canadian society where there is strong resistance to economic aggressiveness, social informality, and unabashed materialism. A leading Canadian historian, Arthur Lower, has argued that "Henry Ford was a figure who could hardly have been other than American. Canada did not provide a stage for such as he. Yet this was not on account of lack of opportunities here [in Canada] for accumulating wealth, but rather because that process called for more betting on the sure thing than was necessary across the border."[17] The muted effect of the achievement pattern in Canada is also observed by an English commentator: "Canadian 'quietness' extends also to the worlds of both business and politics…the rat race exists, of course; the North American urge to get ahead, to keep up with the Jones's, is all there, but in Canada, it seems to be kept to a healthier mean."[18]

The emphasis on achievement in the United States is strongly linked to universalism. For instance, in the United States there is a proclaimed need to treat everyone according to the same standard. This universalistic objective underlies the concept of the "melting pot" which holds that no one should be disqualified from full participation on the grounds of ethnic origin or other social distinctions. The melting-pot concept is achievement orientation applied to entire ethnic groups.[19] In contradistinction to the melting pot of the United States, Canadians speak of their society as a "mosaic," a concept which embodies in theory the "right to sustained collective individuality."[20] Vincent Massey, a former Governor General, has expressed the Canadian stress on the presentation of particularistic values:

> We have been successful in our manner of adjusting the relations of the varied communities making Canada their home. About one out of three speaks French as his mother tongue. He is no minority assimilated within a common Canadianism, but rather a partner sharing equally in the joint project of Confederation. Then there are the "new Canadians" of whom two million from Great Britain and from Europe have reached our shores since 1945.... We try to fit in the newcomers much as they are, as pieces in the Canadian mosaic.[21]

Canadian particularism has been demonstrated also in the requirement, in existence until recently, that Canadian passports indicated ethnic origin, for example, a Canadian of German origin even though the German origin may go back more than a century. The Canadian Census not only records religious data gathered from each individual, but also reports the national origins of every Canadian, except for Jews. Jews, regardless of country of paternal ancestry, are classified as such under both religion and national origin.

Canada's political party system has witnessed the rise of a number of "particularistic" third parties, various French-Canadian nationalist or separatist movements, plus the Progressives, Social Credit, and the Co-operative Commonwealth Federation (CCF). The latter, a socialist party, has recently joined with the Canadian Labour Congress to form the New Democratic Party which, based on trade unions, is the largest contemporary "third" party. This pattern of Canadian politics—that is, the continued presence of strong particularistic third parties—is consistent with the assumption that Canada is more particularistic (group-attribute conscious) than the seemingly more universalistic United States.

THE ROOTS OF TWO DEMOCRACIES

Many writers seeking to account for value differences between the United States and Canada suggest that they stem in large part from the revolutionary origins of the United States and the counter-revolutionary history of Canada, from two disparate founding ethos. The Loyalist *émigrés* from the American Revolution and Canada's subsequent and repeated fears of encroachment by the United States fostered the institutionalization of a counter-revolutionary or conservative ethos.[22] By contrast the core values of the United States are linked to the idealistic ideology which emerged during the Revolution and were codified in the Declaration of Independence and elaborated in the principles successfully pressed by the Jeffersonian Democrats in the first formative post-Revolutionary decades.

In Canada's counter-revolutionary beginnings we find the clue to the continuance of British ascriptive and elitist value patterns. The Canadian historian, Arthur Lower, has pointed out that "in its new wilderness home and its new aspect of British North Americanism, colonial Toryism made its second attempt to erect on American soil a copy of the English social edifice. From one point of view this is the most significant thing about the Loyalist movement; it withdrew a class concept of life from the south, moved it up north and gave it a second chance."[23] The anti-revolutionary and anti-American character of Canada's political and social development helped strengthen ethnic particularism. The English rulers of French Canada opposed assimilation as a means of resisting Americanization. Falconer indicates that "as late as 1822 Lord Dalhousie favored the French Canadians of the lower province as a make-weight against Americanizing tendencies which he discerned in Upper Canada."[24] Similarly, the unification of the British North American colonies was procured by Empire-oriented Canadian Conservatives who feared expansion by the United States across the border. The decision to provide

Canada with a much stronger central government than that of the United States was based on anti-American feeling.[25]

In distinction to Canada, the United States is a result of a successful Revolution and prolonged War of Independence organized around an ideology which proclaimed the validity of a specific system of equalitarian and universalistic social relations. Populist beliefs were at the root of early demands from the citizenry that the franchise be extended to everyone. Such populist tendencies lead to the "conviction that government should reflect the will of the people.... [It] breeds a suspicion of strong leaders...."[26] The populist demands on American politicians to be competent and deliver rewards to the people were as natural in the Revolutionary era as they are today.

In addition to the norms directly derived from or linked to political concepts, American values have fostered strong positive orientations to hard work and economic development. The emphasis on equality and achievement reinforced the belief that one could and should get ahead by continuous hard work, frugality, self-discipline, and individual initiative. The absence of an aristocratic model in the nation as a whole after the Revolution left the United States free to develop a socially as well as economically dominant class of merchants and manufacturers whose desire for wealth was uninhibited by norms denigrating hard work and the accumulation of capital.

The special character of American religion has been of considerable significance in the development of the related values of equalitarianism and achievement. Much of the United States was heir to a Calvinistic Puritanism, supplanted by Arminian religious beliefs by the early nineteenth century. According to the Arminian doctrines of free will, free grace, and unlimited hope for the conversion of all men, a devout man was an ambitious man and righteousness was to be rewarded both in this life and in the next.[27] It has been argued that this change occurred because "in a period when special privileges of individuals were being called into question or being

destroyed, there would naturally be less favor for that form of theology which was dominated by the doctrine of special election of a part of mankind, a growing favor for forms which seemed more distinctly to be based upon the idea of the natural equality of all men."[28]

The abolition of religious establishment in the United States which followed on the Revolution and the political successes of the Democrats fostered a strong commitment to voluntarism. This commitment, together with the early dominance of the dissenting anti-statist Methodist and Baptist denomination, meant that religion not only contributed to the economic ethos of the country, but reinforced the egalitarian and democratic social ethic as well.

The ecclesiastical character of Canadian religions greatly inhibited the development of achievement and equalitarian values. Religion in Canada, being related to the state, has provided that country with a control hierarchical mechanism rooted in tradition, which is wholly lacking in the history of the United States. Because of the strong tie between church and state in Canada, religious development there, in contrast to religious movements in the United States, has been less prone to fundamentalism and experimentalism.[29]

Some of the flavour of the social distinctions between Canada and the United States which reflect the greater strength of traditionalist and more conservative values in Canada may be traced also to a Canadian frontier fashioned in a spirit of cautious defensiveness against American expansionist tendencies. Rarely did Canada leave its borders unprotected or its frontier communities autonomous. Law and order in the form of the centrally controlled North West Mounted Police moved into frontier settlements before and along with the settlers. Not only did this establish respect for institutions of law and order, but the special constabulary force which followed on the heels of the frontiersman in Canada also meant that the Mounted Police dominated the frontier scene.[30] In addition, the presence of national government controls on the Canadian frontier weakened the development of excessive individualism.

In the United States on the other hand, frontier agricultural, ranching, and mining areas, unrelated for long periods to any central government or policing system, provided uncontrolled opportunities and encouraged settlers to use their own resources as they saw fit. The cowboy, the frontiersman, and even the vigilante, not the uniformed Mountie, are the heroes of western settlement in the United States.

THE PROBLEM OF CANADIAN IDENTITY

It is not unusual for Americans to refer to Canada as if it had no special independent national character; in fact, Americans frequently think of Canada as a northern extension of their own country, a place for fishing in the summer, hunting in the fall, and skiing in the winter. This attitude towards Canada is aptly described by Douglas LePan, a former Canadian diplomat, who once called upon a United States Senator to discuss the building of a bridge across one of the rivers along the border only to find the Senator oblivious to the need for a boundary at all. He reports that he was rather taken aback when the Senator blithely stated: "You know, I have never been able to see why there should be a border between us at all, our two countries so much alike." LePan, remarking on his feelings, reports that "the Senator, for all his generous good nature, seemed quite unaware that if the boundary were obliterated, the result in the case of a country of some 19 million people living alongside a much richer and more powerful country of almost 190 million people would not be some kind of union; it would be simply absorption."[31] The United States views Canada through a myopia of ethnocentrism in which "in a large country…people find it hard to understand that a much smaller country [in terms of population] is just as mature, viable, well-established, and distinct as the larger. Add to this the relatively small overt differences of culture and language, and one gets a situation in which the larger is inclined to assume that the smaller is an accident which will soon fade away. English Canadians seem to assume that French Canada will go away, that it won't always be French. Americans seem to imply, by many words and deeds, that Canada will not always be Canada."[32]

The existing Canadian national identity is in large part a reaction against a long-term supposed threat to its independence and traditions, against absorption into the American republic.[33] Loyalty to the British Crown has been one effective means of providing sentiment against American intervention and control. The social consequence of Canadian allegiance to a British monarch has been the acceptance of a national purpose based on the principle of "indivisibility of the Commonwealth." As Vincent Massey has put it:

There are some people in Canada with strong nationalist feelings who think that their end could only be achieved through a republican reform of government. There are, happily, very few persons with such views, and they are profoundly misguided in labouring under the delusion that as a republic we could remain an independent nation. We could not. The Crown-in-Parliament is the supreme symbol of our nationhoood and our greatest defense against absorption into a continental state.[34]

There is at present extensive American capital investment in Canada, high consumption of American goods, and a wide audience for American communication media. Many have rebelled against this American penetration into Canadian life.[35] The Canadian nationalist points to such facts as proof of "domination" by the United States.[36]

Nationalism in English-speaking Canada has undergone some curious changes from the time when it represented a left-wing, often pro–United States protest against the Imperial connection, and the closed economic-political-ecclesiastical system sustained by this connection. Today it is often the left-winger who is most anti-American and pro-British. The more traditional form of Canadian nationalism would seem to continue in the French-Canadian protest movements with their anti-English and anti-Establishment overtones directed at those within Canadian borders who represent English cultural, political, and economic domination. As English-speaking Canadians seek to isolate Canada from the United States, French Canadians look for means to assure the safety of their own culture, surrounded as it is by two hundred million English speakers. In a sense both English-speaking and French-speaking Canadians have similar objectives: to protect two minority cultures from being absorbed by more powerful neighbours.[37]

The problem of changing Canadian and American identities is clearly linked to the broad topic of this paper, the nature and sources of the differences in values and institutions of the two North American democracies. In the past decades the image of the United States has changed drastically. Relatively few in the rest of the world still see the United States as it sees itself, the champion of democratic and egalitarian ideals. To the leaders of the underdeveloped nations and the Communist world, and of many others, including Canada, the United States is now the leading defender of conservative traditional social forms, and is governed from within by an oligarchy of power-*élite*. Many Canadians now seek to defend the integrity of Canada against the United States by defining their own country as more humane, more equalitarian, more democratic, and more anti-imperialist than the United States. Many Canadians now view their country as more "leftist" or liberal in its institutions and international objectives than the United States. Whether this shift in the definition of the character of the United States, Canada's chief reference group, will also affect Canadian values remains to be seen. For anyone interested in Canada or in the general problem of how a nation maintains or changes its basic identity, the situation provides a fascinating question for observation and study.

CRITICAL THINKING QUESTIONS

1. Do you believe that Canadian and American values are different? What evidence do you have to support your position?

2. If Canadian and American values are different, do you feel they are becoming more or less alike over time?

3. Are the concepts of "mosaic" and "melting pot" still useful for defining national differences in how Canadians and Americans treat minority groups? What examples can you offer to support your position?

4. Given recent terrorist events (e.g., the 11 September 2001, attacks) do you agree with Lipset's assertion that the United States is *revolutionary* and Canada *counter-revolutionary*? Why or why not?

NOTES

1. S. M. Lipset, *The First New Nation* (New York, 1963), n.b. 248–73.

2. Because of the absence of clear indicators and the overlap with the equalitarian-elitist dimension, the specificity-diffuseness pattern variable is not discussed in this paper. For reasons of parsimony, I ignore Parsons' other pattern variables—affectivity, affectivity-neutrality and instrumental-consummatory distinctions. See Talcott Parsons, *The Social System* (Glencoe, Ill., 1951), 58–67. See also Parsons' recent elaboration of the pattern variables in "Pattern Variables Revisited," *American Sociological Review*, xxv, 4, 1960, 467–83.

3. Kaspar D. Naegele, "Canadian Society: Some Reflections," in Bernard Blishen, Frank Jones, Kaspar Naegele, and John Porter, eds., *Canadian Society* (Toronto, 1961), 27. This article is an excellent effort to summarize the general value system of Canada. Naegele argues convincingly that Canada on many matters lies "in the middle between America and England" and that it both accepts and rejects various aspects of the English and American models.

4. The educational data are calculated from materials in UNESCO, *Basic Facts and Figures*, 1960 (Paris, 1963); United Nations *Demographic Yearbook*, 1960 (New York, 1960); 2nd United Nations Compendium of Social Statistics (New York, 1963).

5. Dennis Wrong, *American and Canadian Viewpoints* (Washington, 1955), 20; Wilson Woodside, *The University Question* (Toronto, 1958), 21–2.

6. One of the more subtle signs of certain status distinctions was noted by A. R. M. Lower, *Canadians in the Making* (Toronto, 1958), 446, n. 11, who observed that, to his astonishment, in one midwestern university in the United States known to him, students and faculty actually share the same lavatory. Dennis Wrong points out that "with respect to the position of women, greater conservatism exists in Canada than in the United States...relatively fewer women have achieved prominence as public figures." *American and Canadian Viewpoints*, 11.

7. Wrong, *American and Canadian Viewpoints*, 36–7.

8. Canada: Dominion Bureau of Statistics, *Police Administration Statistics*, 1961, 19; United States: Federal Bureau of Investigation, *Uniform Crime Report*—1961, 20, 110, Table 36, and *Uniform Crime Report*—1963, 33–4. Dennis Wrong notes that "one finds less of the frequent American distrust of lawyers as 'shysters,' or as ambitious politicians, in English-speaking Canada and a greater sense of remoteness and majesty of the law." Wrong argues that the contrast between the popular-culture heroes of American and Canadian frontier expansion indicate the respect among Canadians for the law and the converse for Americans: "...in the United States it is the cowboy, a rugged individualist whose relationship to the forces of law and order was at least ambiguous, who has come to symbolize the frontier, while in Canada the 'mountie,' a policeman who clearly stands for law and order and traditional institutional authority, is the corresponding symbol of Canadian westward expansion." *Wrong, American and Canadian Viewpoints*, 38.

9. S. M. Lipset, *The First New Nation*, 264–65.

10. For example, S. D. Clark has pointed out that McCarthyism, a populist movement expressing political intolerance, is not likely to emerge in Canada. "In Canada it would be hard to conceive of a state of political freedom great enough to permit the kind of attacks upon responsible leaders of the government which have been carried out in the United States." S. D. Clark, "The Frontier and Democratic Theory," *Transactions of the Royal Society of Canada*, XLVIII, June 1954, 72. Regarding judiciary appointments, see Henry H. Bull, "The Career Prosecutor of Canada," *Journal of Criminal Law, Criminology, and Police Science*, LIII, 1962, 89–96.

11. Wrong, *American and Canadian Viewpoints*, 38.

12. Ibid., 29.

13. Alistair Horne, *Canada and the Canadians* (London, 1961), 248–49. It might be added that hotels are owned by the CNR, and now all provinces except Quebec have hospitalization insurance plans; Canada also has Family Allowances of $6 per month for every child under 10, and $8 for those between 10 and 15 (see Horne, 250).

14. Maurice Lamontagne, "The Role of Government," in G. P. Gilmour, ed., *Canada's Tomorrow* (Toronto, 1954), 125. See also James Byrce's discussion on Canada's resistance to the policy of *laissez-faire: Modern Democracies*, vol. I (London, 1921), 471.

15. S. D. Clark, "The Canadian Community," in G. Brown, ed., *Canada* (Berkeley, California, 1950), 386–87.

16. Horne, *Canada and the Canadians*, 245.

17. Lower, *Canadians in the Making*, 426. In Quebec, also, there has been notable Catholic resistance to aggressive business enterprise, due primarily to the strength of religious and traditionalist views. See Wrong, *American and Canadian Viewpoints*, 29–30.

18. A. Horne, *Canada and the Canadians*, 9.

19. "In the United States the Briton hastened to become a good American; in Canada he has been encouraged to remain a good Briton. Nor has any vigorous effort been made to assimilate continental European peoples in Canada, except through the public school; as with the French Canadians, the break of continental Europeans from their cultural past has tended to expose them to European influences." S. D. Clark, "The Canadian Community," 386–87.

20. Kaspar Naegele, "Canadian Society: Some Reflections," in Blishen et al., *Canadian Society*, 44.

21. Vincent Massey, *Canadians and Their Commonwealth* (Oxford, 1961), 5–6.

22. See J. M. S. Careless, *Canada: A Story of Challenge* (Cambridge, 1963), 111, 112, 113. Even since World War II, as Careless argues, Canada has remained more conservative than the United States: "In comparison with the rich and restless republic [the United States], Canada was a cautious and conservative country: cautious because her path was harder, more conservative because of her closer bonds with the Old World, and the stronger power of traditions brought from Britain and France" (p. 405).

23. Arthur Lower, *From Colony to Nation* (Toronto, 1946), 114.

24. Sir Robert Falconer, *The United States as a Neighbour* (Cambridge, 1925), 23.

25. W. L. Morton, "The Extension of the Franchise in Canada," *Report of the Canadian Historical Association* (Toronto, 1943), 76.

26. Wrong, *American and Canadian Viewpoints*, 31–2.

27. See Philip Schaff, *America: A Sketch of the Political, Social and Religious Character of the United States of North America* (New York, 1855), 259.

28. Franklin Jameson, *The American Revolution Considered as a Social Movement* (Princeton, 1926), 157.

29. S. D. Clark, *The Developing Canadian Community* (Toronto, 1962), 178. Clark remarks: "Political pressures have forced the community to come to the support of organized religion and such support has placed a definite limitation upon sectarian activity. With the collective weight of the community brought to bear upon them, the sects have been forced either to retreat behind a wall of isolation or build themselves into an integral part of the community, or else to seek denominational supports by aligning themselves with the state and with the traditional institutions of the community."

30. Clark, *The Developing Canadian Community*, 386–87.

31. Douglas V. LePan, "The Outlook for the Relationship," in John Sloan Dickey, ed., *The United States and Canada* (Englewood Cliffs, N.J., 1964), n.b. 155–56.

32. Everett C. Hughes, " A Sociologist's View," in John Sloan Dickey, *The United States and Canada*, 18.

33. "Canadian national life can almost be said to take its rise in the negative will to resist absorption in the American republic. It is largely about the United States as an object that the consciousness of Canadian national unity has grown up..." S. D. Clark, "The Importance of Anti-Americanism in Canadian National Feeling," in H. F. Angus, ed., *Canada and Her Great Neighbor* (Toronto, 1938), 243.

34. Vincent Massey, *Canadians and Their Commonwealth*, 19.

35. The concern of Canadians with the large amount of American investment is not merely based on the historical insecurity of Canada vis-à-vis its more powerful neighbour. It is interesting to note that Americans owned 44 per cent of Canadian manufacturing industry in 1959 and that the United States has more money invested in Canada than in any other area in the world. See Norman L. Nicholson, *Canada in the American* Community (Princeton, N.J., 1963), 119.

36. Harry G. Johnson, "Problems of Canadian Nationalism," *International Journal* (Summer, 1961), 238–49.

37. S. D. Clark, "Canada and Her Great Neighbour," paper presented at the meeting of the *American Sociological Association* (Montreal, Canada), September 3, 1964.

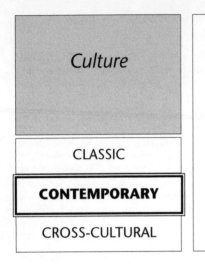

10

Culture

CLASSIC

CONTEMPORARY

CROSS-CULTURAL

Investigating Canadian and American Value Differences Through an Analysis of Media Portrayals of Native Issues

Bruce Ravelli

In this article, Bruce Ravelli tests Seymour Martin Lipset's predictions about the differences between Canadian and American values by analyzing each country's print media presentations of Native issues. The analysis fails to find support for many of Lipset's arguments but does reveal some interesting differences between media portrayals.

CULTURE

One of sociology's defining interests is the study of the relationship between the individual and society (Brym with Fox, 1989: 4). A critical component of this investigation is the attempt to understand the role culture plays in defining people's perception of their social environment.

The first section of this article reviews the defining characteristics of culture and many of the concepts that sociologists use to analyze and study it. The second section investigates Canadian and American cultural values, to determine whether they are different. The purpose of this article then is twofold: the first is to acquaint you with the sociological analyses of culture, and the second is to compare and contrast Canadian and American cultures in the hope of helping you appreciate what it means to be Canadian.

DEFINING ELEMENTS OF CANADIAN CULTURE

Before we begin our analysis, it is important to define what sociologists mean when they refer to a society's *culture* and *values*.[1] *Culture* is defined as a broad spectrum of beliefs, values, and material objects that help people define their way of life. For example, Canadians' appreciation of multiculturalism and support for universal health care are two defining attributes of what it means to be Canadian. *Values* are defined in more general terms and involve standards, principles, and broad guidelines as to how people should try to live their lives. For example, a Canadian value might be the belief that it is better to compete fairly and lose than to cheat and win. As we will see, Canadian culture and values are shaped by an intricate and diverse set of physical and social circumstances.

Physically, Canada is the second-largest country in the world (Countries of the World, 2002). Although it boasts a rich and diverse supply of natural resources, it also endures challenging, cold winters. Noted Canadian writer Margaret Atwood believes that Canada's adaptation to its harsh physical environment defines Canadian culture and, to some extent, what it means to be Canadian (Atwood, 1970: 33, cited in Lipset, 1986: 124). Socially, Canadian culture has been defined by the coexistence of, and at times conflict between, the English and the French (Hiller, 1996). The fact that 87 percent of the people living in Quebec identify French as their mother tongue suggests that on this criterion at least, Quebec is certainly *distinct* from the rest of the country (Statistics Canada, 2002). However, Quebec's distinctiveness does not rest solely on language; it also rests on its people's shared history, symbols, ideas, and perceptions of reality (McGuigan, 1997: 52). Clearly, Canada's physical and social environments have influenced its culture, but arguably, they have also influenced its values as well.

Canadian values were of primary interest to a 1991 federal commission called the Citizens' Forum on Canada's Future, or the Spicer Commission (CFCF, 1991: 35–45). In its report, the commission identified seven primary cultural values:

1. *Equality and fairness in a democratic society:* Canadians believe in treating all citizens equally (e.g., people with disabilities).
2. *Consultation and dialogue:* Canadians try to settle differences peacefully through discussion and collective problem solving (e.g., Aboriginal self-government initiatives).
3. *Importance of accommodation and tolerance:* Canadians attempt to accommodate the traditions and customs of various ethnic populations (e.g., Aboriginal peoples and the French in Quebec).
4. *Appreciation for diversity:* Canadians support diversity (e.g., regional, ethnic, linguistic, or cultural differences).
5. *Compassion and generosity:* Canadians value their social safety net as an attempt to provide a fair and accessible society for all (e.g., universal health care, pension plans, economic development programs, openness to refugees, and commitment to reducing regional disparities).
6. *Attachment to Canada's natural beauty:* Canadians believe they have a close connection to the natural environment and feel that governments should do more to protect it from pollution and other forms of industrialization (e.g., environmental protection legislation).
7. *Commitment to freedom, peace, and nonviolent change:* Canadians see themselves as peaceful people who maintain an active role in international peacekeeping (e.g., Canada's support for UN-sponsored peacekeeping initiatives) (Macionis, Jansson, & Benoit, 2002: 36).

Clearly, Canadian culture and values are a culmination of many physical and social forces, and studying Canadian–American differences fascinates Canadians (Lipset, 1999: 124; 1990: 53; 1986: 123) and Canadian sociologists in particular (Arnold & Tigert, 1974; Brym & Saint-Pierre, 1997; Clark, 1942; Clement, 1975; Hull, 1998: 4; Porter, 1965; Ravelli, 1994; Reitz & Breton, 1994). Seymour Martin Lipset (an American) has based his career on the study of what makes Canadians and Americans different (Tiryakian, 1991: 1040; Waller, 1990: 380). Lipset's book *Continental Divide* (1990) summarizes and consolidates his almost forty-five years of research on Canadian–American differences; in it he justifies his research, arguing that

Knowledge of Canada or the United States is the best way to gain insight into the other North American country. Nations can only be understood in comparative perspective. And the more similar the units being compared, the more possible it should be to isolate the factors responsible for differences between them. Looking intensively at Canada and the United States sheds light on both of them. (1990: xiii)

Canadians, historically at least, defined themselves by what they were not—Americans (Lipset: 1990: 53; 1986: 123). For Lipset, the primordial event that generated the different founding ideologies of Canada and the United States was the American Revolution (Lipset, 1990: 8; 1986: 114; 1985: 160; 1963: 239). The United States emerged from the Revolution as a manifestation of the classic liberal state, rejecting all ties to the throne, ascriptive elitism, noblesse oblige, and communitarianism (1986: 114). English Canada, however, fought to maintain its imperial ties through the explicit rejection of liberal revolutions (Lipset, 1986: 115). Canadian identity was not defined by a successful revolution, but instead a successful counterrevolution (Lipset, 1993: 161; 1990: 42). America, conversely, was defined by a rigid and stable ideology Lipset called Americanism (1950: 181).[2]

Lipset offers evidence that Canadian and American founding ideologies are present in each country's literature (1986: 123). For example, American literature concentrates on themes of winning, opportunism, and confidence, while Canadian writing focuses on defeat, difficult physical circumstances, and abandonment by Britain (Lipset, 1990: 1; 1986: 123). Lipset cites well-known Canadian novelist Margaret Atwood, who suggests that national symbols reveal a great deal about the cultural values a nation embraces. For Atwood, the defining symbol for America was "the frontier," which inspired images of vitality and unrealized potential, while the symbol of "survival" summed up Canada's national character: "Canadians are forever taking the national pulse like doctors at a sickbed; the aim is not to see whether the patient will live well but simply whether he will live at all" (Atwood, 1970: 33, cited in Lipset, 1986: 124). Lipset suggests that the symbols, attitudes, and values of a people do not exist in a vacuum; rather, social and political institutions embody and reinforce them (Lipset, 1990: xiv; 225; 1986: 114, 119; Baer, Grabb, & Johnston, 1990a: 693). For Lipset, values are the basis on which society builds its social and political structures, and different value systems manifest themselves in all social realms, not just literature. (Lipset, 1990: xiv)

Lipset argues that social structures reflect a society's values and beliefs (Baer, Grabb, & Johnston, 1990a: 693; Grabb & Curtis, 1988: 129, 137; Lipset, 1963: 210). To understand the importance of culture in determining a society's social structure, Lipset incorporated Talcott Parsons' (1952) pattern variables typology into his research (Lipset, 1963: 210). Parsons' pattern variables provide researchers with a method for classifying social values that is more sensitive to cultural variation than the older polar concepts of sociology, such as core–periphery, folk–urban, mechanical–organic, and primary–secondary.

Lipset's thesis of cross-national value differences suggests that Canadians are more elitist and ascriptive; appreciate racial and ethnic variation; and are more community-oriented than Americans. Although Lipset is a dominant figure in North American sociology,[3] his Canadian–American research has been the subject of much interest and debate. Various researchers (see Baer, Grabb, & Johnston, 1990a, 1990b, 1990c, 1993; Curtis, Grabb, & Baer, 1992; Grabb & Curtis, 1988) have attempted to test Lipset's thesis but have faced several difficulties, the most challenging being the following:

- Lipset's research is based on subjective data that are difficult, if not impossible, to test systematically.
- Lipset's pattern variables are at times contradictory and often suggest Canadian–American differences that are opposite to what his thesis would predict.
- Lipset fails to recognize how contemporary social change may influence Canadian and American values.
- Lipset's approach ignores regional variations.
- Lipset fails to offer alternative explanations for Canadian and American value differences.

In spite of such pointed criticism, sociologists generally agree that Lipset's fundamental proposition that Canadian and American cultural values are different, is sound (see Brym with Fox, 1989: 16–8; Clark, 1975: 26; Baer, Grabb, & Johnston, 1990a: 708; 1990c: 276; McGuigan, 1990: 127; Ogmundson & Fisher, 1994: 196). One area of investigation that may shed a contemporary light on Canadian–American differences is an analysis of each country's media, looking for evidence of national value differences.[4]

THE MEDIA'S INFLUENCE ON DEFINING CULTURE

In *Inventing Reality* (1993), Michael Parenti argues that although the media may not mould our every opinion, they do mould *opinion visibility* (Parenti, 1993: 23; see also Gamson & Modigliani, 1989: 3). In effect, journalists, reporters, and news anchors set our *perceptual agenda* (a view shared by Adams, 1978: 30; and Smith, 1992: 210). Parenti states, "The media may not always be able to tell us what to think, but they are strikingly successful in telling us what to think about" (1993: 23; see also Smith, 1992: 210). It is not so much that the media construct opinion; it is enough that they give legitimacy to certain views and illegitimacy to others (Parenti, 1993: 24). This ability has important implications for how the media define and reflect our perceptions and guide our interactions with the social world by effectively constructing news that reflects dominant values (Parenti, 1993: 69). Edward Herman and Noam Chomsky explore this issue in *Manufacturing Consent* (1988).

Herman and Chomsky suggest that the media intentionally create a social environment favourable to the dominant classes by *manufacturing consent* through the filtering of stories (Herman & Chomsky, 1988: xi, 2). This filtering takes two forms: (1) deciding not to cover a story and (2) presenting a story in such a way as to diffuse or bias its objective content. This filtering influences how people see and interpret the social world because it defines their reality. Herman and Chomsky suggest that the primary role of mainstream media is to ensure popular support for the economic, social, and political agenda of the privileged classes (1988: 298). Their *propaganda* model reveals many of the techniques media use to manufacture consent.

One way to find evidence for Canadian and American cultural differences would be to study a single social phenomenon common to both countries, such as how the media present a common and familiar issue. This brief review of how the media reflect and define a society's values reinforces the selection of media as one avenue by which to investigate Lipset's thesis of cross-national value differences in more detail. As argued by many, the media are becoming *the* conduit through which much of the world defines and reflects its cultural values (see Adams, 1978: 30; Campbell, 1999; Gamson & Modigliani, 1989: 3; Gitlin, 1980; Herman & Chomsky, 1988: 2; Parenti, 1993: 23; Smith, 1992: 210; Tetzlaff, 1992). My approach uses Native issues as a social phenomenon for study since both Canada and the United States have a long history of Native–White contact (see Berelson & Salter, 1946; Grenier, 1993; Singer, 1982; Skea, 1993).[5]

To test Lipset's thesis, I employed a fifty-year longitudinal study of Canadian and American media and how they presented Native issues. The medium I chose for the comparison was newsmagazines, in particular, *Maclean's* in Canada and *Newsweek* in the United States.[6] These newsmagazines were selected because they are regarded as journalistic leaders (see Roy, 1990: 510; van Driel & Richardson, 1988: 38) and attract national audiences. Thus, they should present national values to the extent that they exist. To test Lipset's theory, I formulated seven hypotheses flowing directly out of his four pattern variables (see Table 10.1).

My sampling frame included all articles referring to Natives in *Maclean's* and *Newsweek* from 1943 to 1993.[7] After locating the articles, I conducted a content analysis to determine whether there were systematic differences between each magazine's coverage of Native issues.

My analysis of *Maclean's* and *Newsweek* incorporated two complementary perspectives, the first a quantitative examination testing whether Lipset's value differences were evident (see Appendix A), and the second a qualitative exploration to detect themes speaking to Lipset's thesis (see Appendix B). The quantitative analysis provides a rudimentary statistical assessment of Lipset's thesis, while the qualitative has greater sensitivity to themes appearing in the articles pertaining to cultural differences. By coding the articles from both quantitative and qualitative perspectives, I hoped to gain a more complete appreciation of their portrayals of Native issues than would be possible by using either approach independently.

Results suggest little quantitative or qualitative support for Lipset's thesis of Canadian–American value differences (see Table 10.2).

TABLE 10.1 Testing Lipset's Thesis

Lipset's Pattern Variable	Hypothesis
Elitism–Egalitarianism	1a: Canadians will view political leaders more positively than Americans.
	1b: Canadians will view minority leaders more critically than Americans.
Ascription–Achievement	2a: Canadians will support government-sponsored redistribution programs more than Americans.
	2b: Canadians will criticize lawlessness more than Americans.
Particularism–Universalism	3: Canadians will support the mosaic perspective more than Americans.
Diffuseness–Specificity	4a: Canadians will support the collectivist perspective more than Americans.
	4b: Canadians will criticize minority challenges to the collective more than Americans.

TABLE 10.2 Qualitative/Quantitative Results Summary

Pattern Variable	Hypothesis	Quantitative Results	Qualitative Results
Elitism versus Egalitarianism	1a: Political Leadership	Reject	Reject
	1b: Native Leadership	Reject	Reject
Ascription versus Achievement	2a: Redistribution Programs	Reject	Support
	2b: Native Lawlessness	Reject	Reject
Particularism versus Universalism	3: Mosaic Perspective	Support	Support
Diffuseness versus Specificity	4a: Collectivist Perspective	Reject	Support
	4b: Native Challenge to the Collective	Reject	Reject

Table 10.2 illustrates that six of the seven quantitative results fail to support Lipset's thesis. Statistical differences existed between *Maclean's* and *Newsweek* and their presentation of Native issues, but the differences were often in the opposite direction of what Lipset's thesis would predict. Qualitative results were similar to the quantitative in that four of the seven hypotheses rejected Lipset's thesis.

1. Elitism versus Egalitarianism is **not supported** as all four tests reject Lipset's hypothesis.
2. Ascription versus Achievement is **not supported** as three of the four tests refute Lipset's hypothesis.
3. Particularism versus Universalism is **supported** as both tests support Lipset's hypothesis.
4. Diffuseness versus Specificity is **not supported** as three of the four tests reject Lipset's hypothesis.

My findings suggest that Canadian and American cultural values do vary, but not in a manner consistent with Lipset's pattern variable thesis. The only pattern variable to be supported was *Particularism versus Universalism*, which suggests that Canadians do recognize and encourage racial and ethnic diversity more than Americans. Although my research found little support for the three remaining pattern variables, it did find evidence to support the common experience that Canadian and American cultures differ (see Reitz & Breton, 1994).

CONCLUSION

After reading almost 400 magazine articles, on at least three separate occasions, I was struck by how often *Maclean's* presented Native issues with emotion and passion and how rarely any empathy was shown for the plight of American Natives in *Newsweek*. For me, this suggests one of the defining differences between Canadians and Americans—the belief in, and support for, multiculturalism. Granted, Canada's record of dealing with Native populations has often been strained and difficult; however, the dialogue between the parties has played a central and defining role in constructing our national value systems. This level of public debate and discussion between American Natives and the larger American society has not yet occurred. Canadians, however, must appreciate that just saying that Canada is a multicultural society is not enough. All people in Canada need to know, and be shown, that for Canadians, multiculturalism is not just an abstract philosophy; it is one of the defining elements of who we are as a people—multiculturalism means nothing if we don't practise what we preach.

APPENDIX A

My quantitative coding tested Lipset's overall thesis of cross-national value differences by comparing how each article portrayed issues that were relevant to Lipset's pattern variables. For example, when an article discussed political leaders (pertinent to hypothesis 1a), I noted every reference to political leaders as positive, negative, or indeterminate in the margins of the article. Positive statements about political leaders were coded as PL+, negative as PL–, and indeterminate as PL? When I completed the coding, I added the number of positive, negative, and indeterminate references and determined an overall coding for that article. That is, if the article had 15 positive statements about the political leader, 3 negative, and 0 indeterminate, I concluded that the article presented a supportive portrayal of political leaders. The statistical analyses were based on these comparisons. An obvious concern at this point is how confident I am that my coding of the articles was reliable.

Research is deemed reliable when the particular research technique, applied repeatedly to the same phenomenon, yields the same results (Babbie, 1995: 124). I am confident that my coding was reliable for two reasons. First, totals for the three possible codings (i.e., PL+, PL–, PL?) were never within 10 percent of each other. This indicates that the article's editorial bias (or lack of one) was readily apparent. Second, even though I was the only person coding the articles, I re-coded a 10 percent random sample of the articles (30 articles from *Maclean's*, 10 from *Newsweek*) six months after I completed my initial coding. The coefficient of reliability between the codings was 72 percent (coefficient of reliability = number of units in identical category/total number of units). Since coefficient values higher than 60 percent are deemed reliable (Jackson, 1995: 72), I am confident that my coding reliably reflects the articles' (and by extension, the newsmagazines') editorial bias.

APPENDIX B

Content analysis is a set of procedures used to study text (Weber, 1990: 9) and is appropriate for most forms of communication (Babbie, 1995: 307). Using content analysis I was able to investigate themes in media content that went beyond those explicitly stated. Robert Weber (1990: 9) suggests that content analysis of media can reveal international differences and uncover the cultural patterns of groups, institutions, or societies. The ability to look beyond the text makes content analysis well suited for a cross-national analysis of culture differences in media (Babbie, 1995: 315).

CRITICAL THINKING QUESTIONS

1. What are pattern-variables? Do you feel they are useful concepts when investigating national value differences? Why?
2. Mass media play an important role in our lives today. What are some ways in which mass media influence your world view that was not possible in your parents' generation?
3. An ongoing debate for researchers is whether media actively *define* our reality or alternatively, simply *reflect* it. Which do you feel is the more convincing position? Why?

NOTES

1. The majority of the following analysis is a consolidation of my doctoral dissertation, "Canadian–American Value Differences: Media Portrayals of Native Issues" (1997), unpublished manuscript, Department of Sociology, University of Victoria.
2. An ideology is a system of beliefs, common ideas, perceptions, and values held in common by members of a collective (Parsons, 1952: 349). Ideology can be thought of as the filter through which we interpret our social world.
3. As demonstrated, in part, by his election as president of the American Sociological Association for 1993–94.
4. My working assumption behind this analysis is the belief that media content will reflect national values to secure the widest audience possible and, by extension, the greatest financial benefit for its shareholders.
5. The term "Native" is used to describe the indigenous populations of North America. This terminology was selected over others (e.g., Aboriginal, First Nations, Amerindian, Indian) as it is the standard in contemporary literature (see Francis, 1992: 9).
6. Electronic media are too recent to study and print media lend themselves to better contextual analysis (see Neumann, Just, & Crigler, 1992: 58–9; Vipond, 1992: 27, 78, 128).
7. To locate the articles, I first consulted the Library of Congress subject heading Indians of North America. I then

manually searched the *Reader's Guide to Periodical Literature* (Reader's Guide) and the *Canadian Periodical Index* (CPI) for references to the subject title. This strategy located 296 articles in *Maclean's* and 96 in *Newsweek*.

REFERENCES

Adams, W. C. 1978. Network news research in perspective: A bibliographic essay. In *Television network news: Issues in content research*. Washington, DC: George Washington University Press.

Arnold, S. J., and D. J. Tigert. 1974. Canadians and Americans: A comparative analysis. *International Journal of Comparative Sociology*, 15: 68–83.

Atwood, M. 1970. *The journals of Suzanna Moodie: Poems*. Toronto: Oxford University Press.

Babbie, E. 1995. *The practice of social research*, 7th ed. Belmont, Calif.: Wadsworth Publishing Company.

Baer, D., E. Grabb, and W. A. Johnston. 1990a. *The values of Canadians and Americans: A critical analysis and reassessment*. Social Forces, 68(3): 693–713.

———. 1990b. Reassessing differences in Canadian and American values. In *Images of Canada: The sociological tradition*, eds. J. Curtis, and L. Tepperman, 86–97. Scarborough, Ont.: Prentice-Hall Canada.

———. 1990c. The values of Canadians and Americans: A rejoinder. *Social Forces*, 69(1): 273–77.

———. 1993. National character, regional culture, and the values of Canadians and Americans. *Canadian Review of Sociology and Anthropology*, 30(1): 13–36.

Berelson, B., and P. J. Salter. 1946. Majority and minority Americans: An analysis of magazine fiction. *Public Opinion Quarterly*, 10.

Brym, R. J., with B. J. Fox. 1989. *From culture to power: The sociology of English Canada*. Toronto: Oxford University Press.

Brym, R., and C. Saint-Pierre. 1997. Canada: Canadian sociology. *Contemporary Sociology*, 26(5): 543–46.

Campbell, K. 1999. Why we must protect Canadian culture from the U.S. juggernaut. In *Canadian communications: Issues in contemporary media culture*, eds. B. Szuchewycz, and J. Sloniowski, 214–18. Scarborough, Ont.: Prentice Hall/Allyn and Bacon Canada.

CFCF (Citizen's Forum on Canada's Future). 1991. *Report to the People and Government of Canada*. Ottawa: Supply and Services Canada.

Clark, S. D. 1942. *The social development of Canada: An introductory study with select documents*. Toronto: University of Toronto Press.

———. 1975. The post–Second World War Canadian society. *The Canadian Review of Sociology and Anthropology*, 12(1).

Clement, W. 1975. *The Canadian corporate elite: An analysis of economic power*. Toronto: McClelland and Stewart.

Countries of the World. 2002. Country statistics at a glance. [Online]. Available: **http://www.infoplease.com/ipa/A0762380.html**. Accessed July 17, 2002.

Curtis, J. E., E. G. Grabb, and D. E. Baer. 1992. Voluntary association membership in fifteen countries: A comparative analysis." *American Sociological Review*, 57(April): 139–52.

Francis, D. 1992. *The imaginary Indian: The image of the Indian in Canadian culture.* Vancouver: Arsenal Pulp Press.

Gamson, W. A., and A. Modigliani. 1989. Media discourse and public opinion on nuclear power: A constructionist approach." *American Journal of Sociology*, 95(1) : 1–37.

Gitlin, T. 1980. *The whole world is watching.* Berkeley: University of California Press.

Grabb, E. G., and J. E. Curtis. 1988. English Canadian–American differences in orientation toward social control and individual rights. *Sociological Focus*, 21(2): 127–40.

Grenier, M. 1993. Native Indians in the English-Canadian press: The case of the Oka Crisis. *Media, Culture and Society*, 16 (April): 313–36.

Herman, E. S., and N. Chomsky. 1988. *Manufacturing consent: The political economy of the mass media.* New York: Pantheon Books.

Hiller, H. 1996. *Canadian society: A macro analysis*, 3rd ed. Scarborough, Ont.: Prentice Hall Canada.

Hull, J. P. 1998. From many, two: A bibliographic history of Canadian–American relations. *American Studies International*, 36(2): 4–22.

Jackson, W. 1995. *Methods: Doing social research.* Scarborough, Ont.: Prentice Hall Canada.

Lipset, S. M. 1950. *Agrarian socialism: The Cooperative Commonwealth Federation in Saskatchewan.* Berkeley and Los Angeles: University of California Press.

———. 1963. *The first new nation: The United States in historical and comparative perspective.* New York: Basic Books.

———. 1985. Canada and the United States: The cultural dimension. *In Canada and the United States*, eds. C. F. Doran, and J. H. Sigler, 109–160. Englewood Cliffs, N.J.: Prentice Hall.

———. 1986. Historical traditions and national characteristics: A comparative analysis of Canada and the United States. *Canadian Journal of Sociology* 11(2): 113–55.

———. 1990. Continental divide: The values and institutions of the United States and Canada. New York: Routledge.

———. 1993. Revolution and counterrevolution: The United States and Canada. In *A passion for identity: An introduction to Canadian studies*, eds. D. Taras, B. Rasporich, and E. Mandel, 150–61. Scarborough, Ont.: Nelson Canada.

———. 1999. American union density in comparative perspective. *Contemporary Sociology*, 27(2): 123–25.

Macionis, J. J., S. M. Jansson, and C. M. Benoit. 2002. *Society: The basics*, 2nd Cdn ed. Toronto: Pearson Education Canada.

McGuigan, B. 1990. *The comparative sociology of Seymour Martin Lipset: An analysis and critique.* Unpublished master's thesis. University of Calgary.

———. 1997. Issues in Canadian culture. In *Issues in Canadian sociology*, 2nd ed., eds. M. Kanwar, and D. Swenson, 35–60. Dubuque, Iowa: Kendall/Hunt Publishing.

Neumann, R. W., M. R. Just, and A. N. Crigler. 1992. *Common knowledge: News and the construction of political meaning.* Chicago: University of Chicago Press.

Ogmundson, R. L., and L. Fisher. 1994. Beyond Lipset and his critics: An initial reformulation. *Canadian Review of Sociology and Anthropology*, 31(2): 196–99.

Parenti, M. 1993. *Inventing the politics of news media reality*, 2nd ed. New York: St. Martin's Press.

Parsons, T. 1952. *The social system.* London: Tavistock Publications Ltd.

Porter, J. 1965. *The vertical mosaic: An analysis of social class and power in Canada.* Toronto: University of Toronto Press.

Ravelli, B. 1994. Health care in the United States and Canada. In *The Sociological Outlook: A Text with Readings*, 4th ed., ed. R. Luhman, 467–68. San Diego: Collegiate Press.

Reitz, J. G., and R. Breton. 1994. *The illusion of difference: Realities of ethnicity in Canada and the United States.* Toronto: C.D. Howe Institute.

Roy, D. 1990. The U.S. print media and the conventional military balance in Europe. *Armed Forces & Society*, 16(4): 509–28.

Singer, B. D. 1982. Minorities in the media: A content analysis of Native Canadians in the daily press. *Canadian Review of Sociology and Anthropology*, 19(3): 348–59.

Skea, W. H. 1993. The Canadian newspaper industry's portrayal of the Oka Crisis. *Native Studies Review*, 9(1): 15–31.

Smith, R. L. 1992. Media networking: Toward a model for the global management of sociocultural change. In *Mass media effects across cultures*, eds. F. Korzenny et al., 201–28. Newbury Park, Calif.: Sage.

Statistics Canada. 2002. Population by home language, 2001 Census. [Online]. Available: **http://www.statcan.ca/ english/Pgdb/demo29b.htm.** Accessed July 16, 2002.

Tetzlaff, D. 1992. Popular culture and social control in late capitalism. *In Culture and power: A media, culture and society reader*, eds. P. Scannell, P. Schlesinger, and C. Sparks, 48–72. London: Sage.

Tiryakian, E. A. 1991. Book review of *Continental divide: The values and institutions of the United States and Canada* by S. M. Lipset. *American Journal of Sociology*, 96(4): 1040–42.

Van Driel, B., and Richardson, J. T. 1988. *Print media coverage of new religious movements: A longitudinal study.* Journal of Communication, 38(3): 37–61.

Vipond, M. 1992. *The mass media in Canada.* Toronto: James Lorimer & Company.

Waller, H. M. 1990. Book review of *Continental divide: The values and institutions of the United States and Canada* by S. M. Lipset. *Canadian Journal of Political Science*, 23: 380–81.

Weber, R. P. 1990. *Basic content analysis*, 2nd ed. Newbury Park, Calif.: Sage Publications.

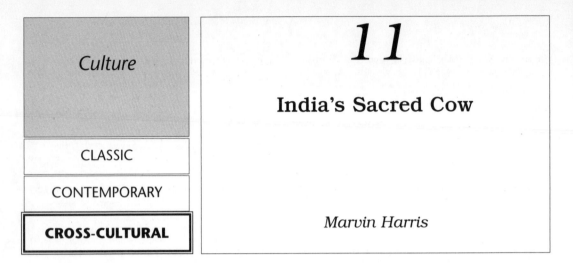

Culture

CLASSIC

CONTEMPORARY

CROSS-CULTURAL

11

India's Sacred Cow

Marvin Harris

Anthropologist Marvin Harris uses the cultural ecology approach to investigate how exotic and seemingly inexplicable cultural patterns may turn out to be strategies for human survival in a particular natural environment. In this article, he offers his own favourite example: Why do people in India—many of whom are hungry—refuse to eat beef from the "sacred cows" that are found most everywhere?

Whenever I get into discussions about the influence of practical and mundane factors on lifestyles, someone is sure to say, "But what about all those cows the hungry peasants in India refuse to eat?" The picture of a ragged farmer starving to death alongside a big fat cow conveys a reassuring sense of mystery to Western observers. In countless learned and popular allusions, it confirms our deepest conviction about how people with inscrutable Oriental minds ought to act. It is comforting to know—somewhat like "there will always be an England"—that in India spiritual values are more precious than life itself. And at the same time it makes us feel sad. How can we ever hope to understand people so different from ourselves? Westerners find the idea that there might be a practical explanation for Hindu love of the cow more upsetting than Hindus do.

Source: From *Cows, Pigs, Wars, and Witches: The Riddles of Culture* by Marvin Harris. Copyright © 1974 by Marvin Harris, Random House. Reprinted with permission of Random House, Inc.

The sacred cow—how else can I say it?—is one of our favorite sacred cows.

Hindus venerate cows because cows are the symbol of everything that is alive. As Mary is to Christians the mother of God, the cow to Hindus is the mother of life. So there is no greater sacrilege for a Hindu than killing a cow. Even the taking of human life lacks the symbolic meaning, the unutterable defilement, that is evoked by cow slaughter.

According to many experts, cow worship is the number one cause of India's hunger and poverty. Some Western-trained agronomists say that the taboo against cow slaughter is keeping one hundred million "useless" animals alive. They claim that cow worship lowers the efficiency of agriculture because the useless animals contribute neither milk nor meat while competing for croplands and foodstuff with useful animals and hungry human beings....

It does seem that there are enormous numbers of surplus, useless, and uneconomic animals, and that this situation is a direct result of irrational

Hindu doctrines. Tourists on their way through Delhi, Calcutta, Madras, Bombay, and other Indian cities are astonished at the liberties enjoyed by stray cattle. The animals wander through the streets, browse off the stalls in the market place, break into private gardens, defecate all over the sidewalks, and snarl traffic by pausing to chew their cuds in the middle of busy intersections. In the countryside, the cattle congregate on the shoulders of every highway and spend much of their time taking leisurely walks down the railroad tracks.

To Western observers familiar with modern industrial techniques of agriculture and stock raising, cow love seems senseless, even suicidal. The efficiency expert yearns to get his hands on all those useless animals and ship them off to a proper fate. And yet one finds certain inconsistencies in the condemnation of cow love. When I began to wonder if there might be a practical explanation for the sacred cow, I came across an intriguing government report. It said that India had too many cows but too few oxen. With so many cows around, how could there be a shortage of oxen? Oxen and male water buffalo are the principal source of traction for plowing India's fields. For each farm of ten acres or less, one pair of oxen or water buffalo is considered adequate. A little arithmetic shows that as far as plowing is concerned, there is indeed a shortage rather than a surplus of animals. India has 60 million farms, but only 80 million traction animals. If each farm had its quota of two oxen or two water buffalo, there ought to be 120 million traction animals—that is, 40 million more than are actually available.

The shortage may not be quite so bad since some farmers rent or borrow oxen from their neighbors. But the sharing of plow animals often proves impractical. Plowing must be coordinated with the monsoon rains, and by the time one farm has been plowed, the optimum moment for plowing another may already have passed. Also, after plowing is over, a farmer still needs his own pair of oxen to pull his oxcart, the mainstay of the bulk transport throughout rural India. Quite possibly private ownership of farms, livestock, plows, and oxcarts lowers the efficiency of Indian agriculture, but this, I soon realized, was not caused by cow love.

The shortage of draft animals is a terrible threat that hangs over most of India's peasant families. When an ox falls sick a poor farmer is in danger of losing his farm. If he has no replacement for it, he will have to borrow money at usurious rates. Millions of rural households have in fact lost all or part of their holdings and have gone into sharecropping or day labor as a result of such debts. Each year hundreds of thousands of destitute farmers end up migrating to the cities, which already teem with unemployed and homeless persons.

The Indian farmer who can't replace his sick or deceased ox is in much the same situation as an American farmer who can neither replace nor repair his broken tractor. But there is an important difference: Tractors are made by factories, but oxen are made by cows. A farmer who owns a cow owns a factory for making oxen. With or without cow love, this is a good reason for him not to be too anxious to sell his cow to the slaughterhouse. One also begins to see why Indian farmers might be willing to tolerate cows that give only 500 pounds of milk per year. If the main economic function of the zebu cow is to breed male traction animals, then there's no point in comparing her with specialized American dairy animals, whose main function is to produce milk. Still, the milk produced by zebu cows plays an important role in meeting the nutritional needs of many poor families. Even small amounts of milk products can improve the health of people who are forced to subsist on the edge of starvation.

Agriculture is part of a vast system of human and natural relationships. To judge isolated portions of this "ecosystem" in terms that are relevant to the conduct of American agribusiness leads to some very strange impressions. Cattle figure in the Indian ecosystem in ways that are easily overlooked or demeaned by observers from industrialized, high-energy societies. In the United States, chemicals have almost completely replaced animal manure as the principal source of farm fertilizer. American farmers stopped using manure when they began to plow with tractors rather than mules or horses. Since tractors excrete poisons rather than fertilizers, a commitment to large-scale machine farming is almost of necessity a commitment to the use of chemical fertilizers. And around the world today there has in fact grown up a vast integrated petrochemical-tractor-truck industrial complex that produces farm machinery, motorized transport, oil and gasoline, and chemical fertilizers and pesticides upon which new high-yield production techniques depend.

For better or worse, most of India's farmers cannot participate in this complex, not because they worship their cows, but because they can't afford to buy tractors. Like other underdeveloped nations, India can't build factories that are competitive with the facilities of the industrialized nations nor pay for large quantities of imported industrial products. To convert from animals and manure to tractors and petrochemicals would require the investment of incredible amounts of capital. Moreover, the inevitable effect of substituting costly machines for cheap animals is to reduce the number of people who can earn their living from agriculture and to force a corresponding increase in the size of the average farm. We know that the development of large-scale agribusiness in the United States has meant the virtual destruction of the small family farm. Less than 5 percent of U.S. families now live on farms, as compared with 60 percent about a hundred years ago. If agribusiness were to develop along similar lines in India, jobs and housing would soon have to be found for a quarter of a billion displaced peasants.

Since the suffering caused by unemployment and homelessness in India's cities is already intolerable, an additional massive build-up of the urban population can only lead to unprecedented upheavals and catastrophes.

With this alternative in view, it becomes easier to understand low-energy, small-scale, animal-based systems. As I have already pointed out, cows and oxen provide low-energy substitutes for tractors and tractor factories. They also should be credited with carrying out the functions of a petrochemical industry. India's cattle annually excrete about 700 million tons of recoverable manure. Approximately half of this total is used as fertilizer, while most of the remainder is burned to provide heat for cooking. The annual quantity of heat liberated by this dung, the Indian housewife's main cooking fuel, is the thermal equivalent of 27 million tons of kerosene, 35 million tons of coal, or 68 million tons of wood. Since India has only small reserves of oil and coal and is already the victim of extensive deforestation, none of these fuels can be considered practical substitutes for cow dung. The thought of dung in the kitchen may not appeal to the average American, but Indian women regard it as a superior cooking fuel because it is finely adjusted to their domestic routines. Most Indian dishes are prepared with clarified butter known as *ghee,* for which cow dung is the preferred source of heat since it burns with a clean, slow, long-lasting flame that doesn't scorch the food. This enables the Indian housewife to start cooking her meals and to leave them unattended for several hours while she takes care of the children, helps out in the fields, or performs other chores. American housewives achieve a similar effect through a complex set of electronic controls that come as expensive options on late-model stoves.

Cow dung has at least one other major function. Mixed with water and made into a paste, it is used as a household flooring material. Smeared over a dirt floor and left to harden into a smooth surface, it keeps the dust down and can be swept clean with a broom.

Because cattle droppings have so many useful properties, every bit of dung is carefully collected. Village small fry are given the task of following the family cow around and of bringing home its daily petrochemical output. In the cities, sweeper castes enjoy a monopoly on the dung deposited by strays and earn their living by selling it to housewives....

During droughts and famines, farmers are severely tempted to kill or sell their livestock. Those who succumb to this temptation seal their doom, even if they survive the drought, for when the rains come, they will be unable to plow their fields. I want to be even more emphatic: Massive slaughter of cattle under the duress of famine constitutes a much greater threat to aggregate welfare than any likely miscalculation by particular farmers concerning the usefulness of their animals during normal times. It seems probable that the sense of unutterable profanity elicited by cow slaughter has its roots in the excruciating contradiction between immediate needs and long-term conditions of survival. Cow love with its sacred symbols and holy doctrines protects the farmer against calculations that are "rational" only in the short term. To Western experts it looks as if "the Indian farmer would rather starve to death than eat his cow."... They don't realize that the farmer would rather eat his cow than starve, but that he will starve if he does eat it....

Do I mean to say that cow love has no effect whatsoever on...the agricultural system? No. What I am saying is that cow love is an active element in a complex, finely articulated material and cultural order. Cow love mobilizes the latent capacity of human beings to persevere in a low-energy ecosystem in which there is little room for waste or indolence. Cow love contributes to the adaptive resilience of the human population by preserving temporarily dry or barren but still useful animals; by discouraging the growth of an energy-expensive beef industry; by protecting cattle that fatten in the public domain or at landlords' expense; and by preserving the recovery potential of the cattle population during droughts and famines....

Wastefulness is more a characteristic of modern agribusiness than of traditional peasant economies....

Automobiles and airplanes are faster than oxcarts, but they do not use energy more efficiently. In fact, more calories go up in useless heat and smoke during a single day of traffic jams in the United States than is wasted by all the cows of India during an entire year. The comparison is even less favorable when we consider the fact that the stalled vehicles are burning up irreplaceable reserves of petroleum that it took the earth tens of millions of years to accumulate. If you want to see a real sacred cow, go out and look at the family car.

CRITICAL THINKING QUESTIONS

1. What evidence does Harris offer to support his argument that defining the cow as sacred is a necessary strategy for human survival in India?
2. If survival strategies make sense when we take a close look at them, why do they become so encased in elaborate cultural explanations?
3. Does India's recognition of the sacred cow help or hurt that nation's natural environment?
4. Following Harris's logic, can you think of reasons that people in some parts of the world (the Middle East, for instance) do not eat pork?

Society

12

CLASSIC

CONTEMPORARY

CROSS-CULTURAL

Manifesto of the Communist Party

Karl Marx and Friedrich Engels

Karl Marx, collaborating with Friedrich Engels, produced the "Manifesto" in 1848. This document is a well-known statement about the origin of social conflict in the process of material production. The ideas of Marx and Engels have been instrumental in shaping the political lives of more than one-fifth of the world's population, and, of course, they have been instrumental in the development of the social-conflict paradigm in sociology.

BOURGEOIS AND PROLETARIANS[1]

The history of all hitherto existing society[2] is the history of class struggles.

Freeman and slave, patrician and plebeian, lord and serf, guild-master[3] and journeyman, in a word, oppressor and oppressed, stood in constant opposition to one another, carried on an uninterrupted, now hidden, now open fight, a fight that each time ended, either in a revolutionary reconstitution of society at large, or in the common ruin of the contending classes.

In the earlier epochs of history, we find almost everywhere a complicated arrangement of society into various

Source: From *Manifesto of the Communist Party,* Part I, by Karl Marx and Friedrich Engels.

orders, a manifold gradation of social rank. In ancient Rome we have patricians, knights, plebeians, slaves; in the Middle Ages, feudal lords, vassals, guild-masters, journeymen, apprentices, serfs; in almost all of these classes, again, subordinate gradations.

The modern bourgeois society that has sprouted from the ruins of feudal society has not done away with class antagonisms. It has but established new classes, new conditions of oppression, new forms of struggle in place of the old ones.

Our epoch, the epoch of the bourgeoisie, possesses, however, this distinctive feature; it has simplified the class antagonisms. Society as a whole is more and more splitting up into two great hostile camps, into two great classes directly facing each other: Bourgeoisie and Proletariat.

From the serfs of the Middle Ages sprang the chartered burghers of the earliest towns. From these burgesses the first elements of the bourgeoisie were developed.

The discovery of America, the rounding of the Cape, opened up fresh ground for the rising bourgeoisie. The East Indian and Chinese markets, the [colonization] of America, trade with the colonies, the increase in the means of exchange, and in commodities generally, gave to commerce, to navigation, to industry, an impulse never before known, and thereby, to the revolutionary element in the tottering feudal society, a rapid development.

The feudal system of industry, under which industrial production was monopolized by close guilds, now no longer sufficed for the growing wants of the new markets. The manufacturing system took its place. The guild-masters were pushed on one side by the manufacturing middle class; division of labor between the different corporate guilds vanished in the face of division of labor in each single workshop.

Meantime the markets kept ever growing, the demand, ever rising. Even manufacture no longer sufficed. Thereupon, steam and machinery revolutionized industrial production. The place of manufacture was taken by the giant, Modern Industry, the place of the industrial middle class, by industrial millionaires, the leaders of whole industrial armies, the modern bourgeois.

Modern industry has established the world-market, for which the discovery of America paved the way. This market has given an immense development to commerce, to navigation, to communication by land. This development has, in its turn, reacted on the extension of industry; and in proportion as industry, commerce, navigation, railways extended, in the same proportion the bourgeoisie developed, increased its capital, and pushed into the background every class handed down from the Middle Ages.

We see, therefore, how the modern bourgeoisie is itself the product of a long course of development, of a series of revolutions in the modes of production and of exchange.

Each step in the development of the bourgeoisie was accompanied by a corresponding political advance of that class. An oppressed class under the sway of the feudal nobility, an armed and self-governing association in the mediæval commune,[4] here independent urban republic (as in Italy and Germany), there taxable "third estate" of the monarchy (as in France), afterwards, in the period of manufacture proper, serving either the semi-feudal or the absolute monarchy as a counterpoise against the nobility, and, in fact, cornerstone of the great monarchies in general, the bourgeoisie has at last, since the establishment of modern industry and of the world-market, conquered for itself, in the modern representative State, exclusive political sway. The executive of the modern State is but a committee for managing the common affairs of the whole bourgeoisie.

The bourgeoisie, historically, has played a most revolutionary part.

The bourgeoisie, wherever it has got the upper hand, has put an end to all feudal, patriarchal, idyllic relations. It has pitilessly torn asunder the motley feudal ties that bound man to his "natural superiors," and has left remaining no other nexus between man and man than naked self-interest, than callous "cash payment." It has drowned the most heavenly ecstasies of religious fervour, of chivalrous enthusiasm, of philistine sentimentalism, in the icy water of egotistical calculation. It has resolved personal worth into exchange value, and in place of the numberless indefeasible chartered freedoms, has set up that single, unconscionable freedom—Free Trade. In one word, for exploitation, veiled by religious and political illusions, it has substituted naked, shameless, direct, brutal exploitation.

The bourgeoisie has stripped of its halo every occupation hitherto honoured and looked up to with reverent awe. It has converted the physician, the lawyer, the priest, the poet, the man of science, into its paid [wage-laborers].

The bourgeoisie has torn away from the family its sentimental veil, and has reduced the family relation to a mere money relation.

The bourgeoisie has disclosed how it came to pass that the brutal display of vigour in the Middle Ages, which reactionists so much admire, found its fitting complement in the most slothful indolence. It has been the first to show what man's activity can bring about. It has accomplished wonders far surpassing Egyptian pyramids, Roman aqueducts, and Gothic cathedrals; it has conducted expeditions that put in the shade all former Exoduses of nations and crusades.

The bourgeoisie cannot exist without constantly revolutionizing the instruments of production, and thereby the relations of production, and with them the whole relations of society. Conservation of the old modes of production in unaltered form, was, on the contrary, the first condition of existence for all earlier industrial classes. Constant revolutionizing of production, uninterrupted disturbance of all social conditions, everlasting uncertainty and agitation distinguish the bourgeois epoch from all earlier ones. All fixed, fast-frozen relations, with their train of ancient and venerable prejudices and opinions, are swept away, all new-formed ones become antiquated before they can ossify. All that is solid melts into air, all that is holy is profaned, and man is at last compelled to face with sober senses, his real conditions of life, and his relations with his kind.

The need of a constantly expanding market for its products chases the bourgeoisie over the whole surface of the globe. It must nestle everywhere, settle everywhere, establish [connections] everywhere.

The bourgeoisie has through its exploitation of the world-market given a cosmopolitan character to production and consumption in every country. To the great chagrin of reactionists, it has drawn from under the feet of industry the national ground on which it stood. All old-established national industries have been destroyed or are daily being destroyed. They are dislodged by new industries, whose introduction becomes a life and death question for all civilised nations, by industries that no longer work up indigenous raw material, but raw material drawn from the remotest zones; industries whose products are consumed, not only at home, but in every quarter of the globe. In place of the old wants, satisfied by the productions of the country, we find new wants, requiring for their satisfaction the products of distant lands and climes. In place of the old local and national seclusion and self-sufficiency, we have intercourse in every direction, universal interdependence of nations. And as in material, so also in intellectual production. The intellectual creations of individual nations become common property. National one-sidedness and narrow-mindedness become more and more impossible, and from the numerous national and local literatures there arises a world-literature.

The bourgeoisie, by the rapid improvement of all instruments of production, by the immensely facilitated means of communication, draws all, even the most barbarian, nations into civilization. The cheap prices of its commodities are the heavy artillery with which it batters down all Chinese walls, with which it forces the barbarians' intensely obstinate hatred of foreigners to capitulate. It compels all nations, on pain of extinction, to adopt the bourgeois mode of production; it compels them to introduce what it calls civilization into their midst, i.e., to become bourgeois themselves. In a word, it creates a world after its own image.

The bourgeoisie has subjected the country to the rule of the towns. It has created enormous cities, has greatly increased the urban population as compared with the rural, and has thus rescued a considerable part of the population from the idiocy of rural life. Just as it has made the country dependent on the towns, so it has made barbarian and semi-barbarian countries dependent on the civilised ones, nations of peasants on nations of bourgeois, the East on the West.

The bourgeoisie keeps more and more doing away with the scattered state of the population, of the means of production, and of property. It has agglomerated population, centralized means of production, and has concentrated property in a few hands. The necessary consequence of this was political centralization. Independent, or but loosely connected provinces, with separate interests, laws, governments and systems of taxation, became lumped together in one nation, with one government, one code of laws, one national class-interest, one frontier and one customs-tariff.

The bourgeoisie, during its rule of scarce one hundred years, has created more massive and more colossal productive forces than have all preceding generations together. Subjection of Nature's forces to man, machinery, application of chemistry to industry and agriculture, steam-navigation, railways, electric telegraphs, clearing of whole continents for cultivation, canalization of rivers, whole populations conjured out of the ground—what earlier century had even a presentiment that such productive forces slumbered in the lap of social labor?

We see then: The means of production and of exchange on whose foundation the bourgeoisie built itself up were generated in feudal society. At a certain stage in the development of these means of production and of exchange, the conditions under which feudal society produced and exchanged, the feudal organization of agriculture and manufacturing industry, in one word, the feudal relations of property became no longer compatible with the already developed productive forces; they became so many fetters. They had to burst asunder; they were burst asunder.

Into their places stepped free competition, accompanied by a social and political constitution adapted to it, and by the economical and political sway of the bourgeois class.

A similar movement is going on before our own eyes. Modern bourgeois society with its relations of production, of exchange and of property, a society that has conjured up such gigantic means of production and of exchange is like the sorcerer who is no longer able to control the powers of the nether world whom he has called up by his spells. For many a decade past the history of industry and commerce is but the history of the revolt of modern productive forces against modern conditions of production, against the property relations that are the conditions for the existence of the bourgeoisie and of its rule. It is enough to mention the commercial crises that by their periodical return put on its trial, each time more threateningly, the existence of the entire bourgeois society. In these crises a great part not only of the existing products, but also of the previously created productive forces, are periodically destroyed. In these crises there breaks out an epidemic that, in all earlier epochs, would have seemed an absurdity—the epidemic of overproduction. Society suddenly finds itself put back into a state of momentary barbarism; it appears as if a famine, a universal war of devastation had cut off the supply of every means of subsistence; industry and commerce seem to be destroyed; and why? Because there is too much civilization, too much means of subsistence, too much industry, too much commerce. The productive forces at the disposal of society no longer tend to further the development of the conditions of bourgeois property; on the contrary, they have become too powerful for these conditions, by which they are fettered, and so [as] soon as they overcome these fetters, they bring disorder into the whole of bourgeois society, endanger the existence of bourgeois property. The conditions of bourgeois society are too narrow to comprise the wealth created by them. And how does the bourgeoisie get over these crises? On the one hand by enforced destruction of a mass of productive forces; on the other, by the conquest of new markets, and by the more thorough exploitation of the old ones. That is to say, by paving the way for more extensive and more destructive crises, and by diminishing the means whereby crises are prevented.

The weapons with which the bourgeoisie felled feudalism to the ground are now turned against the bourgeoisie itself.

But not only has the bourgeoisie forged the weapons that bring death to itself; it has also called into existence the men who are to wield those weapons—the modern working class— the proletarians.

In proportion as the bourgeoisie, i.e., capital, is developed, in the same proportion is the proletariat, the modern working class, developed, a class of laborers, who live only so long as they find work, and who find work only so long as their labor increases capital. These laborers, who must sell themselves piecemeal, are a commodity, like every other article of commerce, and are consequently exposed to all the vicissitudes of competition, to all the fluctuations of the market.

Owing to the extensive use of machinery and to division of labor, the work of the proletarians has lost all individual character, and, consequently, all charm for the workman. He becomes an appendage of the machine, and it is only the most simple, most monotonous and most easily acquired knack that is required of him. Hence, the cost of production of a workman is restricted, almost entirely, to the means of subsistence that he requires for his maintenance, and for the propagation of his race. But the price of a commodity, and also of labor, is equal to its cost of production. In proportion, therefore, as the repulsiveness of the work increases, the wage decreases. Nay more, in proportion as the use of machinery and division of labor increases, in the same proportion the burden of toil also increases, whether by prolongation of the working hours, by increase of the work enacted in a given time, or by increased speed of the machinery, etc.

Modern industry has converted the little workshop of the patriarchal master into the great factory of the industrial capitalist. Masses of laborers, crowded into the factory, are organized like soldiers. As privates of the industrial army they are placed under the command of a perfect hierarchy of officers and sergeants. Not only are they the slaves of the bourgeois class, and of the bourgeois State, they are daily and hourly enslaved by the machine, by the over-looker, and, above all,

by the individual bourgeois manufacturer himself. The more openly this despotism proclaims gain to be its end and aim, the more petty, the more hateful and the more embittering it is.

The less the skill and exertion or strength implied in manual labor, in other words, the more modern industry becomes developed, the more is the labor of men superseded by that of women. Differences of age and sex have no longer any distinctive social validity for the working class. All are instruments of labor, more or less expensive to use, according to their age and sex.

No sooner is the exploitation of the laborer by the manufacturer, so far, at an end, that he receives his wages in cash, than he is set upon by the other portions of the bourgeoisie, the landlord, the shopkeeper, the pawnbroker, etc.

The lower strata of the middle class—the small tradespeople, shopkeepers, and retired tradesmen generally, the handicraftsmen and peasants—all these sink gradually into the proletariat, partly because their diminutive capital does not suffice for the scale on which Modern Industry is carried on, and is swamped in the competition with the large capitalists, partly because their specialised skill is rendered worthless by new methods of production. Thus the proletariat is recruited from all classes of the population.

The proletariat goes through various stages of development. With its birth begins its struggle with the bourgeoisie. At first the contest is carried on by individual laborers, then by the workpeople of a factory, then by the operatives of one trade, in one locality, against the individual bourgeois who directly exploits them. They direct their attacks not against the bourgeois conditions of production, but against the instruments of production themselves; they destroy imported wares that compete with their labor, they smash to pieces machinery, they set factories ablaze, they seek to restore by force the vanished status of the workman of the Middle Ages.

At this stage the laborers still form an incoherent mass scattered over the whole country, and broken up by their mutual competition. If anywhere they unite to form more compact bodies, this is not yet the consequence of their own active union, but of the union of the bourgeoisie, which class, in order to attain its own political ends, is compelled to set the whole proletariat in motion, and is moreover yet, for a time, able to do so. At this stage, therefore, the proletarians do not fight their enemies, but the enemies of their enemies, the remnants of absolute monarchy, the landowners, the non-industrial bourgeois, the petty bourgeoisie. Thus the whole historical movement is concentrated in the hands of the bourgeoisie; every victory so obtained is a victory for the bourgeoisie.

But with the development of industry the proletariat not only increases in number, it becomes concentrated in greater masses, its strength grows, and it feels that strength more. The various interests and conditions of life within the ranks of the proletariat are more and more equalized, in proportion as machinery obliterates all distinctions of labor, and nearly everywhere reduces wages to the same low level. The growing competition among the bourgeois, and the resulting commercial crises, make the wages of the workers ever more fluctuating. The unceasing improvement of machinery, ever more rapidly developing, makes their livelihood more and more precarious; the collisions between individual workmen and individual bourgeois take more and more the character of collisions between two classes. Thereupon the workers begin to form combinations (Trades' Unions) against the bourgeois; they club together in order to keep up the rate of wages; they found permanent associations in order to make provision beforehand for these occasional revolts. Here and there the contest breaks out into riots.

Now and then the workers are victorious, but only for a time. The real fruit of their battles lies, not in the immediate result, but in the ever expanding union of the workers. This union is helped on by the improved means of communication that are created by modern industry, and that place the workers of different localities in contact with one another. It was just this contact that was needed to centralize the numerous local struggles, all of the same character, into one national struggle between classes. But every class struggle is a political struggle. And that union, to attain which the burghers of the Middle Ages, with their miserable highways, required centuries, the modern proletarians, thanks to railways, achieve in a few years.

This organization of the proletarians into a class, and consequently into a political party, is continually being upset again by the competition between the workers themselves. But it ever rises up again, stronger, firmer, mightier. It compels legislative recognition of particular interests of the workers, by taking advantage of the divisions among the bourgeoisie itself. Thus the ten-hours'-bill in England was carried.

Altogether collisions between the classes of the old society further, in many ways, the course of development of the proletariat. The bourgeoisie finds itself involved in a constant battle. At first with the aristocracy; later on, with those portions of the bourgeoisie itself, whose interests have become antagonistic to the progress of industry; at all times, with the bourgeoisie of foreign countries. In all these battles it sees itself compelled to appeal to the proletariat, to ask for its help, and thus, to drag it into the political arena. The bourgeoisie itself, therefore, supplies the proletariat with its own elements of political and general education, in other words, it furnishes the proletariat with weapons for fighting the bourgeoisie.

Further, as we have already seen, entire sections of the ruling classes are, by the advance of industry, precipitated into the proletariat, or are at least threatened in their conditions of existence. These also supply the proletariat with fresh elements of enlightenment and progress.

Finally, in times when the class-struggle nears the decisive hour, the process of dissolution going on within the ruling class, in fact within the whole range of old society, assumes such a violent, glaring character, that a small section of the ruling class cuts itself adrift, and joins the revolutionary class, the class that holds the future in its hands. Just as, therefore, at an earlier period, a section of the nobility went over to the bourgeoisie, so now a portion of the bourgeoisie goes over to the proletariat, and in particular, a portion of the bourgeois ideologists, who have raised themselves to the level of comprehending theoretically the historical movements as a whole.

Of all the classes that stand face to face with the bourgeoisie today, the proletariat alone is a really revolutionary class. The other classes decay and finally disappear in the face of modern industry; the proletariat is its special and essential product.

The lower-middle class, the small manufacturer, the shopkeeper, the artisan, the peasant, all these fight against the bourgeoisie, to save from extinction their existence as fractions of the middle class. They are therefore not revolutionary, but conservative. Nay more, they are reactionary, for they try to roll back the wheel of history. If by chance they are revolutionary, they are so, only in view of their impending transfer into the proletariat, they thus defend not their present, but their future interests, they desert their own standpoint to place themselves at that of the proletariat.

The "dangerous class," the social scum, that passively rotting mass thrown off by the lowest layers of old society, may, here and there, be swept into the movement by a proletarian revolution; its conditions of life, however, prepare it far more for the part of a bribed tool of reactionary intrigue.

In the conditions of the proletariat, those of old society at large are already virtually swamped. The proletarian is without property; his relation to his wife and children has no longer anything in common with the bourgeois family-relations; modern industrial labor, modern subjection to capital, the same in England as in France, in America as in Germany, has stripped him of every trace of national character. Law, morality, religion, are to him so many bourgeois prejudices, behind which lurk in ambush just as many bourgeois interests.

All the preceding classes that got the upper hand sought to fortify their already acquired status by subjecting at large to their conditions of appropriation. The proletarians cannot become masters of the productive forces of society, except by abolishing their own previous mode of appropriation, and thereby also every other previous mode of appropriation. They have nothing of their own to secure and to fortify; their mission is to destroy all previous securities for, and insurances of, individual property.

All previous historical movements were movements of minorities, or in the interest of minorities. The proletarian movement is the self-conscious, independent movement of the immense majority, in the interest of the immense majority. The proletariat, the lowest stratum of our present society, cannot stir, cannot raise itself up, without the whole superincumbent strata of official society being sprung into the air.

Though not in substance, yet in form, the struggle of the proletariat with the bourgeoisie is at first a national struggle. The proletariat of each country must, of course, first of all settle matters with its own bourgeoisie.

In depicting the most general phases of the development of the proletariat, we traced the more or less veiled civil war, raging within existing society, up to the point where that war breaks out into open revolution, and where the violent overthrow of the bourgeoisie, lays the foundation for the sway of the proletariat.

Hitherto, every form of society has been based, as we have already seen, on the antagonism of oppressing and oppressed classes. But in order to oppress a class, certain conditions must be assured to it under which it can, at least, continue its slavish existence. The serf, in the period of serfdom, raised himself to membership in the commune, just as the petty bourgeois, under the yoke of feudal absolutism, managed to develop into a bourgeois. The modern laborer, on the contrary, instead of rising with the progress of industry, sinks deeper and deeper below the conditions of existence of his own class. He becomes a pauper, and pauperism develops more rapidly than population and wealth. And here it becomes evident, that the bourgeoisie is unfit any longer to be the ruling class in society, and to impose its conditions of existence upon society as an overriding law. It is unfit to rule, because it is incompetent to assure an existence to its slave within his slavery, because it cannot help letting him sink into such a state, that it has to feed him, instead of being fed by him. Society can no longer live under this bourgeoisie, in other words, its existence is no longer compatible with society.

The essential condition for the existence, and for the sway of the bourgeois class, is the formation and augmentation of capital; the condition for capital is wage-labor. Wage-labor rests exclusively on competition between the laborers. The advance of industry, whose involuntary promoter is the bourgeoisie, replaces the isolation of the laborers, due to competition, by their involuntary combination, due to association. The development of modern industry, therefore, cuts from under its feet the very foundation on which the bourgeoisie produces and appropriates products. What the bourgeoisie therefore produces, above all, are its own grave-diggers. Its fall and the victory of the proletariat are equally inevitable.

CRITICAL THINKING QUESTIONS

1. What are the distinguishing factors of "class conflict"? How does class conflict differ from other kinds of conflict, as between individuals or nations?

2. Why do Marx and Engels argue that understanding society in the present requires investigating the society of the past?

3. On what grounds did Marx and Engels *praise* industrial capitalism? On what grounds did they *condemn* the system?

NOTES

1. By *bourgeoisie* is meant the class of modern capitalists, owners of the means of social production and employers of wage-labor. By *proletariat,* the class of modern wage-laborers who, having no means of production of their own, are reduced to selling their labor-power in order to live.

2. That is, all written history. In 1847, the prehistory of society, the social organization existing previous to recorded history, was all but unknown. Since then, Haxthausen discovered common ownership of land in Russia. Maurer proved it to be the social foundation from which all Teutonic races started in history, and by and by village communities were found to be, or to have been, the primitive form of society everywhere from India to Ireland. The inner organization of this primitive Communistic society was laid bare, in its typical form, by Morgan's crowning discovery of the true nature of the gens and its relation to the tribe. With the dissolution of these primæval communities society begins to be differentiated into separate and finally antagonistic classes. I have attempted to retrace this process of dissolution in "Der Ursprung der Familie, des Privateigenthums und des Staats," 2d ed. Stuttgart 1886.

3. Guild-master, that is, a full member of a guild, a master within, not a head of, a guild.

4. "Commune" was the name taken, in France, by the nascent towns even before they had conquered from their feudal lords and masters, local self-government and political rights as "the Third Estate." Generally speaking, for the economical development of the bourgeoisie, England is here taken as the typical country, [and] for its political development, France.

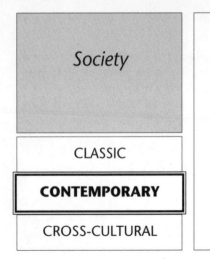

Society

CLASSIC

CONTEMPORARY

CROSS-CULTURAL

13

How the Internet Nurtures Long-Distance Relationships and Local Ties

John B. Horrigan

During the late 1990s, many sociologists, journalists, and other observers predicted that the Internet would replace close, offline relationships (including phone calls and snail mail) with impersonal and hurried e-mail messages. Many of the writers worried that university students would spend more time online than attending classes. In this selection, John B. Horrigan's analysis of a national study of 3002 adults, eighteen and older, challenges many of these pessimistic concerns. Despite gloomy predictions, little evidence exists that the Internet is creating alienation, isolation, and a disengagement from our interpersonal relationships.

BACKGROUND

When ARPANET, the Internet's precursor, came online in 1969, it did not have a foundational moment like the telephone's, where Alexander Graham Bell ordered his associate Thomas Watson: "Mr. Watson, come here, I want you." That sentence signaled an era of person-to-person communication over distance. In contrast, ARPANET connected a community. In its earliest days, it was a community of computer researchers at major U.S. universities working on similar problems.[1] Since then, the Internet's capability of allowing many-to-many communications has fostered communities of various sizes and sorts.

Source: "Online Communities: Networks that Nurture Long-Distance Relationships and Local Ties," by John B. Horrigan, Pew Internet & American Life Project, October 31, 2001. **http://www.pewinternet.org/reports/toc.asp?Report=47**, pp. 8–19 (accessed January 6, 2002). Reprinted with permission.

In this report, we assess the scope of online communities in the United States and the impact they are having on people's lives. We examine two kinds of communities—those that are primarily cyber-based with no inherently geographic aspect (i.e., online communities) and those in which people use the Internet to connect with groups based in the community in which they live (i.e., communities online). We call members of the former group *Cyber Groupies*. We define people who belong to any group having to do with their community as *Local Groupies* and analyze how they use the Internet to stay in touch with local affairs.

Our survey suggests that going online to connect with a group is a central part of Americans' Internet experience. More people have used the Internet to contact an online group than have done extremely popular activities, such as getting news online, health information, or financial information. More people participate in online groups than have bought things online. Fully 84 percent of all Internet users have contacted an online group at one time or another.... There are about 90 million of these [Cyber Groupies]. Some 79 percent of Cyber Groupies identify a particular group with which they remain in contact. Additionally, Cyber Groupies often surf to more than one online group; the average Cyber Groupie has gone to about four different online groups at one time or another. Finally, a quarter of Internet users (26 percent) say they have used email and the Web to contact or get information about groups and organizations in their communities. These Local Groupies number more than 28 million....

The broad appeal of online groups and the youthful tilt of the Cyber Groupie population—especially among those active in online groups and those who have recently joined them—suggests that the Internet is providing an important place for associational activity for some of the most enthusiastic online Americans. This is occurring in the context of widespread worry that Americans are less and less willing to get involved in community affairs and group activities. It is too soon to say that use of the Internet is

reversing that trend. But the findings from this survey indicate that group activity is flourishing online and it is a place that attracts Internet users to new group activity (see Table 13.1).

THE INTERNET, COMMUNITIES, AND THE VIRTUAL "THIRD PLACE"

Social scientists cite any number of indicators to illustrate that Americans' level of civic engagement is on the decline. Membership in organizations whose health may be seen as an indicator of strong community involvement—such as the Parent-Teachers Association (PTA)—has declined steadily over the past several decades.[2] The share of Americans voting in presidential elections has fallen since the 1960s, with voting rates in some local elections no higher than 10 percent.[3] There has been some evidence of growth in certain kinds of organization called *tertiary associations*, but that has not been encouraging to those who worry about the decline of community in America. Tertiary organizations have members spread throughout the country, rarely have local chapters, and usually ask members only for a membership

Table 13.1   The Cyber Groupie Population

Percent of Internet Users in Each Group Who Are...	Cyber Groupies (%)	Non-Cyber Groupies (%)
Sex		
Male	51	40
Female	49	60
Age		
18–24	17	15
25–34	24	19
35–44	28	22
45–54	20	16
55+	11	28
Internet Experience		
Online in last 6 months	8	19
Online for about 1 year	17	23
Online for 2–3 years	33	32
Online for > 3 years	41	25
Number of Observations	$N = 1,426$	$N = 271$

Source: Pew Internet & American Life Project, Jan.–Feb. 2001 Survey, Internet users, *n* = 1,697. Margin of error is ±3%.

check in exchange for an occasional newsletter. These organizations expect little of their members besides their financial contributions.

While concurring that community involvement is on the wane, many activists believe that the Internet might be able to reverse the trend. Since the early days of the Web, activists have argued that "community networks" could bind increasingly fragmented communities together and provide a voice for segments of society that have been traditionally ignored. Such electronic communities can lower the barriers to democratic participation. Advocates hope lower barriers, coupled with deliberate activities that bring all segments of a town or city into the planning process for building community networks, can help revive the community spirit in America.[4] These advocates do not argue that it is inevitable that the Internet will create community involvement, but rather that the Internet presents an opportunity to build community at a time when the need is great....[5]

The findings of the Pew Internet & American Life Project survey indicate that something positive is afoot with respect to the Internet and community life in the United States. People's use of the Internet to participate in organizations is not necessarily evidence of a revival of civic engagement, but it has clearly stimulated new associational activity. And, because they have been both physical and virtual, these group interactions are richer than those found in tertiary associations. This type of activity might be likened to what sociologist Ray Oldenburg calls the "third place"— the corner bar, café, or bookstore where people hang out to talk about things that are going on in their lives and neighborhood.[6]

Although Oldenburg very clearly has physical interaction in mind in talking about third places, the Internet has spurred in cyberspace the types of conversations that Oldenburg describes in third places. Our survey suggests that significant numbers of Cyber Groupies are enjoying new relationships because of their use of the Internet. One-quarter (27 percent) of Cyber Groupies say the Net has helped them connect with people of different

economic and ethnic backgrounds, and 37 percent say it has helped them connect with people of different generations. Whether through cyber groups or online groups grounded in local communities, the Internet's "virtual third places" appear to be building bridges among their participants.

Patterns of Chatter

If online communities are to have "third place" characteristics, chatter and connection have to be part of what is occurring when people access these groups. Our survey findings suggest that online communities, far from having passive members who lurk on email lists, are environments where a healthy number of members email others and interact on a frequent basis. This is especially true for nonlocal cyber communities, where a quarter of members routinely email other members (see Table 13.2).

Approximately 23 million Internet users engage in email exchanges with other online group members several times a week. This is about one-quarter of Cyber Groupies. While much of this emailing (76 percent) is simply seeking out membership news and group information, a lot of it (68 percent) involves discussing issues with other group members. And half (49 percent) of those who email an online group say that one of their main reasons to do so is to create or maintain personal relationships with members.

For Local Groupies—the 68 percent of Internet users who belong to a group with some connection to the community where they live— there are lower levels of online chatter, perhaps because physical proximity enables face-to-face communication. Three out of eight (38 percent) Local Groupies use email to communicate with others in the group. This is conspicuously less than the 60 percent who email nonlocal cyber groups. Of these local emailers, however, one-third (33 percent) send messages to other group members at least several times a week. This means that one in eight (13 percent) members of online groups that are close to home routinely

Table 13.2   How People Engage with Their Online Groups

Percent of Each Group Who Responded "Yes" to the Following Questions	*Cyber Groupies (%)*	*LocalGroupies (%)*
Did you belong to this group before you startedcommunicating with them online?	42	80
Do you ever send or receive email with this group or its members?	60	38
Do you email your online group at least several times a week?	43	33
Has communicating with this group through the Internet allowed you to get to know people you otherwise would not have met?	50	35
Does your group or association have a Web site?	73	40
Do you find your group's Web site very useful?	50	40
Number of observations	*N* = 1,350	*N* = 438

Source: Pew Internet & American Life Project, Jan.–Feb. 2001 Survey, Internet users, *n* = 1,697. Margin of error is ±3% for Cyber Groupies, ±5% for Local Groupies.

exchange e-communications with group members. That comes to 10 million Americans.

It is not surprising that Local Groupies report lower levels of engagement with their online groups than do Cyber Groupies. Local groups can rely on physical proximity for interaction, and members may be accustomed to face-to-face or telephone contact. Most Local Groupies belonged to their principal local organization *before* they started using the Internet to deal with the group, while most Cyber Groupies did not belong to their main group before they started communicating with it online. Still, one-third (35 percent) of Local Groupies who go to their group's Web site or email the group say that participation online with a favorite local group has enabled them to meet new people. This is not as striking as the 50 percent of Cyber Groupies who report they have gotten to know someone new through their online group, but it illustrates that even in local areas many people use the Internet to make new contacts....

Reasons for Chatter

Internet users were also asked about the reasons they communicate with their principal online group. They were most likely to report that [they] liked discussing issues with others and creating and maintaining personal relationships with other group members. About two-thirds say an important reason they email others in the group is to discuss issues affecting the group, while half say emailing the group helps build relationships with others in the group (see Table 13.3).

NEW COMMUNITY PARTICIPANTS

Net Joiners: The People Who Find Groups on the Internet, Then Become Members

In addition to fostering chatter, the Net is drawing people to groups they had not previously encountered. In part of our survey we asked

TABLE 13.3 Why People Communicate with
Online Groups

Reasons Cited by Cyber Groupies for Emailing an Online Group	Percent Who Say It Is Important
Getting general membership news and information	76
Getting involved with or learning more about group activities	71
Discussing issues with others	68
Creating or maintaining relationships with others in group	49

Source: Pew Internet & American Life Project,
Jan.–Feb.2001 Survey, Internet users, *n* = 1,697. Margin of
error is ±3%.

TABLE 13.4 Cyber Groupies: Online Groups Net
Joiners and Long-timers Go To

Which of These Groups Are You Most in Contact with through the Internet?	All Cyber Groupies (%)	Net Joiners* (%)	Long-timers** (%)
Trade association or professional group	21	17	30
A group for people who share a hobby or interest	17	23	18
A religious organization	6	3	8
A group of people who share your lifestyle	6	5	6
A fan group of a particular team	6	7	6
A sports team or league in which you participate	5	5	6
A group of people who share your beliefs	4	3	5
A local community group or association	4	2	5
A political group	3	2	4
A fan group of a TV show or entertainer	3	10	3
A support group for a medical condition orpersonal problem	2	6	2
Ethical or cultural group	1	2	2
Labor union	1	1	1
Not in contact with any particular group	16	16	9

Source: Pew Internet & American Life Project, Jan.–Feb.
2001 Survey, Internet users, *n* = 1,697.

*Those who join online groups after they encounter the
group online.

**Those who belong to a group before they use the Internet
to communicate with it.

Margin of error is ±3%.

respondents about the online group they most frequently contacted via the Internet. We enquired whether they belonged to this group before they started using the Internet. More than half of Cyber Groupies (56 percent) joined the group after having begun communicating with it over the Internet. For Local Groupies, 20 percent joined the group after they began communicating with it on the Internet. We call the people who have joined a group after being in contact via the Internet *Net Joiners*. The people who already belong to a group and who then begin to use the Internet to stay in touch with group activities are *Long-timers* (see Table 13.4).

Net Joiners generally have less Internet experience than Long-timers. Net Joiners are also more demographically diverse than long-time group members. Notably, the joiners as a group are younger than the overall Internet population. Although Net Joiners tend to report lower levels of frequent participation in online groups than Long-timers do, there does not appear to be pervasive lurking among either Net Joiners or Long-timers. Many people, when thinking about the group with which they are most involved, report they are active participants in online discussions.

Joiners of online groups, whether they are cyber groups or local groups, have different membership patterns. Net Joiners are drawn principally to hobbyist groups, whereas Long-timers are most involved with trade or professional associations. For Local Groupies, the differences are more striking. While most long-time members of local groups are most engaged with religious groups, Net Joiners are evenly split among religious groups and local youth groups. Moreover, they are interested in charitable groups, neighborhood associations, and local sports leagues.

On average, Cyber Groupies are most likely to say that a trade or professional group is the online group with which they most closely stay in touch (21 percent say this), followed closely by hobby groups (17 percent). In contrast, Net Joiners of online groups are most involved with a group having to do with a hobby.

Net Joiners are less involved with their online group than Long-time members if involvement is measured by email traffic with the group, new acquaintances made, and perceptions about over-all engagement with the group (see Table 13.5). About half of all Net Joiners (49 percent) say they use email to communicate with an online group, well below the three-quarters (78 percent) of Long-timers who use the Internet to keep in touch with it. However, when measured by frequency of email contact, Net Joiners are about as likely as the long-time members to send or receive an email from the group at least several times a week (41 percent for Net Joiners to 45 percent for Long-timers)....

Demographically, Net Joiners of cyber groups are more likely than Long-timers to be female, young, nonwhite, come from house-holds with modest incomes, and relatively new to the Internet. Net Joiners are far less likely to have a college education than Long-timers and twice as likely to be in a household making less than $30,000 per year. Net Joiners are also about twice as likely as Long-timers to be Hispanic or African American. Another notable difference comes in Internet experience. These figures suggest that not only are cyber groups a magnet for Internet users, they are especially attractive to novice Internet users....

Building New Ties; Strengthening Existing Ones

For millions, use of the Internet cuts two ways in their social lives: It helps them find others who share their passions or lifestyles or professional interests. It also helps them feel more connected to groups or people they already know.

TABLE 13.5 Profile of Net Joiners of Cyber Groups and Long-timers in Those Groups

	Net Joiners* (%)	Long-timers** (%)
Where they live		
Rural areas	20	17
Suburban areas	46	54
Urban areas	33	29
Sex		
Male	48	53
Female	52	47
Age		
18–24	21	13
25–34	25	24
35–44	27	29
44–55	16	23
55+	10	11
Race/ethnicity		
White, not Hispanic	74	81
Black, not Hispanic	10	6
Hispanic	11	5
Other	4	6
Education		
High school grad or less	39	25
Some college	30	27
College grad	30	48
Income		
Less than 30K	22	11
$30K–$50K	24	21
$50K–$75K	16	21
Over $75K	17	25
Don't know/refused	20	21
Internet experience		
Online in last 6 months	11	5
Online for about 1 year	18	5
Online for 2–3 years	33	34
Online for years	38	47
Number of observations	N = 798	N = 613

Source: Pew Internet & American Life Project, Jan.–Feb. 2001 Survey.

*Those who join online groups **after** they encounter the group online.

Those who belong to a group **before they use the Internet to communicate with it.

Table 13.6 summarizes Internet users' perspectives on how the Internet allows them to connect to different groups or people. The Internet's strongest bridges are relatively short ones. Online

Americans most often say that the Internet has helped them connect to groups with which they are already involved or people or groups with common interests. Still, between one-quarter and one-third of Cyber Groupies say that the Net has helped them connect with people of different ages, ethnic backgrounds, or economic backgrounds. One bridge that the Internet does not build, at least to a large extent, is to local community groups. Of the 26 percent of Cyber Groupies who say it has helped connect them to nearby groups, only 6 percent say it has helped them "a lot" in getting them in touch with locally based groups.

Cyber Groupies who are active in their online group are more likely to use the Net to connect with new people or groups. These users—defined as those who are members of a local and cyber group *and* who exchange emails with the group—are substantially more likely than other Internet users to report that the Internet has deepened their ties to groups to which they already belong or to local community groups. They enjoy a kind of "participatory premium."

The effect is also significant when survey respondents are asked how effective the Internet is in helping them find people who share their interests or beliefs. Those active in online communities are more likely than other Internet users to say their online activities help them connect with people of different backgrounds. Given that the pool of active online community members is among the Internet elite (the technology's early adopters who tend to be white, wealthy, and educated), this last finding is understandable. These users are accustomed to talking to those people and groups with whom they have conversed since they came to the Internet. On average, these people are not too different from each other.

As Internet adoption continues, it might be the case that new users are more likely to connect with people of different backgrounds than are their predecessors, in large part because the Internet population continues to diversify. Although difficult to predict, there is some evidence that this broadening of users' social universes might increase as the Internet population grows.

The behavior of Local Groupies who joined an online community after making initial Internet contact illustrates this hopeful scenario. They are a fairly diverse set of Internet veterans, with 11 percent Hispanics, 10 percent African Americans, and 68 percent whites. This subset of Local Groupies is much more likely than active online community members in general to connect with people of different backgrounds. When asked whether the Internet has helped them connect with people from different generations, 53 percent said it had "a lot" or "some"; 41 percent said it had helped them connect with people from different racial or ethnic backgrounds; and 46 percent said the Internet had helped them connect with people from different economic backgrounds. And more than half (54 percent) said the Internet helped them connect to groups in their local community.

TABLE 13.6 How the Internet Makes Them Feel Connected

Percent Who Say Their Use of the Internet Has Helped Them "a Lot" or "Some"	Cyber Groupies (%)	Very Active Online Community Members (%)
Find people or groups who share your interests	49	61
Become more involved with organizations or groups to which you already belong	40	58
Connect with people of different ages or generations	37	44
Find people or groups who share your beliefs	32	46
Connect with people from different economic backgrounds	29	37
Connect with people from different racial or ethnic backgrounds	27	33
Connect with groups based in your local community	26	43

Source: Pew Internet & American Life Project, Jan.–Feb. 2001 Survey, Internet users, $n = 1,697$. Margin of error is ±3%.

In each case, these numbers represent about a 10-point increase over the average for active online community members.

The Internet is also a bridge builder for younger members of online communities. Many in the 18-to-24 age bracket say the Internet helps them reach out to people of different ages, economic backgrounds, and ethnicity. Nearly half (47 percent) of online community members between the ages of 18 and 24 say the Internet helps "a lot" or "some" to connect them to people in different generations, 42 percent say it has helped make connections with people in different ethnic groups, and 36 percent say it has helped them reach out to people from different economic backgrounds. Twenty-nine percent say it has helped them connect to groups in their local community. For the young who are quite active in online communities (i.e., those who email their groups), the results are more striking. Fully 60 percent say the Internet has helped connect them to people of different generations, 54 percent say that about ethnic groups, and 44 percent say it has helped them connect to local community groups.

In sum, online communities are enabling Internet users to build bridges to other groups and people, while at the same time deepening ties to groups and ideas with which people are already involved. As the Internet draws people to online groups, it is notable that these people (i.e., Net Joiners among Local Groupies) are ethnically more diverse than other Internet users. As the Internet disseminates more broadly throughout the population, there are signs that online groups may facilitate new connections across ethnic, economic, and generational categories. It is also worth underscoring that young people seem especially interested in taking advantage of the Internet's bridge-building potential in online groups. As noted at the outset, there is pervasive worry that young people shy away from group activity and civic engagement. With the online groups drawing young people into groups involved with their local community, this survey suggests that the Internet may develop into an important new avenue for civic engagement among young people.

CRITICAL THINKING QUESTIONS

1. How do Cyber Groupies differ from Local Groupies? Do you belong to either group? If so, which one? Why? If you don't belong to either group, why not?
2. How do "patterns of chatter" on the Internet create a community of participants between the Net Joiners and the Long-timers? Does Horrigan's discussion of these groups characterize your Internet participation? Why or why not?
3. What are the weaknesses of the Internet in building local community groups among Cyber Groupies and Local Groupies? What are some of the strengths?

NOTES

1. Michael Hiltzik, *Dealers of Lightning: Xerox PARC and the Dawn of the Computer Age.* (New York: Harper Collins, 1999), p. 43.
2. Robert D. Putnam, *op. cit.* p. 57. About 47% of families with children belonged to the PTA in 1960, while 18% belonged in 1997.
3. *Ibid.* p. 31–3. Putnam points out that 63% of eligible voters cast ballots in 1960, and 49% did so in 1996.
4. Douglas Schuler, *New Community Networks: Wired for Change.* (New York: Addison-Wesley Publishing, 1996), p. 142.
5. Steven E. Miller, *Civilizing Cyberspace: Policy, Power, and the Information Superhighway.* (New York: Addison-Wesley Publishing, 1996), p. 329.
6. Ray Oldenburg, *The Great Good Place: Cafés, Coffee Shops, Bookstores, Bars, Hair Salons, and Other Hangouts at the Heart of a Community,* 3rd ed. (New York: Marlowe & Company, 1999). For Oldenburg, people's "first place" is home and "second place," work.

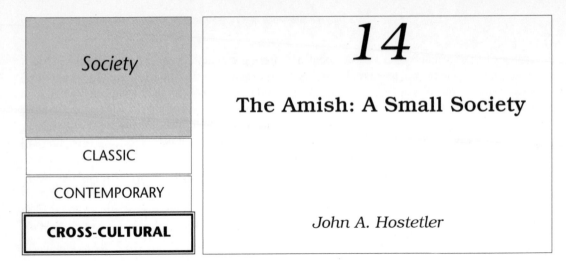

Society

CLASSIC

CONTEMPORARY

CROSS-CULTURAL

14

The Amish: A Small Society

John A. Hostetler

Some 100 000 Old Order Amish live in the rolling farmland of Pennsylvania, Ohio, Indiana, and southern Ontario. These descendants of sixteenth-century Germans, who fled persecution for their religious beliefs, constitute a distinctive "small society" that keeps the larger world at arm's length. This description of the Amish suggests the extent of cultural diversity within North America and raises questions about why some people would reject the "advantages" that many others take for granted.

Small communities, with their distinctive character—where life is stable and intensely human—are disappearing. Some have vanished from the face of the earth, others are dying slowly, but all have undergone changes as they have come into contact with an expanding machine civilization. The merging of diverse peoples into a common mass has produced tension among members of the minorities and the majority alike.

The Old Order Amish, who arrived on American shores in colonial times, have survived in the modern world in distinctive, viable, small communities. They have resisted the homogenization process more successfully than others. In planting and harvest time one can see their bearded men working the fields with horses and their women hanging out the laundry in neat rows to dry. Many American people have seen Amish families, with the men wearing broad-brimmed

black hats and the women in bonnets and long dresses, in railway depots or bus terminals. Although the Amish have lived with industrialized America for over two and a half centuries, they have moderated its influence on their personal lives, their families, communities, and their values.

The Amish are often perceived by other Americans to be relics of the past who live an austere, inflexible life dedicated to inconvenient and archaic customs. They are seen as renouncing both modern conveniences and the American dream of success and progress. But most people have no quarrel with the Amish for doing things the old-fashioned way. Their conscientious objection was tolerated in wartime, for after all, they are meticulous farmers who practice the virtues of work and thrift.

...The Amish are a church, a community, a spiritual union, a conservative branch of Christianity, a religion, a community whose members practice simple and austere living, a familistic entrepreneuring system, and an adaptive human community....

Source: From *Amish Society,* 3rd ed., by John A. Hostetler (Baltimore: The Johns Hopkins University Press, 1980), pp. 3–12. Reprinted with permission.

The Amish are in some ways a little commonwealth, for their members claim to be ruled by the law of love and redemption. The bonds that unite them are many. Their beliefs, however, do not permit them solely to occupy and defend a particular territory. They are highly sensitive in caring for their own. They will move to other lands when circumstances force them to do so.

Commonwealth implies a place, a province, which means any part of a national domain that geographically and socially is sufficiently unified to have a true consciousness of its unity. Its inhabitants feel comfortable with their own ideas and customs, and the "place" possesses a sense of distinction from other parts of the country. Members of a commonwealth are not foot-loose. They have a sense of productivity and accountability in a province where "the general welfare" is accepted as a day-to-day reality. Commonwealth has come to have an archaic meaning in today's world, because when groups and institutions become too large, the sense of commonwealth or the common good is lost. Thus it is little wonder that the most recent dictionaries of the American English language render the meaning of commonwealth as "obsolescent." In reality, the Amish are in part a commonwealth. There is, however, no provision for outcasts.

It may be argued that the Amish have retained elements of wholesome provincialism, a saving power to which the world in the future will need more and more to appeal. Provincialism need not turn to ancient narrowness and ignorance, confines from which many have sought to escape. A sense of province or commonwealth, with its cherished love of people and self-conscious dignity, is a necessary basis for relating to the wider world community. Respect for locality, place, custom, and local idealism can go a long way toward checking the monstrous growth of consolidation in the nation and thus help to save human freedom and individual dignity.

…Anthropologists, who have compared societies all over the world, have tended to call semi-isolated peoples "folk societies," "primitives," or merely "simple societies." These societies constitute an altogether different type in contrast to the industrialized, or so-called civilized, societies.

The "folk society," as conceptualized by Robert Redfield,[1] is a small, isolated, traditional, simple, homogeneous society in which oral communication and conventionalized ways are important factors in integrating the whole life. In such an ideal-type society, shared practical knowledge is more important than science, custom is valued more than critical knowledge, and associations are personal and emotional rather than abstract and categoric.

Folk societies are uncomfortable with the idea of change. Young people do what the old people did when they were young. Members communicate intimately with one another, not only by word of mouth but also through custom and symbols that reflect a strong sense of belonging to one another. A folk society is *Gemeinschaft*-like; there is a strong sense of "we-ness." Leadership is personal rather than institutionalized. There are no gross economic inequalities. Mutual aid is characteristic of the society's members. The goals of life are never stated as matters of doctrine, but neither are they questioned. They are implied by the acts that constitute living in a small society. Custom tends to become sacred. Behavior is strongly patterned, and acts as well as cultural objects are given symbolic meaning that is often pervasively religious. Religion is diffuse and all-pervasive. In the typical folk society, planting and harvesting are as sacred in their own ways as singing and praying.

The folk model lends itself well to understanding the tradition-directed character of Amish society. The heavy weight of tradition can scarcely be explained in any other way. The Amish, for example, have retained many of the customs and small-scale technologies that were common in rural society in the nineteenth century. Through a process of syncretism, Amish religious values have been fused with an earlier period of simple country living when everyone farmed with horses and on a scale where family members could work together. The Amish exist as a folk or "little" community in a rural subculture within the modern state.... The outsider who drives through an Amish settlement cannot help but recognize them by their clothing, farm homes, furnishings, fields, and other material traits of culture. Although they speak perfect English with outsiders, they speak a dialect of German among themselves.

Amish life is distinctive in that religion and custom blend into a way of life. The two are inseparable. The core values of the community are religious beliefs. Not only do the members worship a deity they understand through the revelation of Jesus Christ and the Bible, but their patterned behavior [also] has a religious dimension. A distinctive way of life permeates daily life, agriculture, and the application of energy to economic ends. Their beliefs determine their conceptions of the self, the universe, and man's place in it. The Amish world view recognizes a certain spiritual worth and dignity in the universe in its natural form. Religious considerations determine hours of work and the daily, weekly, seasonal, and yearly rituals associated with life experience. Occupation, the means and destinations of travel, and choice of friends and mate are determined by religious considerations. Religious and work attitudes are not far distant from each other. The universe includes the divine, and Amish society itself is considered divine insofar as the Amish recognize themselves as "a chosen people of God." The Amish do not seek to master nature or to work against the elements, but try to work with them. The affinity between Amish society and nature in the form of land, terrain, and vegetation is expressed in various degrees of intensity.

Religion is highly patterned, so one may properly speak of the Amish as a tradition-directed group. Though allusions to the Bible play an important role in determining their outlook on the world, and on life after death, these beliefs have been fused with several centuries of struggling to survive in community. Out of intense religious experience, societal conflict, and intimate agrarian experience, a mentality has developed that prefers the old rather than the new. While the principle seems to apply especially to religion, it has also become a charter for social behavior. "The old is the best, and the new is of the devil" has become a prevalent mode of thought. By living in closed communities where custom and a strong sense of togetherness prevail, the Amish have formed an integrated way of life and a folklike culture. Continuity of conformity and custom is assured and the needs of the individual from birth to death are met within an integrated and shared system of meanings. Oral tradition, custom, and conventionality play an important part in maintaining the group as a functioning whole. To the participant, religion and custom are inseparable. Commitment and culture are combined to produce a stable human existence.

...A century ago, hardly anyone knew the Amish existed. A half-century ago they were viewed as an obscure sect living by ridiculous customs, as stubborn people who resisted education and exploited the labor of their children. Today the Amish are the unwilling objects of a thriving tourist industry on the eastern seaboard. They are revered as hard-working, thrifty people with enormous agrarian stamina, and by some, as islands of sanity in a culture gripped by commercialism and technology run wild.

CRITICAL THINKING QUESTIONS

1. In what ways does this description of the Amish way of life make you think about your own way of life differently?
2. Why would the Amish reject technological advances that most members of our society hold to be invaluable?
3. What might the majority of the North American population learn from the Amish?

NOTE

1. Robert Redfield, "The Folk Society," *American Journal of Sociology,* 52 (Jan. 1947), 293–308. See also his book *The Little Community* (Chicago: University of Chicago Press, 1955).

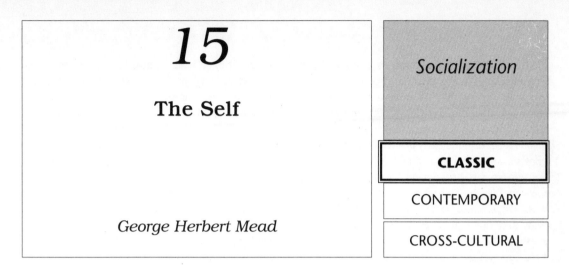

15

The Self

George Herbert Mead

Socialization

CLASSIC

CONTEMPORARY

CROSS-CULTURAL

The self is not the body but arises in social experience. Explaining this insight is perhaps George Herbert Mead's greatest contribution to sociology. Mead argues that the basic shape of our personalities is derived from the social groupings in which we live. Note, too, that even the qualities that distinguish each of us from others emerge only within a social community.

In our statement of the development of intelligence we have already suggested that the language process is essential for the development of the self. The self has a character which is different from that of the physiological organism proper. The self is something which has a development; it is not initially there, at birth, but arises in the process of social experience and activity, that is, develops in the given individual as a result of his relations to that process as a whole and to other individuals within that process....

Source: From *Mind, Self and Society: From the Standpoint of a Social Behaviorist* by George Herbert Mead (Chicago: University of Chicago Press, 1934), pp. 135–42, 144, 149–56, 158, 162–64. Copyright © 1934 by The University of Chicago Press. Reprinted with permission of the University of Chicago Press.

We can distinguish very definitely between the self and the body. The body can be there and can operate in a very intelligent fashion without there being a self involved in the experience. The self has the characteristic that it is an object to itself, and that characteristic distinguishes it from other objects and from the body. It is perfectly true that the eye can see the foot, but it does not see the body as a whole. We cannot see our backs; we can feel certain portions of them, if we are agile, but we cannot get an experience of our whole body. There are, of course, experiences which are somewhat vague and difficult of location, but the bodily experiences are for us organized about a self. The foot and hand belong to the self. We can see our feet, especially if we look at them from the wrong end of an opera glass, as strange things which we have difficulty in recognizing as our own. The parts of the body are quite distinguishable from the self. We can lose parts of the body without any serious invasion of the self. The mere ability to experience different parts of the body is not different from the experience of a table. The table presents a different feel from what the hand does when one hand feels another, but it is an experience of something with which we come definitely into contact. The body does not experience itself as a whole, in the sense in which the self in some way enters into the experience of the self.

It is the characteristic of the self as an object to itself that I want to bring out. This characteristic is represented in the word "self," which is a reflexive, and indicates that which can be both subject and object. This type of object is essentially different from other objects, and in the past it has been distinguished as conscious, a term which indicates an experience with, an experience of, one's self. It was assumed that consciousness in some way carried this capacity of being an object to itself. In giving a behavioristic statement of consciousness we have to look for some sort of experience in which the physical organism can become an object to itself.[1]

When one is running to get away from someone who is chasing him, he is entirely occupied in this action, and his experience may be swallowed up in the objects about him, so that he has, at the time being, no consciousness of self at all. We must be, of course, very completely occupied to have that take place, but we can, I think, recognize that sort of a possible experience in which the self does not enter. We can, perhaps, get some light on that situation through those experiences in which in very intense action there appear in the experience of the individual, back of this intense action, memories and anticipations. Tolstoi as an officer in the war gives an account of having pictures of his past experience in the midst of his most intense action. There are also the pictures that flash into a person's mind when he is drowning. In such instances there is a contrast between an experience that is absolutely wound up in outside activity in which the self as an object does not enter, and an activity of memory and imagination in which the self is the principal object. The self is then entirely distinguishable from an organism that is surrounded by things and acts with reference to things, including parts of its own body. These latter may be objects like other objects, but they are just objects out there in the field, and they do not involve a self that is an object to the organism. This is, I think, frequently overlooked. It is that fact which makes our anthropomorphic reconstructions of animal life so fallacious. How can an individual get outside himself (experientially) in such a way as to become an object to himself? This is the essential psychological problem of selfhood or of self-consciousness; and its solution is to be found by referring to the process of social conduct or activity in which the given person or individual is implicated. The apparatus of reason would not be complete unless it swept itself into its own analysis of the field of experience; or unless the individual brought himself into the same experiential field as that of the other individual selves in relation to whom he acts in any given social situation. Reason cannot become impersonal unless it takes an objective, noneffective attitude toward itself; otherwise we have just consciousness, not *self*-consciousness. And it is necessary to rational conduct that the individual should thus take an objective, impersonal attitude toward himself, that he should become an object to himself. For the individual organism is obviously an essential and important fact or constituent element of the empirical situation in which it acts; and without taking objective account of itself as such, it cannot act intelligently, or rationally.

The individual experiences himself as such, not directly, but only indirectly, from the particular standpoints of other individual members of the same social group, or from the generalized standpoint of the social group as a whole to which he belongs. For he enters his own experience as a self or individual, not directly or immediately, not by becoming a subject to himself, but only insofar as he first becomes an object to himself just as other individuals are objects to him or in his experience; and he becomes an object to himself only by taking the attitudes of other individuals toward himself within a social environment or context of experience and behavior in which both he and they are involved.

The importance of what we term "communication" lies in the fact that it provides a form of behavior in which the organism or the individual may become an object to himself. It is that sort of communication which we have been discussing—not communication in the sense of the cluck of the hen to the chickens, or the bark of a wolf to the pack, or the lowing of a cow, but communication in the sense of significant symbols, communication which is directed not only to others but also to the individual himself. So far as that type of communication is a part of behavior it at least introduces a self. Of course, one may hear without listening; one may see things that he does not realize; do things that he is not really aware of. But it is where one does respond to that which he addresses to another and where that response of his own becomes a part of his conduct, where he not only hears himself but responds to himself, talks and replies to himself as truly as the other person replies to him, that we have behavior in which the individuals become objects to themselves....

The self, as that which can be an object to itself, is essentially a social structure, and it arises in social experience. After a self has arisen, it in a certain sense provides for itself its social experiences, and so we can conceive of an absolutely solitary self. But it is impossible to conceive of a self arising outside of social experience. When it has arisen we can think of a person in solitary confinement for the rest of his life, but who still has himself as a companion, and is able to think and to converse with himself as he had communicated with others. That process to which I have just referred, of responding to one's self as another responds to it, taking part in one's own conversation with others, being

aware of what one is saying and using that awareness of what one is saying to determine what one is going to say thereafter—that is a process with which we are all familiar. We are continually following up our own address to other persons by an understanding of what we are saying, and using that understanding in the direction of our continued speech. We are finding out what we are going to say, what we are going to do, by saying and doing, and in the process we are continually controlling the process itself. In the conversation of gestures what we say calls out a certain response in another and that in turn changes our own action, so that we shift from what we started to do because of the reply the other makes. The conversation of gestures is the beginning of communication. The individual comes to carry on a conversation of gestures with himself. He says something, and that calls out a certain reply in himself which makes him change what he was going to say. One starts to say something, we will presume an unpleasant something, but when he starts to say it he realizes it is cruel. The effect on himself of what he is saying checks him; there is here a conversation of gestures between the individual and himself. We mean by significant speech that the action is one that affects the individual himself, and that the effect upon the individual himself is part of the intelligent carrying-out of the conversation with others. Now we, so to speak, amputate that social phase and dispense with it for the time being, so that one is talking to one's self as one would talk to another person.[2]

This process of abstraction cannot be carried on indefinitely. One inevitably seeks an audience, has to pour himself out to somebody. In reflective intelligence one thinks to act, and to act solely so that this action remains a part of a social process. Thinking becomes preparatory to social action. The very process of thinking is, of course, simply an inner conversation that goes on, but it is a conversation of gestures which in its completion implies the expression of that which one thinks to an audience. One separates the significance of what he is saying to others from the actual speech and gets it ready before saying it. He thinks it out, and perhaps writes it in the form of a book; but it is still a part of social intercourse in which one is addressing other persons and at the same time addressing one's self, and in which one controls the address to other persons by the response made to one's own gesture. That the person should be responding to himself is necessary to the self, and it is this sort of social conduct which provides behavior within which that self appears. I know of no other form of behavior than the linguistic in which the individual is an object to himself, and, so far as I can see, the individual is not a self in the reflexive sense unless he is an object to himself. It is this fact that gives a critical importance to communication, since this is a type of behavior in which the individual does so respond to himself.

We realize in everyday conduct and experience that an individual does not mean a great deal of what he is doing and saying. We frequently say that such an individual is not himself. We come away from an interview with a realization that we have left out important things, that there are parts of the self that did not get into what was said. What determines the amount of the self that gets into communication is the social experience itself. Of course, a good deal of the self does not need to get expression. We carry on a whole series of different relationships to different people. We are one thing to one man and another thing to another. There are parts of the self which exist only for the self in relationship to itself. We divide ourselves up in all sorts of different selves with reference to our acquaintances. We discuss politics with one and religion with another. There are all sorts of different selves answering to all sorts of different social reactions. It is the social process itself that is responsible for the appearance of the self; it is not there as a self apart from this type of experience.

A multiple personality is in a certain sense normal, as I have just pointed out....

The unity and structure of the complete self reflects the unity and structure of the social process as a whole; and each of the elementary selves of which it is composed reflects the unity and structure of one of the various aspects of that process in which the individual is implicated. In other words, the various elementary selves which constitute, or are organized into, a complete self are the various aspects of the structure of that complete self answering to the various aspects of the structure of the social process as a whole; the structure of the complete self is thus a reflection of the complete social process. The organization and unification of a social group is identical with the organization and unification of any one of the selves arising within the social process in which that group is engaged, or which it is carrying on.[3]

...Another set of background factors in the genesis of the self is represented in the activities of play and the game.... We find in children...imaginary companions which a good many children produce in their own experience. They organize in this way the responses which they call out in other persons and call out also in themselves. Of course, this playing with an imaginary companion is only a peculiarly interesting phase of ordinary play. Play in this sense, especially the stage which precedes the organized games, is a play at something. A child plays at being a mother, at being a teacher, at being a policeman; that is, it is taking different roles, as we say. We have something that suggests this in what we call the play of animals: A cat will play with her kittens, and dogs play with each other. Two dogs playing with each other will attack and defend, in a process which if carried through would amount to an actual fight. There is a combination of responses which checks the depth of the bite. But we do not have in such a situation the dogs taking a definite role in the sense that a child deliberately takes the role of another. This tendency on the part of children is what we are working with in the kindergarten where the roles which the children assume are made the basis for training. When a child does assume a role he has in himself the stimuli which call out that particular response or group of responses. He may, of course, run away when he is chased, as the dog does, or he may turn around and strike back just as the dog does in his play. But that is not the same as playing at something. Children get together to "play Indian." This means that the child has a certain set of stimuli that call out in itself the responses that they would call out in others, and which answer to an Indian. In the play period the child utilizes his own responses to these stimuli which he makes use of in building a self. The response which he has a tendency to make to these stimuli organizes them. He plays that he is, for instance, offering himself something, and he buys it; he gives a letter to himself and takes it away; he addresses himself as a parent, as a teacher; he arrests himself as a policeman. He has a set of stimuli which call out in himself the sort of responses they call out in others. He takes this group of responses and organizes them into a certain whole. Such is the simplest form of being another to one's self. It involves a temporal situation. The child says something in one character and responds in another character, and then his responding in another character is a stimulus to himself in the first character, and so the conversation goes on. A certain organized structure arises in him and in his other which replies to it, and these carry on the conversation of gestures between themselves.

If we contrast play with the situation in an organized game, we note the essential difference that the child who plays in a game must be ready to take the attitude of everyone else involved in that game, and that these different roles must have a definite relationship to each other. Taking a very simple game such as hide-and-seek, everyone with the exception of the one who is hiding is a person who is hunting. A child does not require more than the person who is hunted and the one who is hunting. If a child is playing in the first sense he just goes on playing, but there is no basic organization gained. In that early stage he passes from one to another just as a whim takes him. But in a game where a number of individuals are involved, then the child taking one role must be ready to take the role of everyone else. If

he gets in a ball game he must have the responses of each position involved in his own position. He must know what everyone else is going to do in order to carry out his own play. He has to take all of these roles. They do not all have to be present in consciousness at the same time, but at some moments he has to have three or four individuals present in his own attitude, such as the one who is going to throw the ball, the one who is going to catch it, and so on. These responses must be, in some degree, present in his own make-up. In the game, then, there is a set of responses of such others so organized that the attitude of one calls out the appropriate attitudes of the other.

This organization is put in the form of the rules of the game. Children take a great interest in rules. They make rules on the spot in order to help themselves out of difficulties. Part of the enjoyment of the game is to get these rules. Now, the rules are the set of responses which a particular attitude calls out. You can demand a certain response in others if you take a certain attitude. These responses are all in yourself as well. There you get an organized set of such responses as that to which I have referred, which is something more elaborate than the roles found in play. Here there is just a set of responses that follow on each other indefinitely. At such a stage we speak of a child as not yet having a fully developed self. The child responds in a fairly intelligent fashion to the immediate stimuli that come to him, but they are not organized. He does not organize his life as we would like to have him do, namely, as a whole. There is just a set of responses of the type of play. The child reacts to a certain stimulus, and the reaction is in himself that is called out in others, but he is not a whole self. In his game he has to have an organization of these roles; otherwise he cannot play the game. The game represents the passage in the life of the child from taking the role of others in play to the organized part that is essential to self-consciousness in the full sense of the term.

…The fundamental difference between the game and play is that in the former the child must have the attitude of all the others involved in that game. The attitudes of the other players which the participant assumes organize into a sort of unit, and it is that organization which controls the response of the individual. The illustration used was of a person playing baseball. Each one of his own acts is determined by his assumption of the action of the others who are playing the game. What he does is controlled by his being everyone else on that team, at least insofar as those attitudes affect his own particular response. We get then an "other" which is an organization of the attitudes of those involved in the same process.

The organized community or social group which gives to the individual his unity of self may be called "the generalized other." The attitude of the generalized other is the attitude of the whole community.[4] Thus, for example, in the case of such a social group as a ball team, the team is the generalized other insofar as it enters—as an organized process or social activity—into the experience of any one of the individual members of it.

If the given human individual is to develop a self in the fullest sense, it is not sufficient for him merely to take the attitudes of other human individuals toward himself and toward one another within the human social process, and to bring that social process as a whole into his individual experience merely in these terms: He must also, in the same way that he takes the attitudes of other individuals toward himself and toward one another, take their attitudes toward the various phases or aspects of the common social activity or set of social undertakings in which, as members of an organized society or social group, they are all engaged; and he must then, by generalizing these individual attitudes of that organized society or social group itself, as a whole, act toward different social projects which at any given time it is carrying out, or toward the various larger phases of the general social process which constitutes its life and of which these projects are specific manifestations. This getting of the broad activities of any given social whole or organized society as such within the experiential field of any one of the individuals involved or included in that whole is,

in other words, the essential basis and prerequisite of the fullest development of that individual's self: Only insofar as he takes the attitudes of the organized social group to which he belongs toward the organized, cooperative social activity or set of such activities in which that group as such is engaged, does he develop a complete self or possess the sort of complete self he has developed. And on the other hand, the complex cooperative processes and activities and institutional functionings of organized human society are also possible only insofar as every individual involved in them or belonging to that society can take the general attitudes of all other such individuals with reference to these processes and activities and institutional functionings, and to the organized social whole of experiential relations and interactions thereby constituted—and can direct his own behavior accordingly.

It is in the form of the generalized other that the social process influences the behavior of the individuals involved in it and carrying it on, i.e., that the community exercises control over the conduct of its individual members; for it is in this form that the social process or community enters as a determining factor into the individual's thinking. In abstract thought the individual takes the attitude of the generalized other[5] toward himself, without reference to its expression in any particular other individuals; and in concrete thought he takes that attitude insofar as it is expressed in the attitudes toward his behavior of those other individuals with whom he is involved in the given social situation or act. But only by taking the attitude of the generalized other toward himself, in one or another of these ways, can he think at all; for only thus can thinking—or the internalized conversation of gestures which constitutes thinking—occur. And only through the taking by individuals of the attitude or attitudes of the generalized other toward themselves is the existence of a universe of discourse, as that system of common or social meanings which thinking presupposes at its context, rendered possible.

…I have pointed out, then, that there are two general stages in the full development of the self. At the first of these stages, the individual's self is considered simply by an organization of the particular attitudes of other individuals toward himself and toward one another in the specific social acts in which he participates with them. But at the second stage in the full development of the individual's self that self is constituted not only by an organization of these particular individual attitudes, but also by an organization of the social attitudes of the generalized other or the social group as a whole to which he belongs.… So the self reaches its full development by organizing these individual attitudes of others into the organized social or group attitudes, and by thus becoming an individual reflection of the general systematic pattern of social or group behavior in which it and the others are all involved—a pattern which enters as a whole into the individual's experience in terms of these organized group attitudes which, through the mechanism of his central nervous system, he takes toward himself, just as he takes the individual attitudes of others.

…A person is a personality because he belongs to a community, because he takes over the institutions of that community into his own conduct. He takes its language as a medium by which he gets his personality, and then through a process of taking the different roles that all the others furnish he comes to get the attitude of the members of the community. Such, in a certain sense, is the structure of a man's personality. There are certain common responses which each individual has toward certain common things, and insofar as those common responses are awakened in the individual when he is affecting other persons he arouses his own self. The structure, then, on which the self is built is this response which is common to all, for one has to be a member of a community to be a self. Such responses are abstract attitudes, but they constitute just what we term a man's character. They give him what we term his principles, the acknowledged attitudes of all members of the community toward what are the values of that community. He is putting himself in the place of the generalized other, which represents the organized responses of all the members of the group. It is that which guides conduct controlled by principles, and a person who has such an organized group of responses is a man who we say has character, in the moral sense.

…I have so far emphasized what I have called the structures upon which the self is constructed, the framework of the self, as it were. Of course we are not only what is common to all: Each one of the selves is different from everyone else; but there has to be such a common structure as I have sketched in order that we may be members of a community at all. We cannot be ourselves unless we are also members in whom there is a community of attitudes which control the attitudes of all. We cannot have rights unless we have common attitudes. That which we have acquired as self-conscious persons makes us such members of society and gives us selves. Selves can only exist in definite relationships to other selves. No hard-and-fast line can be drawn between our own selves and the selves of others, since our own selves exist and enter as such into our experience only insofar as the selves of others exist and enter as such into our experience also. The individual possesses a self only in relation to the selves of the other members of his social group; and the structure of his self expresses or reflects the general behavior pattern of this social group to which he belongs, just as does the structure of the self of every other individual belonging to this social group.

CRITICAL THINKING QUESTIONS

1. How does Mead distinguish between the body and the self? What makes this a radically *social* view of the self?
2. How is the self both a subject and an object to itself? How is the ability to assume the role of the other vital to our humanity?

3. The idea that socialization produces conformity is easy to understand, but explain Mead's argument that individual distinctiveness is also a result of social experience.

NOTES

1. Man's behavior is such in his social group that he is able to become an object to himself, a fact which constitutes him a more advanced product of evolutionary development than are the lower animals. Fundamentally it is this social fact—and not his alleged possession of a soul or mind with which he, as an individual, has been mysteriously and supernaturally endowed, and with which the lower animals have not been endowed—that differentiates him from them.

2. It is generally recognized that the specifically social expressions of intelligence, or the exercise of what is often called "social intelligence," depend upon the given individual's ability to take the roles of, or "put himself in the place of," the other individuals implicated with him in given social situations; and upon his consequent sensitivity to their attitudes toward himself and toward one another. These specifically social expressions of intelligence, of course, acquire unique significance in terms of our view that the whole nature of intelligence is social to the very core—that this putting of one's self in the places of others, this taking by one's self of their roles or attitudes, is not merely one of the various aspects or expressions of intelligence or intelligent behavior, but is the very essence of its character. Spearman's "X factor" in intelligence—the unknown factor which, according to him, intelligence contains—is simply (if our social theory of intelligence is correct) this ability of the intelligent individual to take the attitude of the other, or the attitudes of others, thus realizing the significations or grasping the meanings of the symbols or gestures in terms of which thinking proceeds; and thus being able to carry on with himself the internal conversation with these symbols or gestures which thinking involves.

3. The unity of the mind is not identical with the unity of the self. The unity of the self is constituted by the unity of the entire relational pattern of social behavior and experience in which the individual is implicated, and which is reflected in the structure of the self; but many of the aspects or features of this entire pattern do not enter into consciousness, so that the unity of the mind is in a sense an abstraction from the more inclusive unity of the self.

4. It is possible for inanimate objects, no less than for other human organisms, to form parts of the generalized and organized—the completely socialized—other for any given human individual, insofar as he responds to such objects socially or in a social fashion (by means of the mechanism of thought, the internalized conversation of gestures). Any thing—any object or set of objects, whether animate or inanimate, human or animal, or merely physical—toward which he acts, or to which he responds, socially, is an element in what for him is the generalized other; by taking the attitudes of which toward himself he becomes conscious of himself as an object or individual, and thus develops a self or personality. Thus, for example, the cult, in its primitive form, is merely the social embodiment of the relation between the given social group or community and its physical environment—an organized social means, adopted by the individual members of that group or community, of entering into social relations with that environment, or (in a sense) of carrying on conversations with it; and in this way that environment becomes part of the total generalized other for each of the individual members of the given social group or community.

5. We have said that the internal conversation of the individual with himself in terms of words or significant gestures—the conversation which constitutes the process or activity of thinking—is carried on by the individual from the standpoint of the "generalized other." And the more abstract that conversation is, the more abstract thinking happens to be, the further removed is the generalized other from any connection with particular individuals. It is especially in abstract thinking, that is to say, that the conversation involved is carried on by the individual with the generalized other, rather than with any particular individuals. Thus it is, for example, that abstract concepts are concepts stated in terms of the attitudes of the entire social group or community; they are stated on the basis of the individual's consciousness of the attitudes of the generalized other toward them, as a result of his taking these attitudes of the generalized other and then responding to them. And thus it is also that abstract propositions are stated in a form which anyone—any other intelligent individual—will accept.

16

The Importance of the Family as an Agent of Socialization: Developmental Pathways and Crime Prevention

Michael C. Boyes, Nancy A. Ogden, and Joseph P. Hornick

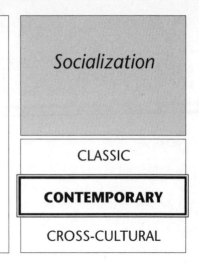

Socialization

CLASSIC

CONTEMPORARY

CROSS-CULTURAL

After a brief review of the key elements of human socialization, Boyes, Ogden, and Hornick describe a new approach to helping to reduce human suffering by curtailing the development of criminal activity. As you read, think about your own assumptions about the program and its potential for further success.

We will discuss a specific program that operates at the level of the individual family in an attempt to reduce human suffering, both today and in the future, by curtailing the development of criminal activity, particularly violent criminal activity. Considerable evidence supports the existence of a relationship between child maltreatment and subsequent delinquency and criminality. Programs that provide children with healthier beginnings early in life endeavour to prevent such children from choosing the maladaptive pathways that commonly lead to criminality, substance abuse, or both. We'll begin by outlining the basic premises on which such assumptions are based, follow with a discussion about general programs, and conclude with a specific Canadian program and its early findings.

Source: Reprinted by permission of the authors, 2002.

INFLUENCES AT THE BEGINNING OF LIFE

Every human being is a product of their biology as well as their individual and sociocultural experiences. Our genetic blueprint, our heredity, provides us with the basic material for our development but does not absolutely determine our behaviour. Although the self has a strong biological element, most social scientists agree that social influence is critical for creating truly human individuals. In fact, few behaviours are not socially influenced. Sociologists use the term *socialization* to refer to lifelong social experiences through which individuals develop a self-identity and learn culture: the physical, mental, and social skills needed for the survival of both the individual and the society. Human beings create and maintain their own culture and transmit it from one generation to the next through socialization. Socialization serves as the fundamental connection between the individual and society and as such is essential for maintaining the stability of society. Therefore, to support and sustain the existing social structure, individual members of a society must be socialized.

How does society ensure that its newest members receive appropriate socialization? Teaching the infant and young child—and eventually the older child, adolescent, and adult—what they need to know to participate in society is the task of persons, groups, or institutions that are collectively called *agents of socialization*. These agents come in many forms: schools, media, peers, families, and so on. Fitting children into their sociocultural environment is an important responsibility for socialization agents. For most individuals the family is the first and most important agent of socialization and is the centre of the infant and young child's world. Parents are our earliest teachers, transmitting cultural and social values to us. The family provides infants with their first social interactions and is likely to be children's primary contact with the world during the early years. Moreover, the family context places children within society in terms of class, religion, race, and ethnicity. Individuals of various social classes demonstrate different expectations for their children's behaviours. For example, working class parents are more likely to demand obedience and conformity from their children than are middle-class parents.

This socialization process is most effective when individuals adhere to the accepted norms and values of society because they come to recognize the function and importance of those norms and values. Ideally, parents help their children learn to be caring and contributing members of society. "Successfully" socialized children grow into adults who act as their own socialization agents. They choose not to break the rules because to do so would be "wrong." This implies that very early in their lives, children develop a warm and trusting relationship with a parent and *want* to please that parent by doing the things the parent considers "right" or "good." How then does a parent establish such a relationship with a young infant?

The Importance of Early Relationships

The initial love and nurturing children receive from their families, usually their parents, are central to their cognitive, emotional, and physical development. If infants live in such an environment, they learn to trust their caregivers; this makes infants feel secure. Security is vitally important for children's sense of well-being. When infants feel safe, they explore the environment, using the caregiver as a secure base. This pattern is part of the normal development of infants and very young children and is essential for healthy growth and development. Most children are nurtured by their parents and live in secure, loving, trusting environments. But the sad truth is that not all infants and children feel safe. Large numbers of infants and children experience maltreatment at the hands of those whom they depend upon, those whom they cannot leave or reject. These children are insecure. Documented cases of child abuse and neglect indicate that human infants without adequate social interaction with other human beings are unable to fully develop healthy human characteristics.

Child maltreatment includes physical, emotional, and sexual abuse, as well as neglect. Research on the community, family, and individual causes of violence in the lives of children and youth emphasizes the importance of the family as an agent of socialization. Deprivation, poor parenting practices, and dysfunctional family interaction are associated with the development of antisocial and delinquent behaviour (Snyder & Patterson, 1987).

Perhaps you are thinking of someone you know who lived in a dysfunctional environment, yet is not abusing any substances and is not involved in any criminal activity. Perhaps this person is you. Not everyone from an abusive, dysfunctional, or violent home will experience these outcomes. The relationship among family violence, substance abuse, and criminal behaviour is not absolute; these consequences are not inevitable. To determine just who *is* at risk, researchers assess the presence or absence of two types of variables: risk factors and protective factors.

In infants' and children's lives, risk factors in their family, school, and community include variables such as discrimination, family violence and dysfunction, poverty, lack of supervision, violent neighbourhoods, and multiple moves. The presence of any of these risk factors significantly increases children's later risk for negative outcomes such as depression, mental illness, conduct problems, suicide, delinquency and criminality, substance abuse, and aggressive or violent behaviour. The greatest risk factor for the development of nearly all forms of behavioural problems is poverty. The number of children living in poverty continues to increase in most industrialized nations, including Canada (Canadian Council on Social Development, 1997). The National Longitudinal Survey of Children and Youth (in Canadian Council on Social Development, 1997) reports that poverty has a negative impact on family functioning and school performance. Family dysfunction and parental depression are significantly higher in families living below the poverty line.

The presence of four or more risk factors increases the risk of negative outcomes tenfold (Sameroff et al., 1987; Smith et al., 1995). The prevalence of serious delinquency and substance abuse is strongly associated with increased numbers of risk factors. Many risk factors are interrelated. For example, family breakdown is related to high levels of juvenile delinquency, high conflict, lowered income, and parent absence, which are in turn each related to juvenile delinquency (Garbarino, 1999). Thus, the factors involved in criminal offending are complex, cumulative, and can be explained through both individual and social history.

An excellent example of the interrelationship between individual and sociocultural influences is the relatively recent research documenting the destructive consequences of children's exposure to community violence (Bell & Jenkins, 1993;

Osofsky et al., 1993; Sheidow et al., 2001). Of course, substantial discrepancy exists in the degree and extent of exposure to violence among children and youth living in inner-city communities. Nevertheless, the Canadian Council on Social Development reports that one in four Canadian children lives in an area that is considered unsafe after dark (Canadian Council on Social Development, 1997). Characteristics of the neighbourhood (such as the percentages of families working or living below the poverty level and the stability of the neighbourhood) and family functioning are important influences on how children function within their local community environments. How important is the family as an agent of socialization in violent communities? Unfortunately, the importance of family functioning is not independent of neighbourhood characteristics; Sheidow et al. (2001) report that in inner-city communities without positive social processes, the risk of exposure to violence cannot be assuaged by family functioning. That is, for many children exposed to violence within their communities, it does not matter how their family is functioning; these children are at risk simply by living within their community. Children in functional families are at risk; children in dysfunctional families are *more* at risk. These observations underscore the importance of understanding the social ecology of development for identifying how risk factors relate to outcomes (Gorman-Smith, Tolan, & Henry, 1999; National Crime Prevention Council, 1995) and serve as an important reminder that the family is not the *only* agent of socialization affecting children.

The impact of violence on children differs with the type of violence, the pattern of violence, the presence of supportive adult caretakers and other support systems, and the age of the child (Perry, 1995). Children at risk at an early age are in greater jeopardy for multiple negative outcomes later in life. This is due in part to the fact that younger children have fewer defensive capabilities (Grizenko & Fisher, 1992; Perry, 1995).

Early Risk and Resilience

Children at risk for later negative outcomes can be identified through particular sets of risk factors. Are researchers equally adept at identifying those factors that will protect children from inferior environments? The answer is, in part, yes. Factors such as high intelligence, secure attachment, average to above average family income, educated parents, and so on, can serve as protection for children in destitute environments, causing them to be more resilient. In fact, most studies of protective factors (see, for example, Losel & Bliesener, 1990) suggest that under adverse circumstances, 80 percent of children will "bounce back" from developmental challenges. This assumption is proving to be overly optimistic (Garbarino, 2001; Perry, 1994). For instance, resilience is drastically diminished under conditions of extreme risk accumulation or if children receive inadequate care in the first two years. Garbarino (2001) suggests that these observations could be interpreted to mean that the children and youth best able to survive functionally are those who have the least to lose morally and psychologically. The data yielded by his conversations with youths incarcerated for murder and other acts of violent crime confirm his theory. He reports that the crimes were unaffected by moral compunction or emotional responsibility for others.

How can this be? The work of Perry and his colleagues (1994, 1995) documents the impact of early neglect and abuse on the development of the brain. This research contends that infant's and children's brains are more plastic (i.e., receptive to inputs from the environment) than more mature brains are: the infant or child is most vulnerable to disadvantaged environments during the first three or four years. These developmental experiences determine how the brain will be organized and therefore how it will function. Early trauma can produce inadequate development of the brain's cortex (the part of the brain that controls higher abilities such as abstract reasoning and impulse control) by stimulating a stress-related hormone—cortisol—that impedes brain growth.

These findings have implications for research, intervention, and prevention. For example, the earlier an intervention occurs, the more effective and preventative it is likely to be (Blair, Ramey, & Hardin, 1995; Kiser, Heston, & Millsap, 1991; McFarlane, 1987) and thus the more enduring its impact. Furthermore, insightful sociocultural and public policy implications should arise from understanding the critical role that early experience plays in socializing children as they mature and acculturate or identify as traumatized and maladapted, thereby affecting our society for ill or good. Perry forcefully argues that we must stop accepting the myth that children are resilient; evidence contradicts such assertions, and children are irrevocably affected by maltreatment. "Persistence of the pervasive [political acceptance of] maltreatment of children in the face of devastating global and national resources will lead, inevitably, to sociocultural devolution" (Perry, 1994: 12).

In Canada, where children and youth compose 23 percent of the population, nearly one-quarter of police-reported assaults are visited on children and youth (Statistics Canada, 1996). This statistic is disturbing enough; however, of greater concern is the belief of officials that many incidents of maltreatment are not documented because they are either not observed or reported, leading to an underestimate of the extent of the problem. Factors such as the secrecy surrounding the issue, the dependency of the victim on the abuser, and the lack of knowledge about potential sources for help also contribute to underreporting.

We can conclude that the ramifications of the maltreatment of children involve tremendous personal and sociocultural costs. The financial costs are also staggering. In its report *Preventing Crimes by Investing in Families* (1996), the National Crime Prevention Council conservatively estimates that the annual cost of crime in Canada is in the range of 46 *billion* dollars (of which approximately one-quarter may be attributed to youth crime). Family violence escalates social and economic costs to the health care system, affects the civil and criminal justice systems, and creates immeasurable human suffering. The prevention of crime translates into meaningful reductions in human anguish, community victimization, and money spent on services for young offenders and their families. Society must rethink its priorities with respect to dedicating adequate time, energy, and resources to every aspect of prevention. Programs that support families and parents of very young children can significantly reduce child abuse and juvenile crime.

Secure attachments have recently been used to ascertain levels of vulnerability for those at risk of serious criminal behaviour. Many young offenders have been abused or have witnessed abuse in their homes. As already discussed, family violence is a problem that creates lasting physical, psychological, or economic repercussions for children and for society. The impacts of child abuse are experienced throughout the individual's lifetime. For example, 50 percent of those who were abused as children reported also being abused as adults (McCauley et al., 1997).

A DEVELOPMENTAL APPROACH TO CRIME PREVENTION

Over the past few decades, the focus on crime prevention has shifted from treatment and punishment to preventative initiatives targeting the family and parenting skills, using a multisystemic, developmental approach. It is essential to turn individuals from harmful pathways before maladaptive patterns of behaviour are well established. Thus, early prevention is the most effective strategy. Early intervention approaches involve various aspects of the family and those outside factors that influence family functioning. Willing participation in intensive, high-quality early intervention programs has been shown to be associated with improved developmental outcomes for high-risk children (Ramey & Ramey, 1994). For the first three years of children's lives, home-visiting programs are a successful way to reach high-risk children and their families and to promote resiliency (Luthar & Ziglar, 1991). Farrington (1994) summarizes research evidence attesting to the positive impact that early intervention programs have on deflecting criminal behaviour and other social problems. Interventions at crucial developmental transition points can have a major positive effect on at-risk families and their children, improving quality of life and potentially preventing criminal activity.

The saying "it takes a village to raise a child" does more than simply suggest that raising children requires a lot of work. What it points to is the essential importance of considering *both* the direct contacts that children have as they develop *and* the multiple contexts in which those contacts occur to properly see what facilitates or hampers optimal development. There have been several attempts to capture a broader perspective on development using ecological developmental models. Based on Bronfenbrenner's (1979) pioneering work, ecological models identify the familial and contextual influences that contribute to abuse. However, these influences are transactional; that is, the individual and the immediate and larger social contexts are viewed as actively influencing one another.

From this ecological developmental model perspective, opportunities for risk reduction must be considered in the contexts comprising the child and his or her immediate family, friends, neighbourhood, spiritual community, and school. Other influential contexts include aspects of social and physical geography such as weather, local and national laws, social conventions, and cultural and subcultural values and ideals. How all these contextual forces interact with the child's physical makeup determines the actual developmental course taken by an individual child (Garbarino, 1990).

Interventions for Reducing Risks and Bolstering Protective Factors: The Healthy Families Example

Creating specific programs aimed at reducing stress, enhancing family functioning, and promoting child development was the logical first step in implementing theoretical developmental models. The Healthy Start program in Hawaii was designed to improve family coping skills, as well as family functioning, and promoted positive parenting. The stated purpose of the Hawaii Healthy Start program was to reduce child abuse and neglect. The program identified families at high risk for abuse or neglect by screening newborns and their families in hospital and followed up with home visits from community-based family support services. Families were linked to family physicians or to nursing clinics and connected to a number of community services. Families were followed until the child was five years old. Evaluation of the program revealed that the high-risk families that participated in the program had half the state average for child maltreatment and abuse, whereas the rate of abuse for high-risk families that did not participate in the program was twice the state average.

Since their inception in 1992, Healthy Families America Inc. has modelled their programs on Hawaii's groundbreaking initiative, and has implemented nearly 200 programs throughout the United States. However, escalating health costs in a country without socialized medicine caused the Healthy Families America program interventions to became increasingly focused on helping low income, at-risk families to access state-funded health services. The Health Insurance Association of America (1999) estimates that by the year 2007, 53.5 million people in the United States will be uninsured, and more than one-third of these people will be children. This, coupled with the fact that at both the state and federal levels child and family services (i.e., Child Welfare) are less broadly organized in the American system, indicated that modifications to the Healthy Families initiative would be necessary if the program were to come to Canada. Canada has a system of socialized medicine that guarantees universal health care and is strongly supported through efficient community public health support. In fact, Canadian children at all income levels make the same average number of visits to doctors, whereas insured American children are eight times more likely to visit a doctor than are uninsured children (Canadian Council on Social Development, 1997). Moreover, Canada boasts more formally organized child and family ministries. These differences enabled Canadian researchers to redefine program objectives and allowed them to focus more intensely and more broadly on the other issues involved in assessing risk.

The Department of Justice Canada, through the National Crime Prevention Centre (NCPC), financed a Healthy Families demonstration project. The main goal of the investment is to establish effective programs for reducing delinquency and crime. Three programs were chosen to pilot the project: "Best Start" in Prince Edward Island, "Healthy Families" in Yukon, and "Success by 6 Healthy Families" in Alberta. Each program and the people they serve were chosen because they represent very different types of communities. The Prince Edward Island program is in a small urban centre with a large rural population, the Yukon program serves an Aboriginal community, and the Edmonton program serves a large urban community. In 1999, the Canadian Research institute for Law and the Family (CRILF), located in Alberta, began a three-year project to complete process and outcome evaluations of these Healthy Families programs.

The Healthy Families program utilized trained paraprofessional visitors to provide home visitation services to families identified by the public health system as requiring assistance. Healthy Families programs administer initial and follow-up screenings and establish schedules for home visits. The model requires that the entire child-raising system be assessed. Evaluators from CRILF used existing measures and developed measures to assess for each child the risk and protective factors that could influence a less than optimal developmental trajectory, potentially influencing the child's vulnerability to delinquent and criminal behaviour.

The overall mandate of all Healthy Families Programs is to optimize the development of young at-risk children and their families and to increase the children's opportunities for later success through early screening, assessment, and intervention. The Canadian focus has been on the transition to parenting, enabling parents to become more effective caregivers. First, the program empowers parents and enables them to access a broad range of community programs and resources (e.g., community kitchens, library reading programs, parenting support groups). Second, the program has an intense focus on the interaction between the parent and the child, with an eye to identifying issues and facilitating positive parent–child interaction and healthy growth and development for both. Program personnel are trained to identify and address maladaptive parenting attitudes and behaviours.

A key issue underlying the Healthy Families project in Canada (and the United States) is whether early experience and intervention make a difference to later occurrence of delinquency or crime. The answer in a recent comprehensive longitudinal review of developmental and early intervention approaches conducted in Australia is unequivocally "yes" (National Crime Prevention, 1999). In Canada, this question will remain unanswered until the young children involved in the Healthy Families project reach adulthood, but initial data from the project are causing researchers to be cautiously optimistic.

Early outcome data from the Canadian project suggest that if at-risk families are involved in a Healthy Families program, they have a reduced likelihood of Child Welfare involve-ment (both contacts and apprehensions). For example, data from Prince Edward Island indicate Child Welfare involvement in less than 2 percent of the families involved in the program compared with more than 25 percent of families in a matched comparison group. This is of particular note given that the number of children apprehended by Child Welfare agencies across Canada has increased (Canadian Council on Social Development, 1997). Outcomes will not actually be known for another twenty years, but existing data on welfare apprehension and crime suggest that a reduction in apprehensions should lead to better developmental outcomes, which in turn should lower rates of violent crime and incarceration. In the short term, kindergarten teachers will assess every child associated with the Healthy Families program for school readiness, as this is considered a strong indicator of a young child's early developmental experiences, especially whether the child received the enrich-ment and support that they needed.

To summarize, the foundations for crime are laid early, within the broad social and economic early environment of the child. If society is determined to reduce crime and victimization, it must support families and provide, maintain, and enhance opportunities for children from the beginning of their lives. As Canadians, we need many more proactive strategies of intervention when children are at risk. We should enable child welfare services to be proactively engaged at the moment when children and families need them most. We need to emphasize prevention not punishment, because by the time society intervenes to punish, it is already too late. Programs that work to optimize the socialization of the next generation of Canadians hold the most promise for reducing rates of abuse and crime and brightening Canada's future. The greatest protection society can give itself is to ensure that every individual has access to basic necessities: health care, childcare, housing, education, job training, employment, and recreation.

CRITICAL THINKING QUESTIONS

1. What are the agents of socialization? Which do you feel is the most important for the healthy development of children? Support your answer.

2. With reference to the article, discuss the adage, "it takes a village to raise a child."

3. As argued in the article, instead of placing our limited social wealth into punishing the perpetrators of crime, we should invest more effort and resources into prevention. Discuss this assertion with examples from your own community.

REFERENCES

Bell, C. C., & E. J. Jenkins. 1993. Community violence and children on Chicago's southside, *Psychiatry,* 56: 46–54.

Blair, C., C. T. Ramey, & J. M. Hardin. 1995. Early intervention for low birthweight, premature infants: Participation and intellectual development. *American Journal on Mental Retardation*, 99: 542–54.

Bronfenbrenner, U. 1979. *The ecology of human development: Experiments by nature and design.* Cambridge, Mass.: Harvard University Press.

Canadian Council on Social Development. 1997. *The progress of Canada's children,* Ottawa: SSCD Publications.

Farrington, D. P. 1994. Early developmental prevention of juvenile delinquency. *Child Behavior and Mental Health*, 4: 209–27.

Garbarino, J. 1990. The human ecology of early risk. In *Handbook of early childhood intervention*, eds. S. J. Meisels, and J. P. Shonkoff. New York: Cambridge University Press.

———. 2001. An ecological perspective on the effects of violence on children. *Journal of Community Psychology,* 29(3): 361–78.

Gorman-Smith, D., P. H. Tolan, & D. B. Henry. 1999. The relation of community and family to risk among urban poor adolescents. In *Where and when: Influence of historical time and place on aspects of psychopathology,* eds. P. Cohen, L. Robins, & C. Slomskoski. Hillsdale, N.J.: Erlbaum.

Grinzenko, N., & Fischer, C. 1992. Review of studies of risk and protective factors for psychopathology in children. *Canadian Journal of Psychiatry*, 37: 711–21.

Health Insurance Association of America. 1999. "Patient protection" bills give short shrift to the uninsured. [Online]. Available: **http://www.hiaa.org/search/content.cfm?ContentID=304**. Accessed July 10, 2002.

Kiser, L., J. Heston, & P. Millsap. 1991. Physical and sexual abuse in childhood: Relationship with post-traumatic stress disorder. *Journal of the American Academy of Child and Adolescent Psychiatry,* 30(2): 776–83.

Losel, F., & T. Bliesener. 1990. Resilience in adolescence: A study on the generalizability of protective factors. In *Health Hazards in Adolescence*, eds. K. Hurrelmann, & F. Losel. New York: Walter de Gruyter.

Luther, S. S., & E. Zigler. January 1991. Vulnerability and competence: A review of research on resilience in childhood. *American Journal of Orthopsychiatry,* 61: 6–22.

McCauley, J., D. Kern, K. Kolodner, L. Dill, A. F. Schroeder, H. K. DeChant, J. Ryden, L. R. Derogatis, and E. B. Bass. 1997. Clinical characteristics of women with a history of child abuse. *Journal of the American Medical Association,* 277(17): 1362–68.

McFarlane, A. C. 1987. Post-traumatic phenomena in a longitudinal study of children following a natural disaster. *Journal of American Academy of Child and Adolescent Psychiatry*, 26: 764–69.

National Crime Prevention Council of Canada (NCPC). 1996. Preventing crime by investing in families: An integrated approach to promote positive outcomes in children. [Online]. Available: **http://www.crime-prevention.org/english/publications/children/family/index.html**. Accessed July 10, 2002.

———. 1995. *Resiliency in young children.* Ottawa: NCPC/CNPC.

———. 1999. *Pathways to prevention: Developmental and early intervention approaches to crime in Australia.* Ottawa: National Crime Prevention, Attorney-General's Department, Canberra.

Ontario Association of Children's Aid Societies. 1998. Child protection: Pay now or pay later, *OACAS Journal,* 42(3): 14–5.

Osofsky, J. D., S. Wewers, D. M. Hann, & A. C. Fick. 1993. Chronic community violence: What is happening to our children? *Psychiatry,* 56: 36–45.

Perry, B. D. 1994. Neurobiological sequelae of childhood trauma: Post-traumatic stress disorders in children. In *Catecholamine function in posttraumatic stress disorder: Emerging concepts,* ed. M. Murburg. Washington: American Psychiatric Press.

———. 1995. Incubated in terror: Neurodevelopmental factors in the "cycle of violence." In *Children, youth, and violence: Searching for solutions*, ed. J. D. Osofsky. New York: Guilford Press.

Ramey, C. T., & S. L. Ramey. 1994. Which children benefit the most from early intervention? *Pediatrics,* 94: 1064–66.

Sameroff, A., R. Seifer, R. Barocas, M. Zax, & S. Greenspan. 1987. Intelligence quotient scores of 4-year-old children: Socio-environmental risk factors. *Pediatrics,* 79: 343–50.

Sheidow, A. J., D. Gorman-Smith, P. H. Tolan, & D. B. Henry. 2001. Family and community characteristics: Risk factors for violence exposure in inner-city youth, *Journal of Community Psychology*, 29(3): 345–60.

Smith, C., A. J. Lizotte, T. P. Thornberry, & M. D. Krohn. 1995. Resilient youth: Identifying factors that prevent high-risk youth from engaging in delinquency and drug use. In *Current perspectives on aging and the life cycle, Volume 4: Delinquency and disrepute in the life course,* eds. Z. S. Blau & J.Hagan, 217–47. London: JAI Press Inc.

Snyder, J., & G. Patterson. 1987. Family interaction and delinquent behaviour. In *Handbook of juvenile delinquency,* ed. H. C. Quay. New York: Wiley Publishing.

Statistics Canada. 1996. *Crime statistics.* [Online]. Available: **http://www.StatCan.ca.Daily.English/970730/d97/0730.htm**. Accessed July 10, 2002.

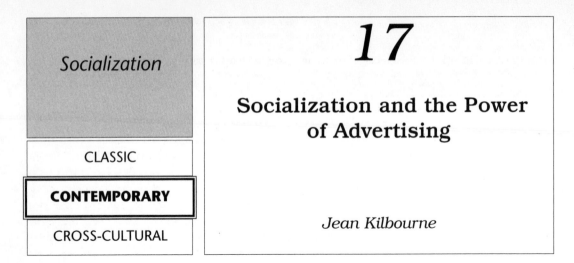

17

Socialization and the Power of Advertising

Jean Kilbourne

Can parents just turn off the TV to protect their kids from the negative impact of advertising? No, claims Jean Kilbourne. Because advertising permeates our environment, she claims, "We cannot escape it." Advertisers customize ads for subscribers of magazines, attract children to Web sites with games and prizes, and bombard us with products on billboards, public transportation systems, and the sides of buildings, trucks, and shopping carts. As a result, Kilbourne argues, advertising continues to persuade people of all ages that the way to be happy is to buy, buy, buy.

If you're like most people, you think that advertising has no influence on you. This is what advertisers want you to believe. But, if that were true, why would companies spend over $200 billion a year on advertising? Why would they be willing to spend over $250,000 to produce an average television commercial and another $250,000 to air it? If they want to broadcast their commercial during the Super Bowl, they will gladly spend over a million dollars to produce it and over one and a half million to air it. After all, they might have the kind of success that Victoria's Secret did during the 1999 Super Bowl. When they paraded bra-and-panty-clad models across TV screens for a mere thirty seconds, 1 million people turned away from the game to log on to the Website promoted in the ad. No influence?...

Source: Reprinted with the permission of The Free Press, a Division of Simon & Schuster Adult Publishing Group, from *Deadly Persuasion: Why Women and Girls Must Fight the Addictive Power of Advertising* by Jean Kilbourne, Copyright © 1999 by Jean Kilbourne.

Through focus groups and depth interviews, psychological researchers can zero in on very specific target audiences—and their leaders. "Buy this 24-year-old and get all his friends absolutely free," proclaims an ad for MTV directed to advertisers. MTV presents itself publicly as a place for rebels and nonconformists. Behind the scenes, however, it tells potential advertisers that its viewers are lemmings who will buy whatever they are told to buy.

The MTV ad gives us a somewhat different perspective on the concept of "peer pressure." Advertisers, especially those who advertise tobacco and alcohol, are forever claiming that advertising doesn't influence anyone, that kids smoke and drink because of peer pressure. Sure, such pressure exists and is an important influence, but a lot of it is created by advertising. Kids who exert peer pressure don't drop into high schools like Martians. They are kids who tend to be leaders, whom other kids follow for good or for bad. And they themselves are mightily influenced by advertising, sometimes very deliberately, as in the

MTV ad. As an ad for *Seventeen* magazine, picturing a group of attractive young people, says, "Hip doesn't just happen. It starts at the source: *Seventeen.*" In the global village, the "peers" are very much the same, regardless of nationality, ethnicity, culture. In the eyes of the media, the youths of the world are becoming a single, seamless, soulless target audience—often cynically labeled Generation X, or, for the newest wave of teens, Generation Y. "We're helping a soft drink company reach them, even if their parents can't," says [a newspaper ad] featuring a group of young people. The ad continues, "If you think authority figures have a hard time talking to Generation X, you should try being an advertiser," and goes on to suggest placing ads in the television sections of newspapers....

Home pages on the World Wide Web hawk everything from potato chips to cereal to fast food—to drugs. Alcohol and tobacco companies, chafing under advertising restrictions in other media, have discovered they can find and woo young people without any problem on the Web.

Indeed, children are especially vulnerable on the Internet, where advertising manipulates them, invades their privacy, and transforms them into customers without their knowledge. Although there are various initiatives pending, there are as yet no regulations against targeting children online. Marketers attract children to Web sites with games and contests, and then extract from them information that can be used in future sales pitches to the child and the child's family. They should be aware that this information might be misleading. My daughter recently checked the "less than $20,000" household income box because she was thinking of her allowance.

Some sites offer prizes to lure children into giving up the email addresses of their friends too. Online advertising targets children as young as four in an attempt to develop "brand loyalty" as early as possible. Companies unrelated to children's products have Web sites for children, such as Chevron's site, which features games, toys, and videos touting the importance of—surprise!—the

oil industry. In this way, companies can create an image early on and can also gather marketing data. As one ad says to advertisers, "Beginning this August, Kidstar will be able to reach every kid on the planet. And you can, too."

The United States is one of the few industrialized nations in the world that thinks that children are legitimate targets for advertisers. Belgium, Denmark, Norway, and the Canadian province of Quebec ban all advertising to children on television and radio, and Sweden and Greece are pushing for an end to all advertising aimed at children throughout the European Union. An effort to pass similar legislation in the United States in the 1970s was squelched by a coalition of food and toy companies, broadcasters, and ad agencies. Children in America appear to have value primarily as new consumers. As an ad for juvenile and infant bedding and home accessories says, "Having children is so rewarding. You get to buy childish stuff and pretend it's for them." [America's] policy—or lack thereof—on every children's issue, from education to drugs to teen suicide to child abuse, leaves many to conclude that [America is] a nation that hates its children.

However, the media care about them. The Turner Cartoon Network tells advertisers, "Today's kids influence over $130 billion of their parent's spending annually. Kids also spend $8 billion of their own money. That makes these little consumers big business." Not only are children influencing a lot of spending in the present, they are developing brand loyalty and the beginnings of an addiction to consumption that will serve corporations well in the future. According to Mike Searles, president of Kids 'R' Us, "If you own this child at an early age, you can own this child for years to come. Companies are saying, 'Hey, I want to own the kid younger and younger.' " No wonder Levi Strauss & Co. finds it worthwhile to send a direct mailing to seven- to twelve-year-old girls to learn about them when they are starting to form brand opinions. According to the senior advertising manager, "This is more of a long-term relationship that we're trying to explore." There may not seem much harm in this until we consider that the tobacco and alcohol industries are also interested in long-term relationships beginning in childhood—and are selling products that can indeed end up "owning" people.

Advertisers are willing to spend a great deal on psychological research that will help them target children more effectively. Nintendo U.S. has a research center which interviews at least fifteen hundred children every week. Kid Connection, a unit of the advertising agency Saatchi & Saatchi, has commissioned what the company calls "psychocultural youth research" studies from cultural anthropologists and clinical psychologists. In a recent study, psychologists interviewed young people between the ages of six and twenty and then analyzed their dreams, drawings, and reactions to symbols. Meanwhile, the anthropologists spent over five hundred hours watching other children use the Internet.

Children are easily influenced. Most little children can't tell the difference between the shows and the commercials (which basically means they are smarter than the rest of us). The toys sold during children's programs are often based on characters in the programs. Recently, the Center for Media Education asked the Federal Trade Commission to examine "kidola," a television marketing strategy in which toy companies promise to buy blocks of commercial time if a local broadcast station airs programs associated with their toys.

One company has initiated a program for advertisers to distribute samples, coupons, and promotional materials to a network of twenty-two thousand day care centers and 2 million preschool children. The editor-in-chief of *KidStyle*, a kids' fashion magazine that made its debut in 1997, said, "It's not going to be another parenting magazine. This will be a pictorial magazine focusing on products."

Perhaps most troubling, advertising is increasingly showing up in our schools, where ads are emblazoned on school buses, scoreboards, and book covers, where corporations provide "free" material for teachers, and where many children are a captive audience for the commercials on Channel One, a marketing program that gives video equipment to desperate schools in exchange for the right to broadcast a "news" program studded with commercials to all students every morning. Channel One is hardly free, however—it is estimated that it costs taxpayers $1.8 billion in lost classroom time. But it certainly is profitable for the owners who promise advertisers "the largest teen audience around" and "the undivided attention of millions of teenagers for 12 minutes a day." Another ad for Channel One boasts, "Our relationship with 8.1 million teenagers lasts for six years [rather remarkable considering most of theirs last for…like six days]." Imagine the public outcry if a political or religious group offered schools an information package with ten minutes of news and two minutes of political or religious persuasion. Yet we tend to think of commercial persuasion as somehow neutral, although it certainly promotes beliefs and behavior that have significant and sometimes harmful effects on the individual, the family, the society, and the environment.

"Reach him at the office," says an ad featuring a small boy in a business suit, which continues, "His first day job is kindergarten. Modern can put your sponsored educational materials in the lesson plan." Advertisers are reaching nearly 8 million public-school students each day.

Cash-strapped and underfunded schools accept this dance with the devil. And they are not alone. As many people become less and less willing to pay taxes to support public schools and other institutions and services, corporations are only too eager to pick up the slack—in exchange for a captive audience, of course. As one good corporate citizen, head of an outdoor advertising agency, suggested, "Perhaps fewer libraries would be closing their doors or reducing their services if they wrapped their buildings in tastefully done outdoor ads."

According to the Council for Aid to Education, the total amount corporations spend on "educational" programs from kindergarten through high school has increased from $5 million in 1965 to about $500 million today. The Seattle School Board recently voted to aggressively pursue advertising and corporate sponsorship. "There can be a Nike concert series and a Boeing valedictorian," said the head of the task force. We already have market-driven educational materials in our schools, such as Exxon's documentary on the beauty of the Alaskan coastline or the McDonald's Nutrition Chart and a kindergarten curriculum that teaches children to "Learn to Read through Recognizing Corporate Logos."

No wonder so many people fell for a "news item" in *Adbusters* (a Canadian magazine that critiques advertising and commercialism) about a new program called "Tattoo You Too!," which pays schools a fee in exchange for students willing to be tattooed with famous corporate logos, such as the Nike "swoosh" and the Guess question mark. Although the item was a spoof, it was believable enough to be picked up by some major media. I guess nothing about advertising seems unbelievable these days. There are penalties for young people who resist this commercialization. In the spring of 1998 Mike Cameron, a senior at Greenbrier High School in Evans, Georgia, was suspended from school. Why? Did he bring a gun to school? Was he smoking in the boys' room? Did he assault a teacher? No. He wore a Pepsi shirt on a school-sponsored Coke day, an entire school day dedicated to an attempt to win ten thousand dollars in a national contest run by Coca-Cola.

Coke has several "partnerships" with schools around the country in which the company gives several million dollars to the school in exchange for a longterm contract giving Coke exclusive rights to school vending machines. John Bushey, an area superintendent for thirteen schools in Colorado Springs who signs his correspondence "The Coke Dude," urged school officials to "get next year's volume up to 70,000 cases" and suggested letting students buy Coke throughout the day and putting vending machines "where they are accessible all day."

Twenty years ago, teens drank almost twice as much milk as soda. Today they drink twice as much soda as milk. Some data suggest this contributes to broken bones while they are still teenagers and to osteoporosis in later life....

ADVERTISING IS OUR ENVIRONMENT

Advertisers like to tell parents that they can always turn off the TV to protect their kids from any of the negative impact of advertising. This is like telling us that we can protect our children from air pollution by making sure they never breathe. Advertising is our *environment*. We swim in it as fish swim in water. We cannot escape it. Unless, of course, we keep our children home from school and blindfold them whenever they are outside of the house. And never let them play with other children. Even then, advertising's messages are inside our intimate relationships, our homes, our hearts, our heads.

Advertising not only appears on radio and television, in our magazines and newspapers, but also surrounds us on billboards, on the sides of buildings, plastered on our public transportation. Buses now in many cities are transformed into facsimiles of products, so that one boards a bus masquerading as a box of Dunkin' Donuts (followed, no doubt, by a Slimfast bus). The creators of this atrocity proudly tell us in their ad in *Advertising Age*, "In your face...all over the place!" Indeed.

Trucks carry advertising along with products as part of a marketing strategy. "I want every truck we have on the road making folks thirsty for Bud Light," says an ad in *Advertising Age*, which refers to a truck as a "valuable moving billboard." Given that almost half of all automobile crashes are alcohol-related, it's frightening to think of people becoming thirsty for Bud Light while driving their cars. A Spanish company has paid the drivers of seventy-five cars in Madrid to turn their cars into Pall Mall cigarette packages, and hopes to expand its operation throughout Spain. Imagine cars disguised as bottles of beer zipping along our highways. If we seek to escape all this by taking a plane, we become a captive audience for in-flight promotional videos.

Ads are on the videos we rent, the shopping carts we push through stores, the apples and hot dogs we buy, the online services we use, and the navigational screens of the luxury cars we drive. A new device allows advertisers to print their messages directly onto the sand of a beach. "This is my best idea ever—5,000 imprints of Skippy Peanut Butter jars covering the beach," crowed the inventor. Added the promotion director, "I'm here looking at thousands of families with kids. If they're on the beach thinking of Skippy, that's just what we want." Their next big idea is snow imprinting at ski resorts. In England the legendary white cliffs of Dover now serve as the backdrop for a laser-projected Adidas ad. American consumers have recently joined Europeans in being offered free phone calls if they will also listen to commercials. Conversations are interrupted by brief ads, tailored to match the age and social profiles of the conversants. And beer companies have experimented with messages posted over urinals, such as "Time for more Coors" or "Put used Bud here."

The average American is exposed to at least three thousand ads every day and will spend three years of his or her life watching television commercials. Advertising makes up about 70 percent of our newspapers and 40 percent of our mail. Of course, we don't pay direct attention to very many of these ads, but we are powerfully influenced, mostly on an unconscious level, by the experience of being immersed in an advertising culture, a market-driven culture, in which all our institutions, from political to religious to educational, are increasingly for sale to the highest bidder. According to Rance Crain, editor-in-chief of *Advertising Age*, the major publication of the advertising industry, "Only eight percent of an ad's message is received by the conscious mind; the rest is worked and reworked deep within the recesses of the brain, where a product's positioning and repositioning takes shape." It is in this sense that advertising is subliminal: not in the sense of hidden messages embedded in ice cubes, but in the sense that we aren't consciously aware of what advertising is doing.

Children who used to roam their neighborhoods now often play at McDonald's. Families go to Disneyland or other theme parks instead of state and national parks—or to megamalls such as the Mall of America in Minneapolis or Grapevine Mills in Texas, which provide "shoppertainment." One of the major tourist destinations in historic Boston is the bar used in the 1980s hit television series *Cheers*. The Olympics today are at least as much about advertising as athletics. We are not far off from the world David Foster Wallace imagined in his epic novel *Infinite Jest*, in which years are sponsored by companies and named after them, giving us the Year of the Whopper and the Year of the Tucks Medicated Pad.

Commercialism has no borders. There is barely any line left between advertising and the rest of the culture. The prestigious Museum of Fine Arts in Boston puts on a huge exhibit of Herb Ritts, fashion photographer, and draws one of the largest crowds in its history. In 1998 the museum's Monet show was the most popular exhibit in the world. Museum officials were especially pleased by results of a survey showing 74 percent of visitors recognized that the show's sponsor was Fleet Financial Group, which shelled out $1.2 million to underwrite the show.

Bob Dole plays on his defeat in the presidential election in ads for Air France and Viagra, while Ed Koch, former mayor of New York City, peddles Dunkin' Donuts' bagels. Dr. Jane Goodall, doyenne of primatology, appears with her chimpanzees in an ad for Home Box Office, and Sarah Ferguson, the former duchess of York, gets a million dollars for being the official spokeswoman for Weight Watchers (with a bonus if she keeps her weight down)....

The unintended effects of advertising are far more important and far more difficult to measure than those effects that are intended. The important question is not "Does this ad sell the product?" but rather "What else does this ad sell?" An ad for Gap khakis featuring a group of acrobatic swing dancers probably sold a lot of pants, which, of course, was the intention of the advertisers. But it also contributed to a rage for swing dancing. This is an innocuous example of advertising's powerful unintended effects. Swing dancing is not binge drinking, after all.

Advertising often sells a great deal more than products. It sells values, images, and concepts of love and sexuality, romance, success, and, perhaps most important, normalcy. To a great extent, it tells us who we are and who we should be. We are increasingly using brand names to create our identities. James Twitchell argues that the label of our shirt, the make of our car, and our favorite laundry detergent are filling the vacuum once occupied by religion, education, and our family name....

CRITICAL THINKING QUESTIONS

1. Advertisers maintain that people rely on commercials and ads to make informed decisions about the products and services they buy. Do you agree or disagree with advertisers' claims that they are providing a service to consumers by educating them about their market choices? Use the material in this chapter to support your answer.

2. What does Kilbourne mean when she says that advertising "sells much more than products"? How, for example, does advertising influence our values and lifestyles? Does advertising affect children's and adolescents' attitudes about tobacco, alcohol, food, and their self-image?

3. Belgium, Denmark, Norway, and other countries have banned all television and radio advertising directed at children. Should Canada pass similar legislation?

REFERENCES

Angier, N. 1996. Who needs this ad most? *New York Times,* (November 24): 4E.

Associated Press. 1998. Pepsi prank goes flat. *Boston Globe,* (March 26): A3.

Austen, I. 1999. But first, another word from our sponsors. *New York Times,* (February 18): E1, E8.

Bidlake, S. 1997. Commercials support free phone calls. *Advertising Age International,* (September): 147, 149.

Carroll, J. 1996. Adventures into new territory. *Boston Globe,* (November 24): D1, D5.

Cortissoz, A. 1998. For young people, swing's the thing. *Boston Globe,* (July 25): A2, A10.

Crain, R. 1997. Who knows what ads lurk in the hearts of consumers? The inner mind knows. *Advertising Age,* (June 9): 25.

Foreman, J. 1999. Sugar's "empty calories" pile up. *Boston Globe* (March 1): C1, C4.

Grunwald, M. 1997. Megamall sells stimulation. *Boston Globe,* (December 9): A1, A26.

Harris, R. 1989. Children who dress for excess: Today's youngsters have become fixated with fashion. *Los Angeles Times,* (November 12): A1.

Jacobson, M. F. and L. A. Mazur. 1995. *Marketing madness: A survival guide for a consumer society.* Boulder, CO: Westview Press.

Jhaly, S. 1998. *Advertising and the end of the world* (a video). Northampton, MA: Media Education Foundation.

Kerwin, A. M. 1997. "KidStyle" crafts customized ad opportunities. *Advertising Age,* (April 28): 46.

Koranteng, J. 1999. Sweden presses EU for further ad restrictions. *Advertising Age International,* (April 12): 2.

Krol, C. 1998. Levi's reaches girls as they develop opinions on brands. *Advertising Age,* (April 20): 29.

Lewis, M. 1997. Royal scam. *New York Times Magazine,* (February 9): 22.

Liu, E. 1999. Remember when public space didn't carry brand names? *USA Today,* (March 25): 15A.

McCarthy, C. 1990. In thingdom, laying waste our powers. *Washington Post,* (November 11): F3.

McLaren, C. 1997. The babysitter's club. *Stay Free!* (Spring): 8–11.

Mohl, B. 1999. Lend them your ear, and your call is free. *Boston Globe,* (January 13): A1, A10.

Monet show sets world record. 1999. *Boston Globe,* (February 2): E2.

Not for Sale! 1997 (spring). Oakland, CA: Center for Commercial-Free Public Education.

Not for Sale! 1999 (winter). Oakland, CA: Center for Commercial-Free Public Education.

Orlando, S. 1999. A material world: Defining ourselves by consumer goods. [Online]. Available: **http://www.sciencedaily.com/releases/1999/05/990518114815.htm**.

Reading, Writing…and TV commercials. 1999. *Enough!* 7(10) (Spring).

Rich, F. 1997. howdydoodycom. *New York Times,* (June 8): E15.

Rosenberg, A. S. 1999. Ad ideas etched in sand. *Boston Globe,* (February 1): A3.

Sharkey, J. 1998. Beach-blanket Babel: Another reason to stay at the pool. *New York Times,* (July 5): 2.

Twitchell, J. B. 1996. *Adcult USA: The triumph of advertising in American culture.* New York: Columbia University Press.

U.S. Department of Transportation. 1999. National Highway Traffic Safety Administration. [Online]. Available: **http://www.nhtsa.dot.gov/people/ncsa/FactPreve/alc96.html**.

Wallace, D. F. 1996. *Infinite jest.* Boston: Little Brown.

Weber, J. 1997. Selling to kids: At what price? *Boston Globe,* (May 18): F4.

18

Parents' Socialization of Children in Global Perspective

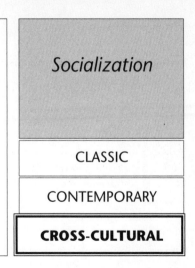

Socialization

CLASSIC

CONTEMPORARY

CROSS-CULTURAL

D. Terri Heath

One of the most important functions of the family is the socialization of children. Although parents might receive help from others (such as relatives, neighbours, and professional caregivers), most communities expect parents themselves to raise their children to be productive and responsible adults. Across vastly different cultural environments, D. Terri Heath shows the universal importance of closeness with parents in children's "life satisfaction, psychological well-being, lack of substance use, and absence of delinquent behavior."

THE BENEFITS OF CLOSE PARENT–YOUTH RELATIONSHIPS IN ADOLESCENCE

This article...[describes] how a positive relationship between parents and children later enhances the life satisfaction and psychological well-being of older youths and protects them from juvenile delinquency and substance abuse. As the cross-cultural examples illustrate, youth who perceive a close relationship with their parents exhibit more positive outcomes in each of these four areas. Life satisfaction and psychological well-being are described first, followed by illustrative cross-cultural examples. Next is a description of the impact of close parent–child relationships and their protective value on the substance abuse and juvenile delinquency of adolescents.

Source: From *Families in Multicultural Perspective,* eds. Bron B. Ingoldsby and Suzanna Smith, pp. 161–86. Copyright © 1995 Guilford Press, NY. Reprinted by permission of Guilford Press.

Relevant, illustrative cross-cultural examples conclude this section.

Life satisfaction is a subjective measure of an individual's perception of his/her quality of life. Rather than objective measures of income, education, accumulation of wealth, and home ownership, life satisfaction is the level of individual satisfaction each person perceives in his/her own life: that which is privately known and privately evaluated. A multitude of factors influence life satisfaction, and because it is a personal evaluation, these factors differ for individuals. A study of life satisfaction among Hong Kong adolescents illustrates the profound effects peers and parents can exert on an adolescent's life satisfaction.

Psychological well-being is a measure of multiple submissions: self-esteem, locus of control, anxiety, loneliness, and sociability. Persons who exhibit high self-esteem, an internal locus of control, low anxiety and loneliness, and high sociability are considered to have strong psychological well-being. Just as with life satisfaction, many factors can influence psychological well-being, but this section focuses specifically on the association between strong relationships with parents and positive outcomes for youth and young adults.

Hong Kong

Adolescence is a transitional period in the life cycle. Associations with family and peers are changing, and adolescents often feel increased pressure to succeed in social relationships outside their families. Their level of attachment, identification, and frequency of consultation with parents relative to that with peers influences the life satisfaction of adolescents in general and, specifically, their satisfaction with school, family, and others. Hong Kong, on the south coast of China, is heavily influenced by current political and economic changes in China. Chinese culture, with its emphasis on family and community over individual independence, continues to play a significant role in the culture of Hong Kong. Because the orientation of adolescents toward their peers and parents has important implications for their satisfaction with life, Hong Kong offers a unique look at this relationship in a rapidly developing society. In a study of 1,906 students, ages thirteen to sixteen, adolescents who were more oriented toward their parents, as well as those who were more oriented toward their peers, were equally satisfied with school, their acceptance by others, the government, and the media. However, those adolescents who are most oriented toward their parents were additionally satisfied with life in general, their families, and the environment (Man, 1991). Man (1991) concludes that "in a predominantly Chinese society like Hong Kong, the family remains a highly important determinant of the adolescents' life satisfaction" (p. 363).

Iran

Parents continue to influence the lives of their children as young adults through parental interactions, guidance, and shared history. When young adults are dissatisfied with their parents,

their adult psychological well-being appears to be negatively influenced. When Iranian students, ages seventeen to thirty-nine, studying at universities in Iran and the United States, were asked about their childhood dissatisfactions with their parents, an interesting pattern emerged. Those adults who perceived the most childhood dissatisfaction with parents were most likely to experience current loneliness, anxiety, external locus of control, misanthropy, neurosis, and psychosis when compared to adults who scored low on the dissatisfaction scale. They were also more likely to experience lower self-esteem and lower sociability, as well as decreased satisfaction with peer relationships, than were adults who had perceptions of childhood satisfaction with parents (Hojat, Borenstein, & Shapurian, 1990). There were no differences between the Iranian students studying at U.S. universities and those studying at Iranian institutions. The authors conclude that when a child's needs for closeness, attachment, and intimacy are not fulfilled to the child's satisfaction in early childhood, the result can be adult dissatisfactions with peer relationships and decreased psychological well-being in adulthood.

Puerto Rico

Can a child's need for closeness and intimacy be adequately fulfilled when the parents of the child are either alcohol dependent or mentally ill? By comparing three groups of children—those with an alcoholic parent, with a mentally ill parent, and with other parents without obvious diagnoses—researchers in Puerto Rico believe that children and adolescents, ages four to sixteen, with alcoholic or mentally ill parents are more likely than other children to be exposed to adverse family environments, such as stressful life events, marital discord, and family dysfunction. In addition, the children in these families were more maladjusted than were children in families without a diagnosed parent, according to reports by psychiatrists, parents, and the children themselves (Rubio-Stipec et al., 1991).

(However, the teachers of these three groups of children were unable to detect differences in child behavior, probably because 43 percent of them rated their familiarity with the child as "not good.") It appears from this research that children of alcoholic or mentally ill parents suffer negative consequences during childhood, and these consequences are readily apparent to psychiatrists, their parents, and even the children themselves.

In many cultures, adolescence is a period of rapid psychological growth and a shift in orientation from parents to peers. Adolescents move through this period from childhood at the beginning to adulthood at the end. Most choose educational and career paths during this period. Many choose marriage partners. They move from residing with their parents to residing with peers, with spouses, or by themselves. Because this is a time of such change, some adolescents cope with the transitions by engaging in problematic behaviors (e.g., drug and alcohol abuse and juvenile delinquency). This section presents some of the factors that contribute to problematic behaviors for youth in Canada and three subcultures in the United States: Native American, white, and Hispanic.

Canada

Social control theorists contend that adolescent alcohol consumption is influenced by the degree to which youth are influenced by peers more than parents. A study of alcohol consumption by Canadian eleventh and twelfth graders demonstrates this relationship (Mitic, 1990). Students were divided into three groups: (1) those who drank only with their parents, (2) those who drank only with their peers, and (3) those who drank both with and without their parents. The consumption rates of this last group were further divided into the amount of drinking with and without parents. As might be expected, students who drank only with parents consumed the least amount of alcohol. Those who drank with both parents and peers consumed the most alcohol and drank more heavily when they were with peers. It appears that what

parents model for their children regarding alcohol consumption has only a small influence in the youths' consumption behaviors when the parents are not present.

Hispanics and Whites in the United States

Researchers found that Hispanic and white youth (ages nine to seventeen) in the United States are also significantly influenced in their drug and alcohol consumption by their relationships with friends and parents. For white and Hispanic adolescents who used either licit substances (e.g., cigarettes and alcohol), marijuana, or other illicit substances (e.g., cocaine, heroin, and prescription drugs used for recreational purposes), the single most important influence was the percentage of friends who used marijuana. Those youths who had higher percentages of friends who used marijuana were more likely to use each category of drug (licit, marijuana, and other illicit) than were youths who had fewer friends who used marijuana; this is equally true for both Hispanic and white youth. Although both users and abstainers were more affiliated with their parents than their peers, users were more strongly influenced by their peers; more likely to disregard parental objections to their friends; more likely to believe that their friends, rather than their parents, understand them best; and more likely to respect the ideas of their friends in difficult situations. The only cultural difference was that, in general, Hispanic youths respected their parents' views more than did white youths, regardless of whether they used or abstained from drugs and alcohol (Coombs, Paulson, & Richardson, 1991). Coombs et al. conclude that "youths having viable relationships with parents are less involved with drugs and drug-oriented peers" (p. 87).

Ojibway Native Americans

Delinquent behavior represents a dysfunctional response to stressors and strains in adolescence. On Native American reservations in the United

States, an orientation toward parents and tribal elders appears to protect some youth from these negative behaviors. High percentages of Native American Ojibway adolescents, ages twelve to eighteen, reported inappropriate or illegal activities, such as using alcohol (85 percent), stealing something (70 percent), skipping school (64 percent), smoking marijuana (53 percent), and intentional damage to property (45 percent). However, those who spent more time with their family in chores, recreation, family discussions, and meals were less involved in negative behaviors. As expected, those youth who spent more time in activities away from their families—such as listening alone to the radio, and partying with drugs and alcohol—were at greatest risk for delinquent behaviors and court adjudications (Zitzow, 1990). Ojibway youths who spent more time in activities with parents and tribal elders were less likely to engage in delinquent behaviors resulting in court adjudications.

Summary

This last section focuses on how close parent–youth relationships are associated with the life satisfaction, psychological well-being, lack of substance use, and absence of delinquent behavior in adolescents. Without exception, adolescents in all six studies benefit from increased involvement with healthy parents. Parental involvement enhanced life satisfaction among adolescents in Hong Kong and contributed to psychological well-being among Iranian college students and Puerto Rican youths. The presence of parents was associated with less alcohol consumption among Canadian adolescents, a strong bond with parents was associated with less drug consumption by Hispanic and white youth in the United States, and spending time with parents and tribal elders was associated with less involvement in delinquent behaviors for Native American adolescents in the United States.

CONCLUSION

In reviewing the literature on cross-cultural research on parent–child relations for this chapter, a clear trend became increasingly apparent. When parents are more involved and/or have greater expectations of their children's behavior, children demonstrate better outcomes. As is apparent from the illustrative examples, greater parental involvement is an active involvement, not a passive one. It is acquired not simply by the amount of time parents and children spend together but rather by how the time is spent. An involved parent is not one who spends the majority of the day near his/her child but rarely interacting with the child. It is, instead, the parent who uses opportunities to share activities such as teaching the child a local trade, reading together, or fostering a close, supportive relationship through companionship. This active, involved parent appears much more likely to rear a successful child. Illustrative cross-cultural examples...of high-quality interaction between parents and children, such as spending time reading together in Great Britain, establishing firm limits and offering support in China, and engaging adolescents in activities with parents and tribal elders in the United States, has been associated with better child outcomes. These patterns emerged even when examining parent–son versus parent–daughter relations, relationships among family members in developing versus developed countries, or parent–child relationships in families that resided in Western cultures versus Eastern ones....

CRITICAL THINKING QUESTIONS

1. According to Heath, are there greater differences or similarities across cultures in the relationship between parent–child closeness and adolescent behaviour?
2. What are some of the factors that contribute to the problematic behaviour of adolescents both cross-culturally and within Canada?

3. What does Heath mean by "parental involvement"? What other variables might have an impact on parent–child relationships that are not discussed in this section?

REFERENCES

Coombs, R. H., M. J. Paulson, and M. A. Richardson. 1991. Peer versus parental influence in substance use among Hispanic and Anglo children and adolescents. *Journal of Youth and Adolescence*, 20(1): 73–88.

Hojat, M., B. D. Borenstein, and R. Shapurian. 1990. Perception of childhood dissatisfaction with parents and selected personality traits in adulthood. *Journal of General Psychology*, 117(3): 241–53.

Man, P. 1991. The influence of peers and parents on youth life satisfaction in Hong Kong. *Social Indicators Research*, 24(4): 347–65.

Mitic, W. 1990. Parental versus peer influence on adolescents' alcohol consumption. *Psychological Reports*, 67: 1273–74.

Rubio-Stipec, M., H. Bird, G. Canino, and M. Alegria. 1991. Children of alcoholic parents in the community. *Journal of Studies on Alcohol*, 52(1): 78–88.

Zitzow, D. 1990. Ojibway adolescent time spent with parents/elders as related to delinquency and court adjudication experiences. *American Indian and Alaska Native Mental Health Research*, 4(1): 53–63.

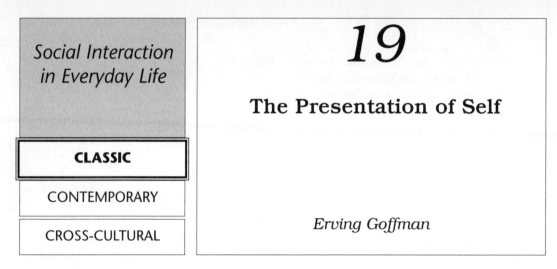

Social Interaction in Everyday Life

CLASSIC

CONTEMPORARY

CROSS-CULTURAL

19

The Presentation of Self

Erving Goffman

Face-to-face interaction is a complex process by which people both convey and receive information about one another. In this selection, Erving Goffman presents basic observations about how everyone tries to influence how others perceive them. In addition, he suggests ways in which people can evaluate how honestly others present themselves.

When an individual enters the presence of others, they commonly seek to acquire information about him or to bring into play information about him already possessed. They will be interested in his general socioeconomic status, his conception of self, his attitude toward them, his competence, his trustworthiness, etc. Although some of this information seems to be sought almost as an end in itself, there are usually quite practical reasons for acquiring it. Information about the individual helps to define the situation, enabling others to know in advance what he will expect of them and what they may expect of him. Informed in these ways, the others will know how best to act in order to call forth a desired response from him.

For those present, many sources of information become accessible and many carriers (or "sign-vehicles") become available for conveying this

Source: From *The Presentation of Self in Everyday Life* by Erving Goffman, copyright © 1959 by Erving Goffman, Bantam Doubleday Dell Publishing Group, Inc. Reprinted with permission.

information. If unacquainted with the individual, observers can glean clues from his conduct and appearance which allow them to apply their previous experience with individuals roughly similar to the one before them or, more important, to apply untested stereotypes to him. They can also assume from past experience that only individuals of a particular kind are likely to be found in a given social setting. They can rely on what the individual says about himself or on documentary evidence he provides as to who and what he is. If they know, or know of, the individual by virtue of experience prior to the interaction, they can rely on assumptions as to the persistence and generality of psychological traits as a means of predicting his present and future behavior.

However, during the period in which the individual is in the immediate presence of the others, few events may occur which directly provide the others with the conclusive information they will need if they are to direct wisely their own activity. Many crucial facts lie beyond the time and place of interaction or lie concealed within it. For example, the "true" or "real" attitudes, beliefs, and emotions of the individual can be ascertained only indirectly, through his avowals or through what appears to be involuntary expressive behavior. Similarly, if the individual offers the others a product or service, they will often find that during the interaction there will be no time and place immediately available for eating the pudding that the proof can be found in. They will be forced to accept some events as conventional or natural signs of something not directly available to the senses. In Ichheiser's terms,[1] the individual will have to act so that he intentionally or unintentionally *expresses* himself, and the others will in turn have to be *impressed* in some way by him.

The expressiveness of the individual (and therefore his capacity to give impressions) appears to involve two radically different kinds of sign activity: the expression that he *gives,* and the expression that he *gives off.* The first involves verbal symbols or their substitutes which he uses admittedly and solely to convey the information that he and the others are known to attach to these symbols. This is communication in the traditional and narrow sense. The second involves a wide range of action that others can treat as symptomatic of the actor, the expectation being that the action was performed for reasons other than the information conveyed in this way. As we shall have to see, this distinction has an only initial validity. The individual does of course intentionally convey misinformation by means of both of these types of communication, the first involving deceit, the second feigning.

...Let us now turn from the others to the point of view of the individual who presents himself before them. He may wish them to think highly of him, or to think that he thinks highly of them, or to perceive how in fact he feels toward them, or to obtain no clear-cut impression; he may wish to ensure sufficient harmony so that the interaction can be sustained, or to defraud, get rid of, confuse, mislead, antagonize, or insult them. Regardless of the particular objective which the individual has in mind and of his motive for having this objective, it will be in his interests to control the conduct of the others, especially their responsive treatment of him. This control is achieved largely by influencing the definition of the situation which the others come to formulate, and he can influence this definition by expressing himself in such a way as to give them the kind of impression that will lead them to act voluntarily in accordance with his own plan. Thus, when an individual appears in the presence of others, there will usually be some reason for him to mobilize his activity so that it will convey an impression to others which it is in his interests to convey. Since a girl's dormitory mates will glean evidence of her popularity from the calls she receives on the phone, we can suspect that some girls will arrange for calls to be made, and Willard Waller's finding can be anticipated:

> It has been reported by many observers that a girl who is called to the telephone in the dormitories will often allow herself to be called several times, in order to give all the other girls ample opportunity to hear her paged.[2]

Of the two kinds of communication—expressions given and expressions given off—this report will be primarily concerned with the latter, with the more theatrical and contextual kind, the nonverbal, presumably unintentional kind, whether this communication be purposely engineered or not. As an example of what we must try to examine, I would like to cite at length a novelistic incident in which Preedy, a vacationing Englishman, makes his first appearance on the beach of his summer hotel in Spain:

> But in any case he took care to avoid catching anyone's eye. First of all, he had to make it clear to those potential companions of his holiday that they were of no concern to him whatsoever. He stared through them, round them, over them—eyes lost in space. The beach might have been empty. If by chance a ball was thrown his way, he looked surprised; then let a smile of amusement lighten his face (Kindly Preedy), looked round dazed to see that there *were* people on the beach, tossed it back with a smile to himself and not a smile *at* the people, and then resumed carelessly his nonchalant survey of space.

But it was time to institute a little parade, the parade of the Ideal Preedy. By devious handlings he gave any who wanted to look a chance to see the title of his book—a Spanish translation of Homer, classic thus, but not daring, cosmopolitan too—and then gathered together his beach-wrap and bag into a neat sand-resistant pile (Methodical and Sensible Preedy), rose slowly to stretch at ease his huge frame (Big-Cat Preedy), and tossed aside his sandals (Carefree Preedy, after all).

The marriage of Preedy and the sea! There were alternative rituals. The first involved the stroll that turns into a run and a dive straight into the water, thereafter smoothing into a strong splashless crawl towards the horizon. But of course not really to the horizon. Quite suddenly he would turn on to his back and thrash great white splashes with his legs, somehow thus showing that he could have swum further had he wanted to, and then would stand up a quarter out of water for all to see who it was.

The alternative course was simpler, it avoided the cold-water shock and it avoided the risk of appearing too high-spirited. The point was to appear to be so used to the sea, the Mediterranean, and this particular beach, that one might as well be in the sea as out of it. It involved a slow stroll down and into the edge of the water—not even noticing his toes were wet, land and water all the same to *him!*—with his eyes up at the sky gravely surveying portents, invisible to others, of the weather (Local Fisherman Preedy).[3]

The novelist means us to see that Preedy is improperly concerned with the extensive impressions he feels his sheer bodily action is giving off to those around him. We can malign Preedy further by assuming that he has acted merely in order to give a particular impression, that this is a false impression, and that the others present receive either no impression at all, or, worse still, the impression that Preedy is affectedly trying to cause them to receive this particular impression. But the important point for us here is that the kind of impression Preedy thinks he is making is in fact the kind of impression that others correctly and incorrectly glean from someone in their midst....

There is one aspect of the others' response that bears special comment here. Knowing that the individual is likely to present himself in a light that is favorable to him, the others may divide what they witness into two parts; a part that is relatively easy for the individual to manipulate at will, being chiefly his verbal assertions, and a part in regard to which he seems to have little concern or control, being chiefly derived from the expressions he gives off. The others may then use what are considered to be the ungovernable aspects of his expressive behavior as a check upon the validity of what is conveyed by the governable aspects. In this a fundamental asymmetry is demonstrated in the communication process, the individual presumably being aware of only one stream of his communication, the witnesses of this stream and one other. For example, in Shetland Isle one crofter's wife, in serving native dishes to a visitor from the mainland of Britain, would listen with a polite smile to his polite claims of liking what he was eating; at the same time she would take note of the rapidity with which the visitor lifted his fork or spoon to his mouth, the eagerness with which he passed food into his mouth, and the gusto expressed in chewing the food, using these signs as a check on the stated feelings of the eater. The same woman, in order to discover what one acquaintance (A) "actually" thought of another acquaintance (B), would wait until B was in the presence of A but engaged in conversation with still another person (C). She would then covertly examine the facial expressions of A as he regarded B in conversation with C. Not being in conversation with B, and not being directly observed by him, A would sometimes relax usual constraints and tactful deceptions, and freely express what he was "actually" feeling about B. This Shetlander, in short, would observe the unobserved observer.

Now given the fact that others are likely to check up on the more controllable aspects of behavior by means of the less controllable, one can expect that sometimes the individual will try to exploit this very possibility, guiding the impression he makes through behavior felt to be reliably informing.[4] For example, in gaining admission to a tight social circle, the participant observer may not only wear an accepting look while listening to an informant, but may also be careful to wear the same look when observing the informant talking to others; observers of the observer will then not as easily discover where he actually stands. A specific illustration may be cited from Shetland Isle. When a neighbor dropped in to have a cup of tea, he would ordinarily wear at least a hint of an expectant warm smile as he passed through the door into the cottage. Since lack of physical obstructions outside the cottage and lack of light within it usually made it possible to observe the visitor unobserved as he approached the house, islanders sometimes took pleasure in watching the visitor drop whatever expression he was manifesting and replace it with a sociable one just before reaching the door. However, some visitors, in appreciating that this examination was occurring, would blindly adopt a social face a long distance from the house, thus ensuring the projection of a constant image.

This kind of control upon the part of the individual reinstates the symmetry of the communication process, and sets the stage for a kind of information game—a potentially infinite cycle of concealment, discovery, false revelation, and rediscovery. It should be added that since the others are likely to be relatively unsuspicious of the presumably unguided aspects of the individual's conduct, he can gain much by controlling it. The others of course may sense that the individual is manipulating the presumably spontaneous aspects of his behavior, and seek in this very act of manipulation some shading of conduct that the individual has not managed to control. This again provides a check upon the individual's behavior, this time his presumably uncalculated behavior, thus re-establishing the asymmetry of the communication process. Here I would like only to add the suggestion that the arts of piercing an individual's effort at calculated unintentionality seem better developed than our capacity to manipulate our own behavior, so that regardless of how many steps have occurred in the information game, the witness is likely to have the advantage over the actor, and the initial asymmetry of the communication process is likely to be retained....

In everyday life, of course, there is a clear understanding that first impressions are important. Thus, the work adjustment of those in service occupations will often hinge upon a capacity to seize and hold the initiative in the service relation, a capacity that will require subtle aggressiveness on the part of the server when he is of lower socioeconomic status than his client. W. F. Whyte suggests the waitress as an example:

> The first point that stands out is that the waitress who bears up under pressure does not simply respond to her customers. She acts with some skill to control their behavior. The first question to ask when we look at the customer relationship is, "Does the waitress get the jump on the customer, or does the customer get the jump on the waitress?" The skilled waitress realizes the crucial nature of this question....
> The skilled waitress tackles the customer with confidence and without hesitation. For example, she may find that a new customer has seated himself before she could clear off the dirty dishes and change the cloth. He is now leaning on the table studying the menu. She greets him, says, "May I change the cover, please?" and, without waiting for an answer, takes his menu away from him so that he moves back from the table, and she goes about her work. The relationship is handled politely but firmly, and there is never any question as to who is in charge.[5]

When the interaction that is initiated by "first impressions" is itself merely the initial interaction in an extended series of interactions involving the same participants, we speak of "getting off on the right foot" and feel that it is crucial that we do so. Thus, one learns that some teachers take the following view:

> You can't ever let them get the upper hand on you or you're through. So I start out tough. The first day I get a new class in, I let them know who's boss.... You've got to start off tough, then you can ease up as you go along. If you start out easy-going, when you try to get tough, they'll just look at you and laugh.[6]

...In stressing the fact that the initial definition of the situation projected by an individual tends to provide a plan for the cooperative activity that follows—in stressing this action point of view—we must not overlook the crucial fact that any projected definition of the situation also has a distinctive moral character. It is this moral character of projections that will chiefly concern us in this report. Society is organized on the principle that any individual who possesses certain social characteristics has a moral right to expect that others will value and treat him in an appropriate way. Connected with this principle is a second, namely that an individual who implicitly or explicitly signifies that he has certain social characteristics ought in fact to be what he claims he is. In consequence, when an individual projects a definition of the situation and thereby makes an implicit or explicit claim to be a person of a particular kind, he automatically exerts a moral demand upon the others, obliging them to value and treat him in the manner that persons of his kind have a right to expect. He also implicitly forgoes all claims to be things he does not appear to be[7] and hence forgoes the treatment that would be appropriate for such individuals. The others find, then, that the individual has informed them as to what is and as to what they *ought* to see as the "is."

One cannot judge the importance of definitional disruptions by the frequency with which they occur, for apparently they would occur more frequently were not constant precautions taken. We find that preventive practices are constantly employed to avoid these embarrassments and that corrective practices are constantly employed to compensate for discrediting occurrences that have not been successfully avoided. When the individual employs these strategies and tactics to protect his own projections, we may refer to them as "defensive practices"; when a participant employs them to save the definition of the situation projected by another, we speak of "protective practices" or "tact." Together, defensive and protective practices [compose] the techniques employed to safeguard the impression fostered by an individual during his presence before others. It should be added that while we may be ready to

see that no fostered impression would survive if defensive practices were not employed, we are less ready perhaps to see that few impressions could survive if those who received the impression did not exert tact in their reception of it.

In addition to the fact that precautions are taken to prevent disruption of projected definitions, we may also note that an intense interest in these disruptions comes to play a significant role in the social life of the group. Practical jokes and social games are played in which embarrassments which are to be taken unseriously are purposely engineered.[8] Fantasies are created in which devastating exposures occur. Anecdotes from the past—real, embroidered, or fictitious—are told and retold, detailing disruptions which occurred, almost occurred, or occurred and were admirably resolved. There seems to be no grouping which does not have a ready supply of these games, reveries, and cautionary tales, to be used as a source of humor, a catharsis for anxieties, and a sanction for inducing individuals to be modest in their claims and reasonable in their projected expectations. The individual may tell himself through dreams of getting into impossible positions. Families tell of the time a guest got his dates mixed and arrived when neither the house nor anyone in it was ready for him. Journalists tell of times when an all-too-meaningful misprint occurred, and the paper's assumption of objectivity or decorum was humorously discredited. Public servants tell of times a client ridiculously misunderstood form instructions, giving answers which implied an unanticipated and bizarre definition of the situation.[9] Seamen, whose home away from home is rigorously he-man, tell stories of coming back home and inadvertently asking mother to "pass the fucking butter."[10] Diplomats tell of the time a near-sighted queen asked a republican ambassador about the health of his king.[11]

To summarize, then, I assume that when an individual appears before others he will have many motives for trying to control the impression they receive of the situation.

CRITICAL THINKING QUESTIONS

1. How does the "presentation of self" contribute to a definition of a situation in the minds of participants? How does this definition change over time?

2. Apply Goffman's approach to the classroom. What are the typical elements of the instructor's presentation of self? a student's presentation of self?

3. Can we evaluate the validity of people's presentations? How?

NOTES

1. Gustav Ichheiser, "Misunderstandings in Human Relations," supplement to *The American Journal of Sociology* 55 (Sept., 1949), 6–7.

2. Willard Waller, "The Rating and Dating Complex," *American Sociological Review* 2, 730.

3. William Sansom, *A Contest of Ladies* (London: Hogarth, 1956), pp. 230–32.

4. The widely read and rather sound writings of Stephen Potter are concerned in part with signs that can be engineered to give a shrewd observer the apparently incidental cues he needs to discover concealed virtues the gamesman does not in fact possess.

5. W. F. Whyte, "When Workers and Customers Meet," chap. 7, *Industry and Society,* ed. W. F. Whyte (New York: McGraw-Hill, 1946), pp. 132–33.

6. Teacher interview quoted by Howard S. Becker, "Social Class Variations in the Teacher–Pupil Relationship," *Journal of Educational Sociology* 25, 459.

7. This role of the witness in limiting what it is the individual can be has been stressed by Existentialists, who see it as a basic threat to individual freedom. See Jean-Paul Sartre, *Being and Nothingness,* trans. Hazel E. Barnes (New York: Philosophical Library, 1956), pp. 365ff.

8. Goffman, op. cit., pp. 319–27.

9. Peter Blau, "Dynamics of Bureaucracy" (Ph.D. dissertation, Department of Sociology, Columbia University, forthcoming, University of Chicago Press), pp. 127–29.

10. Walter M. Beattie, Jr., "The Merchant Seaman" (unpublished M.A. Report, Department of Sociology, University of Chicago, 1950), p. 35.

11. Sir Frederick Ponsonby, *Recollections of Three Reigns* (New York: Dutton, 1952), p. 46.

Social Interaction in Everyday Life

CLASSIC

CONTEMPORARY

CROSS-CULTURAL

20

The Body Beautiful: Adolescent Girls and Images of Beauty

Beverly J. Matthews

Matthews investigates the social world of adolescent girls and the role it plays in defining their physical selves. Her interviews suggest that young women's self-perception is the result of complex interactions between diverse social influences.

INTRODUCTION

The tyranny of appearance norms have long been recognized in the lives of women (see Brownmiller, 1984; Greer, 1970; or Freedman, 1986, for example). Both academic literature and the popular media have examined factors which underlie the intense pressure women experience to adhere to a cultural ideal and the price they pay for either attempting to comply or failing to do so (see Chernin, 1981; Shute, 1992; Hesse-Biber, 1996; Bordo, 1993). While we are aware of the problem among older teenagers and adult women, recent studies indicate that even girls in early adolescence are prone to eating problems and a preoccupation with food (Pipher, 1996; Brumberg, 1997). Some of the literature in this

Source: "The Body Beautiful: Adolescent Girls and Images of Beauty," by Beverly J. Matthews. In Lori G. Beaman (Ed.), *New Perspectives on Deviance: The Construction of Deviance in Everyday Life* (pp. 208–19). Toronto: Prentice Hall, 2000. Reprinted by permission.

area focuses on media images and unhealthy portrayals of beauty and the ways in which women are influenced by such portrayals (Wolf, 1991). While this has been a fruitful line of inquiry, it is incomplete. It implies that women uncritically, or helplessly, follow a cultural ideal, simply because it is prescribed by society. The findings of this research study into the social world of adolescent girls reveal that straining to conform to the "ideal look" is not always an end in itself, that it is often a purposeful act designed to achieve social goals.

Young women are surrounded by images which define attractiveness as a very particular, thin, "perfect" ideal. While many strive to achieve this goal, they do not all do so out of blind conformity, or simply because they have negative images of themselves. The problem is more complex: many girls use appearance as a means for achieving social status and power; they conform to avoid the costs associated with deviating from the ideal. They experience the gender system in a unique way, because of their stage in life, which compounds the pressures all women experience around appearance; however, these girls are not all misguided individuals passively following a societal definition of beauty. Just like older women, adolescents are working to negotiate and achieve their individual goals within a micro and macro gender structure. They are actively finding their location within the peer arena and their relationships with food and appearance play a key role in this endeavor. In this research, in-depth interviews with adolescent women reveal much about the adolescent world and the importance of appearance norms within it.

EXAMINING THE MULTILEVEL GENDER SYSTEM AND THE SOCIAL WORLD OF ADOLESCENT GIRLS

When studying the social world it is essential to recognize the interplay between the individual and the social context. Although women have the freedom to make their own choices, these choices are constrained by the socially created structures which surround them. Sociologists have long recognized the existence of social structures and have worked to explain their relation to individuals: "social structures create social persons who (re)create social structures who create social persons who (re)create…ad infinitum" (Stryker, 1980: 53). They also recognize that such structures operate on two levels. "[W]e inhabit the *micro-world* of our immediate experience with others in face-to-face relations. Beyond that, with varying degrees of significance and continuity, we inhabit a *macro-world* consisting of much larger structures…. Both worlds are essential to our experience of society" (Berger & Berger, 1975: 8). Sociologists and feminists have studied the creation of the social person and the role that gender plays in that development. They have also examined the gendered dimensions of social structures and their impact upon

members of the society (see Risman & Schwartz, 1989; Smith, 1987; Bem, 1993).

Through my research into gender and social behaviour (Matthews & Beaujot, 1997; Matthews, 1997), it has become clear that the gender system can be more fully understood by acknowledging that it operates on several levels at one time. And that analyses are more complete when three levels are integrated into the explanatory framework. This tri-level model of the gender system includes the individual gender role orientation, a micro structure, and a macro structure. On the most basic level, men and women have individual gender role orientations, which they have developed through socialization and interaction over the course of their lives. These orientations consist of their beliefs about the appropriate roles for women and men and serve as guidelines for choices regarding presentation of self, relationships, and activities, as well as attitudes and values. However, these gender role orientations alone do not determine behaviour. Women's choices about how to behave, and how to present themselves, are also influenced by the micro level gender structure, where they encounter others in daily interaction and negotiate their roles. Conforming to expectations is an integral part of interaction; people play roles in order to facilitate communication and joint action. They are also influenced by the macro level gender structure: the societal context which provides a landscape within which people act out their choices. It is my contention that the combination of the three levels and the way in which they interact, sometimes complementary and sometimes contradictory, can advance our understanding of the gender system and of young women's actions concerning weight and appearance.

For women making decisions about weight, food, and dieting, it is apparent that all three levels of the gender system influence their choices and behaviour. The macro structure, which has evolved over time, emphasizes the importance of appearance for women. While women's accomplishments are many, they continue to be judged by their appearance. It provides media images of "perfect bodies" and advertising which constantly criticizes and undermines women with appearance "flaws" (i.e., extra pounds, "problem" skin, gray hair). On the micro level, appearance is also salient. Because slenderness is the norm, there is some pressure in daily interaction to achieve it. Friends and family often encourage, and occasionally coerce, women into dieting and following the cultural ideal. Choosing not to diet, not following the ideal, seems to imply either slovenliness— "she's really let herself go"—or a personal statement about her unwillingness to conform. It is rarely accepted as a woman choosing to be comfortable with herself as she is. Thus interaction with others is influenced by their interpretation of her appearance. At the individual level, women's understanding of themselves is filtered through the existing social structures. Women know that they may be afforded more attention and respect if they follow the ideal;[1] they may also have internalized the societal standards throughout their lives. Thus, not "measuring up" to the ideal may cause personal anguish.

Women's decisions to diet are bound up with several levels of gender and must be considered in this light. The three levels of gender may be complementary or contradictory. That is, while people all live in a social world that appears to appreciate and promote only one body type, individual micro structures or individual gender role orientations may be in agreement or at odds with this standard. Women may be surrounded by people who disregard the cultural ideal and thus feel less pressure to conform in their interactions. They may have developed a critical stance to the societal ideal and experience no internal misgivings about weight and appearance. Or they may experience pressure on all three levels to follow the ideal. Clearly, in order to understand women's relationships to food and diet it is insufficient to focus on only one level. Women's social contexts and their individual gender role orientations are unique and must be considered as such.

Adolescence compounds the imperatives of the gender system. While all people feel the effects of the gender systems in which they operate, adolescents face unique challenges; adolescence is (1) a time of identity construction and (2) a time to find one's own location in the social world. They must navigate their ways through the layers of gender, making their choices and moderating their behaviours based on the context in which they live. And because individuals in this age group do not necessarily have a strong gender role orientation guiding their choices and actions, they are more vulnerable to the influences of the micro and macro gender structures. Also, because they have moved into a new "adolescent world," they can no longer rely on the "borrowed identity" from their childhood or the social status of their families. They must construct a unique self and establish their own position within the social world. This new self will largely be based on measures of status determined by peer groups and the broader youth culture.

Scholars and clinicians have developed a body of literature which discusses adolescent experience in great detail. We can trace study in this area back to Erikson's theory of stages. He argued that adolescence is a time of identity construction (Erikson, 1956). Until adolescence, identity is acquired through the family; individuals are socialized to see themselves much as the family sees them. In childhood, attitudes, values, and definitions are accepted uncritically. During adolescence, the earlier "borrowed" identity is questioned. Individuals ask themselves whether they agree with what they have been told, what they have learned. While reconstructing themselves, adolescents rely less on families (who played an important role in defining their childhood selves) and, in an effort to become independent and autonomous, turn towards their peers and societal standards. Part of this identity construction is, of course, the gender role orientation. Not just "who am I?" but "who am I as a woman?" "What does this involve?" "How should I act? think?" By the time these girls become adults, most have developed a sense of who they are as women. Therefore, when they are confronted with external stressors—for example, pressure from conflicts among individual, micro, and macro levels of the gender system—they have an internal sense of self that provides direction, which is lacking during early adolescence.

During adolescence, peers play a critical role. They are all experiencing similar changes, though at varying paces. By observing each other, they gain a sense of what is considered desirable and appropriate. While they observe, they are painfully aware that they are also being observed. The "imaginary audience" hypothesis suggests that adolescents are so sensitive to the evaluation/judgement of others that they perceive an audience, and behave accordingly, even when they are not being observed (Elkind & Bowen, 1979). As each adolescent is looking at others she is gathering the "raw resources" to shape her "self." Seltzer calls this the "comparative act" (Seltzer, 1989). Through the evaluation and critique and assessment of peers as well as imitation and experimentation, an adolescent gains the materials necessary to construct her "self." The knowledge that one is both judging and being judged makes adolescents highly conscious of their social desirability. Seltzer describes the adolescent world as the "peer arena," the micro structure where identity is constructed.

A further aspect of adolescence is finding one's location; that is, answering the question "where do I fit in?" This clearly is associated with the "social desirability" mentioned above. Just as the adult society is stratified—around class, race, and gender, for example—and one gains social power through position based on resources, the adolescent world is also hierarchical and also involves social power. The young person must find his or her place in this social structure. The social class from which the adolescent has come is still prevalent, but it is not sufficient to define who has power in the peer arena, because it is based on the parent's resources and not on the adolescent's own characteristics. So the hierarchy

among adolescents is based largely on personal resources. Because a significant part of constructing the self at this point is coming to understand gender role orientation and sexuality, the adolescent hierarchy is based in large part on one's presentation of manhood or womanhood. That is to say, the more "manly" men, displaying evidence of the strength, courage, and competence stereotypically expected of males, are considered more desirable than others. And among women, appearance and desirability are key attributes.

The powerful effect of the peer arena determines where any individual will fit in the social world. And in this arena, status is linked to appearance. Do you look the part? Or, as important, are you "playing" the part by dieting and making appearance a key part of your conversations and social world? Drawing messages from the larger macro gender structure, peers set the rules for "fitting in." And the unstable aspect of individual adolescents' own sense of self and their incomplete individual gender role orientation makes withstanding the pressure to conform difficult. By later adolescence, the tendency to conform is reduced (Berndt, 1979); individuals are more sure of themselves, have established their identities and gender role orientations, and may be, therefore, less vulnerable to the pressures of the micro and macro structures.

THIS STUDY

We undertook a qualitative research project in the summer of 1997 in Southern Alberta entitled "Growing Up Female." Through 25 depth interviews and focus groups with 6 girls, we explored adolescents' own perceptions of the challenges they face and how they navigate through the peer arena. The analysis was based on the principles of grounded theory (Glaser & Strauss, 1967; Strauss, 1987). That is, rather than trying to verify a specific hypothesis, we attempted to see their world as adolescents see it and discover how the three levels of the sex/gender system interact in their lives. From listening to the girls, reviewing the tapes, and examining transcripts, patterns emerged. The patterns were then explored more fully in subsequent interviews. The goal was not to quantify, but rather to get a sense of the importance of conforming to appearance norms within the adolescent social hierarchy.

The study began with a "typical" sample of young women chosen to represent different ages, social classes, and family arrangements. We quickly came to recognize that one's location in the hierarchy—insider, outsider, popular, outcast, etc.—was a critical variable and that the sample needed to reflect this diversity as well. (The girls' location in the hierarchy was also seen to influence them in terms of vulnerability to outside pressure and suggestion, but not in the ways one might predict.) The girls interviewed were from junior high, high school (one of whom attended an all girl's high school), post-secondary institutions, and "drop outs" (many of whom had moved to alternative schools).

The importance of qualitative studies is that they can answer the question "why?" While quantitative studies can measure patterns to determine how many suffer from eating disorders and/or depression, and can assess the correlation [among] class, race, family and behaviour numerically, one must look deeper to understand the underlying causal connection between these behaviours and the social factors in the girls' lives. One must try to understand their social world as they define and live it. It is vital for the researchers to avoid directing the discussions so as not to artificially focus on "constraints." Questions about what boys do to them or what society does to them denies the agency of the young women. Instead, this study asked the girls what they did to get along in their world. What are the rules in their world? Where did the rules come from?

Once we had collected information from all of the respondents, we identified patterns and came to understand how fully social hierarchy, and therefore social power, influenced their

lives and how salient appearance is within that hierarchy. The best way to convey these findings is through case studies. In the following section, I will present the cases of women located in each of the various positions in the adolescent hierarchy, allowing each to speak about where they fit and how they came to hold that position. (Obviously, names have been changed but other details are unaltered.)

FINDINGS

Not surprisingly, the study indicates that for adolescent girls, appearance is salient and notions about what is a desirable appearance are influenced by cultural norms: the macro structure provides powerful images and pressures. However, the girls made it clear that they were not all victims blindly following a goal set by the larger society without thought. And not all were dissatisfied with their appearances—not even all of those who spent a considerable amount of time and energy complaining about themselves and dieting. As they explained, appearance equals status. "Life would be easier if you looked like that [like the women on *Melrose Place*] because people give you an easier time if you are pretty. If more guys like you, the girls give you an easier time,…I don't think it should be that way, but I think society puts a lot of importance on your looks and size." And dieting and "fat" talk are also linked to status. The girls say they hate their bodies, or themselves, but when they discuss it more fully they often acknowledge that these statements are a means of fitting in.[2] They see that being part of the group means "obsessing" about their bodies, and group membership leads to success and social power. Those who fit the appearance criteria belong to the elite group, have power, know they have it, and enjoy wielding it. They reinforce their own position by deliberately making others feel inadequate. In fact, the power that they gain from their elite status is the power to exclude others. Their actions enhance their own positions while making appearance more salient for all girls (that is, making the micro structure extremely appearance-based).

The findings indicate that the most difficult time for young women was during junior high school, sooner than most people would like to believe is the case. Why should twelve-year-olds be caught up in issues about body and appearance? Are they trying to attract boys or men? Not really. They perceive other girls as both their audience and their harshest critics. Therefore, their preoccupation with weight and body is not about being desirable to the boys so much as gaining acceptance within the hierarchy. Boys can certainly exacerbate the pressure through name-calling and harassment, but this is only one part of the larger issue: finding your place in the social world is based on playing a role and looking the part. Even girls who attended "all girl schools" were subject to appearance pressures.

By later adolescence, women have already begun to develop a stronger sense of self and [have] grown less vulnerable to the group's definition of who they are. By the end of high school, most girls had worked through much of their confusion and vulnerability. While they continued to talk about dieting and eating, about shape and size, this was much less about really planning to change their physical appearance than about "playing the game." Those who wanted to fit into the social hierarchy recognized that playing by these rules was necessary. However, by this stage, many girls had found their own groups of friends and set their own goals and challenges; they felt freer express their own gender role orientations rather than following the group's definition of "woman."[3]

But in early adolescence, in junior high, most girls are just beginning the process of becoming independent and autonomous. There is a shift from living with the self-image that your parents and family defined for you to finding your "own" self with the assistance of peers. The peers' opinions count for a great deal because they form the social world in which this new self must establish

herself. This is for most girls the period of most intense pressure to be autonomous and independent, greatest confusion about self, and therefore greatest vulnerability. And in this setting, young adolescent girls are becoming themselves, adults, and "women."

As indicated, most of the girls had worked through and beyond this understanding that their self worth and status as women was tied to appearance by the time they reached the end of high school. But some girls did not get past this stage as easily as others. They continued to measure themselves by their appearance.

The Elite Group

The first group of those who had trouble moving beyond the adolescent definitions of desirability is made up of girls who were popular in junior high and high school; they were at the top of the social hierarchy. They seemed to be the winners who enjoyed the power that accompanied their status. They basked in the attention of all: other girls, boys, and most teachers. Two of the respondents talked about their experiences at the top of this hierarchy.

Jillian said that she is so good at being part of the group that she has no very clear sense of who she is. While in high school she knew exactly where she belonged. "I was definitely one of the popular ones." She said bluntly, "I consider myself to be pretty, that might have something to do with it [her popularity]. All my friends were popular." In fact, she revelled in the attention she received. She was teased by the boys about her looks ("I have big boobs") but found this flattering rather than intimidating or threatening. Being a part of the elite group was not a problem while in the insulated world of the high school, but she feels completely lost since leaving school. She found that the attributes that had given her power were no longer as valuable and she had no sense of direction. Jillian had allowed herself to be defined by the micro structure of her peer group and did not develop her own identity. She adopted the norms of the group without truly developing her own gender role orientation. Now that she has moved into a new environment, and without the guidance of her own individual gender role orientation, she feels aimless. "Where I stand now I'm not going anywhere. I'm not moving forward, I'm not moving backward, I'm just not going anywhere."

Reva was also very popular in high school, but [she] recognized even at the time that this popularity had no solid foundation. She tried to hang on to status and popularity via appearance but was constantly concerned about it. "I was insecure but I don't know if other people knew it." She was unsure of her "self" and her true desirability. She recognized that popularity in high school was all about "material things, the way things look, everything on the outside." And she knew that she and her friends maintained their position by belittling others: "I think we were back stabbers and snobby, pretty snobby." But at the time this seemed reasonable. Having a boyfriend was an affirmation of Reva's status and her desirability. When she and her boyfriend broke up, she believed that she need only lose weight to regain her social position. "Actually, there were a couple of us that wanted to like, starve ourselves, try to lose weight so we just wouldn't eat." As a result, she developed an eating disorder. Eventually, she went into counselling and slowly has come to recognize the damage that her bulimia caused. But at the time, being thin made sense and gaining a even a little bit of weight "really stressed me out."

Being in the elite group is no guarantee of success or well-being. While it worked for some in the short-term because they really did attain power—the power to exclude others—it did not bring long-term contentment. Upon graduation, the micro structure which had given girls power and a valued position was disbanded, leaving them directionless. Even within high school, all was not well. While this group appeared to dictate what was the appropriate appearance around the school, this was often a reflection of media images.

"Popular" respondents mentioned TV shows and magazines that influenced their "style." And maintaining their social position involved a constant effort to keep up with the cultural ideal. For some this seemed easy, but for others like Reva, it was both difficult and undermining.

The "Wannabes"

While this seems like a pejorative term, it's how these girls describe themselves. They believe they will be in the most popular group if they just make a few changes; as a result, they spend their adolescent years struggling to reach the top of the pyramid. Kim is a member of this group. She says she understands the hierarchy and knows how it works: "The pressure increases as you move towards the popular group. You always have to prove yourself—based on how you look." She also knows that she is very close to the top and believes she could get there if she could just play the game right. And despite acknowledging that being popular doesn't always allow you to be a good person—"Popular people are jerks, they don't care about others, are very competitive, and treat people badly"—this doesn't stop her from wanting to be one of them. She works hard to win favour, to accept the rules. She believes that she could be popular if she was just a bit thinner. People in her group tend to diet for real, thinking they are just ten pounds away from having social power. She said the whole group began smoking on the same day when one person found out that it suppressed appetite. "We always talked about weight and how to lose it—drink Slimfast®, take Dexatrim®." Expending so much energy on reaching the top of the social hierarchy means that Kim spends little time trying to find her own direction or "self." She just knows she isn't happy. She feels "insecure, always beating myself up" and says "trying to fit in is limiting." She does not have a strong sense of self and therefore accepts the peer arena as the ultimate arbiter. The unquestioning acceptance of the peer arena and of the validity of the social hierarchy leaves people in this group, like those in the group "above" them on the popularity scale, vulnerable to a gender system which focuses on appearance. Their gender role orientation reflects this desire to achieve the ideal appearance: being a woman means looking the part.

Life in the Middle

The girls on the next level "down" on the hierarchical scale are the least vulnerable. While girls in this group still cope with pressure in the peer arena, they know they will never be at the top. As a result, they tend to examine it more critically, asking whether increased popularity is worth achieving. The answer is usually no. These girls form their own rules, have outside interests, and define "self" by a standard other than that of the hierarchy. One result of this alternate definition of self is that appearance is less salient than ability.

The individuals in this group often have outside interests—music, sports, religion, or the guiding movement, for example—that seem to help them find a self worth regardless of their status at school. And at school they either are not picked on or don't let it bother them because they know that it isn't real. They construct their "self" based on what they are, not on what someone tells them they should be. Jana is never going to be at the top of the social hierarchy; she knows it and doesn't care. Her parents are of different races and she perceives that being biracial makes her "different." But it isn't a problem for her, she says, she just has to find her own way. When listening to Jana, she convinces you that this makes her stronger. She sees other "kids who try their hardest to be like another person and follow what they do" but distinguishes herself. She says unequivocally, "I am who I am." Racial slurs don't bother her, she makes a joke of it. When her best friend goes on and on about being fat, Jana believes "she does it just for attention." She isn't affected by media images either: "I'm not saying they're not beautiful but I'm saying that you don't know what's

under all that make-up, that's four hours of make-up put on. I could look like that too." In essence, Jana isn't caught up in the gender system because she is not trying to prove herself in the peer arena. She has a strong sense of self and does not accept the salience of appearance. However, she also notes that "I've never gotten fat so it has never been an issue for me." She can be truly comfortable with herself even when others in her world are striving to attain an ideal.

Una is also in this middle group. She is involved in both music and sports and spends much of her time with these activities. She says, "there's no pressure in my group. We don't have to spend time on make-up and hair." They don't want to be skinny partly because "the coach encourages us to stay fit." "I just don't have the time or the money to keep up." But she does acknowledge that it was harder to "be yourself" in junior high: "People were starting to form groups and you were left out if you didn't follow the group." But her close circle of friends didn't value the "popular" behaviours and didn't try to look the part.

Freedom from the tyranny of the gender system—which offers an almost impossible beauty standard—seems much more attainable for these young women. Because they do not have an opportunity to join the elite group, and because they have other qualities which make them strong, they are less vulnerable to its dictates. Not being part of the "in" crowd enables them to critique the hierarchy and its norms. In essence, these girls have developed gender role orientations which conflict with the macro structure and most of them have found a group of peers who also reject the salience of appearance.

On The Fringe

The next group—the "lowest" on the scale I have identified—is that of individuals who define themselves as "outsiders." They believe they are excluded because of their size and shape (though some of them have other characteristics which also contribute to their exclusion). These girls don't have the ability to break out of the outsider role into which they have been cast. For adolescents in this group, not fitting in really hurts; they feel rejected, ridiculed, isolated. Because they are so far from the norm—often very overweight or dealing with severe acne—they feel that they are suffering at the hands of their peers.

Some do come to hate themselves because they are treated so cruelly. Rachel describes one hurtful experience "I was trying to walk through the crowd when one guy said 'R, you don't belong in this crowd.' There was another girl who told me to f— off. I was watching them I guess. I was pretty shy too. But I think *it* made me shy" The "it" she refers to is being excluding for not looking the "right" way. She feels very alone, even though there are several other girls on the "outside." She now "rejects the image thing" because she knows she doesn't fit ("I'm big boned like my dad") but she tried really hard in junior high. She really hated herself, even though she believed she was good on the inside, because of the way she was treated, because her body was devalued. In fact, Rachel feels pressure from her family to try harder to fit in—her mom would like her to change her appearance but she says she "just gave up trying."

Terry was also on the outside because of her weight. She had a couple of close friends "but the rest just left me out." Unlike Rachel, though, she "successfully" lost weight and reaped the rewards of following the group standard. She wanted to be small no matter what and simply stopped eating. At first everyone was pleased. She got more attention at school. People noticed her and talked to her. Initially, Terry liked being popular. "I felt better for a while but then came to realize that my life still sucked. Even when I was skinny I wasn't happy." She came to hate being popular because she could see more clearly than most how artificial the distinction was. Terry believes being skinny actually made her feel worse because the "popular Terry" wasn't the "real Terry." Her peers only saw her outside and still didn't recognize her

true worth. Her family and few close friends became worried and did not support her dieting. And "I got tired of measuring every mouthful, having everyone watching and measuring every mouthful, so I started eating again." She gained the weight back and is now more comfortable with herself. "A whole new world opened up when I left school." Both Terry and Rachel understood how the social hierarchy worked. They knew how to gain power by following the mandate of the peer group. But they both chose not to. They lost status within the micro structure but grew more comfortable with themselves.

Karla was in a similar situation and it was terribly damaging. She started out in the popular group but " I found you had to stoop quite low to become popular. You had to be willing to be rude to all the other people." She wanted to be friendly to everyone and eventually the popular crowd turned their backs on her. They began to harass her and single her out; most of the insults were based on her appearance. "After a while, when so many people tell you something, you know you start to believe it's true, like you get it from enough people it starts to seem true, so I got enough people telling me I was ugly enough times, it kind of makes you believe it." Eventually she quit school because it became unbearable. She'd like to go back but "it's hard to get started up again if you live in the same place and you stay in the same place because everyone knows your past.... I can't start over again because the people who knew me, knew me as a geek, a freak." She feels better about herself now but doesn't want to face that kind of pressure again.

Examining the fringe group in terms of the three levels of gender, the "hell" for these girls was the micro gender structure of the peer arena; however, the values of the microsystem seemed to be reinforced—though not caused—by the larger macro structure. Our society is far more conscious of racism and sexism than of "lookism," especially as it is manifested in the adolescent world. Rachel and Karla internalized the negative messages directed at them by their peers. And they both came to hate themselves. Fortunately, they also both were able to overcome those feelings and recognize that their value was determined neither by their appearance nor by the critics in the peer arena.

IMPLICATIONS

Why is appearance so salient for adolescent girls? This study reinforces the understanding that at this period in her life, a girl has few measuring sticks and no long list of personal accomplishments. She must seek some means of reassuring herself that she is becoming an adult, a woman, an individual separate from her earlier, family-defined self. The larger macro gender structure of fashion magazines and advertisement sends messages that appearance is an important feature of power and desirability. This notion is adopted by adolescent girls in part because it is a field over which many feel they have some control (however illusory such a perception might be). They think that they can change their bodies, their clothing, their hairstyles. And they recognize that a specific kind of beauty is valued by the society at large. Thus appearance becomes a standard. This means that appearance actually does serve as a means of attaining social acceptability and power within the peer arena. As the study revealed, becoming a woman has less to do with the role one might play and more to do with the body. An interesting—perhaps startling—paradox emerged when we asked the respondents to define "woman." On the one hand, being a woman, they said, does not constrain career choices. They believe women can become anything they want. As available "sexual" roles grow, women are not defined by filling a specific role—for example, wife or mother. And as they perceive that more and more options are available in the work world, no particular job defines "woman." On the other hand, something distinguishes women from men. And that something is appearance. It is the girl's body that makes her a woman. Therefore, being a woman means one should be preoccupied with one's body and making one's body fit the part. None of the girls we spoke to was trying to diet to avoid growing up into womanhood; indeed, they were dieting to *achieve* womanhood, which they have come to accept is characterized by a very particular physical stature.

Young women are not all passive recipients of society's messages about the body. They perceive that they are not victims, that they are not trying to achieve certain appearances because men or boys want them to. Instead, they see themselves as actively involved in struggles with other women. Their female peers are the harshest critics. Among these critics, appearance brings social power, even if it is only the power to exclude others. They want the right body in order to attain social power and to prove themselves as women. Having a "boyfriend" is important in part because it sends a message to the peer arena that one has successfully achieved the requisite look. This becomes part of the measuring stick.

When the three levels of the gender system—the individual, micro, and macro levels—all agree that appearance is salient, the girl who experiences this will strive to attain the beauty standard. She believes that achieving this look will bring her social acceptance and membership into the elite group. If she fails to measure up to the standard, she faces the painful realization that she will be devalued by those with power in the peer arena. However, if she also learns that the imperatives of the peer arena are not absolute, and she is able to develop her own gender role orientation, then appearance loses its salience, and the elite group loses its power over her. If the three levels do not all agree, if girls have developed gender role orientations which do not incorporate the societal beauty ideal, or they belong to micro structures (as adolescents, perhaps a group of friends, sports team, or social club apart from the school-based peer arena) which value ability rather than appearance, then they are less subject to the appearance standards.

While adolescent girls face an exaggerated version of the gender system, all women are subject to the same forces. We must find our way within a societal landscape that valorizes beauty often above ability. And frequently we must do so in micro structures (in the work place and in our homes) which adopt this standard and devalue our actions. Like these adolescent girls, we remain strong if we develop gender role orientations which do not centre around appearance, and if we foster relationships and micro structures which value women for their strength and skill rather than their outward appearance. The results of this study are suggestive—not yet detailed enough or broad enough to be conclusive—but give us some insight into girls' own perceptions of their world and perhaps into the roots of gender role uncertainty that continues for some women into adulthood.

CRITICAL THINKING QUESTIONS

1. What are some of the characteristics that define a "Wannabe"?
2. Why do you think the girls' social positions influenced their perceptions of their physical selves?
3. Given Matthews' findings, do you think that adolescent boys face similar social pressures concerning their appearance? What examples from your own experiences help support your opinion?
4. In your view, are the social pressures on young women's appearance becoming more or less powerful over time? Why do you think that is the case?

NOTES

1. Obviously, this is a generalization. An important point of this argument is that individual women—especially adult women—move in microstructures and have developed "selves" that allow them to function effectively in a way inconsistent with the "body beautiful" standards…society.

2. This is not to say that…[none of the] girls…experience[d] genuine pain and self-hatred—their situations will be explored more fully in subsequent sections. It does mean that many girls are not as negative about themselves as it might appear from listening to their conversations among their peers.

3. It is possible that for university women, living in dormitories, food, eating, and weight once again become salient as a new social hierarchy must be established. While this was not investigated in this study, we are currently interviewing women in residences to see if the pattern re-emerges.

REFERENCES

Bem, S. 1993. *The lenses of gender.* New Haven: Yale University Press.

Berger, P., and B. Berger. 1975. *Sociology: A biographical approach.* New York: Basic Books.

Berndt, T. 1979. Developmental changes in conformity to peers and parents." *Developmental Psychology,* 15: 606–16.

Bordo, S. 1993. *Unbearable weight: Feminism, western culture and the body.* Los Angeles: University of California Press.

Brownmiller, S. 1984. *Femininity.* New York: Linden Press.

Brumberg, J. 1997. *The body project: An intimate history of American girls.* New York: Random House.

Chernin, K. 1981. *The obsession: Reflections on the tyranny of slenderness.* New York: Harper and Row.

Elkind, D., and Bowen. 1979. Imaginary audience behaviour in children and adults. *Developmental Psychology,* 15: 33–44.

Erikson, E. 1956. The problem of ego identity. *Journal of the American Psychoanalytic Association,* 4: 56–121.

Freedman, R. 1986. *Beauty bound.* Lexington, Mass.: D.C. Heath and Company.

Glaser, B., and A. Strauss. 1967. *Am I thin enough yet?: The cult of thinness and the commercialization of identity.* New York: Oxford University Press.

Greer, G. 1970. *The female eunuch.* London: MacGibbon & Kee.

Hesse-Biber, S. 1996. *Am I thin enough yet? The cult of thinness and the commercialization of identity.* New York: Oxford University Press.

Matthews, B. 1997. *The gender system and fertility: An examination of the hidden links.* Population Studies Centre: Working Paper.

Matthews, B., and R. Beaujot. 1997. Gender orientations and fertility strategies. *Canadian Review of Sociology and Anthropology,* 34(4): 415–28.

Pipher, M. 1996. *Reviving Ophelia: Saving the selves of adolescent girls.* New York: Ballantine Books.

Risman, B., and P. Schwartz. 1989. *Gender in intimate relationships: A microstructural approach.* Belmont: Wadsworth Publishing Co.

Seltzer, V. 1989. *The psychosocial worlds of the adolescent: Public and private.* New York: John Wiley and Sons.

Shute, J. 1992. *Life size.* New York: Avon Books.

Smith, D. 1987. *The everyday world as problematic: A feminist sociology.* Toronto: University of Toronto Press.

Strauss, A. 1987. *Qualitative analysis for social scientists.* New York: Cambridge University Press.

Stryker, S. 1980. *Symbolic interactionism: A social structural version.* Menlo Park: Benjamin Cummings Publishing.

Wolf, N. 1991. *The beauty myth.* New York: Morrow Books.

21

The DOs and TABOOs of Body Language Around the World

Roger E. Axtell

In a world that grows smaller every year, it is easy to offend others simply by being ourselves—gestures that we take as innocent may be seen by someone else as deeply insulting. This selection suggests the extent of the problem and, in an age of global business dealings, the need to cultivate cultural sensitivity.

THREE GREAT GAFFES OR ONE COUNTRY'S GOOD MANNERS, ANOTHER'S GRAND FAUX PAS

In Washington they call protocol "etiquette with a government expense account." But diplomacy isn't just for diplomats. How you behave in other people's countries reflects on more than you alone. It also brightens—or dims—the image of where you come from and whom you work for. The Ugly American about whom we used to read so much may be dead, but here and there the ghost still wobbles out of the closet.

Three well-traveled Americans tell how even an old pro can sometimes make the wrong move in the wrong place at the wrong time.

Source: From *DOs and TABOOs around the World*, 3rd ed., by Roger Axtell. Copyright © 1993 Parker Pen Company. A Benjamin Book distributed by John Wiley & Sons, Inc. Reprinted by permission of John Wiley & Sons, Inc.

A Partner in One of New York's Leading Private Banking Firms

When the board chairman is Lo Win Hao, do you smile brightly and say, "How do you do, Mr. Hao?" or "Mr. Lo"? Or "Mr. Win"?

I traveled nine thousand miles to meet a client and arrived with my foot in my mouth. Determined to do things right, I'd memorized the names of the key men I was to see in Singapore. No easy job, inasmuch as the names all came in threes. So, of course, I couldn't resist showing off that I'd done my homework. I began by addressing top man Lo Win Hao with plenty of well placed Mr. Hao's—and sprinkled the rest of my remarks with a Mr. Chee this and a Mr. Woon that. Great show. Until a note was passed to me from one man I'd met before, in New York. Bad news. "Too friendly too soon, Mr. Long," it said. Where diffidence is next to godliness, there I was, calling a roomful of VIPs, in effect, Mr. Ed and Mr. Charlie. I'd remembered everybody's name—but forgotten that in Chinese the surname comes *first* and the given name *last*.

An Associate in Charge of Family Planning for an International Human Welfare Organization

The lady steps out in her dazzling new necklace and everybody dies laughing. (Or what not to wear to Togo on a Saturday night.)

From growing up in Cuba to joining the Peace Corps to my present work, I've spent most of my life in the Third World. So nobody should know better than I how to dress for it. Certainly one of the silliest mistakes an outsider can make is to dress up in "native" costume, whether it's a sari or a sombrero, unless you really know what you're doing. Yet, in Togo, when I found some of the most beautiful beads I'd ever seen, it never occurred to me not to wear them. While I was up-country, I seized the first grand occasion to flaunt my new find. What I didn't know is that locally the beads are worn not at the neck but at the waist—to hold up a sort of loincloth under the skirt. So, into the party I strutted, wearing around my neck what to every Togolese eye was part of a pair of underpants.

An Account Executive at an International Data Processing and Electronics Conglomerate

Even in a country run by generals, would you believe a runny nose could get you arrested?

A friend and I were coming into Colombia on business after a weekend in the Peruvian mountains touring Machu Picchu. What a sight that had been. And what a head cold the change in temperature had given my friend. As we proceeded through customs at the airport, he was wheezing and blowing into his handkerchief like an active volcano. Next thing I knew, two armed guards were lockstepping him through a door. I tried to intercede before the door slammed shut, but my spotty Spanish failed me completely. Inside a windowless room with the guards, so did his. He shouted in English. They shouted in Spanish. It was beginning to look like a bad day in Bogotá when a Colombian woman who had seen what happened burst into the room and finally achieved some bilingual understanding. It seems all that sniffling in the land of the infamous coca leaf had convinced the guards that my friend was waltzing through their airport snorting cocaine.

CUDDLY ETHNOCENTRICS

If only the world's customs inspectors could train their German shepherds to sniff out the invisible baggage we all manage to slip with us into foreign countries. They are like secret little land mines of the mind. Set to go off at the slightest quiver, they can sabotage a five-minute stroll down the Champs-Élysées or a $5 million tractor sale to Beijing. Three of our most popular national take-alongs:

Why Don't They Speak English? For the same reason we don't speak Catalan or Urdu. The wonder, in fact, is that so many people do speak so many languages. Seldom is a Continental European fluent in fewer than three, often more. Africans grow up with language of the nation that once colonized theirs plus half a dozen different tribal dialects. Japan has three distinct Japanese languages, which even the lowliest street sweeper can understand. Middle Eastern businesspeople shift effortlessly from their native tongue(s) to Oxford English to Quai d'Orsay French. Yet most of the English-speaking world remains as cheerfully monolingual as Queen Victoria's parakeet. If there are any complaints, then, it is clear they should not be coming from the American/English-speaking traveler.

Take Me to Your Burger King. In Peoria a Persian does not go looking for pot-au-feu. Alone among travelers, Americans seem to embark like astronauts—sealed inside a cozy life-support system from home. Scrambled eggs. Rent-a-cars. Showers. TV. Nothing wrong with any of it back home, but to the rest of the universe it looks sadly like somebody trying to read a book with the cover closed. Experiment! Try the local specialties.

American Know-How to the Rescue! Our brightest ideas have taken root all over the world—from assembling lines in Düsseldorf to silicone chips in Osaka to hybrid grains that are helping to nourish the Third World. Nonetheless, bigger, smarter, and faster do not inevitably add up to better. Indeed, the desire to take on shiny new American ways has been the downfall of nations whose cultures were already rich in art and technology when North America was still a glacier. As important as the idea itself is the way it is presented.

A U.S. doctor of public health recently back from West Africa offers an example of how to make the idea fit the ideology. "I don't just pop over and start handing out antimalarial pills on the corner," she says. "First I visit with the village chief. After he gives his blessing, I move in with the local witch doctor. After she shows me her techniques and I show her mine—and a few lives are saved—maybe then we can get the first native to swallow the first pill."

This is as true at the high-tech level as at the village dispensary. "What is all this drinking of green tea before the meeting with Mitsubishi?" The American way is to get right down to business. Yet if you look at Mitsubishi's bottom line, you have to wonder if green tea is such a bad idea after all.

It should come as no surprise that people surrounded by oceans rather than by other people end up ethnocentric. Even our biggest fans admit that America often strikes the rest of the world as a sweet-but-spoiled little darling, wanting desperately to please, but not paying too much attention to how it is done. Ever since the Marshall Plan, we seemed to believe that *our* games and *our* rules were the only ones in town. Any town. And that all else was the Heart of Darkness.

Take this scene in a Chinese cemetery. Watching a Chinese reverently placing fresh fruit on a grave, an American visitor asked, "When do you expect your ancestors to get up and eat the fruit?" The Chinese replied, "As soon as your ancestors get up and smell the flowers."

HANDS ACROSS THE ABYSS

Our bad old habits are giving way to a new when-in-Rome awareness. Some corporations take it so seriously that they put employees into a crash course of overseas cultural immersion. AT&T, for instance, encourages—and pays for—the whole family of an executive on the way to a foreign assignment to enroll in classes given by experts in the mores and manners of other lands.

Among the areas that cry out loudest for international understanding are how to say people's names, eat, dress, and talk. Get those four basics right and the rest is a piece of kuchen.

Basic Rule #1: What's in a Name?

…The first transaction between even ordinary citizens—and the first chance to make an impression for better or worse—is, of course, an exchange of names. In America there usually is not very much to get wrong. And even if you do, so what?

Not so elsewhere. Especially in the Eastern Hemisphere, where name frequently denotes social rank or family status, a mistake can be an outright insult. So can switching to a given name without the other person's permission, even when you think the situation calls for it.

"What would you like me to call you?" is always the opening line of one overseas deputy director for an international telecommunications corporation. "Better to ask several times," he advises, "than to get it wrong." Even then, "I err on the side of formality until asked to 'Call me Joe.'" Another frequent traveler insists his company provide him with a list of key people he will meet, country by country, surnames underlined, to be memorized on the flight over.

Don't Trust the Rules. Just when you think you have broken the international name code, they switch the rules on you. Take Latin America. Most people's names are a combination of the father's and mother's, with only the father's name used in conversation. In the Spanish-speaking countries the father's name comes first. Hence, Carlos Mendoza-Miller is called Mr. Mendoza. *But* in Portuguese-speaking Brazil it is the other way around, with the mother's name first.

In the Orient the Chinese system of surname first, given name last does not always apply.

The Taiwanese, many of whom were educated in missionary schools, often have a Christian first name, which comes before any of the others—as in Tommy Ho Chin, who should be called Mr. Ho or, to his friends, Tommy Ho. Also, given names are often officially changed to initials, and a Y. Y. Lang is Y. Y.; never mind what it stands for. In Korea, which of a man's names takes a Mr. is determined by whether he is his father's first or second son. Although in Thailand names run backwards, Chinese style, the Mr. is put with the *given* name, and to a Thai it is just as important to be called by his given name as it is for a Japanese to be addressed by his surname. With the latter, incidentally, you can in a very friendly relationship respond to his using *your* first name by dropping the Mr. and adding *san* to his last name, as in Ishikawa-san.

Hello. Are you still there? Then get ready for the last installment of the name game, which is to disregard all of the above—sometimes. The reason is that many Easterners who deal regularly with the West are now changing the order of their names to un-confuse us. So, while to one another their names remain the same, to us the given name may come before the surname. Then again, it may not.

The safest course remains: Ask.

Basic Rule #2: Eat, Drink, and Be Wary

…[M]ealtime is no time for a thanks-but-no-thanks response. Acceptance of what is on your plate is tantamount to acceptance of host, country, and company. So, no matter how tough things may be to swallow, swallow. Or, as one veteran globe-girdler puts it, "Travel with a cast-iron stomach and eat everything everywhere."

Tastiness Is in the Eye of the Beholder. Often, what is offered constitutes your host country's proudest culinary achievements. What would we Americans think of a Frenchman who refused a bite of homemade apple pie or

sizzling sirloin? Squeamishness comes not so much from the thing itself as from our unfamiliarity with it. After all, an oyster has remarkably the same look and consistency as a sheep's eye, and at first encounter a lobster would strike almost anybody as more a creature from science fiction than something you dip in melted butter and pop into your mouth.

Incidentally, in Saudi Arabia sheep's eyes are a delicacy, and in China it's bear's paw soup.

Perhaps the ultimate in exotic dining abroad befell a family planning expert on a trip for an international human welfare organization. It was a newly emerged African country where the national dish—in fact, the *only* dish eleven months of the year—is yam. The visitor's luck, however, was to be there the *other* month, when gorillas come in from the bush to steal the harvest. Being the only available protein, gorilla meat is as prized as sirloin is over here, and the village guest of honor was served a choice cut. Proudly, a platter of the usual mashed yams was placed before her—but with a roast gorilla hand thrusting artfully up from the center.

Is there any polite way out besides the back door?

Most experienced business travelers say no, at least not before taking at least a few bites. It helps, though, to slice whatever the item is very thin. This way, you minimize the texture—gristly, slimy, etc.—and the reminder of whence it came. Or, "Swallow it quickly," as one traveler recommends. "I still can't tell you what sheep's eyeballs taste like." As for dealing with taste, the old canard that "it tastes just like chicken" is often mercifully true. Even when the "it" is rodent, snake—or gorilla.

Another useful dodge is not knowing what you are eating. What's for dinner? Don't ask. Avoid poking around in the kitchen or looking at English-language menus. Your host will be flattered that you are following his lead, and who knows? Maybe it really is chicken in that stew.…

Bottoms Up—or Down? Some countries seem to do it deliberately, some inadvertently, except for

Islam, where they don't do it at all. Either way, getting visitors as tipsy as possible as fast as possible stands as a universal sign of hospitality, and refusal to play your part equals rebuff. Wherever you go, toasts are as reciprocal as handshakes: If one does, all do. "I don't drink, thank you" rarely gets you off gracefully. Neither does protesting that you must get up early. (So must everyone else.)

"I try to wangle a glass of wine instead of the local firewater," one itinerant American says. "The only trouble is, the wine is usually stronger than the hard stuff." Mao-tai, Chinese wine made from sorghum, is notorious for leaving the unsuspecting thoroughly shanghaied. The Georgian wine so popular in Russia is no ladylike little Chablis either. In Nordic lands proper form for the toast is to raise the glass in a sweeping arc from belt buckle to lips while locking stares with your host. It takes very few akvavit-with-beer-chasers before you both start seeing northern lights.

In Africa, where all the new countries were once old European colonies, it is often taken for granted that if you are white you must have whiskey or gin or whatever the colonials used to like. A traveler to a former French possession describes the dilemma of being served a large gourdful of Johnnie Walker Red at nine in the morning. The host was simply remembering how the French had always loved their Scotch. *When* they drank it and *how much* were details he had never noticed. Yet there was no saying no without giving offense. A few sips had to be taken and a promise made to finish the rest later.

Basic Rule #3: Clothes Can Also *Un*make the Man

…Wherever you are, what you wear among strangers should not look strange to *them*. Which does not mean, "When in Morocco wear djellabas," etc. It means wear what you look natural in—and know how to wear—that also fits in with your surroundings.

For example, a woman dressed in a tailored suit, even with high heels and flowery blouse, looks startlingly masculine in a country full of

diaphanous saris. More appropriate, then, is a silky, loose-fitting dress in a bright color—as opposed to blue serge or banker's gray.

In downtown Nairobi, a safari jacket looks as out of place as in London. With a few exceptions (where the weather is just too steamy for it), the general rule everywhere is that for business, for eating out, even for visiting people at home, you should be very buttoned up: conservative suit and tie for men, dress or skirt-suit for women. To be left in the closet until you go on an outdoor sight-seeing trek:

jeans, however haute couture
jogging shoes
tennis and T-shirts
tight-fitting sweaters (women)
open-to-the-navel shirts (men)
funny hats (both)

Where you *can* loosen up, it is best to do it the way the indigenes do. In the Philippines men wear the barong tagalog—a loose, frilly, usually white or cream-colored shirt with tails out, no jacket or tie. In tropical Latin American countries the counterpart to the barong is called a *guayabera* and, except for formal occasions, is acceptable business attire. In Indonesia they wear *Batiks*—brightly patterned shirts that go tieless and jacketless everywhere. In Thailand the same is true for the collarless Thai silk shirt. In Japan dress is at least as formal as in Europe (dark suit and tie for a man, business suit or tailored dress for a woman) except at country inns (called *ryokans*), where even big-city corporations sometimes hold meetings. Here you are expected to wear a kimono. Not to daytime meetings but to dinner, no matter how formal. (Don't worry—the inn always provides the kimono.)

One thing you notice wherever you go is that polyester is the mark of the tourist. The less drip-dry you are, the more you look as if you have come to do serious business, even if it means multiple dry-cleaning bills along the way.

Take It Off or Put It On—Depending. What you do or do not wear can be worse than bad taste—ranging from insulting to unhygienic to positively sinful. Shoes are among the biggest offenders in the East, even if you wear a 5AAA. They are forbidden within Muslim mosques and Buddhist temples. Never wear them into Japanese homes or restaurants unless the owner insists, and in Indian and Indonesian homes, if the host goes shoeless, do likewise. And wherever you take your shoes off, remember to place them neatly together facing the door you came in. This is particularly important in Japan....

In certain conservative Arab countries, the price for wearing the wrong thing can hurt more than feelings. Mullahs have been known to give a sharp whack with their walking sticks to any woman whom they consider immodestly dressed. Even at American-style hotels there, do not wear shorts, skirts above the knee, sleeveless blouses, or low necklines—much less a bikini at the pool....

CRITICAL THINKING QUESTIONS

1. Historically, people in North America have been rather indifferent to the dangers of inadvertently offending others. Why do you think this has been the case?

2. Have you ever offended others—or been offended—in the way depicted by Axtell? If so, how? How did you and others respond?

3. Can the type of cultural conflict Axtell describes occur here in Canada? How?

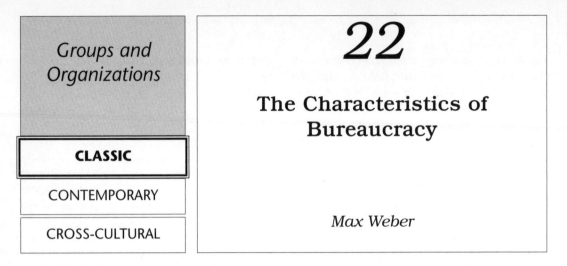

Groups and
Organizations

22

The Characteristics of Bureaucracy

CLASSIC

CONTEMPORARY

CROSS-CULTURAL

Max Weber

According to Max Weber, human societies have historically been oriented by tradition of one kind or another. Modernity, in contrast, is marked by a different form of human consciousness: a rational world view. For Weber, there is no clearer expression of modern rationality than bureaucracy. In this selection, Weber identifies the characteristics of this organizational form.

Modern officialdom functions in the following specific manner:

I. There is the principle of fixed and official jurisdictional areas, which are generally ordered by rules, that is, by laws or administrative regulations. (1) The regular activities required for the purposes of the bureaucratically governed structure are distributed in a fixed way as official duties. (2) The authority to give the commands required for the discharge of these duties is distributed in a stable way and is strictly delimited by rules concerning the coercive means, physical, sacerdotal, or otherwise, which may be placed at the disposal of officials. (3) Methodical provision is made for the regular and continuous fulfillment of these duties and for the execution of the corresponding rights; only persons who have the generally regulated qualifications to serve are employed.

In public and lawful government these three elements constitute "bureaucratic authority." In private economic domination, they constitute bureaucratic "management." Bureaucracy, thus understood, is fully developed in political and ecclesiastical communities only in the modern state, and, in the private economy, only in the most advanced institutions of capitalism. Permanent and public office authority, with fixed jurisdiction, is not the historical rule but rather the exception. This is so even in large political structures such as those of the ancient Orient, the Germanic, and Mongolian empires of conquest, or of many feudal structures of state. In all these cases, the ruler executes the most important measures through personal trustees, table-companions, or court-servants. Their commissions and authority are not precisely delimited and are temporarily called into being for each case.

II. The principles of office hierarchy and of levels of graded authority mean a firmly ordered system of super- and subordination in which there is a supervision of the lower offices by the

Source: From *Max Weber: Essays in Sociology,* by Max Weber, ed. H. H. Gerth and C. Wright Mills. Copyright ©1946 by Max Weber. Used by permission of Oxford University Press, Inc.

higher ones. Such a system offers the governed the possibility of appealing the decision of a lower office to its higher authority, in a definitely regulated manner. With the full development of the bureaucratic type, the office hierarchy is monocratically organized. The principle of hierarchical office authority is found in all bureaucratic structures: in state and ecclesiastical structures as well as in large party organizations and private enterprises. It does not matter for the character of bureaucracy whether its authority is called "private" or "public."

When the principle of jurisdictional "competency" is fully carried through, hierarchical subordination—at least in public office—does not mean that the "higher" authority is simply authorized to take over the business of the "lower." Indeed, the opposite is the rule. Once established and having fulfilled its task, an office tends to continue in existence and be held by another incumbent.

III. The management of the modern office is based upon written documents ("the files"), which are preserved in their original or draft form. There is, therefore, a staff of subaltern officials and scribes of all sorts. The body of officials actively engaged in a "public" office, along with the respective apparatus of material implements and the files, make up a "bureau." In private enterprise, "the bureau" is often called "the office."

In principle, the modern organization of the civil service separates the bureau from the private domicile of the official, and, in general, bureaucracy segregates official activity as something distinct from the sphere of private life. Public monies and equipment are divorced from the private property of the official.... In principle, the executive office is separated from the household, business from private correspondence, and business assets from private fortunes. The more consistently the modern type of business management has been carried through, the more are these separations the case. The beginnings of this process are to be found as early as the Middle Ages.

It is the peculiarity of the modern entrepreneur that he conducts himself as the "first official" of his enterprise, in the very same way in which the ruler of a specifically modern bureaucratic state spoke of himself as "the first servant" of the state. The idea that the bureau activities of the state are intrinsically different in character from the management of private economic offices is a continental European notion and, by the way of contrast, is totally foreign to the American way.

IV. Office management, at least all specialized office management—and such management is distinctly modern—usually presupposes a thorough and expert training. This increasingly holds for the modern executive and employee of private enterprises, in the same manner as it holds for the state official.

V. When the office is fully developed, official activity demands the full working capacity of the official, irrespective of the fact that his obligatory time in the bureau may be firmly delimited. In the normal case, this is only the product of a long development, in the public as well as in the private office. Formerly, in all cases, the normal state of affairs was reversed: Official business was discharged as a secondary activity.

VI. The management of the office follows general rules, which are more or less stable, more or less exhaustive, and which can be learned. Knowledge of these rules represents a special technical learning which the officials possess. It involves jurisprudence, or administrative or business management.

The reduction of modern office management to rules is deeply embedded in its very nature. The theory of modern public administration, for instance, assumes that the authority to order certain matters by decree—which has been legally granted to public authorities—does not entitle the bureau to regulate the matter by commands given for each case, but only to regulate the matter abstractly. This stands in extreme contrast to the regulation of all relationships through individual privileges and bestowals of favor, which is absolutely dominant in patrimonialism, at least insofar as such relationships are not fixed by sacred tradition.

All this results in the following for the internal and external position of the official.

I. Office holding is a "vocation." This is shown, first, in the requirement of a firmly prescribed course of training, which demands the entire capacity for work for a long period of time, and in the generally prescribed and special examinations which are prerequisites of employment. Furthermore, the position of the official is in the nature of a duty. This determines the internal structure of his relations, in the following manner: Legally and actually, office holding is not considered a source to be exploited for rents or emoluments, as was normally the case during the Middle Ages and frequently up to the threshold of recent times.... Entrances into an office, including one in the private economy, is considered an acceptance of a specific obligation of faithful management in return for a secure existence. It is decisive for the specific nature of modern loyalty to an office that, in the pure type, it does not establish a relationship to a *person,* like the vassal's or disciple's faith in feudal or in patrimonial relations and authority. Modern loyalty is devoted to impersonal and functional purposes....

II. The personal position of the official is patterned in the following way:

(1) Whether he is in a private office or a public bureau, the modern official always strives and usually enjoys a distinct *social esteem* as compared with the governed. His social position is guaranteed by the prescriptive rules of rank order and, for the political official, by special definitions of the criminal code against "insults of officials" and "contempt" of state and church authorities.

The actual social position of the official is normally highest where, as in old civilized countries, the following conditions prevail: a strong demand for administration by trained experts; a strong and stable social differentiation, where the official predominantly derives from socially and economically privileged strata because of the social distribution of power; or where the costliness of the required training and status conventions are binding upon him. The possession of educational certificates—to be discussed elsewhere—are usually linked with qualification for office. Naturally, such certificates or patents enhance the "status element" in the social position of the official....

Usually the social esteem of the officials as such is especially low where the demand for expert administration and the dominance of status conventions are weak. This is especially the case in the United States; it is often the case in new settlements by virtue of their wide fields for profit-taking and the great instability of their social stratification.

(2) The pure type of bureaucratic official is *appointed* by a superior authority. An official elected by the governed is not a purely bureaucratic figure. Of course, the formal existence of an election does not by itself mean that no appointment hides behind the election—in the state, especially, appointment by party chiefs. Whether or not this is the case does not depend upon legal statutes but upon the way in which the party mechanism functions. Once firmly organized, the parties can turn a formally free election into the mere acclamation of a candidate designated by the party chief. As a rule, however, a formally free election is turned into a fight, conducted according to definite rules, for votes in favor of one of two designated candidates....

(3) Normally, the position of the official is held for life, at least in public bureaucracies; and this is increasingly the case for all similar structures. As a factual rule, *tenure for life* is presupposed, even where the giving of notice or periodic reappointment occurs. In contrast to the worker in a private enterprise, the official normally holds tenure. Legal or actual life-tenure, however, is not recognized as the official's right to the possession of office, as was the case with many structures of authority in the past. Where legal guarantees against arbitrary dismissal of transfer are

developed, they merely serve to guarantee a strictly objective discharge of specific office duties free from all personal considerations....

(4) The official receives the regular *pecuniary* compensation of a normally fixed *salary* and the old age security provided by a pension. The salary is not measured like a wage in terms of work done, but according to "status," that is, according to the kind of function (the "rank") and, in addition, possibly, according to the length of service. The relatively great security of the official's income, as well as the rewards of social esteem, make the office a sought-after position....

(5) The official is set for a *"career"* within the hierarchical order of the public service. He moves from the lower, less important, and lower paid to the higher positions. The average official naturally desires a mechanical fixing of the conditions of promotion: if not of the offices, at least of the salary levels. He wants these conditions fixed in terms of "seniority," or possibly according to grades achieved in a developed system of expert examinations....

CRITICAL THINKING QUESTIONS

1. In what respects is bureaucracy impersonal? What are some of the advantages and disadvantages of this impersonality?
2. Through most of human history, kinship has been the foundation of social organization. Why is kinship missing from Weber's analysis of bureaucracy? On what other basis are people selected for bureaucratic positions?
3. Why does bureaucracy take a hierarchical form? Do you think formal organization must be hierarchical?

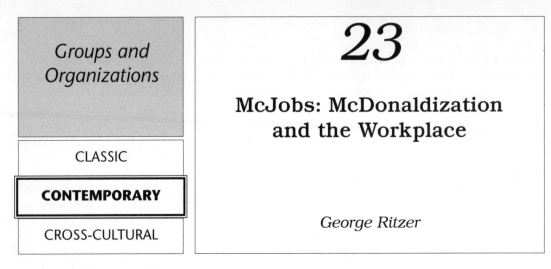

Groups and Organizations

CLASSIC

CONTEMPORARY

CROSS-CULTURAL

23

McJobs: McDonaldization and the Workplace

George Ritzer

A decade ago, George Ritzer coined the term "McDonaldization" to refer to a set of organizational principles—including efficiency, uniformity, predictability, and control— that play an important part in today's society. Here, he describes the way McDonald's and similar organizations control not just their workers, but also their customers.

In recent years the spread of McDonaldized systems has led to the creation of an enormous number of jobs. Unfortunately, the majority of them can be thought of as McDonaldized jobs, or "McJobs." While we usually associate these types of positions with fast-food restaurants, and in fact there are many such jobs in that setting (over 2.5 million people worked in that industry in the United States in 1992 [Van Giezen, 1994]), McJobs have spread throughout much of the economy with the growing impact of McDonaldization on work settings which had previously experienced relatively little rationalization.

It is worth outlining some of the basic realities of employment in the fast-food industry in the United States since those jobs serve as a model for employment in other McDonaldized settings (Van Giezen, 1994). The large number of people

employed in fast-food restaurants accounts for over 40 percent of the approximately 6 million people employed in restaurants of all types. Fast-food restaurants rely heavily on teenage employees—almost 70 percent of their employees are twenty years of age or younger. For many, the fast-food restaurant is likely to be their first employer. It is estimated that the first job for one of every fifteen workers was at McDonald's; one of every eight Americans has worked at McDonald's at some time in his or her life. The vast majority of employees are part-time workers: The average work week in the fast-food industry is 29.5 hours. There is a high turnover rate: Only slightly more than half the employees remain on the job for a year or more. Minorities are over-represented in these jobs—almost two-thirds of employees are women and nearly a quarter are non-white. These are low-paid occupations, with many earning the minimum wage, or slightly more. As a result, these jobs are greatly affected by changes in the minimum wage: An upward

Source: Reprinted by permission of Sage Publications Ltd. from George Ritzer, *The McDonaldization Thesis: Explorations and Extensions,* copyright © 1998 Sage Publications.

revision has an important effect on the income of these workers. However, there is a real danger that many workers would lose their positions as a result of such increases, especially in economically marginal fast-food restaurants.[1]

Although the McDonaldization of society is manifest at all levels and in all realms of the social world, the work world has played a particularly pivotal role in this. On the one hand, it is the main source of many of the precursors of McDonaldization, including bureaucracies, scientific management, assembly lines, and so on. More contemporaneously, the kinds of jobs, work procedures, and organizing principles that have made McDonald's so successful have affected the way in which many businesses now organize much of their work. In fact, it could well be argued that the primary root of the McDonaldization of the larger society is the work world. On the other hand, the McDonaldization of the larger society has, in turn, served to further rationalize the work world. We thus have a self-reinforcing and enriching process that is speeding the growth and spread of McDonaldization.

The process of McDonaldization is leading to the creation of more and more McJobs.[2] The service sector, especially at its lower end, is producing an enormous number of jobs, most of them requiring little or no skill. There is no better example of this than the mountain of jobs being produced by the fast-food industry. However, new occupational creation is not the only source of McJobs: Many extant low-level jobs are being McDonaldized. More strikingly, large numbers of middle-level jobs are also being deskilled and transformed into McJobs.

McJobs are characterized by the five dimensions of McDonaldization. The jobs tend to involve a series of simple tasks in which the emphasis is on performing each as efficiently as possible. Second, the time associated with many of the tasks is carefully calculated and the emphasis on the quantity of time a task should take tends to diminish the quality of the work from the point of view of the worker. That is, tasks are so simplified

and streamlined that they provide little or no meaning to the worker. Third, the work is predictable: employees do and say essentially the same things hour after hour, day after day. Fourth, many nonhuman technologies are employed to control workers and reduce them to robotlike actions. Some technologies are in place, and others are in development, that will lead to the eventual replacement of many of these "human robots" with computerized robots. Finally, the rationalized McJobs lead to a variety of irrationalities, especially the dehumanization of work. The result is the extraordinarily high turnover rate described above and difficulty in maintaining an adequate supply of replacements.[3]

The claim is usually made by spokespeople for McDonaldized systems that they are offering a large number of entry-level positions that help give employees basic skills they will need in order to move up the occupational ladder within such systems (and many of them do). This is likely to be true in the instances in which the middle-level jobs to which they move—for example shift leader, assistant manager, or manager of a fast-food restaurant—are also routinized and scripted. In fact, it turns out that this even holds for the positions held by the routinized and scripted instructors at [McDonald's training program at] Hamburger University who teach the managers, who teach the employees, and so on. However, the skills acquired in McJobs are not likely to prepare one for, help one to acquire, or help one to function well in, the far more desirable postindustrial occupations which are highly complex and require high levels of skill and education. Experience in routinized actions and scripted interactions do not help much when occupations require thought and creativity....

At the cultural level, large numbers of people in the United States, and increasingly throughout much of the rest of the world, have come to value McDonaldization in general, as well as its fundamental characteristics. McDonaldization, as well as its various principles, has become part of our value system. That value system has, in turn, been translated into a series of principles that have been exported to, adopted by, and adapted to, a wide range of social settings....

...For example, the behavior of customers at fast-food restaurants is being affected in much the same way as the behavior of those who work in those restaurants....

The constraints on the behavior of employees and customers in McDonaldized systems are of both a structural and a cultural nature. Employees and customers find themselves in a variety of McDonaldized structures that demand that they behave in accord with the dictates of those structures. For example, the drive-through window associated with the fast-food restaurant (as well as other settings such as banks) structures both what customers in their cars and employees in their booths can and cannot do. They can efficiently exchange money for food, but their positions (in a car and a booth) and the press of other cars in the queue make any kind of personal interaction virtually impossible. Of course, many other kinds of behavior are either made possible, or prohibited, by such structures. In Giddens's (1984) terms, such structures are both enabling and constraining.

At a cultural level, both employees and customers are socialized into, and have internalized, the norms and values of working and living in a McDonaldized society. Employees are trained by managers or owners who are likely, themselves, to have been trained at an institution like McDonald's Hamburger University (Schaaf, 1991). Such institutions are as much concerned with inculcating norms and values as they are with the teaching of basic skills. For their part, customers are not required to attend Hamburger University, but they are "trained" by the employees themselves, by television advertisements, and by their own children who are often diligent students, teachers, and enforcers of the McDonald's way. This "training," like that of those employees who attend Hamburger University, is oriented not only to teaching the "skills" required to be a customer at a fast-food restaurant (e.g. how to queue up in order to order food), but also the norms and values

of such settings as they apply to customers (e.g. customers are expected to dispose of their own debris; they are not expected to linger after eating). As a result of such formal and informal training, both employees and customers can be relied on to do what they are supposed to, and what is expected of them, with little or no personal supervision....

...McJobs are not simply the deskilled jobs of our industrial past in new settings; they are jobs that have a variety of new and distinctive characteristics.... Industrial and McDonaldized jobs both tend to be highly routinized in terms of what people do on the job. However, one of the things that is distinctive about McDonaldized jobs, especially since so many of them involve work that requires interaction and communication, especially with consumers, is that what people *say* on the job is also highly routinized. To put this another way, McDonaldized jobs are tightly scripted: They are characterized by *both* routinized actions (for example, the way McDonald's hamburgers are to be put down on the grill and flipped [Love, 1986: 141–2]) and scripted interactions (examples include, "May I help you?"; "Would you like a dessert to go with your meal?"; "Have a nice day!"). Scripts are crucial because, as Leidner (1993) points out, many of the workers in McDonaldized systems are interactive service workers. This means that they not only produce goods and provide services, but they often do so in interaction with customers.

The scripting of interaction leads to new depths in the deskilling of workers. Not only have employee actions been deskilled; employees' ability to speak and interact with customers is now being limited and controlled. There are not only scripts to handle general situations, but also a range of subscripts to deal with a variety of contingencies. Verbal and interactive skills are being taken away from employees and built into the scripts in much the same way that manual skills were taken and built into various technologies. At one time distrusted in their ability to *do* the right thing, workers now find themselves no longer trusted to *say* the right thing. Once able to create distinctive interactive styles, and to adjust them to different circumstances, employees are now asked to follow scripts as mindlessly as possible....

One very important, but rarely noted, aspect of the labor process in the fast-food restaurant and other McDonaldized systems is the extent to which customers are being led, perhaps even almost required, to perform a number of tasks without pay that were formerly performed by paid employees. For example, in the modern gasoline station the driver now does various things for free (pumps gas, cleans windows, checks oil, even pays through a computerized credit card system built into the pump) that were formerly done by paid attendants. In these and many other settings, McDonaldization has brought the customer *into* the labor process: The customer *is* the laborer! This has several advantages for employers such as lower (even nonexistent) labor costs, the need for fewer employees, and less trouble with personnel problems: Customers are far less likely to complain about a few seconds or minutes of tedious work than employees who devote a full work day to such tasks. Because of its advantages, as well as because customers are growing accustomed to and accepting of it, I think customers are likely to become even more involved in the labor process.

This is the most revolutionary development, at least as far as the labor process is concerned, associated with McDonaldization. As a result of this dramatic change, the analysis of the labor process must be extended to what customers do in McDonaldized systems. The distinction between customer and employee is eroding, or in postmodern terms "imploding," and one can envision more and more work settings in which customers are asked to do an increasing amount of "work." More dramatically, it is also likely that we will see more work settings in which there are no employees at all! In such settings customers, in interaction with nonhuman technologies, will do *all* of the human labor. A widespread example is the ATM in which customers (and the technol-

ogy) do all of the work formerly done by bank tellers. More strikingly, we are beginning to see automated loan machines which dispense loans as high as $10,000 (Singletary, 1996). Again, customers and technologies do the work and, in the process, many loan-officer positions are eliminated. Similarly, the new automated gasoline pumps allow (or force) customers to do all of the required tasks; in some cases and at certain times (late at night) no employees at all are present.

In a sense, a key to the success of McDonaldized systems is that they have been able to supplement the exploitation of employees with the exploitation of customers. Lest we forget, Marx "put at the heart of his sociology—as no other sociology does—the theme of exploitation" (Worsley, 1982: 115). In Marxian theory, the capitalists are seen as simply paying workers less than the value produced by the workers, and as keeping the rest for themselves. This dynamic continues in contemporary society, but capitalists have learned that they can ratchet up the level of exploitation not only by exploiting workers more, but also by exploiting a whole new group of people—consumers. In Marxian terms, customers create value in the tasks they perform for McDonaldized systems. And they are not simply paid less than the value they produce, they are paid *nothing at all*. In this way, customers are exploited to an even greater degree than workers....

While no class within society is immune to McDonaldization, the lower classes are the most affected. They are the ones who are most likely to go to McDonaldized schools, live in inexpensive, mass-produced tract houses, and work in McDonaldized jobs. Those in the upper classes have much more of a chance of sending their children to non-McDonaldized schools, living in custom-built homes, and working in occupations in which they impose McDonaldization on others while avoiding it to a large degree themselves.

Also related to the social class issue...is the fact that the McDonaldization of a significant portion of the labor force does not mean that all, or even most, of the labor force is undergoing this process. In fact, the McDonaldization of some of the labor force is occurring at the same time that another large segment is moving in a postindustrial, that is, more highly skilled, direction (Hage & Powers, 1992). Being created in this sector of society are relatively high-status, well-paid occupations requiring high levels of education and training. In the main, these are far from McJobs and lack most, or all, of the dimensions discussed at the beginning of this [reading]. The growth of such postindustrial occupations parallels the concern in the labor process literature with flexible specialization occurring side by side with the deskilling of many other jobs. This points to a bifurcation in the class system. In spite of appearances, there is no contradiction here; McDonaldization and postindustrialization tend to occur in different sectors of the labor market. However, the spread of McJobs leads us to be dubious of the idea that we have moved into a new postindustrial era and have left behind the kind of deskilled jobs we associate with industrial society.

CRITICAL THINKING QUESTIONS

1. Describe ways in which McDonaldization is evident in many familiar settings (not just the workplace, but perhaps shopping malls and even university campuses). What elements of McDonaldization can you find?
2. In what ways does a McDonaldized setting control not just workers but also customers? Why do organizations want to control customers?
3. Why does McDonaldization seem to appeal to many people? Do you think this process is good or harmful for society as a whole? Why?

NOTES

This chapter combines a paper, "McJobs," published in Rich Feller and Garry Walz (eds.), *Career Transitions in Turbulent Times* (Greensboro, N.C.: ERIC/CASS Publications, 1996) and the Invited Plenary Address, International Labour Process Conference, Blackpool, England, April, 1995.

1. Although a study by Katz and Krueger (1992) indicates an employment *increase* accompanying a rise in the minimum wage.
2. As we will see below, other kinds of high-status, high-paying postindustrial occupations are also growing.
3. There are, of course, many other factors involved in turnover.

REFERENCES

Giddens, A. 1984. *The constitution of society: Outline of the theory of structuration.* Berkeley: University of California Press.

Hage, J., and C. H. Powers. 1992. *Post-industrial lives: Roles and relationships in the 21st century.* Newbury Park, Calif.: Sage.

Leidner, R. 1993. *Fast food, fast talk: Service work and the routinization of everyday life.* Berkeley: University of California Press.

Love, J. 1986. *McDonald's: Behind the arches.* Toronto: Bantam Books.

Schaaf, D. 1994. Inside Hamburger University. *Training*, December: 18–24.

Singletary, M. 1996. Borrowing by the touch. *Washington Post*, (30 March): C1, C2.

Van Giezen, R. W. 1994. Occupational wages in the fast-food restaurant industry. *Monthly Labor Review*, August: 24–30.

Worsley, P. 1982. *Marx and Marxism.* Chichester: Ellis Horwood.

24

Japanese Etiquette and Ethics in Business

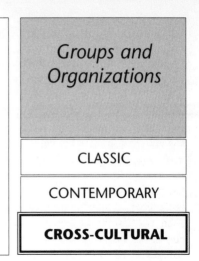

Groups and Organizations

CLASSIC

CONTEMPORARY

CROSS-CULTURAL

Boye De Mente

Businesses in different cultures vary in managerial style and organizational philosophy. North Americans have a growing interest in the organizational practices of Japan, a nation that has had remarkable economic success in recent decades. Because the economies of Japan and Canada are increasingly linked, there are practical benefits to understanding the cultural patterns of this economic superpower.

SHU-SHIN KOYO *(IT'S FOR LIFE)*

Probably the most talked about and notorious facet of Japan's family-patterned company system is *shu-shin koyo* (shuu-sheen koe-yoe), or "lifetime employment," which applies, however, to only an elite minority of the nation's workers. Although a direct descendant of feudal Japan, when peasants and craftsmen were attached to a particular clan by birth, the lifetime employment system did not become characteristic of large-scale modern Japanese industry until the 1950s. In the immediate postwar period, losing one's job was tantamount to being sentenced to starvation. To prevent employees from being fired or arbitrarily laid off, national federation union leaders took advantage of their new freedom and the still weak position of industry to force adoption of

Source: From *Japanese Etiquette and Ethics in Business,* 5th ed., by Boye De Mente (Lincolnwood, Ill.: NTC Business Books, 1987), pp. 71–81, 84–89, 91–97. Copyright © 1987. Reprinted with permission.

the lifetime employment system by the country's major enterprises.

Under the lifetime employment system, all *permanent* employees of larger companies and government bureaus are, in practice, hired for life. These organizations generally hire only once a year, directly from schools. Well before the end of the school year, each company and government ministry or agency decides on how many new people it wants to bring in. The company or government bureau then invites students who are to graduate that year (in some cases only from certain universities) to take written and oral examinations for employment.

One company, for example, may plan on taking 200 university graduates as administrative trainees, and 500 junior and senior high school graduates for placement in blue-collar work. Since "permanent" employment is "for life," companies are careful to select candidates who have well-rounded personalities and are judged most likely to adjust to that particular company or agency's philosophy and "style."

This method of employee selection is known as *Shikaku Seido* or "Personal Qualifications System." This means that new employees are selected on the basis of their education, character, personality, and family backgrounds; as opposed to work experience or technological backgrounds.

A larger Japanese company hiring new employees, as well as firms entering into new business tie-ups, are sometimes compared to *miai kekkon* or "arranged marriages." The analogy is a good one. Both employment and joint-venture affiliations are, in principle, for life. Therefore, both parties want to be sure not only of the short-term intentions of the potential partner but also of the character and personality—even if there are any "black sheep" in the family. Thus both prospective employee and potential business partner must undergo close scrutiny. When the Japanese commit themselves, the commitment is expected to be total.

Choosing employees on the basis of personal qualifications is especially important to Japanese supervisors and managers, because they personally cannot hire, fire, or hold back promotions. They must acquire and keep the trust, goodwill, and cooperation of their subordinates, and manage by example and tact.

Besides exercising control over employee candidates by allowing only students from certain universities to take their entrance examinations, many companies in Japan also depend upon well-known professors in specific universities to recommend choice candidates to them each year. The reputations of some professors, especially in the physical sciences, are often such that they can actually "parcel out" the best students from their graduating classes to top firms in their field.

NENKO JORETSU *(THE "MERIT OF YEARS")*

Once hired by a larger company, the permanent Japanese employee who is a university graduate is on the first rung of a pay/promotion escalator system that over the years will gradually and auto-matically take him to or near the upper management level. This is the famous (or infamous) *nenko joretsu* (nane-koe joe-ray-t'sue), "long-service rank" or seniority system, under which pay and promotions are primarily based on longevity.

Not surprisingly, the employee, at least in administrative areas, is considered more important than the job in the Japanese company system. As a result, job classifications on the administrative level may be clear enough, but specific duties of individuals tend to be ill-defined or not defined at all. Work is more or less assigned on a collective basis, and each employee tends to work according to his or her ability and inclinations. Those who are capable, diligent, and ambitious naturally do most of the work. Those who turn out to be lazy or incompetent are given tasks befitting their abilities and interests.

Young management trainees are switched from one job to another every two or three years, and in larger companies they are often transferred to other offices or plants. The reason for this is to expose them to a wide range of experiences so they will be more valuable to the company as they go up the promotion ladder. Individuals are "monitored" and informally rated, and eventually the more capable are promoted faster than the other members of their age group. The ones promoted the fastest usually become managing directors; and one of their number generally becomes president.

During the first twelve to fifteen years of employment, the most capable junior managers accrue status instead of more pay raises and faster promotions. If they prove to be equally capable in their personal relations with others, they are the ones who are eventually singled out to reach the upper levels of the managerial hierarchy.

The seniority system in Japanese companies takes ordinary, even incapable, people who have toed the company line and made no blunders, to the head of departments, and occasionally to the head of companies. But their limitations are recognized, and the department or company is run by competent people below them, with little or no damage to the egos of the less capable executives or to the overall harmony within the firm.

Each work-section of a Japanese company is three-layered, consisting of young, on-the-job trainees (a status that often lasts for several years); mature, experienced workers who carry most of the burden; and older employees whose productivity has fallen off due to their age.

Direct, specific orders do not set well with the members of these work-sections. Such orders leave them with the impression they are not trusted and that management has no respect for them. Even the lowest clerk or delivery boy in a company is very sensitive about being treated with respect. The Japanese say they prefer general "ambiguous" instructions. All that work-groups want from management "are goals and direction."

Because human relations are given precedence in the Japanese management system, great importance is attached to the "unity of employees" within each of these groups. The primary responsibility of the senior manager in a group is not to direct the people in their work but to make "adjustments" among them in order to maintain harmonious relations within the group.

"What is required of the ideal manager," say the Japanese, "is that he know how to adjust human relations rather than be knowledgeable about the operation of his department or the overall function of the company. In fact, the man who is competent and works hard is not likely to be popular with other members of his group and as a result does not make a good manager," they add.

Besides "appearing somewhat incompetent" as far as work is concerned while being skilled at preventing interemployee friction, the ideal Japanese manager has one other important trait. He is willing to shoulder all the responsibility for any mistakes or failings of his subordinates—hoping, of course, there will be no loss of face.

The efficient operation of this group system is naturally based on personal obligations and trust between the manager and his staff. The manager must make his staff obligated to him in order to keep their cooperation and in order to ensure that none of them will deliberately do anything or leave anything undone that would cause him embarrassment. Whatever knowledge and experience are required for the group to be productive is found among the manager's subordinates if he is weak in this area.

SEISHIN *(TRAINING IN SPIRIT)*

The Japanese associate productivity with employees having *seishin* (say-e-sheen), or "spirit," and being imbued with "Japanese morality." Company training, therefore, covers not only technical areas but also moral, philosophical, aesthetic, and political factors. Each of the larger companies has its own particular company philosophy and image, which are incorporated into its training and indoctrination programs. This is one of the prime reasons…major Japanese companies prefer not to hire older, experienced "outsiders"; it is assumed that they could not wholly accept or fit into the company mold.

ONJO SHUGI *("MOTHERING" EMPLOYEES)*

The amount of loyalty, devotion, and hard work displayed by most Japanese employees is in direct proportion to the paternalism, *onjo shugi* (own-joe shuu-ghee), of the company management system. The more paternalistic (maternalistic would seem to be a better word) the company, the harder working and the more devoted and loyal employees tend to be. Japanese-style paternalism includes the concept that the employer is totally responsible for the livelihood and well-being of all employees and must be willing to go all the way for an employee when the need arises.

The degree of paternalism in Japanese companies varies tremendously, with some of them literally practicing cradle-to-grave responsibility for employees and their families. Many managers thus spend a great deal of time participating in social events involving their staff members—births, weddings, funerals, and so on.

Fringe benefits make up a very important part of the income of most Japanese workers, and they include such things as housing or housing subsidies, transportation allowances, family allowances, child allowances, health services, free recreational facilities, educational opportunities, retirement funds, etc.

The wide range of fringe benefits received by Japanese employees is an outgrowth of spiraling inflation and an increasingly heavy income tax system during the years between 1945 and 1955. Companies first began serving employees free lunches. Then larger companies built dormitories, apartments, and houses. Eventually, recreational, educational, and medical facilities were added to employee benefits.

Japan's famous twice-a-year bonuses, *shoyo* (show-yoe), were originally regarded as a fringe benefit by employees and management, but workers and unions have long since considered them an integral part of wages. Unions prefer to call the bonuses *kimatsu teate* (kee-mot-sue tay-ah-tay), or "seasonal allowances." The bonuses, usually the equivalent of two to six or eight months of base wages, are paid in midsummer just before *Obon* (Oh-bone), a major Buddhist festival honoring the dead, and just before the end of the calendar year in December.

RINJI SAIYO *(THE OUTSIDERS)*

Not all employees of Japanese companies, including the larger ones, are hired for life or come under the *nenko joretsu* system of pay and promotion. There are two distinct categories of employees in most Japanese companies: those who are hired as permanent employees under the *shu-shin koyo* and *nenko joretsu* systems, and those hired under the *rinji saiyo* or "temporary appointment" system. The latter may be hired by the day or by the year, but they cannot be hired on contract for more than one year at a time. They are paid at a lower scale than permanent employees and may be laid off or fired at any time.

The *rinji saiyo* system of temporary employees is, of course, a direct outgrowth of the disadvantages of a permanent employment system, which at most is viable only in a booming, continuously growing economy.

The rapid internationalization of Japan's leading corporations is also having a profound effect on their policies regarding young Japanese who have graduated from foreign universities. Until the mid-1980s most Japanese companies simply would not consider hiring someone who had been partly or wholly educated abroad. Their rationale was that such people were no longer 100 percent Japanese and, therefore, would not fit into the training programs or the environment of Japanese companies.

Now a growing number of Japanese corporations with large international operations are looking for young people who have been educated abroad, speak a foreign language, and already have experience in living overseas. Ricoh, for example, now has a regular policy of hiring some of its annual crop of new employees from the group of Japanese students attending American universities.

Several Japanese employment agencies are now active among Japanese students in the U.S., providing them with information about job opportunities with Japanese companies overseas.

JIMUSHO NO HANA *("OFFICE FLOWERS")*

Women, mostly young, make up a highly visible percentage of Japan's labor force, particularly in offices (where they are often referred to as *jimusho no hana* or "office flowers") and in light manufacturing industries requiring precision handwork. Most of these young women are expected to leave the work force when they get married, but increasing numbers of them are staying on after marriage, at least until they begin having children, and are returning to the labor force after their children are raised. Equally significant is that, little by little, women are beginning to cross the barrier between staff and management, and participate in the heady world of planning and decision-making.

While female managers are still generally confined to such industries as public relations, advertising, publishing, and retailing, economic and social pressures are gradually forcing other industries as well to begin thinking about desegregating their male-only management systems.

Another highly conspicuous phenomenon in Japan today is the growing number of women who head up their own successful companies in such areas as real estate, cosmetics, apparel, and the food business.

The world of Japanese business is still very much a male preserve, however, with many of the relationships and rituals that make up a vital part of daily business activity still closed to women. There are virtually no women in the numerous power groups, factions, clubs, and associations that characterize big business in Japan.

Foreign women who choose to do business in or with Japan face most of the same barriers that handicap Japanese women. They are unable to participate in the ritualistic after-work drinking and partying that are a major part of developing and maintaining effective business relations within the Japanese system. They cannot transcend their sex and be accepted as businesspersons first and foremost. They are unable to deal with other women on a managerial level in other companies simply because there generally are none.

They must also face the fact that most Japanese executives have had no experience in dealing with female managers, have no protocol for doing so, and are inclined to believe that women are not meant to be business managers in the first place.

This does not mean that foreign women cannot successfully engage in business in Japan, but they must understand the barriers, be able to accept them for what they are, and work around them. If they come on strong, as women or as managers, to Japanese businessmen who are traditionally oriented, they will most likely fail. They must walk a much finer line than men.

At the same time, a foreign woman who is both attractive and really clever in knowing how to use her femininity to manipulate men can succeed in Japan where others fail. This approach can be especially effective if the woman concerned is taken under the wing of an older, powerful Japanese businessman who likes her and takes a personal interest in her success.

Perhaps the most important lesson the foreign businesswoman in Japan must learn is that the Japanese regard business as a personal matter, and believe that the personal element must be satisfied before any actual business transpires. This means she must go through the process of establishing emotional rapport with her male Japanese counterparts, and convince them that she is a knowledgeable, experienced, trustworthy, and dependable businessperson.

It is often difficult for foreign men to develop this kind of relationship with Japanese businessmen, particularly when language is a problem, so the challenge to foreign women who want to do business in Japan (unless they go just as buyers or artists, etc.) is formidable.

The type of foreign woman who is most likely to do well in the Japanese environment is one who has a genuine affinity for the language and the culture, and appreciates both the opportunities and challenges offered by the situation. She must also have an outstanding sense of humor, be patient, and be willing to suppress some of her rational, liberal feelings.

RINGI SEIDO *(PUTTING IT IN WRITING)*

In addition to the cooperative-work approach based on each employee contributing according to his or her ability and desire, many large Japanese companies divide and diversify management responsibility by a system known as *ringi seido* (reen-ghee say-ee-doe), which means, more or less, "written proposal system." This is a process by which management decisions are based on proposals made by lower level managers, and it is responsible for the "bottom-up" management associated with many Japanese companies.

Briefly, the *ringi* system consists of proposals written by the initiating section or department that are circulated horizontally and vertically to all layers of management for approval. Managers and executives who approve of the proposal stamp the document with their *hanko* (hahn-koe) name seals in the prescribed place. Anyone who disapproves either passes the document on without stamping it or puts his seal on it sideways or upside down to indicate conditional approval.

When approval is not unanimous, higher executives may send the document back with recommendations that more staff work be done on it or that the opinions of those who disapprove be taken into consideration. Managers may attach comments to the proposal if they wish.

In practice, the man who originates a *ringi-sho* (written proposal document) informally consults with other managers before submitting it for official scrutiny. He may work for weeks or months in his efforts to get the idea approved unofficially. If he runs into resistance, he will invariably seek help from colleagues who owe him favors. They in turn will approach others who are obligated to them.

The efficiency and effectiveness of the *ringi seido* varies with the company. In some it is little more than a formality, and there is pressure from the top to eliminate the system altogether. In other companies the system reigns supreme, and there is strong opposition to any talk of eliminating it. The system is so deeply entrenched in both the traditional management philosophy of the Japanese and the aspirations and ambitions of younger managers that it will no doubt be around for a long time.

The foreign businessman negotiating with a Japanese company should be aware that his proposals may be the subject of one or more *ringi-sho* which not only takes up a great deal of time (they must be circulated in the proper chain-of-status order), it also exposes them to the scrutiny of as many as a dozen or more individuals whose interests and attitudes may differ.

Whether or not a *ringi* proposal is approved by the president is primarily determined by who has approved it by the time it gets to him. If all or most of the more important managers concerned have stamped the *ringi-sho,* chances are the president will also approve it.

While this system is cumbersome and slow, generally speaking it helps build and maintain a cooperative spirit within companies. In addition, it assures that when a policy change or new program is initiated, it will have the support of the majority of managers.

As can be seen from the still widespread use of the *ringi seido,* top managers in many Japanese companies are not always planners and decision-makers. Their main function is to see that the company operates smoothly and efficiently as a team, to see that new managers are nurtured within the system, and to "pass judgment" on proposals made by junior managers.

NEMAWASHI *(BEHIND THE SCENES)*

Just as the originator of a *ringi* proposal will generally not submit it until he is fairly sure it will be received favorably, Japanese managers in general do not, unlike their foreign counterparts, hold formal meetings to discuss subjects and make decisions. They meet to agree formally on what has already been decided in informal discussions behind the scenes.

These informal discussions are called *nemawashi* (nay-mah-wah-she) or "binding up the roots"—to make sure a plant's roots are protected when it is transplanted.

Nemawashi protocol does not require that all managers who might be concerned be consulted. But agreement must always be obtained from the "right" person—meaning the individual in the department, division, or upper echelon of the company management—who really exercises power....

MIBUN *(THE RIGHTS HAVE IT)*

Everybody in Japan has his or her *mibun* (me-boon), "personal rights" or "station in life," and every *bun* has its special rights and responsibilities. There are special rights and special restrictions applying to managers only, to students only, to teachers only, to workers only, etc. The restrictions of a particular category are usually clear-cut and are intended to control the behavior of the people within these categories at all times—for example, the office employee even when he is not working or the student when he isn't in school.

The traditional purpose of the feudalistic *mibun* concept was to maintain harmony within and between different categories of people. A second purpose was to prevent anyone from bringing discredit or shame upon his category or his superiors.

A good example of the *mibun* system at work was once told by Konosuke Matsushita, founder of the huge Matsushita Electric Company (Panasonic, National, etc.). At the age of ten, Matsushita was apprenticed to a bicycle shop, which meant that he was practically a slave, forced to work from five in the morning until bedtime.

In addition to his regular duties, Matsushita had to run to a tobacco store several times a day for customers who came into the bicycle shop. Before he could go, however, he had to wash. After several months of this, he hit upon the idea of buying several packs of cigarettes at one time, with his own meager savings, so that when a customer asked for tobacco, he not only could hand it to him immediately but also profit a few *sen* on each pack, since he received a discount by buying twenty packs at a time.

This pleased not only the bicycle shop customers but also Matsushita's master, who complimented him highly on his ingenuity. A few days later, however, the master of the shop told him that all the other workers were complaining about his enterprise and that he would have to stop it and return to the old system.

It was not within the *bun* of a mere flunky to demonstrate such ability.

The aims of foreign businessmen are often thwarted because they attempt to get things done by Japanese whose *bun* does not allow them to do whatever is necessary to accomplish the desired task. Instead of telling the businessmen they cannot do it or passing the matter on to someone who can, there is a tendency for the individual to wait a certain period, or until they are approached again by the businessmen, then announce that it is impossible.

In any dealings with a Japanese company, it is especially important to know the *bun* of the people representing the firm. The Japanese businessman who does have individual authority is often buttressed behind subordinates whose *bun* are strictly limited. If the outsider isn't careful, a great deal of time can be wasted on the wrong person.

It is the special freedoms or "rights" of the *bun* system that cause the most trouble. As is natural everywhere, the Japanese minimize the responsibilities of their *bun* and emphasize the rights, with the result that there are detailed and well-known rules outlining the rights of each category, but few rules covering the responsibilities.

As one disillusioned bureaucrat-turned-critic put it, "The rights of government and company bureaucrats tend to be limitless, while responsibilities are ignored or passed on to underlings. The underlings in turn say they are powerless to act without orders from above—or that it isn't their responsibility." The same critic also said that the only ability necessary to become a bureaucrat was that of escaping responsibility without being criticized.

A story related by a former editor of one of Japan's better known intellectual magazines illustrates how the *mibun* system penetrates into private life. While still an editor with the magazine, Mr. S went out one night for a few drinks with a very close writer-friend. While they were drinking, another writer, the noted Mr. D, came into the bar and joined them.

Mr. S continues: "I was not 'in charge' of Mr. D in my publishing house and didn't know him very well, but according to Japanese etiquette I should have bowed to him, paid him all kinds of high compliments, and told him how much I was obligated to him. But it was long after my working hours and I was enjoying a drink with a friend who was also a writer, so I just bowed and paid little attention to him.

"At this, Mr. D became angry and commanded me in a loud voice to go home. I refused to move, and he began shouting curses at me. I shouted back at him that I was drinking with a friend and it was none of his business, but he continued to abuse me loudly until my friend finally managed to quiet him down. Of course, I would have been fired the next day except that my friend was able to keep Mr. D from telling the directors of my company."

In doing business with a Japanese firm, it is important to find out the rank of each individual you deal with so you can determine the extent of his *bun*. It is also vital that you know the status of his particular section or department, which has its own ranking within the company.

There are other management characteristics that make it especially difficult for the uninitiated foreigner to deal with Japanese companies, including barriers to fast, efficient communication between levels of management within the companies. Everything must go through the proper chain of command, in a carefully prescribed, ritualistic way. If any link in this vertical chain is missing—away on business or sick—routine communication usually stops there. The ranking system does not allow Japanese management to delegate authority or responsibility to any important extent. Generally, one person cannot speak for another.

In fact, some Japanese observers have begun criticizing the consensus system of business and political management, saying its absolute power represents a major threat to Japan in that it prevents rapid decision-making and often makes it impossible for the Japanese to react swiftly enough to either problems or opportunities.

HISHOKAN *(WHERE ARE ALL THE SECRETARIES?)*

As most Western businessmen would readily admit, they simply could not get along without their secretaries. In many ways, secretaries are as important, if not more so, than the executives themselves. In Japan only the rare businessman has a secretary whose role approximates the function of the Western secretary.

The reason for the scarcity of secretaries in Japan is many-fold. The style of Japanese management—the collective work-groups, decision-making by consensus, face-to-face communication, and the role of the manager as harmony-keeper instead of director—practically precludes the secretarial function. Another factor is the language itself, and the different language levels demanded by the subordinate-superior system. Japanese does not lend itself to clear, precise instructions because of the requirements of etiquette. It cannot be transcribed easily or quickly, either in shorthand or by typewriter—although the appearance of Japanese-language computers in the early 1980s [began] to change that.

As a result, the Japanese are not prepared psychologically or practically for doing business through or with secretaries. The closest the typical Japanese company comes to having secretaries in the American sense are receptionists—usually pretty, young girls who are stationed at desks in building lobbies and in central floor and hall areas. They announce visitors who arrive with appointments and try to direct people who come in on business without specific appointments to the right section or department. When a caller who has never had any business with the company, and has no appointment, appears at one of the reception desks, the girl usually tries to line him up with someone in the General Affairs (*Somu Bu*) Department.

Small Japanese companies and many departments in larger companies do not have receptionists. In such cases, no specific individual is responsible for greeting and taking care of callers.

The desks nearest the door are usually occupied by the lowest ranking members in the department, and it is usually up to the caller to get the attention of one of them and make his business known.

SHIGOTO *(IT'S NOT THE SLOT)*

The importance of face-to-face meetings in the conduct of business in Japan has already been mentioned. Regular, personal contact is also essential in maintaining "established relations" (the ability to *amaeru*) with business contacts. The longer two people have known each other and the more often they personally meet, the firmer this relationship.

This points up a particular handicap many foreign companies operating in Japan inadvertently impose on themselves by switching their personnel every two, three, or four years. In the normal course of business in Japan, it takes at least two years and sometimes as many as five years before the Japanese begin to feel like they really know their foreign employer, supplier, client, or colleague.

It also generally takes the foreign businessman transferred to Japan anywhere from one to three years or so to learn enough to really become effective in his job. Shortly afterward, he is transferred, recalled to the head office, is fired, or quits, and is replaced by someone else.

American businessmen in particular tend to pay too little attention to the disruption caused by personnel turnover, apparently because they think more in terms of the "position" or "slot" being filled by a "body" that has whatever qualifications the job calls for. Generally speaking, they play down the personality and character of the person filling the position and often do not adequately concern themselves with the role of human relations in business.

This, of course, is just the opposite of the Japanese way of doing things, and it accounts for a great deal of the friction that develops between Japanese and Westerners in business matters....

SEKININ SHA *(FINDING WHERE THE BUCK STOPS)*

In Western countries there is almost always one person who has final authority and responsibility, and it is easy to identify this person. All you have to do is ask, "Who is in charge?" In Japanese companies, however, no one individual is in charge. Both authority and responsibility are dispersed among the managers as a group. The larger the company, the more people are involved. When there are mistakes or failures, Japanese management does not try to single out any individual to blame. They try to focus on the cause of the failing in an effort to find out why it happened. In this way, the employee who made the mistake (if one individual was involved) does not lose face, and all concerned have an opportunity to learn a lesson.

Ranking Japanese businessmen advise that it is difficult to determine who has real authority and who makes final decisions in a Japanese company. Said a Sony director: "Even a top executive must consult his colleagues before he 'makes' a decision because he has become a high executive more by his seniority than his leadership ability. To keep harmony in his company he must act as a member of a family." Sony's co-founder Akio Morita adds that because of this factor, the traditional concept of promotion by seniority may not have much of a future in Japan. He agrees, however, that it is not something that can be changed in a short period of time.

In approaching a Japanese company about a business matter, it is therefore almost always necessary to meet and talk with the heads of several sections and departments on different occasions. After having gone through this procedure, you may still not get a clear-cut response from anyone, particularly if the various managers you approached have not come to a favorable consensus among themselves. It is often left up to you to synthesize the individual responses you receive and draw your own conclusions.

It is always important and often absolutely essential that the outsider (foreign or Japanese) starting a new business relationship with a Japanese company establish good rapport with each level of management in the company. Only by doing so can the outsider be sure his side of the story, his needs and expectations, will get across to all the necessary management levels.

Earle Okumura, a Los Angeles-based consultant, and one of the few Americans who is bilingual and bicultural and has had extensive business experience in Japan, suggests the following approach to establishing "lines of communication" with a Japanese company when the project concerns the introductions of new technology to be used by the Japanese firm:

Step I. Ask a director or the head of the Research and Development [R&D] Department to introduce you to the *kacho* (section chief) who is going to be directly in charge of your project within his department. Take the time to develop a personal relationship with the *kacho* (eating and drinking with him, etc.) then ask him to tell you exactly what you should do, and how you should go about trying to achieve and maintain the best possible working relationship with the company.

Step II. Ask the R&D *kacho,* with whom you now have at least the beginning of an *amae* relationship, to introduce you to his counterparts in the Production Department, Quality Control, and Sales Departments, etc., and go through the same get-acquainted process with each of them, telling them about yourself, your company, and your responsibilities. In all of these contacts, care must be taken not to pose any kind of threat or embarrassment to the different section managers.

Step III. After you have established a good, working relationship with the various *kacho* concerned, thoroughly explained your side of the project, and gained an understanding of their thinking, responsibilities, and capabilities, the third step is to get an appointment with the managing director or president of the company for a relaxed, casual conversation about policies, how

much you appreciate being able to work with his company, and the advantages that should accrue to both parties as a result of the joint venture.

Do not, Okumura cautions, get involved in trying to pursue details of the project with the managing director or president. He will most likely not be familiar with them and, in any event, will be more concerned about your reliability, sincerity, and ability to deal with the company.

Before an American businessman commits himself to doing business with another company, he checks out the company's assets, technology, financial stability, etc. The Japanese businessman is first interested in the character and quality of the people in the other company and secondarily interested in its facilities and finances. The Japanese put more stock in goodwill and the quality of interpersonal relationships in their business dealings.

MIZU SHOBAI *(THE "WATER BUSINESS")*

Mizu shobai (Mee-zoo show-bye), literally "water business," is a euphemism for the so-called entertainment trade—which is another euphemism for the hundreds of thousands of bars, cabarets, night clubs, "soap houses" (formerly known as Turkish baths), hotspring spas, and geisha inns that flourish in Japan. The term *mizu* is applied to this area of Japanese life because, like pleasure, water sparkles and soothes, then goes down the drain or evaporates into the air (and the business of catering to fleshly pleasures was traditionally associated with hot baths). *Shobai* or "business" is a very appropriate word, because the *mizu shobai* is one of the biggest businesses in Japan, employing some 5 million men and women.[1]

Drinking and enjoying the companionship of attractive young women in *mizu shobai* establishments is an important part of the lives of Japanese businessmen. There are basically two reasons for their regular drinking. First, ritualistic drinking developed into an integral part of religious life in ancient times, and from there it was carried over into social and business life.

Thus, for centuries, no formal function or business dealing of any kind has been complete without a drinking party (*uchiage*) (uu-chee-ah-gay) to mark the occasion. At such times, drinking is more of a duty than anything else. Only a person who cannot drink because of some physical condition or illness is normally excused.

The second reason for the volume of customary drinking that goes on in Japan is related to the distinctive subordinate-superior relationships between people and to the minutely prescribed etiquette that prevents the Japanese from being completely informal and frank with each other *except when drinking.*

Because the Japanese must be so circumspect in their behavior at all "normal" times, they believe it is impossible to really get to know a person without drinking with him. The sober person, they say, will always hold back and not reveal his true character. They feel ill at ease with anyone who refuses to drink with them at a party or outing. They feel that refusing to drink indicates a person is arrogant, excessively proud, and unfriendly. The ultimate expression of goodwill, trust, and humility is to drink to drunkenness with your coworkers and with close or important business associates in general. Those who choose for any reason not to go all the way must simulate drunkenness in order to fulfill the requirements of the custom.

Enjoying the companionship of pretty, young women has long been a universal prerogative of successful men everywhere. In Japan it often goes further than that. It has traditionally been used as an inducement to engage in business as well as to seal bargains, probably because it is regarded as the most intimate activity men can share.

When the Japanese businessman offers his Western guest or client intimate access to the charms of attractive and willing young women—something that still happens regularly—he is not "pandering" or engaging in any other "nasty" practice. He is merely offering the Western businessman a form of hospitality that has been popular in Japan since ancient times. In short, Japanese businessmen do openly and without guilt feelings what many Western businessmen do furtively.

The foreign businessman who "passes" when offered the opportunity to indulge in this honorable Japanese custom, either before or after a bargain is struck, may be regarded as foolish or prudish for letting the opportunity go by, but he is no longer likely to be accused of insincerity.

Many Westerners find it difficult to join in wholeheartedly at the round of parties typically held for them by their Japanese hosts, especially if it is nothing more than a drinking party at a bar or cabaret. Westerners have been conditioned to intersperse their drinking with jokes, boasting, and long-winded opinions—supposedly rational—on religion, politics, business, or what-have-you.

Japanese businessmen, on the other hand, do not go to bars or clubs at night to have serious discussions. They go there to relax emotionally and physically—to let it all hang out. They joke, laugh, sing, dance, and make short, rapid-fire comments about work, their superiors, personal problems, and so on; but they do not have long, deep discussions.

When the otherwise reserved and carefully controlled Japanese businessman does relax in a bar, cabaret, or at a drinking party, he often acts—from a Western viewpoint—like a high school kid "in his cups" for the first time.

At a reception given by a group of American dignitaries at one of Tokyo's leading hotels, my table partner was the chief of the research division of the Japanese company being honored. The normally sober and distinguished scientist had had a few too many by the time the speeches began, and he was soon acting in the characteristic manner of the Japanese drunk. All during the speeches he giggled, sang, burped, and whooped it up, much to the embarrassment of both sides.

Most Japanese businessmen, particularly those in lower and middle management, drink regularly and have developed an extraordinary capacity to drink heavily night after night and keep up their day-to-day work. Since they drink to loosen up and enjoy themselves, to be hospitable and to get to know their drinking partners, they are suspicious of anyone who drinks and remains formal and sober. They call this "killing the *sake*," with the added connotation that it also kills the pleasure.

During a boisterous drinking bout in which they sing and dance and trade risqué banter with hostesses or geisha, Japanese businessmen often sober up just long enough to have an important business exchange with a guest or colleague and then go back to the fun and games.

Foreign businessmen should be very cautious about trying to keep up with their Japanese hosts at such drinking rituals. It is all too common to see visiting businessmen being returned to their hotels well after midnight, sodden drunk. The key to this important ceremony is to drink moderately and simulate drunkenness.

In recent years, inflation has dimmed some of the nightly glow from geisha houses, the great cabarets, the bars, and the "in" restaurants in Japan's major cities. The feeling is also growing that the several billion dollars spent each year in the *mizu shobai* is incompatible with Japan's present-day needs. But like so many other aspects of Japanese life, the *mizu shobai* is deeply embedded in the overall socioeconomic system, as well as in the national psyche. It is not about to disappear in the foreseeable future.

Most of the money spent in the *mizu shobai* comes from the so-called *Sha-Yo Zoku* (Shah-Yoe Zoe-kuu), "Expense-Account Tribe"—the large number of salesmen, managers, and executives who are authorized to entertain clients, prospects, and guests at company expense. Japanese companies are permitted a substantial tax write-off for entertainment expenses to begin with, and most go way beyond the legal limit (based on their capital), according to both official and unofficial sources.

CRITICAL THINKING QUESTIONS

1. Akio Morita, a founder of Sony Corporation, once commented that Japanese companies look more like social organizations than business enterprises (De Mente, 1987: 61). What evidence in this selection can be used to assess this observation?

2. How do Japanese business organizations differ from the ideal model of Western bureaucracy described by Max Weber in Reading 22?

3. What elements of Japanese business organizations explain the relatively slow entry of women into the work force, and especially into management positions?

NOTE

1. For more about the subject of *mizu shobai,* see *Bachelor's Japan* by Boye De Mente. Rutland, Vt.: Tuttle, 1967 (© 1962).

REFERENCE

De Mente, B. 1987. *Japanese etiquette and ethics in business.* Lincolnwood, Ill.: NTC Business Books.

25

The Functions of Crime

Emile Durkheim

Deviance

CLASSIC

CONTEMPORARY

CROSS-CULTURAL

Common sense leads us to view crime, and all kinds of deviance, as pathological—that is, as harmful to social life. Despite the obvious social costs of crime, however, Durkheim argues that crime is normal because it is part of all societies. Furthermore, he claims that crime makes important contributions to the operation of a social system.

...Crime is present not only in the majority of societies of one particular species but in all societies of all types. There is no society that is not confronted with the problem of criminality. Its form changes; the acts thus characterized are not the same everywhere; but, everywhere and always, there have been men who have behaved in such a way as to draw upon themselves penal repression.... There is, then, no phenomenon that presents more indisputably all the symptoms of normality, since it

appears closely connected with the conditions of all collective life. To make of crime a form of social morbidity would be to admit that morbidity is not something accidental, but, on the contrary, that in certain cases it grows out of the fundamental constitution of the living organism; it would result in wiping out all distinction between the physiological and the pathological. No doubt it is possible that crime itself will have abnormal forms, as, for example, when its rate is unusually high. This excess is, indeed, undoubtedly morbid in nature. What is normal, simply, is the existence of criminality....

Here we are, then, in the presence of a conclusion in appearance quite paradoxical. Let us make no mistake. To classify crime among the phenomena of

Source: Reprinted with permission of The Free Press, a Division of Simon & Schuster, from *The Rules of Sociological Method* by Emile Durkheim, translated by S. A. Solovay and John H. Mueller. Edited by George E. G. Catlin. Copyright © 1938 by George E. Catlin; copyright renewed 1966 by Sarah A. Solovay, John H. Mueller, and George E. G. Catlin.

normal sociology is not to say merely that it is an inevitable, although regrettable, phenomenon, due to the incorrigible wickedness of men; it is to affirm that it is a factor in public health, an integral part of all healthy societies. This result is, at first glance, surprising enough to have puzzled even ourselves for a long time. Once this first surprise has been overcome, however, it is not difficult to find reasons explaining this normality and at the same time confirming it.

In the first place crime is normal because a society exempt from it is utterly impossible. Crime, we have shown elsewhere, consists of an act that offends certain very strong collective sentiments. In a society in which criminal acts are no longer committed, the sentiments they offend would have to be found without exception in all individual consciousnesses, and they must be found to exist with the same degree as sentiments contrary to them. Assuming that this condition could actually be realized, crime would not thereby disappear; it would only change its form, for the very cause which would thus dry up the sources of criminality would immediately open up new ones.

Indeed, for the collective sentiments which are protected by the penal law of a people at a specified moment of its history to take possession of the public conscience or for them to acquire a stronger hold where they have an insufficient grip, they must acquire an intensity greater than that which they had hitherto had. The community as a whole must experience them more vividly, for it can acquire from no other source the greater force necessary to control these individuals who formerly were the most refractory. For murderers to disappear, the horror of bloodshed must become greater in those social strata from which murderers are recruited; but, first it must become greater throughout the entire society. Moreover, the very absence of crime would directly contribute to produce this horror; because any sentiment seems much more respectable when it is always and uniformly respected.

One easily overlooks the consideration that these strong states of the common consciousness cannot be thus reinforced without reinforcing at the same time the more feeble states, whose violation previously gave birth to mere infraction of convention—since the weaker ones are only the prolongation, the attenuated form, of the stronger. Thus robbery and simple bad taste injure the same single altruistic sentiment, the respect for that which is another's. However, this same sentiment is less grievously offended by bad taste than by robbery; and since, in addition, the average consciousness has not sufficient intensity to react keenly to the bad taste, it is treated with greater tolerance. That is why the person guilty of bad taste is merely blamed, whereas the thief is punished. But, if this sentiment grows stronger, to the point of silencing in all consciousnesses the inclination which disposes man to steal, he will become more sensitive to the offenses which, until then, touched him but lightly. He will react against them, then, with more energy; they will be the object of greater opprobrium, which will transform certain of them from the simple moral faults that they were and give them the quality of crimes. For example, improper contracts, or contracts improperly executed, which only incur public blame or civil damages, will become offenses in law.

Imagine a society of saints, a perfect cloister of exemplary individuals. Crimes, properly so called, will there be unknown; but faults which appear venial to the layman will create there the same scandal that the ordinary offense does in ordinary consciousnesses. If, then, this society has the power to judge and punish, it will define these acts as criminal and will treat them as such. For the same reason, the perfect and upright man judges his smallest failings with a severity that the majority reserve for acts more truly in the nature of an offense. Formerly, acts of violence against persons were more frequent than they are today, because respect for individual dignity was less strong. As this has increased, these crimes have become more rare; and also, many acts violating this sentiment have been introduced into the penal law which were not included there in primitive times.[1]

...Crime is, then, necessary; it is bound up with the fundamental conditions of all social life, and by that very fact it is useful, because these conditions of which it is a part are themselves indispensable to the normal evolution of morality and law.

Indeed, it is no longer possible today to dispute the fact that law and morality vary from one social type to the next, nor that they change within the same type if the conditions of life are modified. But, in order that these transformations may be possible, the collective sentiments at the basis of morality must not be hostile to change, and consequently must have but moderate energy. If they were too strong, they would no longer be plastic. Every pattern is an obstacle to new patterns, to the extent that the first pattern is inflexible. The better a structure is articulated, the more it offers a healthy resistance to all modification; and this is equally true of functional, as of anatomical, organization. If there were no crimes, this condition could not have been fulfilled; for such a hypothesis presupposes that collective sentiments have arrived at a degree of intensity unexampled in history. Nothing is good indefinitely and to an unlimited extent. The authority which the moral conscience enjoys must not be excessive; otherwise no one would dare criticize it, and it would too easily congeal into an immutable form. To make progress, individual originality must be able to express itself. In order that the originality of the idealist whose dreams transcend his century may find expression, it is necessary that the originality of the criminal, who is below the level of his time, shall also be possible. One does not occur without the other.

Nor is this all. Aside from this indirect utility, it happens that crime itself plays a useful role in this evolution. Crime implies not only that the way remains open to necessary changes but that in certain cases it directly prepares these changes. Where crime exists, collective sentiments are sufficiently flexible to take on a new form, and crime sometimes helps to determine the form they will take. How many times, indeed, it is only an anticipation of future morality—a step toward what will be! According to Athenian law, Socrates was a criminal, and his condemnation was no more than just. However, his crime, namely, the independence of his thought, rendered a service not only to humanity but to his country....

From this point of view the fundamental facts of criminality present themselves to us in an entirely new light. Contrary to current ideas, the criminal no longer seems a totally unsociable being, a sort of parasitic element, a strange and unassimilable body, introduced into the midst of society. On the contrary, he plays a definite role in social life.

CRITICAL THINKING QUESTIONS

1. On what grounds does Durkheim argue that crime should be considered a "normal" element of society?
2. Why is a society devoid of crime an impossibility?
3. What are the functional consequences of crime and deviance?

NOTE

1. Calumny, insults, slander, fraud, etc.

Deviance

CLASSIC

CONTEMPORARY

CROSS-CULTURAL

26

The Rebels: A Brotherhood of Outlaw Bikers

Daniel R. Wolf

Using a classic social research strategy, fieldwork, Wolf reviews his experiences as a member of the outlaw biker gang, the Rebels.

ENTERING THE WORLD OF THE OUTLAW

All the world likes an outlaw. For some damn reason they remember 'em.

(Jesse James)

A midnight run shatters the night air. Thirty Harley-Davidson motorcycles stretch out for a quarter-mile, thundering down the highway. The pack moves in tight formation, advancing as a column of staggered twos. Veteran riders make sure there are fifteen yards between themselves and the bikes they are riding behind, three yards and a 45-degree angle between themselves and the bikes they are riding beside. Thirty men ride in boots and jeans, leathers and cut-off denim jackets, beards and long hair, tattoos and earrings, buck knives and chain belts. Each rider follows the grimacing skull on the back patch of the rider in front of him. Some ride with their ol' ladies, "jamming in the wind" with a laid-back coolness bordering on arrogance, a combination of speed, grace, and power. The lead biker snaps his wrist to full throttle and the super-charged V-twin engines heat up and pound out the challenge. Each biker is locked into the tunnel vision of his own world. He feels the heavy metal vibrations in every joint of his body, but he can no longer hear the rumble of his own machine, just a collective roar. Headlamps slice open just enough darkness to let the sculptured metal of extended front ends slide through. Cool blackness clips over high-rise handlebars, whips their faces, then quickly swallows the red glare of taillights. A grey blur of pavement that represents instant oblivion passes six inches beneath the soles of their boots. At a hundred miles an hour the inflections of the road surface disappear, eye sockets are pushed back, and tears flow. Riders hurtle down the highway, in total control of their own destinies, wrapped in the freedom of high sensation. They are the Rebels: Caveman, Blues, Tiny, Wee Albert, Gerry, Slim, Tramp, Danny,

Source: From *The Rebels: A Brotherhood of Outlaw Bikers* by Daniel R. Wolf. Toronto: University of Toronto Press, 1991, pp. 3–21. Reprinted by permission of the publisher.

Onion, Jim Raunch, Ken, Voodoo, Larry, Killer, Whimpy, Clayton, Steve, Indian, Armand, Crash, Big Mike, Smooth Ed, Yesnoski, Snake, Dale the Butcher, Saint, and Terrible Tom.

Outlaw motorcycle clubs originated on the American west coast following the Second World War. With names such as the Booze Fighters and their parent club the 13 Rebels, the Galloping Gooses, Satan's Sinners, and the Winos, they rapidly spread across the United States and into Canada in the early 1950s; Canada's first outlaw club was the Canadian Lancers in Toronto, Ontario. Today, outlaw motorcycle clubs are an international social phenomenon. As of 1990 the outlaw club subculture had spread into eleven other countries, including the European nations of Great Britain, West Germany, France, Switzerland, Austria, Belgium, Denmark, and the Netherlands in the mid-sixties and early seventies, and then into Australia, New Zealand, and Brazil in the mid-seventies and early eighties.

What is or is not considered deviant by society, and how society reacts to that deviance, always involves the process of social definition. Technically, the label "outlaw motorcycle club" designates a club that is not registered with the American Motorcycle Association (AMA) or the Canadian Motorcycle Association (CMA), which are the respective governing bodies for the sport of motorcycling in the United States and Canada. The AMA and CMA are themselves affiliated with the Fédération Internationale Motorcycliste (FIM), the international coordinating body for motorcycling whose headquarters are located in Paris, France. A motorcycle club that is registered with the AMA or CMA obtains a club charter from those parent bodies that allows the club and its members to participate in or sponsor sanctioned motorcycle events—mainly racing competitions. AMA or CMA registration further aligns the club with the legal and judicial elements of the host society; some clubs will go one step further and incorporate themselves as "registered societies" with the local state or provincial authorities. Non-registered clubs are labelled

"outlaw" and considered as the 1 per cent deviant fringe that continues to tarnish the public image of both motorcycles and motorcyclists. For its part, the outlaw-biker community graciously accepted the AMA's "one percenter" label as a means of identifying a "righteous outlaw." Today, many outlaw club members wear 1% badges as a supplement to their club colours; or, as Sonny Barger, president of the Hell's Angels, first did in the sixties, they make a very personal and uncompromising statement on where they stand on the issue of being an outlaw by having the 1% logo tattooed on their shoulders.

Historically, the initial and most dramatic definition of outlaw clubs occurred in response to the world's first motorcycle riot in the rural town of Hollister, California, on 4 July 1947. Approximately five hundred non-affiliated bikers disrupted an AMA-sponsored Gypsy Tour and competition events involving 2500 affiliated bikers by drinking and racing in the streets of the host town of Hollister. The ineffective efforts of a numerically insufficient seven-man police force, in conjunction with the sometimes provocative vigilante tactics of indignant local residents, caused the motorcyclists to coalesce as a mob. At the height of the riot, bikers rode their motorcycles into bars and restaurants and through traffic lights, tossed bottles out of upper-floor windows, and got rid of the beer they had been drinking in the streets (indecent exposure). The unruly behaviour lasted for approximately thirty-six hours, from July 4th to 5th; the world's first motorcycle riot ended with the departure of many of the partyers on the evening of the first day and the arrival on the second of an auxiliary police force of thirty-two officers.

The national exposure that was given the Hollister incident by *Life* magazine and others resulted in the stigmatization of an image: the motorcyclist as deviant. *Life's* account started a mass-media chain reaction that saw the Hollister incident grow considerably in its sensationalistic portrayal, and, as a result, the image of the motorcyclist as deviant become more defined and immutable. In 1949, Frank Rooney wrote a short narrative entitled "Cyclist Raid," based on *Life's* one-hundred-and-fifteen-word documentary, in 1951, "Cyclist Raid" was published in *Harper's* magazine. The *Harper's* serial was read by Stanley Kramer, a Hollywood producer, who immortalized the "motorcycle riot" in the movie *The Wild One,* released in 1953. The anti-hero image of the motorcyclist was cast in the person of Marion Brando, while Lee Marvin personified the motorcyclist as villain. Interestingly enough, the striped shirt that Lee Marvin wore in the movie was later bought by a member of the Hell's Angels Motorcycle Club (MC)—a symbolic indication of events to come. The movie was to titillate the North American media with its "factual" account of a "menacing element of modern youth": A little bit of the surface of contemporary American life is scratched in Stanley Kramer's "The Wild One"…and underneath is opened an ugly, debauched and frightening view of a small, but particularly significant and menacing element of modern youth.…

The subject of its examination is a swarm of youthful motorcyclists who ride through the country in wolf-pack fashion and terrorize the people of one small town.… These "wild ones" resent discipline and show an aggressive contempt for common decency and the police. Reckless and vandalistic, they live for sensations, nothing more—save perhaps the supreme sensation of defying the normal world. (Crowther, *New York Times,* 31 December 1953)

Audiences who like their facts dished up with realism, no matter how painful, might pay attention to "The Wild One"—a picture that is factual.… It displays a group of hoodlums, motorcyclists who ride around the country with a contempt for the law and a fondness for annoying people, who take over a small town…a slice of contemporary Americana at its worst. (Hartung, *Commonweal,* 3 February 1954)

The above "factual" accounts were based on viewing a Stanley Kramer movie production whose script was written by John Paxton; Paxton's script was based on Kramer's reading of Frank Rooney's serialized story in *Harper's* magazine; Rooney's short story was in turn based

on his reading of *Life's* one-hundred-and-fifteen-word report—complete with photo—which itself was originally construed by adding four major distortions to a brief press-wire release.

By contemporary standards the amount of property damage and civic duress incurred in Hollister was minimal. In actuality there were only thirty-eight arrests (out of approximately three or four thousand bikers), fighting was mostly confined to the bikers, and no one was killed, maimed, or even gang-kissed. "Wino Willie" Forkner is a biker who has ridden Harleys since he was a teenager in the 1930s. He had returned from the Second World War after fighting the Japanese as a waist gunner and engineer for the American Seventh Air Force. He attended the Hollister incident as a charter member of the Booze Fighters MC:

The worst thing that happened was that a bunch of guys wanted to break Red Daldren out of jail. I was in a bar and somebody came in and said there were about 500 bikers ready to break him out, and I thought, "Shit, that's all we need, something like that." So I ran down to where the crowd was assembling and told 'em, "Hell, old Red's drunk and he needs a good night's sleep. Leave him stay—he'll be out in the morning." Then I turned around and went back to the bar, and damned if the cops didn't come and nail me for inciting a riot [the charges were dropped]…but no big bad things happened. There were a few broken windows that we paid for. ("Wino Willie" Faukner, interview in *Easyriders,* September 1986: 107)

However, as *Life* was to point out twenty-five years after the Hollister riot, the significance of the media chain reaction was its very real consequences: "The *Wild One* became a milestone in movie history, launching the cult of gang violence in films. It also helped create an image of motorcycling that non-violent bike riders have been trying to live down for a quarter of a century now" *(Life,* September 1972: 32). After the Hollister incident and, more to the point, after the movie, the AMA issued its now famous statement about 1 per cent of the motorcycling public, specifically clubs like the Booze Fighters, being a deviant criminal fringe element.

There is a tendency to view the Hollister motorcycle riot and its subsequent national media coverage as the genesis of the "outlaw biker"—it was the birth of an image. In effect, the outlaw biker image that was created served as a frame of reference for many young and restless rebels who copied the celluloid vision in search of both a thrill and a cause. Historically, outlaw motorcycle clubs have operated in the shadows of several different media stereotypes, all of which have been variations on the theme of "social menace." In the 1950s bikers were depicted as social rebels and deviants; in the sixties and seventies the clubs were seen as subcultures of violence and drugs. The contemporary image adds a spectre of organized crime. In 1984 the Criminal intelligence Service of Canada (CISC) declared that outlaw motorcycle gangs had become as much of an organized-crime threat to Canada as the traditional Mafia. According to the CISC report, outlaw clubs "are involved in practically all major crime activities from murder to white-collar crime." At the annual meeting of Canadian police chiefs in 1985, outlaw motorcycle clubs were again acknowledged as the number-one concern in the area of organized crime; media headlines carried the claim: "Bikers more powerful than Mafia" (Canadian Press release, *Edmonton Journal,* 15 August 1985: A12). How law-enforcement agencies have come to view outlaw motorcycle clubs is summarized in the following profile contained in an application for a search warrant made out by a member of the City of Calgary police department's Special Strike Force:

Outlaw Motorcycle Gangs have over the years evolved into highly sophisticated "organized crime" bodies, involved in drug manufactured/distribution/trafficking, prostitution, "gun running," fencing of stolen property and strong arm debt collection.

Law enforcement agencies across Canada have recognized that outlaw motorcycle gangs as "organized crime" bodies pose the single most serious threat to the country.

An outlaw motorcycle gang is "Any group of motorcycle enthusiasts who have voluntarily made a commitment to band together and abide by their organization's rigorous rules enforced by violence, who engage in activities that bring them and their club into serious conflict with society and the law."

It is their involvement as a group in criminal activities and antisocial behaviour which sets them apart from other organized groups. (Detective Brendan Alexander Kapuscinski, City of Calgary police force, "Application for Warrant to Search and Seize," 1988: 2)

"If the Cops are the Good Guys," writes the representative of an American federal law-enforcement training centre, "then it's hard to imagine a more archetypal Bad Guy than the outlaw motorcyclist!" (Ayoob, 1982: 26). North Americans typically react with an interesting mixture of apprehension and fascination to the fearsome images of aggression, revolt, anarchy, and criminal abandon that are used to portray outlaw-biker gangs.

Ironically, the appeal of outlaw clubs to their members is very different from what the public understands. Outlaw bikers view themselves as nothing less than frontier heroes, living out the "freedom ethic" that they feel the rest of society has largely abandoned. They acknowledge that they are antisocial, but only to the extent that they seek to gain their own unique experiences and express their individuality through their motorcycles. Their "hogs" become personal charms against the regimented world of the "citizen." They view their club as collective leverage that they can use against an establishment that threatens to crush those who find conventional society inhibiting and destructive of individual character. In an interesting twist of stereotypes the citizen becomes the bad guy, or at least weak, and the outlaw becomes the hero. Bikers make much of the point that the differential treatment—harassment—accorded outlaw clubs by law-enforcement agencies runs counter to the basic principles of self-determination. They protest that a truly democratic society should be able to tolerate diversity and accommodate an awareness that drifting away from society's conventions is very different from opting out of society's laws. Somewhere between the convenient stereotype of "criminal deviants" used by the police and the stylized self-conscious image outlaws have of themselves as "frontier heroes" lies the story of real people.

The Rebels Motorcycle Club is an outlaw club. It began in 1969 as a small club of motorcycle enthusiasts who rode their Harley-Davidsons on the streets of Edmonton, Alberta, a mid-sized Canadian city with a population of approximately 700,000 people. Today (1990), the Rebels MC is a federation of four clubs—located in the provinces of Alberta and Saskatchewan—that maintains informal social and political ties with the Hells Angels MC. Becoming a Rebel means being part of a tightly knit voluntary association that operates as a secret society within an organizational framework that includes a political structure, a financial base, a geographical territory, a chain of command, a constitution, an elaborate set of rules, and internal mechanisms for enforcing justice and compliance from within.

At its best a veteran club will operate with the internal discipline and precision of a paramilitary organization, which is completely necessary if it hopes to beat the odds and survive. These men close their world to the outside, turning to each other for help and guidance. They protect themselves with a rigid code of silence that cloaks their world in secrecy. Thus, despite the fact that outlaw motorcycle clubs are found in every major urban centre in Canada and the United States—there are approximately 900 clubs—*the subculture had remained ethnographically unexplored.*

As a doctoral graduate student in anthropology at the University of Alberta, Edmonton, I wanted to study the "Harley tribe." It was my intent to obtain an insider's perspective on the emotions and the mechanics that underlie the outlaw bikers' creation of a subcultural alternative. My interest in outlaw motorcycle clubs was not entirely theoretical; it was also a personal challenge. Brought up on the streets of a lower-class neighbourhood, I saw my best friend—with whom I broke into abandoned buildings as a kid—sent to prison for grand theft auto, and then shot down in an attempted armed robbery. Rather than be crushed

like that, I worked in meat-packing plants and factories for thirteen hours a day and put myself through university. I also bought myself a British-made Norton motorcycle. My Norton Commando became a "magic carpet ride" of thrills and excitement that I rode with lean women who were equally hungry to get their share. But it was more than that. I rode my motorcycle in anger; for me it became a show of contempt and a way of defying the privileged middle class that had put me down and had kept my parents "in their place." I felt that the Establishment had done me no favours and that I owed it even less. At that time I saw outlaw bikers as a reflection of my own dark side. I made them the embodiment of my own youthful rebellion and resentment. In retrospect, I believe that it was this aspect of my non-academic background—the fact that I had learned to ride and beat the streets—that made it possible for me to contemplate such a study, and eventually to ride with the Rebels.

At the time of beginning my fieldwork I had been riding British-made motorcycles for three years and had talked briefly to members of the King's Crew MC in Calgary. But this was not enough to comprehend the outlaw-biker community or to study it. My impression of outlaw bikers was narrow and incomplete and, in that sense, almost as misleading as the stereotype held by most "citizens." I was physically close to the scene, but far removed from a balanced understanding; that understanding would only come from "being there."

I customized my Norton, donned some biker clothing, and set off to do some fieldwork. My first attempts at contacting an outlaw club were near disasters. In Calgary, I met several members of the King's Crew MC in a motorcycle shop and expressed an interest in "hanging around." But I lacked patience and pushed the situation by asking too many questions. A deviant society, especially one that walks on the wild side of illegal activities, will have its own information network for checking out strangers. I found out quickly that outsiders, even bikers, do not rush into a club, and that anyone who doesn't show the proper restraint will be shut out. That was mistake number one. Days later, I carelessly got into an argument with a club "striker," a probationary member, that led to blows in a bar-room skirmish. He flattened my nose and began choking me. Unable to get air down my throat and breathing only blood through my nostrils, I managed a body punch that luckily found his solar plexus and loosened his grip. I then grabbed one of his hands and pulled back on the thumb till l heard the joint break. Mistake number two. It was time to move on. I packed my sleeping-bag on my Norton and headed west for Vancouver with some vague and ridiculous notion of meeting up with the Satan's Angels, now a chapter of the Hell's Angels.

Riding into Burnaby (Greater Vancouver) I discovered that an outlaw biker has to learn a whole new set of rules for dealing with the law. I had decided to modify my public identity in order to facilitate participant observation of a deviant group; I could not expect any favours from legal authorities and I would have to learn how to cope with what might be termed differential treatment—bikers use the term "harassment"—on the part of police officers. I saw the flashing red light in my rear-view mirror moments before l heard the siren. I had been looking for the Admiral Hotel, a bar where the Satan's Angels hung out. I started to gear down when I noticed that the RCMP (Royal Canadian Mounted Police) cruiser was only three feet from my rear tire. I continued to slow down and hoped that he knew what he was doing. I pulled into the parking lot behind the Admiral bar, got of my bike, and turned around to approach the officer. As I reached for my wallet he immediately ordered me to turn around and put my hands behind my head. I froze in what was probably 90 per cent uncertainty and 10 per cent defiance. When I didn't move he unlatched the holster that held his pistol; he gripped the weapon and then reached inside his car and grabbed the radio mike to call for a backup. Within moments a second cruiser was on the scene. He lined me up with the car's headlights, turned on the high beams, and then began the standard shakedown. Upon request I produced my operator's licence, vehicle registration, and insurance, and was then asked where I was from, what club I rode with, if I had a criminal record, and if I had ever been in trouble with the law before. As I answered the questions, wondering what kind of trouble I was in now, a third cruiser pulled up, turned on its bright lights, and two more officers joined in. At that time some of my identification read "Daniel" and some read "Danny," which prompted a series of questions about aliases and a radio check about outstanding arrest warrants and vehicle registration. When this failed to produce any evidence against me, I was asked if I was carrying any weapons or drugs. The answer to both questions was "no" and the whole situation began to seem absurd. I was being put on stage under the spotlights of three police cruisers in a back alley drama directed by five RCMP officers. Meanwhile, the Satan's Angels that I'd come to meet were relaxing and having some cool beers in the bar across the alley. I began to laugh at the irony, which was mistake number three. "Put your hands up against that wall!" yelled a constable who was angered by my apparent disdain for he law. One officer searched through the pockets of my leathers and jeans while another rummaged through the leather saddle-bags on my bike. After the bike and body search, I asked the officers if motorcycle clubs were a major problem in their area. I was told they weren't, "but some guys figure they're king shit when you pull them over, and you've got to remember that no matter how tough you are, there's always someone tougher!" I was then asked how long I was staying, and I replied that it depended on my financial situation. I answered straightforwardly and stated that I was carrying credit cards and a little more than three hundred dollars, as the police already knew—having counted it. Only then did one of the officers explain: "When he asked you how long you're staying, what he's saying is that this road leads to Harvey Avenue, which leads to the highway out of town!"

I had sewn a secret pocket into the sleeve of my leather jacket. It contained a letter from the [Social Sciences and Humanities Research Council]…(SSHRC) addressed to the RCMP that identified myself and my research. The officers failed to find it, and I wasn't about to reveal it. My research goal was to find out and experience what happens within the outlaw-biker scene, not be told what happens from the outside. Three days earlier I had talked to a Vancouver city police officer who knew me as a researcher: "I'll save you a whole lot of trouble, maybe even your neck, and explain this whole biker thing to you," he said. "They're all just psychologically unstable. That's all you have to know; otherwise none of it makes any sense."

"Those cops [at the Admiral Hotel] were setting you up," Steve, the Rebels MC sergeant at arms, would explain some months later. "They were just waiting for you to make a stupid move and they've got you by the balls. They could have beaten the shit outta you, and you'd have five cops as witnesses. Well, it would've been tough shit for you!" I learned that one does not play the role of Jesse James when being pulled over by "the man," especially on a "club run," or motorcycle tour, where police can make a shakedown last up to two hours. One learns to avoid all eye contact and restrict all verbal responses to a monosyllabic "no" or "yes." Over the next few years I got lots of practice; that first summer I was pulled over and interrogated fifteen times— on only one of these occasions was I actually charged with an offence, a speeding violation.

While touring through the British Columbia interior I joined up with three members of the Tribesmen MC from Squamish, BC, whom I met at a Penticton hamburger stand. From the Tribesmen I learned that gaining entry into a club would take time. The time factor meant that my best chance of success lay in studying the Rebels in the familiar confines of my own back yard in Edmonton. "You don't make friends with members of a club," cautioned Lance of the Tribesmen. "You let them make friends with

you." Lance pointed out that in order to ride with a club I would have to be accepted by all the members, get to know some of the members personally, and at least one member well enough that he would be willing to sponsor me and take responsibility for my actions. A critical suggestion emphatically made by all three Tribesmen was "Get yourself a hog [Harley-Davidson]!"

These first experiences "in the field" made it clear that I couldn't study any club I wanted, at any time that suited me. There was a good reason for this, as I discovered later. Restricting contacts with non-club members was a key to club survival. With time I realized that maintaining strict boundaries is a central theme that underlies all aspects of club life. This fact presented a major ethical dilemma. I could not do a study if I explained my research goal at the outset. However, an "undercover" strategy contravened a fundamental ethical tenet in which I believed, that no research should be carried out without the informants' full awareness. I devised an alternative strategy that satisfied myself, my thesis committee, and the guidelines that the University of Alberta had set down for ethical research. The plan was that initially I would attempt to establish contact with the Rebels as a biker who also happened to be a university— anthropology—student. If I were successful in achieving sufficient rapport and mutual trust with club members, I would officially ask the Rebels MC for permission to conduct a study. The bottom line was that it would be the Rebel club members I rode with who would make the final decision as to whether or not the study would go beyond my personal files.

This strategy was not without risks. Outlaw clubs are aware that they are under constant police surveillance, often by special police units, such as the RCMP's E-squad in Vancouver or the City of Calgary's Strike Force. I learned that the Edmonton Rebels suspected that a biker who had recently attempted to gain entry into their club as a "striker" was an agent of the RCMP. After repeated attempts, the police have long since discovered that infiltrating an outlaw club is a long, arduous, and risky process when it is being done for "professional" reasons. "Infiltration of the gangs is difficult. 'They have an internal discipline that makes it dangerous,' said a police officer. 'It's an area we have trouble infiltrating. The conditions of initiation make it almost impossible....' 'They are scary,' said one police intelligence officer, who asked not to be identified. 'We've had two or three informants killed, found tied to trees up north with bullet holes in them'" (Canadian Press release, *Edmonton Journal,* 29 September 1979).

In the United States the FBI had gone so far as to have several agents start up their own club in order to bypass the striker (probation) period that screens out bogus bikers. The Edmonton police play a wide variety of angles in order to update their information on the Rebels. On one occasion, two plain-clothes officers wore media badges at a biker rally protesting mandatory helmet legislation in order to move freely among the club members and take pictures. If the Rebels discovered my research motive before I was ready to tell them, it would have been difficult to communicate any good intentions, scientific or otherwise. There existed the distinct possibility that more than just the study would have been terminated prematurely. I lived with that possibility for three years.

I fine-tuned my image before I approached the Rebels. This was going to be my final make-it-or-forget-it attempt. I purchased an old 1955 Harley-Davidson FL, a "panhead," which I customized but later sold in favour of a mechanically more reliable 1972 Electraglide, a "shovelhead." I had grown shoulder-length hair and a heavy beard. I bought a Harley-Davidson leather jacket and vest, wore studded leather wristbands and a shark's-tooth pendant, and sported a cut-off denim jacket with assorted Harley-Davidson pins and patches, all symbolic of the outlaw-biker world-view. While I was still very nervous about approaching the Rebels, I had become more comfortable with

myself. My public image expressed what I now felt was my personal character. There was no pretension. As far as I was concerned, I was a genuine biker who was intrigued with the notion of riding with an outlaw club.

I discovered that I was a lot more apprehensive than I thought as I sat at the opposite end of the Kingsway Motor inn and watched the Rebels down their drinks. The loud thunder of heavy-metal rock music would make initiating a delicate introduction difficult if not impossible; and there were no individual faces or features to be made out in the smoky haze, only a series of Rebel skull patches draped over leather jackets in a corner of the bar that outsiders seemed to warily avoid. It was like a scene out of a western movie: hard-faced outlaws in the bar, downing doubles while waiting for the stagecoach to arrive. I decided to go outside and devise an approach strategy, including how I would react if one of the Rebels turned to me and simply said, "Who invited you?" I had thought through five different approaches when Wee Albert of the Rebels MC came out of the bar to do a security check on the "Rebel iron" in the parking lot. He saw me leaning on my bike and came over to check me out. For some time Wee Albert and I stood in the parking lot and talked about motorcycles, riding in the wind, and the Harley tradition. He showed me some of the more impressive Rebel choppers and detailed the jobs of customizing that members of the club had done to their machines. He then checked out my "hog," gave a grunt of approval, and invited me to come in and join the Rebels at their tables. Drinking at the club bar on a regular basis gave me the opportunity to get to know the Rebels and gave them an opportunity to size me up and check me out on neutral ground. I had made the first of a long sequence of border crossings that all bikers go through if they hope to get close to a club.

Wee Albert became a good buddy of mine, and he sponsored my participation in club runs and at club parties. In addition to my having a Sponsor, my presence had to be voted on by the membership as a whole at their weekly Wednesday meeting, if two of the twenty-five members voted "no," then I wasn't around. The number of close friends that I had in the club increased and I was gradually drawn into the Rebel brotherhood. Measured in terms of social networking, brotherhood meant being part of a high frequency of interpersonal contacts that were activated over a wide range of social situations. Among the activities that I took part in were drinking and carousing in the club bar, assisting members in the chopping (customizing) and repair of motorcycles, loaning and borrowing money, shooting pool and "bullshitting" at the clubhouse, exchanging motorcycle parts along with technical information and gossip at a motorcycle shop owned by two club members, going on a duck hunt and on fishing trips, making casual visits and receiving dinner invitations to members' homes, general partying and riding together, providing emotional support, and, when necessary, standing shoulder-to-shoulder in the face of physical threat. Brotherhood, I came to learn, is the foundation of the outlaw-club community. It establishes among members a sense of moral, emotional, and material interdependence; feelings of commitment arise out of a sense of sharing a common fate. The enduring emotion of brotherhood is comradeship. To a "patch holder" (club member) brotherhood means being there when needed; its most dramatic expression occurs when brothers defend each other from outside threats. I vividly remember sitting with the Rebels in the Kingsway Motor inn bar, trying to sober up quickly while I mentally acted out what I thought would be my best martial-arts moves. I looked down at my hand: I had sprained my thumb the night before while sparring in karate. My right hand was black, blue, swollen, and useless. I watched nervously as sixty-five members of the Canadian Airborne Regiment strutted into the bar. Their walk said that they were looking for us and a brawl. I came to view brotherhood as both a privilege and a tremendous personal responsibility.

I watched my own identity change as the result of experiences I had on my own as a biker and those I shared with club members. These often involved the process of public identification, or labelling, and other reactions by outsiders. I learned that a lone biker on the highway is vulnerable. I was run off the road three times over a four-year period. On one of those occasions I was forced off a mountain road into the side of a cliff and nearly catapulted into oblivion. Another lesson was that an outlaw biker has to be ready for "the heat to come down" at the most unexpected times. For instance, while I was washing my bike at a car wash, the owner phoned the police about a suspicious-looking biker. The police came, searched my bike, and I was arrested and charged with carrying a concealed and illegal weapon—a switch-blade. I felt sure that I would have a criminal record long before, and maybe instead of, a PhD. Fortunately, I discovered that a good lawyer, who is "owed a favour" by the crown prosecutor, can get the charges dropped—in this case, three minutes prior to the start of the trial. I learned that a police officer will follow an outlaw biker for five miles to give him a ticket for doing 35 mph in a 30-mph zone. A biker could be given a ticket for a balding tire or because his custom handlebars were one-half of an inch too high above the motorcycle's seat. I recall being turned down by insurance companies for vehicle coverage, refused admittance to private camp-grounds, and kicked off a public beach by Penticton police who thought we intended to incite a riot. I found that associating with outlaw patch holders could be an invitation to danger. While riding with the club, I and some patch holders were pulled over by a cruiser and warned that members of the Highway Kings MC were out gunning for Rebels with shotguns. None of these situations could have been acted out in a detached manner. My involvement demanded the intensity of a highly emotional reaction. Each encounter was an escalation towards an outlaw-biker identity. My record of personal encounters with citizens and the police, especially those that were threatening, enabled me to understand and articulate the biker's perspective on drifting away from the Establishment and being drawn into the club. Sometimes, as I watched the faces of the Rebels, I could see the hardening of an attitude—"us-against-the-world."

Gradually my status changed from being a "biker" with a familiar face to being a "friend of the club." There were no formal announcements. Tiny just yelled across at me one afternoon while we were starting up our bikes, "Hey! 'Coyote!' No way I'm riding beside you. Some farmer is going to shoot our asses off and then say he was shooting at varmints." This was a reference to the coyote skin I had taken to wearing over my helmet. Wee Albert looked at me, grinned, and said "That's it, 'Coyote.' From now on that'll be your club name." Most of the patch holders had club names, such as Spider or Greaser. These names are reminders of club association. More important, they separate the individual from his past, giving him the opportunity to build a new persona in terms of group-valued traits. Pseudonyms give members an aura; they draw upon a collective power. They are no longer just Rick, Allan, or Bill; they are Blues, Terrible Tom, and Caveman; they are outlaw bikers!

As a "friend of the club" I took part informally in political rhetoric concerning the club's future, such as debates concerning the hot issue of club expansion. This position of trust with the Rebels brought me into contact with other outlaw clubs such as the King's Crew of Calgary, the Spokesmen of Saskatoon, the Bounty Hunters of Victoria, the Gypsy Wheelers of White Rock, and the Warlords of Edmonton. Through these inter-club contacts I became familiar with the political relationships of conflict and alliance that exist among outlaw clubs. Meeting members of different clubs also provided me with the comparative data I needed to isolate those aspects of behaviour and organization that were shared by all clubs, and helped to explain how some clubs were different and why. My long-term association with the Rebels gave me a valuable historical perspective that included insights into the developmental sequence of clubs. I was able to describe how new clubs form, why few emergent clubs beat the odds and survive, and how a chosen few clubs achieved long-term success and expansion while all that remains of other clubs is their colours hanging upside down as trophies on the wall of a rival's clubhouse.

If the Rebels had at any time refused permission for the study, I would have destroyed all the data I had collected and closed the investigation. The fact that I had established myself as a friend of the club was no reason for the members to agree to become scientific units of analysis. Rejection of the study appeared more and more imminent as I grew to sense and share members' distrust of outsiders. I had come to appreciate some of the multifaceted advantages of having a negative public stereotype—however unrealistic. When outsiders look at an outlaw biker, they do not see an individual, all they see is the club patch that he wears on the back of his leathers. The negative image that comes with the Rebel skull patch discourages unnecessary intrusions by outsiders. "That way I'm not bothered," explained Steve of the Rebels, "and I don't have to tell the guy 'Fuck off, cunt!'" The patch becomes part of the biker's threat display: it effectively keeps violence to a minimum by warding off those outsiders who might otherwise choose to test the mettle of the bikers. For the majority of outsiders, the prospect of having to initiate even the briefest of encounters with an outlaw biker brings forth emotions ranging from uneasiness to sheer dread. Ironically, the more I got to know the members and the greater the bonds of trust and brotherhood, the less I expected that they would approve of the study. "The best public relations for us," according to Indian of the Rebels, "is no public relations!" I found it increasingly difficult to live with the fact that the closer I came to my destination of knowing the Rebels, the further distant became my goal of doing an ethnographic study.

One night, during a three-week Rebel run to the west coast, I was sharing a beer with Tiny while sitting on the porch of the Bounty Hunters' club-house. We were watching officers of the Victoria police force who were watching us from their cruisers in the street and from a nearby hotel—binoculars between closed curtains. "You know, Coyote," grumbled a 6-foot, 275-pound Tiny in a very personable tone, "I've talked with some of the guys and we think that you should strike [enter probationary membership] for the club. The way I see it, it shouldn't take you more than a year to earn your colours [club patch]." The pressure was now on and building for me to make a move that would bring me even closer to the club. I had made a commitment to myself that under no circumstances would I attempt to become a full-fledged member without first revealing my desire to do a study on the club. It was time to disengage. It was time for me to sell my study to the Rebels, but I was at a loss as to what to say. I had been a brother through good times and bad, thick and thin; but to distance myself from the Rebels by announcing a study done for outsiders of a way of life I had shared with them against the world seemed nothing short of a betrayal. Entering the field as a biker and main-taining relations of trust and friendship during the course of fieldwork prevented my leaving the field with my notes. I had accomplished what I had hoped to during my fieldwork, but at this point there was no way out. There was no formula for disengagement of the field project. As far as I was concerned, I had lost a three-year gamble.

Weeks of personal frustration and near-depression later, I had an incredible stroke of luck. Wee Albert, who took great pleasure in talk-ing about "what it means to be a Rebel and a brother," approached me and said, "Being an anthropologist you study people, right? Well, have you ever thought of maybe doing a study on the club? Chances are it probably wouldn't carry [club approval], but maybe. I'd like to see it happen." I told Wee Albert that I'd consider it and approach the executive members with the proposal. The door of disengagement was open; Wee Albert had provided me with an honourable way out. Whether or not it would be a successful

disengagement—the approval of an ethnogra-phy—remained to be seen.

I first talked to Ken and Steve about the prospect of "doing an anthropological study." Ken, president, and Steve, sergeant at arms, were both friends of mine and well-respected club offi-cers, but their most positive response was a shrug of the shoulders and "We'll see." Ken decided to bring up the proposed study at a meeting of the club executive. The officers of the club discussed the proposal among themselves and determined that no harm would be done if they presented it one week later to the general membership at a club meeting. For me it was the longest night of the year as I waited for the decision. The issue was hotly debated, a vote was held, and the study approved. Why? Granting me permission for the study was done as a "personal favour": "You have come into favour with a lot of the members and been nothing but good to the club. All in all you've been a pretty righteous friend of the club. But there was a lot of opposition to your study, especially from guys like T.T. [Terrible Tom] and Blues. The way I see it the vote went the way it did because you were asking us a favour. You didn't come in promising us the moon, you know, money from books and that sort of thing. You promised us nothing so we did it as a personal favour" (Wee Albert). Any offers of economic remuneration on my part would have been inter-preted as an insult; the Rebels were doing me a favour. I strongly suspect that any researcher who buys his or her way into a closed society—with promises of money or royalties—will garner information that is at best forced, at worst fabri-cated. However, I did give the "victims" of the four-and-one-half-hour questionnaire a twenty-six-ounce bottle of Alberta Springs (Old Time Sipping Whisky) and a Harley-Davidson beer mug. "Fair return" for the club as a whole was a bound copy of my thesis, which found a home in the Rebels' clubhouse.

I continued to ride with the Rebels for another year and a half, during which time I carried out formal data-gathering procedures. These included extensive open-ended interviews with a number of Rebel patch holders and ended with the administration of a four-hour-long structured questionnaire to six members. Interestingly enough, Blues, a Rebel who was both a friend and a staunch opponent of the study, was one of the six. "The club is all I have. It means everything to me. It's with me all the time. I feel leery about talking to anybody about it. If I wasn't 100 per cent for you I wouldn't be here. If you'd been asking these questions three years ago [when I initially made contact with the Rebels MC], well no fucking way. We've been burned before, but never again!" Blues's trust and vote of confidence brought me a tremendous degree of personal satisfaction.

The theoretical framework and methodological approach that I use in [my] book are based on a cognitive definition of culture. Culture is here defined as the rules and categories of meaning and action that are used by individuals to both interpret and generate appropriate behaviour. I therefore view the outlaw-biker subculture as a human experience. It is a system of meaning in which I, as an anthropologist, had to involve myself in order to develop an adequate explanation of what was being observed. That is, in order to understand the biker subculture, or any culture for that matter, one must first try to understand it as it is experienced by the bikers themselves. Only then can one comprehend both the meaning of being an outlaw and how that meaning is constructed and comes to be shared by bikers. Only by first seeing the world through the eyes of the outlaws can we then go on to render intelligible the decisions that they make and the behaviours they engage in. Those meanings, decisions, and behaviours may lead you to applaud outlaw bikers as heroes. Alternatively, they may lead you to condemn them as villains. Labelling them as heroes or villains is a subsequent value judgment that the reader has the option of making. That value judgment is quite separate from first knowing outlaw bikers – my job as an ethnographer.

In order to operationalize this theoretical position of capturing an insider's perspective, I adopted a research methodology that closely resembles that of a symbolic interactionist. That is, within the overall framework of participant observation I emphasize analysis that is proximate—events are described in terms of variables that are close to the immediate situation in which the actors find themselves; processual—events are viewed as an emerging step-by-step reality whose completion requires actors to meet a series of contingencies; and phenomenological—events are explained in a manner that pays serious attention to how the actors experience them (Lofland, 1969: 296–97). By blending the methodological strategy of participant observation with the perspective of symbolic interactionism (Visano, 1989: 3, 29), I hope to replicate for the reader the experienced natural world as it unfolds for the outlaw biker.

CRITICAL THINKING QUESTIONS

1. Discuss the significance of the "one percenter" label for bikers.
2. Do you think that the image of the "biker" has changed since the Hollister incident in 1947? If so, in what ways? If not, why do you feel that the image has remained stable over time?
3. Has Wolf's presentation of the Rebels changed how you look at bike gangs? If so, how? If not, why not?

REFERENCES

Agar, M. 1986. *Speaking of ethnography.* Beverly Hills, Calif.: Sage.

Ayoob, M. 1982. Outlaw bikers. *Police Product News*, 6(5).

Forkner, W. 1986. "Wino" Willie Forkner: All the old romance retold. *Easyriders* 16(159).

Kapuscinski, B. A. 1988. Application for warrant to search and seize. Attorney-General of the Province of Alberta: 2.

Keiser, L. R. 1979. *The Vice Lords: Warriors of the streets.* Toronto: Holt, Rinehart and Winston. Lofland, J. 1969. *Deviance and identity.* Englewood Cliffs. N.J.: Prentice-Hall.

Maanen, J. van. 1988. *Tales of the field: On writing ethnography.* Chicago: University of Chicago Press.

Visano, L. 1989. Researching deviance: An interactionist account. Paper presented at the Canadian Sociology and Anthropology Association annual conference, Quebec City.

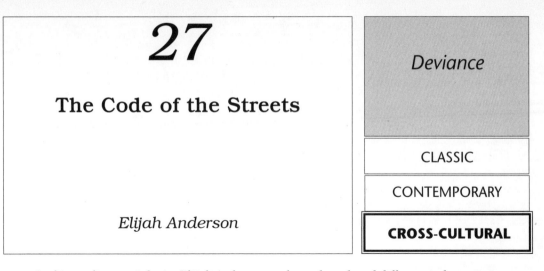

27

The Code of the Streets

Elijah Anderson

Deviance

CLASSIC

CONTEMPORARY

CROSS-CULTURAL

In this reading, sociologist Elijah Anderson explores the cultural differences that exist in our inner cities. Alongside mainstream cultural values, he explains, exists a "code of the streets," which leads some young people to engage in crime and violence. From this point of view, crime is not so much a matter of breaking the rules as it is playing by a different set of rules.

Of all the problems besetting the poor inner-city black community, none is more pressing than that of interpersonal violence and aggression. It wreaks havoc daily with the lives of community residents and increasingly spills over into downtown and residential middle-class areas. Muggings, burglaries, carjackings, and drug-related shootings, all of which may leave their victims or innocent bystanders dead, are now common enough to concern all urban and many suburban residents. The inclination to violence springs from the circumstances of life among the ghetto poor— the lack of jobs that pay a living wage, the stigma of race, the fallout from rampant drug use and drug trafficking, and the resulting alienation and lack of hope for the future.

Simply living in such an environment places young people at special risk of falling victim to

aggressive behavior. Although there are often forces in the community which can counteract the negative influences, by far the most powerful being a strong, loving, "decent" (as inner-city residents put it) family committed to middle-class values, the despair is pervasive enough to have spawned an oppositional culture, that of "the streets," whose norms are often consciously opposed to those of mainstream society. These two orientations—decent and street—socially organize the community, and their coexistence has important consequences for residents, particularly children growing up in the inner city. Above all, this environment means that even youngsters whose home lives reflect mainstream values—and the majority of homes in the community do—must be able to handle themselves in a street-oriented environment.

This is because the street culture has evolved what may be called a code of the streets, which amounts to a set of informal rules governing interpersonal public behavior, including violence. The

Source: From *Code of the Street: Decency, Violence, and the Moral Life of the Inner City* by Elijah Anderson. Copyright © 1999 by Elijah Anderson. Used by permission of W.W. Norton & Co., Inc.

rules prescribe both a proper comportment and a proper way to respond if challenged. They regulate the use of violence and so allow those who are inclined to aggression to precipitate violent encounters in an approved way. The rules have been established and are enforced mainly by the street-oriented, but on the streets the distinction between street and decent is often irrelevant; everybody knows that if the rules are violated, there are penalties. Knowledge of the code is thus largely defensive; it is literally necessary for operating in public. Therefore, even though families with a decency orientation are usually opposed to the values of the code, they often reluctantly encourage their children's familiarity with it to enable them to negotiate the inner-city environment.

At the heart of the code is the issue of respect—loosely defined as being treated "right," or granted the deference one deserves. However, in the troublesome public environment of the inner city, as people increasingly feel buffeted by forces beyond their control, what one deserves in the way of respect becomes more and more problematic and uncertain. This in turn further opens the issue of respect to sometimes intense interpersonal negotiation. In the street culture, especially among young people, respect is viewed as almost an external entity that is hard-won but easily lost, and so must constantly be guarded. The rules of the code in fact provide a framework for negotiating respect. The person whose very appearance—including his clothing, demeanor, and way of moving—deters transgressions feels that he possesses, and may be considered by others to possess, a measure of respect. With the right amount of respect, for instance, he can avoid "being bothered" in public. If he is bothered, not only may he be in physical danger but he has been disgraced or "dissed" (disrespected). Many of the forms that dissing can take might seem petty to middle-class people (maintaining eye contact for too long, for example), but to those invested in the street code, these actions become serious indications of the other person's intentions. Consequently, such people become very sensitive to advances and slights, which could well serve as warnings of imminent physical confrontation.

This hard reality can be traced to the profound sense of alienation from mainstream society and its institutions felt by many poor inner-city black people, particularly the young. The code of the streets is actually a cultural adaptation to a profound lack of faith in the police and the judicial system. The police are most often seen as representing the dominant white society and not caring to protect inner-city residents. When called, they may not respond, which is one reason many residents feel they must be prepared to take extraordinary measures to defend themselves and their loved ones against those who are inclined to aggression. Lack of police accountability has in fact been incorporated into the status system: The person who is believed capable of "taking care of himself" is accorded a certain deference, which translates into a sense of physical and psychological control. Thus the street code emerges where the influence of the police ends and personal responsibility for one's safety is felt to begin. Exacerbated by the proliferation of drugs and easy access to guns, this volatile situation results in the ability of the street-oriented minority (or those who effectively "go for bad") to dominate the public spaces.

DECENT AND STREET FAMILIES

Although almost everyone in poor inner-city neighborhoods is struggling financially and therefore feels a certain distance from the rest of America, the decent and the street family in a real sense represent two poles of value orientation, two contrasting conceptual categories. The labels "decent" and "street," which the residents themselves use, amount to evaluative judgments that confer status on local residents. The labeling is often the result of a social contest among individuals and families of the neighborhood. Individuals of the two orientations often coexist in the same extended family. Decent residents judge themselves to be so while judging others to be of the street, and street individuals often present themselves as decent, drawing distinctions between themselves and other people. In addition, there is quite a bit of circumstantial behavior—that is, one person may at different times exhibit both decent and street orientations, depending on the circumstances. Although these designations result from so much social jockeying, there do exist concrete features that define each conceptual category.

Generally, so-called decent families tend to accept mainstream values more fully and attempt to instill them in their children. Whether married couples with children or single-parent (usually female) households, they are generally "working poor" and so tend to be better off financially than their street-oriented neighbors. They value hard work and self-reliance and are willing to sacrifice for their children. Because they have a certain amount of faith in mainstream society, they harbor hopes for a better future for their children, if not for themselves. Many of them go to church and take a strong interest in their children's schooling. Rather than dwelling on the real hardships and inequities facing them, many such decent people, particularly the increasing number of grandmothers raising grandchildren, see their difficult situation as a test from God and derive great support from their faith and from the church community.

Extremely aware of the problematic and often dangerous environment in which they reside, decent parents tend to be strict in their child-rearing practices, encouraging children to respect authority and walk a straight moral line. They have an almost obsessive concern about trouble of any kind and remind their children to be on the lookout for people and situations that might lead to it. At the same time, they are themselves polite and considerate of others, and teach their children to be the same way. At home, at work, and in church, they strive hard to maintain a positive mental attitude and a spirit of cooperation.

So-called street parents, in contrast, often show a lack of consideration for other people and have a rather superficial sense of family and community. Though they may love their children, many of them are unable to cope with the physical and emotional demands of parenthood, and find it difficult to reconcile their needs with those of their children. These families, who are more fully invested in the code of the streets than the decent people are, may aggressively socialize their children into it in a normative way. They believe in the code and judge themselves and others according to its values.

In fact the overwhelming majority of families in the inner-city community try to approximate the decent-family model, but there are many others who clearly represent the worst fears of the decent family. Not only are their financial resources extremely limited, but what little they have may easily be misused. The lives of the street-oriented are often marked by disorganization. In the most desperate circumstances people frequently have a limited understanding of priorities and consequences, and so frustrations mount over bills, food, and, at times, drink, cigarettes, and drugs. Some tend toward self-destructive behavior; many street-oriented women are crack-addicted ("on the pipe"), alcoholic, or involved in complicated relationships with men who abuse them. In addition, the seeming intractability of their situation, caused in large part by the lack of well-paying jobs and the persistence of racial discrimination, has engendered deep-seated bitterness and anger in many of the most desperate and poorest blacks, especially young people. The need both to exercise a measure of control and to lash out at somebody is often reflected in the adults' relations with their children At the least, the frustrations of persistent poverty shorten the fuse in such people—contributing to a lack of patience with anyone, child or adult, who irritates them.

In these circumstances a woman—or a man, although men are less consistently present in children's lives—can be quite aggressive with children, yelling at and striking them for the least little infraction of the rules she has set down. Often little if any serious explanation follows the verbal and physical punishment. This response teaches children a particular lesson. They learn that to solve any kind of interpersonal problem one must quickly resort to hitting or other violent behavior. Actual peace and quiet, and also the appearance of calm, respectful children conveyed to her neighbors and friends, are often what the young mother most desires, but at times she will be very aggressive in trying to get them. Thus she may be quick to beat her children, especially if they defy her law, not because she hates them but because this is the way she knows to control them. In fact, many street-oriented women love their children dearly. Many mothers in the community subscribe to the notion that there is a "devil in the boy" that must be beaten out of him or that socially "fast girls need to be whupped." Thus much of what borders on child abuse in the view of social authorities is acceptable parental punishment in the view of these mothers.

Many street-oriented women are sporadic mothers whose children learn to fend for themselves when necessary, foraging for food and money any way they can get it. The children are sometimes employed by drug dealers or become addicted themselves. These children of the street, growing up with little supervision, are said to "come up hard." They often learn to fight at an early age, sometimes using short-tempered adults around them as role models. The street-oriented home may be fraught with anger, verbal disputes, physical aggression, and even mayhem. The children observe these goings-on, learning the lesson that might makes right. They quickly learn to hit those who cross them, and the dog-eat-dog mentality prevails. In order to survive, to protect oneself, it is necessary to marshal inner resources and be ready to deal with adversity in a hands-on way. In these circumstances physical prowess takes on great significance.

In some of the most desperate cases, a street-oriented mother may simply leave her young children alone and unattended while she goes out. The most irresponsible women can be found at local bars and crack houses, getting high and socializing with other adults. Sometimes a troubled woman will leave very young children alone for days at a time. Reports of crack addicts abandoning their children have become common in drug-infested inner-city communities. Neighbors or relatives discover the abandoned children, often hungry and distraught over the absence of their mother.

After repeated absences, a friend or relative, particularly a grandmother, will often step in to care for the young children, sometimes petitioning the authorities to send her, as guardian of the children, the mother's welfare check, if the mother gets one. By this time, however, the children may well have learned the first lesson of the streets: Survival itself, let alone respect, cannot be taken for granted; you have to fight for your place in the world.

CAMPAIGNING FOR RESPECT

These realities of inner-city life are largely absorbed on the streets. At an early age, often even before they start school, children from street-oriented homes gravitate to the streets, where they "hang"—socialize with their peers. Children from these generally permissive homes have a great deal of latitude and are allowed to "rip and run" up and down the street. They often come home from school, put their books down, and go right back out the door. On school nights eight- and nine-year-olds remain out until nine or ten o'clock (and teenagers typically come in whenever they want to). On the streets they play in groups that often become the source of their primary social bonds. Children from decent homes tend to be more carefully supervised and are thus likely to have curfews and to be taught how to stay out of trouble.

When decent and street kids come together, a kind of social shuffle occurs in which children have a chance to go either way. Tension builds as a child comes to realize that he must choose an orientation. The kind of home he comes from influences but does not determine the way he will ultimately turn out—although it is unlikely that a child from a thoroughly street-oriented family will easily absorb decent values on the streets. Youths who emerge from street-oriented families but develop a decency orientation almost always learn those values in another setting—in school, in a youth group, in church. Often it is the result of their involvement with a caring "old head" (adult role model).

In the street, through their play, children pour their individual life experiences into a common knowledge pool, affirming, confirming, and elaborating on what they have observed in the home and matching their skills against those of others. And they learn to fight. Even small children test one another, pushing and shoving, and are ready to hit other children over circumstances not to their liking. In turn, they are readily hit by other children, and the child who is toughest prevails. Thus the violent resolution of disputes, the hitting and cursing, gains social reinforcement. The child in effect is initiated into a system that is really a way of campaigning for respect.

In addition, younger children witness the disputes of older children, which are often resolved through cursing and abusive talk, if not aggression or outright violence. They see that one child succumbs to the greater physical and mental abilities of the other. They are also alert and attentive witnesses to the verbal and physical fights of adults, after which they compare notes and share their interpretations of the event. In almost every case the victor is the person who physically won the altercation, and this person often enjoys the esteem and respect of onlookers. These experiences reinforce the lessons the children have learned at home: Might makes right, and toughness is a virtue, while humility is not. In effect they learn the social meaning of fighting. When it is left virtually unchallenged, this understanding becomes an ever more important part of the child's working conception of the world. Over time the code of the streets becomes refined.

Those street-oriented adults with whom children come in contact—including mothers, fathers, brothers, sisters, boyfriends, cousins, neighbors, and friends—help them along in forming this understanding by verbalizing the messages they are getting through experience: "Watch your back." "Protect yourself." "Don't punk out." "If somebody messes with you, you got to pay them back." "If someone disses you, you got to straighten them out." Many parents actually impose sanctions if a child is not sufficiently aggressive. For example, if a child loses a fight and comes home upset, the parent might respond, "Don't you come in here crying that somebody beat you up; you better get back out there and whup his ass. I didn't raise no punks! Get back out there and whup his ass. If you don't whup his ass, I'll whup your ass when you come home." Thus the child obtains reinforcement for being tough and showing nerve.

While fighting, some children cry as though they are doing something they are ambivalent about. The fight may be against their wishes, yet they may feel constrained to fight or face the consequences—not just from peers but also from caretakers or parents, who may administer another beating if they back down. Some adults recall receiving such lessons from their own parents and justify repeating them to their children as a way to toughen them up: Looking capable of taking care of oneself as a form of self-defense is a dominant theme among both street-oriented and decent adults who worry about the safety of their children. There is thus at times a convergence in their child-rearing practices; although the rationales behind them may differ.

SELF-IMAGE BASED ON "JUICE"

By the time they are teenagers, most youths have either internalized the code of the streets or at least learned the need to comport themselves in accordance with its rules, which chiefly have to do with interpersonal communication. The code revolves around the presentation of self. Its basic requirement is the display of a certain predisposition to violence. Accordingly, one's bearing must send the unmistakable if sometimes subtle message to "the next person" in public that one is capable of violence and mayhem when the situation requires it, that one can take care of oneself. The nature of this communication is largely determined by the demands of the circumstances but can include facial expressions, gait, and verbal expressions—all of which are geared mainly to deterring aggression. Physical appearance, including clothes, jewelry, and grooming, also plays an important part in how a person is viewed; to be respected, it is important to have the right look.

Even so, there are no guarantees against challenges, because there are always people around looking for a fight to increase their share of respect—or "juice," as it is sometimes called on the street. Moreover, if a person is assaulted, it is important, not only in the eyes of his opponent but also in the eyes of his "running buddies," for him to avenge himself. Otherwise he risks being "tried" (challenged) or "moved on" by any number of others. To maintain his honor he must show he is not someone to be "messed with" or "dissed." In general, the person must "keep himself straight" by managing his position of respect among others; this involves in part his self-image, which is shaped by what he thinks others are thinking of him in relation to his peers.

Objects play an important and complicated role in establishing self-image. Jackets, sneakers, gold jewelry, reflect not just a person's taste, which tends to be tightly regulated among adolescents of all social classes, but also a willingness to possess things that may require defending. A boy wearing a fashionable, expensive jacket, for example, is vulnerable to attack by another who covets the jacket and either cannot afford to buy one or wants the added satisfaction of depriving someone else of his. However, if the boy forgoes the desirable jacket and wears one that isn't "hip," he runs the risk of being teased and possibly even assaulted as an unworthy person. To be allowed to hang with certain prestigious crowds, a boy must wear a different set of expensive clothes—sneakers and athletic suit—every day. Not to be able to do so might make him appear socially deficient. The youth comes to covet such items—especially when he sees easy prey wearing them.

In acquiring valued things, therefore, a person shores up his identity—but since it is an identity based on having things, it is highly precarious. This very precariousness gives a heightened sense of urgency to staying even with peers, with whom the person is actually competing. Young men and women who are able to command respect through their presentation of self—by allowing their possessions and their body language to speak for them—may not have to campaign for regard but may, rather, gain it by the force of their manner. Those who are unable to command respect in this way must actively campaign for it—and are thus particularly alive to slights.

One way of campaigning for status is by taking the possessions of others. In this context, seemingly ordinary objects can become trophies imbued with symbolic value that far exceeds their monetary worth. Possession of the trophy can symbolize the ability to violate somebody—to "get in his face," to take something of value from him, to "dis" him, and thus to enhance one's own worth by stealing someone else's. The trophy does not have to be something material. It can be another person's sense of honor, snatched away with a derogatory remark. It can be the outcome of a fight. It can be the imposition of a certain standard, such as a girl's getting herself recognized as the most beautiful. Material things, however, fit easily into the pattern. Sneakers, a pistol, even somebody else's girlfriend, can become a trophy. When a person can take something from another and then flaunt it, he gains a certain regard by being the owner, or the controller, of that thing. But this display of ownership can then provoke other people to challenge him. This game of who controls what is thus constantly being played out on inner-city streets, and the trophy—extrinsic or intrinsic, tangible or intangible—identifies the current winner.

An important aspect of this often violent give-and-take is its zero-sum quality. That is, the extent to which one person can raise himself up depends on his ability to put another person down. This underscores the alienation that permeates the inner-city ghetto community. There is a generalized sense that very little respect is to be had, and therefore everyone competes to get what affirmation he can of the little that is available. The craving for respect that results gives people thin skins. Shows of deference by others can be highly soothing, contributing to a sense of security, comfort, self-confidence, and self-respect. Transgressions by others which go unanswered diminish these feelings and are believed to encourage further transgressions. Hence one must be ever vigilant against the transgressions of others or even *appearing* as if transgressions will be tolerated. Among young people, whose sense of self-esteem is particularly vulnerable, there is an especially heightened concern with being disrespected. Many inner-city young men in particular crave respect to such a degree that they will risk their lives to attain and maintain it.

The issue of respect is thus closely tied to whether a person has an inclination to be violent, even as a victim. In the wider society people may not feel required to retaliate physically after an attack, even though they are aware that they have been degraded or taken advantage of. They may feel a great need to defend themselves *during* an attack, or to behave in such a way as to deter aggression (middle-class people certainly can and do become victims of street-oriented youths), but they are much more likely than street-oriented people to feel that they can walk away from a possible altercation with their self-esteem intact. Some people may even have the strength

of character to flee, without any thought that their self-respect or esteem will be diminished.

In impoverished inner-city black communities, however, particularly among young males and perhaps increasingly among females, such flight would be extremely difficult. To run away would likely leave one's self-esteem in tatters. Hence people often feel constrained not only to stand up and at least attempt to resist during an assault but also to "pay back"—to seek revenge—after a successful assault on their person. This may include going to get a weapon or even getting relatives involved. Their very identity and self-respect, their honor, is often intricately tied up with the way they perform on the streets during and after such encounters. This outlook reflects the circumscribed opportunities of the inner-city poor. Generally people outside the ghetto have other ways of gaining status and regard, and thus do not feel so dependent on such physical displays.

BY TRIAL OF MANHOOD

On the street, among males these concerns about things and identity have come to be expressed in the concept of "manhood." Manhood in the inner city means taking the prerogatives of men with respect to strangers, other men, and women—being distinguished as a man. It implies physicality and a certain ruthlessness. Regard and respect are associated with this concept in large part because of its practical application: If others have little or no regard for a person's manhood, his very life and those of his loved ones could be in jeopardy. But there is a chicken-and-egg aspect to this situation: One's physical safety is more likely to be jeopardized in public *because* manhood is associated with respect. In other words, an existential link has been created between the idea of manhood and one's self-esteem, so that it has become hard to say which is primary. For many inner-city youths, manhood and respect are flip sides of the same coin; physical and psychological well-being are inseparable, and both require a sense of control, of being in charge.

The operating assumption is that a man, especially a real man, knows what other men know—the code of the streets. And if one is not a real man, one is somehow diminished as a person, and there are certain valued things one simply does not deserve. There is thus believed to be a certain justice to the code, since it is considered that everyone has the opportunity to know it. Implicit in this is that everybody is held responsible for being familiar with the code. If the victim of a mugging, for example, does not know the code and so responds "wrong," the perpetrator may feel justified even in killing him and may feel no remorse. He may think, "Too bad, but it's his fault. He should have known better."

So when a person ventures outside, he must adopt the code—a kind of shield, really—to prevent others from "messing with" him. In these circumstances it is easy for people to think they are being tried or tested by others even when this is not the case. For it is sensed that something extremely valuable is at stake in every interaction, and people are encouraged to rise to the occasion, particularly with strangers. For people who are unfamiliar with the code—generally people who live outside the inner city—the concern with respect in the most ordinary interactions can be frightening and incomprehensible. But for those who are invested in the code, the clear object of their demeanor is to discourage strangers from even thinking about testing their manhood. And the sense of power that attends the ability to deter others can be alluring even to those who know the code without being heavily invested in it—the decent inner-city youths. Thus a boy who has been leading a basically decent life can, in trying circumstances, suddenly resort to deadly force.

Central to the issue of manhood is the widespread belief that one of the most effective ways of gaining respect is to manifest "nerve." Nerve is shown when one takes another person's possessions (the more valuable the better), "messes with" someone's woman, throws the first punch, "gets in someone's face," or pulls a trigger. Its proper display helps on the spot to check others who would violate one's person and also helps to build a reputation that works to prevent future challenges. But since such a show of nerve is a forceful expression of disrespect toward the person on the receiving end, the victim may be greatly offended and seek to retaliate with equal or greater force. A display of nerve, therefore, can easily provoke a life-threatening response, and the background knowledge of that possibility has often been incorporated into the concept of nerve.

True nerve exposes a lack of fear of dying. Many feel that it is acceptable to risk dying over the principle of respect. In fact, among the hardcore street-oriented, the clear risk of violent death may be preferable to being "dissed" by another. The youths who have internalized this attitude and convincingly display it in their public bearing are among the most threatening people of all, for it is commonly assumed that they fear no man. As the people of the community say, "They are the baddest dudes on the street." They often lead an existential life that may acquire meaning only when they are faced with the possibility of imminent death. Not to be afraid to die is by implication to have few compunctions about taking another's life. Not to be afraid to die is the quid pro quo of being able to take somebody else's life—for the right reasons, if the situation demands it. When others believe this is one's position, it gives one a real sense of power on the streets. Such credibility is what many inner-city youths strive to achieve, whether they are decent or street-oriented, both because of its practical defensive value and because of the positive way it makes them feel about themselves. The difference between the decent and the street-oriented youth is often that the decent youth makes a conscious decision to appear tough and manly; in another setting—with teachers, say, or at his part-time job—he can be polite and deferential. The street-oriented youth, on the other hand, has made the concept of manhood a part of his very identity; he has difficulty manipulating it—it often controls him.

GIRLS AND BOYS

Increasingly, teenage girls are mimicking the boys and trying to have their own version of "manhood." Their goal is the same—to get respect, to be recognized as capable of setting or maintaining a certain standard. They try to achieve this end in the ways that have been established by the boys, including posturing, abusive language, and the use of violence to resolve disputes, but the issues for the girls are different. Although conflicts over turf and status exist among the girls, the majority of disputes seem rooted in assessments of beauty (which girl in a group is "the cutest"), competition over boyfriends, and attempts to regulate other people's knowledge of and opinions about a girl's behavior or that of someone close to her, especially her mother.

A major cause of conflicts among girls is "he say, she say." This practice begins in the early school years and continues through high school. It occurs when "people," particularly girls, talk about others, thus putting their "business in the streets." Usually one girl will say something negative about another in the group, most often behind the person's back. The remark will then get back to the person talked about. She may retaliate or her friends may feel required to "take up for" her. In essence this is a form of group gossiping in which individuals are negatively assessed and evaluated. As with much gossip, the things said may or may not be true, but the point is that such imputations can cast aspersions on a person's good name. The accused is required to defend herself against the slander, which can result in arguments and fights, often over little of real substance. Here again is the problem of low self-esteem, which encourages youngsters to be highly sensitive to slights and to be vulnerable to feeling easily "dissed." To avenge the dissing, a fight is usually necessary.

Because boys are believed to control violence, girls tend to defer to them in situations of conflict. Often if a girl is attacked or feels slighted, she will get a brother, uncle, or cousin to do her fighting for her. Increasingly, however, girls are doing their own fighting and are even asking their male relatives to teach them how to fight. Some girls form groups that attack other girls or take things from them. A hard-core segment of inner-city girls inclined toward violence seems to be developing. As one thirteen-year-old girl in a detention center for youths who have committed violent acts told me, "To get people to leave you alone, you gotta fight. Talking don't always get you out of stuff." One major difference between girls and boys: Girls rarely use guns. Their fights are therefore not life-or-death struggles. Girls are not often willing to put their lives on the line for "manhood." The ultimate form of respect on the male-dominated inner-city street is thus reserved for men.

"GOING FOR BAD"

In the most fearsome youths such a cavalier attitude toward death grows out of a very limited view of life. Many are uncertain about how long they are going to live and believe they could die violently at any time. They accept this fate; they live on the edge. Their manner conveys the message that nothing intimidates them; whatever turn the encounter takes, they maintain their attack—rather like a pit bull, whose spirit many such boys admire. The demonstration of such tenacity "shows heart" and earns their respect.

This fearlessness has implications for law enforcement. Many street-oriented boys are much more concerned about the threat of "justice" at the hands of a peer than at the hands of the police. Moreover, many feel not only that they have little to lose by going to prison but that they have something to gain. The toughening-up one experiences in prison can actually enhance one's reputation on the streets. Hence the system loses influence over the hard core who are without jobs, with little perceptible stake in the system. If mainstream society has done nothing *for* them, they counter by making sure it can do nothing *to* them.

At the same time, however, a competing view maintains that true nerve consists in backing down, walking away from a fight, and going on with one's business. One fights only in self-defense. This view emerges from the decent philosophy that life is precious, and it is an important part of the socialization process common in decent homes. It discourages violence as the primary means of resolving disputes and encourages youngsters to accept nonviolence and talk as confrontational strategies. But "if the deal goes down," self-defense is greatly encouraged. When there is enough positive support for this orientation, either in the home or among one's peers, then nonviolence has a chance to prevail. But it prevails at the cost of relinquishing a claim to being bad and tough; and therefore sets a young person up as at the very least alienated from street-oriented peers and quite possibly a target of derision or even violence.

Although the nonviolent orientation rarely overcomes the impulse to strike back in an encounter, it does introduce a certain confusion and so can prompt a measure of soul-searching, or even profound ambivalence. Did the person back down with his respect intact or did he back down only to be judged a "punk"—a person lacking manhood? Should he or she have acted? Should he or she have hit the other person in the mouth? These questions beset many young men and women during public confrontations. What is the "right" thing to do? In the quest for honor, respect, and local status—which few young people are uninterested in—common sense most often prevails, which leads many to opt for the tough approach, enacting their own particular versions of the display of nerve. The presentation of oneself as rough and tough is very often quite acceptable until one is tested. And then that presentation may help the person pass the test, because it will cause fewer questions to be asked about what he did and why. It is hard for a person to explain why he lost the fight or why he backed down. Hence many will strive to appear to "go for bad," while hoping they will never be tested. But

when they are tested, the outcome of the situation may quickly be out of their hands, as they become wrapped up in the circumstances of the moment.

AN OPPOSITIONAL CULTURE

The attitudes of the wider society are deeply implicated in the code of the streets. Most people in inner-city communities are not totally invested in the code, but the significant minority of hard-core street youths who are have to maintain the code in order to establish reputations, because they have—or feel they have—few other ways to assert themselves. For these young people the standards of the street code are the only game in town. The extent to which some children—particularly those who through upbringing have become most alienated and those lacking in strong and conventional social support—experience, feel, and internalize racist rejection and contempt from mainstream society may strongly encourage them to express contempt for the more conventional society in turn. In dealing with this contempt and rejection, some youngsters will consciously invest themselves and their considerable mental resources in what amounts to an oppositional culture to preserve themselves and their self-respect. Once they do, any respect they might be able to garner in the wider system pales in comparison with the respect available in the local system; thus they often lose interest in even attempting to negotiate the mainstream system.

At the same time, many less alienated young blacks have assumed a street-oriented demeanor as a way of expressing their blackness while really embracing a much more moderate way of life; they, too, want a nonviolent setting in which to live and raise a family. These decent people are trying hard to be part of the mainstream culture, but the racism, real and perceived, that they encounter helps to legitimate the oppositional culture. And so on occasion they adopt street behavior. In fact, depending on the demands of the situation, many people in the community slip back and forth between decent and street behavior; a vicious cycle has thus been formed. The hopelessness and alienation many young inner-city black men and women feel, largely as a result of endemic joblessness and persistent racism, fuels the violence they engage in. This violence serves to confirm the negative feelings many whites and some middle-class blacks harbor toward the ghetto poor, further legitimating the oppositional culture and the code of the streets in the eyes of many poor young blacks. Unless this cycle is broken, attitudes on both sides will become increasingly entrenched, and the violence, which claims victims black and white, poor and affluent, will only escalate.

CRITICAL THINKING QUESTIONS

1. Describe the major elements of what Anderson calls "the code of the streets." How does this code oppose mainstream values?
2. How is the code of the streets a product of the disadvantages, social isolation, and racism faced by many inner-city people?
3. Why do most inner-city people—even those who are poor—reject the street code?

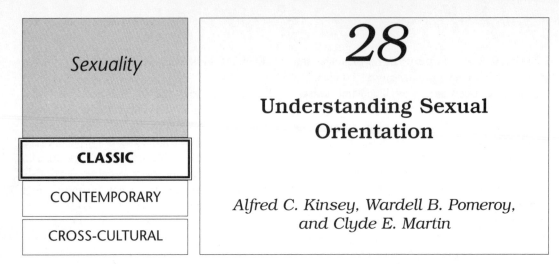

28

Understanding Sexual Orientation

Sexuality

CLASSIC

CONTEMPORARY

CROSS-CULTURAL

Alfred C. Kinsey, Wardell B. Pomeroy, and Clyde E. Martin

In 1948, Alfred Kinsey and his colleagues published the first modern study of sexuality in the United States—and they raised plenty of eyebrows. For the first time, people began talking openly about sex, questioning many common stereotypes. Here Kinsey reports his finding that sexual orientation is not a matter of clear-cut differences between heterosexuals and homosexuals, but is better described as a continuum by which most people combine elements of both.

THE HETEROSEXUAL-HOMOSEXUAL BALANCE

Concerning patterns of sexual behavior, a great deal of the thinking done by scientists and laymen alike stems from the assumption that there are persons who are "heterosexual" and persons who are "homosexual," that these two types represent antitheses in the sexual world, and that there is only an insignificant class of "bisexuals" who occupy an intermediate position between the other groups. It is implied that every individual is innately—inherently—either heterosexual

or homosexual. It is further implied that from the time of birth one is fated to be one thing or the other, and that there is little chance for one to change his pattern in the course of a lifetime.

It is quite generally believed that one's preference for a sexual partner of one or the other sex is correlated with various physical and mental qualities, and with the total personality which makes a homosexual male or female physically, psychically, and perhaps spiritually distinct from a heterosexual individual. It is generally thought that these qualities make a homosexual person obvious and recognizable to anyone who has a sufficient understanding of such matters. Even psychiatrists discuss "the homosexual personality" and many of them believe that

Source: From *Sexual Behavior in the Human Male* by Alfred C. Kinsey, Wardell B. Pomeroy, and Clyde E. Martin. Philadelphia: W. B. Saunders Company, 1948, pp. 636–39.

Figure 28.1 Heterosexual-homosexual rating scale

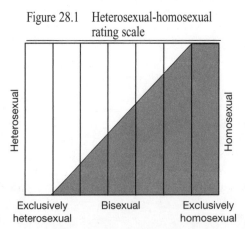

Heterosexual

Homosexual

Exclusively heterosexual

Bisexual

Exclusively homosexual

preferences for sexual partners of a particular sex are merely secondary manifestations of something that lies much deeper in the totality of that intangible which they call the personality.

It is commonly believed, for instance, that homosexual males are rarely robust physically, are uncoordinated or delicate in their movements, or perhaps graceful enough but not strong and vigorous in their physical expression. Fine skins, high-pitched voices, obvious hand movements, a feminine carriage of the hips, and peculiarities of walking gaits are supposed accompaniments of a preference for a male as a sexual partner. It is commonly believed that the homosexual male is artistically sensitive, emotionally unbalanced, temperamental to the point of being unpredictable, difficult to get along with, and undependable in meeting specific obligations. In physical characters there have been attempts to show that the homosexual male has a considerable crop of hair and less often becomes bald, has teeth which are more like those of the female, a broader pelvis, larger genitalia, and a tendency toward being fat, and that he lacks a linea alba. The homosexual male is supposed to be less interested in athletics, more often interested in music and the arts, more often engaged in such occupations as bookkeeping, dress design, window display, hairdressing, acting, radio work, nursing, religious service, and social work. The converse to all of these is supposed to represent the typical heterosexual male. Many a clinician attaches considerable weight to these things in diagnosing the basic heterosexuality or homosexuality of his patients. The characterizations are so distinct that they seem to leave little room for doubt that homosexual and heterosexual represent two very distinct types of males....

It should be pointed out that scientific judgments on this point have been based on little more than the same sorts of impressions which the general public has had concerning homosexual persons. But before any sufficient study can be made of such possible correlations between patterns of sexual behavior and other qualities in the individual, it is necessary to understand the incidences and frequencies of the homosexual in the population as a whole, and the relation of the homosexual activity to the rest of the sexual pattern in each individual's history.

The histories which have been available in the present study make it apparent that the heterosexuality or homosexuality of many individuals is not an all-or-none proposition. It is true that there are persons in the population whose histories are exclusively heterosexual, both in regard to their overt experience and in regard to their psychic reactions. And there are individuals in the population whose histories are exclusively homosexual, both in experience and in psychic reactions. But the record also shows that there is a considerable portion of the population whose members have combined, within their individual histories, both homosexual and heterosexual experience and/or psychic responses. There are some whose heterosexual experiences predominate, there are some whose homosexual experiences predominate, there are some who have had quite equal amounts of both types of experience [see Figure 28.1].

Some of the males who are involved in one type of relation at one period in their lives may have only the other type of relation at some later period. There may be considerable fluctuation of patterns from time to time. Some males may be involved in both heterosexual and homosexual activities within the same period of time. For instance, there are some who engage in both heterosexual and homosexual activities in the same year, or in the same month or week, or even in the same day. There are not a few individuals who engage in group activities in which they may make simultaneous contact with partners of both sexes.

Males do not represent two discrete populations, heterosexual and homosexual. The world is not to be divided into sheep and goats. Not all things are black nor all things white. It is a fundamental of taxonomy that nature rarely deals with discrete categories. Only the human mind invents categories and tries to force facts into separated pigeon-holes. The living world is a continuum in each and every one of its aspects. The sooner we learn this concerning human sexual behavior the sooner we shall reach a sound understanding of the realities of sex.

CRITICAL THINKING QUESTIONS

1. Why do you think people have long thought of heterosexuality and homosexuality as opposite and mutually exclusive (that is, only in terms of "exclusively heterosexual" or "exclusively homosexual" in the Figure 28.1 on page 180)?
2. Kinsey suggests that anyone's sexual orientation may well change over time. Do you agree? Why or why not?
3. Why do people tend to label someone with any degree of homosexual experience as a "homosexual"? (After all, we don't do the same in the case of any heterosexual experience.)

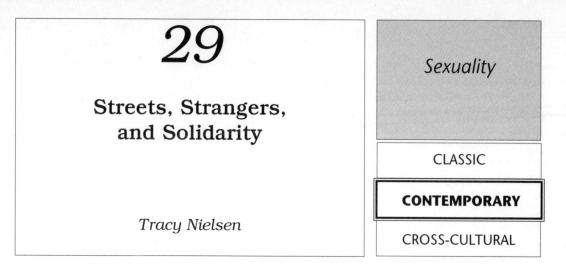

29

Streets, Strangers, and Solidarity

Tracy Nielsen

Sexuality

CLASSIC

CONTEMPORARY

CROSS-CULTURAL

Nielsen offers many important and engaging insights into the social experiences found in the lesbian subculture. By investigating lesbian interaction in public places, Nielsen reveals how lesbians build nonintimate solidarity through highly sensitive and accurate gaydar.

In New York City, my girlfriend and I were walking, holding hands, down a busy East Village sidewalk. We passed a couple of lesbians. All four of us exchanged quick (knowing) glances and subtle nods. The more femme looking one held my gaze for a prolonged moment and smiled. I remarked, jokingly, to my partner that she must have liked me. A few seconds after we passed each other, we all turned our heads to look back at each other. Being caught in the act of obvious recognition was both exhilarating and a bit embarrassing. My partner called out, "Hey, she's mine." We all laughed and then kept on our way. This passing exchange, so seemingly inconsequential that most people on the street did not notice it, created a surge of validation for four lesbians on a New York City sidewalk. In a world surrounded by heterosexual norms, complete strangers shared a moment of "queer pride."

(Fieldnotes)

Source: Reprinted by permission of the author, 2002.

As unexceptional as this incident may appear, the interactions within it are sociologically significant. The essential role of strangers in building social solidarity in cities has been greatly underestimated. Urban public places have traditionally been viewed as populated by anti-social types who care little about the fellow human beings with whom they share space.

Such an anti-urban attitude is based on a profound misunderstanding of the way urbanites operate. Studious observation of interaction between strangers reveals that, far from being interactional wastelands, public places are sites of rich and dynamic social life (Lofland, 1990). It is difficult to grasp the meaning of fleeting engagements between strangers, such as the one described above, not only because they are short lived, but also because they are so routine that they are often engaged in unconsciously. Marginalized people are necessarily more conscious of their actions than members of dominant groups. I have drawn on this heightened consciousness to illustrate the ways lesbians build nonintimate solidarity, thereby stressing the significance of stranger interaction in the urban public realm.

As an insider in the lesbian subculture, I was able to use a unique empirical method to study the interactional patterns of this group. I actively engaged in participant observation of lesbians in public places in a number of North American cities. After detecting other lesbians on the streets and sharing acknowledgment rituals with them, I stopped them to talk about what had occurred between us and asked them to take part in a survey that I had designed to encourage lesbians to think about their public realm experiences. The empirical materials for this article came from my fieldnotes on these unusual encounters, informal interviews, and completed questionnaires from 38 participants.[1]

SEXUAL IDENTITY AND URBAN SPACES

For gay people, the urban public realm is both challenging and rewarding (Gardner, 1994). In heterosexually dominated urban spaces, gay people often experience the magnified vulnerability and sense of isolation that accompany a stigmatized identity. However, like members of other minorities, when gay people connect, they are more likely to experience moments of heightened civility than people whose identities are in sync with the dominant reality.

Lesbians often possess an enhanced awareness of the presence of other gay people in public places. Interactionally, it is possible to turn this awareness to their advantage. However, lesbians must always be vigilant about the risks that accompany being "out" in a homophobic society.[2] These risks range from breaches in civility, such as staring and harassment, to more serious attacks, such as physical assault. Interesting subcultural rituals have developed over time, as lesbians negotiate the dual processes of building solidarity by recognizing and responding to each other, while dealing with issues of trust and risk. Strategies used by lesbians revolve around the interrelated concepts of *recognition, acknowledgment,* and *encounters.* Signals of recognition (gaydar) and acknowledgment (lesbian interaction rituals) that pass between lesbians often lead to prolonged and more spontaneous engagement (encounters). These interactional episodes, often strategically subtle, have profound effects on the lesbian subculture.

READING STRANGERS' IDENTITIES

The public realm is the world of strangers. City life would not be possible if strangers did not categorize each other so as to define situations and to know how to act toward each other. Habitually drawing on stereotypes or typifications to categorize strangers is a ubiquitous urban phenomenon.[3] Because much of this "ordering of the urban populace" (Lofland, 1973) is automatic and relatively unproblematic, many people are unaware of the influence that these everyday categorization processes have on subsequent social actions and interactions.

Lesbians, however, can take little for granted with respect to their sexual identities. Because a lesbian identity is largely indiscernible, most strangers will assume the "default sexuality" (heterosexuality) unless a lesbian identity is clearly presented to the public world. Although most urbanites tend to have a sophisticated grasp of the diverse identities of the strangers they encounter, based, for example, on age, race, class, and occupation, many are unaware of the signals and cues that represent a lesbian identity.

It would be a mistake to assume that public realm invisibility is an objective for lesbians. The ability to "pass" as straight can be desirable for lesbians who are not out or who feel vulnerable about their sexual orientation. However, it is also common for lesbians to claim that they are troubled by the omnipresent assumption of heterosexuality and therefore to challenge it by designing their presentation of self (Goffman, 1959) towards lesbian visibility. As indicated by this Vancouver lesbian's struggle to explain her presentation of self, impression management is never simple.

> I always prefer that people identify me as lesbian—to experience interaction in any other way makes me feel that I am being "accepted" based on an incorrect assumption of heterosexuality. For years I presented myself as a stereotypical dyke, accentuating every possible visual and spatial cue to ensure that I would be recognized by all members of the public. Interestingly, though, I now identify as a more femme lesbian and it rarely occurs to me that I may appear straight. Although I wear make up and have grown my hair to a considerable length, I generally take up a great deal of energy or space in many public settings. I have an open stance, very strong (I hesitate to say masculine) gait and sit most frequently with my legs apart. I also perceive my shoes to be a give-away. I always wear "comfortable" (read: masculine or male-identified) shoes.

The desire to be visible to other lesbians has resulted in an elaborate impression management system in the lesbian subculture. The signalling and receiving behaviour that takes place between gay people in the public realm has been playfully named "gaydar" by the gay/lesbian subculture. Many heterosexuals express disbelief when gay people say they can, in the words of one survey participant, "*spot the queers a mile away*."[4] Those who do think they can detect lesbians often rely on superficial stereotypes. However, lesbians are aware that reading a lesbian identity requires a more finely tuned grasp of coding signals than the presence of masculine traits on a female body. Lesbians are a diverse subculture. If lesbians relied on simplistic readings to detect other lesbians, they would overlook the majority of lesbians in public places. A survey participant discusses the complexity of the New York City subculture.

> In New York, there are so many types of lesbians that gaydar is quite complicated. There are the women who wear baggy pants and oversized shirts. Then you have the ones who dress alternatively and have many piercings and tattoos. Then I also see the business/professional types. Then you have the athletic types.... Come to think of it, lesbians are just as diverse as heterosexuals.

Although gaydar is unique to the gay subculture, this concept illustrates the tentative and contingent nature of stranger interaction in general. In attempting to make sense of situations, urbanites continually test their conceptions of strangers.[5] Through expressions given and given off (Goffman, 1959), lesbians signify their identities to an audience (i.e., lesbian strangers). The presence of "surface signs" may make a lesbian take a second look at a stranger for more "subtle signs" to confirm a gaydar reading. Surface signs are those more obvious cues signifying a lesbian identity that even some outsiders can discern (e.g., very short hair, a butch appearance or public displays of affection between women). Subtle signs include those cues whose meanings are clear mainly to insiders (e.g., strong stance, lesbian insignia, or prolonged eye contact).

Strangers assess each other's roles and identities using cues based on appearance (e.g., clothing, hairstyles, and jewellery), behaviour (e.g., actions, facial expressions, and body language) and space (e.g., where they are located in the city).[6] A lesbian from New York City made the following humorous observation about appearential cues.

> Sometimes I need a set of cues for my gaydar to go off. Short hair, of course, makes me think twice, especially if it is spiky, slicked back, anything butch. In NYC it can get tricky because straight women have co-opted many dyke looks. If a woman has long hair but has piercings in places other than her ears or tattoos I might think she's a dyke. The other things that make me think "hmmm" are clunky black shoes or boots, those damn rainbows, shirts that say "dyke" are pretty easy, baggy jeans hanging off someone's hips, thick black leather belts, torn clothing that looks like it was found under a rock and anything that is considered, by the outside world, as belonging to men.

Although strangers often gain first impressions from appearance cues, appearances can be deceiving. Thus, deeper cues must often be used. A Winnipeg lesbian stressed the importance of assessing behavioural cues.

> I think there is more than just clothes and hair—it is a combination that includes body language. A

straight woman can wear masculine attire but I have my doubts that she is gay because the *cues are broader*. For example, I have a co-worker who I am sure is a lesbian (it turns out she has a female "roommate" and they seem more involved than sharing house bills). This woman will wear stereotypical feminine clothing but her "sporty" gait makes me think she'd be more comfortable in a ball field. She seems a bit more masculine in voice, manner and body movement. To me this is a common giveaway. Straight women rarely express their body language in that way (and when they do I usually think they are bisexual or closeted).

Like all urbanites, lesbians also assess spatial cues in making lesbian identity placements. As gay/lesbian spaces become more popular as hangouts, these cues can be misleading. As a New Yorker points out:

I am more likely to assume that someone is queer if she is in a lesbian space (i.e., bar, bookstore, pride march) but in the East Village of Manhattan, I do recognize that there are many queer-friendly exceptions even within those spaces.

With the exception of very clear cues such public displays of affection (PDAs) between women, most signals of a lesbian identity are ambiguous. Perhaps for this reason, many lesbians find themselves looking beyond appearential, behavioural, and spatial cues for an attitudinal variable. A lesbian from Toronto put it this way:

I believe there are a thousand hidden cues that we give to one another that we then interpret as a feeling. But there is a feeling I get when I discover another lesbian. I am having a hard time narrowing it down.... It's a look, a feeling, a vibe that they send you that says, I see you, I recognize you. Now I don't believe in ESP so I think it must be a form of nonverbal communication, but it's hard to put my finger on exactly what it is.

All urbanites interpret signals from strangers that are so subtle that describing them is very difficult. These cues are often picked up subconsciously. Because lesbians are motivated to recognize other lesbians, they find it easier to verbalize the nature of these intangible cues. Lesbians often say that their radar picks up a "dyke energy" or "lesbian vibe." A Winnipeg lesbian expressed it

this way: "I identify women as lesbian (I admit it) based on hair, clothes, and mannerisms but also their 'essence.' Lesbians have an indescribable trait that just screams 'I'm a lesbian!'"

A critical reader might ask why lesbians are so concerned about recognizing other lesbians in public places. Although it might be tempting to dismiss gaydar as a frivolous notion, the emotional responses elicited by sighting other lesbians captures the significance of gaydar for the lesbian community. Consider these comments from survey respondents from Minneapolis, Toronto, and New York, respectively.

I feel affirmed, energized and empowered and proud of myself and the lesbians I encounter. It makes me feel that I'm not alone in the world and that I am okay.

I look for lesbians everywhere. Especially at straight functions. It's kind of a game and it makes the experience less lonely. I get thrilled to see lesbians and will work to connect with them in some manner. There is definitely a feeling I get when I discover another lesbian. It's so damn exciting!

Seeing a queer person in a crowd of strangers is like seeing a friend, even if we don't connect, I feel comforted and less alone.

If lesbians engage their "dyke spotting" abilities and invest these sightings with a heightened importance, can we conclude that the process of gaydar ends with recognition and the fleeting "warm and fuzzy" feelings that accompany spotting a "friend" in a crowd of hostile strangers?

ACKNOWLEDGING STRANGERS

The assessment of strangers' identities is, in fact, simply one step in a dynamic interactional process. Symbolic interactionists suggest that all social action stems from these initial categorizations. However, a strong urban norm dictates that strangers appear to pay little heed to each other. Goffman's (1963) concept of "civil inattention" describes the urban interaction ritual in which trust and mutual respect are routinely secured in instances of co-presence between strangers. In a quick scanning of a stranger's eyes, we assess the other's identity and in an equally quick "dimming of the lights" (looking away) we convey respect for the sacredness of the other's self.

Using gaydar can lead to situations of heightened civility where gay strangers momentarily eschew the norms of civil inattention that structure the urban world as they become more attentive to each other based on shared marginalized sexual identity. This "reciprocal responsiveness" (Couch, 1989) takes varied forms. The smallest exchanges between lesbian strangers involve ritualistic mutual acknowledgement. I refer to these actions as "acknowledgement rituals" to capture their habitual nature.

Returning to the scenario described at the beginning of the article, we find that once the four lesbians had read each other's identities, a number of actions followed. These rituals would not likely have been shared among heterosexual strangers. Six lesbian interaction rituals took place on the New York City sidewalk: prolonged eye contact, nodding, smiling, subtle checking out, brief words, and low-level flirting. These rituals have developed historically in lesbian subcultures as ways to show that recognition has occurred and to take that recognition further by displaying solidarity. A Winnipeg lesbian described a number of these rituals.

It is all in the eyes! Initially eye contact and then a subtle smile. If possible, then a longer look to figure out why I think she is or isn't. If I am with another queer person, then we play the "Is She or Isn't She?" game. If it is at all appropriate in the setting, I will engage in low-level flirting. Some lesbians of course carefully avoid any acknowledgment but those who have at least some comfort with who they are make eye contact, smile knowingly, nod hello.

Rituals of acknowledgement in public places are not unique to lesbians. Strangers often find occasion to nod or smile at each other and even to exchange brief greetings. It is the motivation behind the increased interactional civility between lesbians that is unique. In a world where lesbian identity can be problematic, strangers send signals of identity validation to each other

through mutual acknowledgment in the form of small gestures filled with amplified meaning. Certain characteristics of these rituals make them specific to the subculture as in the "Is She or Isn't She?" game described above. The persistent use of folk terms such as "the knowing smile," "the butch nod," or "the subtle check out" to describe the ways lesbians respond to each other suggests their ubiquity in the lesbian subculture.

The interactions described in the opening scenario could not have taken place without the most basic of rituals: eye contact. Mutual eye contact is "perhaps the most direct and purest reciprocity which exists anywhere" (Simmel, 1970: 301). In the simplest gestures the most profound messages are sent. It is for this reason that the eye is said to be the window to the soul.

Civil inattention is often altered when lesbians are co-present. Lesbians repeatedly state that they can detect another lesbian by the intensity of the eye contact she makes. Despite the apparent simplicity and brevity of this ritual, its message is profound and its effects in guiding social action enormous. Folk terms for this slightly longer eye contact include "the knowing look," "the prolonged glance," or "the lingering gaze." In a very short time, lasting only a second or two, lesbians convey in "the look" that a secret knowledge is shared. As a Toronto resident put it, "If you catch a woman looking at you (twice or in a cautious but lingering way—apart from the 'through you' stares of public transit) then it is a signal that you are being checked out and read as queer or whatever."

Due to its secretive nature, lesbians often describe intense or prolonged eye contact as exciting. A Winnipeg lesbian observes, "Making eye contact with dykes conjures up feeling of pleasure, delight, a sense of power that we know something about each other that maybe other people on the street don't recognize—or if they recognize it they are not part of it."

Eye contact is both a behavioural cue of recognition and an action of acknowledgment. One way that lesbians determine the accuracy of a gaydar reading is by assessing the quality and length of eye contact they receive from a stranger. In the scenario below, described by a Toronto lesbian, eye contact is the only cue available. It is such a powerful cue, however, that it is enough to solidify a gaydar reading.

My first experience recognizing a lesbian came about when I was 16 years old. A new teacher had come to our school. She dressed femmy, had a good figure and long blond hair. I was in the empty hall going through my locker when she came out of her classroom. It was just she and me in the hallway. I looked up at her and our eyes locked. And I knew, and I knew that she knew. I was almost knocked over with the surprise of it all. I started to laugh and she started to laugh and we just stood there in the hallway smiling and laughing and seeing each other. The bell rang and the hallway filled with students. So what was it? It wasn't her look or anything she wore. It wasn't situational, the high-school hallway. It was the way she looked at me. Like she knew who I was. Like we shared something. It was also wild to know this thing that I was sure no one else in the school knew. That she was willing to let herself be recognized by recognizing me. That was my first real experience with recognizing a lesbian stranger: it was strange and joyful. Later when I told my gay friends about the experience, I couldn't really explain how I knew, but I was and still am 100% certain. I knew because she told me [in the way she looked at me].

Few lesbians, I suspect, would read this story without emotion. This moment, described so lucidly, captures the essence of what gaydar means to many lesbians. Neither of the lesbians in the scenario was "out," in the full meaning of the term, and yet they shared a brief moment of solidarity that placed them outside the heterosexual norm.

Prolonged or intense eye contact seals an identity placement made through assessment of cues. Further rituals (e.g., smiling, nodding, or exchanging greetings) follow eye contact. If the situation is conducive, more spontaneous actions, such as low-level flirting, may take place.[7] These rituals of recognition and acknowledgement temporarily imbue public places with lesbian meaning. Hence, they can ease the difficulties that lesbians experience in negotiating a heterosexist society. Are engagements between lesbian strangers always so subtle and ritualistic?

ENCOUNTERS

Anti-urbanites view the idea of stranger interaction as an oxymoron (Lofland, 1990). The following quote sums up an attitude toward the public realm that continues to influence both the sociological imagination (Mills, 1959) and common-sense beliefs about urbanite interaction:

On the street, in the subway, on the bus [the city dweller] comes in contact with hundreds of people. But these brief incidental associations are based neither on sharing of common values nor on a co-operation for a common purpose. They are formal in the most complete sense of the term in that they are empty of content. (Spykman, 1926: 58)

Is this pessimistic conjecture a reality? Not so, according to urban ethnographers.[8] On the contrary, a moral order underlies the apparent chaos and impersonality of city streets. This "interaction order" (Goffman, 1983) is sustained differently from the morality found in primary groups. Strangers on city streets do not display the kinds of close interaction found in smaller settings; that would be impossible. Yet civil intentions can be detected between strangers, affirming the existence of a collective urban civility.

Being openly gay in public places carries a degree of risk. Despite this fact, or perhaps because of it, gay people may find more opportunities than heterosexuals to engage in encounters. Heightened civility between lesbian strangers, then, moves beyond politeness and a collective effort to sustain an orderly society. Such actions also send messages of solidarity. Once the transitory actions of mutual acknowledgement take place, openings in the norms of silence between strangers may be created where lesbians make contacts that are spontaneous and enduring in nature. These encounters range from small gestures of helping behaviour to more sustained interactions, such as making friends or romantic connections.

Lesbians often state that they are more willing to help a stranger if they perceive her to be gay. They may look for reasons to assist a woman they have tagged as lesbian in order to connect. Two lesbians, from Minneapolis and Vancouver, respectively, illustrate this point.

I always try to be extra nice to the dykes who checkout at my register (give them free stuff, talk more, flirt, etc.). There is a lot of negativity and homophobia out there, so I smile and make eye contact a lot. Sometimes I try to start conversation if it is reasonable.

I decided in my mind which of the staff at a bookstore I shopped at in Vancouver were lesbians based on which ones were more overtly friendly to me when I was buying or browsing through lesbian-themed books. When I worked in retail and lesbians (or women I assumed or suspected were lesbians) came into the store, I was much more friendly to them than to general customers.

Always aware of safety issues, lesbians are often subtle in their interactions with lesbian strangers. Although the events described below by a New Yorker do not typify normal subway riding behaviour, the incident is unexceptional. Though no words are exchanged, the meaning of the nonverbal communication is clear.

My girlfriend and I were riding the subway home, and it was fairly late. A very interesting couple sat across from us holding hands. The younger of the two was an androgynous, butchy dyke, and her girlfriend was much older and clearly femme. My girlfriend was holding my hand and we all very subtly, casually glanced at each other. They were getting off the subway at the same stop as us, and when the subway doors opened, the butchy dyke stood at the opening *holding the door* until her girlfriend, *my* girlfriend and *myself* had safely exited. The funny thing is, we would have made it through the door just fine on our own, I mean we'd definitely done it many times before…*but*, it was simply the *beauty*, and *respect* and *recognition* and *pride* of the gesture that really struck me. The subway is definitely one of the scariest places to be out, because you are surrounded by some of the scariest people in New York ya know? It was just so beautiful how this woman *without* words made such as huge statement to me and my girl, by showing concern and recognizing us.

The exchange among the four subway riders can be interpreted as a silent honouring of the boldness of being "out" in one of the cities "scariest places." In a marginalized subculture, signals of solidarity are political in nature, even when not intended as political statements. Through displays of solidarity, the subculture is strengthened and heterosexual hegemony is challenged.

Political and safety issues aside, strangers connect for the pure pleasure of engaging with fellow human beings (Lofland, 1990). Nonintimate social interaction, although qualitatively different from intimate social interaction, can be deeply satisfying. In fact, these encounters have certain advantages, not the least of which are that differences are not immediately threatening and group dynamics do not come into play. Jane Jacobs has referred to "sidewalk terms" to capture the nature of these types of social engagements. In public places, it is possible to connect with people "without unwelcome entanglements, without boredom, necessity for excuses, explanations, fears of giving offence, embarrassments respecting impositions or commitments and all such paraphernalia of obligations which accompany less limited relationships. It is possible to be on excellent sidewalk terms with people who are very different from oneself" (Jacobs, 1961: 62).

Sidewalk connections are made easily among lesbians because they share a symbolic culture that facilitates the breaking down of boundaries. A New Yorker recalls an encounter with a stranger that transformed her bus riding experience. Take notice of the way the interaction unfolded. The mutual reading of identity cues (assisted by subtle actions) was followed by acknowledgement, which led to an encounter.

I was on a city bus. It was extremely crowded with people pushing and shoving their way home. A woman sat down next to me and, although we did not initially acknowledge one another, I read her as a dyke right away. She was middle-aged, with a short haircut and style that I read as 70s feminist lesbian. I realize that I did something I often do when I see others I perceive as queer. I picked up my backpack so that the rainbow beads on the zipper were visible. Whether or not any conversation takes place, I feel a sense of connection with others when I know they've recognized a common sign. I got out my book and began reading. I noticed the woman next to me peering over at the page. Normally I'd be irritated by this, but I was interested to connect with this woman I perceived to be "family" in this straight crowd. I acknowledged her glance by looking back in a friendly way. She mentioned her surprise to see the book and said she [had known] the author long ago. We spoke about the book and about where one might buy the book and she mentioned that she hosts a poetry night at Bluestockings [a lesbian bookstore collective] once a month. We got off the bus at the same stop and went our separate ways...but, speaking with her even just briefly created a sense of connection to the community in me that stayed with me the whole day.

The fact that this episode took place in an ordinary public place is important. The creation of "free territories" in the city is a resistance tactic of marginalized people (Lyman & Scott, 1970). Lesbian territories are spaces where lesbians can interact, free from heterosexual constraints. In more restrictive times, lesbians and gays forged urban spaces in underground places such as bars (Nestle, 1997). With the advent of the gay rights movement, many lesbian spaces, such as coffee shops, bookstores, and urban neighbourhoods with large numbers of lesbians living in them, have become available (Valentine, 1995). Recently, however, the gay community, refusing to be ghettoized, has emphasized the right to be "out" in heterosexually dominated public places.

Considering the historical restriction of lesbian interaction to specified spaces, it is no surprise that interacting as lesbians in nongay public places is exciting. This strategy of being visible in public has become progressively, politically significant.

Such visibility reacts against the confined space of the "closet," which has been perhaps the most compelling metaphor for visibility and identity within gay and lesbian narratives. The closet symbolizes the space of denial, darkness, confinement. To come out depends on emerging from the spatial structures of the closet and into the public, onto the street. Therefore, the process of attaining an authentic gay identity relies on the movement from one space to another—from the closet to the street (Polchin, 1997: 386).

As lesbians struggle to express themselves freely in public places, the connection between lesbian visibility and street level solidarity continues to grow in importance. Each time lesbians engage with each other in public places, they strengthen the subculture and challenge the right of heterosexuals to dominate those spaces. These interactions infuse a lesbian reality into a society that would otherwise render lesbians invisible. The significance of gaydar and the interactions that follow, then, cannot be underestimated nor dismissed as the trivial imaginings of an elitist subculture. They are parts of the dynamic identity and community building processes that occur on city streets. As Giddens (1984) has argued, it is through the collective actions of individual social actors that structures of society are created and recreated. Indeed Goffman (1967: 91) expressed it best when he observed: "The gestures which we sometimes call empty are perhaps in fact the fullest things of all."

CRITICAL THINKING QUESTIONS

1. What is gaydar and how would a person know when they have it?
2. Nielsen suggests that lesbians often find interactions with other lesbians in a nongay public place exciting. As a budding sociologist, how would you explain such a reaction?
3. What rituals do heterosexual couples use to signal their interest in or attraction to each other? Do you believe these cues have changed over time? If so, how? If not, why not?
4. With reference to the article, discuss the quotation, "the gestures which we sometimes call empty are perhaps in fact the fullest things of all."

NOTES

1. This article is drawn from my Ph.D. dissertation. For details of the methodology, theoretical outcomes, and in-depth quotations from participants see Nielsen (2002), "Streets Strangers and Solidarity: A Study of Lesbian Interaction in the Public Realm." Unpublished dissertation. The University of Manitoba.
2. The word "out" is used by gays and lesbians to refer to being open (i.e., "out of the closet") about their sexual identity.

3. Outright condemnation of stereotyped thinking is unrealistic. Although it is tempting to relegate stereotyping to the rigid attitudes of prejudiced people, in reality all people must employ stereotypes to organize the kaleidoscopic flow of events around them. A more realistic approach is to confront the dual reality of these "enabling conventions" (Goffman, 1971) as both distorters of reality and doorways to social engagement.

4. Note that as part of the "gay pride" movement, gays and lesbians have re-appropriated pejorative labels such as queer, dyke, fag, and homo. By adopting these labels for their own use, the subculture has reduced their power to stigmatize.

5. Turner's (1990) concept of "role making" describes the way that social actors impose meanings on situations through the process of testing the inferences they make about others in social situations.

6. For a detailed analysis of the ways that strangers use these different types of cues (appearential, behavioural, and spatial) in making sense of the chaotic "world of strangers" see Lofland (1973).

7. For an explanation of why low-level flirting takes on ritualistic qualities in the lesbian subculture as both a gaydar cue and a recognition strategy, see Nielsen (2002). The dissertation outlines the details of these rituals and the situational variables that affect whether they take place (i.e., safety, spatial concerns, racial variables, and outness levels).

8. Urban ethnographers have steadily chipped away at the pervasive belief in the emptiness of urban interaction. See Lofland (1998) for an overview of these ethnographic studies.

REFERENCES

Couch, C. 1989. *Social processes and relationships*. New York: General Hall.

Giddens, A. 1984. *The constitution of society: Outline of the theory of structuration*. Cambridge: Polity Press.

Gardner, C. B. 1994. A family among strangers: Kinship claims among gay men in public places. In *The community of the streets*, eds. L. Lofland, and S. Cahill, 95–120. London: JAI Press Inc.

Goffman, E. 1959. *The presentation of self in everyday life*. New York: Anchor.

———. 1963. *Behavior in public places*. New York: Free Press of Glencoe.

———. 1967. *Interaction ritual*. New York: Pantheon Books.

———. 1971. *Relations in public*. New York: Basic Books.

———. 1983. The interaction order. *American Sociological Review*, 48: 1–17.

Jacobs, J. 1961. *The death and life of great American cities*. New York: Vintage Books.

Lofland, L. 1973. *A world of strangers: Order and action in urban public space*. New York: Basic Books.

———. 1990. Social interaction: Continuities and complexities in the study of nonintimate sociality. In *Sociological perspectives on social psychology*, eds. K. Cook, G. Fine, and J. House, 176–201. Boston: Allyn and Bacon.

———. 1998. *The public realm: Exploring the city's quintessential social territory*. New York: Basic Books.

Lyman, S., and M. Scott. 1970. Territoriality: A neglected sociological dimension. In *Social psychology through symbolic interactionism*, eds. G. Stone, and H. Faberman, 214–26. Massachusetts: Xerox College Publishing.

Mills, C. W. 1959. *The sociological imagination*. London: Oxford University Press.

Nestle, J. 1997. Restriction and reclamation: Lesbian bars and beaches in the 1950s. In *Queers in space: Communities, public places, resistance*, eds. G. Ingram, A. Bouthilette, and Y. Retter, 61–8. Seattle: Bay Press.

Nielsen, T. 2002. Streets, strangers and solidarity: A study of lesbian interaction in the public realm. Unpublished dissertation. Winnipeg: University of Manitoba.

Polchin, J. 1997. Having something to wear: The landscape of identity on Christopher Street. In *Queers in space: Communities, public places, resistance*, eds. G. Ingram, A. Bouthilette, and Y. Retter, 381–90. Seattle: Bay Press.

Simmel, G. 1970. On visual interaction. In *Social psychology through symbolic interactionism*, eds. G. Stone, and H. Farberman, 300–02. Massachusetts: Xerox College Publishing.

Spykman, N. 1926. A social philosophy of the city. In *The urban community: Selected papers from the proceedings of the American Sociological Society*, ed. E. Burgess. Chicago: University of Chicago Press.

Turner, R. 1990. Role-taking: Process versus conformity. In *Life as theatre: A dramaturgical sourcebook*, eds. D. Brissett, and C. Edgley, 85–100. New York: Aldine de Gruyter.

Valentine, G. 1995. Out and about: Geographies of lesbian landscapes. *International Journal of Urban and Regional Research*, 19: 96–112.

Sexuality	30
CLASSIC	**Homosexual Behavior in Cross-Cultural Perspective**
CONTEMPORARY	
CROSS-CULTURAL	*J. M. Carrier**

Although sexuality is a biological process, the meaning of sexuality is culturally variable. Carrier shows that attitudes toward homosexuality are far from uniform around the world. Some societies are quite accommodating about sexual practices that other societies punish harshly.

The available cross-cultural data clearly show that the ways in which individuals organize their sexual behavior vary considerably between societies (Westermarck, 1908; Ford & Beach, 1951; Broude & Greene, 1976). Although biological and psychological factors help explain variations of sexual behavior between individuals within a given society, intercultural variations in patterns of human sexual behavior are mainly related to social and cultural differences occurring between societies around the world. The purpose of this chapter is to consider what kinds of variations in homosexual behavior occur between societies, and to determine which sociocultural factors appear to account for the variance of the behavior cross-culturally.[1]

*The author is particularly indebted to Evelyn Hooker for her invaluable comments and criticism; and to the Gender Identity Research Group at UCLA for an early critique of the ideas presented in this paper.

THE CROSS-CULTURAL DATA

Data available on homosexual behavior in most of the world's societies, past or present, are meager. Much is known about the dominant middle-class white populations of the United States, England, and northern European countries where most scientific research on human sexual behavior has been done, but very little is known about homosexual behavior in the rest of the world. The lack of knowledge stems from the irrational fear and prejudice surrounding the study of human sexual behavior, and from the difficulties associated with the collection of information on a topic that is so personal and highly regulated in most societies.

Most of the cross-cultural information on sexual behavior has been gathered by Western anthropologists. The quality of the information collected and published, however, varies considerably. Based on a survey of the literature, Marshall and Suggs (1971) report that: "Sexual behavior is occasionally touched upon in anthropological publications but is seldom the topic of either articles or monographs by anthropologists." Broude and Greene (1976), after coding the sexual attitudes and practices in 186 societies using the Human Relations Area Files, note:[2]

…information of any sort on sexual habits and beliefs is hard to come by.… [W]hen data do exist concerning sexual attitudes and practices, they are often sketchy and vague; what is more, such information is usually suspect in terms of its reliability, either because of distortions on the part of the subjects or because of biases introduced by the ethnographer.…

Cross-cultural data on homosexual behavior is further complicated by the prejudice of many observers who consider the behavior unnatural, dysfunctional, or associated with mental illness, and by the fact that in many of the societies studied the behavior is stigmatized and thus not usually carried out openly. Under these circumstances, the behavior is not easily talked about. At the turn of the twentieth century such adjectives as disgusting, vile, and detestable were still being used to describe homosexual behavior; and even in the mid-1930s some anthropologists continued to view the behavior as unnatural. In discussing sodomy with some of his New Guinea informants, Williams (1936), for example, asked them if they "had ever been subjected to an unnatural practice." With the acceptance of the view in the mid-1930s that homosexual behavior should be classified as a mental illness (or at best dysfunctional), many anthropologists replaced "unnatural" with the medical model. This model still finds adherents among researchers at present, especially those in the branch of anthropology referred to as psychological anthropology.

Because of the prejudice with which many researchers and observers approached the subject, statements about the reported absence of homosexual behavior, or the limited extent of the behavior where reported, should be viewed with some skepticism. Mead (1961) suggests that statements of this kind "can only be accepted with the greatest caution and with very careful analysis of the personality and training of the investigator." She further notes that: "Denials of a practice

cannot be regarded as meaningful if that practice is verbally recognized among a given people, even though a strong taboo exists against it."

This chapter will mainly utilize the published research findings of empirical studies which have considered homosexual behavior in some detail. It will examine homosexual behavior in preliterate, peasant, and complex modern societies in all the major geographical regions of the world.[3] Where necessary, these findings will be supplemented with information found in accounts given by travelers, missionaries, and novelists.

SOCIOCULTURAL FACTORS

A number of sociocultural factors help explain variations of homosexual behavior between societies. Two of the most important are cultural attitudes and proscriptions related to cross-gender behavior, and availability of sexual partners.[4] The latter is in turn related to such variables as segregation of sexes prior to marriage, expectations with respect to virginity, age at marriage, and available economic resources and/or distribution of income.

Cross-Gender and Homosexual Behavior

Different expectations for male persons as opposed to female persons are culturally elaborated from birth onward in every known society. Although behavioral boundaries between the sexes may vary culturally, male persons are clearly differentiated from female persons; and progeny is assured by normative societal rules which correlate male and female gender roles with sexual behavior, marriage, and the family. There is a general expectation in every society that a majority of adult men and women will cohabit and produce the next generation. Social pressure is thus applied in the direction of marriage. The general rule is that one should not remain single.

The cross-cultural data on human sexual behavior suggest that a significant relationship exists between much of the homosexual behavior reported cross culturally and the continuing need of societies to deal with cross-gender behavior. Feminine male behavior, and the set of anxieties associated with its occurrence in the male part of the population, appears to have brought about more elaborate cultural responses temporally and spatially than has masculine female behavior. There are no doubt many reasons why this is so, but it appears to be related in general to the higher status accorded men than women in most societies; and, in particular, to the defense role that men have historically played in protecting women and children from outsiders.

Societies in which homosexual behavior can be linked to cultural responses to cross-gender behavior may be categorized according to the type of response made. Three major cultural types have been identified: those societies which make a basic accommodation to cross-gender behavior, those societies which outlaw the behavior as scandalous and/or criminal, and those societies which neither make an accommodation to such behavior nor outlaw it but instead have a cultural formulation which tries to ensure that cross-gender behavior does not occur.

Accommodating Societies

Societies making an accommodation to cross-gender behavior in one form or another have been reported in many different parts of the world. Munroe et al. (1969), for example, put together a list of societies having what they call "institutionalized male transvestism…the permanent adoption by males of aspects of female dress and/or behavior in accordance with customary expectations within a given society." Their list includes Indian societies in North and South America, island societies in Polynesia and Southeast Asia, and preliterate and peasant societies in mainland Asia and Africa. Although reported for both sexes, male cross-gender behavior appears in the literature more often than female.

A folk belief exists in some of these societies that in every generation a certain number of individuals will play the gender role of the opposite sex, usually beginning at or prior to puberty and often identified at a very early age. The Mohave Indians of the American Southwest, for example, used to hold the following belief—typical of many Indian societies in North America—about cross-gender behavior of both sexes:

> Ever since the world began at the magic mountain…it was said that there would be transvestites. In the beginning, if they were to become transvestites, the process started during their intrauterine life. When they grew up they were given toys according to their sex. They did not like these toys however. (Devereux, 1937)

In southern Mexico one group of Zapotec Indians believes that "effeminate males" are born not made: "Typical comments include: But what can we do; he was born that way; he is like God made him. A related belief also exists that…it is a thing of the blood" (Royce, 1973). In Tahiti, the belief exists that there is at least one cross-gender behaving male, called a *mahu* in all villages: "When one dies then another substitutes…. God arranges it like this. It isn't allowed (that there should be) two *mahu* in one place" (Levy, 1973).

Cross-gender behavior is accepted in other societies because it is believed that some supernatural event makes people that way prior to birth, or that the behavior is acquired through some mystical force or dream after birth. In India, for example, the following belief exists about the *Hijadas,* cross-gender behaving males thought to be impotent at birth who later have their genitals removed:

> When we ask a *Hijada* or an ordinary man in Gujarat "Why does a man become a *Hijada?*" the usual reply is "One does not become a *Hijada* by one's own will; it is only by the command of the *mata* that one becomes a *Hijada.*" The same idea is found in a myth about the origin of the *Hijadas.* It is said that one receives the *mata's* command either in dreams or when one sits in meditation before her image. (Shah, 1961)

Among the Chukchee of northeastern Asia, a role reversal was accepted because of an unusual dream or vision:

Transformation takes place by the command of the *ka'let* (spirits) usually at the critical age of early youth when shamanistic inspiration first manifests itself. (Bogores, 1904)

Among the Lango in Africa:

A number of Lango men dress as women, simulate menstruation, and become one of the wives of other males. They are believed to be impotent and to have been afflicted by some supernatural agency. (Ford & Beach, 1951)

Although not necessarily accepted gladly, the various folk beliefs make the behavior accept-able, and a certain number of cross-gender behaving individuals are to be expected in every generation. Expectations about the extent to which the opposite gender role is to be played, however, appear to have changed over time with acculturation. Affected individuals in the past often were required to make a public ritualized change of gender and cross-dress and behave in accordance with their new identity. Among the Mohave, for example, there was an initiation ceremony and it was important for the initiate "to duplicate the behavior pattern of his adopted sex and make 'normal' individuals of his anatomic sex feel toward him as though he truly belonged to his adopted sex" (Devereux, 1937). The *mahu* in Tahiti were described in the latter part of the eighteenth century as follows:

These men are in some respects like the Eunichs [*sic*] in India but are not castrated. They never cohabit with women but live as they do. They pick their beard out and dress as women, dance and sing with them and are as effeminate in their voice. (Morrison, 1935)

Affected individuals in most societies at pres-ent are allowed a choice as to the extent they want to play the role; e.g., how far they want to identify with the opposite sex, whether they want to cross-dress or not, etc. Levy (1973) notes, for example, that in Tahiti: "Being a *mahu* does not now usually entail actually dressing as a woman." The North American Indian societies who used to have initiation ceremonies discon-tinued them long ago; and, although expectations

about cross-gender behaving individuals persist, only remnants of the original belief system are remembered currently. They continue, however, to be tolerant and "there apparently is no body of role behavior aimed at humiliating boys who are feminine or men who prefer men sexually" (Stoller, 1976).

The link between cross-gender behavior and homosexual behavior is the belief that there should be concordance between gender role and sexual object choice. When a male behaves like a female, he should be expected therefore to want a male sexual partner and to play the female sex role—that is, to play the insertee role in anal intercourse or fellatio. The same concor-dance should be expected when a female behaves like a male. As a result of beliefs about concordance, it is important to note that a soci-ety may not conceptualize the sexual behavior or its participants as "homosexual."

There is some evidence in support of this linking of gender role and homosexual behavior in societies making an accommodation and providing a social role for cross-gender behaving individuals. Kroeber (1940), for example, concluded from his investigations that: "In most of primitive northern Asia and North America, men of homosexual trends adopted women's dress, work, and status, and were accepted as nonphysiological but institutionalized women." Devereux's Mohave informants said that the males who changed their gender role to female had male husbands and that both anal inter-course and fellatio were practiced, with the participants playing the appropriate gender sex role. The informants noted the same concor-dance for females who behaved like males.

Unfortunately, the anthropological data do not always make clear whether cultural expectations in a given society were for concordance between gender role and erotic object; or, in terms of actual behavior, how many cross-gender behav-ing individuals chose same sex, opposite sex, or both sexes as erotic objects. In the paper I just quoted, Kroeber also concluded: "How far invert erotic practices accompanied the status is not always clear from the data, and it probably varied. At any rate, the North American attitude toward the berdache stresses not his erotic life but his social status; born a male, he became accepted as a woman socially."

Many anthropologists and other observers confounded their findings by assuming an equivalence between "transvestite" and "homosexual."[5] Thus, when an informant described cross-gender behavior, they may have concluded without foundation that a same-sex erotic object choice was part of the behavior being described, and that they were eliciting information on "homosexuals." Angelino and Shedd (1955) provide supporting evidence. They reviewed the literature on an often used anthropological concept, berdache, and concluded that the "term has been used in an exceedingly ambiguous way, being used as a synonym for homosexualism, hermaphroditism, transvestism, and effeminism." They also note that the meaning of berdache changed over time; going from kept boy/male prostitute, to individuals who played a passive role in sodomy, to males who played a passive sex role and cross-dressed.

In spite of the confusion between "transvestite" and "homosexual," the available data suggest that in many of the societies providing a social role for cross-gender behavior, the selection of sexual partners was based on the adopted gender role; and, though they might be subjected to ridicule, neither partner in the sexual relationship was penalized for the role played.

The *mahu* role in Tahiti provides a contemporary look at how one Polynesian society continues to provide a social role for cross-gender behavior. According to Levy (1973), villagers in his area of study do not agree on the sexual behavior of the *mahu*—some "believe that *mahu* do not generally engage in homosexual intercourse." Information from both *mahu* and *non-mahu* informants, however, leads to the conclusion that probably a majority of the *mahus* prefer adolescent males with whom they perform "ote

moa" (literally, "penis sucking"). The following are some aspects of the role and the community response to it:

It is said to be exclusive. Its essential defining characteristic is "doing woman's work," that is, a role reversal which is *publicly demonstrated*—either through clothes or through other public aspects of women's role playing. Most villagers approve of, and are pleased by, the role reversal. But homosexual behavior is a covert part of the role, and it is disapproved by many villagers. Men who have sexual relations with the *mahu*...do not consider themselves abnormal. Villagers who know of such activities may disapprove, but they do not label the partners as unmanly. The *mahu* is considered as a substitute woman for the partner. A new word, *raerae,* which reportedly originated in Papeete, is used by some to designate nontraditional types of homosexual behavior. (Levy, 1973)

It should also be noted that in Levy's village of study *mahus* were the only adult men reported to be engaging in homosexual intercourse.

Another contemporary example of a social role for cross-gender behavior is the *Hijada* role provided cross-gender behaving males in northwestern India. Given slightly different names by different observers (*Hijaras, Hinjras,* and *Hijiras*), these males appear to be playing the same role. There is general agreement on the fact that they cross-dress, beg alms, and collect dues at special ceremonies where they dance and sing as women. There is a considerable difference of opinion, however, as to whether they engage in homosexual intercourse or in any sexual activity for that matter. From the available data, it appears that they live mostly in towns in communes, with each commune having a definite jurisdiction of villages and towns "where its members can beg alms and collect dues" (Shah, 1961). They are also reported to live separately by themselves. From the findings of Carstairs (1956) and Shah (1961), one can at least conclude that the *Hijadas* living alone are sexually active:

Carstairs is wrong in considering all the Hijadas as homosexual, but there seems to be some truth in his information about the homosexuality of the Deoli Hijada (Note: Deoli is the village of Carstairs' study.)

Faridi and Mehta also note that some Hijadas practice "sodomy." This, however, is not institutionalized homosexuality. (Shah, 1961)

The finding by Opler (1960) that "they cannot carry on sexual activities and do not marry" may apply to the majority of *Hijadas* living in communes. The question of what kind of sexual behavior the *Hijadas* practice, if any, cannot be answered definitively with the data available. That they are still a viable group in India is confirmed by a recent Associated Press release:

About 2000 eunuchs dressed in brightly colored saris and other female garb were converging on this northern town from all over India this weekend for a private convention of song, dance and prayer.

Local reaction to the gathering was mixed. "They're perverts," commented a local peanut vendor. "We should have nothing to do with them. They should be run out of town."

A New Delhi social worker...said they sometimes supplement their income as paid lovers of homosexuals. (Excerpts from AP, February 6, 1979)

Disapproving Societies

Societies in which cross-gender behavior produces strong emotional negative reactions in large segments of the population tend to have the following commonalities: (1) negative reactions produced by the behavior are essentially limited to the male part of the population and relate mainly to effeminate males; (2) cross-gender behavior is controlled by laws which prohibit cross-dressing, and by laws and public opinion which consider other attributes associated with the behavior as scandalous; (3) gender roles are sharply dichotomized; and (4) a general belief exists that anyone demonstrating cross-gender behavior is homosexual.

A number of complex modern and peasant societies in the Middle East, North Africa, southern Europe, and Central and South America have the commonalities listed. The author's research in Mexico (Carrier, 1976 and 1977) illustrates how homosexual behavior in these societies appears to be linked to social responses to cross-gender behavior. The comments that follow are limited to male homosexual behavior. Female homosexuality is known to exist in these societies, but too little is known about the behavior to be included in the discussion.

Mexican Homosexual Behavior. The Mexican mestizo culture places a high value on manliness. One of the salient features of the society is thus a sharp delimitation between the roles played by males and females. Role expectations in general are for the male to be dominant and independent and for the female to be submissive and dependent. The continued sharp boundary between male and female roles in Mexico appears to be due in part to a culturally defined hypermasculine ideal model of manliness, referred to under the label *machismo*. The ideal female role is generally believed to be the reciprocal of the macho (male) role.[6]

As a consequence of the high status given manliness, Mexican males from birth onward are expected to behave in as manly a way as possible. Peñalosa (1968) sums it up as follows: "Any signs of feminization are severely repressed in the boy." McGinn (1966) concludes: "The young Mexican boy may be severely scolded for engaging in feminine activities, such as playing with dolls or jacks. Parents verbally and physically punish feminine traits in their male children." The importance of manly behavior continues throughout the life span of Mexican males.

One result of the sharp dichotomization of male and female gender roles is the widely held belief that effeminate males basically prefer to play the female role rather than the male. The link between male effeminacy and homosexuality is the additional belief that as a result of this role preference effeminate males are sexually interested only in masculine males with whom they play the passive sex role. Although the motivations of males participating in homosexual encounters are without question diverse and complex, the fact remains that in Mexico cultural pressure is brought to bear on effeminate males to play the passive insertee role in sexual intercourse, and a kind of de facto cultural approval is given (that is, no particular stigma is attached to) masculine males who want to play the active insertor role in homosexual intercourse.

The beliefs linking effeminate males with homosexuality are culturally transmitted by a vocabulary which provides the appropriate labels, by homosexually oriented jokes and word games (*albures*), and by the mass media. The links are established at a very early age. From early childhood on, Mexican males are made aware of the labels used to denote male homosexuals and the connection is always clearly made that these homosexual males are guilty of unmanly effeminate behavior.

The author's data also support the notion that prior to puberty effeminate males in Mexico are targeted as sexual objects for adolescent and adult males, and are expected to play the passive insertee sex role in anal intercourse. Following the onset of puberty, they continue to be sexual targets for other males because of their effeminacy. The consensus of my effeminate respondents in Mexico is that regardless of whether they are at school, in a movie theater, on the downtown streets, in a park, or in their own neighborhood, they are sought out and expected to play the anal passive sex role by more masculine males. As one fourteen-year-old respondent put it, in response to the question of where he had looked for sexual contacts during the year prior to the interview: "I didn't have to search for them…they looked for me."

The other side of the coin is represented by masculine male participants in homosexual encounters. Given the fact that effeminate males in Mexico are assumed homosexual and thus considered available as sexual outlets, how do the cultural factors contribute to the willingness of masculine males to play the active insertor sex role? The available data suggest that, insofar as the social variables are concerned, their willingness to participate in homosexual encounters is due to the relatively high level of sexual awareness that exists among males in the society, to the lack of stigmatization of the insertor sex role, and to the restraints that may be placed on alternative

sexual outlets by available income and/or by marital status. The only cultural proscriptions are that "masculine" males should not play the passive sex role and should not be exclusively involved with homosexual intercourse.

The passive sex role is by inference—through the cultural equivalence of effeminacy with homosexuality—prescribed for "effeminate" males. It becomes a self-fulfilling prophecy of the society that effeminate males (a majority?) are eventually, if not from the beginning, pushed toward exclusively homosexual behavior. Some do engage in heterosexual intercourse, and some marry and set up households; but these probably are a minority of the identifiably effeminate males among the mestizos of the Mexican population.

Brazilian Homosexual Behavior. Both Young (1973) and Fry (1974) note the relationship between cross-gender behavior and homosexuality in Brazil.

> Brazilians are still pretty hung-up about sexual roles. Many Brazilians believe in the *bicha/bofe* (femme/butch) dichotomy and try to live by it. In Brazil, the average person doesn't even recognize the existence of the masculine homosexual. For example, among working-class men, it is considered all right to fuck a *bicha,* an accomplishment of sorts, just like fucking a woman. (Young, 1973)
>
> In the simplest of terms, a male is a man until he is assumed or proved to have "given" in which case he becomes a *bicha.* With very few exceptions, males who "eat" *bichas* are not classified as anything other than "real men." Under this classificatory scheme they differ in no way from males who restrict themselves to "eating" females. (Note: the male who gives is an insertee, the one who eats is an insertor.) (Fry, 1974)

Southern European Homosexual Behavior. Contemporary patterns of male homosexual behavior in Greece appear similar to those observed by the author in Mexico. An American anthropologist who collected data on homosexual behavior in Greece while working there on an archaeological project (Bialor, 1975) found, for example, that preferences for playing one sex role or the other (anal insertor or anal insertee) appear to be highly developed among Greek males. Little or no stigma is attached to the masculine male who plays the active insertor role. The social setting in modern Greece also appears to be strikingly similar to that in modern Mexico. Karlen (1971) describes it as follows:

> The father spends his spare time with other men in cafes; society is a male club, and there all true companionship lies. Women live separate, sequestered lives. Girls' virginity is carefully protected, and the majority of homicides are committed over the "honor" of daughters and sisters. In some Greek villages a woman does not leave her home unaccompanied by a relative between puberty and old age. Women walk the street, even in Athens, with their eyes down; a woman who looks up when a man speaks to her is, quite simply, a whore. The young male goes to prostitutes and may carry on homosexual connections; it is not unusual for him to marry at thirty having had no sexual experience save with prostitutes and male friends. (p. 16)

In an evaluation of the strategy of Turkish boys' verbal dueling rhymes, Dundes, Leach, and Ozkok (1972) make the following observations about homosexual behavior in Turkey:

> It is extremely important to note that the insult refers to *passive* homosexuality, not to homosexuality in general. In this context there is nothing insulting about being the active homosexual. In a homosexual relationship, the active phallic aggressor gains status; the passive victim of such aggression loses status. It is important to play the active role in a homosexual relationship; it is shameful and demeaning to be forced to take the passive role.

Moroccan Homosexual Behavior. The author does not know of any formal studies of homosexual behavior in Morocco. The available information suggests, however, that contemporary patterns of homosexual behavior in Morocco are similar to those in Mexico; that is, as long as Moroccan males play the active, insertor sex role in the relationship, there is never any question of their being considered homosexual. Based on his field work in Morocco shortly after the turn of the century, Westermarck (1908) believed that "a very large proportion of the men" in some parts of the country were involved in homosexual

activity. He also noted that: "In Morocco active pederasty is regarded with almost complete indifference, whilst the passive sodomite, if a grown-up individual, is spoken of with scorn. Dr. Polak says the same of the Persians." Contemporary patterns of homosexual behavior in the Islamic Arab countries of North Africa are probably similar to those in Morocco....

DISCUSSION

Heterosexual intercourse, marriage, and the creation of a family are culturally established as primary objectives for adults living in all of the societies discussed above. Ford & Beach (1951) concluded from their cross-cultural survey that "all known cultures are strongly biased in favor of copulation between males and females as contrasted with alternative avenues of sexual expression." They further note that this viewpoint is biologically adaptive in that it favors perpetuation of the species and social group, and that societies favoring other nonreproductive forms of sexual expression for adults would not be likely to survive for many generations.

Homosexual intercourse appears to be the most important alternative form of sexual expression utilized by people living around the world. All cultures have established rules and regulations that govern the selection of a sexual partner or partners. With respect to homosexual behavior, however, there appear to be greater variations of the rules and regulations. And male homosexual behavior generally appears to be more regulated by cultures than female homosexual behavior. This difference may be the result of females being less likely than males to engage in homosexual activity; but it may also just be the result of a lack of data on female as compared with male homosexual behavior cross-culturally.

Exclusive homosexuality, however, because of the cultural dictums concerning marriage and the family, appears to be generally excluded as a sexual option even in those societies where homosexual behavior is generally approved. For example, the two societies where all male individuals are free to participate in homosexual activity if they choose, Siwan and East Bay, do not sanction exclusive homosexuality.[7] Although nearly all male members of these two societies are reported to engage in extensive homosexual activities, they are not permitted to do so exclusively over their adult life span. Davenport (1965) reports "that East Bay is a society which permits men to be either heterosexual or bisexual in their behavior, but denies the possibility of the exclusively homosexual man." He notes that "they have no concept and therefore no word for the exclusive homosexual." There are not much data available on the Siwans, but it has been reported that whether single or married Siwan males "are expected to have both homosexual and heterosexual affairs" (Ford & Beach, 1951).

In East Bay there are two categories of homosexual relationships. One category appears similar to that found in a number of Melanesian societies; an older man plays the active (insertor) sex role in anal intercourse with younger boys "from seven to perhaps eleven years of age." Davenport notes:

> The man always plays the active role, and it is considered obligatory for him to give the boy presents in return for accommodating him. A man would not engage his own son in such a relationship, but fathers do not object when friends use their young sons in this way, provided the adult is kind and generous. (p. 200)

The other category is between young single men of the same age group who play both sex roles in anal intercourse. The young men, however, "are not regarded as homosexual lovers. They are simply friends or relatives, who, understanding each other's needs and desires, accommodate one another thus fulfilling some of the obligations of kinship and friendship." This category may be related to several social factors which limit heterosexual contacts of young single men. First, the population is highly masculine with a male/female ratio of 120:100 in the fifteen- to twenty-five-year-old age group. Second, females have historically been brought in as wives for those who could afford the bride price. Third, sexual relations between unmarried individuals and adultery are forbidden. Both relationships are classed as larcenies and "only murder carries a more severe punishment." At first marriage a bride is expected to be a virgin. Chastity is highly valued in that it indicates adultery is less likely to occur after marriage. And fourth, there is "an extensive system for separating the sexes by what amounts to a general social avoidance between men and women in all but a few situations." From early adolescence on, unmarried men and boys sleep and eat in the men's house; and married men spend much of their time there during the day. Davenport notes that both masturbation and anal copulation are socially approved and regarded as substitutes for heterosexual intercourse by members of the society. Female homosexual activity is not reported in East Bay.

Among Siwan males the accepted homosexual relationship is "between a man and a boy but not between adult men or between two young boys" (Bullough, 1976). They are reported to practice anal intercourse with the adult man always playing the active (insertor) sex role. In this society, boys are more valued than girls. Allah (1917) reports that

> …[the] bringing up of a boy costs very little whereas the girl needs ornaments, clothing, and stains. Moreover the boy is a very fruitful source of profit for the father, not for the work he does, but because he is hired by his father to another man to be used as a catamite. Sometimes two men exchange their sons. If they are asked about this, they are not ashamed to mention it.

Homosexual activity is not reported for Siwan females.

The way in which cross-gender behavior is linked to homosexual behavior, and the meaning ascribed to the "homosexual" behavior by participants and significant others, differ between the three categories of societies identified in this study. What is considered homosexuality in one culture may be considered appropriate behavior within prescribed gender roles in another, a homosexual act only on the part of one participant in another, or a ritual act involving growth and masculinity in still another. Care must therefore be taken when judging sexual behavior cross-culturally with such culture-bound labels as "homosexual" and "homosexuality."

From a cultural point of view, deviations from sexual mores in a given society appear most likely to occur as a result of the lack of appropriate sexual partners and/or a result of conditioning in approved sexual behavior which is limited by age or ritual (for example, where homosexual intercourse is only appropriate for a certain age group and/or ritual time period and inappropriate thereafter). Homosexual activity initiated by sociocultural variables may over time through interaction with personality variables, produce an outcome not in accordance with the sexual mores of the society.

The findings presented in this chapter illustrate the profound influence of culture on the structuring of individual patterns of sexual behavior. Whether from biological or psychological causation, cross-gender behaving individuals in many societies must cope with a cultural formulation which equates their behavior with homosexual activity and thus makes it a self-fulfilling prophecy that they become homosexually involved. There are also individuals in many societies who might *prefer* to be exclusively homosexual but are prevented from doing so by cultural edicts. From whatever causes that homosexual impulses originate, whether they be biological or psychological, culture provides an additional dimension that cannot be ignored.

CRITICAL THINKING QUESTIONS

1. What type of society tends to be accepting of homosexuality? What kind of society is disapproving of this sexual orientation? Why?
2. What insights can be drawn from this article that help to explain violence and discrimination directed toward gay people in Canadian society?

3. Are data about sexuality easily available to researchers? Why not?

NOTES

1. Homosexual behavior or activity will be used here to describe sexual behavior between individuals of the same sex; it may have nothing to do with sexual object choice or sexual orientation of the individual involved. Additionally, the terms "sex role" and "gender role" will be used to describe different behavioral phenomena. As Hooker (1965) points out, they "are often used interchangeably, and with resulting confusion." Following her suggestion the term "sex role," when homosexual practices are described, will refer to typical sexual performance only. "The gender connotations (M-F) of these performances need not then be implicitly assumed." The term "gender role" will refer to the expected attitudes and behavior that distinguish males from females.

2. The Human Relations Area Files (HRAF) contain information on the habits, practices, customs, and behavior of populations in hundreds of societies around the world. These files utilize accounts given not only by anthropologists but also by travelers, writers, missionaries, and explorers. Most cross-cultural surveys of sexual behavior, like those of Ford and Beach and Broude and Greene, have been based on HRAF information. A major criticism of the HRAF information on sexual behavior relates to the difficulty of assessing the reliability of the data collected in different time periods by different people with varying amounts of scientific training as observers.

3. "Preliterate" refers to essentially tribal societies that do not have a written language; "peasant" refers to essentially agrarian literate societies; and "complex modern" refers to highly industrialized societies.

4. In one of the first scholarly surveys of homosexual behavior done by an anthropologist, Westermarck (1908) concluded that: "A very important cause of homosexual practices is absence of the other sex."

5. The confounding of transvestism with homosexuality still occurs. For example, Minturn, Grosse, and Haider (1969) coded male homosexuality with transvestism in a recent study of the patterning of sexual beliefs and behavior, "because it is often difficult to distinguish between the two practices, and because they are assumed to be manifestations of the same psychological processes and to have similar causes."

6. The roles described represent the normative cultural ideals of the mestizoized national culture. Mestizos are Mexican nationals of mixed Indian and Spanish ancestry. They make up a large majority of the population, and their culture is the dominant one.

7. Both societies are small, each totaling less than 1,000 inhabitants. The Siwans live in an oasis in the Libyan desert. The people of East Bay (a pseudonym) live in a number of small coastal villages in an island in Melanesia.

REFERENCES

Allah, M. 1917. Siwan customs. *Harvard African Studies,* 1: 7.

Angelino, A., and C. Shedd. 1955. A note on berdache. *American Anthropologist,* 57: 121–25.

Associated Press. 1979. Eunuchs gather for convention in India. *Panipat,* February 6, 1979.

Bialor, P. 1975. Personal communication.

Bogores, W. 1904. The Chukchee. *Memoirs of American Museum of Natural History,* 2: 449–51.

Broude, G., and S. Greene. 1976. Cross-cultural codes on twenty sexual attitudes and practices. *Ethnology,* 15(4): 410–11.

Bullough, V. 1976. *Sexual variance in society and history,* 22–49. New York: John Wiley.

Carrier, J. 1976. Cultural factors affecting urban Mexican male homosexual behavior. *Archives of Sexual Behavior,* 5(2): 103–24.

———. 1977. Sex-role preference as an explanatory variable in homosexual behavior. *Archives of Sexual Behavior,* 6(1): 53–65.

Carstairs, G. 1956. Hinjra and Jiryan: Two derivatives of Hindu attitudes to sexuality. *British Journal of Medical Psychology,* 2: 129–32.

Davenport, W. 1965. Sexual patterns and their regulation in a society of the southwest Pacific. In *Sex and behavior,* 164–207. New York: John Wiley.

Devereux, G. 1937. Institutionalized homosexuality of the Mohave Indians. In *The problem of homosexuality in modern society,* 183–226. New York: E. P. Dutton.

Dundes, A., J. Leach, and B. Ozkok. 1972. The strategy of Turkish boys' verbal dueling. In *Directions in sociolinguistics: The ethnography of communication.* New York: Holt.

Ford, C. S., and F. A. Beach. 1951. *Patterns of sexual behavior.* New York: Harper & Row.

Fry, P. 1974. Male homosexuality and Afro-Brazilian possession cults. Unpublished paper presented to Symposium on Homosexuality in Crosscultural Perspective, 73rd Annual Meeting of the American Anthropological Association, Mexico City.

Hooker, E. 1965. An empirical study of some relations between sexual patterns and gender identity in male homosexuals. In *Sex research: New developments,* 24–5. New York: Holt.

Karlen, A. 1971. *Sexuality and homosexuality: A new view.* New York: W. W. Norton.

Kroeber, A. 1940. Psychosis or social sanction. *Character and Personality,* 8: 204–15. Reprinted in *The nature of culture,* 313. Chicago: University of Chicago Press, 1952.

Levy, R. 1973. *Tahitians.* Chicago: University of Chicago Press.

Marshall, D., and R. Suggs. 1971. *Human sexual behavior,* 220–21. New York: Basic Books.

McGinn, N. 1966. Marriage and family in middle-class Mexico. *Journal of Marriage and Family Counseling,* 28: 305–13.

Mead, M. 1961. Cultural determinants of sexual behavior. In *Sex and internal secretions,* 1433–79. Baltimore: Williams & Wilkins.

Minturn, L., M. Grosse, and S. Haider. 1969. Cultural patterning of sexual beliefs and behavior. *Ethnology,* 8(3): 3.

Morrison, J. 1935. *The journal of James Morrison.* London: Golden Cockeral Press.

Munroe, R., J. Whiting, and D. Hally. 1969. Institutionalized male transvestism and sex distinctions. *American Anthropologist,* 71: 87–91.

Opler, M. 1960. The Hijadas (hermaphrodites) of India and Indian national character: A rejoinder. *American Anthropologist,* 62(3): 505–11.

Peñalosa, F. 1968. Mexican family roles. *Journal of Marriage and Family Counseling,* 30: 680–89.

Royce, A. 1973. Personal communication.

Shah, A. 1961. A note on the Hijadas of Gujarat. *American Anthropologist,* 63(6): 1325–30.

Stoller, R. 1976. Two feminized male American Indians. *Archives of Sexual Behavior,* 5(6): 536.

Westermarck, E. 1908. On homosexual love. In *The origin and development of the moral ideas.* London: Macmillan.

Williams, F. 1936. *Papuans of the trans-fly.* London: Oxford University Press.

Young, A. 1973. Gay gringo in Brazil. In *The gay liberation book,* eds. L. Richmond and G. Noguera, 60–7. San Francisco: Ramparts Press.

31

The Vertical Mosaic: An Analysis of Social Class and Power in Canada

John Porter

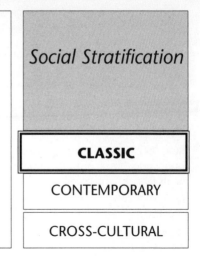

Social Stratification

CLASSIC

CONTEMPORARY

CROSS-CULTURAL

In this chapter from the highly regarded book The Vertical Mosaic, *Porter highlights the importance of studying Canadian social class structures. Porter traces the Canadian belief that there are no clearly defined classes in Canada back to the frontier environment and the settlement of Canada.*

THE CANADIAN MIDDLE CLASS IMAGE

One of the most persistent images that Canadians have of their society is that it has no classes. This image becomes translated into the assertion that Canadians are all relatively equal in their possessions, in the amount of money they earn, and in the opportunities which they and their children have to get on in the world. An important element in this image of classlessness is that, with the absence of formal aristocracy and aristocratic institutions, Canada is a society in which equalitarian values have asserted themselves over authoritarian values. Canada, it is thought, shares not only a continent with the United States, but also a democratic ideology which rejects the historical class and power structures of Europe.

Source: From *The Vertical Mosaic* by John Porter. Toronto: University of Toronto Press, 1965, pp. 3–6. Reprinted with the permission of the publisher.

Social images are one thing and social realities another. Yet the two are not completely separate. Social images are not entirely fictional characters with only a coincidental likeness to a real society, living or dead. Often the images can be traced to an earlier historical period of the society, its golden age perhaps, which, thanks to the historians, is held up, long after it has been transformed into something else, as a model way of life. As well as their historical sources, images can be traced to their contemporary creators, particularly in the world of the mass media and popular culture. When a society's writers, journalists, editors, and other image-creators are a relatively small and closely linked group, and have more or less the same social background, the images they produce can, because they are consistent, appear to be much more true to life than if their group were larger, less cohesive, and more heterogeneous in composition.

The historical source of the image of a class-less Canada is the equality among pioneers in the frontier environment of the last century. In the early part of the [twentieth] century there was a similar equality of status among those who were settlers in the west, although, as we shall see, these settlers were by no means treated equally. A rural, agricultural, primary producing society is a much less differentiated society than one which has highly concentrated industries in large cities. Equality in the rural society may be much more apparent than real, but the rural environment has been for Canada an important source of the image of equality. Later we shall examine more closely how the historical image has become out of date with the transformation of Canadian society from the rural to the urban type.

Although the historical image of rural equality lingers, it has gradually given way in the urban industrial setting to an image of a middle level classlessness in which there is a general uniform-mity of possessions. For families these posses-sions include a separate dwelling with an array of electrical equipment, a car, and perhaps a summer cottage. Family members, together or as individuals, engage in a certain amount of ritual-istic behaviour in churches and service clubs. Modern advertising has done much to standard-ize the image of middle class consumption levels and middle class behaviour. Consumers' maga-zines are devoted to the task of constructing the ideal way of life through articles on child-rearing, homemaking, sexual behaviour, health, sports, and hobbies. Often, too, corporations which do not produce family commodities directly will have large advertisements to demonstrate how general social well-being at this middle level is an outcome of their own operations.

That there is neither very rich nor very poor in Canada is an important part of the image. There are no barriers to opportunity. Education is free. Therefore, making use of it is largely a question of personal ambition. Even university education is available to all, except that it may require for some a little more summer work and thrift. There is a view widely held by many university gradu-ates that they, and most other graduates, have worked their way through college. Consequently it is felt anyone else can do the same.

In some superficial respects the image of middle class uniformity may appear plausible. The main values of the society are concerned with the consumption of commodities, and in the so-called affluence that has followed World War II there seem to have been commodities for everybody, except, perhaps, a small group of the permanently poor at the bottom. Credit facilities are available for large numbers of low-income families, enabling them, too, to be consumers of commodities over and above the basic necessi-ties of life. The vast array of credit facilities, some of them extraordinarily ingenious, have inequalities built into them, in that the cost of borrowing money varies with the amount already possessed. There are vast differences in the quality of goods bought by the middle income levels and the lower income levels. One commodity, for instance, which low-income families can rarely purchase is privacy, particu-larly the privacy of a house to themselves. It is perhaps the value of privacy and the capacity to afford it which has become the dividing line between the real and the apparent middle class.

If low-income families achieve high consump-tion levels it is usually through having more than one income earner in the household. Often this is the wife and mother, but it may be an older child who has left school, and who is expected to contribute to the family budget. Alternatively, high consumption levels may be achieved at a cost in leisure. Many low-income family heads have two jobs, a possibility which has arisen with the shorter working day and the five-day week. This "moonlighting," as it is called in labour circles, tends to offset the progress which has been made in raising the level of wages and reducing the hours of work. There is no way of knowing how extensive "moonlighting" is, except that we know that trade unions denounce it as a practice which tends to take away the gains which have been obtained for workers. For large segments of the population, therefore, a high level of consumption is obtained by means which are alien to a true middle class standard. [When]…we…examine closely the distribution of income, we …see what a small proportion of Canadian families were able to live a middle class style of life in the middle 1950s, the high tide of post-war affluence.

At the high end of the social class spectrum, also in contrast to the middle level image, are the families of great wealth and influence. They are not perhaps as ostentatious as the very wealthy of other societies, and Canada has no "celebrity world" with which these families must compete for prestige in the way Mills has suggested is important for the very rich in American society.[1]

Almost every large Canadian city has its wealthy and prominent families of several generations. They have their own social life, their children go to private schools, they have their clubs and associations, and they take on the charitable and philanthropic roles which have so long been the "duty" of those of high status. Although this upper class is always being joined by the new rich, it still contributes, as we shall see later, far more than its proportionate share to the elite of big business.

The concentration of wealth in the upper classes is indicated by the fact that in Canada in 1955 the top one per cent of income recipients received about 40 per cent of all income from dividends.

Images which conflict with the one of middle class equality rarely find expression, partly because the literate middle class is both the producer and the consumer of the image. Even at times in what purports to be serious social analysis, middle class intellectuals project the image of their own class onto the social classes above and below them. There is scarcely any critical analysis of Canadian social life upon which a conflicting image could be based. The idea of class differences has scarcely entered into the stream of Canadian academic writing despite the fact that class differences stand in the way of implementing one of the most important values of western society, that is equality.[2] The fact, which we shall see later, that Canada draws its intellectuals either from abroad or from its own middle class, means that there is almost no one producing a view of the world which reflects the experience of the poor or the underprivileged. It was as though they did not exist. It is the nature of these class differences and their consequences for Canadian society that [we]…seek to explore.

Closely related to differences in class levels are differences in the exercising of power and decision-making in the society: Often it is thought that once a society becomes an electoral democracy based on universal suffrage, power becomes diffused throughout the general population so that everyone participates somehow in the selection of social goals. There is, however, a whole range of institutional resistances to the transfer of power to a democratic political system.…

CRITICAL THINKING QUESTIONS

1. Is Porter's assertion that Canadians believe they exist within a classless society still valid today? Why or why not?
2. Porter's work was published in 1965. Do any of his observations continue to be revealing in a contemporary analysis of Canadian society?
3. According to Porter, does democracy ensure the equal allocation of power and influence within society? Why or why not?

NOTES

1. C. W. Mills, *The Power Elite* (New York, 1956), chap. 4.
2. Nor does class appear as a theme in Canadian literature. See R. L. McDougall, "The Dodo and the Cruising Auk," *Canadian Literature*, no. 18 (Autumn 1963).
3. For a comparative study of social mobility see S. M. Lipset and R. Bendix, *Social Mobility in Industrial Society* (Berkeley, 1959).

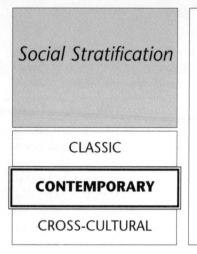

32

Social Stratification

CLASSIC

CONTEMPORARY

CROSS-CULTURAL

Does the Vertical Mosaic Still Exist? Ethnicity and Income in Canada, 1991*

Jason Z. Lian and David Ralph Matthews

Lian and Matthews review Porter's work and explore it using contemporary data. The authors find that race (particularly visible minorities) has become the fundamental basis for income inequality in Canada.

This paper updates our knowledge about the relationship between ethnicity and social class in Canada using *The Public Use Microdata File for Individuals* drawn from the 1991 Census of Canada. We provide three levels of analysis. First, we examine the relationship between ethnicity and education by ethnic group. Second, we examine the "return to education" in terms of income for those of various ethnic groups. Third, we use log-linear regression to examine the relationship between ethnicity, education, and income while controlling for the effects of a variety of other social variables. We find that, at

*This is a revised version of a paper presented at the Canadian Ethnic Studies Association, Biennial Meeting, Gimli, Manitoba, October 1995. We thank Margaret Denton, John Fox, and Wulong Gu for helpful suggestions and comments. The manuscript of this article was submitted in February 1997 and accepted in July 1997.

Source: Jason Z. Lian and David Matthews. 1998. Does the Vertical Mosaic Still Exist? Ethnicity and Income in Canada, 1991. *The Canadian Review of Sociology and Anthropology*, 35(4), 461–81. Reprinted by permission of the Canadian Sociology and Anthropology Association.

most educational levels, Canadians of French ethnicity now earn significantly more than those of British ethnicity when other variables are controlled. With this exception, for those of European ethnic backgrounds there are now virtually no significant differences in income within educational levels when other social variables are controlled. However, those who belong to visible minorities have significantly lower incomes than other Canadians at all educational levels. Race is now the fundamental basis of income inequality in Canada.

In 1965, John Porter described Canadian society as a "vertical mosaic" stratified along ethnic lines (1965: 60–103). Porter argued that the British and French, as the first ethnic groups to come into Canada, became the "charter groups" and to a considerable extent dictated the circumstances under which other ethnic groups were subsequently permitted to enter. He argued that "entrance status" was generally granted to those of other ethnic groups who were willing to accept lower level occupational roles (63–73) and that, as a result, "immigration and ethnic affiliation...have been important factors in the formation of social classes in Canada" (73). Porter used census data from the 1931 to 1961 period to demonstrate that the British dominated the French in all of the most prestigious occupational categories, and that other ethnic groups were generally distributed in a hierarchy below them.

Since then, considerable effort has been expended by researchers to support or refute Porter's thesis and to examine the extent to which ethnic social class mobility has occurred as previous immigrants overcame their "entrance status" and moved up the social class hierarchy. Proponents of the vertical mosaic thesis have argued that differences in occupational status among Canadian ethnic groups remain substantial. Over the past thirty years, they have demonstrated that, for the two charter groups, the occupational status of the British has remained significantly higher than that of the French (Royal Commission, 1969: 34–45; Breton & Roseborough, 1971; Boyd et al., 1981). They have argued that among other groups, Jews and those from the north and west of Europe are generally in favourable positions, South Europeans and visible minorities are generally in disadvantaged positions, and Aboriginal Peoples are at the bottom of the Canadian occupational hierarchy (Reitz, 1980; Porter, 1985; Jabbra & Cosper, 1988; Li, 1988; Lautard & Guppy, 1990). Thus, in 1984, Lautard and Loree could still claim that "occupational inequality is still substantial enough to justify the use of the concept 'vertical mosaic' to characterize this aspect of ethnic relations in Canada" (343).

In contrast, a number of other researchers have argued that the influence of ethnicity in the process of social mobility was and/or is minimal in Canada, and that ethnic affiliation did not operate as a significant block to social mobility as Porter had suggested. Most such works have examined the relationship between ethnicity and occupation, while controlling for a range of other variables. Using such methods, they have argued that the association between ethnicity and

occupational status was minimal and declining (Pineo, 1976; Darroch, 1979; Ornstein, 1981) and that the contention of the vertical mosaic thesis that the status of immigrants groups has been rigidly preserved is "patently false" (Tepperman, 1975: 156). Other researchers have suggested that a convergence process in occupational status among ethnic groups in Canada has become more apparent since Porter's original analysis (Reitz, 1980: 150–53), the relationship between ethnic origin and class position has been in flux (Nakhaie, 1951), and that gains by non-charter groups have been significantly greater than those of the charter groups (Boyd et al., 1981; Pineo & Porter, 1985: 382–83). Porter, himself, has argued that the situation he described in 1965 may have been in existence only for a relatively short period in Canadian history (Pineo & Porter, 1985: 390). It is also argued that, to the extent that any ethnic status hierarchy remains, Porter's status hierarchy of ethnic groups has changed dramatically with the British dropping from the top to the middle and the Asians moving to the top with the Jews (Herberg, 1990). As a result, it has been stated recently that ethnicity is no longer a drawback for social mobility in Canada (Isajiw, Sev'er & Driedger, 1993).

In many such works, the relation of education and ethnicity has come under considerable scrutiny. Thus, proponents of the ethnic inequality thesis have argued that the Canadian education system has been a mechanism to reproduce social inequality (Shamai, 1992: 44–5) and that educational opportunity was not equally accessible to all groups (Li, 1988: 77–96). Alternatively, those who have been critical of the ethnic inequality thesis have argued that there is little evidence of ethnic inequality in education in Canada and that a *"contest-achieved"* system of status attainment is operating (Herberg, 1990). Indeed, Porter was himself involved in work which argued that non-charter groups have gained significantly in educational achievement compared to the

British (Pineo & Porter, 1985: 384) and that the educational system has worked to help minority Canadians overcome the disadvantages of their background (391).

The general conclusion of this body of work would seem to be that there is a collapsing of the vertical mosaic. However, there is growing evidence (see Li, 1988; Reitz, 1980; Agocs & Boyd, 1993) that Canada has retained what Geschwender and Guppy have called a "colour-coded vertical mosaic" (1995: 2). Such works suggest that, whereas ethnic stratification has lessened among white European groups, differences between racial groups have persisted and that, in effect, Canada's mosaic has been reduced to a division based principally on skin colour (1995: 2).

This paper will examine the evidence for and against ethnic inequality in Canada with respect to income distribution, using *The Public Use Microdata Files for Individuals* (PUMFI) provided by Statistics Canada, which constitutes a 3% sample of the 1991 Census. Such files have been made available since 1971, but the 1991 PUMFI provides both a more extensive list of ethnic groups and a more detailed categorization of other variables that may be employed as controls than were available in previous issues. Thus, the present paper is able to provide more current information on the relationship between ethnicity and income than most previous studies, and also is able to identify ethnicity more precisely and use more stringent control variables in the analysis.

To carry out the analysis we have used those respondents in the PUMFI who were in the "working population," and from this group have eliminated those respondents for whom data were not available or who had zero or negative earnings.[1] These latter reductions reduce the number of respondents in the working population sample by 4.78%, nearly half of whom had zero or negative earnings in 1990. As a result of these adjustments, the average earnings of the sample increased by approximately 4%, but the ethnic composition

changed very little.... Thus, for purposes of the present study which focuses on ethnicity, our sample was not affected significantly.

ETHNICITY AND EDUCATION

In any study of ethnic stratification and mobility, education is seen as a critically important intervening variable between ethnicity and income. A fundamental question in such studies is whether educational achievement is distributed equally among ethnic groups. Earlier we noted the diverging positions on this subject in Canada— some argued that the educational system has functioned to reproduce the existing socio-economic hierarchy in favour of the dominant groups (Li, 1988: 73–7; Shamai, 1992: 53–5), and others argued that the educational system has functioned as a source of upward mobility for Canadian minority groups since the early decades of this century (Herberg, 1990).

It is not possible to test this issue fully using data from a single time period. However, data from the 1991 PUMFI show a considerable variation in education among ethnic groups when compared with the Canadian average and this variation remains even when one separates out the Canadian born from the foreign born. This indicates that, among native-born Canadians, educational achievement is unevenly distributed by ethnicity....

In 1991, approximately 30% of the employed labour force in Canada had less than secondary education, just over 54% had secondary or non-university post-secondary education, and almost 17% had post-secondary education. About two-thirds of the European groups and half of the visible minority groups were close to this Canadian average. However, several Southern European groups (Italians, Greeks, Portuguese), Vietnamese, and Aboriginal Peoples had proportionally more persons with this lower educational level while Arabs, West Asians, Jews and Filipinos were under-represented in the lower educational groups.

At the other extreme, in terms of post-secondary (university) education most European groups were around the national average, Poles were moderately above and Jews were nearly three times likely to have a university degree than were those of European origin *per se*. With the exception of the Black/Caribbean and Aboriginal groups who ranked substantially below the national level, the remaining visible minority groups had high rates of university education. This was particularly the case for those of Arab, West Asian, South Asian, Chinese, Filipino and Other East and Southeast Asian ethnic backgrounds.

To some considerable degree this latter finding is a reflection of Canadian immigration policy since the 1970s, which has favoured those with high levels of education and training. Thus, Arab, West Asian, South Asian, Filipino, and Vietnamese foreign born were generally better educated than their Canadian-born counterparts. This relationship held for most other groups with the notable exception of the Greek, Italian, and Balkan ethnic groups among whom the native born were generally better educated than recent immigrants.

EDUCATION AND INCOME DIFFERENCES AMONG ETHNIC GROUPS

While differences in education by ethnic group, particularly among the Canadian-born, are an indication of possible ethnic discrimination, the more significant indication is whether the "returns for education" are also unequal among ethnic groups. That is, does similar education (at whatever level) generate significantly different incomes among the ethnic groups?…

At the national level, those with secondary education earned about 50% more than those without secondary education and those with university education earned about 150% more than those without secondary education…. However, there are extreme ethnic differences at all three educational levels.

The following analyses are all based on comparisons with the national average for each of the educational categories. Looking first at the two "charter groups," workers of British origin with non-secondary education earned 3% more than the national average for this educational level, those with secondary education earned 7% more, while those with university education earned 8% more. In comparison, workers of French ethnicity with non-secondary education earned 12% more than the national average, those with secondary education earned 1% less and those with university education earned 4% more. Thus, in contrast to Porter's finding that the French were rewarded significantly less than the British for their educational achievement, at the lower educational level they now have a significant edge over the British, and are above the national average in income at the higher educational levels.

Those of Western European ethnic background earned considerably higher incomes than the Canadian average in each of the education categories, the exception being university educated persons of Dutch and German ethnic backgrounds who earned only marginally more. Eastern Europeans also tended to earn more than the Canadian average, with Hungarians and Ukrainians earning substantially more at all levels. Persons of Polish ethnicity with lower as well as middle levels of education earned more than average, but better educated persons of Polish ethnicity earned less.

For those whose Jewish ethnic background was recorded, those with the lowest level of education earned 9% more than the Canadian average income for that level, while those with university education earned 19% more than the Canadian university educated average income. However, those with secondary education earned 4% less than the average Canadians at their educational level.

The pattern for Southern Europeans is mixed. At the lowest educational level, most of these ethnic groups earned above the Canadian average income with those of Italian, Portuguese, Greek, and Balkan origin earning considerably higher than that average. However, at higher educational levels Southern Europeans were generally disadvantaged.

However, it is when we consider visible minorities that the largest discrepancies between education and income are apparent. At the lower education levels all 10 visible minority groups earned less than an average Canadian with similar education, ranging from 5% less for those of Arab ethnicity to 33% less for those of Filipino ethnic background and 42% less for Aboriginal Peoples. Likewise, among those with secondary education, all 10 visible minority groups earned substantially less than the comparable Canadian average. Similarly, amongst those with post-secondary education, while those of Black and Chinese ethnicity earned only somewhat less than the Canadian average, those in the other eight visible minority groups received earning[s] substantially below that level.

The overall conclusion to be drawn from these two tables is that persons of European background generally receive above average income for their educational level with the exception of persons with higher education from some Eastern and Southern European ethnic groups. Indeed, persons from many such ethnic backgrounds now receive incomes relative to education that are higher than for either of the two "charter groups." *However, for visible minorities a very different picture emerges. For all visible ethnic groups and at all educational levels, the rewards for education are substantially below the Canadian average.*

ETHNICITY AND INCOME DIFFERENCES WITHIN EDUCATIONAL CATEGORIES, TAKING INTO ACCOUNT OTHER VARIABLES

Although the preceding analysis has provided strong indications that the rewards for education vary by ethnic group and particularly that workers of visible minorities receive comparatively less than other workers with similar education, it is possible that these results are not due to ethnicity *per se* but to a range of other factors such as the age composition, marital status, or

period of immigration of workers from various ethnic groups. Thus, if one wants to measure directly the effect of ethnicity on earnings within educational categories, it is necessary to take into account the effect of these other earnings-related variables.

To do this, we developed a semi-logarithmic regression model of earnings determination with interaction terms constructed of ethnicity and education, controlling for gender; age and age squared; marital status; province of residence; metropolitan versus non-metropolitan area of residence; geographic mobility in the past five years; period of immigration; knowledge of official languages; occupational level; industrial sector; weeks worked and weeks worked squared; and full versus part-time weeks worked. Controlling for these factors in a semi-logarithmic regression yields an adjusted R square of 0.58007, indicating that 58% of the variations in log earnings have been accounted for by the variables included in the model.

Because of the dominant position of the British in Canadian society both numerically and socio-economically, we have used them as the base line category in the regression for an estimation of the net log earnings of the other ethnic groups at each educational level. While persons of British ethnicity with "no degree, certificate, or diploma" were used as the reference category for all other inter-active categories of ethnicity and education in the regression, for easy interpretation, we have converted the partial coefficients for the other ethnic groups as deviations from those of their category of "no degree, certificate, or diploma" for the British. The coefficients derived in this manner have been converted into percentages and displayed in Table 32.1

As an example of how to interpret the table, we would note that the 3.1% in the cell for French with "no degree, certificate, or diploma" indicates that workers of French ethnic origin earned 3.1% more than their British counterparts with comparable education when all the dimensions in our model have been taken into account. Similarly,

TABLE 32.1 Adjusted Earnings[1] of Persons of Different Ethnic Origins[2] as Percentage Differences from Those of Persons of British Origin by Educational Level, Canada, 1990

Ethnic Origin	No Degree, Certificate, or Diploma	High School Graduation Certificate	Trades Certificate	Other Non-University Certificate	University Certificate below Bachelor Level	Bachelor's Degree(s)	University Certificate above Bachelor Level	Masters Degree(s)	Earned Doctorate	Degree in Medicine[3]
British[4]	3 1**	13.2**	16.8**	21.3**	27.3**	39.6**	47.4**	58.3**	76.6**	141.7**
French	0.5	1.7**	3 0**	5.3**	8 1**	2.3*	2.8	1.2	5.4	4.2
Dutch	2.8	2.8	1.6	-2.0	-18.4**	-3.9	-3.9	-12.4*	1.9	-40.6**
German	3.7**	-0.5	-2.1	0.7	3.7	-2.6	-3.4	-7.0	-3.4	-14.7
Other W European	14.0**	5.2	1.0	14.3**	16.2	0.9	-7.4	2.4	6.1	-24.4
Hungarian	-2.4	-2.1	-1.3	-11.3**	-18.7	-2.0	4.4	11.4	-17.0	8.3
Polish	-3.6	-1.1	1.8	1.1	-19.2*	0.6	-3.0	-14.4*	-6.1	-12.5
Ukrainian	2.7	3.1	2.7	4.0**	-14.4**	5.6*	-2.2	-3.4	-13.8	6.3
Balkan	2.4	-3.6	-2.0	5.3	4.6	-2.1	-5.6	-5.8	-8.6	-3.4
Greek	-6.3**	-6.6**	0.4	-1.7	-32.5**	-9.3	-15.7	-2.4	-25.9	-50.1**
Italian	-0.6	2.7*	-0.0	7.1**	8.3	-1.1	-2.1	3.6	-1.8	-26.4*
Portuguese	11.0**	3.1	4.8	2.8	-22.5**	-4.9	5.3	0.6	–	41.7
Spanish	4.1	-14.4**	0.7	-6.0	-13.1	-14.7	0.5	-20.2	48.5	14.6
Jewish	21.9**	8.0**	3.3	3.1	3.2	4.4	6.7	0.7	6.7	-2.2
Arab	1.4	-6.2*	-12.6**	1.6	-22.7**	-17.8**	-22.3**	-18.1**	1.6	-27.7**
West Asian	-5.4	-10.4**	-5.3	-0.6	-10.2	-7.5	-15.6	-18.2**	-25.7	-30.5*
South Asian	2.9	-3.9*	-8.6**	-4.1	-0.7	-17.7**	-12.8**	-18.9**	-6.8	-15.9*
Chinese	-4.4**	5.3**	-3.3	-5.6**	-6.6	-7.3**	-14.1**	-10.3**	-26.3**	-15.2*
Filipino	-6.4	-2.1	-12.5**	-8.2*	-7.5	-12.4**	-12.5	-20.9*	–	13.0
Vietnamese	0.8	-11.9**	-19.7**	3.2	-19.3**	-12.7	-39.2**	-6.9	-7.0	-42.7**
Other E & SE Asian	-4.2	-10.2**	-3.7	-6.8	20.2*	-14.6**	-10.1	-12.1	-27.5	-35.1**
Latin American	3.7	-11.7**	-2.3	-29.8**	-7.8	-24.4**	-31.1**	-18.7	-30.4	-40.6
Black	-8.1**	-3.1	-3.3	-10.4**	-3.7	-10.0**	10.6	-12.4	-10.3	-10.2
Aboriginal	-18.8**	-16.0**	-20.0**	-24.7**	-1.9	-8.0	-24.2	-20.2	-49.4	-76.7**
Others	-2.7**	-0.3	-1.7*	-0.9	0.3	-3.7**	-2.5	-6.7**	-2.6	-7.2

Source: Public Use Microdata File for Individuals, 1991 Census of Canada.

  1. Controlling for gender, age, marital status, province of residence, metropolitan/non-metropolitan area, geographic mobility, period of immigration, knowledge of official languages, occupation, industrial sector, weeks worked, and part-time/full-time weeks worked.
  2. The earnings of workers of various ethnic origins are expressed as percentage differences from the earnings of workers of British origin in the same educational category....
  3. Including degrees in medicine, dentistry, veterinary medicine, and optometry.
  4. The category of "no degree, certificate, or diploma" for the British is the base category for other categories for the British....
*Significant at 0.10
**Significant at 0.05

persons of British origin with "no degree, certificate, or diploma" are used as the base category for their British counterparts at other levels of education. Thus, for example, workers of British origin with "high school graduate certificates" earned 13.2% more than their counterparts of British origin, who had "no degree, certificate, or diploma," when all the other factors in our [regression] were taken into account. As also noted, this difference is significant at the 0.05 level.

Looking first at the two "charter groups," it is obvious that the net economic returns to education for workers of British origin is significant, with each advancing educational category providing progressively higher returns. It is clear that the economic value of education for persons of British origin in the Canadian labour market is beyond doubt.

However, of more significance is the somewhat surprising finding that, after the other factors are controlled, persons of French origin at *all* educational levels had earnings above that for persons of British origin. Moreover, at the Bachelor's degree level and below, these differences of income between the French and the British are statistically significant. Hence, whatever may have been the situation in the past, it is clear that any suggestion that today the French are discriminated against in terms of the returns they receive for their education, is clearly not the case. Indeed, especially at lower levels, the French are significantly favoured over the British in terms of this relationship.

Among Europeans, whether from the north, east, or south of Europe, most ethnic groups had approximately the same income levels as their British counterparts with similar education. Notable exceptions were the Dutch and Poles who, in several of the upper educational levels earned significantly less, and those of Jewish ethnicity in the lowest educational categories who earned significantly more. The most significant discrepancies occurred, not in relation to any ethnicity, but in terms of certain educational categories. Thus, where respondents held either a "university certificate below the bachelor's level" or a "degree in medicine," persons from continental Europe were quite likely to have incomes significantly below that of the British when other factors were taken into account. The frequency of such discrepancies in these two categories suggests that this may have to do with the evaluation of educational qualification at these levels rather than just ethnicity.

In sharp contrast to the situation for Europeans, adjusted earnings of visible minorities were much lower than for the British at most educational levels. Compared to their British counterparts, out of the 10 educational categories, most visible minority groups earned less than their British counterparts in the majority of categories. Moreover, in many of the educational categories, visible minorities earned *significantly* less than their British counterparts.

Given this obvious evidence of discrimination against all visible minority groups, it is difficult to single out any one or two groups as being more hard done by than others. Perhaps persons of Chinese background might fit this category as they earned less than those of British ethnicity in all 10 educational categories and significantly less than the British in 8 of the 10 educational categories. However, Aboriginal Peoples and West Asians also earned less in 10 categories, and most other visible minority groups earned less in nine of them. While the Arabs might seem better off amongst visible minorities in that they earned lower in only 7 categories, they were significantly less in all 7, a level of earnings discrimination surpassed only by those of Chinese ethnicity.

Whereas one might have thought that increased level of education would lead to lower levels of discrimination, there is little in Table 32.1 to support such a position. From high school to doctorate there is clear evidence of lower earnings amongst visible minorities compared to their British counterparts at the same educational level. Thus, all visible minorities earned less than the British at the high school graduate level, at the level of bachelors degree holder, master's degree holder and, with the exception of Arabs, at the level of doctorate degree holder. Likewise, all visible minorities who held degrees in medicine earned less than their British counterparts, as did all but the Blacks among those who held a university certificate above bachelor's but below master's level. Moreover, in the majority of cases *these differences were either significant or highly significant. In sum, it is clear from these findings that educational achievement at any level fails to protect persons of visible minority background from being disadvantaged in terms of the income they receive.*

SUMMARY AND DISCUSSION

We began this paper with the question, "Does the 'vertical mosaic' still exist?" It has been our assumption that the most appropriate place to look for evidence to either support or refute the vision of Canadian society as a "vertical mosaic" is through an examination of the relationship between ethnicity and income, first controlling for educational level, and then controlling for other key social variables so that this relationship can be measured more directly and precisely.

Our conclusion is that, by 1991, for the majority of ethnic groups in Canada there is no evidence that the traditionally accepted image of a vertical mosaic still remains. Among the two charter groups, the French now earn more for comparable education than their British counterparts when other factors are controlled. Likewise, many ethnic groups from all parts of Europe who had entered Canada with generally little education and hence occupied lower income positions, have now moved up the educational and income hierarchies and there is very little evidence of discrimination against any such ethnic groups.

On the other hand, there is also clear evidence that visible minorities have not fared well. When education and a range of other social variables are controlled, Aboriginal Peoples still remain

mired at the bottom of Canadian society. Almost all Asian groups and most of those of Latin American and Middle Eastern ethnicity were also similarly disadvantaged.

In sum, the evidence indicates that similar educational qualifications carried different economic values in the Canadian labour market for individuals of different "racial" origins. All visible minority groups had below-average earnings in each of the categories, while most of those of European ethnicity had above-average earnings.

It is possible that there are some other variables than "race" which systematically operate to discriminate against people of colour in Canadian society. However, the 1991 *Public Use Microdata File for Individuals* permits more "controls" for other possible variables than has ever previously been possible in such a large data set based on Canadian society. Thus, we have controlled for most of the other competing factors and their interaction effects which might conceivably affect the fundamental relationship between education and income that lies at the centre of our analysis. If there are other factors which might affect this relationship, we cannot easily discern what these might be. More importantly, the large literature on the relationship between education, income, and ethnicity in Canada which we have reviewed provides no clue of any other factor or factors which might have such a significant influence.

Consequently, whereas we began this paper with the question, "Does the vertical mosaic still exist?," we must end it with an even more serious question, namely, "Is Canada a racist society?" Canadians have long prided themselves on their policy of ethnic pluralism in contrast to the "melting pot" of the United States. We have also generally seen ourselves as a more racially tolerant society than the American one. However, our data suggest that there are limits to our tolerance of cultural and racial divisions. While we are apparently willing to accept cultural differences (particularly from a wide range of European cultures) in terms of the income received relative to level of education, we show no such tolerance for those who are racially "visible" from the white majority in Canadian society. All our evidence suggests that, while our traditional "vertical mosaic" of ethnic differences may be disappearing, it has been replaced by a strong "coloured mosaic" of racial differences in terms of income rewards and income benefits. While this does not necessarily mean that we have racial discrimination when it comes to other social benefits such as location of residence, access to public facilities, and the extreme forms of discrimination that have characterized some other societies, our evidence leads us to conclude that there *is* some considerable level of racial discrimination in Canada in terms of financial rewards for educational achievement. In this respect at least, yes, we are a racist society.

CRITICAL THINKING QUESTIONS

1. Does contemporary data support Porter's original work in *The Vertical Mosaic*? If so, how? If not, why not?
2. Given the evidence presented in the article, do you feel that Canada is a racist society? What evidence from your own community supports your position?
3. What role, if any, does a person's level of education have on income in Canada?

NOTES

1. The analysis is based on 425,107 cases. The 1991 PUMFI contains 809,654 cases. Respondents who did not work in 1990 (nearly half of whom were under age 15) have been excluded, thereby dropping the sample to 446,478 cases representing the working population of Canada in 1990. A small number of persons were on employment authorizations or Minister's permits or were refugee claimants. As the income of such persons could have been significantly affected by factors atypical of the Canadian labour market, they have been excluded, thereby reducing the sample to 443,161 cases. Also eliminated were a small number of cases with missing information on education, age, marital status, geographic mobility, and period of immigration (i.e., the factors of

earning determination used in this study), thereby reducing the sample to 439,959 cases. Finally, to estimate the net effect of ethnicity on earnings with educational categories, we employed linear least-squares regression with logarithms of earnings as the dependent variable..., and this meant persons with zero or negative earnings had to be eliminated. This further reduced the sample to 425,107 persons.

REFERENCES

Agocs, C., and M. Boyd. 1993. The Canadian ethnic mosaic recast for the 1990s. In *Social inequality in Canada: Patterns, problems, policies,* eds. J. Curtis, E. Grabb, and N. Guppy, 330–60. Scarborough, Ont.: Prentice-Hall Canada Inc..

Barringer, H., and G. Kassebaum. 1989. Asian Indians as a minority in the United States: The effects of education, occupations and gender on income. *Sociological Perspectives,* 32(4): 501–20.

Beggs, J. J. 1995. The institutional environment: Implications for race and gender inequality in the U.S. labour market. *American Sociological Review,* 60 (August): 612–33.

Boyd, M., J. Goyder, F. E. Jones, H. A. McRoberts, P. C. Pineo, and J. Porter. 1981. Status attainment in Canada: Findings of the Canadian mobility study. *Canadian Review of Sociology and Anthropology,* 18(5): 657–73.

Breton, R., and H. Roseborough. 1971. Ethnic differences in status. In *Canadian society: Sociological perspectives,* eds. B. R. Blishen, F. E. Jones, K. D. Naegele, and J. Porter, 450–68. Toronto: Macmillan of Canada Ltd.

Darroch, A. G. 1979. Another look at ethnicity, stratification and social mobility in Canada. *Canadian Journal of Sociology,* 4(1): 1–24.

Featherman, D. L., and R. M. Hauser. 1978. *Opportunity and change.* New York: Academic Press.

Fox, B. J. and J. Fox. 1986. Women in the labour market, 1931–81: Exclusion and competition. *The Canadian Review of Sociology and Anthropology,* 23(1): 1–21.

Geschwender, J. A., and N. Guppy. 1995. Ethnicity, educational attainment and earned income among Canadian-born men and women. *Canadian Ethnic Studies,* 27(1): 67–84.

Halvorsen, R., and R. Palmquist. 1980. The interpretation of dummy variables in semilogarithmic equations. *American Economic Review,* 70(3): 474–75.

Herberg, E. N. 1990. The ethno-racial socioeconomic hierarchy in Canada: Theory and analysis of the new vertical mosaic. *International Journal of Comparative Sociology,* 31(3–4): 206–20.

Isajiw, W. W., A. Sev'er, and L. Dreidger. 1993. Ethnic identity and social mobility: A test of the "drawback model." *Canadian Journal of Sociology,* 18(2): 177–96.

Jabbra, N. W., and R. L. Cosper. 1988. Ethnicity in Atlantic Canada: A survey. *Canadian Ethnic Studies,* 20(3): 6–27.

Lautard, E. H., and N. Guppy. 1990. The vertical mosaic revisited: Occupational differentials among Canadian ethnic groups. In *Race and ethnic relations in Canada,* ed. P. S. Li, 189–208. Toronto: Oxford University Press.

Lautard, E. H., and D. J. Loree. 1984. Ethnic stratification in Canada, 1931–1971. *Canadian Journal of Sociology,* 9: 333–43.

Li, P. S. 1988. *Ethnic inequality in a class society.* Toronto: Thompson Educational Publishing Inc.

Nakhaie, M. R. 1995. Ownership and management position of Canadian ethnic groups in 1973 and 1989. *Canadian Journal of Sociology,* 20(2): 167–92.

Ornstein, M. D. 1981. The occupational mobility of men in Ontario. *The Canadian Review of Sociology and Anthropology,* 18(2): 181–215.

Pineo, P. C. 1976. Social mobility in Canada: The current picture. *Sociological Focus,* 9(2): 109–23.

Pineo, P. C., and J. Porter. 1985. Ethnic origin and occupational attainment. In *Ascription and achievement: Studies in mobility and status attainment in Canada,* eds. M. Boyd, J. Goyder, F. E. Jones, H. A. McRoberts, P. C. Pineo, and J. Porter, 357–92. Ottawa: Carleton University Press.

Porter, J. 1965. *The vertical mosaic.* Toronto: University of Toronto Press.

Reitz, J. G. 1980. *The survival of ethnic groups.* Toronto: McGraw-Hill Ryerson, Ltd.

Royal Commission on Bilingualism and Biculturalism, Canada. 1969. *Report of the Royal Commission on Bilingualism and Biculturalism,* Vol. 3A. Ottawa: Queen's Printer.

Sandefur, G. D., and W. J. Scott. 1983. Minority group status and the wages of Indian and Black males. *Social Science Research,* 12(1): 44–68.

Shamai, S. 1992. Ethnicity and educational achievement in Canada: 1941–1981. *Canadian Ethnic Studies,* 24(1): 41–57.

Statistics Canada. 1993. *Standard occupational classification, 1991.* Ottawa: Ministry of Industry, Science and Technology.

———. 1994. *User documentation for public use microdata file for individuals, 1991 Census.* Catalogue No.: 48-030E. Ottawa: Statistics Canada.

Tepperman, L. 1975. *Social mobility in Canada.* Toronto: McGraw-Hill Ryerson.

Winn, C. 1988. The socio-economic attainment of visible minorities: Facts and policy implications. In *Social inequality in Canada: Patterns, problems, policies,* eds. J. Curtis, E. Grabb, N. Guppy, and S. Gilbert, 195–213. Scarborough, Ont.: Prentice-Hall Canada.

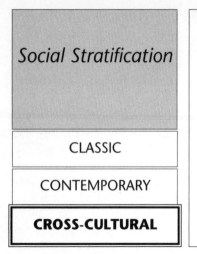

Social Stratification

CLASSIC

CONTEMPORARY

CROSS-CULTURAL

33

The Uses of Global Poverty: How Economic Inequality Benefits the West

Daina Stukuls Eglitis

Why don't rich nations do more to reduce the severe poverty that paralyzes much of the world? This selection argues that people in rich countries, including the United States, actually benefit from global poverty in several ways.

In the global village, there stand a wide variety of homes, from the stately mansion on the hill, to the modest abode blessed with electricity and running water, to the adequate but unheated (or uncooled) hut, to the flood-prone, tattered shanty cobbled together from gathered scrap. Those who live on the hill are aware of their neighbors, as their neighbors are aware of them. Most inhabitants of the global village recognize that wealth and the accompanying opportunities for education, health care, and consumption are not evenly divided and that a substantial gap exists between the more and less materially blessed populations. Not everyone agrees on why that is the case.

Consider the following comparisons of life in the global village: In 1999, the gross national income in purchasing power parity (GNI PPP)[1] in the United States was $31,910. In Germany the figure was $23,510, and in Australia, $23,850. By contrast, the GNI PPP of China was $3,550, in Indonesia it was $2,660, and in Pakistan, $1,860. On the bottom tier of states, we find countries like

Source: Prepared by the author for this book.

Nigeria with a GNI of $770 and Sierra Leone with just $440. If we use the GNI PPP as a yardstick of economic power and the well-being of populations, we may begin to construct a picture of a global system characterized by the massive maldistribution of wealth, economic security, and purchasing power. Our village is one characterized by deep and fundamental stratification.

What have been the responses of well-off states to this global class system with its extremes of wealth and poverty? Not surprisingly, perhaps, political rhetoric has consistently elevated the goal of spreading the prosperity enjoyed by the advanced industrial states of the West around the globe. In remarks made at the United States Coast Guard Academy commencement ceremony in 1989, President George Bush phrased it this way: "What is it that we want to see? It is a growing community of democracies anchoring international peace and stability, and a dynamic free-market system generating prosperity and progress on a global scale.... If we succeed, the next decade and the century beyond will be an era of unparalleled growth, an era which sees the flourishing of freedom, peace, and prosperity around the world."

If shared global prosperity was the goal, it seems safe to say that while there was some modest progress made in areas like Latin America, Eastern Europe, and parts of Asia, "we" did not really succeed, because the global wealth gap is still massive and growing. The rich countries remain rich, and the poor countries, for the most part, remain trapped in desperate, dire poverty.

This has not changed.

Another thing that has not changed is the rhetorical commitment to spreading the wealth.

In a speech in Coventry, England, in December 2000, President Bill Clinton laid out a "prescription for how the United States might help close the gap between rich and poor nations." And in his farewell address to the nation in January 2001, the President declared that "the global gap requires more than compassion. It requires action." As of 2002, President George W. Bush has not addressed the question of non-Western development specifically, though it seems relatively safe to say that he too will join the political chorus of support for global prosperity, although his administration seems destined to be defined by a focus on war rather than development.

Western rhetoric, assistance programs, and advice seem to support the goal of global prosperity and its extension to the 1.3 billion who live on less than $1 per day and those millions or even billions more who eke out a sparse existence just above the threshold of absolute poverty. But the reality of prosperity has touched only a relative few countries, while the struggle to meet basic needs touches many more. Social indicators like the GNI PPP highlight the differences we find in our village. But what explains them? Why does global poverty exist and persist? Why does a global class system with a thin layer of rich states and a broad strata of poor countries exist and persist? What explains why some villagers inhabit houses on the mount while others squat in mud huts below? Possible answers are many. This article explores one way

of understanding the yawning gap between the planet's wealthiest and poorest states.

In 1971, sociologist Herbert Gans published an article entitled "The Uses of Poverty: The Poor Pay All."[2] In the article, Gans utilized a conservative theoretical perspective in sociology, functionalism, to inquire about the persistence of poverty in America. The functionalist perspective takes as its starting point the position that essentially all institutions and social phenomena that exist in society contribute in some manner to that society—that is, they are functional for society. If they did not contribute to the social order, the functionalists maintain, they would disappear. Using this perspective, functionalists may inquire about, for instance, the functions, both obvious and hidden (or manifest and latent, to use sociologist Robert Merton's terms), of institutions like the education system or the family or social phenomena like punishment for deviance. These social theorists assume that institutions or phenomena exist because they are functional, and hence their guiding question is, What function do they serve?

Gans posed a similar question about poverty, asking, What are the uses of poverty? Clearly, the notion that poverty is functional for society as a whole is ludicrous: Who would suggest that it is functional for those who endure economic deprivation? So Gans offered a modified functionalist analysis: "...instead of identifying functions for an entire social system, I shall identify them for the interest groups, socioeconomic classes, and other population aggregates with shared values that 'inhabit' a social system. I suspect that in a modern heterogeneous society, few phenomena are functional or dysfunctional for the society as a whole, and that most result in benefits to some groups and costs to others."

Gans sought to explain the existence and persistence of poverty in modern, wealthy America by highlighting the way that the existence of poverty has benefits for the nonpoor—not just "evil" individuals like the loan shark or the slum lord, but for "normal" members of nonpoor classes. He identified thirteen "uses" of poverty, including the notions that the existence of a poor class "ensures that society's 'dirty work' will be done," that "the poor buy goods others do not want and thus prolong the economic usefulness of such goods," and "the poor can be identified and punished as alleged or real deviants in order to uphold the legitimacy of conventional norms." He was not arguing that poverty is good. He was suggesting that understanding poverty's existence and persistence mean recognizing that the poor have positive social and economic functions for the nonpoor. Thus, one would conclude that the elimination of poverty, while elevated as a societal goal, would be, in practice, costly to the nonpoor.

While Gans's theoretically based inquiry into poverty was focused on America's poor, the same question might be asked about the existence of global poverty: What are the "uses" of global poverty for the better-off countries of the world economic system? The purpose of such an inquiry would be, as it was in Gans's inquiry, not to use a functionalist analysis to legitimate poverty or the highly skewed distribution of wealth in the global system, but to contribute to a deeper understanding of why it continues to exist by explaining how its persistence confers benefits on well-off states and their inhabitants.

The argument is not that advanced states are consciously conspiring to keep the poor states destitute: Well-off countries have historically sought to offer help to less developed countries. In reality, however, there are limited incentives for the better-off states to support the full industrial and technological (and even democratic) development of all the states in the global system. To the degree that the existence of a class of poor states is positively functional for wealthy states, we can begin to imagine why development and assistance programs that help ensure survival, but not prosperity, for poor populations are quite characteristic of Western policy.

This article notes eleven "uses" of global poverty. Global poverty is not, from this perspective, functional for the global community as a whole. The notion that the poverty of billions who live in economically marginal states is globally "useful" would be absurd. But it is not absurd to ask how the existence of a class of poor states serves wealthy states. In fact, asking such a question might contribute to a better understanding of the dual phenomena of global poverty and the global "class" system.

Point 1: The existence of global poverty helps ensure the wealth of affordable goods for Western consumers.

The cornucopia of decently priced goods of reasonable quality enjoyed by Western consumers is underpinned by the low-wage work done in low-income countries. The labels on the clothing you are wearing right now likely contain the familiar words "Made in China" or perhaps "Made in Pakistan." Your clothing is probably of reasonable quality, and you likely paid a reasonable (but not necessarily cheap) price for it.

The Western consumer of textiles such as off-the-rack clothing is a beneficiary of a globalized manufacturing process that has seen the movement of manufacturing to low-wage areas located in poor states that provide ready pools of workers needy enough to labor for pittance. In China, the average hourly wage of apparel workers is about 23 cents. This benefits the consumer of that apparel. The worker herself (workers in this industry are usually female) derives less benefit: The average hourly wage needed to meet basic needs in China, according to Women's Edge, an advocacy group, is 87 cents.[3]

Another way that the impoverished workers of the third world help reduce the cost of goods coming to Western consumers is through their agricultural labor. For instance, the comparably (and sometimes illegally) low wages paid to many poor migrant farm workers from Mexico and Central America in states like California contribute to America's ample and reasonably priced food supply.

Stories about low-wage workers in developing countries have, in recent years, emerged in the Western press and provoked some expressions of outrage and the formation of groups like United Students Against Sweatshops. These expressions have been small and limited. Imagine, however, the outrage if popular sports shoes, already pricey, climbed another $50 in cost as a result of manufacturers opting for well-paid, unionized labor. Or imagine if the price of a head of iceberg lettuce, America's favorite vegetable, suddenly doubled in price to $3.00. Which outrage would be more potent?

Point 2: The existence of global poverty benefits Western companies and shareholders in the form of increased profit margins.

Labor costs typically constitute a high percentage of a company's expenditures. By reducing labor costs, companies can both keep prices reasonable (which benefits, as noted, the consumer) and raise profit margins. Not surprisingly, then, companies are not likely to locate in—and are more likely to leave—locations where wages are relatively high. The use of poor female workers in the third world is, in this respect, especially "beneficial" to companies. Women comprise about 80 percent of workers in Export Processing Zones and are often paid 20 percent to 50 percent less than male counterparts. The less costly the workforce, the greater the opportunity for profit. Not coincidentally, countries with an ample supply of poor workers willing to work for miserable wages are also countries with lax safety and environmental regulations, which also keeps down the costs to the Western employer and pushes up the profits. Hence, companies benefit directly from the existence of economically deprived would-be workers willing (or not in a position to be unwilling) to work for paltry wages in potentially hazardous, or at least very unpleasant, conditions.

Point 3: The existence of global poverty fosters access to resources in poor states that are needed in or desired by the West.

Poor states may sell raw goods at low prices to Western states, which can transform the resource into a more valuable finished product. The position of the poor states in the world economy makes it less likely that they can derive the full benefit of the resources they possess for the government and people. The case of oil in resource-rich but desperately poor Nigeria is an example. Seven major foreign oil companies operate in Nigeria, all representing interests in wealthy states. The vast majority of benefits from Nigeria's oil has accrued not to the country's people, but to the companies (and consumers) of the wealthy states. There is no attempt to hide this: John Connor, head of Texaco's worldwide exploration and production, talking about a massive oil strike in January 2000, stated that the successful conclusion of the well test "sets the stage for development of a world-class project that will add substantially to the company's resource base."[4] Clearly, the failure of Nigeria's people to benefit from the country's resources is also linked to a succession of corrupt governments, but the poverty of the masses and the powerful position of oil companies help to ensure that resistance to exploitation of resources for the benefit for non-Nigerian interests will be marginal.

Point 4: The existence of global poverty helps support Western medical advances.

The poor provide a pool of guinea pigs for the testing of medicines developed for use primarily in the West. The beneficiaries are not the poor themselves but Western consumers of advanced medicine (60 percent of profits are made in the United States, which leads the world in drug consumption) and the pharmaceutical companies, which stand astride a $350 billion (and growing) industry. A series of reports in the *Washington Post* in December 2000 documents the disturbing practice of conducting drug trials on ill inhabitants of poor states. For instance, an unapproved antibiotic was tested by a major pharmaceutical company on sick children during a meningitis epidemic in Nigeria. The country's lax regulatory oversight, the sense among some doctors that they could not object to experiment conditions for political or economic reasons, the dearth of alternative health care options, combined with the desire of the company to rapidly prepare for the market a potential "blockbuster" drug underpinned a situation in which disease victims were treated as test subjects rather than patients. This case highlights the way that nonpoor states actually benefit from the existence of poor states with struggling, sick populations. A reporter for the series noted that "companies use the tests to produce new product and revenue streams, but they are also responding to pressure from regulators, Congress, and lobbyists for disease victims to develop new medicines quickly. By providing huge pools of human subjects, foreign trials help speed new drugs to the marketplace—where they will be sold mainly to patients in wealthy countries."[5]

Point 5: The existence of global poverty contributes to the advancement of Western economies and societies with the human capital of poor states.

Poorer states like India have become intellectual feeders of well-educated and bright individuals whose skills cannot be fully rewarded in less developed states. The magnetic draw of a better life in economies that amply reward their human capital pulls the brightest minds from their countries of origin, a process referred to as "brain drain." Advanced economies such as the United States and England are beneficiaries of brain drain. The United States has moved to take advantage of the pool of highly educated workers from the developing world: Congress has passed legislation increasing the number of H-1B visas, or "high-tech visas," to bring up to 600,000 workers to the United States over the next several years.

The United States and England offer attractive opportunities to highly educated workers from poorer states. Notably, high-tech companies often pay the foreign workers less than their domestic equivalents would demand.

Point 6: The existence of global poverty may contribute to the pacification of the Western proletariat, or "Workers of the World, A Blue Light Special!"

To some degree, the broad availability of good, inexpensive merchandise may help obscure class divisions in the West, at least in the arena of consumption. It is clear that those with greater wealth can consume more high-quality goods, but low-end "designer" merchandise is accessible to the less well-off in cathedrals of consumption such as Wal-Mart. At K-Mart, for instance, Martha Stewart peddles her wares, intended to transform "homemaking chores…into what we like to call 'domestic art.'" "Thanks in part to the low-wage workers in places like China, these goods are available to the unwashed masses (now washed by Martha's smart and cozy towels) as well as to better-situated homemakers. Consumption appears to be one of the great equalizers of modern society. (It is worth noting, though, that many members of the Western working class are also "victims" of global poverty, since many jobs have gone abroad to low-wage areas, leaving behind, for less educated workers, positions in the less remunerative and less secure service industry or leaving former industrial workers jobless.)

Point 7: Global poverty benefits the West because poor countries make optimal dumping grounds for goods that are dangerous, expired, or illegal.

Wealthy countries and their inhabitants may utilize poorer states as repositories for dangerous or unwanted material such as nuclear waste. The desperation of cash-strapped states benefits better-off countries, which might otherwise have difficulty ridding themselves of the dangerous by-products of their industrial and consumer economies. For instance, in December 2000, the Russian Parliament, in an initial vote on the issue, overwhelmingly supported the amendment of an environmental law to permit the importation of foreign nuclear waste. The alteration of the law was supported by the Atomic Ministry of the Russian Federation, which suggested that over the next decade, Russia might earn up to $21 billion from the importation of spent nuclear fuel from states like Japan, Germany, and South Korea. Likely repositories of the radioactive refuse are Mayak and Krasnoyarsk, already among the most contaminated sites on the planet.

India has also emerged as a dumping ground for hazardous junk from the world's industrial giants. The western Indian city of Alang, for instance, is host to the world's largest shipbreaking yard, where Western-owned ships are sent for dismantling and, ostensibly, recycling. The process of "breaking" the old vessels, however, endangers workers and the environment because it releases asbestos, PCBs, and other toxic wastes.[6]

Point 8: The existence of global poverty provides jobs for specialists employed to assist, advise, and study the world's poor and to protect the "better-off" from them.

Within this group of specialists we find people in a variety of professions. There are those who are professional development workers, operating through organizations like the United States Agency for International Development (USAID) to further "America's foreign policy interests in expanding democracy and free markets while improving the lives of the citizens of the developing world."[7] The Peace Corps is also built around the goal of bringing Western "know-how" to the poor with volunteer programs that promote entrepreneurship and agricultural development.

Academics in fields as diverse as economics, sociology, international affairs, political science,

and anthropology study, write about, and "decipher" the lives of the poor and the condition of poor states. Texts on development, articles debating why poverty persists, and books from university presses are only some of the products of this research. Journalists and novelists can build careers around bringing colorful, compelling representations of the poor to the warm living rooms of literate, well-off consumers. Still others are charged with the task of protecting wealthy states from "invasions" of the poor: U.S. border patrols, for instance, employ thousands to keep those seeking better fortunes out of U.S. territory.

Point 9: Global poverty benefits inhabitants of wealthy countries, who can feel good about helping the global poor through charitable work and charitable giving.

From the celebrity-studded musical production "We are the World" to trick-or-treating for UNICEF, those who inhabit the wealthy corners of the world feel good about themselves for sharing their good fortune. The Web site of World Vision, a faith-based charity that offers the opportunity to sponsor poor children, features a speak-out area for contributors. On that site, a young Canadian sponsor wrote, "A few days ago I woke up early and turned the TV on…looking at those children made me realize I could help them. I thought if I have enough money to pay for the Internet, cell phone, and a couple of other things I didn't need, I said to myself, [then] why not give that money to people who need it instead of spending it all in [*sic*] luxury and things that are not really important.… I immediately picked up the phone and called to sponsor a child! I am happy. I can help someone who needs it!"[8]

Apparently, we need not feel guilt about consuming many times what the unfortunate inhabitants of the world's poor states do if only we are willing to give up a few of our luxuries to help them. Indeed, not only do the poor not inspire guilt, they may inspire positive feelings: As the World Vision writer notes, she feels "happy" because she can "help someone who needs it." No less a figure than the world's richest man, Bill Gates, is also "dedicated to improving people's lives by sharing advances in health and learning with the global community" through the Gates Foundation.[9]

A related point is that the poor we see on television or hear about in news or music give those of us in wealthy countries the opportunity to feel good about ourselves, regardless of our position in the socioeconomic structure of our own states. Consider the memorable lines from the 1985 Band-Aid song, "Do They Know It's Christmas?" which was produced by British pop artist Bob Geldof as a charitable act to raise money for Ethiopia's famine victims: "And the Christmas bells that ring there are the clanging chimes of doom. Well, tonight, thank God, it's them instead of you." Indeed, even the underpaid blue- or pink-collar worker in the West can relate to that sentiment.

Point 10: The poverty of less-developed states makes possible the massive flow of resources westward.

Imagine if large and largely poor countries like China, Nigeria, and India consumed at U.S. rates. At present, Americans consume a tremendously disproportionate share of the world's resources. With their profligate use of all manner of resources, most notably fossil fuels, Americans are the greediest consumers of natural resources on the planet. On both an absolute and per capita basis, most world resources flow westward. Notably, an October 4, 2000, article in the *Seattle Times* reported that bicycles, long a characteristic and popular means of transport for Chinese commuters, are losing popularity: "Increasingly, young Chinese are not even bothering to learn to ride bikes, because growing wealth has unleashed a plethora of transportation choices, public and private."[10] The new transportation of choice is still largely public buses or private taxis; the Chinese have not yet graduated to mass private cars. But it is interesting to ponder whether there would be enough (affordable) oil for everyone if the

Chinese, with their growing population and prosperity, became a country of two-vehicle families or developed a taste and market for gas-guzzling sports utility vehicles. In this case, the West likely benefits from the fact that few can afford (at least at present) to consume at the rate its people do.

Point 11: The poorer countries, which reproduce at rates higher than Western states, are useful scapegoats for real and potential global environmental threats.

What is the bigger environmental threat to our planet? Is it the rapid growth of the populations of developing states or the rapid consumption of resources by the much smaller populations of developed states? The overdevelopment of the West may well be the bigger threat, though the growth of populations in third-world countries, which is often linked to conditions of underdevelopment, such as a lack of birth control and the need to have "extra" children as a hedge against high child mortality rates, makes an attractive alternative explanation for those who would not wish to fault the SUV-driving, disposable-diaper using, BBQ-loving American consumer for threats to the global environment. While some Western policymakers express concern about the environmental threats emerging from rapid population growth or the use of "dirty" technology in developing states, there is comparably little serious attention given to the global threat presented by the profligate consumption by Western states. The poor divert attention from the environmental problems caused by Western overconsumption.

I have talked about eleven ways that the continued existence of global poverty benefits those who reside in wealthy states. The argument I have offered to explain the persistence of a strata of poor states and the yawning global gap highlights the idea that while global poverty (and the status quo) is beneficial to the wealthy West, serious steps to alleviate it will not be taken. It is surely the case that poverty does not have to exist. But while we in the West derive the benefits and bonuses of these economic inequalities, it seems likely that our efforts to support, advise, and assist the less developed states will remain at levels that are financially and politically convenient and feasible, and will target survival rather than true prosperity for those outside our gated, privileged, greedy Western neighborhood. In Gans's words, "Phenomena like poverty can be eliminated only when they become dysfunctional for the affluent or powerful, or when the powerless can obtain enough power to change society."

CRITICAL THINKING QUESTIONS

1. The author describes several ways in which people in rich nations benefit from global poverty. Which do you find most convincing? Why?

2. What weaknesses do you find in the arguments? Explain.

3. Do you think that rich countries provide assistance to poor countries? If so, in what ways? If not, why?

NOTES

1. The figures in this paragraph come from the Population Research Bureau Web site at **http://www.prb.org**, which provides excellent demographic data. According to the PRB, the "GNI PPP per capita is gross national income in purchasing power parity divided by mid-year population.... GNI PPP refers to gross national income converted to 'international' dollars using a purchasing power parity conversion factor. International dollars indicate the amount of goods or services one could buy in the United States with a given amount of money. GNI PPP provides an indicator of the welfare of people that is comparable across countries free of price and exchange rate distortions that occur when GNI is converted using market exchange rates."

2. *Social Policy,* July/August 1971.

3. Information on issues of trade and Chinese women is available at **http://www.womensedge.org**. The information cited is from the April 2000 Web issue of *Notes from the Edge*.

4. "Texaco in massive oil strike in Nigeria" in *The Namibian*, available online at **http://www.namibian.com.na/Netstories/2000/January/Marketplace/texaco.html**.

5. Stephens, Joe, "As Drug Testing Spreads, Profits and Lives Hang in Balance," *Washington Post*, (December 2000): A1.

6. Information on both issues is available at the Web site of the environmental group Greenpeace at **http://www.greenpeace.org**.

7. The Web site address is **http://www.usaid.gov**.

8. The charity's Web site address is **http://www.worldvision.org**.

9. The foundation is at **http://www.gatesfoundation.org**.

10. The article is cited at the Web site of the Competitive Enterprise Institute: **http://www.cei.org/CHNReader.asp?ID=1227**.

34

Sex and Temperament in Three Primitive Societies

Margaret Mead

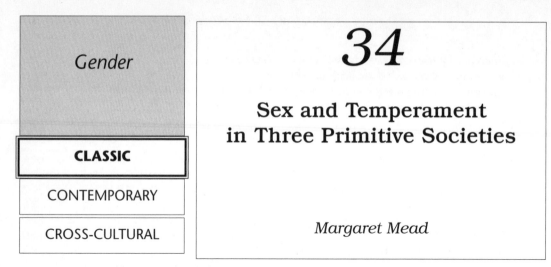

The work of anthropologist Margaret Mead laid the foundation for much of our contemporary sociological research and debate on gender. Are "masculine" and "feminine" traits innate or learned? Do men and women differ because of nature (heredity) or nurture (socialization)? Based on her studies of three "primitive peoples" in New Guinea, Margaret Mead argues that cultural conditioning is more important than biology in shaping behaviour.

We have…considered in detail the approved personalities of each sex among three primitive peoples. We found the Arapesh—both men and women—displaying a personality that, out of our historically limited preoccupations, we would call maternal in its parental aspects, and feminine in its sexual aspects. We found men, as well as women, trained to be cooperative, unaggressive, responsive to the needs and demands of others. We found no idea that sex was a powerful driving force either for men or for women. In marked contrast to these attitudes, we found among the Mundugumor that both men and women developed as ruthless, aggressive, positively sexed individuals, with the maternal cherishing aspects of personality at a minimum. Both men and women approximated to a personality type that we in our culture would find only in an undisciplined and very violent male. Neither the Arapesh nor the Mundugumor profit by a contrast between the sexes; the Arapesh ideal is the mild, responsive man married to the mild, responsive woman; the Mundugumor ideal is the violent aggressive man married to the violent aggressive woman. In the third tribe, the Tchambuli, we found a genuine reversal of the sex attitudes of our own culture, with the woman the dominant, impersonal, managing partner, the man the less responsible and the emotionally dependent person. These three situations suggest, then, a very definite conclusion. If those temperamental attitudes which

we have traditionally regarded as feminine—such as passivity, responsiveness, and a willingness to cherish children—can so easily be set up as the masculine pattern in one tribe, and in another be outlawed for the majority of women as well as for the majority of men, we no longer have any basis for regarding such aspects of behaviour as sex-linked. And this conclusion becomes even stronger when we consider the actual reversal in Tchambuli of the position of dominance of the two sexes, in spite of the existence of formal patrilineal institutions.

The material suggests that we may say that many, if not all, of the personality traits which we have called masculine or feminine are as lightly linked to sex as are the clothing, the manners, and the form of head-dress that a society at a given period assigns to either sex. When we consider the behaviour of the typical Arapesh man or woman as contrasted with the behaviour of the typical Mundugumor man or woman, the evidence is overwhelmingly in favour of the strength of social conditioning. In no other way can we account for the almost complete uniformity with which Arapesh children develop into contented, passive, secure persons, while Mundugumor children develop as characteristically into violent, aggressive, insecure persons. Only to the impact of the whole of the integrated culture upon the growing child can we lay the formation of the contrasting types. There is no other explanation of race, or diet, or selection that can be adduced to explain them. We are forced to conclude that human nature is almost unbelievably malleable, responding accurately and contrastingly to contrasting cultural conditions. The differences between individuals who are members of different cultures, like the differences between individuals within a culture, are almost entirely to be laid to differences in conditioning, especially during early childhood, and the form of this conditioning is culturally determined. Standardized personality differences between the sexes are of this order, cultural creations to which each generation, male and

female, is trained to conform. There remains, however, the problem of the origin of these socially standardized differences.

While the basic importance of social conditioning is still imperfectly recognized—not only in lay thought, but even by the scientist specifically concerned with such matters—to go beyond it and consider the possible influence of variations in hereditary equipment is a hazardous matter. The following pages will read very differently to one who has made a part of his thinking a recognition of the whole amazing mechanism of cultural conditioning—who has really accepted the fact that the same infant could be developed into a full participant in any one of these three cultures—than they will read to one who still believes that the minutiae of cultural behaviour are carried in the individual germ-plasm. If it is said, therefore, that when we have grasped the full significance of the malleability of the human organism and the preponderant importance of cultural conditioning, there are still further problems to solve, it must be remembered that these problems come *after* such a comprehension of the force of conditioning; they cannot precede it. The forces that make children born among the Arapesh grow up into typical Arapesh personalities are entirely social, and any discussion of the variations which do occur must be looked at against this social background.

With this warning firmly in mind, we can ask a further question. Granting the malleability of human nature, whence arise the differences between the standardized personalities that different cultures decree for all of their members, or which one culture decrees for the members of one sex as contrasted with the members of the opposite sex? If such differences are culturally created, as this material would most strongly suggest that they are, if the new-born child can be shaped with equal ease into an unaggressive Arapesh or an aggressive Mundugumor, why do these striking contrasts occur at all? If the clues to the different personalities decreed for men and women in Tchambuli do not lie in the physical constitution of the two sexes—an assumption that we must reject both for the Tchambuli and for our own society—where can we find the clues upon which the Tchambuli, the Arapesh, the Mundugumor, have built? Cultures are manmade, they are built of human materials; they are diverse but comparable structures within which human beings can attain full human stature. Upon what have they built their diversities?

We recognize that a homogeneous culture committed in all of its gravest institutions and slightest usages to a cooperative, unaggressive course can bend every child to that emphasis, some to a perfect accord with it, the majority to an easy acceptance, while only a few deviants fail to receive the cultural imprint. To consider such traits as aggressiveness or passivity to be sex-linked is not possible in the light of the facts. Have such traits, then, as aggressiveness or passivity, pride or humility, objectivity or a preoccupation with personal relationships, an easy response to the needs of the young and the weak or a hostility to the young and the weak, a tendency to initiate sex-relations or merely to respond to the dictates of a situation or another person's advances—have these traits any basis in temperament at all? Are they potentialities of all human temperaments that can be developed by different kinds of social conditioning and which will not appear if the necessary conditioning is absent?

When we ask this question we shift our emphasis. If we ask why an Arapesh man or an Arapesh woman shows the kind of personality that we have considered in the first section of this book, the answer is: Because of the Arapesh culture, because of the intricate, elaborate, and unfailing fashion in which a culture is able to shape each new-born child to the cultural image. And if we ask the same question about a Mundugumor man or woman, or about a Tchambuli man as compared with a Tchambuli woman, the answer is of the same kind. They display the personalities that are peculiar to the cultures in which they were born and educated. Our attention has been on the differences

between Arapesh men and women as a group and Mundugumor men and women as a group. It is as if we had represented the Arapesh personality by a soft yellow, the Mundugumor by a deep red, while the Tchambuli female personality was deep orange, and that of the Tchambuli male, pale green. But if we now ask whence came the original direction in each culture, so that one now shows yellow, another red, the third orange and green by sex, then we must peer more closely. And leaning closer to the picture, it is as if behind the bright consistent yellow of the Arapesh, and the deep equally consistent red of the Mundugumor, behind the orange and green that are Tchambuli, we found in each case the delicate, just discernible outlines of the whole spectrum, differently overlaid in each case by the monotone which covers it. This spectrum is the range of individual differences which lie back of the so much more conspicuous cultural emphases, and it is to this that we must turn to find the explanation of cultural inspiration, of the source from which each culture has drawn.

There appears to be about the same range of basic temperamental variation among the Arapesh and among the Mundugumor, although the violent man is a misfit in the first society and a leader in the second. If human nature were completely homogeneous raw material, lacking specific drives and characterized by no important constitutional differences between individuals, then individuals who display personality traits so antithetical to the social pressure should not reappear in societies of such differing emphases. If the variations between individuals were to be set down to accidents in the genetic process, the same accidents should not be repeated with similar frequency in strikingly different cultures, with strongly contrasting methods of education.

But because this same relative distribution of individual differences does appear in culture after culture, in spite of the divergence between the cultures, it seems pertinent to offer a hypothesis to explain upon what basis the personalities of men and women have been differently standardized so often in the history of the human race. This hypothesis is an extension of that advanced by Ruth Benedict in her *Patterns of Culture.* Let us assume that there are definite temperamental differences between human beings which if not entirely hereditary at least are established on a hereditary base very soon after birth. (Further than this we cannot at present narrow the matter.) These differences finally embodied in the character structure of adults, then, are the clues from which culture works, selecting one temperament, or a combination of related and congruent types, as desirable, and embodying this choice in every thread of the social fabric—in the care of the young child, the games the children play, the songs the people sing, the structure of political organization, the religious observance, the art and the philosophy.

Some primitive societies have had the time and the robustness to revamp all of their institutions to fit one extreme type, and to develop educational techniques which will ensure that the majority of each generation will show a personality congruent with this extreme emphasis. Other societies have pursued a less definitive course, selecting their models not from the most extreme, most highly differentiated individuals, but from the less marked types. In such societies the approved personality is less pronounced, and the culture often contains the types of inconsistencies that many human beings display also; one institution may be adjusted to the uses of pride, another to a casual humility that is congruent neither with pride nor with inverted pride. Such societies, which have taken the more usual and less sharply defined types as models, often show also a less definitely patterned social structure. The culture of such societies may be likened to a house the decoration of which has been informed by no definite and precise taste, no exclusive emphasis upon dignity or comfort or pretentiousness or beauty, but in which a little of each effect has been included.

Alternatively, a culture may take its clues not from one temperament, but from several temperaments. But instead of mixing together into an inconsistent hotchpotch the choices and emphases of different temperaments, or blending them together into a smooth but not particularly distinguished whole, it may isolate each type by making it the basis for the approved social personality for an age-group, a sex-group, a caste-group, or an occupational group. In this way society becomes not a monotone with a few discrepant patches of an intrusive colour, but a mosaic, with different groups displaying different personality traits. Such specializations as these may be based upon any facet of human endowment—different intellectual abilities, different artistic abilities, different emotional traits. So the Samoans decree that all young people must show the personality trait of unaggressiveness and punish with opprobrium the aggressive child who displays traits regarded as appropriate only in titled middle-aged men. In societies based upon elaborate ideas of rank, members of the aristocracy will be permitted, even compelled, to display a pride, a sensitivity to insult, that would be deprecated as inappropriate in members of the plebeian class. So also in professional groups or in religious sects some temperamental traits are selected and institutionalized, and taught to each new member who enters the profession or sect. Thus the physician learns the bedside manner, which is the natural behaviour of some temperaments and the standard behaviour of the general practitioner in the medical profession; the Quaker learns at least the outward behaviour and the rudiments of meditation, the capacity for which is not necessarily an innate characteristic of many of the members of the Society of Friends.

So it is with the social personalities of the two sexes. The traits that occur in some members of each sex are specially assigned to one sex, and disallowed in the other. The history of the social definition of sex-differences is filled with such arbitrary arrangements in the intellectual and artistic field, but because of the assumed congruence between physiological sex and emotional endowment we have been less able to recognize that a similar arbitrary selection is being made among emotional traits also. We have assumed that because it is convenient for a mother to wish to care for her child, this is a trait with which women have been more generously endowed by a carefully teleological process of evolution. We have assumed that because men have hunted, an activity requiring enterprise, bravery, and initiative, they have been endowed with these useful attitudes as part of their sex-temperament.

Societies have made these assumptions both overtly and implicitly. If a society insists that warfare is the major occupation for the male sex, it is therefore insisting that all male children display bravery and pugnacity. Even if the insistence upon the differential bravery of men and women is not made articulate, the difference in occupation makes this point implicitly. When, however, a society goes further and defines men as brave and women as timorous, when men are forbidden to show fear and women are indulged in the most flagrant display of fear, a more explicit element enters in. Bravery, hatred of any weakness, of flinching before pain or danger—this attitude which is so strong a component of *some human* temperaments has been selected as the key to masculine behaviour. The easy unashamed display of fear or suffering that is congenial to a different temperament has been made the key to feminine behaviour.

Originally two variations of human temperament, a hatred of fear or willingness to display fear, they have been socially translated into inalienable aspects of the personalities of the two sexes. And to that defined sex-personality every child will be educated, if a boy, to suppress fear, if a girl, to show it. If there has been no social selection in regard to this trait, the proud temperament that is repelled by any betrayal of feeling will display itself, regardless of sex, by keeping a stiff upper lip. Without an express prohibition of such behaviour the expressive unashamed man or woman will weep, or comment upon fear or suffering. Such attitudes, strongly marked in certain temperaments, may by social selection be

standardized for everyone, or outlawed for everyone, or ignored by society, or made the exclusive and approved behaviour of one sex only.

Neither the Arapesh nor the Mundugumor have made any attitude specific for one sex. All of the energies of the culture have gone towards the creation of a single human type, regardless of class, age, or sex. There is no division into age-classes for which different motives or different moral attitudes are regarded as suitable. There is no class of seers or mediums who stand apart drawing inspiration from psychological sources not available to the majority of the people. The Mundugumor have, it is true, made one arbitrary selection, in that they recognize artistic ability only among individuals born with the cord about their necks, and firmly deny the happy exercise of artistic ability to those less unusually born. The Arapesh boy with a tinea infection has been socially selected to be a disgruntled, antisocial individual, and the society forces upon sunny cooperative children cursed with this affliction a final approximation to the behaviour appropriate to a pariah. With these two exceptions no emotional role is forced upon an individual because of birth or accident. As there is no idea of rank which declares that some are of high estate and some of low, so there is no idea of sex-difference which declares that one sex must feel differently from the other. One possible imaginative social construct, the attribution of different personalities to different members of the community classified into sex-, age-, or caste-groups, is lacking.

When we turn however to the Tchambuli, we find a situation that while bizarre in one respect, seems nevertheless more intelligible in another. The Tchambuli have at least made the point of sex-difference; they have used the obvious fact of sex as an organizing point for the formation of social personality, even though they seem to us to have reversed the normal picture. While there is reason to believe that not every Tchambuli woman is born with a dominating, organizing, administrative temperament, actively sexed and willing to initiate sex-relations, possessive, definite, robust, practical and impersonal in outlook, still most Tchambuli girls grow up to display these traits. And while there is definite evidence to show that all Tchambuli men are not, by native endowment, the delicate responsive actors of a play staged for the women's benefit, still most Tchambuli boys manifest this coquettish play-acting personality most of the time. Because the Tchambuli formulation of sex-attitudes contradicts our usual premises, we can see clearly that Tchambuli culture has arbitrarily permitted certain human traits to women, and allotted others, equally arbitrarily, to men.

CRITICAL THINKING QUESTIONS

1. How do female and male personality traits differ among the Arapesh, the Mundugumor, and the Tchambuli?
2. How does Mead explain these differences? What does she mean, for example, when she states that "human nature is unbelievably malleable to cultural conditions"?
3. Most people in North America still describe men as aggressive, strong, confident, and ambitious while characterizing women as emotional, talkative, romantic, and nurturing. Does this mean that biology is more important than environment in shaping our personality and behaviour?

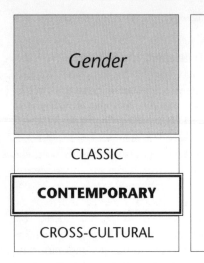

35

Playing by the Rules of the Game: Women's Experiences and Perceptions of Sexual Harassment in Sport

Vivian Krauchek and Gillian Ranson*

In this reading, Krauchek and Ranson investigate the experiences of female athletes in the male-dominated world of elite sport. Through their interviews of female athletes, they uncover a wide variety of examples of gender harassment of female athletes by their male coaches.

This paper explores the experiences and perceptions of sexual harassment among women athletes coached by men in the male-dominated world of elite sport. Drawing on interviews with 32 female athletes, we focus on the women's own interpretations of the behaviours they encounter, and locate their experiences of sexual harassment within the broader context of gender harassment and discrimination which shapes much of their experience in sport. We consider the possibility of challenging sexual harassment in sport by changing the terms of women's participation.

―――――――

*The authors would like to thank Barbara Crow, Leslie Miller, Aysan Sev'er and the CRSA reviewers for helpful comments on an earlier draft of this paper. The manuscript of this article was submitted in June 1999 and accepted in August 1999.

Source: Vivian Krauchek and Gillian Ranson. 1999. Playing by the Rules of the Game: Women's Experiences and Perceptions of Sexual Harassment in Sport. *The Canadian Review of Sociology and Anthropology,* 36(4), 585–600. Reprinted by permission of the Canadian Sociology and Anthropology Association.

Sexual harassment has now been established as not merely a personal trouble for individual women but a social problem "rooted in power dynamics" (Sev'er, 1996: 188). However, in spite of the wide variety of sites in which sexual harassment is experienced, much of the scholarly work on the subject has focussed on workplaces and educational institutions.

In this paper, our interest is in the experience of sexual harassment in an environment that has received much less attention. We report here on a study of female athletes coached by men in the male-dominated world of elite sport. Our study is strategic because of the ways coach–athlete relationships, and the sporting context in which they occur, *differ* in important ways from more conventional workplace or educational relationships and settings. First, the authority exerted by the men as coaches is, self-evidently, over women's bodies and the physical performances of those bodies. Second, while the athletes' performances take place in public, much of the "work" to achieve them is not so public. While coaches may share some accountability for their athletes' performances—the "ends" of the relationship—they are generally not accountable for what happens off the field. Brackenridge (1997) describes several features of the coach–athlete relationship that may make female athletes particularly vulnerable to sexual harassment from male coaches: the dependence of the athlete on the coach's expertise—and the heavy pressure *not* to leave the sport or drop out that is placed on highly talented athletes; the construction of coach and team members as "family" and the special intimacy of the coach–athlete relationship; the apolitical, laissez-faire attitude to inequality that makes sport "a particularly active site of social exploitation" (Brackenridge, 1997: 115). On the latter point, Canadian scholars (e.g., Hall et al., 1989; Lenskyj, 1992; Kirby, 1995; Hall, 1995, 1996) point to the general unwillingness of national sports organizations in Canada to view sexual harassment as an institutional, rather than an individual, problem.

Our particular focus on female athletes is not meant to discount the sexual harassment known to have been perpetrated by male coaches against male athletes. It is rather that, as Tomlinson and Yorganci (1997) point out, the relations of power and control that characterize all coach–athlete interactions are particularly acute when the coach is a man and the athlete—competing in male-dominated terrain—is a woman.

SEXUAL HARASSMENT IN SPORT

...Among the earliest scholarly studies of sexual harassment in sport are Lackey's (1990) survey of 264 Nebraska women college and university athletes, and Yorganci's (1993) survey of 149 female athletes in the U.K. Lackey found that at least 20% of the female athletes he surveyed identified harassment as occurring in each of three categories: profanity, intrusive physical contacts (for example, "slapping on the butt"), and demeaning language, in other words language that is "embarrassing,

derogatory, containing sexual innuendoes that male athletes are superior to females" (Lackey, 1990: 23). However, he found his respondents accepted much of the behaviour as "part of the game"; only 17% acknowledged sexual harassment as a problem. In Yorganci's study, 54% of respondents had experienced or knew of someone who had experienced demeaning language, verbal intrusion, physical contact, fondling or pressure to have sexual intercourse from their male coaches. Of these, 43% felt that the behaviour was not sexual harassment. Similar patterns have been reported by Lenskyj (1992), Kirby and Greaves (cited in Smith, 1996), Tomlinson and Yorganci (1997), and Volkwein et al. (1997).

These studies suggest that women in sport, like those studied in other contexts, are not only unwilling to take formal action against their harassers (Fitzgerald et al., 1988; Cairns, 1997; Thomas & Kitzinger, 1997); they are also unwilling to label as sexual harassment many of the behaviours that would certainly be recognized as such both in law and by researchers studying the issue. The various explanations cited for this anomalous situation centre on a recognition of the sporting world as emphatically masculine, and women's participation in it as contingent on their willingness to accept the (masculine) rules of the game.

Male dominance in sport has been demonstrated in the literature on several fronts. Barriers to women's participation in sports, historically on the grounds that it endangered their feminine physiology, have been only slowly and grudgingly removed (Messner, 1992; Hargreaves, 1994). Feminist critics point to the role of the media in sexualizing and trivializing women's athleticism (Lenskyj, 1987; Messner et al., 1993; Hargreaves, 1994; Burton-Nelson, 1994). Other studies note the absence of women in the hierarchies of authority and administration in sport (White & Brackenridge, 1985; Lenskyj, 1992; Hargreaves, 1994; Hall et al., 1989; Hall, 1995, 1996)....

ISSUES IN THE STUDY OF SEXUAL HARASSMENT

...A major problem for researchers is to decide which behaviours should be included in the definition of sexual harassment. Attempts to specify such behaviours (e.g., Fitgerald et al., 1988) have generally proposed a continuum of severity, ranging from the verbal level of sexist and offensive comments, to the more serious level of actual or attempted intercourse. But more recent work by Fitzgerald and her colleagues (Fitzgerald & Hesson-McInnis, 1989; Fitzgerald & Shullman, 1993) suggests that the continuum model over-simplifies what is a multi-dimensional construct. In particular, they draw attention to *gender* harassment as conceptually distinct from the more commonly identified forms of sexual harassment. Gender harassment is exemplified in sexist behaviour or remarks, or gender favouritism (as in the male professor clearly favouring the male students in a co-ed class). There is some dispute about whether the conceptual distinctiveness of gender harassment actually disqualifies it from inclusion in a study of sexual harassment; Gruber (1992), for example, describing his own category of sexual remarks/comments, considers that sexist comments, while contributing to a hostile environment, are not *technically* instances of sexual harassment. However, Fitzgerald and her colleagues clearly locate sexist behaviour, as well as sexually offensive behaviour, within the general category of sexual harassment behaviours known as "conditions of work" or "environment."[1] They argue that until questions about how to study sexual harassment as a *process* are resolved, "[r]esearchers should inquire about the full range of potentially sexually harassing behaviors, from gender harassment to sexual assault" (Fitzgerald & Shullman, 1993: 9).

Exactly how to conduct such inquiry raises the second methodological (and epistemological) question. Critics of much of the survey research on sexual harassment (e.g., Gruber, 1990, 1992; Arvey & Cavanaugh, 1995; Welsh & Nierobisz,

1997) suggest ways to improve surveys. But while useful in helping us to understand the incidence of particular behaviours among large populations, surveys are not always sensitive to the context in which those behaviours occur. More importantly, they are less appropriate tools for exploring individuals' own interpretations of behaviours and contexts.

We draw from the work of Fitzgerald and her colleagues, described above, the need to take account of a wide range of behaviours and contexts. We argue that, in our particular case, local "contexts" of coach–athlete interaction are part of the institutional context of masculine hegemony in sports in which sexual harassment is almost normative. This commits us to a study of sexual harassment which does not bracket off certain specific behaviours for particular attention, but which attempts to explore behaviours and perceptions of behaviours in *both* the local *and* the broader institutional context. In other words, we need to pay close attention to environment, not merely as a category of sexual harassment, but as the place in which it may be cultivated.

We also take seriously the issues related to women's recognition and acknowledgement of sexually harassing behaviours. These issues are critical if social harassment as a problem is to be effectively addressed. A stable finding in the literature, as noted above, is that women generally do *not* see sexual harassment for what it is. To ask, "Why not?" as we wish to do, clearly commits us to a study which also pays close attention to how women *do* see such behaviour, and how they themselves interpret the details and the context of their relationships.

RESEARCH DESIGN AND METHODOLOGY

Our study design is significantly shaped by the two imperatives noted above: the need to pay attention to context, and the need to hear women's own interpretations of it. Our approach was to use a semi-structured interview in which all questions were open-ended. Details of the interview guide are discussed elsewhere (Krauchek, 1999). Briefly, however, we included questions that addressed issues of power and control in the coach–athlete relationship, as well as questions relating to gender and sexuality. While not explicitly asking about sexual harassment, we provided ample opportunity for a discussion of sexually harassing behaviours to emerge. For example, we asked about the coach's coaching style, what he was like outside of sport, whether the athlete's athletic career (or her life) would have looked different had she not worked with the coach, the athlete's image of an ideal coach (and how well the coach in question measured up), whether she had ever thought of quitting (and why), how she would feel about a daughter (or a son) playing with the coach in question.

Interviews were conducted by the first author, herself an athlete who had competed at provincial, national and international levels in her sport, and whose entire sporting career had involved relationships with male coaches. Clearly this experience also informed the interview guide, and shaped "the discourse between interviewer and respondent as they try to make continuing sense of what they are saying to each other" (Mishler, 1986: 53–4). Interviews took place between March and September 1997. All were taped and transcribed verbatim....

EXPERIENCES OF SEXUAL HARASSMENT

In the context of a discussion of sexual harassment by male coaches, it is important to record that of at least some male coaches, only good things were said. Indeed, about a quarter of the women believed that in at least one of their coaches, they had gained a friend and an important figure in their lives. They spoke of some of these coaches as "father figures" whom "everybody really loved," as men to whom they would entrust their children for coaching.

But what also emerged, for about two-thirds of the women, were experiences along the range of sexually harassing behaviours from gender harassment to what Gruber (1992) would call "sexual imposition." A now-retired athlete reported the most serious incident of the study, as follows:

> We were coming back on the plane, it was my second year with him, and I was sitting next to him on the plane. I was awakened by him fondling me, I kid you not, and I just kept my eyes closed and was thinking, "This cannot be happening—he cannot be doing this." His hands were all over, he was rubbing my legs and my stomach. I thought, "This can't be happening to me." So I just got up really quickly and went to the bathroom and then sat down in another seat. I guess I just never thought he would take advantage of me while I was sleeping. I trusted him.... I never thought he'd do that. That blew anything that ever happened between us and anything he ever said to me after that. I can't believe he stepped over this boundary.... I was shattered.

At the time, she took no action. More than a year later, she changed coaches. But the incident clearly sensitized her to the prevalence of sexual harassment in sport. As a coach herself now, she actively counsels the teenage girls she encounters in her sport about who to avoid on the coaching circuit, because "many coaches are male predators."

Five of the women talked about what they described as "womanizing" behaviour on the part of a coach, summed up by one of them as follows:

> [A]t the banquets when he's got a bit of liquor in him he is incredibly opposite from what he always is. He's flirty and he's always touchy-feely when he's dancing with you. I don't like to dance with him..., he'll take your hand and pull you in anyways.

Though "womanizing" behaviour was described similarly by all five women, their reactions to it varied. One said, albeit with a laugh, "I would charge him." One commented that the behaviour showed a side of the coach that she was "a little sceptical or hesitant about"; it was behaviour that made her "shiver a little bit." One commented that "if someone from the outside was looking in, it might not seem appropriate. She added, however, that as long as the offending coach treated her respectfully as coach to athlete, "I don't have a problem with him." The fourth commented that her coach was "actually pretty fun to be around" even though he could sometimes "cross the line" with behaviour that's "not anything big, just a little peck on the cheek," but "somewhat inappropriate or uncharacteristic for a coach, I think." The fifth remarked that she was really "turned off" by the way a former coach "always went after the athletes on the other teams," and this was one reason why she changed coaches. Yet, asked if she would allow him to coach her daughter, she said, "Oh, yes, I think he's fine."

While all these experiences concerned behaviour that was explicitly sexual, and caused some level of discomfort for all the women concerned, none of them *spoke* of "sexual harassment" even though these were the experiences that ought to have been most likely to warrant the label. And there were some startling differences of interpretation, not only between the individual women, but also in the way individual perceptions could be clearly distinguished from how "someone from the outside" might see things. Knowing that someone else might view certain behaviours as constituting sexual harassment does not necessarily change the insider's view.

The "womanizing behaviour" examples also indicate another dimension of sexual harassment, namely that while individual women may seem to be its overt targets, observation of the behaviour by other women greatly extends its effects. This is one of the ways in which environments become "toxic" (Welsh & Nierobisz, 1997). What is further suggested here is the difficulty of separating "environment" harassment from the more serious forms of sexual intrusion or coercion which target individuals.

Much more common in the interviews, however, were experiences in the category labelled by Fitzgerald and Shullman (1993) as gender harassment, and defined as including sexist remarks and behaviour, and gender favouritism. Some of these comments related to

women's bodies, and so could be seen as verging on more sexualized terrain. For example, Ann[2] reported comments about body weight being directed at women rather than men. "When the guys get bulky you don't hear a whole lot about it, but when a girl starts putting on weight…a lot is said and it's embarrassing for women because I think they beat themselves up enough about it." Nadine agreed:

Just the girls would have to go running after workout because in his words, "they were all fat." …He made little comments, "You're being lazy. You're getting fat." It was never like that for the guys, which drove me insane because there were some fat guys compared to the girls—they didn't have to run.

Traci commented:

He's always, always making little comments, like if you see somebody walk by…he'll say, "Oh, look at that," just really negative toward women in general. And then you wonder what he says about you behind your back.

Other comments and reported behaviours included a wide variety of other forms of gender harassment. For example, Ann reported being upset by her coach when, informed of her education plans, he said, "Oh, you don't want to be a doctor. You'll just be a nurse." Clare heard her coach say that "women aren't as tough as men." Sue elaborated the same basic story:

He would say, "I know women, I know athletic women, when you coach them they're going to cry, they're going to sulk, they're wimps, you have to deal with their emotional side."

Gail spoke of an incident with a swim coach before a competition:

He was doing something on the board and a bunch of us were sitting around the board looking at it and we had lots of time for warm-up, but he chose to yell in our direction, but he only said the female names, "Get in the water!" And he said it really nasty. Meanwhile there were three guys standing with us and he never said a word to them. And he was talking to us as if we were kids.

These are only a few of the very many similar stories that emerged during the interviews.

We see them as illuminating the environment in which the more serious and explicitly sexual episodes of harassment occur. Sexual harassment as a *process*, as Fitzgerald and Shullman (1993) point out, is difficult to assess. But attention to environment and context makes it much easier to understand. The woman whose coach makes her feel embarrassed because of her weight has had a different experience from the woman who watches her coach come on to other team members at a banquet. But both experiences grow out of an environment where women are degraded. And it is the behaviour labelled as gender harassment that produces that degradation on a daily basis.

THE BROADER CONTEXT: PLAYING BY MEN'S RULES

This perspective returns us to the broader context of women's participation in sports. Sexual harassment, according to the theoretical analyses outlined earlier, is a means of upholding the masculine hegemony of sport in the face of increasing participation and challenge by women. Yet even the women who do encroach on this male turf do not participate on the same terms. For heuristic purposes, we can specify three possible ideological positions for the women in the male-dominated elite sporting world of our study. They can adopt the male model of sporting participation by becoming "one of the boys"; they can, in the terms of Disch and Kane (1996), adopt the "apologetic" code of conduct that continues to affirm male supremacy by allowing themselves and other women to be "second-class citizens"; or they can challenge the rules of the game.

These positions have serious implications in terms of how women as athletes might respond, both personally and generally, to the sexual harassment of women in sport. We argue that women who resist the masculine rules of the game, and who want to compete in sport on their own terms, are most likely to challenge and confront sexual harassment in all its forms. This

is the transformative potential described earlier by Birrell and Theberge (1994). On the other hand, we see women who are "one of the boys," or who consent to second-class status, as accepting the rules of the game, and by extension unlikely to challenge sexual harassment. It is beyond the scope of our data and this paper to test these propositions, but we see them as theoretically plausible. And as a first attempt at mapping the terrain of women's resistance to, and accommodation of, sexual harassment in sport, we can certainly offer examples from the interviews of the three positions outlined above.

We begin with the "resisters"—those who challenge the rules of the game. Several comments illustrated women's resistance both to men's rules, and to men's perceptions of women as athletes. Ellen's resistance was to her coach's ideas about body weight:

> I know he doesn't think I'm lean enough. But I told him, "I don't care what you think about that"—it's bad for you to be less. He wants us to be 12% body weight.... That's where you start screwing things up. So I always say, "No, I'm never going to be that low."

...Comments representative of the position of "one of the boys," or of women as second-class athletes, were much more common in the interviews. The extent to which women become "one of the boys" is most clearly demonstrated in their talk about pain and injury. The tenet "no pain, no gain" is widely recognized to be a central ideological component of masculinist sport (Connell, 1990; Kidd, 1990; Sabo, 1994; Young et al., 1994). But our interviews suggest the extent to which elite women athletes are also prepared to "suck it up." In most cases of dealing with injury, they "worked through it," "got used to it," "learned to play with it," and "expected it." As Maureen commented, "you have to sacrifice your body" in order to compete. The interviews yielded a long list of descriptions of injuries, including shoulder strains, groin injuries, chronic back injuries, pulled hamstrings, sprained ankles among many others. Pain and injury were thoroughly normalized. According to Traci, "you take eight ibuprofen and anti-inflammatories and you run." Sue recalled staying on the field to play after pulling a hamstring: "I could hardly walk and I didn't leave. I still thought I could make a difference."

...Nowhere, however, was the articulation of women's lower status in the sporting world made more clear than in the strongly stated preferences of several women for men, rather than women, as coaches. While it must be noted that information about gender preferences was volunteered and not deliberately sought, only three of the nine women who raised the issue could see advantages to having a woman as a coach. Much more typical was Traci's comment:

> I think it's awful to say it but you sort of respect male coaches more...boys especially look up to male coaches. And it's horrible but I think women do too. And that makes it a lot harder for women to be coaches, to get the same recognition and respect as a male coach does. And that's horrible. But I think a lot of people would agree with me.

Others commented that they had only experienced male coaches, and had no basis of comparison. But this only supported the view of another athlete that "it's almost ingrained in a person that the male is the coach."

Having given examples from our study of the discourse representative of the three ideological positions available to female athletes, we note that our concern is to map the ideological terrain rather than assess the relative strength of each position. In any case, individual women at different times during the interview moved across the ideological space from one position to another. That said, the fact that we heard much more accommodation than resistance has implications for the way the serious problems of sexual harassment in sport might be addressed.

IMPLICATIONS FOR CHANGE

This discussion of the broader institutional context in which our athletes and their coaches interact brings us back to the first theoretical proposition informing the study—the radical feminist claim that sexual harassment constitutes a defence of male turf against intrusion by women, and that women's entry into the male-dominated world of elite sport is conditional and on male terms. Our interviews have suggested that the athletes' experiences, which have included sexual harassment in its most inclusive sense, have occurred in a context in which they generally accept the "rules of the game." Our interviews did not produce any evidence of the specific, sexually coercive behaviour known as quid pro quo harassment. But we suggest that women's tolerance of ongoing gender and "environment" harassment as a condition of their participation in sport and because "it's just something that happens" (Thomas & Kitzinger, 1994) is a quid pro quo of a different kind.

What then of the second theoretical proposition, that women's entry into the sporting world represents resistance that brings with it the potential for transformation of the existing structures of power and control? As we have noted, not all women who do enter the world of elite sport participate on the same terms. Women who construct themselves as "one of the boys," or who acquiesce to second-class status, are unlikely to transform power relations unless the prevailing model of masculine behaviour changes also.

Recognition by men in the sports world that the model needs to change would be helpful, and educational efforts in this direction (such as the mandatory workshops now being offered by Calgary's National Sports Centre for all its athletes) are to be commended. So are initiatives like the Coaching Code of Ethics developed by the Canadian Professional Coaches Association. But while continuing to encourage these efforts, we need to acknowledge that those who are well served by the status quo, as we suggest is the case for men in sports, have little motivation to change. We should not pin all our hopes for ending sexual harassment on work with men.

Drawing on some of the findings of our study, we want to suggest that transformation of the power relations which enable sexual harassment in the sporting world could *also* be effected by changing women—but in a way that we hope might be exciting and emancipatory. We have argued earlier that the female athletes most likely to resist sexual harassment, and the model of behaviour which enables it, are those who are not willing to play by men's rules. We gave examples of women—the resisters—who seemed to want to claim their place in sport on their own terms. These were the women who spoke passionately about their love for their sport; who talked in positive terms about their strong, athletic bodies, their size and speed; who relished the hard work and the competition but who most highly valued the friendships they made on the field.

There is much to work with here—at least partly because elements of this discourse of resistance are available to women who in some situations may self-identify more readily as "one of the boys," or continue to think that female athletes "always kind of suck." Clearly what is needed here is perceptual reframing on a fairly large scale, and on (at least) two levels. The more women are able to celebrate their own sporting achievements, and win them on their own terms, the less likely they are to see themselves as inferior. And the more confidently they claim their place in this way, the less willing they will be to tolerate behaviour like sexual harassment that denigrates or impedes their performance.

CRITICAL THINKING QUESTIONS

1. How do *sexual* harassment and *gender* harassment differ?
2. In your opinion, and with reference to the article, why might female athletes be more prone to harassment than other women?
3. Review the three ways that the authors' suggest female athletes can participate in male-dominated elite sports. What other options can you think of? Do you think they are viable?

4. How would you explain the fact that in some of the interviews, most female athletes preferred male coaches even though they were fully aware of their sexist attitudes and behaviours?

NOTES

1. This category is generally contrasted with quid pro quo harassment, defined as sexual cooperation that is coerced by promises of rewards or fear of punishment (Fitzgerald & Hesson-McInnis, 1989: 510).
2. Names have been changed, and other identifying details withheld, to maintain confidentiality.

REFERENCES

Arvey, R., and M. Cavanaugh. 1995. Using surveys to assess the prevalence of sexual harassment: Some methodological problems. *Journal of Social Issues,* 51(1): 39–52.

Birrell, S., and N. Theberge. 1994. Feminist resistance and transformation in sport. In *Women and sport: Interdisciplinary perspectives,* eds. D. Costa, and S. Guthrie, 361–76. Champaign, Ill.: Human Kinetics.

Brackenridge, C. 1997. 'He owned me basically…' Women's experience of sexual abuse in sport. *International Review for the Sociology of Sport,* 32(2): 115–30.

Burton-Nelson, M. 1994. *The stronger women get, the more men love football.* New York: Harcourt Brace & Co.

Cairns, K. 1997. 'Femininity' and women's silence in response to sexual harassment and coercion. In *Sexual harassment: Contemporary feminist perspectives,* eds. A. Thomas, and C. Kitzinger, 91–111. Buckingham: Open University Press.

Connell, R. W. 1990. An iron man: The body and some contradictions of hegemonic masculinity. In *Sport, men and the gender order,* eds. M. Messner and D. Sabo, 83–95. Champaign, Ill.: Human Kinetics Books.

Disch, I., and M. Kane. 1996. When a looker is really a bitch: Lis Olson, sport, and the heterosexual matrix. *Signs,* 21(2): 278–308.

Fitzgerald, L., S. Shullrnan, N. Bailey, M. Richards, J. Swecker, Y. Gold, M. Ormerod, and L. Weitzman. 1988. The incidence and dimensions of sexual harassment in academia and the workplace. *Journal of Vocational Behavior,* 32: 152–75.

Fitzgerald, L., and M. Hesson-Mclnnis. 1989. The dimensions of sexual harassment: A structural analysis. *Journal of Vocational Behavior,* 35: 308–26.

Fitzgerald, L., and S. Shullman. 1993. Sexual harassment: A research analysis and agenda for the 1990s. *Journal of Vocational Behavior,* 42: 5–27.

Gruber, J. 1990. Methodological problems and policy implications in sexual harassment/research. *Population Research and Policy Review,* 9: 235–54.

————. 1992. A typology of personal and environmental sexual harassment: Research and policy implications for the 1990s. *Sex Roles,* 26(11–12): 447–63.

Hall, M. A. 1995. Women and sport: From liberal activism to radical cultural struggle. In *Changing methods,* eds. S. Burr, and L. Code, 265–99. Peterborough, Ont.: Broadview.

————. 1996. *Feminism and sporting bodies: Essays on theory and practice.* Champaign, Ill.: Human Kinetics.

Hall, M. A., D. Cullen, and T. Slack. 1989. Organizational elites recreating themselves: The gender structure of national sports organizations. *Quest,* 41: 28–45.

Hargreaves, J. 1994. *Sporting females: Critical issues in the history and sociology of women's sport.* London: Routledge.

Kidd, B. 1990. The men's cultural centre: Sports and the dynamic of women's oppression/men's repression. In *Sport, Men and the gender order,* eds. M. Messnet and D. Sabo, 31–43. Champaign, Ill.: Human Kinetics.

Kirby, S. 1995. Not in my backyard: Sexual harassment and abuse in sport. *Canadian Woman Studies,* 15(4): 58–62.

Krauchek, V. 1999. In the hands of the coach? Women's interpretations of athleticism and their relationships with men as coaches. Unpublished Master's thesis, Department of Sociology, University of Calgary.

Lackey, D. 1990. Sexual harassment in sports. *Physical Educator,* 47(2): 22–6.

Lenskyj, H. 1987. Canadian women and physical activity. In *From fair sex to feminism: Sport and the socialization of women in the industrial and post-industrial eras,* eds. J. Mangan and R. Park, 208–31. London: Frank Cass and Co. Ltd.

————. 1990. Power and play: Gender and sexuality issues in sport and physical activity. *International Review for the Sociology of Sport,* 25(3): 235–43.

————. 1992. Sexual harassment: Female athletes' experiences and coaches' responsibilities. *Sports,* 12(6): 1–5.

Messner, M. 1992. *Power at play: Sports and the problem of masculinity.* Boston: Beacon Press.

Messner, M., M. Duncan, and K. Jensen. 1993. Separating the men from the girls: The gendered language of televised sport. *Gender & Society,* 7(1): 121–37.

Mishler, E. 1986. *Research interviewing: Context and narrative.* Cambridge: Harvard University Press.

Sabo, D. 1994. Pigskin, patriarchy and pain. In *Sex, violence and power in sports,* eds. M. Messner, and D. Sabo, 82–8. Freedom, Calif.: The Crossing Press.

Sev'er, A. 1996. Mainstream neglect of sexual harassment as a social problem. *Canadian Journal of Sociology,* 21(2): 185–202.

Smith. B. 1996. Abuse prevalent in elite sport, survey indicates. *The Globe and Mail,* (July 17): A1.

Theberge, N. 1994. Toward a feminist alternative to sport as a male preserve. In *Women, sport and culture,* eds. S. Birrell, and C. Cole, 181–92. Champaign, Ill.: Human Kinetics.

Thomas, A., and C. Kitzinger. 1994. "It's just something that happens": The invisibility of sexual harassment in the workplace. *Gender, Work and Organization,* 1(3): 151–61.

————. 1997. Sexual harassment: Reviewing the field. In *Sexual harassment: Contemporary feminist perspectives,* eds. A. Thomas, and C. Kitzinger, 1–18. Buckingham: Open University Press.

Tomlinson, A., and I. Yorganci. 1997. Male coach/female athlete relations: Gender and power relations in competitive sport. *Journal of Sport and Social Issues,* 21(2): 134–55.

Volkwein, K., F. Schnell, D. Sherwood, and A. Livezey. 1997. Sexual harassment in sport: Perceptions and experiences of American female student-athletes. *International Review for the Sociology of Sport,* 32(3): 283–95.

Welsh, S., and A. Nierobisz. 1997. How prevalent is sexual harassment? A research note on measuring sexual harassment in Canada. *Canadian Journal of Sociology,* 22(4): 505–22.

White, A., and C. Brackenridge. 1985. Who rules sport? Gender divisions in the power structure of British sports organizations from 1960. *International Review for the Sociology of Sport,* 20: 1–11.

Yorganci, I. 1993. Preliminary findings from a survey of gender relationships and sexual harassment in sport. In *Body matters: Leisure images and lifestyles,* ed. C. Brackenridge, 197–203. Brighton: Leisure Studies Association.

Young, K., P. White, and B. McTeer. 1994. Body talk: Male athletes reflect on sport, injury, and pain. *Sociology of Sport Journal,* 11: 175–94.

36

Mothers and Children in the World Today

Gender

CLASSIC

CONTEMPORARY

CROSS-CULTURAL

Save the Children

When mothers survive and thrive, so do their children. In its annual report, Save the Children, a nonprofit child-assistance organization, offers critical information on the status of mothers and children in ninety-four countries (seventeen developed countries and seventy-seven developing countries). As the data show, national wealth alone does not guarantee the health and well-being of mothers and children. Although the United States is the world's richest country, for example, it ranks eleventh worldwide on the Mothers' Index. It ranks twenty-second on the Girls' Investment Index—well below several developing countries.

In order to construct the Mothers' Index and Girls' Investment Index, *State of the World's Mothers 2001* cast its net for data as widely as possible. It relies on information published by governments, research institutions, and international agencies.

All countries for which sufficient data were available are included in the study. The Mothers' Index measures and ranks the status of mothers in ninety-four countries; the Girls' Investment Index measures and ranks the status of girls and young women in 140 countries.

The rankings reveal an enormous gap between the highest and lowest scoring countries and point to an urgent need to take action to narrow that gap. While many of the top-ranked countries are also the richest, the data demonstrate that a country's wealth is no guarantee of high performance.

Source: State of the World's Mothers 2001, pp. 20–5. Save the Children, Westport, Connecticut, 2001.

THE MOTHERS' INDEX

The Mothers' Index (see Table 36.1) is based on a composite of separate indices for women's well-being and children's well-being. Of the ninety-four countries included in the study, seventeen are developed countries and seventy-seven are in the developing world.

The six indicators for women's well-being are:

- **Lifetime risk of maternal mortality.** This indicator calculates the risk of death a woman faces from pregnancy or childbirth during her lifetime.
- **Percent of women using modern contraception.** This indicator reflects the percent of women, aged fifteen to forty-nine, married or in union, who use modern contraception to plan the spacing and/or number of their children.
- **Percent of births attended by trained personnel.** This indicator measures the percentage of births attended by physicians, nurses, midwives, or primary health care workers trained in midwifery skills. Trained attendants at childbirth reduce both maternal and newborn mortality by providing a hygienic environment and arranging transportation or referrals for patients when complications arise.

TABLE 36.1 Mothers' Index Rankings

The Mothers' Index reflects how individual countries compare in meeting the needs of mothers. Listed here are the Mothers' Index rankings for all 94 countries included in the survey, along with corresponding rankings for each country's women's and children's indices.

Country	Mothers' Index Rank	Women's Index Rank	Children's Index Rank	Country	Mothers' Index Rank	Women's Index Rank	Children's Index Rank
Sweden	1	1	1	Lesotho	48	44	60
Norway	2	2	2	Jordan	49	51	26
Denmark	3	3	2	Peru	50	46	56
Finland	4	4	7	Lebanon	51	56	26
Netherlands	5	5	5	Nicaragua	52	50	40
Switzerland	6	6	9	Iran, Islamic Rep. of	53	55	30
Canada	7	7	7	Bolivia	54	53	49
Austria	8	8	2	Tunisia	54	58	30
Australia	9	9	5	Botswana	54	47	63
United Kingdom	10	10	18	United Arab Emirates	57	56	50
United States	11	13	9	Turkey	58	54	58
Cuba	12	11	21	Guatemala	59	61	36
Cyprus	12	14	9	Syrian Arab Republic	60	61	52
Costa Rica	14	15	17	Algeria	61	65	45
Argentina	15	12	42	Zambia	62	59	67
Singapore	16	17	15	Egypt	63	69	33
Chile	17	18	13	Kenya	64	59	71
Russian Federation	18	20	22	Uganda	65	63	76
Uruguay	18	22	18	Cameroon	66	66	75
Czech Republic	20	23	14	Tanzania, U. Rep. of	67	64	78
Mexico	21	19	32	Iraq	68	70	64
Korea, Rep. of	22	27	16	Ghana	69	68	74
Colombia	23	24	24	Madagascar	70	70	71
Bulgaria	24	30	12	Papua New Guinea	71	67	85
South Africa	25	16	43	Morocco	71	80	53
Ecuador	26	24	37	Lao People's Dem. Rep.	73	76	66
Moldova, Rep. of	27	34	24	Bangladesh	74	82	61
Venezuela	27	29	34	Senegal	75	75	71
Jamaica	29	27	37	Sudan	76	72	86
Dominican Republic	30	26	45	India	77	79	70
Trinidad and Tobago	31	35	29	Haiti	78	76	80
El Salvador	32	32	43	Mozambique	79	73	82
China	33	33	37	Malawi	80	74	88
Viet Nam	34	20	62	Côte d'Ivoire	81	81	77
Romania	35	36	47	Pakistan	82	87	69
Mauritius	36	39	41	Nepal	83	91	65
Brazil	37	37	57	Eritrea	84	78	90
Paraguay	37	44	35	Benin	85	84	82
Thailand	39	39	48	Central African Republic	86	85	87
Malaysia	40	47	22	Mauritania	87	88	84
Zimbabwe	40	38	54	Burundi	88	86	89
Uzbekistan	42	39	59	Gambia	89	92	79
Sri Lanka	43	42	55	Yemen	90	94	81
Philippines	44	42	50	Mali	91	83	92
Honduras	44	49	26	Ethiopia	92	90	93
Kuwait	46	51	20	Burkina Faso	93	89	94
Namibia	46	31	67	Guinea Bissau	94	93	91

- **Percent of pregnant women with anemia.** This indicator reveals short-comings of diet, nutritional status, possible malaria, worms, and access to prenatal care.
- **Adult female literacy rate.** This measure reflects the percent of women (over age fifteen) who can read and write. It is estimated that two-thirds of the world's 960 million adult illiterates are women.
- **Participation of women in national government.** This indicator represents the percentage of seats in national legislatures or parliament occupied by women. In bicameral legislatures and parliaments, only the lower house is counted (i.e., the U.S. House of Representatives or the British House of Commons).

The four indicators of children's well-being are:

- **Infant mortality rate.** This indicator employs a ratio based on the number of infant deaths per one thousand live births. It provides telling information about nutrition and early child care practices in the home as well as access to preventive health services and appropriate medical care.
- **Gross primary enrollment ratio.** This indicator compares the total number of children enrolled in primary school to the total number of children of primary school age.
- **Percent of population with access to safe water.** This indicator reports the percentage of the population with access to an adequate amount of water from an improved source within a convenient distance from the user's dwelling, as defined by country-level standards.
- **Percent of children under age five suffering from moderate or severe nutritional wasting.** "Wasting" is the term used when a child falls significantly below international recognized weight for height standards. This is a measure of acute malnutrition.

The Top Ten and the Bottom Ten

Sweden, Norway, Denmark, Finland, and the Netherlands top the rankings on the Mothers' Index. The top ten countries, in general, attain very high scores for mothers' health and educational status. Female literacy is above 99 percent in each country. Trained health personnel attend almost all births. The risk of death in child-birth over a

woman's lifetime is less than 1 in 6,000. No more than five infants in 1,000 die before reaching age one. Access to safe drinking water is universal.

However, there are considerable differences in women's access to political power. In Sweden, women comprise 43 percent of the members of parliament, but in the United Kingdom, women comprise only 18 percent.

BOX 36.1: WHAT THE DATA WILL— AND WON'T—TELL YOU!

The Mothers' Index uses data from the UN and other international agencies to present a broad overview of the status of mothers around the world. Nevertheless, there are limitations of this type of data that make it impossible to tell the whole story.

First of all, the great effort (and resources) required for collecting data on a global scale means that many countries only report data for a few general indicators. And often the data are not broken down by gender.

Furthermore, not all countries report data for the same indicators. For example, while many developing countries (with high rates of malnutrition) collect data on a number of malnutrition indicators, developed countries have no such need. On the other hand, countries in the throes of crisis—war, famine, natural disasters—are often unable to gather data in a timely and regular fashion.

It is also important to note that these indicators measure data at the country level. National averages can mask wide variation within a country.

The index can show us patterns among countries, but not among individual women living in disparate regions. The data do, however, show that where countries invest in mothers, children fare better, and motherhood is less likely to be a severe threat to a woman's life and well-being.

BOX 36.2: THE MOTHERS' INDEX

Top Ten
(All Countries)

Rank	Country
1	Sweden
2	Norway
3	Denmark
4	Finland
5	The Netherlands
6	Switzerland
7	Canada
8	Austria
9	Australia
10	United Kingdom

Top Ten
(Developing Countries)

Rank	Country
12	Cuba
12	Cyprus
14	Costa Rica
15	Argentina
16	Singapore
17	Chile
18	Uruguay
21	Mexico
22	Korea, Republic of
23	Colombia

Bottom Ten
(All Countries)

Rank	Country
94	Guinea Bissau
93	Burkina Faso
92	Ethiopia
91	Mali
90	Yemen
89	Gambia
88	Burundi
87	Mauritania
86	Central African Republic
85	Benin

The ten bottom-ranked countries on the Mothers' Index are a mirror image of the top ten, performing poorly on all indicators. Female literacy ranges from a high of 38 percent in Burundi to a low of 13 percent in Burkina Faso. On average, fewer than 3 percent of all women in these countries use modern contraception. The number of women expected to die in pregnancy or during childbirth ranges from a lifetime risk of one in seven in Guinea Bissau to a still-alarming one in twenty-one in the Central African Republic.

- In Burkina Faso, nearly 90 percent of women are illiterate.
- In Burundi, Guinea Bissau, and Mauritania, only 1 percent of women use modern contraception.
- In Nepal, only 9 percent of all births are attended by trained health personnel.
- In India, 88 percent of all pregnant women are anemic.
- In Guinea Bissau, a woman has a one in seven lifetime risk of dying during pregnancy or childbirth.
- In Mali, one out of every seven children dies before his or her first birthday.

This tragedy has clear regional dimensions. All but one of the countries in the bottom ten are in sub-Saharan Africa. With a one in thirty-one lifetime risk of dying in childbirth in sub-Saharan Africa, maternal mortality is 130 times greater than it is in developed countries. Only half of adult women are literate. Trained health personnel are present at fewer than half of all childbirths in this region, and nearly one out of ten infants dies before his or her first birthday. Individual country comparisons are equally dramatic. (See Table 36.2)

THE GIRLS' INVESTMENT INDEX

The new Girls' Investment Index (Table 36.2) measures and ranks the status of girls and young women in 140 countries to gauge how well each country is investing in its future generation of mothers and children. Included

TABLE 36.2 Girls' Investment Index Rankings

By zeroing in on the next generation of mothers, the Girls' Investment Index not only tells us how girls and young women are faring today, but also helps predict how they (the next generation of mothers) and their children will fare tomorrow. Listed here are the Girls' Investment Index rankings for all 140 countries included in the survey.

Country	Rank	Country	Rank	Country	Rank
Finland	1	Moldova, Rep. of	48	Zimbabwe	94
Sweden	1	Kuwait	49	Namibia	96
United Kingdom	3	Lithuania	49	Swaziland	97
Denmark	4	Malaysia	49	Bolivia	98
Australia	5	Poland	49	Guatemala	99
Canada	5	Sri Lanka	49	Myanmar	100
Germany	5	Jamaica	54	Kenya	101
The Netherlands	5	Bahrain	55	Lesotho	102
Belgium	9	Fiji	56	Sudan	103
Singapore	9	Albania	57	Morocco	104
France	11	Panama	58	Papua New Guinea	105
Spain	12	Thailand	59	Madagascar	106
New Zealand	12	Venezuela	60	Ghana	107
Japan	14	Colombia	61	Tanzania, U. Rep. of	108
Iceland	15	Jordan	62	Cameroon	109
Korea, Rep. of	15	Mexico	62	Haiti	109
Norway	15	Romania	62	Comoros	111
Ireland	18	United Arab Emirates	65	India	112
Luxembourg	18	Brazil	66	Djibouti	113
Switzerland	18	Dominican Republic	67	Iraq	113
Slovenia	21	China	68	Zambia	115
Greece	22	Qatar	69	Nigeria	116
Hungary	22	Samoa (Western)	70	Cambodia	117
United States	22	Uzbekistan	71	Pakistan	118
Cyprus	25	Tunisia	72	Rwanda	119
Israel	26	Viet Nam	72	Bangladesh	120
Malta	27	Iran, Islamic Rep. of	74	Togo	121
Italy	28	Paraguay	75	Senegal	122
Czech Republic	29	Saudi Arabia	76	Congo, Dem. Rep. of the	123
Cuba	30	Belize	77	Mauritania	123
Austria	31	El Salvador	77	Côte d'Ivoire	125
Bahamas	31	Philippines	79	Eritrea	126
Costa Rica	31	Tajikistan	80	Uganda	127
Estonia	34	Ecuador	81	Benin	128
Chile	35	South Africa	82	Central African Republic	128
Russian Federation	36	Algeria	83	Burundi	130
Ukraine	36	Oman	84	Malawi	131
Latvia	38	Mongolia	85	Nepal	132
Brunei Darussalam	39	Peru	86	Mozambique	133
Uruguay	39	Syrian Arab Republic	87	Burkina Faso	134
Bulgaria	41	Turkey	88	Yemen	134
Portugal	41	Honduras	89	Ethiopia	136
Trinidad and Tobago	43	Botswana	90	Mali	137
Belarus	44	Nicaragua	91	Guinea Bissau	138
Argentina	45	Indonesia	92	Chad	139
Armenia	45	Cape Verde	93	Niger	140
Mauritius	47	Egypt	97		

are forty-two developed countries and ninety-eight developing countries.

The Girls' Investment Index captures the status of girls and young women from infancy through childbearing age, and presents indicators that reflect women's and children's health status overall. It is composed of twelve different indicators, which are grouped into four investment areas: girls' education, girls' health, young motherhood, and safe motherhood.

Together, these twelve indicators provide an overall measure of those aspects of girls' and young women's well-being that help predict the success of the next generation of mothers and their children. For instance, the age at which a girl marries affects the likelihood that she will complete school, the number and timing of the children she may bear, and the well-being of those children. The indicators are:

Girls' Education

- **Adult female literacy rate.** This measure reflects the percentage of women (over age fifteen) who can read and write. It is estimated that two-thirds of the world's 960 million illiterate adults are women.
- **Female primary school enrollment as percent of male enrollment.** The total number of girls enrolled in primary school—regardless of age—expressed as a percentage of the total number of males enrolled in primary school.
- **Female secondary school enrollment as percent of male enrollment.** The total number of girls enrolled in secondary school—regardless of age—expressed as a percentage of the total number of males enrolled in secondary school.
- **Female youth illiteracy rate.** The percent of women between the ages of fifteen and twenty-four who cannot read and write.

Girls' Health

- **Female infant mortality rate.** This indicator is the number of girls out of one thousand live female births who die in their first year. The rate provides telling information about infant feeding and early

child care practices in the home, accessibility of food, preventive health services, and medical care.
- **Female under-five mortality rate.** This indicator is the number of girls out of one thousand live female births who die before they reach the age of five.

Young Motherhood

- **Births to women fifteen to nineteen years of age.** The adolescent fertility rate is equal to the number of births per one thousand women, aged fifteen to nineteen.
- **Percent of women ages fifteen to nineteen ever married.** This indicator measures the percentage of women ages fifteen to nineteen who have ever been married. Data are from 1991 through 1998.
- **Average age at first marriage (women).** Average age at first marriage may include formal and informal unions.

Safe Motherhood

- **Percent of births attended by trained personnel.** This indicator measures the percentage of births attended by physicians, nurses, midwives, or primary health care workers trained in midwifery skills. Trained attendants at child-birth reduce both maternal and newborn mortality by providing a hygienic environment and arranging transportation or referrals for patients when complications arise.
- **Estimated maternal mortality ratio.** This indicator calculates the number of women who die of pregnancy-related causes per 100,000 live births and is influenced by women's overall health status and their access to safe delivery and emergency obstetric care.
- **Percent of women using modern contraception.** This indicator estimates the percentage of women, aged fifteen to forty-nine, married or in union, who use modern contraception to plan the spacing and/or number of their children.
- In Niger, one out of five girls aged fifteen to nineteen has given birth.
- In Chad, there are only fifty-five girls for every one hundred boys enrolled in primary school.
- In Bangladesh, the average age for a girl at first marriage is fourteen.
- In Mali, nearly one out of every four girls dies before her fifth birthday.

BOX 36.3: THE GIRLS' INVESTMENT INDEX

Top Ten (All Countries)		*Top Ten (Developing Countries)*		*Bottom Ten (All Countries)*	
Rank	*Country*	*Rank*	*Country*	*Rank*	*Country*
1	Finland	9	Singapore	140	Niger
1	Sweden	15	Korea, Republic of	139	Chad
3	United Kingdom	25	Cyprus	138	Guinea Bissau
4	Denmark	30	Cuba	137	Mali
5	Australia	31	Bahamas	136	Ethiopia
5	Canada	31	Costa Rica	134	Burkina Faso
5	Germany	35	Chile	134	Yemen
5	The Netherlands	39	Brunei Darussalam	133	Mozambique
9	Belgium	39	Uruguay	132	Nepal
9	Singapore	43	Trinidad/Tobago	131	Malawi

The Top Ten and The Bottom Ten

Finland and Sweden tie for first place on the Girls' Investment Index, followed by the United Kingdom and Denmark. The ten top-ranked countries on the Investment Index score well on most indicators. Infant and child death rates for girls are low: about five girls in one thousand die before their first birthday; seven girls in one thousand die before the age of five. Nearly the same number of girls and boys are enrolled in primary and secondary school, and all countries—with the exception of Singapore—are above 99 percent for adult female literacy. On average, young women get married for the first time at age twenty-seven; while two out of one hundred teenage girls have children.

In the bottom ten countries, girls and young women (the next generation of mothers) are not faring well. More than one out of ten girls does not live to see her first birthday. Even fewer girls live to enjoy a fifth birthday—almost one out of six girls dies before reaching age five. For those who survive, an average of sixty-six girls for every one hundred boys attend primary school; the proportion drops to forty-nine girls for every one hundred boys in secondary school. In addition, the findings clearly demonstrate that many young girls are already mothers; in Niger, for example, one out of five girls aged fifteen to nineteen has given birth. On average, three quarters of all births take place with no trained health professional present. More than one out of one hundred pregnancies (and births) results in a mother's death. All but two of the ten bottom-ranked countries are in sub-Saharan Africa.

Data on education illuminate these regional discrepancies. With a regional average of 50 percent, sub-Saharan Africa has the lowest female literacy rate of any region, ranging from more than 80 percent in South Africa and Zimbabwe to a low of 17 percent in Guinea-Bissau, 13 percent in Burkina Faso and 7 percent in Niger.

BOX 36.4: COUNTING WHAT REALLY COUNTS...

The Girls' Investment Index highlights four important investment areas: girls' education, girls' health, young motherhood, and safe motherhood. Countries that are willing and able to invest in these areas are much more likely to ensure a high quality of life for the next generation of mothers and their children.

However, there are other areas of investment for which data are not currently available or for which data are not disaggregated by gender or age, which would contribute important information about girls today—and the mothers of tomorrow.

Women's economic status is an important predictor of how future generations of mothers and children will fare.

Unfortunately, data on women's economic status, including data on their share and control of household income and their participation in the formal and informal work sectors, is lacking for many countries of the world.

Violence against women is another area where additional data would contribute to a fuller understanding of women's and girls' lives and their prospects for the future.

While there is a growing body of research in this area, the data is seldom comparable across countries due to national variations in legal and cultural norms and in research techniques.

Additional data collection and analysis, disaggregated by gender and age, is also needed in the areas of HIV/AIDS and women's and girls' unmet nutritional and health care needs.

Individual country comparisons are equally stark:

- In Bangladesh, the average age for a girl at first marriage is fourteen.
- In Malawi, nearly one out of every seven girls dies before the age of one; in Mali, nearly one out of every four girls dies before her fifth birthday.
- In Chad, there are only fifty-five girls for every one hundred boys enrolled in primary school; in Yemen, there are only twenty-six girls for every one hundred boys enrolled in secondary school.
- In the Congo, more than one out of every five girls aged fifteen to nineteen has given birth.

CRITICAL THINKING QUESTIONS

1. Examine the six indicators of the Mothers' Index and the twelve indicators of the Girls' Investment Index. Do these indicators support the report's conclusion that "investment in safe motherhood programs and practices, and in education for girls and women are perhaps the most essential" ingredients in promoting girls' and women's well-being? Explain.

2. Why, according to this report, does the Girls' Investment Index help predict how the next generation of mothers and their children will fare? How, for example, are girls' current educational opportunities and health related to their future roles as mothers?

3. As the data show, the United States does *not* rank in the top ten countries in either mothers' or girls' well-being even though it is the world's richest country. As a Canadian student, why do you feel that this is the case?

37

The Souls of Black Folk

W. E. B. Du Bois

W. E. B. Du Bois, a pioneering U.S. sociologist and the first African American to receive a doctorate from Harvard University, describes how a colour-conscious society casts black people as "strangers in their own homes." One result, Du Bois explains, is that African Americans develop a "double consciousness," seeing themselves as Americans but always gazing back at themselves through the eyes of the white majority, as people set below and apart by colour.

Between me and the other world there is ever an unasked question: unasked by some through feelings of delicacy; by others through the difficulty of rightly framing it. All, nevertheless, flutter round it. They approach me in a half-hesitant sort of way, eye me curiously or compassionately, and then, instead of saying directly, How does it feel to be a problem? they say, I know an excellent colored man in my town; or, I fought at Mechanicsville; or, Do not these Southern outrages make your blood boil? At these I smile, or am interested, or reduce the boiling to a simmer, as the occasion may require. To the real question, How does it feel to be a problem? I answer seldom a word.

Source: From *The Souls of Black Folk* by W. E. B. Du Bois (New York: Penguin, 1982; orig. 1903), pp. 43–53.

And yet, being a problem is a strange experience—peculiar even for one who has never been anything else, save perhaps in babyhood and in Europe. It is in the early days of rollicking boyhood that the revelation first bursts upon one, all in a day, as it were. I remember well when the shadow swept across me. I was a little thing, away up in the hills of New England, where the dark Housatonic winds between Hoosac and Taghkanic to the sea. In a wee wooden schoolhouse, something put it into the boys' and girls' heads to buy gorgeous visiting-cards—ten cents a package—and exchange. The exchange was merry, till one girl, a tall newcomer, refused my card—refused it peremptorily, with a glance. Then it dawned upon me with a certain suddenness that I was different from the others; or like, mayhap, in heart and

247

life and longing, but shut out from their world by a vast veil. I had thereafter no desire to tear down that veil, to creep through; I held all beyond it in common contempt, and lived above it in a region of blue sky and great wandering shadows. That sky was bluest when I could beat my mates at examination-time, or beat them at a foot-race, or even beat their stringy heads. Alas, with the years all this fine contempt began to fade; for the words I longed for, and all their dazzling opportunities, were theirs, not mine. But they should not keep these prizes, I said; some, all, I would wrest from them. Just how I would do it I could never decide: by reading law, by healing the sick, by telling the wonderful tales that swam in my head—some way. With other black boys the strife was not so fiercely sunny: Their youth shrunk into tasteless syco-phancy, or into silent hatred of the pale world about them and mocking distrust of everything white; or wasted itself in a bitter cry, Why did God make me an outcast and a stranger in mine own house? The shades of the prison-house closed round about us all: walls strait and stub-born to the whitest, but relentlessly narrow, tall, and unscalable to sons of night who must plod darkly on in resignation, or beat unavailing palms against the stone, or steadily, half hope-lessly, watch the streak of blue above.

After the Egyptian and Indian, the Greek and Roman, the Teuton and Mongolian, the Negro is a sort of seventh son, born with a veil, and gifted with second-sight in this American world—a world which yields him no true self-consciousness, but only lets him see himself through the revelation of the other world. It is a peculiar sensation, this double-consciousness, this sense of always looking at one's self through the eyes of others, of measuring one's soul by the tape of a world that looks on in amused contempt and pity. One ever feels his twoness—an American, a Negro; two souls, two thoughts, two unreconciled strivings; two warring ideals in one dark body, whose dogged strength alone keeps it from being torn asunder.

The history of the American Negro is the history of this strife, this longing to attain self-conscious manhood, to merge his double self into a better and truer self. In this merging he wishes neither of the older selves to be lost. He would not Africanize America, for America has too much to teach the world and Africa. He would not bleach his Negro soul in a flood of white Americanism, for he knows that Negro blood has a message for the world. He simply wishes to make it possible for a man to be both a Negro and an American, without being cursed and spit upon by his fellows, without having the doors of Opportunity closed roughly in his face.

This, then, is the end of his striving: to be a coworker in the kingdom of culture, to escape both death and isolation, to husband and use his best powers and his latent genius. These powers of body and mind have in the past been strangely wasted, dispersed, or forgotten. The shadow of a mighty Negro past flits through the tale of Ethiopia the Shadowy and of Egypt the Sphinx. Through history, the powers of single black men flash here and there like falling stars, and die sometimes before the world has rightly gauged their brightness. Here in America, in the few days since Eman-cipation, the black man's turning hither and thither in hesitant and doubtful striving has often made his very strength to lose effective-ness, to seem like absence of power, like weak-ness. And yet it is not weakness—it is the contradiction of double aims. The double-aimed struggle of the black artisan on the one hand to escape white contempt for a nation of mere hewers of wood and drawers of water, and on the other hand to plough and nail and dig for a poverty-stricken horde—could only result in making him a poor craftsman, for he had but half a heart in either cause. By the poverty and ignorance of his people, the Negro minister or doctor was tempted toward quackery and demagogy; and by the criticism of the other world, toward ideals that made him ashamed of his lowly tasks. The would-be black *savant* was confronted by the paradox that the knowledge his people needed was a twice-told tale to his white neighbors, while the knowledge which would teach the white world was Greek to his own flesh and blood. The innate love of harmony and beauty that set the ruder souls of his people a-dancing and a-singing raised but confusion and doubt in the soul of the black artist; for the beauty revealed to him was the soul-beauty of a race which his larger audience despised, and he could not articulate the message of another people. This waste of double aims, this seeking to satisfy two unreconciled ideals, has wrought sad havoc with the courage and faith and deeds of ten thousand thousand people, has sent them often wooing false gods and invoking false means of salvation, and at times has even seemed about to make them ashamed of themselves.

Away back in the days of bondage they thought to see in one divine event the end of all doubt and disappointment; few men ever worshipped Freedom with half such unquestioning faith as did the American Negro for two centuries. To him, so far as he thought and dreamed, slavery was indeed the sum of all villainies, the cause of all sorrow, the root of all prejudice; Emancipation was the key to a promised land of sweeter beauty than ever stretched before the eyes of wearied Israelites. In song and exhortation swelled one refrain—Liberty; in his tears and curses the God he implored had Freedom in his right hand. At last it came, suddenly, fearfully, like a dream. With one wild carnival of blood and passion came the message in his own plaintive cadences:

Shout, O children!
Shout, you're free!
For God has bought your liberty!

Years have passed away since then,—ten, twenty, forty; forty years of national life, forty years of renewal and development, and yet the swarthy spectre sits in its accustomed seat at the Nation's feast. In vain do we cry to this our vastest social problem:

Take any shape but that, and my firm nerves
Shall never tremble!

The Nation has not yet found peace from its sins; the freedman has not yet found in freedom his promised land. Whatever of good may have come in these years of change, the shadow of a deep disappointment rests upon the Negro people—a disappointment all the more bitter because the unattained ideal was unbounded save by the simple ignorance of a lowly people.

The first decade was merely a prolongation of the vain search for freedom, the boon that seemed ever barely to elude their grasp, like a tantalizing will-o'-the-wisp, maddening and misleading the headless host. The holocaust of war, the terrors of the Ku-Klux Klan, the lies of carpet-baggers, the disorganization of industry, and the contradictory advice of friends and foes, left the bewildered serf with no new watchword beyond the old cry for freedom. As the time flew, however, he began to grasp a new idea. The ideal of liberty demanded for its attainment powerful means, and these the Fifteenth Amendment gave him. The ballot, which before he had looked upon as a visible sign of freedom, he now regarded as the chief means of gaining and perfecting the liberty with which war had partially endowed him. And why not? Had not votes made war and emancipated millions? Had not votes enfranchised the freedmen? Was anything impossible to a power that had done all this? A million black men started with renewed zeal to vote themselves into the kingdom. So the decade flew away, the revolution of 1876 came, and left the half-free serf weary, wondering, but still inspired. Slowly but steadily, in the following years, a new vision began gradually to replace the dream of political power—a powerful movement, the rise of another ideal to guide the unguided, another pillar of fire by night after a clouded day. It was the ideal of "book-learning"; the curiosity, born of compulsory ignorance, to know and test the power of the cabalistic letters of the white man, the longing to know. Here at last seemed to have been discovered the mountain path to Canaan; longer than the highway of Emancipation and law, steep and rugged, but straight, leading to heights high enough to overlook life.

Up the new path the advance guard toiled, slowly, heavily, doggedly; only those who have watched and guided the faltering feet, the misty minds, the dull understandings, of the dark pupils of these schools know how faithfully, how piteously, this people strove to learn. It was weary work. The cold statistician wrote down the inches of progress here and there, noted also where here and there a foot had slipped or some one had fallen. To the tired climbers, the horizon was ever dark, the mists were often cold, the Canaan was always dim and far away. If, however, the vistas disclosed as yet no goal, no resting-place, little but flattery and criticism, the journey at least gave leisure for reflection and self-examination; it changed the child of Emancipation to the youth with dawning self-consciousness, self-realization, self-respect. In those sombre forests of his striving his own soul rose before him, and he saw himself, darkly as through a veil; and yet he saw in himself some faint revelation of his power, of his mission. He began to have a dim feeling that, to attain his place in the world, he must be himself, and not another. For the first time he sought to analyze the burden he bore upon his back, that dead-weight of social degradation partially masked behind a half-named Negro problem. He felt his poverty; without a cent, without a home, without land, tools, or savings, he had entered into competition with rich, landed, skilled neighbors. To be a man is hard, but to be a poor race in a land of dollars is the very bottom of hardships. He felt the weight of his ignorance, not simply of letters, but of life, of business, of the humanities; the accumulated sloth and shirking and awkwardness of decades and centuries shackled his hands and feet. Nor was his burden all poverty and ignorance. The red stain of bastardy, which two centuries of systematic legal defilement of Negro women had stamped upon his race, meant not only the loss of ancient African

chastity, but also the hereditary weight of a mass of corruption from white adulterers, threatening almost the obliteration of the Negro home.

A people thus handicapped ought not to be asked to race with the world, but rather allowed to give all its time and thought to its own social problems. But alas! while sociologists gleefully count his bastards and his prostitutes, the very soul of the toiling, sweating black man is darkened by the shadow of a vast despair. Men call the shadow prejudice, and learnedly explain it as the natural defence of culture against barbarism, learning against ignorance, purity against crime, the "higher" against the "lower" races. To which the Negro cries Amen! and swears that to so much of this strange prejudice as is founded on just homage to civilization, culture, righteousness, and progress, he humbly bows and meekly does obeisance. But before that nameless prejudice that leaps beyond all this he stands helpless, dismayed, and well-nigh speechless; before that personal disrespect and mockery, the ridicule and systematic humiliation, the distortion of fact and wanton license of fancy, the cynical ignoring of the better and the boisterous welcoming of the worse, the all-pervading desire to inculcate disdain for everything black, from Toussaint to the devil—before this there rises a sickening despair that would disarm and discourage any nation save that black host to whom "discouragement" is an unwritten word.

But the facing of so vast a prejudice could not but bring the inevitable self-questioning, self-disparagement, and lowering of ideals which ever accompany repression and breed in an atmosphere of contempt and hate. Whisperings and portents came borne upon the four winds: Lo! we are diseased and dying, cried the dark hosts; we cannot write, our voting is vain; what need of education, since we must always cook and serve? And the Nation echoed and enforced this self-criticism saying: Be content to be servants, and nothing more; what need of higher culture for half-men? Away with the black man's ballot, by force or fraud—and behold the suicide of a race!

Nevertheless, out of the evil came something of good—the more careful adjustment of education to real life, the clearer perception of the Negroes' social responsibilities, and the sobering realization of the meaning of progress.

So dawned the time of *Sturm und Drang:* Storm and stress today rocks our little boat on the mad waters of the world-sea; there is within and without the sound of conflict, the burning of body and rending of soul; inspiration strives with doubt, and faith with vain questionings. The bright ideals of the past—physical freedom, political power, the training of brains and the training of hands—all these in turn have waxed and waned, until even the last grows dim and overcast. Are they all wrong, all false? No, not that, but each alone was over-simple and incomplete—the dreams of a credulous race-childhood, or the fond imaginings of the other world which does not know and does not want to know our power. To be really true, all these ideals must be melted and welded into one. The training of the schools we need today more than ever—the training of deft hands, quick eyes and ears, and above all the broader, deeper, higher culture of gifted minds and pure hearts. The power of the ballot we need in sheer self-defence—else what shall save us from a second slavery? Freedom, too, the long-sought, we still seek, the freedom of life and limb, the freedom to work and think, the freedom to love and aspire. Work, culture, liberty—all these we need, not singly but together, not successively but together, each growing and aiding each, and all striving toward that vaster ideal that swims before the Negro people, the ideal of human brotherhood, gained through the unifying ideal of Race; the ideal of fostering and developing the traits and talents of the Negro, not in opposition to or contempt for other races, but rather in large conformity to the greater ideals of the American Republic, in order that some day on American soil two world-races may give each to each those characteristics both so sadly lack. We the darker ones come even now not altogether empty-handed: There are today no truer exponents of the pure human spirit of the Declaration of Independence than the American Negroes; there is no true American music but the wild sweet melodies of the Negro slave, the American fairy tales and folklore are Indian and African; and, all in all, we black men seem the sole oasis of simple faith and reverence in a dusty desert of dollars and smartness. Will America be poorer if she replace[s] her brutal dyspeptic blundering with light-hearted but determined Negro humility? or her coarse and cruel wit with loving jovial good-humor? or her vulgar music with the soul of the Sorrow Songs?

Merely a concrete test of the underlying principles of the great republic is the Negro Problem, and the spiritual striving of the freedmen's sons is in the travail of souls whose burden is almost beyond the measure of their strength, but who bear it in the name of an historic race, in the name of this the land of their fathers' fathers, and in the name of human opportunity.

CRITICAL THINKING QUESTIONS

1. What does Du Bois mean by the "double consciousness" of African Americans?
2. Du Bois writes that people of colour aspire to realizing a "better and truer self." What do you think he imagines such a self to be?
3. What are some of the reasons, according to Du Bois, that Emancipation (from slavery in 1863) brought disappointment to former slaves, at least in the short run?
4. Does this essay seem optimistic or pessimistic about the future of race relations? Why?

38

Aboriginal Identity: The Need for Historical and Contextual Perspectives

Jean-Paul Restoule

Restoule explores Canadian Aboriginal identities from legal and historical perspectives as well as the personal and subjective experiences of Aboriginal peoples.

Employing a perspective that distinguishes between "identity" and "identifying" demonstrates the limitations inherent in typical conceptions of cultural identity. Identifying is situational and historical, shaped by the time and place in which it occurs, whereas identity is thought to transcend history and social situations. Identity is represented in the Indian Act and its definition of "Indian." Métis efforts for recognition as an Aboriginal people in their own right is seen as identifying. The potential harm of identity is demonstrated by the Crown's arguments in the case for Gitksan-Wet'suwet'en Aboriginal title.

I recently attended a conference where a number of us were discussing issues concerning Aboriginal identity. We talked about how our

Source: Jean-Paul Restoule. 2000. Aboriginal Identity: The Need for Historical and Contextual Perspectives. *Canadian Journal of Native Education*, 24(2), 102–12. Abridged with the permission of the Canadian Journal of Native Education, University of Alberta and University of British Columbia.

parents had tried to hide any semblance of their Aboriginal identity and how in our experience today it was not only acceptable, but indeed desirable to be Aboriginal. In our experience dreamcatchers were everywhere and Aboriginal plays and events in the city were sold out. "What happened?" we asked each other. Then someone pointed out that where she came from there was not the luxury to talk about identifying as Aboriginal as if it were a choice. Shame about being Aboriginal continued to exist in her community. Most of the people from her community would hide their Aboriginality if possible. For many of them it was not even an option. They were "known" as Aboriginal people. Also, in her experience the issue of drug abuse, AIDS, diabetes, unemployment, spousal abuse, and others were seen as more pressing concerns than identity.

Her words had quite an impact on me. How can some of us talk about the struggle for identity when on a daily basis so many of us struggle just to survive? Is writing about these matters really helping to change anything? I keep coming back to this idea that some of the people in her community would hide their Aboriginality if they could. Understanding what influences our pride or shame in identifying as Aboriginal people is important. How we feel about ourselves contributes to and arises from the issues my colleague felt were more urgent to discuss than identity. I have seen examples where pride in Aboriginal identity is the basis for fighting addiction and where shame in identity is a factor in developing a habit of substance abuse (Restoule, 1999). It is important to explore what identifying as Aboriginal means and what is gained and lost in attempting to erase that identity, as well as what it means to change the referents of what is meant by Aboriginal identity.

IDENTITY AND IDENTIFYING

The term *identity* expressed popularly, as well as in academic circles, implies a fixed nature over a given time period. In psychology, identity is often qualified as, for example, sex-role identity or racial identity (Sutherland, 1989). These qualities are assumed to have some continuity over time for the individual. In Piaget's work, identity refers to a state of awareness that something holds its value despite surface appearances to the contrary (Sutherland, 1989). In logic, identity refers to two words, properties, or statements that are so similar that they can substitute one for the other in an equation without altering the meaning (Sutherland). In sum, identity has been conceived to mean sameness. For social scientists discussing cultural identity, the sameness inherent in the definition of identity refers to the shared norms, traits, and habits of members of a cultural group at one historical moment. Unfortunately, there are educators, lawyers, and policymakers who make the error of assuming Aboriginal identity must hold over several generations.

To talk about Aboriginal identity assumes a sameness and continuity that belies the fluidity and change that Aboriginal people experience and demonstrate. When this assumed permanence of character is run through institutions like the education and court systems "Aboriginal identity" can be constrictive and colonizing. I return to this idea below with a discussion of the case for Gitksan-Wet'suwet'en Aboriginal title. If we change the focus from *identity* to *identifying*, we move from noun to verb and set off a potentially liberating way of conceiving and talking about self-definition. *Identity* implies fixedness; that the "things" that make one Indian remain the same and should be the same as those things associated with Indianness by the Europeans at the time of historical "first" contact. Identity places power in the observer who observes Aboriginal people from the outside and defines them, giving them an identity. *Identifying* shifts control to the self, and motivations come to the fore. This perspective favors a set of referents that are put into action at the historical time one identifies as an Aboriginal person and in the contextual place where one identifies. Identifying is a process of being and becoming what one is in the moment. The power is placed in the self, for the Aboriginal person who emphasizes his or her Indigenous roots at a particular place and time. This allows for the salient components of an Aboriginal identity to be expressed as the actor feels is expedient, allowing for cultural change and adaptation. Identifying is situational and historical, whereas identity is thought to transcend history and social situations.

In this article I use a number of examples to make clearer the distinction between identity and identifying. Dunn's (2001) research on the Métis of the Red River region shows that the tension between identity and identifying existed even in the 1800s. I provide a brief overview of Canadian legislation defining "Indians" as an example of identity as I characterize it above. As a point of contrast, Métis participation in the Constitutional Conferences of the 1980s and the Royal Commission on Aboriginal Peoples (RCAP, 1996) demonstrate identifying.

Employing a perspective that distinguishes between identity and identifying might help us problematize typical conceptions of cultural identity limited in their ability to reflect the situational and contextual identifying that exists in contemporary Aboriginal life. To demonstrate the limitations of an identity perspective, I look at Fitzgerald's (1977) notion of cultural identity as an interplay between color, culture, and class. This conception of cultural identity, I feel, is fairly typical. I refer to work by Valentine (1995) and Pinneault and Patterson (1997) to demonstrate that identity/identifying is indeed contextual and is shaped by the time and place in which it occurs....

LIMITATIONS OF IDENTITY IN ABORIGINAL NORTH AMERICA

Identity is a complicated concept. Cultural identity is often conceived as an interplay between biology, socioeconomic status, and cultural knowledge. Fitzgerald (1977), in his study of Maori students, refers to these three components as color, culture, and class. To Fitzgerald color represents a biological connection to the original peoples. In other words, it is the blood connection, the lineage that can be traced to Aboriginal communities and families. By culture Fitzgerald means knowledge of the traditions, language, and ceremonies or the "markers" of the race. Class stands for socioeconomic position in the greater society. Society is perceived as the greater economic and political entity where many cultures coexist. Each culture participates in the larger society where it is located, although the cultural norms of the group may be distinct from the rest of the society.

Race is often conflated with class, so that a racial group or cultural group is likely to be thought of as occupying a particular class position in relation to the greater society. Power is maintained by barriers that keep racial groups from advancing socioeconomically. Although

certain individuals may succeed in being upwardly mobile, much of the group continues to experience difficulty. As Fitzgerald (1993) observed, "The central tensions between groups do not seem to be essentially cultural but originate in inequalities over power and participation in society. More and more, groups are trying to invent cultures through identity assertions" (p. 221). Identity tends to be more persistent and stable over time, whereas cultures are in a constant state of reinvention. This is because identity often has to do with how the out-group culture views the in-group. Fitzgerald (1977) found that some Maoris he studied validated their right of acceptance in the Maori group by overemphasizing their biological connections and/or class position, especially if they knew little about the culture. I suspect this to be the case among Aboriginal people in Canada. Those who know little about the Aboriginal culture to which they claim a connection probably will emphasize their blood ties to an Aboriginal culture. Claiming to be born "Ojibwe" or "Blackfoot" does not necessarily entail a familiarity with the music, ceremonies, or language. This is a reality of living in a dispersed culture where there have been generations of increased pressure not to exhibit these cultural knowledges.

The interplay of biology, culture, and class cannot maintain its integrity when applied to Aboriginal cultures in North America. Perhaps in the mid-nineteenth century most Aboriginal people could be slotted by class, culture, and biology such that the categories remained relatively stable. Aboriginal persons for the most part were not only able to demonstrate who they were related to (biology), but also could make their way in their culture and were probably lower-class citizens in relation to the class structure of British North America. Today these factors are not necessarily applicable to each Aboriginal person, and it is impossible to predict with any certainty one's placement in each of these categories. For example, today many Aboriginal people may be slotted into lower socioeconomic categories in relation to Canadian class structure, but individual Aboriginal people are not necessarily reducible to a particular class. Also, many people with Aboriginal cultural knowledge have no ties to their home communities or to an officially recognized community. Conversely, many Aboriginal people with blood ties to Aboriginal communities have little or no Aboriginal cultural knowledge. The instability of these categories is evident when one looks at contemporary Aboriginal people on Turtle Island today.

IDENTIFYING AS SITUATIONAL AND CONTEXTUAL

Fitzgerald's (1977) observation that "cultural identity has relevance only in a situation of cultural homogeneity" (p. 59) appears to be supported by the research of both Valentine (1995) and Pinneault and Patterson (1997). Valentine lived and worked among the Anishinabe of Lynx Lake, Ontario where the community is composed almost entirely of Aboriginal families. As Valentine explains,

In southern Ojibwe communities, where forced contact with the White matrix society has been long standing, Native people tend to define themselves vis-à-vis the "other." Thus, if something is "White" then it is necessarily "not-Indian" and vice versa.... In the north, where there has been relatively little and generally recent contact with Whites, the Native people define themselves internally. In a situation such as that in Lynx Lake, it is moot to ask if one element or another is "White" or even "borrowed." If the people are using it, the item is being used "Natively." The question asked by the people of Lynx Lake is "Will X be useful to us?" not "Will the use of X compromise our Nativeness?" (p. 164)

Here the question of what is Aboriginal is raised only in comparison with cultures outside the community.

Contrast the Lynx Lake community with Pinneault and Patterson's (1997) work in urban schools in the Niagara region of Ontario. Here Pinneault and Patterson counsel youth who struggle with debunking myths and labels or with

trying to find where they fit in. Pinneault and Patterson describe the situation thus.

Attempt to put yourself in the following story. You are living in a land which is the first and only foundation of your philosophy, spiritual beliefs, historical patterns, cultural distinction, and ancestral connections. At the same time, you never see a reflection of yourself within the philosophy of others, the educational system, popular culture, or day-to-day events within the community. Stereotyping remains entrenched in most societal situations and you are constantly in a position of needing to defend your rights and position. When you are able to visualize yourself, it is through the interpretation of others who have little understanding of who you are. You are constantly being defined and redefined from an outside system. (p. 27)

Many students in the south are struggling with the creation of safe places to increase self-esteem and build understanding and acceptance of some of the Aboriginal cultural traditions. Obviously identity issues come to the fore when there is sustained contact between culturally different groups, and especially when they are valued differently on the social scale.

Another way to understand the differences between the disparate groups in Niagara and Lynx Lake is to discuss identifying rather than identity. Identifying in Niagara has different meanings and consequences than it does in Lynx Lake. Aboriginal people in Lynx Lake do not identify as "Native" in Lynx Lake because the homogeneous nature of the population makes it redundant to do so. The identity of the people in the distant communities is not different necessarily. Rather the factors that influence an Aboriginal person's choice to identify change from one region to another are different....

LEGISLATIVE DEFINITIONS AS IDENTITY

The Indian Act has been the source of many problems in the history of Aboriginal survival. It has been the legal support for violence enacted against Aboriginal peoples in the form of regulations imposed on personal mobility, language use, and participation in cultural activities. Relevant to this discussion is its peculiar claim of distinction as a rare piece of legislation that sets out in law a definition of a people. This definition has had a profound impact not only in how we are understood by non-Aboriginal people, but also in how we have come to understand ourselves....

In early legislation designed to contain potential violence between Aboriginal people and newcomers, a broad definition of *Indian* was set into law. For example, the 1850 Indian Protection Act defined Indians broadly:

The following classes of persons are and shall be considered as Indians belonging to the Tribe or body of Indians interested in such lands: First—All persons of Indian blood, reputed to belong to the particular Body or Tribe of Indians interested in such lands, and their descendants. Secondly—All persons intermarried with any such Indians and residing amongst them, and the descendants of all such persons. Thirdly—All persons residing among such Indians, whose parents on either side were or are Indians of such Body or Tribe, or entitled to be considered as such: And Fourthly—All persons adopted in infancy by any such Indians, and residing in the Village or upon the lands of such Tribe or Body of Indians, and their descendants.

The only important distinction was between European and Indian. Interestingly enough, early definitions of Indian like this one allowed for men and women of European descent who lived with an Aboriginal community to be considered Indian before the law. What mattered more than blood (although this too was important) was the evidence that one lived as an Indian. One would have to assume this distinction was relatively simple to make in the nineteenth century. Otherwise the definition would have been drafted differently.

As laws governing Indian lands were consolidated, the definition of an Indian in law was redrafted to exclude more Aboriginal people and to encourage the assimilation of registered Indians into the Canadian body politic (RCAP, 1996). Assimilation is genocide according to the United Nations Genocide Convention,

signed by Canada in 1949 and unanimously adopted in Parliament in 1952. Chrisjohn and Young with Maraun (1997) have argued that Canada could be tried in violation of the genocide convention for the operation of residential schools. The Canadian Civil Liberties Union, in debates held before Canada enabled legislation in 1952, recognized the potential for Canada's transfer of Indian children to residential schools to be seen as genocide (Churchill, 1997). Enfranchisement was also a key tool of assimilation or genocide.

Enfranchisement, along with definitions privileging patrilineal descent, reduced the number of Indians eligible for the Register. The children of interracial marriages were counted as Indians only when the father was Indian. Native women who married non-Native men were removed from the Register and often distanced from their communities. Over the years there were many ways Indians could lose their status. Some examples include earning a university degree, requesting the right to vote in a federal election, or requesting removal from the Indian Register for a share of the monies that would have gone to the band on their behalf. Most significantly, Indian women who married non-Indian men were enfranchised involuntarily, and the children of these marriages were ineligible for status. Clearly the goal of the Gradual Enfranchisement Act, and its subsequent absorption into the Indian Act, was assimilation (RCAP, 1996).

The Métis, as an Aboriginal people, found themselves caught in the middle of the changing legal definitions. The numbers of Métis who would have been entitled to receive the benefits of Indian status in 1850 were gradually reduced by arbitrary legislation. Great pains were taken to extinguish Métis claims to Aboriginal title, and they were not accorded any benefits in exchange for the land. This does not mean that only "full-blooded" Indians were entitled to be registered. What mattered was whether it was one's father or mother who was officially recognized as Indian. Often these non-status Indians would align themselves politically with the cultural Métis, who had for the most part been denied any rights as Aboriginal people. This denial occurred despite Métis treaties with Canada in the Manitoba Act and the Dominion Lands Act(s).

BEING AND BECOMING MÉTIS AS AN EXAMPLE OF IDENTIFYING

The Métis provide an interesting example of how colonial definitions are played out and affect self-definitions. Most people believe that Métis means simply "mixed" denoting the mixing of the blood of European and Indian parents in their child. The word has been used to designate various groups with a tie to Aboriginal peoples present on the continent before European settlement. How were the new populations that were a result of the new inter-relationships between Indian and non-Indian characterized or written about in the earliest times? How did Métis, which originally meant simply mixed, come to mean specific kinds of mixes and in specific times and locations?

Dunn (2001), a descendant of the Red River Métis and consultant to the RCAP, has an excellent Web site (www.otherMétis.net) that catalogues the many terms and names that have been used to describe the intermixing of European and Aboriginal peoples. It is important to note that there is little evidence of what these groups of people under discussion preferred to be called in the nineteenth century, and few records of what they called themselves exist. Most of these terms were used by colonial bureaucrats and traders who thought it important enough and necessary to write about this growing and influential population in their particular region.... The diversity of names used indicates at least two important points. First, the groups now known as Métis were seen as a distinct social fact by most of the social

groups sharing the same region. Second, the names accorded these groups of "mixed-race" people are ways for people external to the group to make an identity for them. Obviously some terms are meant to be disparaging. Dunn's ancestors were called Half-breed by the government officials of the day. At the same time, Dunn's great-great-grandfather used the term *Natives of the country* when referring to his group. In any case, as Dunn points out, "the external application of terminology does not guarantee that the term accurately communicates the expression of an internal identity" (para. 22). Identity is a process of being and becoming, and nouns cannot adequately be used to describe identity; rather they merely serve to label and fix a group of persons (Peterson & Brown, 1985). The attributes of the group that make it identifiable as distinct from others are constantly changing, and the words that are used to fix the group also change their referents. The use of the word Métis was taken up by these groups of "mixed blood" or "ancestry" and applied in different ways and for different ends.

At the constitutional conferences in the mid-1980s the leader of the Métis National Council (1986) stated:

> Surely it is more than racial characteristics that makes a people. What about a common history, culture, political consciousness? Our origins, like that of any people when traced back far enough, are mixed, but once we evolved into a distinct aboriginal people, the amount of this much or that much ancestry mattered less than being Métis.

Note that he stressed the acceptance of the community and identification with the community.

This distinction was promoted by the 1996 *Report of the Royal Commission on Aboriginal Peoples*, although it made some concessions for the Congress of Aboriginal Peoples definition of Métis, which is based solely on Aboriginal ancestry (blood). The RCAP (1996) recommendation is as follows:

The Commission recommends that Métis Identity
4.5.2 Every person who (a) identifies himself or
herself as Métis and (b) is accepted as such by the
nation of Métis people with which that person wishes
to be associated, on the basis of criteria and procedures
determined by that nation be recognized as a member
of that nation for purposes of nation-to-nation negotiations and as Métis for that purpose. (vol. 4: 203)

This definition, although leaving the choice of
political affiliation to the individual claimant, is
broad enough to include both Métis National
Council and Native Council of Canada/Congress
of Aboriginal Peoples members.

It should be noted that the Commission's
recommendation above is made in respect to the
sphere of political rights. The Commission (1996)
recognizes that the identification of Aboriginal
communities for legal purposes has taken a different approach. Essentially, after some analysis, the
Commission laid out three elements that seemed
to be acceptable to courts in determining membership in an Aboriginal community:

- some ancestral family connection (not necessarily
  genetic) with the particular Aboriginal people;
- self-identification of the individual with the
  particular Aboriginal people; and
- community acceptance of the individual by the
  particular Aboriginal people. (vol. 4: 297–98)

A fourth element was mentioned as also being
of relevance in some cases: "a rational connection, consisting of sufficient objectively deter-
minable points of contact between the individual
and the particular Aboriginal people" (vol. 4:
298). Acceptable criteria include residence,
family connections, cultural ties, language, and
religion (vol. 4: 298).

In many ways it seems as if we have come
full circle. Early attempts to legislate who is an
Indian were broad and inclusive and allowed for
anyone living in an Aboriginal community to
qualify as Indian under the law. Definitions
became increasingly exclusive, causing inequities and suffering and dissension among
Aboriginal peoples. The RCAP (1996) recommended that all Aboriginal peoples be entitled

to rights as members of an Aboriginal community. But history has seen individuals with
Aboriginal "blood" migrate to urban areas
where they may not live in Aboriginal communities that are located in a tight geographical
configuration. As sound and fair as it may
appear for legal reasoning to recognize only
Aboriginal communities and members of those
communities, in practice it may again turn out to
be a politically expedient way of reducing the
numbers of Aboriginal people whom the
government must recognize. In the end it really
may be up to the individuals in communities of
interest to decide what factors of their personality and culture make them distinctly Aboriginal
and continue a process of being and becoming
that cannot be legislated.

THE IMPACT OF IDENTITY

Once when I was talking to a friend and tenant
at a native housing co-op where I worked, I told
her that my lack of knowledge on a particular
issue was because I was not a politically active
person. She replied, "For an Indian, being born
is political." I realize now that she meant that
from the time we are born, as Indians we are in
a particular relationship with the Canadian state
by virtue of the treaties, the Indian Register,
and the Indian Act. She also meant that because
the state had been seeking our disappearance
for centuries, each time one more of us is born
we are directly in opposition to the goals of the
state. Each of us through our birth proved we
would not disappear. When we are born, we are
defined by the state as a particular kind of
Indian. Either we are eligible for the Indian
Register and designated a Status Indian, or we
are denied the rights that this heritage should
lend itself to. There were times when not being
registered was an advantage because the strict
enforcement of the Indian Act imposed many
measures on recognized Indians. The drawback,
of course, was that many identifiable Indians
were disallowed connections with their

extended families and some of the treaty rights their ancestors had negotiated.

Using strictly the legal view of Indianness, in my family's experience, my father was born an Indian, later "earned the right not to be an Indian" through enfranchisement, and many years later was seen as a Status Indian once again. I was not born an Indian and was given Indian Status only after passage of the amended Indian Act of 1985. Receiving that card in the mail made me question a lot of things, and it caused me to look at my family in a new way. I was confused about how we had an identity decided for us. Why was it not a given that we could define for ourselves who we were?

The issue of Aboriginal identity is most often played out in Canadian law. Aboriginal "difference" from others is used to maintain inequities in power when it is convenient for those with power (Macklem, 1993). However, when our difference results in what is seen as privilege, arguments are made that treating Aboriginal people differently is "un-Canadian" because it is in opposition to the stated goal of equality among individuals before the law. There is a constructed image of what Indians are supposed to be that has to be played into or against in order to make advances in Canadian institutions, especially courts of law (Crosby, 1992; Razack, 1998). If we do not appear Indian enough or do not exhibit enough of the traits that are somewhat expected of Indians, then we will be judged to be no longer different enough from the Euro-Canadian assumption of the mainstream, and thus no longer Aboriginal. We will, in fact, be assumed to have assimilated into the assumed mainstream Canadian norm.

This line of logic has been argued by lawyers for the Crown in the case for Gitksan-Wet'suwet'en Aboriginal title (Crosby, 1992). The Crown argued that because the contemporary Gitksan eat pizza from microwaves and drive cars, they have essentially given up their Aboriginality. Indian rights flow only to those who meet the criteria for authenticity established

by the Eurocentric courts (Crosby, 1992). Sustained colonization has caused many Aboriginal people to move away from a subsistence economy to a market economy, often without their choice. Many of the traditional ways of life seen from the Eurocentric position as "authentic Indian ways" have been altered by the imposition of colonial policies and laws, and then these very charges are used against us as arguments that we are no longer Aboriginal people.

The criteria accepted in the legal system, however, are often limited to material "stuff." What makes one Aboriginal is not the clothes one wears or the food one eats, but the values one holds. There is more to Aboriginal cultures than "fluff and feathers" (Doxtator, 1992). Johnston (1995), an Ojibwe ethnologist, recalls the time a young student in an elementary school, having spent five weeks learning about tipis, buskskin, canoes, and so much other stuff, asked him, "Is that all there is?" Johnston wanted people to know that there was more to Anishinabe culture than mere stuff, and this led him to write books like *Ojibway Heritage* (1976), *Ojibway Ceremonies* (1982), and *The Manitous* (1995). Unfortunately, in museums, movies, and courts of law it is the stuff that is exhibited. We are not Indian unless we prove that we still cling to the stuff that defined us in the eyes of others over 100 years ago. This conception will continue as long as we talk about identity and not identifying.

An interesting exercise is to turn these arguments around and apply them to the Eurocentric arguments for our assimilation. Does the lawyer who said the Gitksan-Wet'suwet'en drive cars realize that Europeans did not drive cars at the point of contact either? Was this lawyer wearing the same clothes his forefathers wore in 1763? Does this lawyer use the number zero? I think the use of zero may be been a case of cultural adoption, not unlike the Aboriginal people who adopt the use of snowmobiles. The culture that made the law is privileged to adapt and change over time, whereas the Aboriginal cultures are denied this same privilege.

Although it may not be the stated objective of the law, the result is often the maintenance of inequitable relations of power. Keeping Indians in the place they had at confederation is a goal of the consolidated Indian Act of 1876.

CONCLUSION

The Indian Act had as its goal nothing less than the assimilation of Aboriginal people in Canada (RCAP, 1996). A key strategy in achieving this goal was increasingly to limit who is an Indian by law and to change the status of those who were already on the list through enfranchisement. In this law "Indians" are identical to one another, but "different" from the Canadian power majority. The writers of legislation did not consider our cultures and histories important. Our identity as Indians was invented. Although at times we have used this identity to our own interests, forming coalitions across cultures to seek political gains (such as inclusion in the Constitution Act, 1982), we have also used these invented identities against one another, allowing these government categories to intrude on our social and cultural affairs (Coates, 1999). In our lives, in our work, in our efforts to educate others, let us identify as Aboriginal people from our inside place, from ourselves, our communities, our traditions. Let us not allow others to decide our identity for us.

ACKNOWLEDGMENTS

I would like to thank the anonymous reviewers of an earlier draft for their comments.

CRITICAL THINKING QUESTIONS

1. From a sociological perspective, why would possessing a positive self-identity influence how you lived your life?
2. With reference to the article, what role has the government played in the development of Aboriginal identity in Canada?

3. Review the similarities and differences between the concepts of *identity* and *identifying*. Why is the distinction important?
4. Review some of the recommendations for the *Report of the Royal Commission on Aboriginal Peoples* (1996) as described in the article. Can you find any examples from your own community where these recommendations have been implemented?

REFERENCES

Chrisjohn, R., & Young, S., with Maraun, M. 1997. *The circle game: Shadows and substance in the Indian residential school experience in Canada*. Penticton, B.C.: Theytus.

Churchill, W. 1997. *A little matter of genocide: Holocaust and denial in the Americas 1492 to the present*. San Francisco, CA: City Lights Books.

Coates, K. 1999. Being Aboriginal. In *Futures and identities: Aboriginal peoples in Canada*, ed. M. Behiels, 23–41. Montreal: Association for Canadian Studies.

Crosby, M. 1992. Construction of the imaginary Indian. In *Vancouver anthology: The institutional politics of art*, ed. S. Douglas, 267–91. Burnaby, B.C.: Talonbooks.

Doxtator, D. 1992. *Fluff and feathers: An exhibit of the symbols of Indianness*. Brantford, Ont.: Woodland Cultural Centre.

Dunn, M. 2001, January. Métis identity—A source of rights? Paper presented at Trent University. [Online]. Available: **http://www.otherMétis.net/index.html/Papers/trent/trent1.html#Terminology**. Retrieved January 4, 2001,

Fitzgerald, T. K. 1977. *Education and identity: A study of the New Zealand Maori graduate*. Wellington: New Zealand Council for Educational Research.

Johnston, B. 1976. *Ojibway heritage*. Toronto: McClelland and Stewart.

———. 1982. *Ojibway ceremonies*. Toronto: McClelland and Stewart.

———. 1995. *The Manitous: The spiritual world of the Ojibway*. Toronto: Key Porter Books.

Macklem, P. 1993. Ethnonationalism, Aboriginal identities, and the law. In *Ethnicity and Aboriginality: Case studies in ethnonationalism*, ed. M. D. Levin, 9–28. Toronto: University of Toronto Press.

Peterson, J., & J. S. H. Brown (eds.). 1985. *The new peoples: Being and becoming Métis in North America*. Winnipeg: University of Manitoba Press.

Pinneault, A., & Patterson, C. 1997. Native support circles in urban schools. *Orbit*, 28(1): 27–9.

Razack, S. 1998. *Looking white people in the eye: Gender, race and culture in courtrooms and classrooms*. Toronto: University of Toronto Press.

Restoule, J. P. 1999. Making movies, changing lives.

Aboriginal film and identity. In *Futures and identities: Aboriginal peoples in Canada,* ed. M. Behiels, 180–89. Montreal: Association for Canadian Studies.

Royal Commission on Aboriginal Peoples. 1996. *Report of the Royal Commission on Aboriginal Peoples.* Ottawa: Ministry of Supply and Services.

Sutherland, N. S. 1989. *The international dictionary of psychology.* New York: Continuum.

The Métis Nation. 1986. 2(1): Winter.

Valentine, L. P. 1995. *Making it their own: Severn Ojibwe communicative practices.* Toronto: University of Toronto Press.

39

Out of Harmony: Health Problems and Young Native American Men

Jennie R. Joe

Despite numerous medical advances, Native American men continue to experience more health problems and shorter life spans than their white counterparts. In this selection, Jennie R. Joe discusses the major health difficulties that confront young Native American men. She maintains that life expectancy rates of Native American men continue to lag behind those of their nonNative counterparts because of demographic and historical differences between these groups. According to Joe, colleges can be especially effective in providing intervention strategies that restore harmony in the lives of many Native American men.

The cultural perception and definition of health in most Native American (the term applies to both American Indians and Alaska Natives) communities are based on the concept of balance or harmony: a healthy state in which one is free of pain or discomfort, is at peace with oneself as well as with others, and is in harmony with all other elements of one's environment. Although these are ideal goals, disease, accidents, and misfortunes are also acknowledged as part of the reality of life. Until recently, very few Native Americans traditionally survived to old age. Such an event is considered a special achievement and the individual is honored and respected.

Reaching old age yesterday or today, however, is not easy. Before the mid-1940s, the average life expectancy for Native Americans was less than 50 years. Today, the life expectancy for Native American men continues to lag behind that of white men (*Regional differences*, 1997). Despite a multitude of medical advances, many Native American men at birth face a risk of premature mortality. This premature death and other indicators of poor health dominate the literature on the health of Native American men. Thus, any discussion of their health often emphasizes poor health and early mortality.

Poverty, poor education, high unemployment, unhealthy lifestyles, and voluntary and forced culture change are among the reasons for the premature mortality of Native American men. Although decades have passed since initial European contact, the consequences of colonization that followed this contact have forever altered tribal lifestyles and, in particular, the traditional role once held by young men.

Source: Jennie R. Joe, "Out of Harmony: Health Problems and Young Native American Men," *Journal of American College Health*, 49 (March, 2001): 237–42.

METHOD

My review of the health of young Native American men is based on a survey of existing literature as well as my knowledge of health care problems and issues that confront contemporary Native Americans.

RESULTS

Demographics

A majority of the Native American population lives in the American West, albeit Indians are present in all 50 states. Recently, the Native American population has been increasing. For example, the most recent 1995 population projection by the Indian Health Service (IHS) is approximately 2.7 million (*Projected American Indian,* 1994). In the 1990 census, Native American women outnumbered the men, 51 percent to 49 percent (1990 Census, 1993; Joe, 1996), and this proportion is not expected to change.

In general, the population profile of Native Americans parallels that of developing countries, namely high birth rates and a young median age. The 1990 census reported that 39 percent of Native Americans were then under the age of 20 years, compared with 29 percent for all races in the United States. The median age reported for the U.S. white population was 33 years, compared with about 27 years for the Native American population (*Projected American Indian,* 1994).

Census data also indicate that in 1990 more than half (56 percent of Native Americans lived in off-reservation communities. The increased rural-to-urban migration also reflects a change in the pattern of family units (Paisano et al., 1994; Snipp, 1997). For example, Sandefur and Liebler (1997) compared 1990 census data with 1980 data and found an increase in the number of Native American children living with one parent. In 1980, 54.4 percent of these children lived with one parent; in 1990, the percentage increased to 62.9. This 8.5 percent increase for Native Americans

was greater than the 6.5 percent increase for the general U.S. population during the same period (Snipp, 1997). Although a majority of the single-parent households among Native Americans are headed by women, it is interesting to note that 9 percent of the single heads of households were fathers (1990 Census, 1993).

Most employed Native American men hold low-paying jobs. This low income is further reflected in the $20,025 median family income reported in the 1990 Census, compared with $31,572 for white families. More Native American families also reported incomes below the national poverty level: 27 percent compared with 7 percent of White households (Gregory, Abello, & Johnson, 1997). Single women were heads of household in most of these low-income families, although poverty is also prevalent in two-parent families.

The lack of employment opportunities and poor wages contribute to high rates of unemployment. Even when employed, Native American men are more likely than Native American women to experience financial setbacks in employment. For example, when Gregory and colleagues compared Native American men's and women's earning levels over a 10-year period, they found that the economic deterioration was more devastating for men, whose earnings fell 12 percent between 1979 and 1989. In addition, these researchers noted that the average hourly earning ratio for Native American men, compared with that for Native American women, decreased 9 percent, yet the annual hours worked decreased by 3 percent (Gregory, Abello, & Johnson, 1997).

Economic downturns are especially damaging to those who have not completed high school. According to Gregory and associates (1997), the real income for these men dropped 22 percent, whereas Native American men with a college education experienced income increases.

Thus, the economic picture for Native American men and their families is greatly influenced by their educational attainments. In comparison with whites, fewer Native Americans complete high school or obtain a college degree. Paisano and colleagues note that only 9 percent of Native Americans (both men and women) hold a bachelor's degree or higher, compared with 22 percent for whites. The 1990 Census data (Paisano et al., 1994) revealed that 14 percent of Native Americans between the ages of eighteen and twenty-four years were enrolled in college in 1989. Although this is a significant number, many of these students do not complete college. Family crises or financial difficulties are frequently cited reasons for leaving school.

Research About Native American Men

Although much of what is reported in ongoing studies of men's health generally may have relevance for Native American men, I know of no current efforts to explore where and how some of these findings can be applied to this population. As I have pointed out, there is almost no research on healthy young Native American men of college age, a population that is of special interest for readers of *The Journal of American College Health*.

The focus of most studies on Native American men has been on various deviant behaviors and health problems in this population: alcoholism, delinquency, suicide, homicide, and criminal behavior (Jensen, Strauss, & Harris, 1977; Bachman, 1992). Whereas much is known about the incidence or prevalence of these problems, few researchers have addressed the reasons why the problems exist or why they persist.

Resources

To present a balanced picture of the overall health picture of young Native American men, one must piece together information from many sources. Unfortunately, the data may exist but are often collected in a way that discourages in-depth analyses. For example, health data collected and reported by IHS consist mainly of information from men who use IHS health facilities. Those data contain morbidity and mortality information by age and gender, but they cannot be examined in terms of other important variables such as years of schooling, socioeconomic status, and degree of acculturation.

That the IHS provides service to only a portion of the Indian population contributes to aspects of the data limitation. Despite these drawbacks, the IHS health data are perhaps the only health data collected routinely and reported annually on a significant percentage of Native Americans and are therefore an important resource when one examines the health of this group.

The IHS, funded by the U.S. Congress, offers health care annually to approximately 1.4 million of the estimated 2 million Native Americans who are members of federally recognized tribes (*Regional differences*, 1997) in 35 small hospitals, 2 large hospitals, and 59 health centers.

In addition, 12 hospitals and 155 health centers are managed by various tribal entities. Provision of services is based on a set of special federal-tribal treaty relationships. The system includes a variety of medical resources that are often the only healthcare in isolated rural communities.

The Health Situation

At different times, researchers such as Broudy and May (1983) and Young (1997) have discussed the changing health pattern of Native Americans, using the three-stage epidemiological model proposed by Omran (1983). The first stage in this model proposes an era of health problems caused by pestilence and famine, followed by an era of receding pandemics. In the third era, most health problems are attributed to the emergence of degenerative and manmade diseases. Olshansky and Ault (1986) have proposed a fourth state, the era of delayed degenerative disease.

Whether and for how long ancestors of most contemporary tribal groups experienced periods of pestilence or famine is not clear because most existing archaeological evidence is inconclusive. The era of pandemics, however, is well known. Following European contact, Native Americans experienced waves of contagious diseases such as smallpox that rapidly depopulated most of the Americas (Stearn & Stearn, 1945). The biological consequences of subsequent tuberculosis epidemics continued for Native Americans well into the first half of the twentieth century (the incidence of tuberculosis is today once again on the increase among Native Americans) (*Projected American Indian,* 1994; *Regional differences,* 1997). Not until the latter half of the last century did the morbidity and mortality picture for Native Americans shift from infectious diseases to domination by chronic diseases and other health behaviors associated with unhealthy lifestyles (U.S. Congress, 1990; Joe & Young, 1994). The consequences of unhealthy living are perhaps best reflected in the rising mortality and morbidity rates associated with unintentional injuries, especially among young Native American men. Most unintentional injuries, usually the result of automobile accidents, tend to be associated with drinking alcohol. Other accidents may result from high-risk occupations or participation in sports such as rodeos (*Injuries among American Indians,* 1990; *Regional differences,* 1997).

The Health of Young Native American Men

The life expectancy at birth (calculated for the period 1992–1994) for American Indian and Alaska Native men is 67.2 years compared with 72.2 for White men, 75.1 for Native American women, and 78.8 for women of all races (*Regional differences,* 1997). Many Native American men die before reaching the age of 30. For example, between 1992 and 1994, the age-specific death rate for young Native American men aged 15 to 24 years was 202.9 per 100,000, compared with the 1993 rate of 2.1 per 100,000 for U.S. men of all races (*Trends in Indian health,* 1994).

Accidents. Accidents, a majority of which involve motor vehicles and alcohol use (James et al., 1993; Kettl & Bixler, 1993; Sugarman & Grossman, 1996), are a major cause of the shortened life expectancy for many of these young Native American men and a leading cause of death for Native American men between the ages of 15 to 44 years. Although accident-related deaths are high for Native men, the rates fluctuate from year to year; they have nevertheless remained higher than the rates in the general U.S. population. Between 1990 and 1994, the adjusted accident-related mortality rate for Native American men of all ages was 94.5 per 100,000, compared with 30.3 per 100,000 for nonNative American men in 1993 (*Regional differences,* 1997). Alcohol is a major contributor to the high accident rate, and there are indications that, for some men, drinking starts early in life. Mail (1995) notes that alcohol consumption for some of these men started during grade school.

Deaths attributable to accidents are most frequent among younger men in the general population, rather than among men over the age of 50 years. The significance of this problem, however, appears to be greater for young Indian men than for others. For example, between 1992 and 1994, the accident death rate for Native American men aged 15 to 24 years was 150 per 100,000, compared with 57.6 for the same age group of men of all races in the United States. Moreover, the ratio of accident death rates for Native American men and women aged 25 and over is 2.8 to 3. The accident death rates for Native American women, however, are two to three times higher than that for other women in the United States (*Regional differences,* 1997).

Frequently, cultural tolerance for using alcohol, driving on poor roads, driving in unsafe vehicles, and acceptance of laws that prohibit the sale or possession of alcohol on reservations contribute to the high rates of alcohol-related motor vehicle accidents. The prohibition on reservation lands forces those who wish to drink to drive great distances to purchase alcohol, consume it on site, and then attempt the long drive home. Drinking behaviors and drinking styles of Native American men are similar to those of young men in other cultures: They are not afraid to take risks, are willing to test or ignore traffic and drinking laws, and believe that they are immortal.

Suicide. Although suicide rates in the U.S. population tend to be highest among persons over the age of 65 years, suicide is the fifth leading cause of death for Native American men over the age of 10 years. When age is included in the analysis, suicide becomes the second leading cause of death for Native American men between the ages of 10 and 24 years (*Projected American Indian,* 1994; *Regional differences,* 1997). Some suicides occur among boys and adolescents; the overall median age of Native Americans who committed suicide between 1979 and 1992 was 26 years (*Homicide and suicide,* 1996).

In their examination of homicide and suicide rates for Native Americans, researchers at the Centers for Disease Control and Prevention (CDC) found that 64 percent of all suicides between 1979 and 1992 were males, aged 15 to 34. The suicide rates for these men was 62 per 100,000 compared with 10 per 100,000 for Native American women in the same age group (*Homicide and suicide,* 1996). Firearms were used in more than half (57 percent of the suicides, with poisoning and strangulation as other frequent means of committing suicide.

Although firearms are the weapons of choice for suicides committed by both Native American men and women, hanging is the second choice for men, whereas poisoning ranks second for Native American women (*Homicide and suicide,* 1996). Reasons for these Native Americans choosing to end their lives are not always known, as is true in the general population. Poverty, family difficulties, poor self-esteem, grief, and an overwhelming sense of hopelessness are among the reasons frequently suggested by the victim's families or friends (Joe, 1996).

Homicide. Between 1990 and 1992, homicide was the third leading cause of years of potential loss of life for Native Americans less than 65 years of age; 28 was the median age of homicide victims (*Homicide and suicide,* 1996). Seven percent of these cases of lost potential years among Native Americans resulted from homicide, a rate that was exceeded only by two other leading causes of death—unintentional injury and heart disease (*Injuries among American Indians,* 1990; Sugarman & Grossman, 1996).

Data on homicide deaths for Native Americans between 1979 and 1992 indicate that men between the ages of 15 and 44 accounted for 60 percent of all Native American homicides. At highest risk were men aged 25 to 34 years. Rates for this age group between 1979 and 1992 were reported as 47 per 100,000. Forty-eight percent of the Native American homicide deaths involve firearms, primarily handguns, but cutting and stabbing also account for significant numbers of homicides (*Homicide and suicide,* 1996).

Approximately 66 percent of the Native American homicide victims between 1988 and 1991 were killed by persons they knew, and 63 percent of male homicide victims were killed by family members or acquaintances, in contrast to 50 percent for the general U.S. population. Between 1988 and 1991, 51 percent of the Native American victims were killed by other Native Americans, and 39 percent were killed by white persons. A majority of these homicides involved men killing men (*Homicide and suicide,* 1996).

Cancer. Cancer incidence and mortality is increasing among American Indians and Alaskan Natives (Greenwald et al., 1996), as is the case among other minority ethnic groups. The American Cancer Society recently reported that cancer incidence rates between 1988 and 1994 for African American men were 560 per 100,000, compared with 469 per 100,000 for white men (*Cancer facts,* 1997). Although rates of cancer in general are lower for Native Americans than for some other racial groups, rates for specific cancers (nasopharyngeal, gall bladder, and stomach) are higher among Indians and Alaska Natives (Haynes & Smedley, 1999). These lower cancer rates may be attributed, in part, to higher mortality from other causes because Native Americans' lifespans are generally shorter than are those of other ethnic groups.

Many factors—late diagnosis, lack of access to treatment, fear of cancer, a belief that cancer is not a problem for Native Americans—contribute to the high cancer mortality of American Indians and Alaska Natives: Although most cancer prevention programs have been initiated for tribal women, some prevention efforts, especially those emphasizing smoking cessation, have begun to target Native American men. A 1994 national health survey revealed that 54 percent of Native American men and 33 percent of women smoked (*Tobacco use*, 1998). Young men are frequently among the very heavy smokers (Cobb & Paisano, 1997).

Cancer incidence rates for Native Americans are generally lower than those for the U.S. population in general; however, cancer is among the leading causes of death for Indian men. The five major sites of cancers that contributed to high mortality among Native men during the years 1992 and 1994 were the lungs (trachea and bronchi), prostate, colon, stomach, and liver. The most recent IHS report indicates that the overall cancer mortality rate for Native American men aged 14 to 25 years was 3.7 compared with 3.3 per 100,000 for same age group of U.S. men, all races (Cobb & Paisano, 1997).

The report indicates that the cancer mortality rates for Native American men are approximately 57 percent greater than the rates for Native American women. Although cancer death rates increase with age among Native American women, cancer mortality occurs among younger men (Cobb & Paisano, 1997).

Diseases of the Heart. Heart disease is the leading cause of death for Native Americans as well as for Asian Americans, Pacific Islanders, and Hispanic Americans (Yu, 1991). One notable exception to these high rates of heart disease

death is found among tribal groups in the Southwest, who have low rates of heart disease in spite of a high prevalence of risk factors, including obesity, diabetes mellitus, and hypertension (*Regional differences,* 1997).

According to the IHS, heart disease death rates for U.S. residents of all races have decreased approximately 20 percent since 1984. Although the leading cause of death among Native Americans is heart disease, the IHS reported that their age-adjusted heart disease death rates have been relatively stable since 1984 (*Regional differences,* 1997). Deaths from heart disease, therefore, have not decreased for these Americans as they have for the U.S. population in general.

When Native Americans' heart disease death rates are examined for the years 1990 to 1992, the age-adjusted rate is 157.6 per 100,000, a rate that is 8 percent higher than the rate for all races in the United States. It should also be noted that during this same period, the age-adjusted death rate for heart disease for Native American men in all age groups was higher than it was for Native American women (*Regional differences,* 1991).

Alcohol and Alcohol Abuse. Alcohol is a frequent confounding factor in many unintended deaths for young Native Americans. During the 1995 fiscal year, alcohol-related hospitalization discharges were 31 per 100,000 of the IHS user population over the age of 15 years, a rate that is 1.6 times greater than the rate for the U.S. population in general (*Regional differences,* 1991).

For many Native American young adults, attitude and perception of alcohol use are established during adolescence, an age when peers are the most powerful determinant of one's behavior (Oetting & Beauvais, 1986; Swaim et al., 1993; Oetting & Donnermeyer, 1998). According to Oetting and Beauvais (1986), the decision of whether to use or not to use alcohol is embedded in adolescents' interactions with close peers. These peer clusters become the setting where "norming" takes place and attitudes and behaviors regarding alcohol use are determined. Beauvais (1998) notes that peer clusters are enmeshed in the larger peer culture and that this larger culture is where certain sociocultural values are learned and parameters are set on how one should behave to fit in with others.

In one earlier study, Swaim and colleagues (1993) found that the dynamic relationship between the influence of peers and parents differs for Native American and other American youth. Peers are important influences for both groups; for Native American youth, the influence of peers is equal to that of their parents.

The problem of alcohol use among the Native American population continues to be studied by researchers in various disciplines. Many theories about alcohol use have evolved from these different perspectives, theories that range from genetic propensity to social deprivation. One explanation held by a number of tribal communities is that the high prevalence of alcohol abuse is a result of the loss of tribal culture or tribal identity, a perspective that has strongly influenced the orientation and interventions strategies offered by prevention and treatment programs.

Beauvais (1998), however, notes that this perspective has not been useful for treating or working with adolescents and young adults. Most of these young people, he writes, have difficulties because they do not yet have the strong cultural identification necessary to want to quit drinking. He therefore concludes that culturally enriched intervention programs may not be meaningful for young Native Americans.

This observation is understandable because colonization either displaced or successfully erased the place for traditional tribal teachings and learning cultural values. Many Native American families, for example, lament that their children or grandchildren do not speak or understand their tribal language (Joe, 1997).

In the past, most Indian parents were purposefully excluded from participating in their children's education and were discouraged from visiting schools where their children were being groomed for the white world. In addition, teachers and administrators made every effort to keep the children from retaining any vestiges of their culture. Students who dared to speak their tribal languages were severely punished; tribal customs were publicly ridiculed, labeled primitive, and were totally unacceptable. It did not take long for many Indian children to become ashamed of their cultural heritage.

COMMENT

The effort to conquer the Americas and its inhabitants displaced and destroyed the culture of many indigenous peoples; the subsequent colonization further altered the traditional lifestyles of those indigenous peoples who survived the warfare, displacement, and repeated waves of devastating communicable diseases. Most of the statistics on poverty, early mortality, and morbidity among young Native American men that I have presented are reminders that significant proportions of each new generation of Native American men continue to suffer long-term consequences of colonization. Unhealthy lifestyles, unintentional accidents, suicide attempts, alcohol abuse, and societal neglect are symptoms of this disenfranchisement.

On the other hand, a significant number of Native American men who enter collegiate communities may be the lucky ones. For a variety of reasons, they have been spared the health problems prevalent in their age group. The collegiate environment, however, does not ensure health. Intense academic, family, or economic stresses have been known to trigger problems that lead to alcohol abuse or other unhealthy lifestyle behaviors.

Some colleges with sizable Native American enrollment have instituted strategies to prevent these problems. Some assist Native American students by designating a space in college residences staffed with peer counselors for incoming students from rural reservation communities. Some colleges and universities promote a Native American resource center, a special place on campus where these students can seek assistance and campus healthcare providers are invited and to speak on specific health topics or be available for health discussions. The latter is especially helpful for young Native American men who are less likely than other students are to use campus health services.

Including campus healthcare providers in student orientation programs is also helpful. In some colleges and universities, Native American student organizations have created resource booklets containing information or names of campus healthcare providers. Efforts such as these help support those students who need this type of individual support from their college healthcare providers.

CRITICAL THINKING QUESTIONS

1. Compare the Native American and white population in terms of median age, income, and employment. How does educational attainment explain some of these variations? Why are such demographic variables inadequate in explaining the overall health picture of Native American men?

2. Researchers have often attributed high and early death rates to "unhealthy lifestyles" during the latter part of the twentieth century. How does unhealthy living increase the mortality rates of young Native American men? Why are car accidents, suicide, homicide, and alcohol abuse higher for Native American men than for their white counterparts?

3. What does Joe mean when she says that the health of most Native American men is "out of harmony"? Out of harmony with what? Why does colonization appear to have had a greater negative impact on the cultural identity and health of Native American men than women? What strategies does Joe propose to restore Native American harmony with themselves and their environment?

REFERENCES

1990 Census of the population: American Indians and Alaska Native areas. 1993. Washington, D.C.: U.S. Dept. of Commerce, Bureau of the Census.

Bachman, R. 1992. *Death and violence on the reservation*. New York: Auburn.

Beauvais, F. 1998. American Indian youth and alcohol: A study in perplexity and ambivalence. *Alcoholic Beverage Medical Research Foundation Journal* (suppl. 3), 8(33): 61–5.

Broudy, D. W., and P. A. May. 1983. Demographic and epidemiological transition among the Navajo Indians. *Social Biology*, 30: 1–6.

Cancer facts and figures—1997. 1997. Atlanta, Ga.: American Cancer Society.

Cobb, N., and R. E. Paisano. 1997. *Cancer mortality among American Indians and Alaska Natives in the United States: Regional differences in Indian health, 1989–1993*. Rockville, Md.: USPHS, Indian Health Service.

Greenwald, J. P., E. F. Borgatte, R. McCorkle, and N. Polissar. 1996. Explaining reduced cancer survival among the disadvantaged. *Milbank Quarterly*, 74: 215–38.

Gregory, G. G., A. C. Abello, and J. Johnson. 1997. The individual economic well-being of Native American men and women during the 1980s: A decade of backwards. *Population Research and Policy Review*, 16: 115–45.

Haynes, M. A., and B. Smedley (eds.). 1999. *The unequal burden of cancer*. Washington, D.C.: National Academy Press.

Homicide and suicide among Native Americans, 1879–1992. 1996. Washington, D.C.: U.S. Dept. of Health and Human Services, Centers for Disease Control, National Center for Injury Prevention and Control.

Injuries among American Indians/Alaska Natives. 1990. Rockville, Md.: USPHS, Indian Health Service.

James, W. H., B. Hutchinson, D. Moore, and A. J. Smith. 1993. Predictors of driving while intoxicated (DWI) among American Indians in the Northwest. *Journal of Drug Education*, 24(4): 317–24.

Jensen, G. F., J. H. Strauss, and V. W. Harris. 1977. Crime, delinquency, and the American Indian. *Human Organization*, 36(3): 252–57.

Joe, J. R. 1996. The health of American Indian and Alaska Native women. *Journal of the American Medical Women's Association*, 51: 141–45.

———. 1997. *Iina ili* (life is valuable): The Hardrock community's efforts to address substance abuse problems. Unpublished report. Tuscan: University of Arizona, Native American Research and Training Center.

Joe, J. R., and R. S. Young. (eds.). 1994. *Diabetes as disease of civilization: The impact of culture change on indigenous peoples*. Berlin: Mouton de Gruyter.

Kettl, P., and E. O. Bixler. 1993. Alcohol and suicide. *American Indian and Alaska Native Mental Health Research*, 5(2): 34–45.

Mail, P. D. 1995. Early modeling of drinking behavior by Native American elementary school children playing drunk. *International Journal of Addiction*, 30(9): 1187–97.

Oetting, E., and F. Beauvais. 1986. Peer clusters theory: Drugs and the adolescent. *Journal of Counseling and Development*, 65(1): 17–22.

Oetting, E., and J. Donnermeyer. 1998. Primary socialization theory: The etiology of drugs and deviance. *Substance Abuse and Misuse*, 33: 995–1026.

Olshansky, S. J., and A. G. Ault. 1986. The fourth stage of epidemiological transition: The age of delayed degenerative disease. *Milbank Quarterly*, 64: 390–91.

Omran, A. R. 1983. The epidemiology transition theory: A preliminary update. *Journal of Tropical Pediatrics*, 29: 305–16.

Paisano, E. L., D. L. Caroll, J. H. Cowles, et al. 1994. *We, the first Americans*. Washington, D.C.: U.S. Dept. of Commerce, Bureau of the Census.

Projected American Indian and Alaska Native population for the United States, 1990–2005. 1994. Rockville, Md.: USPHS, Indian Health Service.

Regional differences in Indian health. 1997. Rockville, Md.: USPHS, Indian Health Service.

Sandefur, G. D., and C. A. Liebler. 1997. The demography of American Indian family. *Population Research and Policy Review*, 16: 95–114.

Snipp, C. M. 1997. The size and distribution of the American Indian population: Fertility, mortality, and residence. *Population Research and Policy Review*, 16: 61–93.

Stearn, E. W., and A. E. Stearn. 1945. *The effects of small-pox on the destiny of Amerindians*. Boston: B. Humphries.

Sugarman, J. R., and D. C. Grossman. 1996. Trauma among American Indians in an urban county. *Public Health Report*, 111(4): 320.

Swaim, R. C., E. R. Oetting, P. J. Thurman, F. Beauvais, and R. W. Edwards. 1993. American Indian adolescent drug use and socialization characteristics: A cross-cultural comparison. *Journal of Cross-Cultural Psychology*, 24(1): 53–70.

Tobacco use among U.S. racial/ethnic minority groups: A report of the Surgeon General. 1998. U.S. Dept. of Health and Human Services: Office of Smoking and Health, Centers for Disease Control.

Trends in Indian health, 1994. 1994. Rockville, Md.: USPHS, Indian Health Service.

U.S. Congress. 1986. *Indian health care*. Washington, D. C.: Office of Technology Assessment. U.S. Government Printing Office.

Young, T. K. 1997. Recent health trends in the Native American population. *Population Research and Policy Review*, 16(1, 2): 147–67.

Yu, P. N. 1991. Heart disease in Asian and Pacific-Islanders, Hispanics, and Native Americans. *Circulation*, 83(4): 1475–77.

40

The Tragedy of Old Age in America

Aging and the Elderly

CLASSIC

CONTEMPORARY

CROSS-CULTURAL

Robert N. Butler

North America has often been described as a "youth culture," in which youth is a measure of personal worth. In this selection, Robert Butler explores the American view of the elderly, which he finds to be fraught with myths and prejudices. He argues that these beliefs not only hurt seniors but also disadvantage everyone.

What is it like to be old in the United States? What will our own lives be like when we are old? Americans find it difficult to think about old age until they are propelled into the midst of it by their own aging and that of relatives and friends. Aging is the neglected stepchild of the human life cycle. Though we have begun to examine the socially taboo subjects of dying and death, we have leaped over that long period of time preceding death known as old age. In truth, it is easier to manage the problem of death than the problem of living as an old person. Death is a dramatic, one-time crisis while old age is a day-by-day and year-by-year confrontation with powerful external and internal

Source: From *Why Survive? Being Old in America* by Robert N. Butler, M.D., pp. 1–2, 6–12, 15–16, copyright © 1975 by Robert N. Butler, M.D., HarperCollins Publishers, Inc. Reprinted with permission of HarperCollins Publishers, Inc.

forces, a bittersweet coming to terms with one's own personality and one's life.

Those of us who are not old barricade ourselves from discussions of old age by declaring the subject morbid, boring, or in poor taste. Optimism and euphemism are other common devices. People will speak of looking forward to their "retirement years." The elderly are described respectfully as "senior citizens," "golden agers," "our elders," and one hears of old people who are considered inspirations and examples of how to "age well" or "gracefully." There is the popularly accepted opinion that Social Security and pensions provide a comfortable and reliable flow of funds so the elderly have few financial worries. Medicare has lulled the population into reassuring itself that the once terrible financial burdens of late-life illnesses are now eradicated. Advertisements and travel folders show relaxed, happy, well-dressed older people enjoying recreation, travel, and their grandchildren. If they are no longer living in the old family home, they are pictured as delighted residents of retirement communities with names like Leisure World and Sun City, with lots of grass, clean air, and fun. This is the American ideal of the "golden years" toward which millions of citizens are expectantly toiling through their workdays.

But this is not the full story. A second theme runs through the popular view of old age. Our colloquialisms reveal a great deal: Once you are old you are "fading fast," "over the hill," "out to pasture," "down the drain," "finished," "out of date," an "old crock," "fogy," "geezer," or "biddy." One hears children saying they are afraid to get old, middle-aged people declaring they want to die after they have passed their prime, and numbers of old people wishing they were dead.

What can we possibly conclude from these discrepant points of view? Our popular attitudes could be summed up as a combination of wishful thinking and stark terror. We base our feelings on primitive fears, prejudice, and stereotypes rather than on knowledge and insight. In reality, the way one experiences old age is contingent upon physical health, personality, earlier-life experiences, the actual circumstances of late-life events (in what order they occur, how they occur, when they occur), and the social supports one receives: adequate finances, shelter, medical care, social roles, religious support, recreation. All of these are crucial and interconnected elements which together determine the quality of late life....

MYTHS AND STEREOTYPES ABOUT THE OLD

In addition to dealing with the difficulties of physical and economic survival, older people are affected by the multitude of myths and stereotypes surrounding old age:

An older person thinks and moves slowly. He does not think as he used to or as creatively. He is bound to

himself and to his past and can no longer change or grow. He can learn neither well nor swiftly and, even if he could, he would not wish to. Tied to his personal traditions and growing conservatism, he dislikes innovations and is not disposed to new ideas. Not only can he not move forward, he often moves backward. He enters a second childhood caught up in increasing egocentricity and demanding more from his environment than he is willing to give to it. Sometimes he becomes an intensification of himself, a caricature of a lifelong personality. He becomes irritable and cantankerous, yet shallow and enfeebled. He lives in his past; he is behind the times. He is aimless and wandering of mind, reminiscing and garrulous. Indeed, he is a study in decline, the picture of mental and physical failure. He has lost and cannot replace friends, spouse, job, status, power, influence, income. He is often stricken by diseases which, in turn, restrict his movement, his enjoyment of food, the pleasures of well-being. He has lost his desire and capacity for sex. His body shrinks, and so too does the flow of blood to his brain. His mind does not utilize oxygen and sugar at the same rate as formerly. Feeble, uninteresting, he awaits his death, a burden to society, to his family and to himself.

In its essentials, this view I have sketched approximates the picture of old age held by many Americans. As in all clichés, stereotypes, and myths there are bits of truth. But many of the current views of old age represent confusions, misunderstandings, or simply a lack of knowledge about old age. Others may be completely inaccurate or biased, reflecting prejudice or outright hostility. Certain prevalent myths need closer examination.

The Myth of "Aging"

The idea of chronological aging (measuring one's age by the number of years one has lived) is a kind of myth. It is clear that there are great differences in the rates of physiological, chronological, psychological, and social aging within the person and from person to person. In fact, physiological indicators show a greater range from the mean in old age than in any other age group, and this is true of personality as well. Older people actually become more diverse rather than more similar with advancing years.

There are extraordinarily "young" eighty-year-olds as well as "old" eighty-year-olds. Chronological age, therefore, is a convenient but imprecise indicator of physical, mental, and emotional status. For the purposes of this book old age may be considered to commence at the conventionally accepted point of sixty-five.

We do know that organic brain damage can create such extensive intellectual impairment that people of all types and personalities may become dull-eyed, blank-faced, and unresponsive. Massive destruction of the brain and body has a "leveling" effect which can produce increasing homogeneity among the elderly. But most older people do not suffer impairment of this magnitude during the greater part of their later life.

The Myth of Unproductivity

Many believe the old to be unproductive. But in the absence of diseases and social adversities, old people tend to remain productive and actively involved in life. There are dazzling examples like octogenarians Georgia O'Keeffe continuing to paint and Pope John XXIII revitalizing his church, and septuagenarians Duke Ellington composing and working his hectic concert schedule and Golda Meir acting as her country's vigorous Prime Minister. Substantial numbers of people become unusually creative for the first time in old age, when exceptional and inborn talents may be discovered and expressed. What is most pertinent to our discussion here, however, is the fact that many old people continue to contribute usefully to their families and community in a variety of ways, including active employment. The 1971 Bureau of Labor Statistics figures show 1,780,000 people over sixty-five working full time and 1,257,000 part time. Since society and business practice do not encourage the continued employment of the elderly, it is obvious that many more would work if jobs were available.

When productive incapacity develops, it can be traced more directly to a variety of losses,

diseases, or circumstances than to that mysterious process called aging. Even then, in spite of the presence of severe handicaps, activity and involvement are often maintained.

The Myth of Disengagement

This is related to the previous myth and holds that older people prefer to disengage from life, to withdraw into themselves, choosing to live alone or perhaps only with their peers. Ironically, some gerontologists themselves hold these views. One study, *Growing Old: The Process of Disengagement*, presents the theory that mutual separation of the aged person from his society is a natural part of the aging experience. There is no evidence to support this generalization. Disengagement is only one of many patterns of reaction to old age.

The Myth of Inflexibility

The ability to change and adapt has little to do with one's age and more to do with one's life-long character. But even this statement has to be qualified. One is not necessarily destined to maintain one's character in earlier life permanently. True, the endurance, the strength, and the stability in human character structure are remarkable and protective. But most, if not all, people change and remain open to change throughout the course of life, right up to its termination. The old notion, whether ascribed to Pope Alexander VI or Sigmund Freud, that character is laid down in final form by the fifth year of life can be confidently refuted. Change is the hallmark of living. The notion that older people become less responsive to innovation and change because of age is not supported by scientific studies of healthy older people living in the community or by everyday observations and clinical psychiatric experience.

A related cliché is that political conservatism increases with age. If one's options are constricted by job discrimination, reduced or fixed income, and runaway inflation, as older people's are, one may become conservative out of economic necessity rather than out of qualities innate in the psyche. Thus an older person may vote against the creation of better schools or an expansion of social services for tax reasons. His property—his home—may be his only equity, and his income is likely to be too low to weather increased taxes. A perfectly sensible self-interest rather than "conservatism" is at work here. Naturally, conservatives do exist among the elderly, but so do liberals, radicals, and moderates. Once again diversity rather than homogeneity is the norm.

The Myth of "Senility"

The notion that old people are senile, showing forgetfulness, confusional episodes, and reduced attention, is widely accepted. "Senility" is a popularized layman's term used by doctors and the public alike to categorize the behavior of the old. Some of what is called senile is the result of brain damage. But anxiety and depression are also frequently lumped within the same category of senility, even though they are treatable and often reversible. Old people, like young people, experience a full range of emotions, including anxiety, grief, depression, and paranoid states. It is all too easy to blame age and brain damage when accounting for the mental problems and emotional concerns of later life.

Drug tranquilization is another frequent, misdiagnosed, and potentially reversible cause of - so-called senility. Malnutrition and unrecognized physical illnesses, such as congestive heart failure, may produce "senile behavior" by reducing the supply of blood, oxygen, and food to the brain. Alcoholism, often associated with bereavement, is another cause. Because it has been so convenient to dismiss all these manifestations by lumping them together under an improper and inaccurate diagnostic label, the elderly often do not receive the benefits of decent diagnosis and treatment.

Actual irreversible brain damage,[1] of course, is not a myth, and two major conditions create mental disorders. One is cerebral arteriosclerosis (hardening of the arteries of the brain); the other,

unfortunately referred to as senile brain disease, is due to a mysterious dissolution of brain cells. Such conditions account for some 50 percent of the cases of major mental disorders in old age, and the symptoms connected with these conditions are the ones that form the basis for what has come to be known as senility. But, as I wish to emphasize again, similar symptoms can be found in a number of other conditions which *are* reversible through proper treatment.

The Myth of Serenity

In contrast to the previous myths, which view the elderly in a negative light, the myth of serenity portrays old age as a kind of adult fairyland Now at last comes a time of relative peace and serenity when people can relax and enjoy the fruits of their labors after the storms of active life are over. Advertising slogans, television, and romantic fiction foster the myth. Visions of carefree, cookie-baking grandmothers and rocking-chair grandfathers are cherished by younger generations. But, in fact, older persons experience more stresses than any other age group, and these stresses are often devastating. The strength of the aged to endure crisis is remarkable, and tranquility is an unlikely as well as inappropriate response under these circumstances. Depression, anxiety, psychosomatic illnesses, paranoia, garrulousness, and irritability are some of the internal reactions to external stresses.

Depressive reactions are particularly widespread in late life. To the more blatant psychotic depressions and the depressions associated with organic brain diseases must be added the everyday depressions that stem from long physical illness or chronic discomfort, from grief, despair, and loneliness, and from an inevitably lowered self-esteem that comes from diminished social and personal status.

Grief is a frequent companion of old age—grief for one's own losses and for the ultimate loss of one's self. Apathy and emptiness are a common sequel to the initial shock and sadness that come with the deaths of close friends and relatives. Physical disease and social isolation can follow bereavement.

Anxiety is another common feature. There is much to be anxious about; poverty, loneliness, and illness head the list. Anxiety may manifest itself in many forms: rigid patterns of thinking and behaving, helplessness, manipulative behavior, restlessness and suspiciousness, sometimes to the point of paranoid states.[2]

Anger and even rage may be seen:

Mary Mack, 73, left her doctor's office irritable, depressed, and untreated. She was angry at the doctor's inattention. She charged that he simply regarded her as a complainer and did not take the necessary time to examine her carefully. She had received the same response from other doctors. Meanwhile her doctor entered the diagnosis in his file: hypochondriasis with chronic depression. No treatment was given. The prognosis was evidently considered hopeless.

John Barber, an elderly black man, spent all his life working hard at low wages for his employers. When he was retired he literally went on strike. He refused to do anything. He would sit all day on his front porch, using his family as the substitute victim of his years of pent-up anger. He had always been seen as mild mannered. Now he could afford to let himself go into rages and describe in vicious detail what he was going to do to people. A social worker viewing his behavior declared to his family that he was "psychotic." But Mr. Barber was not insane; he was angry.

AGEISM—THE PREJUDICE AGAINST THE ELDERLY

The stereotyping and myths surrounding old age can be explained in part by lack of knowledge and by insufficient contact with a wide variety of older people. But there is another powerful factor operating—a deep and profound prejudice against the elderly which is found to some degree in all of us. In thinking about how to describe this, I coined the word "ageism" in 1968:

Ageism can be seen as a process of systematic stereotyping of and discrimination against people because they are old, just as racism and sexism accomplish this with skin color and gender. Old people are categorized as senile, rigid in thought and manner, old-fashioned in morality and skills.... Ageism allows the younger generations to see older people as different from themselves; thus they subtly cease to identify with their elders as human beings.

Ageism makes it easier to ignore the frequently poor social and economic plight of older people. We can avoid dealing with the reality that our productivity-minded society has little use for nonproducers—in this case those who have reached an arbitrarily defined retirement age. We can also avoid, for a time at least, reminders of the personal reality of our own aging and death.

Ageism is manifested in a wide range of phenomena, both on individual and institutional levels—stereotypes and myths, outright disdain and dislike, or simply subtle avoidance of contact; discriminatory practices in housing, employment, and services of all kinds; epithets, cartoons, and jokes. At times ageism becomes an expedient method by which society promotes viewpoints about the aged in order to relieve itself of responsibility toward them. At other times ageism serves a highly personal objective, protecting younger (usually middle-aged) individuals—often at high emotional cost—from thinking about things they fear (aging, illness, death)....

Older people are not always victims, passive and fated by their environment. They, too, initiate direct actions and stimulate responses. They may exploit their age and its accompanying challenges to gain something they want or need, perhaps to their own detriment (for example, by demanding services from others and thus allowing their own skills to atrophy). Exploitation can backfire; excessive requests to others by an older person may be met at first, but as requests increase they are felt as demands—and may indeed be demands. Younger people who attempt to deal with a demanding older person may find themselves going through successive cycles of rage, guilt, and overprotectiveness without realizing they are being manipulated. In addition to his "age," the older person may exploit his diseases and his impairments, capitalizing upon his alleged helplessness. Invalids of all ages do this, but older people can more easily take on the appearance of frailty when others would not be allowed this behavior. Manipulation by older people is best recognized for what it is—a valuable clue that there is energy available which should be redirected toward greater benefit for themselves and others.

It must also be remembered that the old can have many prejudices against the young. These may be a result of their attractiveness, vigor, and sexual prowess. Older people may be troubled by the extraordinary changes that they see in the world around them and blame the younger generation. They may be angry at the brevity of life and begrudge someone the fresh chance of living out a life span which they have already completed.

Angry and ambivalent feelings flow, too, between the old and the middle-aged, who are caught up in the problems unique to their age and position within the life cycle. The middle-aged bear the heaviest personal and social responsibilities since they are called upon to help support—individually and collectively—both ends of the life cycle: the nurture and education of their young and the financial, emotional, and physical care of the old. Many have not been prepared for their heavy responsibilities and are surprised and overwhelmed by them. Frequently these responsibilities trap them in their careers or life styles until the children grow up or their parents die. A common reaction is anger at both the young and the old. The effects of financial pressures are seen primarily in the middle and lower economic classes. But the middle-aged of all classes are inclined to be ambivalent toward the young and old since both age groups remind them of their own waning youth. In addition—with reason—

they fear technological or professional obsolescence as they see what has happened to their elders and feel the pressure of youth pushing its way toward their position in society. Furthermore, their responsibilities are likely to increase in the future as more and more of their parents and grandparents live longer life spans.

CRITICAL THINKING QUESTIONS

1. Butler presents several themes that shape popular views of old age in the United States. What evidence of these do you find in the mass media? What about in your own attitudes and behaviour toward senior citizens?
2. Why do you think North American society has developed unrealistic views of aging?
3. How do seniors themselves sometimes reinforce ageism?

NOTES

1. Human beings react in varying ways to brain disease just as they do to other serious threats to their persons. They may become anxious, rigid, depressed, and hypochondriacal. (Hypochondriasis comprises bodily symptoms or fear of diseases that are not due to physical changes but to emotional concerns. They are no less real simply because they do not have a physical origin.) These reactions can be ameliorated by sensitive, humane concern, talk, and understanding even though the underlying physical process cannot be reversed. Therefore, even the irreversible brain syndromes require proper diagnosis and treatment of their emotional consequences.

2. No less a thinker than Aristotle failed to distinguish between the intrinsic features of aging and the reaction of the elderly to their lives. He considered cowardice, resentment, vindictiveness, and what he called "senile avarice" to be intrinsic to late life. Cicero took a warmer and more positive view of old age. He understood, for example, "If old men are morose, troubled, fretful, and hard to please…these are faults of character and not of age." So he explained in his essay *"De Senectute."*

41

Aging Families:
Have Current Changes and
Challenges Been "Oversold"?

Carolyn J. Rosenthal

Aging
and the
Elderly

CLASSIC

CONTEMPORARY

CROSS-CULTURAL

In this discussion of the changing structure of Canadian families, Rosenthal reviews some apocalyptic predictions about the future in light of recent research findings.

INTRODUCTION

Apocalyptic demography is typically invoked in relation to state-supported pension and health-care programs. Is there also an apocalyptic demography of the family, or what one might call apocalyptic thinking about the family? How is population aging reflected at the level of the family? What aspects of these demographic and associated changes have been "oversold"? Once we have identified how families are changing, we may then ask whether these changes are indeed apocalyptic and, further, what the real challenges are.

Source: Excerpted from "Aging Families: Have Current Changes and Challenges Been 'Oversold'?" by Carolyn J. Rosenthal in *The Overselling of Population Aging: Apocalyptic Demography, Intergenerational Challenges, and Social Policy* edited by Ellen M. Gee and Gloria M. Gutman. Copyright © Oxford University Press Canada 2000. Reprinted by permission of Oxford University Press Canada.

Most, though not all, of the major changes in contemporary families, as compared to families in the past, are related to demographic changes. Over the course of this century, there have been significant changes in family structure, patterns of marriage and divorce, the occurrence and timing of various family life-course events, and women's paid labour force participation. Increases in life expectancy have resulted in families typically including elderly members. The dynamic aspect of this is a much increased overlap of lives between familial generations. During the past century, widowhood became a typical experience for women—a normative life event. Divorce began to increase when Canadian laws were liberalized in the late 1960s. Female employment began to rise sharply in the early 1970s, with a resultant trend to dual-earner families replacing the traditional male breadwinner/female homemaker family as the normative pattern in husband-wife families.

Apocalyptic thinking about these changes in families has focused mainly on caregiving—either the increased likelihood that middle-aged adults will be faced with an older parent who requires care or the increased likelihood that older people who need care will not have family to whom to turn. In various places in this chapter I will argue that empirical research fails to support such apocalyptic thinking and its related claims. At the same time, I will frequently offer the reminder—and plea—that there is more to family life than caregiving and that we very much need research that goes beyond caregiving in studying what these changes mean to families and family life.

THE CHANGING STRUCTURE OF FAMILIES

How has the structure of families changed? What are the challenges associated with these changes? Have these challenges been overstated? Identifying changes in family structure is not simply a matter of academic interest. Policy-makers and the general public are very interested in the implications of these changes. Anne Martin-Matthews and I (1993) have used the term "structural potential" to denote how family structure creates the potential for experiencing various types of family role demands. This is distinguished from actually facing demands and providing help or care, an issue to which I will turn later in this chapter.

The Increasing Likelihood of Having an Older Parent Alive

Almost all young adult Canadians have living parents (Table 41.1). A majority have a living parent until ages 55–9, when about 4 in 10 are still in the adult child role. At ages 60–4, only 2 in 10 still occupy this role. It is also important to note that from age 45 onward, a majority of men and women who do have a parent alive have only one parent, a situation that potentially increases

responsibility on adult children. If one is ultimately interested in the potential burden placed on adult children by having older parents, it is important to consider the structural feature of having a living parent in the context of that parent's age. Table 41.1 shows that among those in their late thirties and early forties, the average age of parents is relatively young. If we take age 75 and older as the time when health downturns typically occur (Marshall et al., 1983), then we may expect Canadian men and women in their thirties and early forties to have healthy parents who do not require help. Even in their late forties, children are unlikely to have mothers whose age suggests the need for help. Fathers are in a vulnerable age group by this time in their children's lives, but, typically, these fathers will still have their wives to provide such help as is needed. Adult children in their early fifties have parents nearing age 80 and very substantial minorities have only one parent. By age 55 and over, a majority have only one parent alive and that parent is typically over age 80. In other words, by age 50 and more clearly by age 55, we might speculate that the structural potential for needing to help parents may well translate into actual help provision.

The Increasing "Generational Overlap" of Lives

To this point I have presented cross-sectional data on the likelihood of having a parent alive at different ages, a likelihood that has increased over the course of this century. This is clearly seen when we examine the increase in the likelihood of a middle-aged adult having a surviving parent. Gee (1990) compares the proportion of three Canadian birth cohorts having a surviving parent at age 50 and age 60. Among Canadians born in 1910, only 33 per cent of individuals at age 50 had a surviving parent. This rose to 49 per cent of those born in 1930 and is expected to rise to 60 per cent of those born in 1960. The likelihood of having a surviving parent at age 60 has

TABLE 41.1: Percentage of Canadians with Parent/s Alive, by Age and Gender

Age	35–9		40–4		45–9		50–4		55–9		60–4	
Number of parents	Women	Men	Women	Men	Women	Men	Women	Men	Women	Men	Women	Men
0	8.9	7.5	14.7	14.6	20.7	26.4	46.6	41.0	60.6	62.3	79.4	82.0
1	35.8	36.1	46.2	41.4	52.2	46.7	39.3	46.2	34.6	33.4	17.6	16.8
2	55.3	56.4	39.1	44.0	27.1	26.8	14.1	12.8	4.8	4.3	2.7	1.2
Age of mother (x)	64.2	65.1	69.8	69.3	74.4	73.3	77.5	78.2	82.0	82.8	85.8	86.4
Age of father (x)	66.8	67.7	72.4	72.0	75.6	76.8	79.0	79.3	82.5	84.1	85.9	86.0

Source: General Social Survey of Canada, 1990.

increased from 8 per cent of those born in 1910 to 16 per cent for those born in 1930 and is predicted to rise to 23 per cent for those born in 1960. It has thus become the majority pattern to have a surviving parent at age 50 and it is becoming more common to have one even at age 60. A related phenomenon is the growing likelihood that young adults still have a grandparent alive. These are, in my view, very positive changes.... The longer duration of grandparents' presence in a family ought to create benefits in terms of family cohesion and continuity. It certainly creates the opportunity to be an adult grandchild and for grandparents to have relationships with their grandchildren that extend into the latter's adulthood. Yet research on adult grandchildren is extremely limited. What are the challenges of having older family members? The one challenge that has received extensive research attention is caregiving—the burden on middle generations imposed by older family members with chronic illness or disability who require care. This is an important issue, but surely caregiving is only one aspect of a broad spectrum of family relations.

Changing Patterns of Marriage, Widowhood, and Divorce

Table 41.2 presents data on marital status at different ages for three cohorts of women in order to provide an indication of changing patterns. Among today's elderly women, widowhood is an expectable life event (Martin-Matthews, 1987), while the normative marital status among older men is married (Table 41.2). Divorce was almost unknown among older women who were aged 65–74 in 1991. Similar patterns are seen in the following cohort (women aged 55–64 in 1991), although members of this cohort are somewhat less likely to be widowed as they enter old age, largely due to the declines in mortality rates of males in mid-life. Among those outside of marriage, however, women in this cohort are somewhat less likely to be widowed and more likely to be divorced compared to the previous cohort (Rosenthal et al., forthcoming).

Since the liberalization of Canadian divorce laws in the late 1960s, divorce rates have increased markedly. Divorce has an impact on older families in two ways—directly (i.e., the individual has experienced divorce) and indirectly (i.e., one's children have experienced divorce). Divorce in the adult child generation may increase needs for support from older parents, particularly for the parents of the custodial child (Gladstone, 1988). Conversely, for others, maintaining contact with grandchildren may become problematic. Some grandparents face serious barriers to maintaining relationships with grandchildren following middle-generation divorce, and indeed we read quite a bit about this situation in articles about the grandparent rights movement. We also read (especially in the U.S. press and literature) about grandparents who

TABLE 41.2 Marital Status Trends, Women, 1961–1991: Percentage Distributions by Cohort and Marital Status

Marital Status	1971	1981	1991	Cohort
Married:				
Age in 1991				
65–74	48.9	51.1	53.9	Born 1917–26
55–64	69.9	72.8	71.8	Born 1927–36
45–54	83.8	83.1	77.2	Born 1937–46
Widowed:				
Age in 1991				
65–74	39.6	37.8	34.8	Born 1917–26
55–64	18.6	17.1	14.6	Born 1927–36
45–54	6.9	5.9	4.7	Born 1937–46
Divorced:				
Age in 1991				
65–74	0.9	2.1	4.0	Born 1917–26
55–64	1.6	3.5	7.1	Born 1927–36
45–54	1.9	5.1	9.2	Born 1937–46

Source: Statistics Canada, *The Nation* (1993), Catalogue No. 93-310, p. 33.

become surrogate parents, for example, when the adult child is a drug addict. Between these two extremes, however, is what I speculate is the majority of grandparents, who join in the struggle that is part of the aftermath of divorce— trying to help adult children through the difficult divorce transition, trying to provide continuity and stability for grandchildren, trying to maintain relationships in non-custodial situations, in short, trying to muddle through.

Divorce may also be experienced directly, not simply as a parent or grandparent. Having the marital status of "divorced" is rare among today's elderly but will be somewhat more common in the cohort about to enter old age. It is difficult to predict precisely the proportion of women in the future who will enter old age as divorced persons because some of today's divorced women will remarry.

What impact will these changes have on older people? Divorce legally severs some kin relationships; for example, daughters-in-law become ex-daughters-in-law. Remarriage, on the other hand, creates new relatives; for example, the remarriage of a daughter brings not only a new son-in-law but perhaps stepgrandchildren. One's own remarriage may bring not only a new spouse but stepchildren. We do not know very much, though, about the extent to which such relationships become attenuated following the dissolution of marriage through death or divorce. Nor do we know much about the extent to which kin acquired later in the life course, that is in mid-life or later life, are supportive and/or remain so following the death of the "linking" person. (For example, if a woman remarries in her fifties and is married for 15 years before her "new" spouse dies, what relationship would be maintained between her and her stepchildren after she is widowed?) Riley and Riley (1993) refer to a "latent matrix of kin relationships," created by increasing longevity and increasing prevalence of divorce and remarriage. Matilda Riley (1983: 451) argues that the "kinship structure has become more extensive and complex, the temporal and spatial boundaries of the family have been altered, and the opportunities for close family relationships have proliferated." Riley's concept of a latent matrix is similar to the concept of "structural potential" that I referred to earlier (Martin-Matthews & Rosenthal, 1993). Uhlenberg (1993), however, argues that although divorce may lead to a larger web of relationships, research suggests that divorce weakens many types of family relationships. Therefore, although there may be notable exceptions, in the general case the expansion of relationships in reconstituted families does not translate into increased support for older people. Having said this, however, I think we need a lot more research on what happens to kin relationships following divorce or death of the "linking" individual. For example, we need research beyond that which simply tells us that this type of relative provides less support than another type of relative (e.g., blood kin).

The "Shrinking" Supply of Children

We hear regularly that the birth rate has fallen and that the average family size (i.e., number of children) has decreased. But what does this mean with respect to actual families, who are not "averages," and to potential support for older people? Uhlenberg (1993: 225) points out that while it is true that over the long term the demographic transition means a reduced average number of children for the elderly, "assertions about the future supply of children for the elderly can be misleading unless two important questions are addressed: What changes in family size make a significant difference? What is the timing of changes in the family size of the elderly?" Uhlenberg argues that:

Although total support received from children is positively related to number of children, the marginal benefits from each additional child beyond the second or third is small. The most critical distinction regarding family size is between having none versus having some, and the second-most important distinction is between having one compared with having two or more. Thus, interest in changing family size should pay less attention to changes in mean number and more attention to proportion with zero or only one child. (Ibid)

...Gee (1995) argues that, in old age, it is the number of surviving children, not the number of children ever born, that is critical. The 1990 Canadian General Social Survey showed that 21 per cent of all men and 24 per cent of all women aged 75 and over have no surviving children (remarkably similar to the U.S. figure for childlessness among women aged 85 and over...). The trends described here indicate that upcoming cohorts of old and middle-aged adults, particularly the parents of the baby boom, will be more likely than their predecessors to be able to draw upon support from children. The challenges engendered by changes in fertility rates need to be viewed in historical perspective (many are not new) and linked to cohort analysis. It is fair to say that alarm calls about the shrinking supply of children are an overstatement—if not a distortion of reality.

The Changing Structure of Multi-generational Families

All of the changes discussed so far combine to produce changes in the generational structure of families. For at least 20 years, social scientists have described the generational structure of families as becoming "long and thin." Bengston et al. (1990) use the term "beanpole" family to describe a family form that contains several generations—four or even five—but relatively few people in each generation. This structure implies a heavy burden on middle generations to care for younger and older generation members, with the prospect of someone in old age caring for someone in very old age. This structure is said to have become increasingly common and, indeed, to be the prototypical family form....

What about the beanpole family type? Uhlenberg asks "how accurate is the often repeated assertion that four- and five-generation families are becoming increasingly common as a result of increased longevity?" He points out that no estimates for the population based on representative samples exist to back up this claim. Rossi and Rossi (1990), based on their study of 1400 adults in Boston, contend that popular beliefs about the prevalence of multi-generational families are exaggerated. Data from the National Survey of Families and Households in the United States (Winsborough et al., 1991) suggest that about one-third of adults aged 45–64 are members of four-generation families. All indications are that very few individuals are or ever will be part of a five-generation family. Moreover, Uhlenberg concludes that the four-generation family will not be the dominant lineage type. Therefore, while the beanpole family, in the sense of generational depth, is probably more common than in the past, we need to be cautious about making sweeping statements about its prevalence....

The Scattering of the Family

Another component of apocalyptic thinking at the level of family change is that, should older people require care, their children will be too far away to provide it. This view encompasses assumptions about both living arrangements and wider geographic dispersion.

Considering living arrangements first. [S]ince about 1960 there has been a trend for older Canadians to live either as a married couple or alone. This trend in living alone is especially pronounced among women (Connidis, 1989; Wister, 1985). Between 1961 and 1991, the proportion of women aged 65 and over living alone more than doubled, from 16 per cent to 34 per cent. Among widowed women, the proportion living alone is close to 80 per cent (Martin-Matthews, 1991: 79). In my view, this is a positive rather than a negative change, one that reflects not only changing norms but, more fundamentally, the opening up of options to women in that Old Age Security and subsidized housing make independent living possible. "One woman, one kitchen" seem to be a strong cultural preference in North America. We have enough evidence that older people like to see their children regularly but do not want to share the same household that we can put to rest arguments promoting shared living between older parents and adult children as an optimal arrangement for most older people....

The fact that most older people do not live in the same household as their children, however, does not necessarily mean that they do not live near their children. Assumptions and statements about the decreasing proximity of older parents and adult children because of increased rates of geographic mobility have perhaps been more common in the U.S. than in Canada, but these statements are not rare in Canada. Proximity is an important issue because it is strongly related to contact and the exchange of help (although much less related to emotional closeness and support). Uhlenberg (1993) shows that mobility rates in the United States were considerably lower in the 1970s and 1980s than they were in the 1950s and 1960s. The data, therefore, do not show a trend that would produce greater dispersion of kin over time. Moreover, the 1987–8 National Survey of

Families and Households found that about three-quarters of older people who have an adult child have a child living within 25 miles. This is almost identical to the percentage of older parents with a child living nearby that was reported by Ethel Shanas in 1968 and—to add some Canadian data—very similar to the percentages Victor Marshall, Jane Synge, and I found in our Hamilton study in 1980 (Rosenthal, 1987). We found that, among people aged 70 and over who had children, about two-thirds lived either in the same household or the same city as a child, and just about 90 per cent lived within an hour and one-half travel time of a child.

This is not to say that older people do not have a child who lives at some distance from them. Most studies only examine the proximity of the nearest child; this obscures the reality that, when people have more than one child, they may have some children close by and others more distant.... In other words, total family dispersion is very unusual, no dispersion beyond one and one-half hours' travel time is characteristics of a large minority of older families, and—importantly—partial dispersion is the most common pattern. We also need to be aware that proximity is something we typically measure at one point in time. In real life, however, proximity is fluid. Adult children may move to another city, only to move back to their city of origin later on. Older parents may make a retirement move to another city. Or, they may move at retirement or later on to be closer to a child. In sum, the geographic dispersion issue seems to have been oversold. My intention here is not to underrate the experience of geographically distant children and parents, particularly when the parents need care; it is simply to emphasize that this is far from the typical experience and it is not on a sharp rise.

Increased Participation of Women in the Paid Labour Force

A well-known trend that must be considered when discussing changing families is the trend towards increased female labour force participation. Consider, for example, women's labour force participation at ages 45–54. Among women who were aged 45–54 in 1991, 72 per cent were in the paid labour force, up from 56 per cent among women of those ages in 1981 and 44 per cent in 1971. Especially noteworthy are the increases in paid employment among married women and women with children at home. These trends mean that combining work and family roles has become much more common than in the past. By 1994, dual-earner families made up 60 per cent of all husband-wife families, compared with 33 per cent in 1967 (Statistics Canada, 1996)....

One major change that has not been overstated with regard to its occurrence is the increased likelihood that adult Canadians will have a parent alive and the related increased generational overlap of lives. These changes create the structural potential for experiencing care-related needs from older parents, but to what degree does this structural potential translate into actually experiencing such demands? Has the extent to which this potential translates into actual demands been oversold? I address this question in the next section.

THE OVERSELLING OF THE DEPENDENCY BURDEN ON FAMILIES

We saw earlier that the structural potential to have aging parents who require help exists for a large percentage of Canadian women. Much media attention is currently given to the potential burden of old family members on those in middle generations. A particularly difficult version of this is the burden and conflict experienced by middle-generation adults who have care responsibilities for family members in both older and younger generations.

While the care-related needs of older parents may present a daunting challenge for families, empirical research suggests that issues of prevalence and burden have been overstated. While the chances are we will all experience the death of

our parents, there is great variability in the need for and extent of involvement of adult children, and in the duration of care. We will not all become primary caregivers, many of us will provide only a little or no care to our parents, some of us will have intense involvement for a very short period of time and still others will have intermittent periods of involvement as parents move in and out of health crises.

The Extent of Provision of Help to Parents

There has been an enormous amount of research on caregiving over the past two decades, but it is important to note that much of this research uses non-representative samples and focuses only on primary caregivers, and only on elders who need substantial amounts of care. This does not give us much of a perspective on how much help adult children typically provide to older parents. Data from the 1990 Canadian General Social Survey (Rosenthal et al., 1996) show that only small proportions of adult Canadian sons and daughters actually help parents once a month or more. Respondents were asked about five kinds of help: housework, transportation, personal care, financial support, and outside work/household maintenance. Across five-year age categories from age 35 to age 64, from 11 to 22 per cent of daughters and 7 to 12 per cent of sons provided at least one of these types of help monthly or more often. Based on these data, we may say that only small minorities of adult children can be considered to be "active" helpers.

Personal care is arguably the most important type of help to examine, both because it may signify that the parent is highly dependent and because it is the most demanding and intensive type of care. Very small percentages of daughters provided personal care monthly or more often, although the percentages increased with age; at ages 35–49, between 1.2 and 2.0 per cent of daughters provided personal care. This rose to 5.6 per cent at ages 50–4 and 7 per cent at ages 55–9, then dropped to 0 per cent at ages 60–4. Among sons, a high of 1 per cent provided personal care at least monthly.

When we talk about dependency and need for help in the family context, we are usually referring to informal care. An additional type of dependency, however, is the need for financial assistance.... Data from the General Social Survey indicate that very small percentages of Canadian daughters or sons provide financial assistance to parents: the highest proportion in any age group to provide financial support monthly or more was 2 per cent of daughters and 3 per cent of sons. The percentages who had provided financial support in the past year were not much higher—4 per cent of daughters and 5 per cent of sons. Whatever increases we might see in the future, this type of help is very uncommon at present, and speculation about the future must be placed in this context. For example, even if the percentages giving this type of help doubled, small proportions of adult children would be involved.

The "Sandwich Generation"

The particular manifestation of the need to help older parents that has caught the public imagination is the woman facing care demands from parents and children—popularly termed the "sandwich generation." David Foot (1996), in his best-selling book, *Boom, Bust, and Echo*, devotes a chapter to how demographics can affect family life, but the only issue specifically related to older family members is the sandwich generation—the increased likelihood that one will have an aged parent in declining health and in need of assistance, occurring in the context of being "sandwiched" or pulled between the needs of one's parents and children. When people read Foot's book—and many Canadians have read it—the message about aging families they receive is that more and more women are being sandwiched. However, Foot makes the leap from the demographic fact that women have the family

structure that makes multiple and conflicting demands potentially possible to the assumption that they actually experience such demands.

It is ironic that Foot highlights the sandwich generation issue as emblematic of the impact of demographic change on older families, since it is becoming well established that this is one aspect of demographic change that has been overstated (Rosenthal et al., 1996; Spitze & Logan, 1990; Uhlenberg, 1993).... In our analysis of 1990 General Social Survey data, Anne Martin-Matthews, Sarah Matthews, and I (Rosenthal et al., 1996) found that the proportion of women with the structural potential to be sandwiched between the roles of adult child and parent of a dependent child (defined as a child in the household) dropped from 71 per cent among women aged 35–9 to 51 per cent among women aged 45–9 and to 24 per cent among women aged 50–4. The most difficult combination of roles is paid worker, adult child, and parent of a dependent child. This role configuration holds the greatest structural potential for competing demands, should an older parent need care. This combination dropped from 42 per cent in the 40–4 age group to 35 per cent for women in their later forties and to very small proportions after that.

Among women with the structural potential to be sandwiched, what proportion actually provides tangible help to parents? Among daughters who had a parent alive and a child at home, the highest percentage in any age group who helped a parent at least monthly was 13 per cent. In the potentially most problematic group, those who had a living parent, a child at home, and a paid job, the highest percentage in any age group who helped a parent at least monthly was 7 per cent....

The fact that few adult children seem to be providing assistance at any one point in time does not mean the family is a great untapped resource that can provide much more free labour so that society can save money on the formal health-care system. Creating this impression is one of the dangers of presenting this kind of data (although, clearly, I have had other purposes in mind)....

Women's Labour Force Participation and the "Caregiving Crunch"

The trend to female employment has led to the concern that women will no longer be available to fulfil their traditional roles of family caregivers to older parents, based on the seemingly logical speculation that employment reduces availability of women to provide family care. Myles (1991) uses the term "caregiving crunch" to refer to the crisis stemming from the decreased supply of informal caregivers as a result of women's increased employment outside the home. Myles refers to a crisis in caregiving, the result of the "dramatic decline in the amount of unpaid working time available to the women who have traditionally performed these tasks." Myles sees this caregiving crunch as the next crisis of the welfare state, one that we are already experiencing. A caregiving crunch is very familiar to women who combine employment with family responsibilities, whether those are for older or younger family members. Research has documented the strains on such women, including the impact of care responsibilities on employment careers (Martin-Matthews & Rosenthal, 1993). It is important to recognize, however, that most employed women whose parents require care continue in paid employment. Further, they appear to provide as much help to parents as their non-employed peers. In other words, the "crunch" does not seem to result in a decreased amount of care to older people. In an analysis of 1996 General Social Survey data (Rosenthal et al., 1999), there were minimal differences between employed and non-employed women in the type of help provided to parents and in the amount of time spent helping parents. This issue needs more examination, and I am not implying that everything is fine because employed women seem to provide care despite their job responsibilities. The point is that the so-called "caregiving crunch," to the extent that it exists, is not yet a crisis for the state; it may well be a crisis, however, for those women faced with these multiple demands. The question becomes one of appropriate policy directions. While policies that provide workplace flexibility and support for employed caregivers are important, it is equally or more important to provide policies that create options to family-provided care.

CONCLUSION

While family structure is changing, some aspects of these changes have been oversold—namely, the shrinking supply of children, the beanpole family, and geographic dispersion. On the other hand, families are more likely to have senior-generation members alive. We have tended to accept speculations about the implications of these changes—implications about the growing dependency burden on families—without testing them against empirical data. In examining three of these assumptions—that most adult children are swamped by the need to help parents, that the sandwich generation is a common predicament, and that women's employment is having a profound impact on care provision—we can see they have been oversold. Demographic change in families is not leading us into the apocalypse. It is important to maintain this perspective, in part because it means government programs to assist people who are in these situations are not likely to face massive hordes of caregivers but rather a comparatively small but highly needy segment of the population at any one point in time.

How do we counteract the tendency towards thinking apocalyptically about changes in older families? First of all, we need to identify carefully what is really happening and to pay attention to cohorts and trends over time. Second, we need to investigate the implications of these trends, rather than simply speculate about what they might be. Third, we need to look beyond averages, a point that is well demonstrated by examining the data on number of children ever born to different cohorts of women. To the extent that we have been able to address these issues, the apocalyptic position appears greatly overstated and indeed unsupportable. This is not to say that families are not changing, for they are changing significantly. The point is rather that they are not changing in ways that set kin relations adrift....

It is important to uncover the realities of social organization and social life, and for this reason we need to understand how the family is changing and what the implications of those changes are. However, there is a real danger that findings may be wrongly interpreted and/or used in support of policies that would not be good for families. I recognize that in much of my own work, for example, work that asks what the changes in family structure mean for support to older people, the implicit or explicit dependent variable is family support. This is a perfectly legitimate and important question. However, it is vital that our questions do not stop there. Whether families are or will be capable of providing needed support to older relatives must take second place to the question of who should be responsible for the care of older people. My position, one that is growing stronger over the years as I continue to learn more about older families, is that the care of the elderly is a public, not a private, issue and that responsibility lies with the state. Within that framework, we may then examine the role families might play if they are able and willing.

CRITICAL THINKING QUESTIONS

1. What are some of the key challenges facing the Canadian family as our population ages?
2. What role, if any, do you feel the Canadian government should take in assisting the elderly?
3. What role, if any, do you feel extended families should take in assisting their aging relatives?
4. In your opinion, who benefits from media attention focusing on the potential burden of older family members on middle-generation adults?

REFERENCES

Bengston, V. L., C. J. Rosenthal, and L. Burton. 1990. Families and aging: Diversity and heterogeneity. In *Handbook of aging and the social sciences,* eds. R. H. Binstock, and L. K. George, 263–87. New York: Academic Press.

Connidis, I. 1989. *Family ties and aging.* Toronto: Butterworths.

Foot, D. K., with Daniel Stoffman. 1996. *Boom, bust, and echo: How to profit from the coming demographic shift.* Toronto: Macfarlane Walter and Ross.

Gee, E. M. 1990. Demographic change and intergenerational relations in Canadian families: Findings and social policy implications. *Canadian Public Policy,* 16(2): 191–99.

———. 1995. Families in later life. In *Family over the life course: Current demographic analysis*, eds. Roderic Beaujot, Gee, Fernando, Rajulton, and Zenaida Ravanera, 7–113. Ottawa: Statistics Canada Demography Division.

Gladstone, J. 1988. Perceived changes in grandmother-grandchild relations following a child's separation or divorce, *Gerontologist,* 28(1): 66–72.

Marshall, V. W., C. J. Rosenthal, and J. Synge. 1983. Concerns about parental health. In *Older women,* ed. Elizabeth W. Markson, 253–73. Lexington, Mass.: Lexington Books.

Martin-Matthews, A. 1987. Widowhood as an expectable life event. In *Aging in Canada: Social Perspectives*, 2nd ed., ed. V. W. Marshall, 343–66. Markham, Ont.: Fitzhenry and Whiteside.

———. 1991. *Widowhood in later life.* Toronto: Butterworths.

Martin-Matthews, A., and C. J. Rosenthal. 1993. Balancing work and family in an aging society: The Canadian experience. In *Annual review of gerontology and geriatrics*, vol. 13, eds. G. Maddox, and M. P. Lawton, 96–119. New York: Springer.

Myles, J. 1991. Women, the welfare state and caregiving. *Canadian Journal on Aging*, 10(2): 82–5.

Riley, M. W. 1983. The family in an aging society: A matrix of latent relationships. *Journal of Family Issues,* 4: 439–54.

Riley, M. W., and J. W. Riley. 1993. Connections: Kin and cohorts. In *The changing contract across generations*, eds. V. L. Bengston, and W. A. Achenbaum. New York: Aldine de Gruyter.

Rosenthal, C. J. 1987. Aging and intergenerational relations in Canada. In *Aging in Canada: Social perspectives*, 2nd ed., ed. V. W. Marshall, 311–42. Markham, Ont.: Fitzhenry and Whiteside.

Rosenthal, C. J., A. Martin-Matthews, and S. Matthews. 1996. Caught in the middle? Occupancy in multiple roles and help to parents in a national probability sample of Canadian adults. *Journal of Gerontology: Social Sciences,* 51B(6): S274–83.

Rosenthal, C. J., A. Martin-Matthews, L. Hayward, and M. Denton. 1999. Women's multiple roles: How constraining is employment on the provision of parent care? Paper presented at the 52nd Annual Scientific Meeting of the Gerontological Society of America, San Francisco.

Rosenthal, C. J., M. Denton, A. Martin-Matthews, and S. French. Forthcoming. Changes in work and family over the life course: Implications for economic security of today's and tomorrow's older women. In *Independence and economic security in old age,* eds. F. Denton, D. Fretz, and B. Spencer. Vancouver: University of British Columbia Press.

Rossi, A. S., and P. H. Rossi. 1990. *Of human bonding: Parent-child relations across the life course.* New York: Aldine de Gruyter.

Spitze, G., and J. R. Logan. 1990. More evidence on women (and men) in the middle. *Research on Aging,* 12: 182–98.

Statistics Canada. 1996. *Characteristics of dual-earner families 1994.* Ottawa: Minister of Industry, Catalogue No. 13-215-XPB.

Uhlenberg, P. 1993. Demographic change and kin relationships in later life. In *Annual Review of Gerontology and Geriatrics,* vol. 13, eds. G. Maddox, and M. P. Lawton, 219–38. New York: Springer.

Winsborough, H., L. Bumpass, and W. Aguilino. 1991. *The death of parents and the transitions to old age.* National Survey of Families and Households Working Paper No. 39. Madison: University of Wisconsin.

Wister, A. 1985. Living arrangement choices among the elderly. *Canadian Journal on Aging,* 4(3): 127–44.

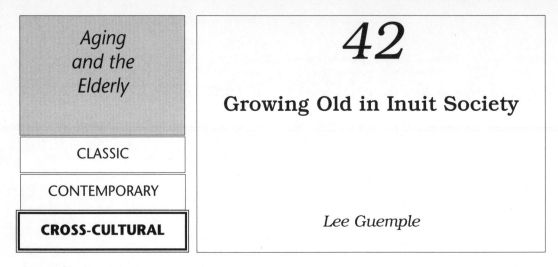

Aging and the Elderly

CLASSIC

CONTEMPORARY

CROSS-CULTURAL

42

Growing Old in Inuit Society

Lee Guemple

Guemple's intention in "Growing Old in Inuit Society" is to investigate how, in precontact Inuit society, the elderly were loved and revered but were also killed or allowed to die by their family and friends. This apparent contradiction, at least to Westerners, allows a glimpse into the rich diversity of human adaptation.

The treatment the Inuit (Eskimo) traditionally accorded their old people during the precontact period has been a source of some consternation to members of the Euro–North American cultural tradition because of a seeming paradox. We know that Inuit lavished care and concern on their old people and invested considerable interest in them. But we also know that they sometimes abandoned them on the trail (Freuchen, 1961: 194–203) and that they stood ready at times even to help them to dispose of themselves by drowning or strangulation (Rasmussen, 1908: 127). Our own notion of what people are like makes it difficult for us to see how they could be so affectionate in one context and cold-hearted in another, when the chips were down.

Source: Reprinted with permission from Guemple, Lee. (1980). Growing Old in Inuit Society. In Victor Marshall (Ed.), *Aging in Canada: Social Perspectives* (pp. 95–101). Fitzhenry and Whiteside Ltd., Markham, Ontario.

The aim of this essay is to try to resolve the paradox; to show how the attitude of love and affection is not incompatible with the idea of killing one's own parents or helping them to kill themselves. To do so we must make a brief foray into the cognitive universe of the Inuit—into their own notion of how the world (of people and things) works. Only then can we fathom how they manage to mix sentiment with seeming cruelty without a sense of contradiction.

First, however, it will be useful to offer some background material on aging in Inuit society. Inuit have no generic term for "senior citizens." Instead, they use one term for an old man, *ituq*, and another for an old woman, *ningiuq*. These terms are used mainly while speaking about the old people, seldom when speaking to them.

It is difficult to establish the age in years at which people are consigned to old age. Like us, Inuit associate adulthood with work status, and old age constitutes a kind of "retirement" from full participation in community affairs. But Inuit do not keep vital statistics like we do. We cannot reckon an age of retirement for them. Besides, everyone is encouraged to continue working for as long as possible so that retirement comes not by convention, but by the gradual process of biological aging. While doing research in the Belcher Islands Inuit community, I was able to calculate the mean age at which men acquire the label of *ituq* at about fifty years of age (Guemple, 1969). Women seem to maintain the status of adult somewhat longer, but will ordinarily pass over into being classed as *ningiuq* at age sixty or so.

Men become old when they can no longer hunt on a year-round basis but pass on the task of routine hunting to younger members of the household—generally a mature son or son-in-law. Hunting in winter is very demanding and because of its importance to the maintenance of life it is the crucial determinate of male status. At somewhere around fifty years of age a man can no longer sustain the strength and stamina to perform this task on a regular basis and will "retire." His withdrawal can be gradual but is often dramatic.

Women's allocated tasks are both more varied and less strenuous with the result that advancing age does not limit their effectiveness nearly as much as it does men's. Women routinely share work among themselves and the heavy work is often passed along to mature girls even in early adulthood while the older women tend to younger children and infants. Loss of strength and agility will not quickly be noticed in a woman. She will simply spend more time at home, performing other routine tasks such as cooking or sewing. The transition to old age is thus more gradual and comes later in the lifecycle than it does for men.

The onset of old age is hastened by debilitating diseases and may be slowed by what I have elsewhere called "renewal" (Guemple, 1969). The major forms of physical impairment that affect premature entry into old age are arthritis and blindness. The cold, damp character of the traditional igloo and tent tend to promote arthritis; and the incidence of blindness due to trachoma and glaucoma is relatively high. Men also suffer a relatively high incidence of corneal abrasion and snow blindness which can often lead to partial impairments of sight. In the recent past tuberculosis has also taken a considerable toll, particularly in those people who have been sent out to hospital to have portions of lungs or bones removed to rid them of infection.

Old age can also be delayed in some instances. Men often accomplish this by extraordinary effort in hunting during the spring and summer seasons when the demands of production are not so great; and they sometimes undergo symbolic renewal by taking younger women as wives in their maturity. Women cannot aspire to marry younger men in their later years; but they can and frequently do assert they are still able to perform their primary functions by seeking to adopt children. It is said that adopting a child makes an old woman feel young again; and while the primary aim of adoption is not stated to be renewal, it is the only reason given that makes very much sense.[1]

Old people are well cared for in Inuit society because they can draw upon two interlocking social institutions as sources of support: the household and the community at large. Members of a household share equitably; so long as there are younger workers in the household to work on behalf of their elders their interests are seen to with great care and devotion (Gubser, 1965: 122; Hawkes, 1916: 117). The rules of residence stipulate that young hunters stay home until they marry, and so an aging elder can expect to have his son do much of his hunting for him. When the daughters marry their husbands will come to live in the household, and they are answerable to their fathers-in-law, at least until after the first child is born. They may also remain in the household of an in-law if there is need and relations between the son-in-law and other household members are cordial.

Old people can expect some support from the community at large so long as they are able to contribute to the fund of resources from which others draw. Inuit rules of sharing enjoin that successful hunters share a portion of their catch with those who were less successful; and mature hunters are generally only too happy to be able to offer support to other community members, since it is the single source of prestige in the local hunting community. In return, the old people offer the produce of the hunting of their sons or sons-in-law or, as circumstances permit, they offer the help in sewing and gathering wood by their daughters, and they themselves will pitch in to help in any way they can to the general good. Men often offer work in repair jobs, executing technically difficult parts of various pieces of technology where knowledge and patience are particularly needed. They go for short hunting trips around camp, and often school young hunters on how to set snares, stalk land animals, etc. Women contribute their domestic labour for sewing, cooking, cleaning, baby tending, and so on. In the evenings, the old people, as keepers of the sacred and secular lore of this non-literate society, maintain a sense of tradition by telling stories and offering advice which experience shows to be particularly applicable to some predicament.

This system seems to work well so long as old people have someone to rely on to make their contribution to the community pool; and the institutional structure appears to break down only when the old people are left stranded by the departure of their children from the household and the community for one reason or another for an extended period of time. In that context, members of the community at large gradually come to view the old couple as parasitic and begin to complain about their dependency. So far as I am aware, community members would not flatly refuse to feed old people in such a situation; but they often receive a lesser share or the least desirable portion. And they may from time to time suffer the indignity of being gossiped about or verbally abused for their failure to contribute adequately.

As the couple grows into old age, one or the other will die leaving the survivor to move in with a son or daughter or with some more distant relative. The children generally accept the added

burden gracefully; though more distant relatives may find it a bit inconvenient to be saddled with a sibling or cousin in old age. The Inuit of the Canadian North never collected material possessions as a form of wealth. The need to be continually on the move prevented the accumulation of luxuries. But men with ambition often collected people as a kind of "wealth"; and old men or women who were not too feeble were generally welcome in the household of an influential hunter if they had no children to care for them. Seldom were old people to be found in utterly desperate straits unless the entire community was impoverished.

If old people were well treated and cared for by their fellows in the traditional culture, they appear also to have been the objects of startling cruelties. Inuit are known to have abandoned their old people on the trail from time to time with very little ceremony; and there are even cases where the children stood ready to help them end their lives if asked to do so. Such behaviour strikes us as terribly inconsistent and begs for an explanation.

The well-documented facts are that Inuit sometimes abandon their old people. This was generally done either by leaving them behind while on the trail or by allowing them to go off on their own to make an end to themselves. When old people were abandoned, it was most often done out of necessity, seldom out of indifference to the old (Burch, 1975: 148–50; Gubser, 1965: 122; Jenness, 1922: 236; Low, 1906: 165; Spencer, 1959: 252), though cases of apparently cruel treatment are known (Stefánsson, 1914: 130).

Freuchen (1961: 200–03) describes a typical case with his usual dramatic flair: a couple is travelling from one community to another accompanied by their immature children and an old woman, the wife's mother. Sometime during the night, the old lady, having faced an arduous day on the trail, decides the burden of living is too heavy for her to carry any longer, that she should now end the struggle to survive, that she has become a millstone to her children and grandchildren. She tells the two adults that she can go on no longer. They try to dissuade her, but she persists. Finally they agree, and in the morning they pack their gear and depart with only a word or two of farewell, leaving the old lady behind in the igloo, alone with her thoughts and her few meagre possessions.

Other examples appear to be even more unfathomable. An old man, perhaps nettled over some incident which has led to a quarrel or an insult to his sense of dignity, calls his two sons to him and tells them that he is old and useless, the butt of community jokes. Because of this, he has decided that, with their help, he will do away with himself. The sons encourage him to think positively, to remember the joys of playing with his grandchildren, and so on, but he insists that he has seen enough of life and wishes to be rid of it. Eventually, they leave off pleading, and under his direction, fetch a seal skin line and, wrapping the middle around his neck a couple of turns, take the ends and strangle him.

The conventional explanation of these situations is that the old are stoic about death and embrace the notion of their dying fearlessly and with resignation, when they feel they are no longer useful. So the sons or daughters accept the old person's decision with very little coaxing.

There are a number of problems with this formulation of their reaction to the possibility of death. For one thing, it assumes that life in the Arctic is a continuous struggle for survival which people perceive and respond to by a sort of stoic resignation. While this notion is one of *our* favourite themes, it is certainly not part of the Inuit repertoire. They do not see their lives as endangered by their marginal situation. They know its hazards well and have what are to them adequate means for coping with them. It is strangeness that creates a sense of threat, not familiarity; so their situation strikes us as threatening. The Inuit do not perceive it to be so.

How then are we to explain their casual acceptance of the death of loved ones, particularly the old? The answer is that old people do not, in Inuit cosmology, really die. In order to understand this statement, it will be necessary to set aside momentarily our consideration of old age as such and examine briefly the Inuit conception of the underlying character of people, whether old or young. That inquiry will provide us with the basis for solving the riddle of their indifference to death.

Inuit believe that the essential ingredient of a human being is its name. The name embodies a mystical substance which includes the personality, special skills, and basic character which the individual will exhibit in life. Without that substance he will die; and should he exchange his name substance for another through a ritualized renaming process, he will become a different person.

The name substance is derived from other humans, but is not thought of as biological in character; and it bears little resemblance to units of heredity such as genes or of some more metaphorical analogue of biological inheritance such as "blood." The name substance is induced into the body within three or four days after birth; and the process of naming a child is viewed by Inuit as one in which a ritual specialist divines what particular name substance has entered its body. Often the name is that of some recently deceased community member, frequently a relative of the child. But it is never the substance of a parent or sibling of the child and the most frequent "choices" of names are those belonging to members of the grandparent generation. The names of children who are sickly are sometimes changed shortly after birth, and shamans and a few others change their names in adulthood and thus become different persons; but most people keep their given names throughout their lifetimes. At death, the name separates from the body but remains within the vicinity of the body or of the place of death for three or four days during which time it is thought to be dangerous to living humans. After that time, it is thought to return to the underworld to wait till it can enter the body of a newborn child. Names thus cycle as do the social identities which are attached to them.

Names are never exclusively held by individuals in Inuit society. Three or sometimes four individuals may bear the same name and thus be the same person in principle. We might express this idea in a different way and say that from the standpoint of the Inuit community at large, the society consists of a limited number of names each having its own social identity—personal history, personality, work skills, attributes, and attitudes, etc.—attached to it. The identities are shared out in the community among its members on roughly a one-for-four basis, and cycle. At birth, individuals step into one of these well-established identities and bear them in latent form until they come to full expression in adulthood. During their lifetimes, they may contribute to their shape; and at death, they pass their part of the identities on to the next generation fully formed. These identities are indestructible; they neither die nor dissipate, but instead go on endlessly cycling through one generation after another.

Since the name substance is not inherited from the parents and not passed on to one's own biological posterity, parents contribute little to the children's identities except body substance which, to Inuit, is of little significance. And, since the social identity comes to the individual fully formed, it is not something the individual or the community were believed to be able to change in any major way, though in special cases it was possible to actually change identities.

We are now in a position to see why Inuit are relatively casual about the death of old people even if they are bound tightly to them in life. Children permit their parents to do away with themselves because they are not attached to them as we are to our parents. Every individual shares a community of spirit with others, but in Inuit society, that community is with those who bear the same name, not those who share the same blood or some metaphorical analogue. Sentiments link parents and children together, but these can never be binding because parents and children share nothing more vital than those sentiments.

A more compelling reason for the seeming indifference to the death of the parents is related to their understandings about the fate of the person concerned. In our cosmology, the death of an individual means at best his departure to another place, at worst the end of all being, the end of all subjective experience of self. In either case, it is a mystery that makes life precious, that makes us rather bear those ills we have than fly to others. In Inuit cosmology, the persona is the one enduring, immutable substance. Whatever else may happen, Inuit know that their persona live on, not in consciousness, but certainly as fully formed social entities. It is this fact of their existence, and not a resigned stoicism, that make them indifferent to death when the body becomes infirm and the will to live weakens.

The treatment of the old we have described here and the cosmological order we have explored to explain what give[s] them confidence and courage in facing old age and death is part of a tradition that is now on the verge of extinction across the Arctic as conversion to Christianity and the transition to modern living conditions gradually replace the aboriginal customs and beliefs. Modern-day old people of the North live in pre-fab homes, draw old age and disability pensions, take their sustenance from the shelf at the store, and receive their medical care from the local nursing station or hospital. These benefits have done much to make old age comfortable materially; and old men and women alike are quick to express their gratitude for these amenities. That the cosmological explanations we offer serve them as well in death as the material comforts we lavish on them in life is a little more difficult to assert with confidence.

CRITICAL THINKING QUESTIONS

1. How do the definitions of old age differ for men and women in traditional Inuit society? Are there similar factors influencing our definitions of old age in contemporary Canadian society?

2. Discuss the significance of a name in Inuit society and how it helps explain their somewhat indifferent approach to death.

3. Guemple concludes by questioning how the transition of Inuit society into a more modern and materialist one may affect their cosmological understanding of death. What do you feel are some of the other costs associated with this transition? Elderly Inuit today benefit from greater material wealth, but do you feel that the benefits outweigh the costs?

NOTE

1. The principal reason given for adoption [of children] by older women is that the adoption will provide someone to take care of the adopter "when they are old." But this same reason is given when the prospective adopter is in her sixties and the child is but one or two years of age. Further, the same reason is given by older women who have numerous children of their own, in some cases children already grown to maturity, and ready to care for the parent.

REFERENCES

Burch, E. 1975. *Eskimo kinsmen: Changing family relationships in Northwest Alaska.* New York: West Publishing Company (American Ethnological Society Monograph No. 59).

Freuchen, P. 1961. *Peter Freuchen's book of the Eskimos.* Cleveland: World.

Gubser, N. J. 1965. *The Nunamiut Eskimo: Hunters of caribou.* New Haven: Yale University Press.

Guemple, L. 1969. Human resource management: The dilemma of the aging Eskimo. *Sociological Symposium,* 2: 59–74.

Hawkes, E. W. 1916. *The Labrador Eskimo: Canada Department of Mines, Geological Survey Memoir 91.* Anthropological Series No. 14. Ottawa: Government Printing Bureau.

Jenness, D. 1922. *The life of the Copper Eskimos. Report of the Canadian Arctic islands.* Ottawa: Government Printing Bureau.

Low, A. P. 1906. *Report on the Dominion Government expedition to Hudson Bay and the Arctic islands.* Ottawa: Government Printing Bureau.

Rasmussen, K. 1908. *People of the polar north.* London: Kegan Paul, Trench, Trubner.

Spencer, R. F. 1959. *The North Alaskan Eskimo.* Washington: Smithsonian Institute. Bureau of American Ethnology, Bulletin 171.

Stefánsson, B. W. A. 1914. *The Stefánsson-Anderson Arctic expedition of the American Museum.* Anthropological Papers of the American Museum of Natural History. Volume 14, Part I.

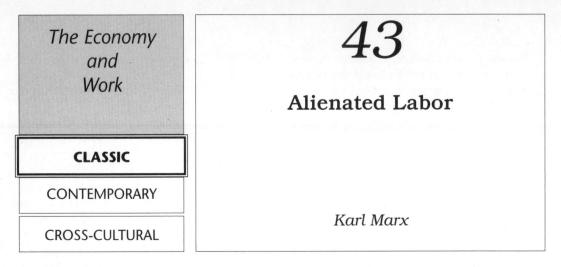

43

Alienated Labor

CLASSIC

CONTEMPORARY

CROSS-CULTURAL

Karl Marx

The human species, argues Karl Marx, is social by nature and expresses that social nature in the act of production. But within the capitalist economic system, Marx claims, the process of production denies human nature, rather than affirming it. The result is what he terms "alienated labor."

...[We] have shown that the worker sinks to the level of a commodity, and to a most miserable commodity; that the misery of the worker increases with the power and volume of his production; that the necessary result of competition is the accumulation of capital in a few hands, and thus a restoration of monopoly in a more terrible form; and finally that the distinction between capitalist and landlord, and between agricultural laborer and industrial worker, must disappear, and the whole of society divide into the two classes of property *owners* and *propertyless* workers....

Source: "Alienated Labor," by Karl Marx from *Karl Marx: Early Writings*, trans. and ed. by T. B. Bottomore. Copyright © 1963, McGraw-Hill Companies. Reprinted by permission of The McGraw-Hill Companies.

Thus we have now to grasp the real connexion between this whole system of alienation—private property, acquisitiveness, the separation of labor, capital and land, exchange and competition, value and the devaluation of man, monopoly and competition—and the system of *money*....

We shall begin from a *contemporary* economic fact. The worker becomes poorer the more wealth he produces and the more his production increases in power and extent. The worker becomes an ever cheaper commodity the more goods he creates. The *devaluation* of the human world increases in direct relation with the *increase in value* of the world of things. Labor does not only create goods; it also produces itself and the worker as a *commodity*, and indeed in the same proportion as it produces goods.

This fact simply implies that the object produced by labor, its product, now stands opposed to it as an *alien being,* as a *power independent* of the producer. The product of labor is labor which has been embodied in an object and turned into a physical thing; this product is an *objectification* of labor. The performance of work is at the same time its objectification. The performance of work appears in the sphere of political economy as a *vitiation*[1] of the worker, objectification as a *loss* and as *servitude to the object,* and appropriation as *alienation.*

So much does the performance of work appear as vitiation that the worker is vitiated to the point of starvation. So much does objectification appear as loss of the object that the worker is deprived of the most essential things not only of life but also of work. Labor itself becomes an object which he can acquire only by the greatest effort and with unpredictable interruptions. So much does the appropriation of the object appear as alienation that the more objects the worker produces the fewer he can possess and the more he falls under the domination of his product, of capital.

All these consequences follow from the fact that the worker is related to the *product of his labor* as to an *alien* object. For it is clear on this presupposition that the more the worker expends himself in work the more powerful becomes the world of objects which he creates in face of himself, the poorer he becomes in his inner life, and the less he belongs to himself. It is just the same as in religion. The more of himself man attributes to God the less he has left in himself. The worker puts his life into the object, and his life then belongs no longer to himself but to the object. The greater his activity, therefore, the less he possesses. What is embodied in the product of his labor is no longer his own. The greater this product is, therefore, the more he is diminished. The *alienation* of the worker in his product means not only that his labor becomes an object, assumes an *external* existence, but that it exists independently, *outside himself,* and alien to him, and that it stands opposed to him as an

autonomous power. The life which he has given to the object sets itself against him as an alien and hostile force.

Let us now examine more closely the phenomenon of *objectification;* the worker's production and the *alienation* and *loss* of the object it produces, which is involved in it. The worker can create nothing without *nature,* without the *sensuous external world.* The latter is the material in which his labor is realized, in which it is active, out of which and through which it produces things.

But just as nature affords the *means of existence* of labor, in the sense that labor cannot *live* without objects upon which it can be exercised, so also it provides the *means of existence* in a narrower sense; namely the means of physical existence for the *worker* himself. Thus, the more the worker *appropriates* the external world of sensuous nature by his labor the more he deprives himself of *means of existence,* in two respects: First, that the sensuous external world becomes progressively less an object belonging to his labor or a means of existence of his labor, and secondly, that it becomes progressively less a means of existence in the direct sense, a means for the physical subsistence of the worker.

In both respects, therefore, the worker becomes a slave of the object; first, in that he receives an *object of work,* i.e., receives *work,* and secondly, in that he receives *means of subsistence.* Thus the object enables him to exist, first as a *worker* and secondly, as a *physical subject.* The culmination of this enslavement is that he can only maintain himself as a *physical subject* so far as he is a *worker,* and that it is only as a *physical subject* that he is a worker.

(The alienation of the worker in his object is expressed as follows in the laws of political economy: The more the worker produces the less he has to consume; the more value he creates the more worthless he becomes; the more refined his product the more crude and misshapen the worker; the more civilized the product the more barbarous the worker; the more powerful the work the more feeble the worker; the more the work manifests intelligence the more the worker declines in intelligence and becomes a slave of nature.)

Political economy conceals the alienation in the nature of labor insofar as it does not examine the direct relationship between the worker (work) and production. Labor certainly produces marvels for the rich but it produces privation for the worker. It produces palaces, but hovels for the worker. It produces beauty, but deformity for the worker. It replaces labor by machinery, but it casts some of the workers back into a barbarous kind of work and turns the others into machines. It produces intelligence, but also stupidity and cretinism for the workers.

The direct relationship of labor to its products is the relationship of the worker to the objects of his production. The relationship of property owners to the objects of production and to production itself is merely a *consequence* of this first relationship and confirms it. We shall consider this second aspect later.

Thus, when we ask what is the important relationship of labor, we are concerned with the relationship of the *worker* to production.

So far we have considered the alienation of the worker only from one aspect; namely, *his relationship with the products of his labor.* However, alienation appears not merely in the result but also in the *process of production,* within *productive activity* itself. How could the worker stand in an alien relationship to the product of his activity if he did not alienate himself in the act of production itself? The product is indeed only the *résumé* of activity, of production. Consequently, if the product of labor is alienation, production itself must be active alienation—the alienation of activity and the activity of alienation. The alienation of the object of labor merely summarizes the alienation in the work activity itself.

What constitutes the alienation of labor? First, that the work is *external* to the worker, that it is not part of his nature; and that, consequently, he does not fulfill himself in his work but denies himself, has a feeling of misery rather than well-being, does not develop freely his mental and physical energies but is physically exhausted and mentally debased. The worker, therefore, feels himself at home only during his leisure time, whereas at work he feels homeless. His work is not voluntary but imposed, *forced labor.* It is not the satisfaction of a need, but only a *means* for satisfying other needs. Its alien character is clearly shown by the fact that as soon as there is no physical or other compulsion it is avoided like the plague. External labor, labor in which man alienates himself, is a labor of self-sacrifice, of mortification. Finally, the external character of work for the worker is shown by the fact that it is not his own work but work for someone else, that in work he does not belong to himself but to another person....

We arrive at the result that man (the worker) feels himself to be freely active only in his animal functions—eating, drinking and procreating, or at most also in his dwelling and in personal adornment—while in his human functions he is reduced to an animal. The animal becomes human and the human becomes animal.

Eating, drinking, and procreating are of course also genuine human functions. But abstractly considered, apart from the environment of human activities, and turned into final and sole ends, they are animal functions.

We have now considered the act of alienation of practical human activity, labor, from two aspects: (1) the relationship of the worker to the *product of labor* as an alien object which dominates him. This relationship is at the same time the relationship to the sensuous external world, to natural objects, as an alien and hostile world; (2) the relationship of labor to the *act of production* within *labor.* This is the relationship of the worker to his own activity as something alien and not belonging to him, activity as suffering (passivity), strength as powerlessness, creation as emasculation, the *personal* physical and mental energy of the worker, his personal life (for what is life but activity?), as an activity which is directed against himself, independent of him and not belonging to him. This is *self-alienation* as against the [afore]mentioned alienation of the *thing.*

We have now to infer a third characteristic of *alienated labor* from the two we have considered. Man is a species-being not only in the sense that he makes the community (his own as well as those of other things) his object both practically and theoretically, but also (and this is simply another expression for the same thing) in the sense that he treats himself as the present, living species, as a *universal* and consequently free being.

Species-life, for man as for animals, has its physical basis in the fact that man (like animals) lives from inorganic nature, and since man is more universal than an animal so the range of inorganic nature from which he lives is more universal. Plants, animals, minerals, air, light, etc. constitute, from the theoretical aspect, a part of human consciousness as objects of natural science and art; they are man's spiritual inorganic nature, his intellectual means of life, which he must first prepare for enjoyment and perpetuation. So also, from the practical aspect, they form a part of human life and activity. In practice man lives only from these natural products, whether in the form of food, heating, clothing, housing, etc. The universality of man appears in practice in the universality which makes the whole of nature into his inorganic body: (1) as a direct means of life; and equally (2) as the material object and instrument of his life activity. Nature is the inorganic body of man; that is to say nature, excluding the human body itself. To say that man *lives* from nature means that nature is his *body* with which he must remain in a continuous interchange in order not to die. The statement that the physical and mental life of man, and nature, are interdependent means simply that nature is interdependent with itself, for man is a part of nature.

Since alienated labor (1) alienates nature from man; and (2) alienates man from himself, from his own active function, his life activity; so it alienates him from the species. It makes *species-life* into a means of individual life. In the first place it alienates species-life and

individual life, and secondly, it turns the latter, as an abstraction, into the purpose of the former, also in its abstract and alienated form.

For labor, *life activity, productive life,* now appear to man only as *means* for the satisfaction of a need, the need to maintain his physical existence. Productive life is, however, species-life. It is life creating life. In the type of life activity resides the whole character of a species, its species-character; and free, conscious activity is the species-character of human beings. Life itself appears only as a *means of life.*

The animal is one with its life activity. It does not distinguish the activity from itself. It is *its activity.* But man makes his life activity itself an object of his will and consciousness. He has a conscious life activity. It is not a determination with which he is completely identified. Conscious life activity distinguishes man from the life activity of animals. Only for this reason is he a species-being. Or rather, he is only a self-conscious being, i.e., his own life is an object for him, because he is a species-being. Only for this reason is his activity free activity. Alienated labor reverses the relationship, in that man because he is a self-conscious being makes his life activity, his *being,* only a means for his *existence.*

CRITICAL THINKING QUESTIONS

1. Does Marx argue that work is inevitably alienating? Why does work within a capitalist economy produce alienation?
2. In what different respects does labour within capitalism alienate the worker?
3. Based on this analysis, under what conditions do you think Marx would argue that labour is not alienating?

NOTE

1. Debasement.

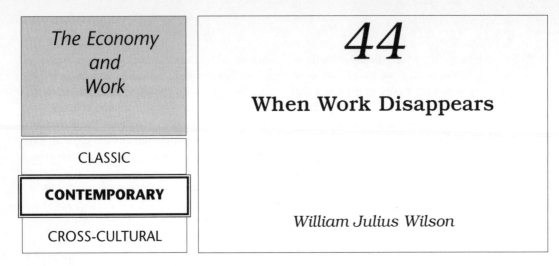

The Economy
and
Work

CLASSIC

CONTEMPORARY

CROSS-CULTURAL

44

When Work Disappears

William Julius Wilson

Many inner-city areas of the United States face catastrophic levels of poverty. Why? In this excerpt from a recent book, William Julius Wilson offers his assessment of the causes of urban decline and makes practical suggestions about how we can solve this pressing problem.

The disappearance of work in the ghetto cannot be ignored, isolated or played down. Employment in America is up. The economy has churned out tens of millions of new jobs in the last two decades. In that same period, joblessness among inner-city blacks has reached catastrophic proportions. Yet in this Presidential election year, the disappearance of work in the ghetto is not on either the Democratic or the Republican agenda. There is harsh talk about work instead of welfare but no talk of where to find it.

The current employment woes in the inner city continue to be narrowly defined in terms of race or lack of individual initiative. It is argued that jobs are widely available, that the extent of inner-city poverty is exaggerated. Optimistic policy analysts—and many African Americans—would prefer that more attention be devoted to the successes and struggles of the black working class and the expanding black middle class. This is understandable. These two groups, many of whom have recently escaped from the ghetto, represent a majority of the African American population. But ghetto joblessness still afflicts a substantial—and increasing—minority: It's a problem that won't go away on its own. If it is not addressed, it will have lasting and harmful consequences for the quality of life in the cities and, eventually, for the lives of all Americans. Solutions will have to be found—and those solutions are at hand.

Source: From *When Work Disappears* by William Julius Wilson. Copyright © 1996 by William Julius Wilson, Alfred A. Knopf, Inc. Reprinted by permission of Alfred A. Knopf, Inc.

For the first time in the twentieth century, a significant majority of adults in many inner-city neighborhoods are not working in a typical week. Inner cities have always featured high levels of poverty, but the current levels of joblessness in some neighborhoods are unprecedented. For example, in the famous black-belt neighborhood of Washington Park on Chicago's South Side, a majority of adults had jobs in 1950; by 1990, only one in three worked in a typical week. High neighborhood joblessness has a far more devastating effect than high neighborhood poverty. A neighborhood in which people are poor but employed is different from a neighborhood in which people are poor and jobless. Many of today's problems in the inner-city neighborhoods—crime, family dissolution, welfare—are fundamentally a consequence of the disappearance of work.

What causes the disappearance of work? There are several factors, including changes in the distribution and location of jobs, and in the level of training and education required to obtain employment. Nor should we overlook the legacy of historic racial segregation. However, the public debate around this question is not productive because it seeks to assign blame rather than recognizing and dealing with the complex realities that have led to economic distress for many Americans. Explanations and proposed solutions to the problem are often ideologically driven.

Conservatives tend to stress the importance of values, attitudes, habits, and styles. In this view, group differences are reflected in the culture. The truth is, cultural factors do play a role; but other, more important variables also have to be taken into account. Although race is clearly a significant variable in the social outcomes of inner-city blacks, it's not the *only* factor. The emphasis on racial differences has obscured the fact that African Americans, whites, and other ethnic groups have many common values, aspirations, and hopes.

An elderly woman who has lived in one inner-city neighborhood on the South Side of Chicago for more than forty years reflects: "I've been here since March 11, 1953. When I moved in, the neighborhood was intact. It was intact with homes, beautiful homes, minimansions, with stores, Laundromats, with Chinese cleaners. We had drugstores. We had hotels. We had doctors over on 39th street. We had doctors' offices in the neighborhood. We had the middle class and upper middle class. It has gone from affluent to where it is today. And I would like to see it come back, that we can have some of the things we had. Since I came in young, and I'm a senior citizen now, I would like to see some of the things come back so I can enjoy them like we did when we first came in."

In the neighborhood of Woodlawn, on the South Side of Chicago, there were more than 800 commercial and industrial establishments in 1950. Today, it is estimated that only about 100 are left. In the words of Loïc Wacquant, a member of one of the research teams that worked with me over the last eight years: "The once-lively streets—residents remember a time, not so long ago, when crowds were so dense at rush hour that one had to elbow one's way to the train station— now have the appearance of an empty, bombed-out war zone. The commercial strip has been reduced to a long tunnel of charred stores, vacant lots littered with broken glass and garbage, and dilapidated buildings left to rot in the shadow of the elevated train line. At the corner of 63d Street and Cottage Grove Avenue, the handful of remaining establishments that struggle to survive are huddled behind wrought-iron bars.... The only enterprises that seem to be thriving are liquor stores and currency exchanges, those 'banks of the poor' where one can cash checks, pay bills and buy money orders for a fee."

The state of the inner-city public schools was another major concern expressed by our urban-poverty study respondents. The complaints ranged from overcrowded conditions to unqualified and uncaring teachers. Sharply voicing her views on these subjects, a twenty-five-year-old married mother of two children from a South Side census tract that just recently became poor stated: "My daughter ain't going to school here. She was going to a nursery school where I paid and of course they took the time and spent it with her, because they was getting the money. But the public schools, no! They are overcrowded and the teachers don't care."

A resident of Woodlawn who had left the neighborhood as a child described how she felt upon her return about the changes that had occurred: "I was really appalled. When I walked down 63d Street when I was younger, everything you wanted was there. But now, coming back as an adult with my child, those resources are just gone, completely.... And housing, everybody has moved, there are vacant lots everywhere."

Neighborhoods plagued by high levels of joblessness are more likely to experience low levels of social organization: The two go hand in hand. High rates of joblessness trigger other neighborhood problems that undermine social organization, ranging from crime, gang violence, and drug trafficking to family breakups. And as these controls weaken, the social processes that regulate behavior change.

Industrial restructuring has further accelerated the deterioration of many inner-city neighborhoods. Consider the fate of the West Side black community of North Lawndale in Chicago: Since 1960, nearly half of its housing stock has disappeared; the remaining units are mostly run-down or dilapidated. Two large factories anchored the economy of this neighborhood in its good days— the Hawthorne plant of Western Electric, which employed more than 43,000 workers, and an International Harvester plant with 14,000 workers. But conditions rapidly changed. Harvester closed its doors in the late 1960s. Sears moved most of its offices to the Loop in downtown Chicago in 1973. The Hawthorne plant gradually phased out its operations and finally shut down in 1984.

"Jobs were plentiful in the past," attested a twenty-nine-year-old unemployed black man who lives in one of the poorest neighborhoods on the South Side. "You could walk out of the house and get a job. Maybe not what you want, but you could get a job. Now, you can't find anything. A lot of people in this neighborhood, they want to work but they can't get work. A few, but a very few, they just don't want to work."

The more rapid the neighborhood deterioration, the greater the institutional disinvestment. In the 1960s and 1970s, neighborhoods plagued by heavy abandonment were frequently redlined (identified as areas that should not receive or be recommended for mortgage loans or insurance); this paralyzed the housing market, lowered property values and encouraged landlord abandonment.

As the neighborhood disintegrates, those who are able to leave depart in increasing numbers; among these are many working- and middle-class families. The lower population density in turn creates additional problems. Abandoned buildings increase and often serve as havens for crack use and other illegal enterprises that give criminals—mostly young blacks who are unemployed—footholds in the community. Precipitous declines in density also make it even more difficult to sustain or develop a sense of community. The feeling of safety in numbers is completely lacking in such neighborhoods.

Problems in the new poverty or high-jobless neighborhoods have also created racial antagonism among some of the high-income groups in the city. The high joblessness in ghetto neighborhoods has sapped the vitality of local businesses and other institutions and has led to fewer and shabbier movie theaters, bowling alleys, restaurants, public parks and playgrounds, and other recreational facilities. When residents of inner-city neighborhoods venture out to other areas of the city in search of entertainment, they come into brief contact with citizens of markedly different racial or class backgrounds. Sharp differences in cultural style often lead to clashes.

Some behavior on the part of residents from socially isolated ghetto neighborhoods—for instance, the tendency to enjoy a movie in a communal spirit by carrying on a running conversation with friends and relatives or reacting in an unrestrained manner to what they see on the screen—is considered offensive by other groups, particularly black and white members of the middle class. Expressions of disapproval, either overt or with subtle hostile glances, tend to trigger belligerent responses from the ghetto residents, who then purposely intensify the behavior that is the source of irritation. The white and even the black middle-class moviegoers then exercise their option and exit, expressing resentment and experiencing intensified feelings of racial or class antagonism as they depart.

The areas surrendered in such a manner become the domain of the inner-city residents. Upscale businesses are replaced by fast-food chains and other local businesses that cater to the new clientele. White and black middle-class citizens complain bitterly about how certain areas of the central city have changed—and thus become "off-limits"—following the influx of ghetto residents.

The negative consequences are clear: Where jobs are scarce, many people eventually lose their feeling of connectedness to work in the formal economy; they no longer expect work to be a regular, and regulating, force in their lives. In the case of young people, they may grow up in an environment that lacks the idea of work as a central experience of adult life—they have little or no labor-force attachment. These circumstances also increase the likelihood that the residents will rely on illegitimate sources of income, thereby further weakening their attachment to the legitimate labor market.

A twenty-five-year-old West Side father of two who works two jobs to make ends meet condemned the attitude toward work of some inner-city black males:

They try to find easier routes and had been conditioned over a period of time to just be lazy, so to speak. Motivation nonexistent, you know, and the society that they're affiliated with really don't advocate hard work and struggle to meet your goals such as education and stuff like that. And they see who's around them and they follow that same pattern, you know.... They don't see nobody getting up early in the morning, going to work or going to school all the time. The guys they be with don't do that...because

that's the crowd that you choose—well, that's been presented to you by your neighborhood.

Work is not simply a way to make a living and support one's family. It also constitutes a framework for daily behavior because it imposes discipline. Regular employment determines where you are going to be and when you are going to be there. In the absence of regular employment, life, including family life, becomes less coherent. Persistent unemployment and irregular employment hinder rational planning in daily life, the necessary condition of adaptation to an industrial economy.

It's a myth that people who don't work don't want to work. One mother in a new poverty neighborhood on the South Side explained her decision to remain on welfare even though she would like to get a job:

I was working and then I had two kids. And I'm struggling. I was making, like, close to $7 an hour.... I had to pay a baby-sitter. Then I had to deal with my kids when I got home. And I couldn't even afford medical insurance.... I was so scared, when my kids were sick or something, because I have been turned away from a hospital because I did not have a medical card. I don't like being on public aid and stuff right now. But what do I do with my kids when the kids get sick?

Working mothers with comparable incomes face, in many cases, even greater difficulty. Why? Simply because many low-wage jobs do not provide health-care benefits, and most working mothers have to pay for transportation and spend more for child care. Working mothers also have to spend more for housing because it is more difficult for them to qualify for housing subsidies. It is not surprising, therefore, that many welfare-reliant mothers choose not to enter the formal labor market. It would not be in their best economic interest to do so. Given the economic realities, it is also not surprising that many who are working in these low-wage jobs decide to rely on or return to welfare, even though it's not a desirable alternative for many of the black single mothers. As one twenty-seven-year-old welfare mother of three children from an impoverished

West Side neighborhood put it: "I want to work. I do not work but I want to work. I don't want to just be on public aid."

As the disappearance of work has become a characteristic feature of the inner-city ghetto, so too has the disappearance of the traditional married-couple family. Only one-quarter of the black families whose children live with them in inner-city neighborhoods in Chicago are husband-wife families today, compared with three-quarters of the inner-city Mexican families, more than one-half of the white families and nearly one-half of the Puerto Rican families. And in census tracts with poverty rates of at least 40 percent, only 16.5 percent of the black families with children in the household are husband-wife families.

There are many factors involved in the precipitous decline in marriage rates and the sharp rise in single-parent families. The explanation most often heard in the public debate associates the increase of out-of-wedlock births and single-parent families with welfare. Indeed, it is widely assumed among the general public and reflected in the recent welfare reform that a direct connection exists between the level of welfare benefits and the likelihood that a young woman will bear a child outside marriage.

However, there is little evidence to support the claim that Aid to Families With Dependent Children plays a significant role in promoting out-of-wedlock births. Research examining the association between the generosity of welfare benefits and out-of-wedlock childbearing and teen-age pregnancy indicates that benefit levels have no significant effect on the likelihood that African American girls and women will have children outside marriage. Likewise, welfare rates have either no significant effect or only a small effect on the odds that whites will have children outside marriage. The rate of out-of-wedlock teen-age childbearing has nearly doubled since 1975—during years when the value of A.F.D.C., food stamps, and Medicaid fell, after adjusting for inflation. And the smallest increases in the number of out-of-wedlock births have not

occurred in states that have had the largest declines in the inflation-adjusted value of A.F.D.C. benefits. Indeed, while the real value of cash welfare benefits has plummeted over the past twenty years, out-of-wedlock childbearing has increased, and postpartum marriages (marriages following the birth of a couple's child) have decreased as well.

It's instructive to consider the social differences between inner-city blacks and other groups, especially Mexicans. Mexicans come to the United States with a clear conception of a traditional family unit that features men as breadwinners. Although extramarital affairs by men are tolerated, unmarried pregnant women are "a source of opprobrium, anguish or great concern," as Richard P. Taub, a member of one of our research teams, put it. Pressure is applied by the kin of both parents to enter into marriage.

The family norms and behavior in inner-city black neighborhoods stand in sharp contrast. The relationships between inner-city black men and women, whether in a marital or nonmarital situation, are often fractious and antagonistic. Inner-city black women routinely say that black men are hopeless as either husbands or fathers and that more of their time is spent on the streets than at home.

The men in the inner city generally feel that it is much better for all parties to remain in a nonmarital relationship until the relationship dissolves rather than to get married and then have to get a divorce. A twenty-five-year-old unmarried West Side resident, the father of one child, expressed this view:

Well, most black men feel now, why get married when you got six to seven women to one guy, really. You know, because there's more women out here mostly than men. Because most dudes around here are killing each other like fools over drugs or all this other stuff.

The fact that blacks reside in neighborhoods and are engaged in social networks and households that are less conducive to employment than those of other ethnic and racial groups in the inner city clearly has a negative effect on their search for work. In the eyes of employers in metropolitan Chicago, these differences render inner-city blacks less desirable as workers, and therefore are reluctant to hire them. The white chairman of a car transport company, when asked if there were differences in the work ethic of whites, blacks, and Hispanics, responded with great certainty:

Definitely! I don't think, I know: I've seen it over a period of thirty years. Basically, the Oriental is much more aggressive and intelligent and studious than the Hispanic. The Hispanics, except Cubans of course, they have the work ethnic [*sic*]. The Hispanics are *mañana, mañana, mañana*—tomorrow, tomorrow, tomorrow.

As for native-born blacks, they were deemed "the laziest of the bunch."

If some employers view the work ethic of inner-city poor blacks as problematic, many also express concerns about their honesty, cultural attitudes and dependability—traits that are frequently associated with the neighborhoods in which they live. A white suburban retail drugstore manager expressed his reluctance to hire someone from a poor inner-city neighborhood. "You'd be afraid they're going to steal from you," he stated. "They grow up that way. They grow up dishonest and I guess you'd feel like, geez, how are they going to be honest here?"

In addition to qualms about the work ethic, character, family influences, cultural predispositions and the neighborhood milieu of ghetto residents, the employers frequently mentioned concerns about applicants' language skills and educational training. They "just don't have the language skills," stated a suburban employer. The president of an inner-city advertising agency highlighted the problem of spelling:

I needed a temporary a couple months ago, and they sent me a black man. And I dictated a letter to him. He took shorthand, which was good. Something like "Dear Mr. So-and-So, I am writing to ask about how your business is doing." And then he typed the letter, and I read the letter, and it's "I am writing to ax about your business." Now you hear them speaking a different language and all

that, and they say "ax" for "ask." Well, I don't care about that, but I didn't say "ax," I said "ask."

Many inner-city residents have a strong sense of the negative attitudes that employers tend to have toward them. A thirty-three-year-old employed janitor from a poor South Side neighborhood had this observation: "I went to a couple jobs where a couple of the receptionists told me in confidence: 'You know what they do with these applications from blacks as soon as the day is over?' They say, 'We rip them and throw them in the garbage.'" In addition to concerns about being rejected because of race, the fears that some inner-city residents have of being denied employment simply because of their inner-city address or neighborhood are not unfounded. A welfare mother who lives in a large public housing project put it this way:

Honestly, I believe they look at the address and the—your attitudes, your address, your surround—you know, your environment has a lot to do with your employment status. The people with the best addresses have the best chances. I feel so, I feel so.

It is instructive to study the fate of the disadvantaged in Europe. There, too, poverty and joblessness are on the increase; but individual deficiencies and behavior are not put forward as the culprits. Furthermore, welfare programs that benefit wide segments of the population like child care, children's allowances (an annual benefit per child), housing subsidies, education, medical care and unemployment insurance have been firmly institutionalized in many Western European democracies. Efforts to cut back on these programs in the face of growing joblessness have met firm resistance from working- and middle-class citizens.

My own belief is that the growing assault on welfare mothers is part of a larger reaction to the mounting problems in our nation's inner cities. When many people think of welfare they think of young, unmarried black mothers having babies. This image persists even though roughly equal numbers of black and white families received

A.F.D.C. in 1994, and there were also a good many Hispanics on the welfare rolls. Nevertheless, the rise of black A.F.D.C. recipients was said to be symptomatic of such larger problems as the decline in family values and the dissolution of the family. In an article published in *Esquire*, Pete Hamill wrote:

> The heart of the matter is the continued existence and expansion of what has come to be called the Underclass…trapped in cycles of welfare dependency, drugs, alcohol, crime, illiteracy and disease, living in anarchic and murderous isolation in some of the richest cities on the earth. As a reporter, I've covered their miseries for more than a quarter of a century.… And in the last decade, I've watched this group of American citizens harden and condense, moving even further away from the basic requirements of a human life: work, family, safety, the law.

> One has the urge to shout, "Enough is enough!"

What can be done? I believe that steps must be taken to galvanize Americans from all walks of life who are concerned about human suffering and the public policy direction in which we are now moving. We need to generate a public-private partnership to fight social inequality. The following policy frameworks provide a basis for further discussion and debate. Given the current political climate, these proposals might be dismissed as unrealistic. Nor am I suggesting that we can or should simply import the social policies of the Japanese, the Germans, or other Western Europeans. The question is how we Americans can address the problems of social inequality, including record levels of joblessness in the inner city, that threaten the very fabric of our society.

CREATE STANDARDS FOR SCHOOLS

Ray Marshall, former [U.S.] Secretary of Labor, points out that Japan and Germany have developed policies designed to increase the number of workers with "higher-order thinking skills." These policies require young people to meet high performance standards before they can graduate

from secondary schools, and they hold each school responsible for meeting these standards.

Students who meet high standards are not only prepared for work but they are also ready for technical training and other kinds of postsecondary education. Currently, there are no mandatory academic standards for secondary schools in the United States. Accordingly, students who are not in college-preparatory courses have severely limited options with respect to pursuing work after high school. A commitment to a system of performance standards for every public school in the United States would be an important first step in addressing the huge gap in educational performance between the schools in advantaged and disadvantaged neighborhoods.

A system of at least local performance standards should include the kind of support that would enable schools in disadvantaged neighborhoods to meet the standards that are set. State governments, with federal support, not only would have to create equity in local school financing (through loans and scholarships to attract more high-quality teachers, increased support for teacher training and reforms in teacher certification) but would also have to insure that highly qualified teachers are more equitably distributed in local school districts.

Targeting education would be part of a national effort to raise the performance standards of all public schools in the United States to a desirable level, including schools in the inner city. The support of the private sector should be enlisted in this national effort. Corporations, local businesses, civic clubs, community centers and churches should be encouraged to work with the schools to improve computer-competency training.

IMPROVE CHILD CARE

The French system of child welfare stands in sharp contrast to the American system. In France, children are supported by three interrelated government programs, as noted by Barbara R. Bergmann, a professor of economics at American University:

child care, income support, and medical care. The child-care program includes establishments for infant care, high-quality nursery schools (*écoles maternelles*), and paid leave for parents of newborns. The income-support program includes child-support enforcement (so that the absent parent continues to contribute financially to his or her child's welfare), children's allowances, and welfare payments for low-income single mothers. Finally, medical care is provided through a universal system of national health care financed by social security, a preventive-care system for children, and a group of public-health nurses who specialize in child welfare.

ESTABLISH CITY-SUBURBAN PARTNERSHIPS

If the other industrial democracies offer lessons for a long-term solution to the jobs problem involving relationships between employment, education, and family-support systems, they also offer another lesson: the importance of city-suburban integration and cooperation. None of the other industrialized democracies have allowed their city centers to deteriorate as has the United States.

It will be difficult to address growing racial tensions in American cities unless we tackle the problems of shrinking revenue and inadequate social services and the gradual disappearance of work in certain neighborhoods. The city has become a less desirable place in which to live, and the economic and social gap between the cities and suburbs is growing. The groups left behind compete, often along racial lines, for declining resources, including the remaining decent schools, housing, and neighborhoods. The rise of the new urban poverty neighborhoods has worsened these problems. Their high rates of joblessness and social disorganization have created problems that often spill over into other parts of the city. All of these factors aggravate race relations and elevate racial tensions.

Ideally, we would restore the federal contribution to city revenues that existed in 1980 and

sharply increase the employment base. Regardless of changes in federal urban policy, however, the fiscal crises in the cities would be significantly eased if the employment base could be substantially increased. Indeed, the social dislocations caused by the steady disappearance of work have led to a wide range of urban social problems, including racial tensions. Increased employment would help stabilize the new poverty neighborhoods, halt the precipitous decline in density, and ultimately enhance the quality of race relations in urban areas.

Reforms put forward to achieve the objective of city-suburban cooperation range from proposals to create metropolitan governments to proposals for metropolitan tax-base sharing (currently in effect in Minneapolis-St. Paul), collaborative metropolitan planning, and the creation of regional authorities to develop solutions to common problems if communities fail to reach agreement. Among the problems shared by many metropolises is a weak public transit system. A commitment to address this problem through a form of city-suburban collaboration would benefit residents of both the city and the suburbs.

The mismatch between residence and the location of jobs is a problem for some workers in America because, unlike the system in Europe, public transportation is weak and expensive. It's a particular problem for inner-city blacks because they have less access to private automobiles and, unlike Mexicans, do not have a network system that supports organized car pools. Accordingly, they depend heavily on public transportation and therefore have difficulty getting to the suburbs, where jobs are more plentiful. Until public transit systems are improved in metropolitan areas, the creation of privately subsidized car-pool and van-pool networks to carry inner-city residents to the areas of employment, especially suburban areas, would be a relatively inexpensive way to increase work opportunities.

The creation of for-profit information and placement centers in various parts of the inner city not only could significantly improve awareness of the availability of employment in the metropolitan area but could also serve to refer workers to employers. These centers would recruit or accept inner-city workers and try to place them in jobs. One of their main purposes would be to make persons who have been persistently unemployed or out of the labor force "job ready."

REINTRODUCE THE W.P.A.

The final proposal under consideration here was advanced by the perceptive journalist Mickey Kaus of *The New Republic,* who has long been concerned about the growth in the number of welfare recipients. Kaus's proposal is modeled on the Works Progress Administration (W.P.A.), the large public-works program initiated in 1935 by President Franklin D. Roosevelt. The public-works jobs that Roosevelt had in mind included highway construction, slum clearance, housing construction, and rural electrification. As Kaus points out:

In its eight-year existence, according to official records, the W.P.A. built or improved 651,000 miles of roads, 953 airports, 124,000 bridges and viaducts, 1,178,000 culverts, 8,000 parks, 18,000 playgrounds and athletic fields, and 2,000 swimming pools. It constructed 40,000 buildings (including 8,000 schools) and repaired 85,000 more. Much of New York City—including La Guardia Airport, F.D.R. Drive, plus hundreds of parks and libraries—was built by the W.P.A.

A neo-W.P.A. program of employment, for every American citizen over eighteen who wants it, would provide useful public jobs at wages slightly below the minimum wage. Like the work relief under Roosevelt's W.P.A., it would not carry the stigma of a cash dole. People would be earning their money. Although some workers in the W.P.A.-style jobs "could be promoted to higher-paying public service positions," says Kaus, most of them would advance occupationally by moving to the private sector. "If you have to work anyway," he says, "why do it for $4 an hour?"

Under Kaus's proposal, after a certain date, able-bodied recipients on welfare would no longer receive cash payments. However, unlike the welfare-reform bill that Clinton has agreed to sign, Kaus's plan would make public jobs available to those who move off welfare. Also, Kaus argues that to allow poor mothers to work, government-financed day care must be provided for their children if needed. But this service has to be integrated into the larger system of child care for other families in the United States to avoid creating a "day-care ghetto" for low-income children.

A W.P.A.-style jobs program will not be cheap. In the short run, it is considerably cheaper to give people cash welfare than it is to create public jobs. Including the costs of supervisors and materials, each subminimum-wage W.P.A.-style job would cost an estimated $12,000, more than the public cost of staying on welfare. That would represent $12 billion for every 1 million jobs created.

The solutions I have outlined were developed with the idea of providing a policy framework that could be easily adopted by a reform coalition. A broad range of groups would support the long-term solutions—the development of a system of national performance standards in public schools, family policies to reinforce the learning system in the schools, a national system of school-to-work transition, and the promotion of city-suburban integration and cooperation. The short-term solutions, which range from job information and placement centers to the creation of W.P.A.-style jobs, are more relevant to low-income people, but they are the kinds of opportunity-enhancing programs that Americans of all racial and class backgrounds tend to support.

Although my policy framework is designed to appeal to broad segments of the population, I firmly believe that if adopted, it would alleviate a good deal of the economic and social distress currently plaguing the inner cities. The immediate problem of the disappearance of work in many inner-city neighborhoods would be confronted. The employment base in these neighborhoods would be increased immediately by the newly created jobs, and income levels would rise because of the expansion of the earned-income tax credit. Programs like universal health care and day care would increase the attractiveness of low-wage jobs and "make work pay."

Increasing the employment base would have an enormous positive impact on the social organization of ghetto neighborhoods. As more people become employed, crime and drug use would subside; families would be strengthened and welfare receipt would decline significantly; ghetto-related culture and behavior, no longer sustained and nourished by persistent joblessness, would gradually fade. As more people became employed and gained work experience, they would have a better chance of finding jobs in the private sector when they became available. The attitudes of employers toward inner-city workers would change, partly because the employers would be dealing with job applicants who had steady work experience and would furnish references from their previous supervisors.

This is not to suggest that all the jobless individuals from the inner-city ghetto would take advantage of these employment opportunities. Some have responded to persistent joblessness by abusing alcohol and drugs, and these handicaps will affect their overall job performance, including showing up for work on time or on a consistent basis. But such people represent only a small proportion of inner-city workers. Most of them are ready, willing, able and anxious to hold a steady job.

The long-term solutions that I have advanced would reduce the likelihood that a new generation of jobless workers will be produced from the youngsters now in school and preschool. We must break the cycle of joblessness and improve the youngsters' preparation for the new labor market in the global economy.

My framework for long-term and immediate solutions is based on the notion that the problems of jobless ghettos cannot be separated from those of the rest of the nation. Although these solutions have wide-ranging application and would alleviate the economic distress of many Americans, their impact on jobless ghettos would be profound. Their most important contribution would be their effect on the children of the ghetto, who would be able to anticipate a future of economic mobility and harbor the hopes and aspirations that for so many of their fellow citizens help define the American way of life.

CRITICAL THINKING QUESTIONS

1. According to Wilson, what is the primary cause of inner-city decline? How does his assessment differ from common notions about this problem?
2. Why have inner-city areas lost so many jobs over the past fifty years?
3. What solutions does Wilson offer? Do you agree with his approach? Why or why not?

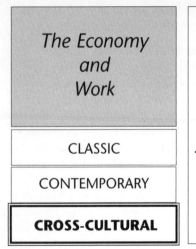

The Economy and Work

CLASSIC

CONTEMPORARY

CROSS-CULTURAL

45

Getting a Job in Harlem: Experiences of African-American, Puerto-Rican, and Dominican Youth

Katherine S. Newman

We often hear that ethnic minorities who live in America's inner cities are society's dregs: They don't want to work, are lazy and immoral, and collect welfare cheques at the expense of the average hard-working taxpayer. In contrast, Katherine S. Newman reached very different conclusions in her study of Black, Puerto Rican, and Dominican workers in Harlem. In this selection, Newman shows that the working poor—especially the youth in poverty-stricken inner-city neighborhoods—work very hard to get and keep minimum-wage jobs that offer little hope for upward mobility.

If you drive around the suburban neighborhoods of Long Island or Westchester County, you cannot miss the bright orange "Help Wanted" signs hanging in the windows of fast-food restaurants. Teenagers who have the time to work can walk into most of these shops and land a job before they finish filling out the application form. In fact, labor scarcity (for these entry-level jobs) is a problem for employers in these highly competitive businesses. Therefore, though it cuts into their profits, suburban and small-town employers in the more affluent parts of the country are forced to raise wages and redouble their efforts to recruit new employees, often turning to the retiree labor force when the supply of willing youths has run out.

Source: Katherine S. Newman, *No Shame in My Game: The Working Poor in the Inner City*, pp. 62–73. New York: Russell Sage Foundation, 1999.

From the vantage point of central Harlem, this "seller's market" sounds like a news bulletin from another planet. Jobs, even lousy jobs, are in such short supply that inner-city teenagers are all but barred from the market, crowded out by adults who are desperate to find work. Burger Barn managers rarely display those orange signs; some have never, in the entire history of their restaurants, advertised for employees. They can depend upon a steady flow of willing applicants coming in the door—and they can be very choosy about whom they sign up. In fact, my research shows that among central Harlem's fast-food establishments, the ratio of applicants to available jobs is fourteen to one. For every fortunate person who lands one of these minimum-wage jobs, there are thirteen others who walk away empty-handed. Since these applicants are also applying to other jobs, we should assume that the overall gap between the supply and demand of workers is not this large. Nonetheless, almost three-quarters of the unsuccessful job-seekers we interviewed were unemployed a year after they applied to Burger Barn, suggesting that the majority were no more successful with their other applications.

Statewide estimates of the gap between the number of people who need jobs (the unemployed plus the welfare recipients) and the number of available jobs in New York approach[es] almost one million.[1] This is a staggering number—which may indeed be an exaggeration, since it includes many people who are unemployed for only a short time, but it should draw our attention to the acute nature of the job problem, especially for low-skilled workers from the inner city.[2]

Long lines of job-seekers depress the wages of those lucky enough to pass through the initial barriers and find a job. Hamburger flippers in central Harlem generally do not break the minimum wage. Longtime workers, like Kyesha Smith, do not see much of a financial reward for their loyalty. After five years on the job, she was earning $5 an hour, only 60 cents more than the minimum wage at the time. Carmen and Jamal had done no better. And this is not because they are not valued; indeed, they are. It is because the supply-and-demand curves familiar to students of Economics 101 are operating with a vengeance in poor communities, as they are on Long Island or in Madison, Wisconsin, where the same jobs are paying more than $7 an hour.

The long odds of landing a job do not stop thousands of inner city residents from trying. When Disneyland took applications after the Rodney King riot in South-Central Los Angeles, some six thousand neatly dressed young people—largely black and Latino—waited in line to apply. In January 1992, when a new Sheraton Hotel complex opened in Chicago, three thousand applicants spent the better part of a day in blowing snow, huddled along the north bank of the Chicago River, hoping for an interview. Four thousand anxious job-seekers stood in lines that wrapped around the block in March 1997 when the Roosevelt Hotel in Manhattan announced it would take applications for seven hundred jobs.

Why do people seek low-wage jobs in places like Burger Barn? How do they go about the task in labor markets that are saturated with willing workers? What separates the success stories, the applicants who actually get jobs, from those who are rejected from these entry-level openings? These are questions that require answers if we are to have a clear picture of how the job market operates in poverty-stricken neighborhoods like Harlem.

WHY WORK?

You know, when I was out, when I wasn't working, I used to get into fights. Well, it wasn't really fights, it was like really arguments…. [Now, my friends] ask me, "Why don't we see you anymore?" Like, I can't. I don't have time. But, you know, I don't really wanna hang around my block anymore 'cuz it's like getting real bad. You know, it's a lot of people fighting around there for no reason. And they shootin' and stuff like that.

Jessica has worked at a fast-food restaurant in the middle of Harlem since she was seventeen, her first private-sector job following several summers as a city employee in a youth program. During her junior and senior year, Jessie commuted forty-five minutes each way to school, put in a full day at school, and then donned her work uniform for an eight-hour afternoon/evening shift.

Exhausted by the regimen, she took a brief break from work toward the end of her senior year, but returned when she graduated from high school. Now, at the age of twenty-one, she is a veteran fast-food employee with an unbroken work record of about three years.

Jessica had several motivations for joining the workforce when she was a teenager, principal among them the desire to be independent of her mother and provide for her own material needs. No less important, however, was her desire to escape the pressures of street violence and what appeared to be a fast track to nowhere among her peers. For in Jessica's neighborhood, many a young person never sees the other side of age twenty. Her own brother was shot in the chest, a victim of mistaken identity. Jessica's mother narrowly escaped a similar fate.

> It had to have been like twelve or one o'clock. My mother was in her room and I was in my room.... I sleep on the top bunk. We started hearing gunshots, so first thing I did, I jumped from my bed to the floor. I got up after the gunshots stopped and went into my mother's room. She was on the floor.... "Are you all right, are you all right?" she said. "Yeah, yeah." The next morning we woke up and it was like a bullet hole in the window in her room. Her bed is like the level of the window. Lucky thing she jumped, I mean went to the floor, because it could have come in through the window.

Incidents of this kind happen every day in Jessica's neighborhood, but contrary to popular opinion, they never become routine, something to be shrugged off as "business as usual." They are the unwelcome and unnatural consequence of a community plagued by a few very troublesome drug dealers, often the only thriving, growth area of the local economy.

Street violence, drive-by shootings, and other sources of terror are obstacles that Jessica and other working-poor people in her community have to navigate around. But Jessica knows that troubles of this kind strike more often among young people who have nothing to do but spend time on the street. Going to work was, for her, a deliberate act of disengagement from such a future. William, who has worked in the same Burger Barn as Jessica, had the same motivation. A short, stocky African American, who was "a fat, pudgy kid" in his teen years, Will was often the butt of jokes and the object of bullying in the neighborhood. Tougher characters were always giving him a hard time, snatching his belongings, pushing him around. They took a special delight in tormenting the "fat boy." William's ego took a pounding.

As he crested into his teenage years, he wanted some way to occupy his time that would keep him clear of the tensions cropping up in his South Bronx housing project. Lots of boys his age were getting into drugs, but Will says, "Fortunately I was never really into that type of thing." After a stint with a summer youth corps job, he found his "own thing": working for Burger Barn. Having a job took him out of the street and into a safe space.

> The job was good.... Just having fun that was unadulterated fun. There was no drugs. It was no pretenses, nobody givin' you a hard time. It was just being ourselves. That was cool.

For Stephanie, the trouble wasn't just in the streets, it was in her house. When she was in her teens, Stephanie's mother began taking in boarders in their apartment, young men and their girlfriends who did not always get along with her. The home scene was tense and occasionally violent, with knives flashing. The worse it got, the more Stephanie turned her attention to her job. She focused on what her earnings could do to rescue her from this unholy home life. Because she had her own salary, she was able to put her foot down and insist that her mother get rid of the troublemakers.

> By the end of the month, I told my mother, if [that guy's] not gone, I'm not never coming home. You don't even have to worry about me. I have this little job, I can pay for myself. I'll get my cousin [to join me] and we'll get a room.... Ever since then, my mother, she trying to do the right thing. She says he's supposed to be out by the end of the month. So by [then] hopefully he'll be gone.

Living where she does, Stephanie is an expert on what happens to people who do not follow the path she has chosen into the legitimate labor market. People she has grown up with, neighbors, and the boyfriends of some of her closest friends have all had brushes with violence and run-ins with the police. It happens alarmingly often in her neighborhood.

> [Gary], my girlfriend's boyfriend, just got shot. Gary and his friends...always used to stand on this corner. Always, it was their hangout spot. Some other friends was hustlin' [drugs] on our block and they went up to Gary, gave him a high five and just passed by. Some other guys came up to Gary and shot him. Shot him right in the leg. They told him, "Ya'll can't hustle on my block." He's lucky because the bullet grazed him, but it was a hollow-tip bullet, so them bullets explode. Blown off a chunk of his knee.

One of the only positive outcomes of these encounters is the resolution Stephanie feels about taking a completely different approach to her own life. She is hardly ignorant of the consequences of getting too close to the drug trade. The knowledge has given her confidence, in the face of many obstacles (not the least of which is a chaotic home life), that an honest job for low pay is preferable to getting mixed up with people in the illegal sector.[3]

Because the working poor have little choice but to live in neighborhoods where rents are low, they often find themselves in social settings like Stephanie's. They have lots of friends and neighbors who are working at real jobs for little income, but they also rub shoulders with criminals who headquarter their enterprises in these poor neighborhoods. Exposure to folks who have taken the wrong fork in the road provides good reason for seeking a safe haven like Burger Barn.

There are many "push factors" that prod Harlem youth to look for work. Yet there are many positive inducements as well. Even as young teens, Jessica, William, and Stephanie were anxious to pay their own way, to free their families from the obligation to take care of all their needs. In this, they are typical of the two hundred Burger Barn workers I tracked, the majority of whom began their work lives when they were thirteen to fifteen years old. This early experience in the labor force usually involves bagging groceries or working off the books in a local bodega, a menial job under the watchful eye of an adult who, more often than not, was a friend of the family or a relative who happened to have a shop.

Taking a job at the age of thirteen is a familiar path for anyone who lived through or has read about the Great Depression of the 1930s, when working-class families fallen on hard times often sent out their young people to find jobs. It stands in sharp contrast to the prevailing expectations of today's middle-class world, in which young teens are told to concentrate on their homework and their soccer leagues and leave the world of work for later in life.[4]

Yet most of the working poor come from homes where the struggles of the 1930s are all too familiar. Poor parents cannot stretch their resources to take care of their children's needs, much less the demands they make when their better-off peers are buying a new CD or a special kind of jacket—the kinds of frills that middle-class families routinely provide for their teens (along with the second telephone line, access to a car, and many other expensive items). Inner-city kids cannot even dream of such luxuries. Even finding the funds to pay for transportation, basic clothing, books, and other necessary expenses is hard for these families.

While middle-class parents would feel they had abrogated a parental responsibility if they demanded that their kids handle these basic costs (not to mention the frills), many poor parents consider the "demand" perfectly normal. Whether American-born or recent immigrants, these parents often began working at an early age themselves and consequently believe that a "good" kid should not be goofing off in his or her free time—summers, after school, and vacations—but should be bringing in some cash to the family.

Burger Barn earnings will not stretch to cover a poor family's larger items like food and shelter, and in this respect entry-level jobs do not underwrite any real independence. They do make it possible for kids like Kyesha and Carmen to participate in youth culture. Many writers have dismissed teenage workers on these grounds, complaining that their sole (read "trivial") motivation for working (and neglecting school) is to satisfy childish desires for "gold chains and designer sneakers."[5] Jessie and Will do want to look good and be cool. But most of their wages are spent providing for basic expenses. When she was still in high school, Jessica paid for her own books, school transportation, lunches, and basic clothing expenses. Now that she has graduated, she has assumed even more of the cost of keeping herself. Her mother takes care of the roof over their heads, but Jessie is responsible for the rest, as well as for a consistent contribution toward the expense of running a home with other dependent children in it. Minimum-wage jobs cannot buy real economic independence; they cannot cover the full cost of living, including rent, food, and the rest of an adult's monthly needs. What Jessica can do with her earnings is cover the marginal cost of her presence in the household, leaving something over every week to contribute to the core cost of maintaining the household. Youth workers, particularly those who are parents themselves, generally do turn over part of their pay to the head of the household as a kind of rent. In this fashion, working-poor youth participate in a pooled-income strategy that makes it possible for households—as opposed to individuals—to sustain themselves. Without their contributions, this would become increasingly untenable, especially in families where Mom is receiving public assistance.[6]

This pattern is even more striking among immigrants and native-born minorities who are not incorporated into the state welfare system. In working-poor households with no connection to the state system, survival depends upon multiple workers pooling their resources.[7] Pressures build early for the older children in these communities to take jobs, no matter what the wages, in order to help their parents make ends meet. Ana Gonzales is a case in point. Having reached twenty-one years old, she had been working since she was fifteen. Originally from Ecuador, Ana followed her parents, who emigrated a number of years before and presently work in a factory in New Jersey. Ana completed her education in her home country and got a clerical job. She emigrated at eighteen, joining two younger brothers and a twelve-year-old sister already in New York. Ana has ambitions for going back to college, but for the moment she works full-time in a fast-food restaurant in Harlem, as does her sixteen-year-old brother. Her sister is responsible for cooking and caring for their five-year-old brother, a responsibility Ana assumes when she is not at work or attending her English as a Second Language class.

The Gonzales family is typical of the immigrant households that participate in the low-wage economy of Harlem and Washington Heights, and it bears a strong resemblance to the Puerto Rican families in other parts of the city.[8] Parents work, adolescent children work, and only the youngest of the children are able to invest themselves in U.S. schooling. Indeed, it is often the littlest who is deputized to master the English language on behalf of the whole family. Children as young as five or six are designated as interpreters responsible for negotiations between parents and landlords, parents and teachers, parents and the whole English-speaking world beyond the barrio.[9]

The social structure of these households is one that relies upon the contributions of multiple earners for cash earnings, child care, and housework.[10] Parents with limited language skills (and often illegal status) are rarely in a position to support their children without substantial contributions from the children themselves. Jobs that come their way rarely pay enough to organize a "child-centered" household in which education and leisure are the predominant activities of the youth until the age of eighteen. Instead, they must rely upon their children and, at most, can look forward to the eventual upward mobility of the youngest of their kids, who may be able to remain in school long enough to move to better occupations in the future.

Older workers, especially women with children to support, have other motives for entering the low-wage labor market. Like most parents, they have financial obligations: rent, clothes, food, and all the associated burdens of raising kids. Among the single mothers working at Burger Barn, however, the options for better-paying jobs are few and the desire to avoid welfare is powerful.[11] This is particularly true for women who had children when they were in their teens and dropped out of school to take care of them.

Latoya, one of Kyesha Smith's closest friends at Burger Barn, had her first child when she was sixteen. She was married at seventeen and then had another. But the marriage was shaky; her husband was abusive and is in jail now. Latoya learned about being vulnerable, and has made sure she will never become dependent again. She lives with Jason, her common-law husband, a man who is a skilled carpenter, and they have a child between them. Jason makes a good living, a lot more money than Latoya can earn on her own. Now that she has three kids, plus Jason's daughter by his first marriage, she has occasionally been tempted to quit work and just look after them. After all, it is hard to take care of four kids, even with Jason's help, and work a full-time job at the same time. She barely has the energy to crawl into bed at night, and crumbles at the thought of the overnight shifts she is obliged to take.

But Latoya's experience with her first husband taught her that no man is worth the sacrifice of her independence.

This was my first real job.... I take it seriously, you know.... It means a lot to me. It give you—what's the word I'm lookin' for? Security blanket. 'Cuz, a lot of married women, like when I was married to my husband, when he left, the burden was left on me. If [Jason] leave now, I can deal with the load because I work. [Jason] help me—we split the bills half and half. But if he leaves, I'm not gonna be, well, "Oh my God, I'm stranded. I have no money." No. I have a little bank account; I got my little nest egg. You know, so it does mean a lot to me. I wouldn't just up and leave my job.

For Latoya, as for many other working mothers, working is an insurance policy against dependence on men who may not be around for the long haul.[12]

FINDING A WAY IN

Tiffany was little more than ten years old when she first tried to find work. She was still living with her mother in the Bedford-Stuyvesant area of Brooklyn at that time, but they were in trouble. "Things were bad," she remembers. "Checks weren't coming in. And what would happen is we needed food.... So I would pack bags and stuff [in a local store] for spare change. And after a full day, I would make enough to buy groceries." Little Tiffany wasn't saving for gold chains, she

was trying to help make ends meet in a family that was falling apart.

But the bagging job wasn't a real, legitimate job. In fact, it was pretty dicey. We was at the whim of the cashiers. Discretion was with the store owner. 'Cause they would run us out sometimes. It was almost like how you see on a larger scale, big-time [crime] organizations.... It was like a little gang thing going on with the packers. There was a lead packer and even he would extort money from the other packers. One time I got beat up by a guy 'cause I was the only female. I was not gonna give none of my money. And he bullied me around. I was scared. I didn't go back for a while.

Still, Tiffany felt she was doing something useful, something important. When customers gave her a tip, she thought she had earned it, and it was more money than she had ever seen. But the whole day might yield no more than fifty cents.

By the time she was thirteen, Tiffany's mother had given her up to a group home in New York's foster care system. In some ways, she had more stability in her life, facing less pressure to provide the food for the table. Yet group homes are regimented, Spartan places, with many rules and regulations. Once school was out for the summer, Tiffany wanted to escape the military atmosphere—the system of infractions and privileges withdrawn, the searches of personal belongings, the single phone call on the weekends—and find something useful to do. She also wanted to earn some money, since her group home was lean on what it deemed "extras," like funds to take in an occasional movie.

Ironically, because she was in foster care, Tiffany had direct access to the city's employment programs for young minorities, collectively known as "summer youth" by most inner-city kids. Through the good offices of her caseworker, she found a job as a clerical assistant in an office that provided assistance to victims of domestic violence. At the age of thirteen, Tiffany was answering the office phone, taking down information from women who had been battered and were seeking shelter. The job gave Tiffany an appreciation for white-collar work: the clean environment, the comfort of air-conditioning (while her friends working for the parks department were outside sweating the hot summer), and the feeling of importance that comes with a little prestige and the ability to help someone in trouble. It focused her desire to work in a social service agency someday.

Working for summer youth, Tiffany discovered one of the liabilities of a paycheck delivered by the government. Like Social Security checks, these salaries were delivered biweekly, on the same Friday, to thousands of kids working throughout the city. Everyone in her neighborhood knew when those checks would be available.

There was a real element of fear involved. Hundreds of other people were getting their checks. There were many people who would steal your check. People would follow you to the check-cashing place and take your money. Waiting on line, you'd usually take a friend with you to pick up your check. If you were smart, you wouldn't cash it right away. You'd go home. You'd wait and go to a check-cashing place in your neighborhood. But you know the young, they wanted their money right away. They wanted to go shopping. So they'd cash it right there and they get hit.

Despite these problems, Tiffany learned a lot from this job that she could apply to other jobs as she got older. She discovered that work involved taking care of responsibilities that were delegated to her and no one else, that it wasn't always fun but had to be done anyway. It taught her that she had to be on time and that completing her work in a defined period of time was an expectation she had to meet. "I had to stay on top of my duties!" Public employment of the kind Tiffany had is often the first gateway into the full-time labor force that inner-city kids experience.[13] They graduate from bagging groceries for tips into these more regular jobs and learn firsthand what it means to report to work daily, handle responsibilities, and be part of an organization.

Job corps initiatives, like the one Tiffany participated in, were born out of a desire to give inner-city kids something constructive to do in the months between school terms, a prophylactic against petty crime during the long hot summers of the War on Poverty years. But they have a much more important, albeit latent, purpose: They are a proving ground for poor youth who need an introduction to the culture of regular (salaried) work. A summer youth position is often the first regular, on-the-books job that an inner-city kid can find, the first refuge from the temporary, irregular, off-the-books employment that kids find on their own.

Larry's first experience with work was handing out advertising flyers on the sidewalk in front of a drugstore. It wasn't a popular occupation in the wintertime; Larry had to stand outside in the freezing slush, waiting for infrequent customers to come by and reluctantly accept the broadsheet thrust at them. It lasted for only a couple of weeks, for the employer decided it wasn't bringing in much business. So Larry followed the advice of his older friends and applied for a summer youth job. He landed one working for the New York City Parks Council, a jack-of-all trades position. "I basically did everything for them," he noted. "Fixed benches, cleaned the park, helped old people. You know, all kinds of things. Paint, Plant, Mop, sweep, all that. Whatever they needed done, I'd do it."[14]

Working for the parks and recreation department, Larry learned some basic carpentry skills. He also learned what all newcomers to the world of work must absorb: how to cooperate with other people, show up on time, take directions, and demonstrate initiative. Most important of all, the job gave Larry a track record he could use when he went out to look for a new job when summer was over.

That Park job did get me my job at [Burger Barn], 'cause they could see that I had work experience, you know. They called and they got good reviews on me. I'm a very hard worker and I'm patient. All of the stuff that they was looking for, you know.

Many of the Burger Barn workers in central Harlem got their start in the public sector. They were able to build on this experience: They could prove to the next employer that they had some experience and drive. This alone put them ahead of many other job-seekers who cannot bring these credentials to bear on the task of finding employment.

The experience also gave them a fount of cultural wisdom about what employers are looking for when they make their choices. Much of the literature on the nation's urban ghetto dwellers tells us that this kind of knowledge has disappeared in high-poverty neighborhoods: Young people are said to be ignorant of what work is like, of what the managers on the other side of the counter "see" when job-seekers from communities like Harlem or the South Bronx walk in the door.[15] Do they see a willing worker who should be given a chance, or do they see a street-smart kid in shades and funky clothes who looks like trouble?

High schools in Harlem and elsewhere in New York have turned some attention to this problem by trying to educate young people about the realities of a tough job market. They pound information into the heads of their students: that they have to dress right, speak right, behave with respect and a certain amount of deference. They have to park all the symbolic baggage of their peer culture at home. Whether we consider the success stories, people who have crossed the barrier of finding a job, or the ones who haven't been so fortunate, we find evidence of widespread knowledge of these stylistic hurdles, and recognition that employers hold the upper hand. Decisions will be theirs to make in a highly competitive market, and one must be prepared to meet their expectations.

These very mainstream attitudes are particularly clear in the voices of Harlem youth who have had some experience with youth employment programs. Larry's days in the parks department gave him a chance to see what management's position was.

If you come to an interview talking that street slang, you lost your chances of getting that job. I think if you want a job, you gotta speak appropriately to the owner, to the employer.

CRITICAL THINKING QUESTIONS

1. What motivates inner-city teenagers to work in "hamburger flipping" jobs (such as the Burger Barn) that many middle-class adolescents avoid?

2. How do applicants who get minimum-wage jobs differ from those who are rejected?

3. Do you feel that these experiences from Harlem can be applied to the employment situation in Canadian cities? If so, how? If not, why?

NOTES

1. The Greater Upstate Law Project and NYC-based Housing Works, both welfare rights advocacy organizations, prepared this analysis from Governor Pataki's administrative reports as well as from NYC Department of Social Services and Department of Labor data. These show that 570,100 New Yorkers are unemployed and 618,628 adults are on AFDC or Home Relief (single cases) for a total of 1.2 million potential job-seekers. Department of Labor, *Occupational Outlook Through 1999* (1995), projects that 242,620 jobs will be available every year between 1996 and 1999. The difference between the potential supply and the potential demand is therefore nearly one million in the state of New York.

2. New York City is experiencing a moderate recovery from a locally severe recession occurring from 1989 to 1992. The City Office of Management and Budget has forecast a net gain of 92,000 payroll jobs from 1995 through 1999. If this forecast is accurate, there will still be a net loss of 200,000 jobs between 1989 and 1999. See "Work to Be Done: Report of the Borough Presidents' Task Force on Education, Employment and Welfare" (August 1995).

3. Drug dealing tends not to be a woman's business. Crime is generally a male enterprise—and an expanding one at that. We know from youth surveys that a large number of young men from poor urban neighborhoods admit that they participate in criminal activity. Richard B. Freeman, "Why Do So Many Young American Men Commit Crimes and What Might We Do About It?" (NBER Working Paper 5451, 1996), argues that the rise in criminal activity among low-skilled young men over the past twenty years is influenced by the job market disincentives of the 1980s and 1990s.

4. Most young students, those in grades six through eight, who hold jobs are from disadvantaged backgrounds. D. C. Gottfredson, "Youth Employment, Crime and Schooling: A Longitudinal Study of a National Sample," *Developmental Psychology* 21 (1985), pp. 419–32. See also Catherine M. Yamoor and Jaylin T. Mortimer, "Age and Gender Differences in the Effects of Employment on Adolescent Achievement and Well-

being," *Youth and Society* 22, no. 2 (December 1990), pp. 225–40. Older teenage workers are just as likely to come from middle-class homes.

5. Academics, too, often focus upon adolescents' expanding interests in acquiring consumer goods as a primary motivation for employment; see Ellen Greenberger and L. Steinberg, *When Teenagers Work* (Basic Books, 1986), and Laurence Steinberg, *Beyond the Classroom* (Simon & Schuster, 1996). This is due, in part, to the changing composition of the teenage workforce, once largely made up of youth from lower classes. See Joseph F. Kett, *Rites of Passage* (Basic Books, 1977).

6. Kathryn Edin's research, based on interviews with 214 AFDC mothers from four cities, makes it exceedingly clear that welfare families cannot make it on state payments alone. Edin found that AFDC, food stamps, and SSI combined make up 63% of the mothers' average total monthly income (which just covers expenses). Contributions from children, family, and friends account for a small but significant 7% of income. See Kathryn Edin, "Single Mothers and Child Support: The Possibilities and Limits of Child Support Policy," *Children and Youth Services Review* 17, no. 102 (1995), pp. 203–30.

7. See Marta Tienda and Jennifer Glass, "Household Structure and Labor Force Participation of Black, Hispanic, and White Mothers," *Demography* 22, no. 3 (1985), pp. 381–94. Through a statistical analysis of 1980 CPA data, Tienda and Glass found that the number and composition of adults in extended families affects their labor force participation. The extended family arrangement alleviates economic hardships by spreading child care and other domestic obligations among more adults, thus allowing greater proportions of wage earners per household.

8. See Mercer Sullivan, *"Getting Paid": Youth, Crime, and Work in the Inner City* (Cornell University Press, 1989), for an account of Puerto Rican families in Sunset Park, Brooklyn.

9. Very young children in immigrant families are also commonly sent "home" to be cared for by relatives who still reside in the country of origin. Patricia Pessar, "The Role of Households in International Migration and the Case of U.S.-Bound Migration from the Dominican Republic,"*International Migration Review* 16, no. 2 (1982), pp. 342–34.

10. For discussion of the cooperative (and strained) structure of immigrant residence and family, see Sarah J. Mahler, *American Dreaming: Immigrant Life on the Margins* (Princeton University Press, 1995); Sherri Grasmuck and Patricia Pessar, *Between Two Islands: Dominican International Migration* (University of California Press, 1991); Lloyd H. Rogler and Rosemary Santana Cooney, *Puerto Rican Families in New York City: Intergenerational Processes* (Waterfront Press, 1984); Nina Glick Schiller, Linda Basch, and Cristina Szanton Blanc, eds., *Towards a Transnational Perspective on Migration: Race,*

Class, Ethnicity, and Nationalism Reconsidered (New York Academy of Sciences, 1992); Alejandro Portes and Ruben G. Rumbaut, *Immigrant America: A Portrait* (University of California Press, 1990); Nancy Foner, ed., *New Immigrants in New York* (Columbia University Press, 1987); and Leo R. Chavez, "Coresidence and Resistance: Strategies for Survival Among Undocumented Mexicans and Central Americans in the United States," *Urban Anthropology* 19, nos. 1–2 (1990), pp. 31–61.

11. Nationwide, unmarried female household heads with children have higher labor force participation rates than married mothers. Tienda and Glass, "Household Structure and Labor Force Participation of Black, Hispanic, and White Mothers," p. 391.

12. This motivation for employment is not uncommon. See Arlie Hochschild, *The Second Shift: Working Parents and the Revolution at Home* (Viking, 1989), pp. 128–41....

13. Currently there are quite a number of demonstration projects around the country that aim to enrich summer youth programs through classroom learning or worksite education, many of which have improved academic outcomes of participants. See Office of the Chief Economist, U.S. Department of Labor, *What's Working (and What's Not): A Summary of Research on the Economic Impacts of Employment and Training Programs* (1995); Jean Baldwin Grossman and Cynthia Sipe, "The Long-Term Impacts of the Summer Training and Education Program" (Philadelphia: Public/Private Ventures); Arnold H. Packer and Marion W. Pines, *School-to-Work* (Princeton: Eye on Education, 1996). Typically, however, participants (a third of whom are 14- and 15-year-olds) in summer programs work for minimum wage in much less structured settings. Many of them get placements at government agencies, schools, and community-based associations doing maintenance or office work while receiving some remedial education.

14. Mayor Giuliani has been an enthusiastic supporter of workfare jobs and has been criticized for substituting these sub-minimum-wage workers for union labor. Funding for summer youth jobs has been progressively curtailed over the years. It is possible that the tasks Larry performed in the parks will become workfare jobs as well. This is important because it may limit the availability of entry-level public-sector positions for young people coming into the labor market.

15. Janice Haaken and Joyce Korschgen, "Adolescents and Conceptions of Social Relations in the Workplace," *Adolescence* 23 (1988), pp. 1–14, reports that adolescents from higher-status backgrounds have a better understanding than adolescents from disadvantaged backgrounds about the workplace expectations of employers. See also James E. Rosenbaum, Takehiko Kariya, Rick Settersten, and Tony Maier, "Market and Network Theories of the Transition from High School to Work: Their Application to Industrialized Societies," *Annual Review of Sociology* 16 (1990), pp. 263–99.

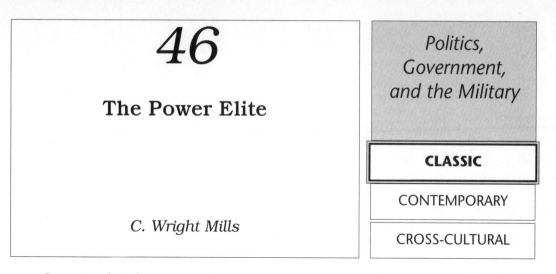

46

The Power Elite

C. Wright Mills

Politics, Government, and the Military

CLASSIC

CONTEMPORARY

CROSS-CULTURAL

Conventional wisdom suggests that our society operates as a democracy, guided by the voice of the people. C. Wright Mills argues that above ordinary people—and even above many politicians—are "the higher circles," those who run the corporations, operate the military establishment, and manipulate the machinery of the state. It is this relative hand-ful of people whom Mills calls "the power elite."

The powers of ordinary men are circumscribed by the everyday worlds in which they live, yet even in these rounds of job, family, and neighborhood they often seem driven by forces they can neither understand nor govern. "Great changes" are beyond their control, but affect their conduct and outlook nonetheless. The very framework of modern society confines them to projects not their own, but from every side, such changes now press upon the men and women of the mass society, who accordingly feel that they are without purpose in an epoch in which they are without power.

Source: From *The Power Elite* by C. Wright Mills. Copyright ©1956 by C. Wright Mills. Renewed 1984 by Yaraslava Mills. Used by permission of Oxford University Press, Inc.

But not all men are in this sense ordinary. As the means of information and of power are centralized, some men come to occupy positions in American society from which they can look down upon, so to speak, and by their decisions mightily affect, the everyday worlds of ordinary men and women. They are not made by their jobs; they set up and break down jobs for thousands of others; they are not confined by simple family responsibilities; they can escape. They may live in many hotels and houses, but they are bound by no one community. They need not merely "meet the demands of the day and hour"; in some part, they create these demands, and cause others to meet them. Whether or not they profess their power, their technical and political experience of it far transcends that of the under-lying population. What Jacob Burckhardt said of "great men," most Americans might well say of their elite: "They are all that we are not."

The power elite is composed of men whose positions enable them to transcend the ordinary environments of ordinary men and women; they are in positions to make decisions having major consequences. Whether they do or do not make such decisions is less important than the fact that they do occupy such pivotal positions: Their failure to act, their failure to make decisions, is itself an act that is often of greater consequence than the decisions they do make. For they are in command of the major hierarchies and organizations of modern society. They rule the big corporations. They run the machinery of the state and claim its prerogatives. They direct the military establishment. They occupy the strategic command posts of the social structure, in which are now centered the effective means of the power and the wealth and the celebrity which they enjoy.

The power elite are not solitary rulers. Advisers and consultants, spokesmen and opinion-makers are often the captains of their higher thought and decision. Immediately below the elite are the professional politicians of the middle levels of power, in the Congress and in the pressure groups, as well as among the new and old upper classes of town and city and region. Mingling with them, in curious ways which we shall explore, are those professional celebrities who live by being continually displayed but are never, so long as they remain celebrities, displayed enough. If such celebrities are not at the head of any dominating hierarchy, they do often have the power to distract the attention of the public or afford sensations to the masses, or, more directly, to gain the ear of those who do occupy positions of direct power. More or less unattached, as critics of morality and technicians of power, as spokesmen of God and creators of mass sensibility, such celebrities and consultants are part of the immediate scene in which the drama of the elite is enacted. But that drama itself is centered in the command posts of the major institutional hierarchies.

The truth about the nature and the power of the elite is not some secret which men of affairs know but will not tell. Such men hold quite various theories about their own roles in the sequence of event and decision. Often they are uncertain about their roles, and even more often they allow their fears and their hopes to affect their assessment of their own power. No matter how great their actual power, they tend to be less acutely aware of it than of the resistances of others to its use. Moreover, most American men of affairs have learned well the rhetoric of public relations, in some cases even to the point of using it when they are alone, and thus coming to believe it. The personal awareness of the actors is only one of the several sources one must examine in order to understand the higher circles. Yet many who believe that there is no elite, or at any rate none of any consequence, rest their argument upon what men of affairs believe about themselves, or at least assert in public.

There is, however, another view: Those who feel, even if vaguely, that a compact and powerful elite of great importance does now prevail in America often base that feeling upon the historical trend of our time. They have felt, for example, the domination of the military event, and from this they infer that generals and admirals, as well as other men of decision influenced by them, must be enormously powerful. They hear that the Congress has again abdicated to a handful of men decisions clearly related to the issue of war or peace. They know that the bomb was dropped over Japan in the name of the United States of America, although they were at no time consulted about the matter. They feel that they live in a time of big decisions; they know that they are not making any. Accordingly, as they consider the present as history, they infer that at its center, making decisions or failing to make them, there must be an elite of power.

On the one hand, those who share this feeling about big historical events assume that there is an elite and that its power is great. On the other hand, those who listen carefully to the reports of men apparently involved in the great decisions often do not believe that there is an elite whose powers are of decisive consequence.

Both views must be taken into account, but neither is adequate. The way to understand the power of the American elite lies neither solely in recognizing the historic scale of events nor in accepting the personal awareness reported by men of apparent decision. Behind such men and behind the events of history, linking the two, are the major institutions of modern society. These hierarchies of state and corporation and army constitute the means of power; as such they are now of a consequence not before equaled in human history— and at their summits, there are now those command posts of modern society which offer us the sociological key to an understanding of the role of the higher circles in America.

Within American society, major national power now resides in the economic, the political, and the military domains. Other institutions seem off to the side of modern history, and, on occasion, duly subordinated to these. No family is as directly powerful in national affairs as any major corporation; no church is as directly powerful in the external biographies of young men in America today as the military establishment; no college is as powerful in the shaping of momentous events as the National Security Council. Religious, educational, and family institutions are not autonomous centers of national power; on the contrary, these decentralized areas are increasingly shaped by the big three, in which developments of decisive and immediate consequence now occur.

Families and churches and schools adapt to modern life; governments and armies and corporations shape it; and, as they do so, they turn these lesser institutions into means for their ends. Religious institutions provide chaplains to the armed forces where they are used as a means of increasing the effectiveness of its morale to kill. Schools select and train men for their jobs in corporations and their specialized tasks in the armed forces. The extended family has, of course, long been broken up by the industrial revolution, and now the son and the father are removed from the family, by compulsion if need be, whenever the army of the state sends out the call. And the symbols of all these lesser institutions are used to legitimate the power and the decisions of the big three.

The life-fate of the modern individual depends not only upon the family into which he was born or which he enters by marriage, but increasingly upon the corporation in which he spends the most alert hours of his best years; not only upon the school where he is educated as a child and adolescent, but also upon the state which touches him throughout his life; not only upon the church in which on occasion he hears the word of God, but also upon the army in which he is disciplined.

If the centralized state could not rely upon the inculcation of nationalist loyalties in public and private schools, its leaders would promptly seek to modify the decentralized educational system. If the bankruptcy rate among the top 500 corporations were as high as the general divorce rate among the 37 million married couples, there would be economic catastrophe on an international scale. If members of armies gave to them no more of their lives than do believers to the churches to which they belong, there would be a military crisis.

Within each of the big three, the typical institutional unit has become enlarged, has become administrative, and, in the power of its decisions, has become centralized. Behind these developments there is a fabulous technology, for as institutions, they have incorporated this technology and guide it, even as it shapes and paces their developments.

The economy—once a great scatter of small productive units in autonomous balance—has become dominated by two or three hundred giant corporations, administratively and politically interrelated, which together hold the keys to economic decisions.

The political order, once a decentralized set of several dozen states with a weak spinal cord, has become a centralized, executive establishment which has taken up into itself many powers previously scattered, and now enters into each and every cranny of the social structure.

The military order, once a slim establishment in a context of distrust fed by state militia, has become the largest and most expensive feature of government, and, although well-versed in smiling public relations, now has all the grim and clumsy efficiency of a sprawling bureaucratic domain.

In each of these institutional areas, the means of power at the disposal of decision makers have increased enormously; their central executive powers have been enhanced; within each of them modern administrative routines have been elaborated and tightened up.

As each of these domains becomes enlarged and centralized, the consequences of its activities become greater, and its traffic with the others increases. The decisions of a handful of corporations bear upon military and political as well as upon economic developments around the world. The decisions of the military establishment rest upon and grievously affect political life as well as the very level of economic activity. The decisions made within the political domain determine economic activities and military programs. There is no longer, on the one hand, an economy, and, on the other hand, a political order containing a military establishment unimportant to politics and to money-making. There is a political economy linked, in a thousand ways, with military institutions and decisions. On each side of the world-split running through central Europe and around the Asiatic rimlands, there is an ever-increasing interlocking of economic, military, and political structures. If there is government intervention in the corporate economy, so is there corporate intervention in the governmental process. In the structural sense, this triangle of power is the source of the interlocking directorate that is most important for the historical structure of the present.

The fact of the interlocking is clearly revealed at each of the points of crisis of modern capitalist society—slump, war, and boom. In each, men

of decision are led to an awareness of the interdependence of the major institutional orders. In the nineteenth century, when the scale of all institutions was smaller, their liberal integration was achieved in the automatic economy, by an autonomous play of market forces, and in the automatic political domain, by the bargain and the vote. It was then assumed that out of the imbalance and friction that followed the limited decisions then possible a new equilibrium would in due course emerge. That can no longer be assumed, and it is not assumed by the men at the top of each of the three dominant hierarchies.

For given the scope of their consequences, decisions—and indecisions—in any one of these ramify into the others, and hence top decisions tend either to become coordinated or to lead to a commanding indecision. It has not always been like this. When numerous small entrepreneurs made up the economy, for example, many of them could fail and the consequences still remain local; political and military authorities did not intervene. But now, given political expectations and military commitments, can they afford to allow key units of the private corporate economy to break down in slump? Increasingly, they do intervene in economic affairs, and as they do so, the controlling decisions in each order are inspected by agents of the other two, and economic, military, and political structures are interlocked.

At the pinnacle of each of the three enlarged and centralized domains, there have arisen those higher circles which make up the economic, the political, and the military elites. At the top of the economy, among the corporate rich, there are the chief executives; at the top of the political order, the members of the political directorate; at the top of the military establishment, the elite of soldier-statesmen clustered in and around the Joint Chiefs of Staff and the upper echelon. As each of these domains has coincided with the others, as decisions tend to become total in their consequence, the leading men in each of the three domains of power—the warlords, the corporation chieftains, the political directorate—tend to come together, to form the power elite of America.

The higher circles in and around these command posts are often thought of in terms of what their members possess: They have a greater share than other people of the things and experiences that are most highly valued. From this point of view, the elite are simply those who have the most of what there is to have, which is generally held to include money, power, and prestige—as well as all the ways of life to which these lead. But the elite are not simply those who have the most, for they could not "have the most" were it not for their positions in the great institutions. For such institutions are the necessary bases of power, of wealth, and of prestige, and at the same time, the chief means of exercising power, of acquiring and retaining wealth, and of cashing in the higher claims for prestige.

By the powerful we mean, of course, those who are able to realize their will, even if others resist it. No one, accordingly, can be truly powerful unless he has access to the command of major institutions, for it is over these institutional means of power that the truly powerful are, in the first instance, powerful. Higher politicians and key officials of government command such institutional power; so do admirals and generals, and so do the major owners and executives of the larger corporations. Not all power, it is true, is anchored in and exercised by means of such institutions, but only within and through them can power be more or less continuous and important.

Wealth also is acquired and held in and through institutions. The pyramid of wealth cannot be understood merely in terms of the very rich; for the great inheriting families, as we shall see, are now supplemented by the corporate institutions of modern society: Every one of the very rich families has been and is closely connected—always legally and frequently managerially as well—with one of the multimillion-dollar corporations.

The modern corporation is the prime source of wealth, but, in latter-day capitalism, the political apparatus also opens and closes many avenues to wealth. The amount as well as the source of income, the power over consumer's goods as well as over productive capital, are determined by position within the political economy. If our interest in the very rich goes beyond their lavish or their miserly consumption, we must examine their relations to modern forms of corporate property as well as to the state; for such relations now determine the chances of men to secure big property and to receive high income.

Great prestige increasingly follows the major institutional units of the social structure. It is obvious that prestige depends, often quite decisively, upon access to the publicity machines that are now a central and normal feature of all the big institutions of modern America. Moreover, one feature of these hierarchies of corporation, state, and military establishment is that their top positions are increasingly interchangeable. One result of this is the accumulative nature of prestige. Claims for prestige, for example, may be initially based on military roles, then expressed in and augmented by an educational institution run by corporate executives, and cashed in, finally, in the political order, where, for General Eisenhower and those he represents, power and prestige finally meet at the very peak. Like wealth and power, prestige tends to be cumulative: The more of it you have, the more you can get. These values also tend to be translatable into one another: The wealthy find it easier than the poor to gain power; those with status find it easier than those without it to control opportunities for wealth.

If we took the 100 most powerful men in America, the 100 wealthiest, and the 100 most celebrated away from the institutional positions they now occupy, away from their resources of men and women and money, away from the media of mass communication that are now focused upon them—then they would be powerless and poor and uncelebrated. For power is not of a man. Wealth does not center in the person of the wealthy. Celebrity is not inherent in any personality. To be celebrated, to be wealthy, to have power requires access to major institutions, for the institutional positions men occupy determine in large part their chances to have and to hold these valued experiences.

The people of the higher circles may also be conceived as members of a top social stratum, as a set of groups whose members know one another, see one another socially and at business, and so, in making decisions, take one another into account. The elite, according to this conception, feel themselves to be, and are felt by others to be, the inner circle of "the upper social classes." They form a more or less compact social and psychological entity; they have become self-conscious members of a social class. People are either accepted into this class or they are not, and there is a qualitative split, rather than merely a numerical scale, separating them from those who are not elite. They are more or less aware of themselves as a social class and they behave toward one another differently from the way they do toward members of other classes. They accept one another, understand one another, marry one another, tend to work and to think if not together at least alike.

Now, we do not want by our definition to prejudge whether the elite of the command posts are conscious members of such a socially recognized class, or whether considerable proportions of the elite derive from such a clear and distinct class. These are matters to be investigated. Yet in order to be able to recognize what we intend to investigate, we must note something that all biographies and memoirs of the wealthy and the powerful and the eminent make clear: No matter what else they may be, the people of these higher circles are involved in a set of overlapping "crowds" and intricately connected "cliques." There is a kind of mutual attraction among those who "sit on the same terrace"—although this often becomes clear to them, as well as to others, only at the point at which they feel the need to draw the line; only when, in their common defense, they come to understand what they have in common, and so close their ranks against outsiders.

The idea of such ruling stratum implies that most of its members have similar social origins, that throughout their lives they maintain a network of informal connections, and that to some degree there is an interchangeability of position between the various hierarchies of money and power and celebrity. We must, of course, note at once that if such an elite stratum does exist, its social visibility and its form, for very solid historical reasons, are quite different from those of the noble cousinhoods that once ruled various European nations.

That American society has never passed through a feudal epoch is of decisive importance to the nature of the American elite, as well as to American society as a historic whole. For it means that no nobility or aristocracy, established before the capitalist era, has stood in tense opposition to the higher bourgeoisie. It means that this bourgeoisie has monopolized not only wealth but prestige and power as well. It means that no set of noble families has commanded the top positions and monopolized the values that are generally held in high esteem; and certainly that no set has done so explicitly by inherited right. It means that no high church dignitaries or court nobilities, no entrenched landlords with honorific accouterments, no monopolists of high army posts have opposed the enriched bourgeoisie and in the name of birth and prerogative successfully resisted its self-making.

But this does *not* mean that there are no upper strata in the United States. That they emerged from a "middle class" that had no recognized aristocratic superiors does not mean they remained middle class when enormous increases in wealth made their own superiority possible. Their origins and their newness may have made the upper strata less visible in America than elsewhere. But in America today there are in fact tiers and ranges of wealth and power of which people in the middle and lower ranks know very little and may not even dream. There are families who, in their well-being, are quite insulated from the economic jolts and lurches felt by the merely prosperous and those farther down the scale. There are also men of power who in quite small groups make decisions of enormous consequence for the underlying population....

CRITICAL THINKING QUESTIONS

1. What institutions form the interlocking triangle in Mills' analysis? Why does he think that these are the most powerful social institutions?
2. Explain Mills' argument that the existence of a power elite is not a consequence of *people* per se but a result of the institutions of society.
3. Do you feel that Mills' arguments, now almost 50 years old, apply to contemporary Canadian society?

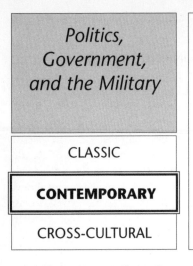

Politics,
Government,
and the Military

CLASSIC

CONTEMPORARY

CROSS-CULTURAL

47

Understanding the
September 11 Terror Attacks:
A Human Rights Approach

Kathryn Sikkink

Terrorism usually strikes unexpectedly, but social scientists have identified some of the root causes of terrorism. This understanding suggests some things that the United States should and should not do in responding to terror tactics.

As we try to come to grips with the tragedy of September 11, [2001] as individuals and as social scientists, a human rights approach can provide some guidance. A human rights approach always begins with, and has as its essence, a concern with individual victims of rights abuses. We turn first to the victims of the September 11 attack and their families and friends. The enormity of the loss of life and the premeditated nature of the attacks on September 11 justifies calling them a crime against humanity. Murder, when "committed as part of a widespread or systematic attack directed against any civilian population" is a crime against humanity.[1] The victims of this crime are entitled not only to our deepest sympathy, but also to justice, either in [American] courts or in an international tribunal.

Often, as social scientists we are trained to explain phenomena using abstract theories. It is second nature to us to immediately ask why and begin the search for deep and proximate causes of puzzling events. It may be useful, especially when speaking to the public, to preface our search for explanations with some prior comments. First, a search for explanation does not imply justification. There is no justification for such acts. Nor does any explanation remove the perpetrators' moral and legal responsibility for these criminal acts. Hannah Arendt was concerned about exactly such a point in the last pages of *Eichmann in Jerusalem*. She wrote:

Another such escape from the area of ascertainable facts and personal responsibility are the countless theories, based on nonspecific, abstract, hypothetical assumptions...which are so general that they explain and justify every event and every deed: No alternative to what actually happened is even considered, and no person could have acted differently from the way he didact.... All these clichés have in common that they make judgment superfluous and that to utter them is devoid of all risk.

She says that such theorizing is a symptom of "the reluctance evident everywhere to make judgments in terms of individual moral responsibility."[2]

In this vein, we need to begin by stating that the crimes of September 11 were consciously committed by individuals who could have chosen to act differently and who bear moral and legal responsibility for their actions. Human rights law provides the international standards to make judgments about individual responsibility.

Having recognized the perspective of the victims, we still need to turn to explanation. I find the literature on the causes of human rights violations useful for thinking about what leads to attacks of this sort. This research tries to identify under what conditions governments and people will commit large-scale murder, torture, and arbitrary imprisonment. It both helps us understand the reasons for such acts and provides some guidance for policies to prevent future human rights violations. The findings indicate that authoritarianism, war, and poverty can lead to large-scale human rights violations.[3] Because authoritarianism and human rights violations are linked, it ultimately is counterproductive to fight terrorism by supporting and arming authoritarian regimes. But we also shouldn't be too optimistic that we can improve the situation quickly simply by encouraging countries to democratize. Although democracies have better human rights records than do authoritarian regimes, during the process of transition to democracy, ethnic conflict and related human rights violations often increase.[4]

Perhaps the strongest finding of the quantitative literature on repression is that there is a strong connection between war and human rights violations. Decades of civil war in Afghanistan flourished prior to the attacks of September 11. The legacy of war, authoritarianism, and poverty will make it difficult for any post-Taliban regime to protect human rights and establish the rule of law.

Certain ideas can also lead to human rights violations. Studies of genocide show how ideas that dehumanize other people can exclude them "from the realm of human obligation."[5] These ideas can help people believe that it is acceptable, even desirable, to kill others. We must be very careful that our response to human rights violations does not serve simultaneously to dehumanize others and in turn make it possible for people to commit crimes against them.

Whatever the deep causes of terrorism, such as war and authoritarianism, the proximate reason is surely a set of ideas—in this case a set of religious ideas. The individuals responsible for the crimes against humanity of September 11 believed that their cause was so righteous that they were called upon to murder others in its name. This belief is not unique to a particular strand of extremist Islam. It was a basis for violence in Christianity for many centuries and is still used by some extremist Christians (for example, those who bomb abortion clinics) to justify violence. These religious ideas are a subset of a wider set of ideas, often utopian ideas, that have been frequently associated with extreme human rights violations. I refer to them as "ends-justify-the-means ideas." Pascal recognized the power of such ideas to generate terror when he said, "Never does man do evil more fully and joyfully than in the service of high ideals." *(Jamais on ne fait le mal si pleinement et si gaiement que quand on le fait par conscience.)*

Not all utopian ideas or high ideals, but those with this familiar "ends-justify-the-means" logic, are suspect. In these ideologies some desired endpoint—Aryan race, pure communist society, or Western and Christian civilization—is so compelling that highly repressive means are seen as necessary for achieving those ends. Studies of ideologies as diverse as Nazism, that of Khmer Rouge of Cambodia, and the National Security Doctrine of the repressive authoritarian regimes in Latin America in the 1970s and 1980s, have identified these ends-justify-the-means processes in action. We might say that this was also the logic behind the U.S. decision to drop the atomic bomb on the civilian populations of Hiroshima and Nagasaki. The goal of bringing World War II to an end was seen as so compelling that it justified dropping bombs on two large cities and killing over 100,000 people, most of them civilians.

What does it mean if the proximate reason for the terrorist attacks is a particular set of ideas, ideas that share a logic with past ideas also associated with devastating violations of human rights? First, our response and the response of our government must not be based on ideas that replicate this same ends-justify-the means logic. We cannot justify dehumanizing our opponents or excluding any individuals from "the realm of human obligation." When the FBI floats the idea of using torture to wrest information [from] detainees, or when we disregard the impact of our bombing campaign on civilians, we too are using an ends-justify-the-means argument.[6] We need to fight these arguments when we find them.

The best way to fight ideas is not to suppress them. Suppressed ideas have an odd way of gaining more power. A human rights approach is committed to free speech, free religion, and a free press. Within this context of free expression, we must intellectually and politically contest ends-justify-the-means ideas, whether held by bin Laden or John Ashcroft. President Bush's statement that "We will make no distinction between the terrorists who committed these acts and those who harbored them," taken to its logical conclusions, also implies an ends-justify-the-means logic. Human Rights Watch recognized this and effectively contested this idea one day later. "Yet distinctions must be made between the guilty and the innocent; between the perpetrators and the civilians who may surround them; between those who commit atrocities and those who may simply share their religious beliefs, ethnicity, and national origin. People committed to justice and law and human rights must never descend to the level of the perpetrators of such acts."

Finally, what does a human rights perspective provide in terms of thinking about responses to the attacks of September 11? A vigorous international and domestic crime-fighting campaign is necessary to investigate the crimes of September 11, bring the perpetrators to justice, and prevent future crimes of this nature. Coordinated international campaigns to track down the criminals, stop their sources of finance and weapons, and break their networks are essential. A human rights approach also reminds us to be especially vigilant about attempts to violate basic rights in this country or in any other country in the name of the struggle against terrorism.

In response to the unprecedented attacks of September 11, the U.S. government has launched a new campaign against terrorism, reminiscent in its breadth and fervor to the anticommunists campaigns of the cold war. We have yet to see clearly how this campaign will play itself out. But the story of U.S. policy towards Latin America over the last twenty-five years has much to offer people thinking about the new campaign against terrorism. In Latin America our government's struggles against communism sometimes led it to commit, support, and justify crimes. With classic ends-justify-the-means logic, we overthrew democratic governments and supported authoritarian ones that murdered their own citizens. The language that some members of our government, press, and members of the public are now using is similar to the language used by authoritarian regimes in Latin America to justify human rights violations. One of the most troubling issues in the wake of the September 11 attacks has been the willingness of certain news commentators to suggest that the United States should use torture to gather information from detainees.[7]

Human rights law permits the suspension of certain rights in cases of "public emergency which threatens the life of the nation." But these suspensions are limited by the requirement that they be "strictly required by the exigencies of the situation." And violations of some rights, such as the right to be free from torture and cruel and unusual punishment, are not permitted in any circumstances. For many decades authoritarian leaders around the world have been saying that torture is necessary to gather information to prevent future terrorist attacks. There is virtually no evidence that torture serves this information-gathering purpose. There is ample evidence, however, that once a government starts to torture, it begins to use it routinely against a range of detainees.

Another clear lesson from Latin America is that covert operations have been the most pernicious exercises of U.S. policy in the region. U.S. covert action against the Allende regime contributed to the rise of Pinochet. The U.S. covert operation that helped overthrow the elected Arbenz government in Guatemala in 1954 set in motion a twenty-five-year cycle of increasingly repressive military regimes that eventually culminated in the genocide of 1980–1982. The 1954 covert operation against Arbenz was the twin of a similar covert operation in 1953 against the democratically elected leftist government of Muhammad Mossadeq in Iran that set into motion a similar downward spiral with far-reaching effects for the Iranian people and the whole region.

In another odd twist linking the two regions, the fundamentalist government of Iran made a willing partner for yet another covert operation, the Iran-Contra clandestine sale of arms to Iran and the diversion of profits to right-wing contra rebels in Nicaragua. This makes me particularly alarmed that some policymakers and academics are calling for a reinvigoration of covert action in U.S. policy.[8] Overt policies [by which] the press, our allies, NGOs, and the American public can observe, critique, or applaud the actions and their consequences are not only more democratic, but they have been more successful in producing viable policy in the long term.

A human rights approach does not necessarily rule out a military response. Indeed, much of the criticism of the failure of the response of the U.N. and of governments to the genocide in Rwanda turns on their refusal to use military force to prevent genocide. But the social science literature showing that war contributes to human rights violations should make us extremely cautious about a military solution. Is the remedy actually exacerbating the very problem it is [trying] to solve?

A human rights approach commits us to deep concern for the civilian victims of the bombing raids in Afghanistan. Under humanitarian law, civilians cannot be military targets, and combatants need to make efforts to protect civilians. The Geneva Conventions empower the Red Cross to act in times of war to protect civilians and medical personnel. Our bombing, not once but twice, of Red Cross warehouses in Kabul is thus deeply symbolic of the more general failure of the bombing campaign to protect and spare civilians. The U.S. military have clarified that they are making efforts to avoid civilian deaths. We judge differently the responsibility of those making efforts to avoid civilian deaths from those whose main goal is provoking civilian deaths. But for the Afghani parent who has lost a child to U.S. bombing raids, such distinctions provide no comfort. Military methods that inevitably lead to significant civilian deaths are inconsistent with a human rights approach, regardless of the intentions of the planners.

The most disturbing recent development is President Bush's announcement that he will order noncitizens to undergo trial in military courts if there is reason to believe that the individual is a member of the Al-Qaida terrorist organization. Not only does this move undermine our commitment to civil liberties and rule of law, but it is unnecessary. In the last decade, states have innovated solutions for pursuing justice for exactly these kinds of crimes, including domestic trials, trials in foreign courts, and international tribunals. The most far-reaching of these—the International Criminal Court—has yet to be established and could not, in any case, try cases that happened before it came into being. The United States has not ratified the ICC Statute, and certain members of the U.S. Congress are actively hostile to the idea. If these crimes had been committed after the Court entered into force, and if the United States had ratified the treaty, the ICC could have been the obvious and most legitimate place to try perpetrators of crimes against humanity.

This should make U.S. policymakers rethink their position on the ICC. We do need international institutions to help us—not only to find the intellectual authors of this crime, but also to bring them to justice with the greatest legitimacy. The security council could set up a special tribunal to try perpetrators of terrorism, much as they set up the ad hoc war crimes tribunals for the former Yugoslavia and Rwanda. A special tribunal would have the virtue of requiring us to think about the tragedy as a crime carried out by specific individuals who have legal responsibility for the act. By thinking about the tragedy as a crime against humanity, we can refrain from thinking about collective guilt of the Afghani people or Islamic fundamentalists. An international tribunal would also underscore that this kind of attack is of concern to all countries, not only to the United States. It would build the confidence of our allies and world public opinion that people accused of terrorism would receive a fair and impartial trial. The struggle we face is not mainly a military one, but a struggle about ideas and public opinion. Our commitment to civil liberties and rule of law is an essential part of our identity and should not be squandered by some of the short-sighted policies of this administration.

CRITICAL THINKING QUESTIONS

1. Summarize the author's argument that *explaining* events such as the September 11 attacks is not the same as *justifying* them. Do you agree or not? Why?
2. What are some factors that the author identifies as contributing to terrorism in the world? What can be done to reduce the extent of terrorism?
3. In what ways, if any, do you feel that the events of September 11 have changed Canadian society?

NOTES

1. Rome Statute of the International Criminal Court, 1998 (U.N. Doc. A/CONF.183/9).
2. Hannah Arendt, *Eichmann in Jerusalem: A Report on the Banality of Evil* (New York: Penguin, 1964), p. 297.
3. See, for example, Steven Poe and C. Neal Tate, "Human Rights and Repression to Personal Integrity in the 1980s: A Global Analysis," *American Political Science Review* 88 (1994): 853–72; and Steven Poe, C. Neal Tate, and Linda Camp Keith, "Repression of the Human Rights to Personal Integrity Revisited: A Global Crossnational Study Covering the Years 1976–1993," *International Studies Quarterly* 43 (1999): 291–315.
4. Jack Snyder, *From Voting to Violence: Democratization and Nationalist Conflict* (New York: W.W. Norton, 2000).
5. Helen Fein, *Genocide: A Sociological Perspective* London: Sage, 1993.
6. "Silence of Four Terror Probe Suspects Poses Dilemma for FBI," *Washington Post* (October 21, 2001), A6.
7. "Torture Seeps into Discussion by News Media," *New York Times* (November 5, 2001), C1.
8. See, for example, John Mearshimer, "Guns Won't Win the Afghan War," *New York Times* (November 4, 2001), calling for diplomacy and covert action to oust Al Qaida.

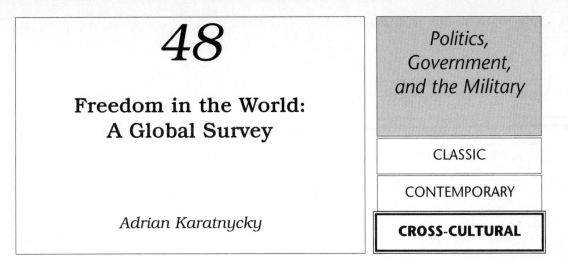

48

Freedom in the World: A Global Survey

Politics, Government, and the Military

CLASSIC

CONTEMPORARY

CROSS-CULTURAL

Adrian Karatnycky

This selection, prepared by the president of Freedom House, a human rights organization, looks at the extent of political freedom in the world during 1998–99. Although the trend is positive, one-third of the world's people live without basic political rights.

MORE FREE COUNTRIES THAN EVER

Despite a year that saw violent civil war in the Republic of the Congo, attempts at ethnic cleansing in Kosovo, ethnic and political violence in Indonesia, and severe economic turbulence in many of the world's emerging markets, freedom made significant strides in 1998. As the year drew to a close, 88 of the world's 191 countries (46 percent) were rated as Free, meaning that they maintain a high degree of political and economic freedom and respect basic civil liberties. This was the largest number of Free countries on record, and represented a net gain of seven from last year—the second-largest increase in the twenty-six-year history of the *Survey*. Another 53 countries (28 percent of the world total) were rated as Partly Free, enjoying more

Source: From *Freedom in the World: The Annual Survey of Political Rights and Civil Liberties, 1998–1999*, ed. Adrian Karatnycky (New York: Freedom House, 1999). Reprinted by permission of Freedom House.

limited political rights and civil liberties, often in a context of corruption, weak rule of law, ethnic strife, or civil war. This represented a drop of four from the previous year. Finally, 50 countries (26 percent of the world total) that deny their citizens basic rights and civil liberties were rated as Not Free. This represented a drop of three from the previous year.

There were seven new entrants into the ranks of Free countries in 1998, including India, which had been rated as Partly Free since 1991, a year that saw the killing of former prime minister Rajiv Gandhi, intense labor strife, and an escalation of intercommunal violence resulting in thousands of deaths. India's return to the ranks of Free countries was the consequence of greater internal stability, fewer instances of intercommunal violence, and the peaceful democratic transfer of power to an opposition-led government. Other entrants into the ranks of Free countries were the Dominican Republic, where a democratically elected government has made efforts to strengthen the administration of justice; Ecuador, which

Table 48.1:   Freedom in the World, 1998–1999

The population of the world this year is estimated at 5,908.7 billion persons, who reside in 191 sovereign states and 61 related and disputed territories—a total of 252 entities. The level of political rights and civil liberties as shown comparatively by the Freedom House Survey is:

Free: 2,354.0 billion (39.84 percent of the world's population) live in 88 of the states and in 44 of the related and/or disputed territories.

Partly Free: 1,570.6 billion (26.59 percent of the world's population) live in 53 of the states and 4 of the related and/or disputed territories.

Not Free: 1,984.1 billion (33.58 percent of the world's population) live in 50 of the states and 13 of the related and/or disputed territories.

A Record of the Survey
(population in billions)

Survey Date	Free		Partly Free		Not Free		World Population
January '81	1,613.0	(35.90%)	970.9	(21.60%)	1,911.9	(42.5%)	4,495.8
January '83	1,665.4	(36.32%)	918.8	(20.04%)	2,000.2	(43.64%)	4,584.1
January '85	1,671.4	(34.85%)	1,117.4	(23.30%)	2,007.0	(41.85%)	4,795.8
January '87	1,842.5	(37.10%)	1,171.5	(23.60%)	1,949.9	(39.3%)	4,963.9
January '89	1,992.8	(38.86%)	1,027.9	(20.05%)	2,107.3	(41.09%)	5,128.0
January '90	2,034.4	(38.87%)	1,143.7	(21.85%)	2,055.9	(39.28%)	5,234.0
January '91	2,088.2	(39.23%)	1,485.7	(27.91%)	1,748.7	(32.86%)	5,322.6
January '92 (a)	1,359.3	(25.29%)	2,306.6	(42.92%)	1,708.2	(31.79%)	5,374.2
January '93	1,352.2	(24.83%)	2,403.3	(44.11%)	1,690.4	(31.06%)	5,446.0
January '94	1,046.2	(19.00%)	2,224.4	(40.41%)	2,234.6	(40.59%)	5,505.2
January '95	1,119.7	(19.97%)	2,243.4	(40.01%)	2,243.9	(40.02%)	5,607.0
January '96	1,114.5	(19.55%)	2,365.8	(41.49%)	2,221.2	(38.96%)	5,701.5
January '97	1,250.3	(21.67%)	2,260.1	(39.16%)	2,260.6	(39.17%)	5,771.0
January '98	1,266.0	(21.71%)	2,281.9	(39.12%)	2,284.6	(39.17%)	5,832.5
January '99 (b)	2,354.0	(39.84%)	1,570.6	(26.59%)	1,984.1	(33.58%)	5,908.7

(a) The large shift in the population figure between 1991 and 1992 is due to India's change from Free to Partly Free.
(b) The large shift in the population figure between 1998 and 1999 is due to India's change from Partly Free to Free.

recently concluded free and fair elections; Nicaragua, where improved relations between civilian authorities and a military formerly dominated by the Sandinistas contributed to the strengthening of democratic stability and where greater attention was paid to the problems of indigenous peoples on the country's Atlantic coast; Papua New Guinea, which saw a January 1998 peace agreement put an end to a destabilizing nine-year secessionist rebellion on Bougainville Island; Slovakia, where free and fair elections brought to power a government dominated by reformers; and Thailand, where the government of Prime Minister Chuan Leekpai has fostered increasing political accountability.

In addition, three countries formerly ranked as Not Free—Indonesia, Nigeria, and Sierra Leone—made tangible progress and are now rated as Partly Free. In Indonesia, the downfall of Suharto has led to the reemergence of political parties and civic groups and the promise of free elections. Although the country's economic crisis has sparked ethnic violence targeting the Chinese minority (and some violence has occurred during student demonstrations), some political controls have loosened, political parties and movements have begun to gain strength, and the media have become more outspoken. In Nigeria, the death of military dictator Sani Abacha has led to a political opening that holds out the promise of multiparty elections and already has seen the reemergence of public debate, a resurgence of political parties, the return of exiled leaders, relatively free and fair local elections, and the rise of an increasingly vibrant press. In Sierra Leone, the defeat of a military coup has put an end to chaos and violence and restored power to the country's democratically elected civilian authorities.

MORE FREE PEOPLE THAN EVER

As a result of the gains in freedom in 1998—especially in India, the world's most populous democracy—2.354 billion people (40 percent of the world's population) now live in Free societies, 1.570 billion (26.5 percent) live in countries that are Partly Free, and 1.984 billion (33.5 percent) live in Not Free countries. The proportion of the world's population living in freedom is the highest in the history of the *Survey*.

In addition to these shifts from one category to another, the 1998 survey recorded more modest improvements in freedom in twenty-one countries. Not all trends for the year were positive. The survey registered more modest declines in freedom in ten countries. These changes are reflected by upward or downward arrows, signifying improvements or declines in a country's score on the freedom scale. One country which registered worrying trends was Argentina, which suffered from the destabilizing effects of political sex scandals and efforts to blackmail political leaders.

Thirteen countries were judged to be the world's most repressive and have received Freedom House's lowest rating: scores of 7 for political rights and 7 for civil liberties. In these states, basic political rights and civil liberties are nonexistent, there is no free press, and independent civic life is suppressed. The most repressive countries, the "world's worst" in terms of freedom, include Iraq, North Korea, Cuba, and Sudan. The others are Afghanistan, Burma, Equatorial Guinea, Libya, Saudi Arabia, Somalia, Syria, Turkmenistan, and Vietnam. It is notable that of

Table 48.2:   The Global Trend

	Free	Partly Free	Not Free
1988–1989	61	39	68
1993–1994	72	63	55
1998–1999	88	53	50

Tracking Democracy

	Number of Democracies
1988–1989	68
1993–1994	108
1998–1999	117

the thirteen least free states, three are one-party Marxist-Leninist states and eight are predominantly Islamic. The number of countries that received Freedom House's lowest rating (7,7) has declined from twenty-one at the close of 1994.

The *Survey of Freedom* also found that at the end of 1998 there were 117 electoral democracies, representing over 61 percent of the world's countries and nearly 55 percent of its population. The Freedom House roster of electoral democracies is based on a stringent standard requiring that all elected national authority must be the product of free and fair electoral processes. Thus, in the estimation of the *Survey*, neither Mexico (whose 1997 national legislative elections were judged free and fair, but whose last national presidential elections failed to meet that standard) nor Malaysia (whose governing United Malays National Organization enjoys huge and unfair advantages in national elections) qualifies as an electoral democracy. After a period in which electoral democracies increased dramatically from 69 in 1987, their number has remained stagnant at 117 since 1995.

The survey team identified five events that represented important gains for freedom in 1988 and five which signaled setbacks for freedom.

The 13 Worst Rated Countries

Afghanistan
Burma
Cuba
Equatorial Guinea
Iraq
Korea, North
Libya
Saudi Arabia
Somalia
Sudan
Syria
Turkmenistan
Vietnam

The Worst Rated Related Territory

Kosovo (Yugoslavia)

The Worst Rated Disputed Territory

Tibet (China)

TOP FIVE GAINS FOR FREEDOM IN 1998

1. *Nigeria:* Developments have moved in a promising direction since the death of the tyrannical General Abacha, with many civil liberties restored, political parties legalized, and national elections pledged for 1999. A good omen was the holding of local elections which were deemed free and fair.

2. *Indonesia:* President Suharto's resignation has been accompanied by indications of changes towards electoral democracy and enhanced civil liberties. On the negative side has been mounting violence against the Chinese minority and bloody clashes between students and the army.

3. *Corruption alert:* The governments of the United States and other leading democracies, along with the World Bank, are focusing increased attention on the role of corruption in undermining political and economic reform in transitional societies. A positive sign: Demands for improvements in the rule of law are increasingly being incorporated into decisions on foreign assistance.

4. *Freedom on the Net:* Several years ago China and other authoritarian regimes announced plans to control the Internet's political content. Those efforts have failed. In the future, the Internet will play a growing role in linking democratic forces within repressive societies and in building a global network of freedom activists.

5. *Dictators beware:* Both current and former dictators had reason for concern. Though controversial, the effort to bring General Pinochet to justice sent a chilling message to tyrants around the world. Yugoslavia's Milosevic was under increased pressure, Indonesia's Suharto resigned, and Congo's Kabila traveled abroad only after securing assurance that he would not be arrested.

TOP FIVE SETBACKS FOR FREEDOM IN 1998

1. *Russia:* The assassination of democracy advocate Galina Staravoitova was the most tragic development in a bad year for Russian reformers. With President Yeltsin enfeebled, a coalition of neo-Communists and hardline nationalists gained increased influence, and succeeded in bringing down a reformist government. A new government, dominated by former Communists, made little progress in stemming corruption or reviving the economy.

2. *Malaysia:* President Mahathir Mohamad responded to his country's economic decline in all the wrong ways: repressing political critics, tightening political control, and placing restrictions on the economy. Here is a prime example of everything that is wrong with "Asian values."

3. *Congo:* Events moved from bad to worse in the Democratic Republic of Congo. President Kabila showed no sign of relaxing his repressive policies. Much of the country remained contested territory, with forces from a half dozen African nations pillaging the countryside and terrorizing the populace.

4. *Religious persecution:* The persecution of religious minorities, especially Christians, remained a serious problem in a number of countries. Among the worst violators: Pakistan, Egypt, China, and Iran. Persecution was most serious in Sudan, where Christians and animists in the southern regions were killed, starved, and forced into exile by forces of the Moslem North.

5. ***Nuclear proliferation:*** The detonation of nuclear devices by India and Pakistan was a jolting reminder of the menace still posed by weapons of mass destruction. Other reasons to worry included Iraq's determination to rebuild its nuclear, chemical, and biological arsenal, North Korea's nuclear saber-rattling, and the role of Russian scientists in the development of weapons for Iran and other states.

ELECTORAL DEMOCRACY AND FREEDOM

Despite the emergence of electoral democracy as the world's predominant form of government, major violations of human rights and civil liberties remain the norm in a majority of countries containing some three-fifths of the world's population. This disjunction arises from the fact that many electoral democracies fall short of being Free. In an influential 1997 article in *Foreign Affairs*, Fareed Zakaria drew on Freedom House data underlining this fact to suggest that the world had entered an era characterized by "The Rise of Illiberal Democracy." Yet there are signs that electoral democracy eventually does have a positive effect on freedom. Particularly notable in the 1998 *Survey* was the growing respect for civil liberties in a number of electoral democracies. In fact, it appears that the trend to which political scientists were pointing had peaked in the first half of the 1990s—a period of rapid democratic expansion in the wake of the collapse of Marxist-Leninist regimes.

Freedom House's most current data suggest that, as the 1990s draw toward a close, we are observing a decline in the number of "illiberal democracies" and an increase in the number and proportion of the world's electoral democracies that are also liberal (i.e., Free) democracies. In 1995, for example, the *Survey* found there were 117 electoral democracies, of which 76 were rated Free (64.9 percent), 40 were judged to be Partly Free (over 34 percent), and one—war-ravaged Bosnia-Herzegovina—was Not Free. Today, out of 117 electoral democracies, 88 (over 75 percent) are Free, while the remaining 29 are Partly Free.

Since 1995, the electoral democracies that have seen a deepening climate of respect for political rights and civil liberties and thus have entered the ranks of Free countries include the Dominican Republic, El Salvador, Honduras, India, Mali, Nicaragua, Papua New Guinea, the Philippines, Romania, Taiwan, and Thailand. These gains have been partly offset by setbacks in some formerly Free electoral democracies, for a net gain of ten Free countries. Ecuador, Slovakia, and Venezuela have oscillated between the Free and Partly Free categories since 1995.

While electoral democracy allows space to emerge for competing political interests and holds out the promise of greater freedom and respect for human rights, the record of some electoral democracies remains marred by political restrictions and violations of civil liberties. Not all these Partly Free democracies suffer from an identical set of problems: Some have weak governments incapable of guaranteeing basic civil liberties in the face of violent political movements (Colombia and Georgia); others must contend with powerful and politically influential militaries (Turkey and Paraguay), or: internal security forces that can act with impunity (Brazil). Some are plagued by powerful oligarchic forces and/or the weak rule of law (Russia and Ukraine); in other cases, democratically elected leaders seek to centralize their power or to exercise power arbitrarily. Yet these phenomena should not obscure the overall global record: Most democratically elected leaders function within the context of effective checks and balances on their power, and most are able to marshal democratic legitimacy in their efforts to govern effectively and responsibly.

At the close of 1998, the Partly Free democracies were twenty-nine in number. The record of the *Survey* in recent years shows that precisely these flawed, Partly Free electoral democracies hold the greatest potential for the expansion of freedom. For where there is free electoral competition among political parties, there is also the possibility for open criticism of government policies and the airing of alternative viewpoints. Many new democracies are just beginning the arduous process of institutionalizing the rule of law; creating a vibrant civil society; instituting procedures that protect minority rights; fostering a sense of moderation and tolerance among competing political forces; developing economically and politically independent broadcast media; and ensuring effective civilian control over the police and the military. All this takes time. It should therefore come as no surprise that most new democracies make more rapid progress in the areas of political processes and political rights than in the area of civil liberties. Nonetheless, though complete freedom may be long in coming, citizens of Partly Free electoral democracies can at least engage in serious debate over public policy—a right rarely, if ever, enjoyed in nondemocratic regimes. Some critics have suggested that electoral democracy leads to bad governance, increases instability, places ethnic minorities at peril, and legitimizes efforts to suppress political opponents. But the record suggests otherwise. There are eighty-eight electoral democracies that successfully protect a broad range of political and civil rights. Moreover, even the twenty-nine electoral democracies that Freedom House rates as only Partly Free are not states that brutally suppress basic freedoms. Rather, they are generally countries in which civic institutions are weak, poverty is rampant, and intergroup tensions are acute. This is not surprising, as many such fragile democracies are emerging from protracted periods of intense civil strife, and some are building new states.

The *Survey* shows evidence of improvements in civil liberties in countries that had previously established democratic electoral practices. This sequence makes sense because free and fair elections take less time to implement than the more complex processes that produce the rule of law and a strong civil society. As the Freedom House data suggest, illiberal democracy tends toward liberal democracy so long as there is internal or external pressure for further reform. Moreover, the regular transfer of power between competing political elites, or even the prospect of such a transfer, appears to improve the chances for the deepening of civil liberties.

Clearly, some Partly Free (or illiberal) democracies lack respect for the rule of law, checks and balances among the branches of government, and protections for the rights of minorities. It is also true that in some circumstances (especially in multiethnic settings) open electoral processes can be occasions for the emergence of political demagogy directed against ethnic minorities. Indeed, almost three in ten electoral democracies fail adequately to safeguard basic freedoms for these sorts of reasons. At the same time, the *Survey of Freedom* suggests that, over the last twenty years, the emergence of electoral democracies has been the best indicator of subsequent progress in the areas of civil liberties and human rights.

ETHNICITY AND NATIONALISM

The Freedom House data also suggest that countries without a predominant ethnic majority are less successful in establishing open and democratic societies than ethnically homogeneous countries. For the purposes of making this comparison, we define countries in which over two-thirds of the population belong to a single ethnic group as mono-ethnic, and those without such a two-thirds majority as multiethnic.

According to this definition, 66 of the 88 Free countries (75 percent) are mono-ethnic, while 22 (25 percent) are multiethnic. Of the 114 countries in the world that possess a dominant ethnic group, 66 (58 percent) are Free, 22 (19 percent) are Partly Free, and 26 (23 percent) are Not Free. By contrast, among multiethnic countries only 22 of 77 (29 percent) are Free, 31 (40 percent) are Partly Free, and 24 (31 percent) are Not Free. A mono-ethnic country, therefore, is twice as likely to be Free as a multiethnic one.

A similar pattern can be found among the 117 electoral democracies, which include 77 mono-ethnic and 40 multiethnic countries. Of the 77 mono-ethnic democracies, 66 (86 percent) are

Free, and 11 (14 percent) are Partly Free. Among multiethnic democracies, 22 (55 percent) are Free and 18 are Partly Free (45 percent). Thus multiethnic democracies are nearly two-and-a-half times more likely to be only Partly Free than are mono-ethnic ones.

In the face of ethnic conflicts in Africa, the former Yugoslavia, and elsewhere, many analysts have recently focused on the destructive power of contemporary nationalism. Yet the fact that nation-states appear to provide the most durable basis for political freedom and respect for civil liberties deserves greater attention. At the same time, while the survey suggests that democracies are more likely to be Free if they do not face significant ethnic cleavages, there also is compelling evidence that multiethnic societies can preserve a broad array of political and civil freedoms. Successful multiethnic societies include established democracies like Canada, Belgium, and Switzerland, as well as such new democracies as Estonia, Latvia, Mali, Namibia, and South Africa. India's return to the ranks of Free countries is an indication that, even in an ethnically charged environment, it is possible for multiethnic societies to establish a climate and framework of significant respect for personal freedoms, the rule of law, and the rights of religious and ethnic minorities.

The set of forty multiethnic electoral democracies merits closer investigation. Are there common characteristics among the Free multiethnic democracies? Is there a significant correlation between certain patterns of population distribution in multiethnic societies and greater freedom? Are homogeneous concentrations of particular ethnic groups more or less conducive to stability and freedom? Is the dispersion of ethnic minorities throughout a country more compatible with democratic stability and the expansion of freedom? Do different forms of state organization contribute to a higher degree of freedom? Are federal arrangements more or less conducive to the development of freedom? When are federal arrangements successful and when do they provoke ethnic conflict or separatism? Under what circumstances do federal arrangements break down? What is the effect of external diasporas and the forces of irredentism on the political development of multiethnic states?

It is clear that in some settings political appeals based on ethnicity make it impossible for democratic systems that feature a regular transfer of power to function. Yet the example of numerous free and democratic multiethnic societies shows that it is possible to transcend ethnic appeals in politics, to avert the permanent disenfranchisement of ethnic minorities, and to establish durable democracies.

In the aftermath of the Cold War, nationalism has come to be identified with violence and intolerance. The *Survey* makes clear, however, that nation-states—many of which are the products of nationalist ideas of state organization—tend to be more compatible with stable democratic rule and political freedom. Indeed, in the 1980s and 1990s, most successful ethnic struggles for national self-determination and even nationhood have been peaceful, involving mass protests, independent civic organization, strikes, and other forms of opposition activity. In the former Soviet bloc, such activism contributed to the downfall of oppressive regimes and the creation of a number of free and democratic states. Where nationalism has led to violence and bloody warfare, another factor has often been present—that of irredentism.

In several instances, ethnic and national aspirations to autonomy or independence have received military support from neighboring nation-states ruled by the very ethnic group that is seeking sovereignty or separation. In such cases (for example, Bosnia's Serb Republic; ethnically Armenian Nagorno-Karabakh in Azerbaijan; the Transdniester Republic in Moldova; to a lesser but considerable degree, the Kosovo Liberation Army; and the Rwandan-aided rebellions in the Republic of the Congo), what is at work may be support provided by an existing state seeking to extend its borders rather than the aspiration to create a new nation-state.

REGIONAL VARIATIONS

Democracy and freedom have been on the upswing since the mid-1970s. Clearly, this trend has been visible across all continents and in most cultures, underscoring that human liberty and democracy are not Western constructs, but universal aspirations. Yet while the expansion of democracy and freedom has been global, it has not everywhere proceeded at the same pace. There have been important geographical and cultural variations that deserve attention and deeper understanding.

At the close of 1998, democracy and freedom are the dominant trends in Western and East-Central Europe, in the Americas, and increasingly in the Asian-Pacific region. In the former Soviet Union the picture is decidedly more mixed, with the growth of freedom stalled and a number of countries evolving into dictatorships. In Africa, too, Free societies and electoral democracies remain a distinct minority. Moreover, there are no democracies or Free societies within the Arab world, and few in other predominantly Muslim societies.

Of the 53 countries in Africa, 9 are Free (17 percent), 21 are Partly Free (40 percent) and 23 are Not Free (43 percent). Only 17 African countries (less than one-third) are electoral democracies. As of the end of 1998, Lesotho's democracy fell, while at the same time, the *Survey* noted positive trends in Nigeria and Sierra Leone.

In Asia, 19 of the region's 38 countries are Free (50 percent), 9 are Partly Free (24 percent), and 10 are Not Free (26 percent). Despite the looming presence of Communist China and the rhetoric of "Asian values," 24 (63 percent) of the region's polities are electoral democracies.

In East-Central Europe and the former USSR, there are growing signs of a deepening chasm. In Central Europe and parts of Eastern Europe, including the Baltic states, democracy and freedom prevail; in the former USSR, however, progress toward the emergence of open societies has stalled or failed. Overall, 19 of the 27 post-Communist countries of East-Central Europe and the former USSR are electoral democracies. Ten of the region's states are Free, 11 are Partly Free, and 6 are Not Free. Of the 12 non-Baltic former Soviet republics, 7 countries are Partly Free, 5 are Not Free, and none are Free.

Among the 35 countries in the Americas, 31 are electoral democracies. Twenty-five states are rated as Free, 9 are Partly Free, and 1—Cuba—is Not Free.

In the Middle East (excluding North Africa), the roots of democracy and freedom are weakest. In this region there is only one Free country, Israel; there are three Partly Free states, Jordan, Kuwait, and Turkey; and there are ten countries that are Not Free. Israel and Turkey are the region's only two electoral democracies.

Western Europe is the preserve of Free countries and democracies, with all twenty-four states both free and democratic.

In addition to these regional breakdowns, Freedom House has examined the state of freedom and democracy in the Arab world. Among the sixteen states with an Arab majority, there are no Free countries, Three predominantly Arab states—Jordan, Kuwait, and Morocco—are Partly Free. There are no electoral democracies in the Arab world.

The *Survey* also reveals some interesting patterns in the relationship between cultures and political development. While there are broad differences within civilizations, and while democracy and human rights find expression in a wide array of cultures and beliefs, the *Survey* shows some important variations in the relationship between religious belief or tradition and political freedom.

Of the eighty-eight countries that are rated Free, seventy-nine are majority Christian by tradition or belief. Of the nine Free countries that are not majority Christian, one is Israel, often considered part of a Judeo-Christian tradition, and two others, Mauritius and South Korea, have significant Christian communities representing at least a third of their population. Of the six remaining Free countries, Mali is predominantly Muslim; nearly half of Taiwan's population is Buddhist; Mongolia and Thailand are chiefly Buddhist; Japan has a majority that observes both Buddhist and Shinto traditions; and India is predominantly Hindu.

While seventy-nine of the eighty-eight Free countries are predominantly Christian, just eleven of the sixty-seven countries with the poorest record in terms of political rights and civil liberties are predominantly Christian. By this indicator, a predominantly Christian country is nearly five-and-a-half times as likely to be Free and democratic as it is to be repressive and non-democratic. There is also a strong correlation between electoral democracy and Hinduism (India, Mauritius, and Nepal), and there are a significant number of Free countries among traditionally Buddhist societies and societies in which Buddhism is the most widespread faith (Japan, Mongolia, Taiwan, and Thailand).

At the close of the twentieth century, the Islamic world remains most resistant to the spread of democracy and civil liberties, especially the Arab countries. Only one country with a Muslim majority—Mali—is Free, fourteen are Partly Free, and twenty-eight are Not Free. Six countries with a predominantly Muslim population are electoral democracies: Albania, Bangladesh, Kyrgyzstan, Mali, Pakistan, and Turkey. Yet the year's trends also showed that the Islamic world is not completely resistant to the expansion of freedom. There was limited progress in Indonesia, the world's most populous Islamic county, and in Nigeria, where half the population is Muslim, there was momentum toward a democratic political opening.

Although we tend to think of civilizations and cultures as fixed and stable entities, it should be kept in mind that political transformations within civilizations can spread rapidly. For example, before the Third Wave of democratization was launched in the 1970s, the majority of predominantly Catholic countries were tyrannies; they included Latin America's oligarchies and military dictatorships, East-Central Europe's Marxist-Leninist states, Iberia's authoritarian-corporalist

systems, and the Philippine dictatorship of Ferdinand Marcos. Social scientists speculated about the influence that Catholicism's hierarchical system of church authority might have on Catholic attitudes toward politics. Today, of course, most Catholic countries have become Free and democratic, and some would argue that it was precisely the internal discipline of the Catholic church which made possible the rapid spread of pro-democratic values following Vatican II and under the papacy of John Paul II.

THE GLOBAL EXPANSION OF FREEDOM

The last quarter century has seen a rapid expansion of democratic governance along with a more gradual expansion of civil society and civil liberties. There is little question that the *Survey's* findings reflect significant gains for human freedom at the dawn of a new millennium. Still, many of the new electoral democracies and newly Free countries remain fragile, and political reversals cannot be excluded. Moreover, there appears to be little forward momentum for democratic change and freedom in many of the Not Free countries. In particular, there is little evidence of progress toward democracy in the Arab world and in the world's remaining Marxist-Leninist states.

The global expansion of political and civic freedoms has coincided with the expansion of market-based economies. Indeed, on the basis of the Freedom House *Survey* and parallel efforts to monitor and assess global economic change, there is growing empirical evidence of the links between economic freedom and political freedom.[1]

Not only does economic freedom help establish the conditions for political freedom by promoting the growth of prosperous middle and working classes, but successful market economies appear to require political freedom as a barrier against economic cronyism, rent seeking, and other anticompetitive and inefficient practices. Open and democratically accountable societies and economies have also shown themselves capable of weathering economic setbacks—a likely consequence of their political legitimacy (rooted in democratic accountability) and economic legitimacy (rooted in property rights). Moreover, while open societies are not immune to corruption scandals, they have strong instruments for combating graft and bribery, including a free press, the separation of powers, alternations in power between various political elites, and independent judicial systems.

While the *Survey* can be used to examine broad trends, it is important that such trends not be equated with iron laws of history or be interpreted one-dimensionally. For example, while the *Survey* findings show that liberal economic change at times leads to liberal political reform, there are also numerous other cases where political openings lead the way to economic liberalization. The more careful conclusion from an examination of the twenty-six-year record of the *Survey* is that both trends manifest themselves in close proximity to one another. Opposition to the dominance of the state in economic life is usually accompanied by opposition to the dominance of the state in personal life and in the life of civil society. Certainly, there appears to be growing awareness of this relationship, as indicated by the growing emphasis on democracy promotion in the foreign assistance policies of the advanced industrial democracies, and by the stress on issues of good governance and effective anti-corruption regimes by multilateral donors like the World Bank.

POLICY IMPLICATIONS

What challenges issue from the *Survey's* findings? What are the policy implications?

The Freedom House findings make it clear that the world is becoming more free. This trend is mainly the consequence of the strengthening of the rule of law, of improvements in civilian control over militaries and police, the successful management of divisive group conflicts, and the growing effectiveness of civil society.

Most of this progress toward respect for political rights and civil liberties is unfolding in countries which have already undergone more limited democratic openings. The *Survey* finds that such societies over time grow receptive to a further deepening of freedom. This suggests that U.S. and international efforts to promote democratic transitions and to give some priority to material and technical assistance to democratic regimes are having a positive effect. But it also means that most progress is occurring in already Partly Free countries. This year, only a small number of Not Free countries registered meaningful progress. Moreover, after a decade of the rapid expansion of electoral democracies, the number of democracies in 1998, 117, is the same as the figure for 1994.

Yet while there is an extremely active and intelligently conceived U.S. policy to promote democratic transitions once limited political openings have occurred, far fewer resources are being directed at promoting democratic openings in the most repressive societies. For example, USAID efforts in closed societies focus mainly on limited technical assistance in support of modest economic reforms, rather than on support for democratic forces in these closed societies. Moreover, USAID does not devote significant resources to promoting political openings in closed societies. Such efforts are primarily undertaken by the independent, Congressionally funded National Endowment for Democracy.

While the United States has something approaching a consistent policy with regard to several rogue and pariah states that also violate basic human rights on a massive scale—Burma, Cuba, Iran, Iraq, Libya, and North Korea specifically—that policy mainly seeks to isolate these countries, and few resources are devoted to efforts that might actively promote change within them.

In the cases of some of the world's most important countries in which basic freedoms are broadly suppressed, U.S. policy consists of occasional—and at times muted—criticism of human rights violations and general expectations that the forces of economic change and trade will somehow inevitably lead to improvements in political and civil liberties. Among the countries in which there is little effort to promote democratic change are China, Vietnam, and—with the exception of the Palestinian National Authority—the Arab world.

Admittedly, some of the world's most closed societies (for example, North Korea) may be impervious to U.S. and other efforts to promote democratic ideas and foster the emergence of democratic movements. But the example of the collapse of communism in Central and Eastern Europe shows that totalitarian societies cannot forever withstand the pressures of an increasingly open and interdependent world.

Moreover, new technologies and the force of modest market-oriented change in some of the most repressive countries suggest that the capacity of the state to exert day-to-day control over information and private life is lessening, even if repression of political dissent is not.

OPENING UP CLOSED SOCIETIES

A comprehensive strategy to open up closed societies should be developed in cooperation with the nongovernmental sector. The mission of USAID should be expanded to allow it to be more active in fostering the development of the nongovernmental sector in closed countries. Aid and assistance for radio broadcasting, book publishing, contact with independent civic forces, and the transfer of information through the Internet should be expanded.

PROTECTING AGAINST REVERSALS

While 1998 saw the expansion of freedom in many parts of the world, forward momentum appears to have stalled in the twelve non-Baltic former republics of the Soviet Union, including Russia and Ukraine. Setbacks for reform and the weakening of reformist voices is likely a temporary phenomenon. It should not be seen as a signal to scale back drastically U.S. engagement. Rather, it requires a more efficient and precise

deployment of resources oriented around assisting reformers in their efforts to win the political battle of ideas.

Reversals of democratic progress should meet with active diplomatic and nongovernmental initiatives. In a period of some economic turmoil and social difficulties in transitional societies, the preservation of gains for civil liberties and political rights must be an urgent priority for U.S. policymakers and the international democratic community.

ECONOMIC FREEDOM AND POLITICAL LIBERTY

The economic crisis that rocked emerging markets in 1998 has not resulted in a reversal of progress toward greater political and economic freedom. Indeed, economic difficulties have not led to a worldwide resurgence of statism. On the contrary, economic failures have rightly been identified with a lack of transparency, cronyism, and corruption. In short, the case for a link between more open and democratically accountable government and economic success is gaining greater credence. The acknowledgment of such a relationship appears to have played a key role in the political openings in Indonesia and Nigeria. The ability of democratic states like the Philippines, Thailand, South Korea, and Brazil to implement policies to address the looming economic crisis have also done much to convince the international financial community that democratic accountability and legitimacy of rule is an important instrument for political reform.

But international donors and financial institutions need to take more resolute policy steps to act on these trends. The changing attitude of some international financial and aid organizations is a positive sign. The World Bank, in particular, has been innovative in its efforts to introduce issues of governance, corruption, and transparency into its programming and to begin to reach out to civil society and nongovernmental groups.

There is growing understanding among some policymakers of the link between the functioning of an effective rule of law system—a system that requires the checks and balances of a free society, a free press, and democratic accountability—and effective economic performance.

INTERNATIONAL STRUCTURES

In 1998, the fiftieth anniversary of the Universal Declaration of Human Rights was celebrated and efforts were made to intensify international action against basic rights violations. There were welcome efforts to arrest and prosecute those guilty of genocide and war crimes, including those guilty of atrocities in Rwanda and in Bosnia.

Many countries—though not the United States, which, for convincing reasons, was opposed—voted to adopt a charter for a far-reaching International Criminal Court. Yet while international action to eradicate rights abuses can be helpful, it must be limited in scope. Above all, international structures should not jeopardize or weaken the ability of democratic states to act to preserve or to protect freedom. Regrettably, many of the provisions in the proposed Criminal Court would have just such an effect.

As the Freedom House findings suggest, freedom is making important gains around the world. Nevertheless, the majority of mankind still lives in societies in which many or all basic freedoms are violated, and in a majority of countries the rule of law is absent or weak. Any body that emerges from an international consensus that includes undemocratic and unfree states is likely to be problematic in its composition. Adequate safeguards must exist to prevent such a court from acting capriciously. The United States is right to object to the current form of the proposed international Criminal Court. A far better policy would be the promotion of new structures made up of the growing community of free and democratic countries that could coordinate cooperation on behalf of human rights and against genocide and war crimes.

CONCLUSIONS

The remarkable expansion of human freedom recorded in the twenty-six years of the *Survey of Freedom* has not proceeded in a straight line. It has featured reversals as well as gains. Therefore, nothing in the findings should suggest that the expansion of democracy and freedom is inevitable. Indeed, much of the progress the *Survey* has recorded is the byproduct of a growing and systematic collaboration between established and new democracies, between democracies and countries in transition, and between established civic groups operating in the context of freedom and their pro-democratic counterparts seeking to promote change in closed societies. The findings of the *Survey* in future years will depend in no small measure on the success of such collaboration and on the elaboration of effective U.S. government policies to extend freedom to parts of the world where it is largely absent.

CRITICAL THINKING QUESTIONS

1. A sharp increase in the number of regions in the world with political freedom came from change in what major nation of the world during 1998?
2. What is the longer-term trend in political rights and freedoms?
3. In which regions of the world is political freedom most widespread? In which is it least widespread?

NOTE

1. Recent comparisons of the relationship between political freedom and economic liberty conducted by Freedom House (Adrian Karatnycky, Alexander Motyl, and Charles Graybow, eds., *Nations in Transit 1998*, New Brunswick, N.J.: Transaction Books, 1998) and the Heritage Foundation (Bryan T. Johnson, "Comparing Economic Freedom and Political Freedom," in Bryan T. Johnson, Kim R. Homes, and Melanie Kirkpatrick. eds., *1999 Index of Economic Freedom*, Washington, D.C.: The Heritage Foundation and Dow Jones Company, Inc., 1999, 29–34), respectively, have found a high correlation between the two variables.

According to the authors of *Nations in Transit 1998*, post-Communist countries that are consolidated democracies also tend to have consolidated their market economies. When these countries' performance with respect to political and economic freedom is related to economic growth, the study found that consolidated democracies and market economies averaged a growth rate of 4.7 percent in 1997, transitional polities and economies registered an average growth rate of 1.4 percent, and consolidated autocracies and statist economies in the region averaged close to a 3 percent drop in GDP. The study similarly found high correlations between more open political systems and lower levels of corruption. Moreover, societies with lower levels of corruption were significantly more successful in generating economic growth. The region's least corrupt countries, for example, grew at an average rate of 4.7 percent in 1997, while states registering high levels of corruption averaged a decline of nearly 1 percent. Researchers at the Heritage Foundation found a high degree of correlation between political rights and civil liberties (as measured by Freedom House) and economic freedom (as measured by the Heritage Foundation's surveys).

49

"His" and "Her" Marriage

Jessie Bernard

Social scientists have found that men and women are not joined at the hip by a wedding ceremony. Rather, their subsequent lives differ in terms of gender roles, power, and ways of communicating. Bernard was among the first sociologists to point out that marriage has a different meaning for women and men. As this selection shows, spouses rarely define reality in the same way, even with regard to simple routines such as sweeping the floor or mowing the lawn.

...[T]here is by now a very considerable body of well-authenticated research to show that there really are two marriages in every marital union, and that they do not always coincide.

"HIS" AND "HER" MARRIAGES

...[T]he differences in the marriages of husbands and wives have come under the careful scrutiny of a score of researchers. They have found that when they ask husbands and wives identical questions about the union, they often get quite different replies. There is usually agreement on the number of children

Source: From *The Future of Marriage* by Jessie Bernard. Copyright © 1972. Reprinted with permission.

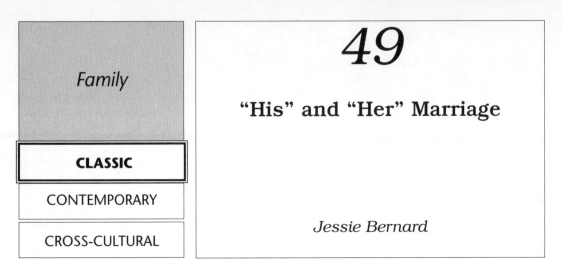

Edward Hopper (1882–1967), *Room in New York*, 1932. Oil on Canvas, 29 x 36 in. UNL-Sheldon Memorial Art Gallery & Sculpture Garden. F.M. Hall Collection, 1932. H-166.

they have and a few other such verifiable items, although not, for example, on length of premarital acquaintance and of engagement, on age at marriage, and interval between marriage and birth of first child. Indeed, with respect to even such basic components of the marriage as frequency of sexual relations, social interaction, household tasks, and decision making, they seem to be reporting on different marriages. As, I think, they are.

In the area of sexual relations, for example, Kinsey and his associates found different responses in from one- to two-thirds of the couples they studied. Kinsey interpreted these differences in terms of selective perception. In the generation he was studying, husbands wanted sexual relations oftener than the wives did, thus "the females may be overestimating the actual frequencies" and "the husbands...are probably underestimating the frequencies." The differences might also have been vestiges of the probable situation earlier in the marriage when the desired frequency of sexual relations was about six to seven times greater among husbands than among wives. This difference may have become so impressed on the spouses that it remained in their minds even after the difference itself had disappeared or even been reversed. In a sample of happily married, middle-class couples a generation later, Harold Feldman found that both spouses attributed to their mates more influence in the area of sex than they did to themselves.

Companionship, as reflected in talking together, he found, was another area where differences showed up. Replies differed on three-fourths of all the items studied, including the topics talked about, the amount of time spent talking with each other, and which partner initiated conversation. Both partners claimed that whereas they talked more about topics of interest to their mates, their mates initiated conversations about topics primarily of interest to themselves. Harold Feldman concluded that projection in terms of needs was distorting even simple, everyday events, and lack of communication was permitting the distortions to continue. It seemed to him that "if these sex differences can occur so often among these generally well-satisfied couples, it would not be surprising to find even less consensus and more distortion in other less satisfied couples."

Although, by and large, husbands and wives tend to become more alike with age, in this study of middle-class couples, differences increased with length of marriage rather than decreased, as one might logically have expected. More couples in the later than in the earlier years, for example, had differing pictures in their heads about how often they laughed together, discussed together, exchanged ideas, or worked together on projects, and about how well things were going between them.

The special nature of sex and the amorphousness of social interaction help to explain why differences in response might occur. But household tasks? They are fairly objective and clear-cut and not all that emotion-laden. Yet even here there are his-and-her versions. Since the division of labor in the household is becoming increasingly an issue in marriage, the uncovering of differing replies in this area is especially relevant. Hard as it is to believe, Granbois and Willett tell us that more than half of the partners in one sample disagreed on who kept track of money and bills. On the question, who mows the lawn? more than a fourth disagreed. Even family income was not universally agreed on.

These differences about sexual relations, companionship, and domestic duties tell us a great deal about the two marriages. But power or decision making can cover all aspects of a relationship. The question of who makes decisions or who exercises power has therefore attracted a great deal of research attention. If we were interested in who really had the power or who really made the decisions, the research would be hopeless. Would it be possible to draw any conclusion from a situation in which both partners agree that the husband ordered the wife to make all the decisions? Still, an enormous literature documents the quest of researchers for answers to the question of marital power. The major contribution it has made has been to reveal the existence of differences in replies between husbands and wives.

The presence of such inconsistent replies did not at first cause much concern. The researchers apologized for them but interpreted them as due to methodological inadequacies; if only they could find a better way to approach the problem, the differences would disappear. Alternatively, the use of only the wife's responses, which were more easily available, was justified on the grounds that differences in one direction between the partners in one marriage compensated for differences in another direction between the partners in another marriage and thus canceled them out. As, indeed, they did. For when Granbois and Willett, two market researchers, analyzed the replies of husbands and wives separately, the overall picture was in fact the same for both wives and husbands. Such canceling out of differences in the total sample, however, concealed almost as much as it revealed about the individual couples who composed it. Granbois and Willett concluded, as Kinsey had earlier, that the "discrepancies…reflect differing perceptions on the part of responding partners." And this was the heart of the matter.

Differing reactions to common situations, it should be noted, are not at all uncommon. They are recognized in the folk wisdom embedded in the story of the blind men all giving different replies to questions on the nature of the elephant. One of the oldest experiments in juridical psychology demonstrates how different the statements of witnesses of the same act can be. Even in laboratory studies, it takes intensive training of raters to make it possible for them to arrive at agreement on the behavior they observe.

It has long been known that people with different backgrounds see things differently. We know, for example, that poor children perceive coins as larger than do children from more affluent homes. Boys and girls perceive differently. A good deal of the foundation for projective tests rests on the different ways in which individuals see identical stimuli. And this perception—or, as the sociologists put it, definition of the situation—is reality for them. In this sense, the realities of the husband's marriage are different from those of the wife's.

Finally, one of the most perceptive of the researchers, Constantina Safilios-Rothschild, asked the crucial question: Was what they were getting, even with the best research techniques, family sociology or wives' family sociology? She answered her own question: What the researchers who relied on wives' replies exclusively were reporting on was the wife's marriage. The husband's was not necessarily the same. There were, in fact, two marriages present:

One explanation of discrepancies between the responses of husbands and wives may be the possibility of two "realities," the husband's subjective reality and the wife's subjective reality—two perspectives which do not always coincide. Each spouse perceives "facts" and situations differently according to his own needs, values, attitudes, and beliefs. An "objective" reality could possibly exist only in the trained observer's evaluation, if it does exist at all.

Interpreting the different replies of husbands and wives in terms of selective perception, projection of needs, values, attitudes, and beliefs, or different definitions of the situation, by no means renders them trivial or incidental or justifies dismissing or ignoring them. They are, rather, fundamental for an understanding of the two marriages, his and hers, and we ignore them at the peril of serious misunderstanding of marriage, present as well as future.

IS THERE AN OBJECTIVE REALITY IN MARRIAGE?

Whether or not husbands and wives perceive differently or define situations differently, still sexual relations are taking place, companionship is or is not occurring, tasks about the house are being performed, and decisions are being made every day by someone. In this sense, some sort of "reality" does exist. David Olson went to the laboratory to see if he could uncover it.

He first asked young couples expecting babies such questions as these: Which one of them would decide whether to buy insurance for the newborn child? Which one would decide the husband's part in diaper changing? Which one would decide whether the new mother would return to work or to school? When there were differences in the answers each gave individually on the questionnaire, he set up a situation in which together they had to arrive at a decision in his laboratory. He could then compare the results of the questionnaire with the results in the simulated situation. He found neither spouse's questionnaire response any more accurate than the other's; that is, neither conformed better to the behavioral "reality" of the laboratory than the other did.

The most interesting thing, however, was that husbands, as shown on their questionnaire response, perceived themselves as having more power than they actually did have in the laboratory "reality," and wives perceived that they had less. Thus, whereas three-fourths (73 percent) of the husbands overestimated their power in decision making, 70 percent of the wives underestimated theirs. Turk and Bell found similar results in Canada. Both spouses tend to attribute decision-making power to the one who has the "right" to make the decision. Their replies, that is, conform to the model of marriage that has characterized civilized mankind for millennia. It is this model rather than their own actual behavior that husbands and wives tend to perceive.

We are now zeroing in on the basic reality. We can remove the quotation marks. For there is, in fact, an objective reality in marriage. It is a reality that resides in the cultural—legal, moral, and conventional—prescriptions and proscriptions and, hence, expectations that constitute marriage. It is the reality that is reflected in the minds of the spouses themselves. The differences between the marriages of husbands and of wives are structural realities, and it is these structural differences that constitute the basis for the different psychological realities.

THE AUTHORITY STRUCTURE OF MARRIAGE

Authority is an institutional phenomenon; it is strongly bound up with faith. It must be believed in; it cannot be enforced unless it also has power. Authority resides not in the person on whom it is conferred by the group or society, but in the recognition and acceptance it elicits in others. Power, on the other hand, may dispense with the prop of authority. It may take the form of the ability to coerce or to veto; it is often personal, charismatic, not institutional. This kind of personal power is self-enforcing. It does not require shoring up by access to force. In fact, it may even operate subversively. A woman with this kind of power may or may not know that she

possesses it. If she does know she has it, she will probably disguise her exercise of it.

In the West, the institutional structure of marriage has invested the husband with authority and backed it by the power of church and state. The marriages of wives have thus been officially dominated by the husband. Hebrew, Christian, and Islamic versions of deity were in complete accord on this matter. The laws, written or unwritten, religious or civil, which have defined the marital union have been based on male conceptions, and they have undergirded male authority.

Adam came first. Eve was created to supply him with companionship, not vice versa. And God himself had told her that Adam would rule over her; her wishes had to conform to his. The New Testament authors agreed. Women were created for men, not men for women; women were therefore commanded to be obedient. If they wanted to learn anything, let them ask their husbands in private, for it was shameful for them to talk in the church. They should submit themselves to their husbands, because husbands were superior to wives; and wives should be as subject to their husbands as the church was to Christ. Timothy wrapped it all up: "Let the woman learn in silence with all subjection. But I suffer not a woman to teach, nor to usurp authority over the man, but to be in silence." Male Jews continued for millennia to thank God three times a day that they were not women. And the Koran teaches women that men are naturally their superiors because God made them that way; naturally, their own status is one of subordination.

The state as well as the church had the same conception of marriage, assigning to the husband and father control over his dependents, including his wife. Sometimes this power was well-nigh absolute, as in the case of the Roman patria potestas—or the English common law, which flatly said, "The husband and wife are as one and that one is the husband." There are rules still lingering today with the same, though less extreme, slant. Diane B. Schulder has summarized the legal framework of the wife's marriage as laid down in the common law:

The legal responsibilities of a wife are to live in the home established by her husband; to perform the domestic chores (cleaning, cooking, washing, etc.) necessary to help maintain that home; to care for her husband and children.... A husband may force his wife to have sexual relations as long as his demands are reasonable and her health is not endangered.... The law allows a wife to take a job if she wishes. However, she must see that her domestic chores are completed, and, if there are children, that they receive proper care during her absence.

A wife is not entitled to payment for household work; and some jurisdictions in the United States expressly deny payment for it. In some states, the wife's earnings are under the control of her husband, and in four, special court approval and in some cases husband's consent are required if a wife wishes to start a business of her own.

The male counterpart to these obligations includes that of supporting his wife. He may not disinherit her. She has a third interest in property owned by him, even if it is held in his name only. Her name is required when he sells property.

Not only divine and civil law but also rules of etiquette have defined authority as a husband's prerogative. One of the first books published in England was a *Boke of Good Manners,* translated from the French of Jacques Le Grand in 1487, which included a chapter on "How Wymmen Ought to Be Gouerned." The thirty-third rule of Plutarch's *Rules for Husbands and Wives* was that women should obey their husbands; if they "try to rule over their husbands they make a worse mistake than the husbands do who let themselves be ruled." The husband's rule should not, of course, be brutal; he should not rule his wife "as a master does his chattel, but as the soul governs the body, by feeling with her and being linked to her by affection." Wives, according to Richard Baxter, a seventeenth-century English divine, had to obey even a wicked husband, the only exception being that a wife need not obey a husband if he ordered her to change her religion. But, again, like Plutarch, Baxter warned that the husband should love his wife; his authority should not be so coercive or so harsh as to destroy love. Among his twelve rules for carrying out the duties of conjugal love, however, was one to the effect that love must not be so imprudent as to destroy authority.

As late as the nineteenth century, Tocqueville noted that in the United States the ideals of democracy did not apply between husbands and wives:

Nor have the Americans ever supposed that one consequence of democratic principles is the subversion of marital power, or the confusion of the natural authorities in families. They hold that every association must have a head in order to accomplish its objective, and that the natural head of the conjugal association is man. They do not therefore deny him the right of directing his partner; and they maintain, that in the smaller association of husband and wife, as well as in the great social community, the object of democracy is to regulate and legalize the powers which are necessary, not to subvert all power.

This opinion is not peculiar to men and contested by women; I never observed that the women of America consider conjugal authority as an unfortunate usurpation [by men] of their rights, nor that they thought themselves degraded by submitting to it. It appears to me, on the contrary, that they attach a sort of pride to the voluntary surrender of their own will, and make it their boast to bend themselves to the yoke, not to shake it off.

The point here is not to document once more the specific ways (religious, legal, moral, traditional) in which male authority has been built into the marital union—that has been done a great many times—but merely to illustrate how different (structurally or "objectively" as well as perceptually or "subjectively") the wife's marriage has actually been from the husband's throughout history.

THE SUBVERSIVENESS OF NATURE

The rationale for male authority rested not only on biblical grounds but also on nature or natural law, on the generally accepted natural superiority of men. For nothing could be more self-evident than that the patriarchal conception of marriage, in which the husband was unequivocally the boss, was natural, resting as it did on the unchallenged superiority of males.

Actually, nature, if not deity, is subversive. Power, or the ability to coerce or to veto, is widely distributed in both sexes, among women as well as among men. And whatever the theoretical or conceptual picture may have been, the actual, day-by-day relationships between husbands and wives have been determined by the men and women themselves. All that the institutional machinery could do was to confer authority; it could not create personal power, for such power cannot be conferred, and women can generate it as well as men.... Thus, keeping women in their place has been a universal problem, in spite of the fact that almost without exception institutional patterns give men positions of superiority over them.

If the sexes were, in fact, categorically distinct, with no overlapping, so that no man was inferior to any woman or any woman superior to any man, or vice versa, marriage would have been a great deal simpler. But there is no such sharp cleavage between the sexes except with respect to the presence or absence of certain organs. With all the other characteristics of each sex, there is greater or less overlapping, some men being more "feminine" than the average woman and some women more "masculine" than the average man. The structure of families and societies reflects the positions assigned to men and women. The bottom stratum includes children, slaves, servants, and outcasts of all kinds, males as well as females. As one ascends the structural hierarchy, the proportion of males increases, so that at the apex there are only males.

When societies fall back on the lazy expedient—as all societies everywhere have done—of allocating the rewards and punishments of life on the basis of sex, they are bound to create a host of anomalies, square pegs in round holes, societal misfits. Roles have been allocated on the basis of sex which did not fit a sizable number of both sexes—women, for example, who chafed at subordinate status and men who could not master superordinate status. The history of the relations of the sexes is replete with examples of such misfits. Unless a modus vivendi is arrived at, unhappy marriages are the result.

There is, though, a difference between the exercise of power by husbands and by wives. When women exert power, they are not rewarded; they may even be punished. They are "deviant." Turk and Bell note that "wives who...have the greater influence in decision making may experience guilt over this fact." They must therefore dissemble to maintain the illusion, even to themselves, that they are subservient. They tend to feel less powerful than they are because they *ought* to be.

When men exert power, on the other hand, they are rewarded; it is the natural expression of authority. They feel no guilt about it. The prestige of authority goes to the husband whether or not he is actually the one who exercises it. It is not often even noticed when the wife does so. She sees to it that it is not.

There are two marriages, then, in every marital union, his and hers. And his...is better than hers. The questions, therefore, are these: In what direction will they change in the future? Will one change more than the other? Will they tend to converge or to diverge? Will the future continue to favor the husband's marriage? And if the wife's marriage is improved, will it cost the husband's anything, or will his benefit along with hers?

CRITICAL THINKING QUESTIONS

1. What evidence does Bernard offer to support her conclusion that there are "his" and "her" marriages rather than "our" marriage?
2. Does the traditional inequality of men and women support or undermine marital roles? How?
3. In your opinion, have marital roles in Canada changed since this article was written in 1972? How?

50

Housework in Canada: The National Picture*

Family

CLASSIC

CONTEMPORARY

CROSS-CULTURAL

M. R. Nakhaie**

Researchers generally agree that women perform the majority of domestic work. Nakhaie looks at this assertion from a Canadian perspective and attempts to address the lack of research on domestic labour in Canada.

Recent survey research indicates that women are still overwhelmingly responsible for, and primarily carry out, the chief household chores (Coverman & Sheley, 1986; Berardo et al., 1987; Michelson, 1988). Most importantly, there appears to be little significant increase in the amount of domestic labour performed by men when their wives take on a second job (i.e., full-time paid work outside the home). Canadian local studies in Vancouver (Meissner et al., 1975), Halifax (Harvey Clarke, 1975), Toronto (Michelson,

1985), Quebec (Bourdais et al., 1987), and Flin Flon (Luxton, 1980; Luxton & Rosenberg, 1986) support these conclusions.

There is, however, no national Canadian research to substantiate these findings. This is a surprising shortcoming, given the persistent conclusion among contributors to the domestic labour debate that there is a great need for empirical research (Fox, 1986: 188; Seccombe, 1986: 207; Armstrong & Armstrong, 1990: 33). In an attempt to contribute to the ongoing debate, this paper provides a multivariate analysis of housework and evaluates its major determinant in the Canadian national setting.

HYPOTHESES

Aside from the importance of capitalism and patriarchy in the institutionalization of gender specific task allocations (see Molyneux, 1979; Fox, 1980; Hamilton & Barrett, 1986; Armstrong & Armstrong, 1990), most theorists agree that the organization of domestic life is a negotiated

*I gratefully acknowledge that the data presented here were drawn from Class Structure and Class Consciousness: Merged Multi-Nation File, the Canadian portion of which was conducted by Professor John Myles of Carleton University with funding from the Social Sciences and Humanities Research Council of Canada. I am indebted to Professors Robert Arnold, James Curtis and Roberta Hamilton, and anonymous reviewers for their helpful and critical comments.

**Department of Sociology, Queen's University, Kingston, Ontario, K7L 3N6, Canada.

Source: M. R. Nakhaie. (1995). Housework in Canada. *Journal of Comparative Family Studies,* 26(3), 409–25. Reprinted with the permission of the Journal of Comparative Family Studies.

process between household occupants.... There is, however, little agreement as to whether this process is power-based or a free choice.

The best-known sociological theory which is concerned with the conjugal power as an explanation of housework performance is that of Wolfe (1959), Blood and Wolfe (1960: 48, 73–4) and Spitze (1986: 691). This theory views power and resources such as income as instrumental in the family structure whereby those members with more income or power are better able to exercise their wills, or to achieve desired goals or outcomes. Davidoff (1976: 124), likewise, argues that the performance of housekeeping and housework are a means of maintaining order and predictability in the immediate environment thus making meaningful patterns of activity, people and material. Cleaning, for example, entails the separation of wanted from unwanted, desirable from undesirable, and is therefore a way of making the environment conform to cultural standards. Those who are powerful, however, can enforce and maintain this order by delegating it to the less powerful. Thus, the resource/power theory suggests that housework is generally undesirable and those with more resources confer power and negotiate or impose household tasks on the powerless. Empirical research has supported this hypothesis (see Bane, 1976; Clark et al., 1978; Nicols and Metzen, 1978; Ericksen et al., 1979; Vanek, 1980; Model, 1982; Bird et al., 1984; Spitze, 1986; Bourdais et al., 1987; but see, Farkas, 1976; Robinson, 1977; Herdesty & Bokemeir, 1989: 263). For example, Ericksen et al. (1979) show a negative relationship between men's income and their hours of housework performance. Similarly, Nicols and Metzen (1978) show that as wives' incomes increase, the number of hours they spend on housework decrease, and that the husbands' housework increases.

The New Home Economics, or Chicago School, builds on the resource/power theory but sees the household operation as based on free choice. It suggests that the household unit seeks to maximize the aggregate utility of the occupants'

labour power in the house and in the market by deciding which commodities to produce in the house and which to purchase from the market. Since women often earn less for the same work as men, this thesis argues that households can maximize utility by adopting a gendered division of labour. This places wives at home doing domestic work while their husbands are involved in the paid work force (Becker, 1974). The traditional sexual division of labour is thus seen as a rational decision made by households which wish to maximize utility (see also Becker, 1976, 1981).

More precisely, this theory is concerned with the "husband-wife earning ratio" as the determinant of home responsibility (Becker, 1974: 303). It suggests that the relative income contribution of spouses to the family signifies the worth of each partner's work in the market and thus is used as the determinant of housework performance. The earliest test of this thesis by Farkas (1976), based on the national U.S. Income Dynamic data, shows that the strength of the net effect of wage-ratio does not appear to warrant the conclusion that the value of human time is the main explanation for spousal contribution to housework. Model (1982), however, revealed that the level of contribution to housework is determined by income differentials between spouses. The latter, in fact, proves to be a better predictor of housework responsibilities than individual income. Similarly, Maret and Finlay's (1984) findings support the hypothesis that the wife's relative economic contribution to the household determines her domestic responsibilities (1984: 362; but see [the] Hardesty and Bokemeir study of rural Kentucky, 1989: 263).

Finally, the time availability hypothesis also sees housework allocation as a negotiated process but not so much based on power or utility maximization. This thesis suggests that husbands and wives perform housework in response to the availability of time after involvement in paid work. Blood and Wolfe (1960: 74), for example, argue that "more household tasks are humdrum and menial in nature," and the most important factor contributing to their performance is available time. Usually the person with the most time is the wife who is not working outside the home. But if she works for pay, the husband incurs a moral obligation to contribute to the housework. Thus, this thesis suggests that as more women work for pay, they have less time to perform housework. Consequently, their husbands have to contribute more to the housework because "the work must be done." Or, alternatively, the more husbands have available free time, because their jobs require fewer hours, the more they will contribute to domestic work.

Several studies point to women's participation in the labour force as the reason for a decrease in their housework and an increase in the home responsibilities of their partners. (Walker, 1970; Epstein, 1971; Holmstrom, 1973; Elliott et al., 1973; Vanek, 1974; Nicols and Metzen, 1978; Pleck, 1979; Sanik, 1981; Berk, 1985; Bourdais et al., 1987; Michelson, 1988; Luxton, 1980). For example, Spitze (1986) uses data from the National Longitudinal Surveys of Young and Mature Women and finds that, as women's hours of employment increases, their share of housework decreases slightly. Similarly, Barnett and Baruch (1987) reveal that women's employment outside the home prompts increased male acceptance of housework.

Despite the positive relationship in the above studies, the impact of wives' employment on husband's housework is also shown to be insignificant (Vanek, 1974; Sanik, 1981), quite small (Walker & Woods, 1976), or at best modest (Nicols & Metzen, 1978). Most importantly, there appears to be little significant increase in men's domestic labour as women take on paid work outside the home. For example, Meissner et al. (1975) studied a random sample of Vancouver couples on a week day and weekend day. They show that women's total workload, involving work both inside and outside the home, increases as they take on paid work, but husbands' does not. While men are reported to spend only a fraction of the time that women spend doing housework, it

is women who are found to adjust their schedules to the changing family situation. Based on a similar study in 1971–72 in Halifax, Harvey and Clarke (1975) also conclude that women, and not men, adjust their work efforts to changing family needs. Michelson's (1985) 1980 survey of Toronto families, based on time-budget data, also shows that full-time paid working women still do far more housework than men. Finally, another local study by Bourdais et al. (1987) in Quebec, reveals that women, on average, contribute three times as many hours as men to household chores. This proportion decreases to twice as much as men's when both partners have a paid job. However, even though a woman's employment decreases her work around the house by nine hours, it increases men's housework by only, one hour (Bourdais et al., 1987).

In sum, American and Canadian local studies reveal that women who work for pay outside the home do not necessarily decrease and their husbands increase their share of housework. Moreover, while homemaking is the largest occupational category in this country (Luxton & Rosenberg, 1986), housework ranks as the most systematically under-researched (Hale, 1990). There have been several very informative studies of local samples, referred to above. The present study will show the generalizability to national data of several results from these earlier local studies. Furthermore, due, perhaps, to differences in research procedures (measures, samples, and the extent of controls), the previous American literature is inconsistent enough in its findings to require further tests. Most American studies rely on a ordinal level of measurement for housework—mostly husband, mostly wife, jointly (Stafford et al., 1977; Clarke et al., 1978; Ericksen et al., 1979; Marret and Finlay, 1984; Bird et al., 1984; Hardesty and Bokemeir, 1989). Other researchers ask respondents to estimate their contribution to housework in terms of the percentage of time or number of hours (Coverman, 1985; Barnett & Baruch, 1987; Berardo et al., 1987). Still other researchers obtain time-use data by a diary of activities kept by each respondent for about 24 hours or a week (Walker, 1970; Walker & Woods, 1976; Robinson et al., 1972; Robinson, 1977; Juster and Stafford, 1985; Coverman and Sheley, 1986). These American studies have also been limited in population coverage to white middle class families (Berardo et al., 1987; Barnet & Baruch, 1987), to women aged 30–44 (Marret & Finlay, 1984), to college students (Stafford et al., 1977), to college and university administrators (Bird et al., 1984), or to local samples (Clarke et al., 1978; Ericksen et al., 1979), although national samples have also been used, as discussed above.[1]

DATA SOURCE

Our data source is the Canadian portion of "The Class Structure and Class Consciousness: Merged Multi-Nation File" (CSCC) which involved in-home personal interviews with a national multi-stage stratified sample of Canadians. The interviews were conducted between November 1982 and April 1983. There were 2576 respondents, 1,810 of whom were married and/or cohabiting and 480 of which both partners worked more than 30 hours per week for pay. The latter subsample is selected to evaluate the findings by Maret and Finlay (1984) that women in dual-earner families continue to bear full responsibility for housework. The sample is weighted to make it representative of the population in terms of gender, age, household size, and community size within provinces.

Dependent Variables

Housework refers to all types of activities which are undertaken to maintain the household, both physically and socially, as well as the maintenance of the physical structure of the house (Clark & Stephenson, 1986: 75). The CSCC survey asked respondents to report how they handle various routine household chores by indicating what percentage of particular tasks is done by them.[2] These tasks, however, were limited to eight, including: looking after children and doing things with them, cooking meals, cleaning after meals, doing laundry, general housecleaning, grocery shopping, yardwork, and house maintenance.

Independent Variables

The measures of personal resource and power include two variables: (1) income scaled from 1 = none to 12 = over $100,000; and (2) perceived power. Blood and Wolfe (1960), in their study of Detroit and Michigan, measured power in terms of an individual's ability to make decisions in critical areas of life (including income and expenditures) and showed that this measure was strongly related to various measures of inequality such as income and prestige. Likewise, the CSCC contained three questions which could measure conjugal power: (1) "who has the most say in making major financial decisions in [the respondent's] household, like a decision to take out a loan or buy a car"; (2) "who has most say about the overall family budget; that is, about how much of the family income goes for different general purposes such as running the house, recreation, new clothes, and so forth"; and (3) "who has the most say in deciding the specific neighborhood where you live now." If the respondents make the decision in any of these areas they receive a score of +1; if their partners make this decision the respondents receive a score of –1 and if both equally decide the respondents receive a score of zero (0). The power variable is created by summing the scores for these questions. Scores range from –3 to +3.

Relative income represents the respondent's relative contribution to the family income. Respondents are asked to report the percentage of annual family income resulting from their spouses' jobs. A score of zero (0) is assigned to those respondents who reported that their spouse does not have a paying job.

There are two measures of time availability. First, the survey asked the respondents to report the number of hours they work per week. This variable ranges from 8 to 97. The second measure evaluates the time availability of spouses. The survey asked the respondents to report their partner's number of hours of paid work per week. This variable ranges from 8 to 87.

In addition to the predictors of homework discussed above we were concerned about the extent to which the presence of children increases women's and men's share of housework (Berk & Berk, 1979; Meissner et al., 1975; Hamilton, 1981). We included the number of children and their ages (under 5, 6–12, 13 plus) to control for children's effect.

RESULTS

Among the total sample, male respondents have a higher mean level of income (about $20K) than females (about $7K) and work more per week (37.4 hours) than females (18.6 hours). Spouses of the male respondents spend 15.44 hours per week in the paid force and contribute 17.3% to the family income, while spouses of the female respondents spend 35.28 hours per week in the paid force and contribute 66.9% to the family income. On average, males score higher in the power construct (.45) than females (–.20). As expected, the magnitude of these gaps declines, though not substantially, among full-time respondents when compared to the total sample. The main differences between males and females in the total and full-time paid working sample are in the income and time availability areas. Among full-time paid working respondents, men's total income does not differ much from that reported by males in the full sample but females' total income increases from about $7K to $13K and their contribution to the family income increases from 17.2 percent to 40.6 percent. The total hours of paid employment for males does increase slightly (from 37.4 to 45.7), but that of females increases substantially (from 18.6 to 40.2). Similarly, when comparing the two groups, males report that their partners' total hours of paid work increase from 15.4 to 40.3 while females report that their partners' total hours of paid work increases from 35.3 to 44.2.

Another expected difference between the two sub-samples is in the numbers of children. Although there is little difference in the number of children reported by either males or females in the total sample, full-time paid working females report fewer children than their male counterparts.

Finally, male respondents reported performing about 33% of the housework, compared to 62% for the female respondents. A similarly large gap in performing housework emerged among full-time paid working respondents. Men increased their housework by about 4% and females decreased theirs by about 3% when compared to the total sample (see Table 50.1). Consistent with previous research, full-time paid work by women does not relieve them from most of the housework (Maret and Finlay, 1984; Meissner et al., 1975; Luxton, 1980)....

DISCUSSION AND CONCLUSIONS

The results of this study support previous findings that relative income, personal resources and time availability as well as the presence of children affect the division of housework. Among these, power, as measured by the ability to make decisions regarding the affairs of the house, receives the least support when compared to the time availability (Meissner et al., 1975: 425; Blood & Wolfe, 1960; Spitze, 1986; Walker, 1970; Epstein, 1971; Holmstrom, 1973; Pleck, 1979; Sanik, 1981; Berk, 1985; Bourdais et al., 1987), relative income (Farkas, 1976: 482; Model, 1982; Maret & Finlay, 1984), presence of children (Hamilton, 1981; Berk & Berk, 1979; Bourdais et al., 1987; Meissner, 1975) and income (Bane, 1976; Nicols & Metzen, 1978; Bourdais et al., 1987) variables. The power measure failed to show the expected effect, probably because it is measured by asking respondents who makes what decisions and therefore indicates perceived authority rather than actual power (McDonald, 1980).

Table 50.1   Mean Scores for the Dependent and Independent Variables by Gender:
Total Sample and Full-Time Paid Working Respondents (Canada, 1983)

	Total Sample		Full-time	
	Males	*Females*	*Males*	*Females*
Power	.45	−.20	−.37	−.08
Income	6.93	3.90	6.81	5.54
Relative income	17.28	66.95	40.46	60.98
# Hours of paid work by spouse	15.44	35.28	40.39	44.23
# Hours of paid work by Resp.	37.40	18.62	45.74	40.24
# Children	1.24	1.25	1.13	1.02
Age of children	10.72	10.82	10.90	9.82
Share of Housework	33.30	62.30	37.50	59.30

Although the New Home Economic model is supported in our study, the impact of the husband-wife earning ratio on doing housework is stronger for males than females. This finding suggests that the economic model, by assuming that people make decisions based on free choice, has ignored power relationships involved in the household. As Coverman (1989) argued, the allocation of household chores is subject to difficult negotiation and conflict among household members. The outcome of these negotiations often depends, however, on the ability and power of the household occupants. Husbands seem to have a structural advantage in this process. Wives, however, have to develop a variety of tactics and strategies to increase their spouses' contributions to housework (Luxton, 1980; see also Hartmann, 1981; Hamilton, 1981).

The suggestion that housework is power-based is also borne out by findings on the relationships between the time availability measures and doing housework. As males increase their hours of paid work per week, they do less housework (particularly among double earner couples), while women do *more* of the housework as they increase their hours of paid work. Moreover, women are more responsive to the increases in their partners' hours of paid work than are men.

Two conclusions can be reached by these findings. First, among the total sample, females do more housework because gender stands as a proxy of a relatively fewer paid hours of work by women compared to men. Thus, among the full-time paid respondents, gender in itself does not have a significant impact on doing housework. Second, there are indications of a "superwomen" (Steinem, 1987: 57; Luxton, 1980) ethic among women who work for long hours in the paid work force and do an even larger share of housework than before. These findings, thus, support the studies in Vancouver (Meissner, 1975), Halifax (Harvey & Clarke, 1975), Flin Flon (Luxton, 1980) and in Quebec (Bourdais et al., 1987) which show that full-time paid working women still do most of the housework, perhaps at the expense of their own leisure and personal care. As these local studies conclude, women's involvement in the paid labour force simply adds to their housework in the family (Anderson, 1988: 165).

The differential impact of the hours of paid work for males and females, particularly among the full-time two income earners, may thus point to Eichler's (1990) argument that the value of time differs systematically in relation to one's power position. Since women as a group are less powerful than men, time spent performing paid work becomes less valuable and cannot easily help reduce their share of housework. This power seems to have been derived from husbands' economic advantage in the labour force, their greater cognitive power in the public domain and from women's cultural mandate, which places priority on the family (Mackie, 1991: 234–235; Luxton & Rosenberg, 1986: 11; Gaskell, 1988).

Finally, one of the persistent findings in this study (and of the previous research) is that gender/sex is the most significant force in accounting for the performance of housework, net of other variables. These consistent findings point to the structural and historical forces which have gradually helped institutionalize a "gender factory" in the house so that each generation of sons learned to do less housework and each generation of daughters continued to be trained in domestic activities. This gendered socialization of housework seems to have been sealed in the best social cement of all: the patterns of daily life and the relationship between parents and children (Cowan, 1983: 86; England & Farkas, 1986; Finley, 1989; Molyneux, 1979; Fox, 1980; Zaretsky, 1982; Hamilton & Barrett, 1986; Armstrong & Armstrong, 1990).

Moreover, the gendered division of labour is passed down to children in the family and schools and through media and religions which portray women as engaged in a narrow range of "female" occupations and household-related tasks (see Russell, 1986; Mackie, 1991). These forces have constructed sex-specific images and stereotypes and have enforced a "tendency for many women to accept as truth the social constraints and mental images which society has prescribed for them" (Pike & Zureik, 1975: 3). Thus, boys' and girls' involvement in housework in their early teens becomes readily distinguishable along gender lines (Benin & Edwards, 1990; White and Brinkerhoff, 1981). Not surprisingly, Gaskell's (1988) study of young girls in their last years of high school in a Vancouver working-class neighborhood revealed that they all assumed that eventually they would

care for their children and do the housework. Young girls seem to have learned that "[c]ooking a nice meal, providing clean sheets or eliminating dull, yellow floor wax" are ways of expressing love (Luxton, 1980: 159). Boys, on the other hand, internalize the male breadwinner ideology as their fundamental gender consciousness (Livingstone & Luxton, 1989).

There are some indications of a shift in Canadian attitudes toward sharing housework. Canadians' support for husbands sharing housework has increased from 57% in 1976 to 81% in 1986 (Wilson, 1991: 56). However, these attitude changes are very slowly translated into changes in behaviour. Although the men of Flin Flon seem to have increased their contribution to housework by 8.3 hours per week between 1976–81, women of this town decreased their contribution to housework by only 4.3 hours per week (Luxton, 1986). Perhaps an equal contribution to housework is possible only if the power relationship between men and women in the wider society and in the house is altered. Simultaneously, gender consciousness should be transcended so that an ideology of breadwinning for males and family priority for females loses its gendered-significance. These, however, may not be easy tasks, given the powerful forces which have split the labour market and have segregated the household as a private domain.

CRITICAL THINKING QUESTIONS

1. Review the *conjugal power* explanation for who performs the majority of housework. Given your own experiences, does this explanation seem accurate?

2. Why do you think there has not been more research into domestic labour in Canada?

3. Do you believe that the gender factory continues to reinforce traditional male and female roles as they relate to domestic labour? If yes, how? If not, why?

NOTES

1. There are substantial differences among the American studies. It is difficult to know to what extent these differences in findings are due to small sample areas, measurement differences and/or differing interpretations of the results. It is plausible that since there is little variation in the amount of housework performed by men, every different analysis will likely conclude with the explanatory importance of different variables.

2. The exact question is: "Now we would like to ask you some questions about how you handle various routine household chores. For each of the following tasks, please tell me roughly what percentage of this task is done by you."

REFERENCES

Armstrong, P., and H. Armstrong. 1990. *Theorizing women's work*. Toronto: Network Basics Series.

Bane, M. J. 1976. *Here to stay: American families in the twentieth century*. New York: Basic Books.

Benin, M. H. and D. A. Edwards. 1990. Adolescents chores: The difference between dual and single-earner families." *Journal of Marriage and the Family*. (52): 361–73.

Barnett, R. C., and G. K. Baruch. 1987. Determinants of father's participation in family work. *Journal of Marriage and the Family*, (49): 29–40.

Becker, G. S. 1974. A theory of marriage. In *Economics of the family*, ed. T. W. Schultz. Chicago: University of Chicago Press.

———. 1976. *The economic approach to human behaviour*. Chicago: University of Chicago Press.

———. 1981. *A treatise on the family*. Harvard, Mass.: Harvard University Press.

Berk, R. 1980. The new home economics: An agenda for sociological research. In *Women and household labour*, ed. S. F. Berk, 113–48. Beverly Hills, Calif.: Sage.

Berk, R., and S. Berk. 1979. *Labour and leisure at home*. Beverly Hills: Sage.

Berk, S. 1985. *The gender factory: The apportionment of work in the American household*, New York: Plenum Press.

Berardo, D. H., C. L. Shehah, and G. R. Leslie. 1987. A residue of tradition: Jobs, careers, and spouses' time in house work. *Journal of Marriage and the Family*, 49: 381–90.

Bird, G. W, G. A. Bird, and M. Scruggs. 1984. Determinants of family task sharing: A study of husbands and wives. *Journal of Marriage and the Family*, 46(2): 345–55.

Blood, R. O., and D. M. Wolfe. 1960. *Husbands and wives: The dynamics of married living*. Glencoe, Ill.: Free Press.

Bourdais, C., P. J. Hamel, and R. Bernard. 1987. Le travail et l'ouvrage: Charge et portage des taches domestiques chez les couples quebecois. *Sociologie et Societes*, XIX(1: Avril): 37–55.

Clark, R. A., F. I. Nye, and V. Gecas. 1978. Work involvement and marital role performance. *Journal of Marriage and the Family*, 40: 9–22.

Clark S., and M. Stephenson. 1986. Housework as real work. In *Work in the Canadian context*, eds. K. L. P. Lundy, and B. Warme, 211–31. Markham, Ont.: Butterworths.

Coverman, S., and J. E. Sheley. 1986. Change in men's housework and child care time 1965–1975. *Journal of Marriage and the Family*, 48: 413–22.

Cowan, R. S. 1983. *More work for mothers: The ironies of household technology from the open hearth to the microwave*. New York: Basic Books.

Davidoff, L. 1976. The rationalization of housework. In *Dependence and exploitation in work and marriage*, eds. D. L. Barker, & S. Allen. London: Longman.

Eichler, M. 1991. Gender and the value of time. In *Images of Canada: The sociological tradition*, eds. J. Curtis, and L. Tepperman. Scarborough, Ont.: Prentice-Hall Canada Inc.

Elliott, D., A. S. Harvey, and D. Procos. 1973. *An overview of Halifax time-budget*. Halifax/Institute of Public Affairs, Dalhousie University.

England. P., and G. Farkas. 1986. *Households, employment, and gender: A social, economic, and Demographic view*. New York: Aldine de Gruyter.

Ericksen, J., W. Yancey, and E. Ericksen. 1979. The division of family roles. *Journal of Marriage and the Family*, 41: 301–14.

Epstein, C. 1971. Law partners and marital partners: Strains and solutions in the dual-career family enterprise" *Human Relations*, 24 (December): 549–64.

Farkas, G. 1976. Education, wage rate and the division of labour between husband and wife. *Journal of Marriage and the Family*, 38: 473–84.

Finley, N. J. 1989. Theories of family labour as applied to gender differences in caregiving for elderly parents. *Journal of Marriage and the Family*, 51: 79–86.

Fox, B. 1980. *Hidden in the household: Women's domestic labour under capitalism*. Oshawa, ON: Women's Press.

Gaskell, J. 1988. The reproduction of family life: Perspectives of male and female adolescents. In *Gender and society: Creating a Canadian women sociology*, ed. A. T. McLaren, 146–68. Toronto: Copp Clark Pitman.

Hale, S. M. 1990. *Controversies in sociology: A Canadian introduction*. Toronto: Copp Clark Pitman Ltd.

Hamilton, R. 1981. Working at home. *Atlantis*, 7(1): 114–26.

Hamilton, R., and M. Barrett. 1986. Introduction. In *The politics of diversity: Feminism, Marxism and nationalism*, eds. R. Hamilton and M. Barrett, 1–35. London: Verso.

Hardesty, C., and J. Bokemeir. 1989. Finding time and making do: Distribution of household labour in non-metropolitan marriages. *Journal of Marriage and the Family*, 51: 253–67.

Hartmann, H. I. 1981. The family as the locus of gender, class, and political struggle: The example of housework. *Signs*, 6(3): 366–94.

Harvey, A. S., and S. Clarke. 1975. *Descriptive analysis of Halifax time-budget data.* Halifax: Institute of Public Affairs, Dalhousie University.

Holmstrom, L. L. 1973. *The two-career family.* Cambridge, Mass.: Schenkman.

Juster, F. T., and F. J. Stafford. 1985. *Time, goods and well-being.* Ann Arbor, Mich.: Survey Research Center, Institute for Social Research, University of Michigan.

Livingstone, D. W., and M. Luxton. 1988. Gender consciousness at work: Modification of the male breadwinner norm among steelworkers and their spouses. *Canadian Review of Sociology and Anthropology*, 26(2): 240–74.

Luxton, M. 1980. *More than a labour of love: Three generations of women's work at home.* Toronto: Women's Press.

Luxton, M., and H. Rosenberg. 1986. *Through the kitchen windows: The politics of home and family.* Toronto: Garamond Press.

Mackie, M. 1991. *Gender relations in Canada: Further exploration.* Markham, Ont.: Butterworths Canada Ltd.

Maret, E., and B. Finlay. 1984. The distribution of household labour among women in dual-earner families. *Journal of Marriage and the Family*, 46: 357–64.

McDonald, G. W. 1980. Family power: The assessment of a decade of theory and research, 1970–1979. *Journal of Marriage and the Family*, 42: 841–54.

Meissner, M., E. W. Humphrey, S. M. Meis, and W. J. Scheu. 1975. No exit for wives: Sexual division of labour and cumulation of household demands. *Canadian Review of Sociology and Anthropology*, 12: 424–39.

Michelson, W. 1985. *From sun to sun: Daily obligations and community structure in the lives of employed women and their families.* Tomwa, N.J.: Rowman & Allanheld Publishers.

———. 1988. The daily routines of employed spouses as a public affairs agenda. In *Readings in sociology: An introduction*, eds. L. Tepperman, and J. Curtis, 400–09. Toronto: McGraw-Hill Ryerson Limited.

Model, S. 1982. Housework by husbands: Determinants and implications. In *Two paychecks: Life in dual earner families*, ed. J. Aldous, 193, 206. Beverly Hills, Calif.: Sage Publications.

Molyneux, M. 1979. Beyond the domestic labour debate. *New Left Review*, 116: 3–27.

Nicols, S., and E. Metzen. 1978. Housework time of husband and wife. *Home Economics Research Journal*, 17: 85–97.

Pike, R., and E. Zuriek. 1975. *Socialization and values in Canadian society.* Toronto: McClelland and Stewart Limited.

Pleck, J. H. 1979. Men's family work: Three perspectives and some new data. *Family Coordinator*, 28: 481–88.

Robinson, J. 1977. *How Americans use time.* New York: Praeger.

Robinson, J., P. Converse, and A. Szali. 1972. Everyday life in the twelve countries. In *The use of time*, ed. A. Szalai. The Hague: Mouton.

Sanik, M. 1981. Division of household work: A decade of comparison, 1967–1977. *Home Economic Research Journal*, 10: 175–80.

Seccombe, W. 1986. Patriarchy stabilized: The construction of male breadwinner wage norm in nineteenth-century Britain. *Social History*, II (1).

Spitze, G. D. 1986. Division of home responsibilities. *Social Forces*, 64: 689–701.

Stafford, R., E. Backman, and R Dibona. 1977. The division of labour among cohabiting and married couples. *Journal of Marriage and the Family*, 39: 43–57.

Steinem, G. 1987. Looking to the future. *Ms.* (July/August): 55–7.

Vanek, J. 1974. Time spent in housework. *Scientific American* (November): 116–21.

Vanek, J. 1980. Household work, wage work and sexual equality. In *Women and household labour*, ed. S. F. Berk, 275–95. Beverly Hills, Calif.: Sage.

Walker, K. E. 1970. *Time-use patterns for household work related to homemaker's employment.* Washington, DC: U.S. Department of Agriculture.

Walker, K. E., and M. E. Woods. 1976. *Time use: A measure of household production of family goods and services.* Washington, DC: Center for the Family of the American Home Economic Association.

White, L. K., and D. B. Brinkerhoff. 1981. Children's work in the family: Its significance and meaning. *Journal of Marriage and the Family*, 81: 789–98.

Wilson, S. J. 1991. *Women, families, and work,* 3rd ed. Toronto: McGraw-Hill Ryerson Limited.

Wolfe,. D. 1959. Power and authority in the family. In *Studies in social power*, ed. D. Cartwright. Ann Arbor, Mich.: University of Michigan Press.

Zaretsky, E. 1982. *Capitalism, the family & personal life.* London: Pluto Press.

51

Mate Selection and Marriage Around the World

Bron B. Ingoldsby

Family

CLASSIC

CONTEMPORARY

CROSS-CULTURAL

The institution of marriage is very popular throughout the world, but how mates are chosen varies considerably from one culture to another. As Bron B. Ingoldsby shows, free-choice mate selection—common in Western countries—is not how couples have been paired with their prospective spouses in most other societies.

MATE SELECTION PROCEDURES

Historically, there have been three general approaches to choosing one's mate: marriage by capture, marriage by arrangement, and free-choice mate selection. I examine each of them in turn.

Marriage by Capture

Although it has probably never been the usual method of obtaining a wife, men have taken women by force in many times and places. This typically occurred in patriarchal societies in which women were often considered property. Often women were seized as part of the spoils of war, and other times a specific woman was forced into marriage because the man wanted her and

could not afford the brideprice or obtain the permission of her parents. The capture and marriage of a woman was legal in England until the reign of Henry VII, who made it a crime to abduct an heiress (Fielding, 1942).

The ancient Hebrews would seize wives under certain circumstances. A dramatic example is recounted in the Old Testament (Judges, chapter 21), where it was arranged for young women to be kidnapped from two different areas to serve as wives so that the tribe of Benjamin would not die out after a war that they had lost.

There was also a formal procedure for dealing with wives captured in warfare:

When thou goest forth to war against thine enemies, and the Lord thy God hath delivered them into thine hands, and thou has taken them captive, And seest among the captives a beautiful woman, and hast a desire unto her, that thou wouldest have her to thy wife; Then thou shalt bring her home to thine house; and she shall shave her head, and pare her nails; And she shall put the raiment of her captivity from off her,

Source: "Mate Selection and Marriage," by Bron B. Ingoldsby, in *Families in Multicultural Perspective,* eds. Bron B. Ingoldsby and Suzanna Smith, pp. 143–57. Copyright © 1995 Guilford Press, NY. Reprinted by permission of Guilford Press.

and shall remain in thine house, and bewail her father and her mother a full month: and after that thou shalt go in unto her, and be her husband, and she shall be thy wife. And it shall be, if thou have no delight in her, then thou shalt let her go whither she will; but thou shalt not sell her at all for money, thou shalt not make merchandise of her, because thou has humbled her. (Deuteronomy 21: 10–14)

At least she was given time to get used to the idea and never sold into slavery! Fielding (1942) cites a number of different cultures, including the Australian aborigines, who frequently resorted to marriage by capture in the recent past. The Yanomamö of Venezuela (an Amazonian tribe) are reported (Peters, 1987) to use capture as one of their mate selection options. One village is often raided by another for the specific purpose of finding wives. If a man captures a young, attractive female, he must be careful as other men from his own village will try to steal her from him.

In the popular musical *Seven Brides for Seven Brothers,* the concept of marriage by capture is acted out, and one of the songs is based on the historical incident of the rape of the Sabine women. There are many cultures that still have remnants of the old practice of marriage by capture in their wedding ceremonies. In each of them, the match is prearranged, but the husband pretends to take his bride by force, and she feigns resistance.

One example are the Roro of New Guinea. On the wedding day, the groom's party surrounds the bride's home and acts out an assault on it. The bride attempts to run away but is caught. Then a sham battle ensues, with the bride's mother leading the way and crying at the loss of her daughter when she is taken off to the groom (Fielding, 1942).

Marriage by Arrangement

It appears that the most common method of mate selection has been by arrangement. Typically, the parents, often with the aid of certain relatives or professional matchmakers, have chosen the spouse for their child. This form of mate choice is more common when extended kin groups are strong and

important. Essentially, marriage is seen as of group, rather than individual, importance, and economics is often the driving force rather than love between the principals.

Arranged marriages have been considered especially important for the rulers of kingdoms and other nobility. Care had to be taken to preserve bloodlines, enhance wealth, and resolve political issues. It is believed, for instance, that the majority of King Solomon's 700 wives and 300 concubines were acquired for the purpose of political alliances.

Stephens (1963) identifies four major reasons that determine mate choice in societies in which marriages are arranged. The first is *price.* The groom's family may need to pay for the bride, with either money or labor. In some cultures, the situation is reversed, with the bride's family paying a dowry to the husband. In other cases, there is a direct exchange, where both families make payments to each other or simply trade women for each other's sons.

The second consideration is *social status.* That is, the reputation of the family from which the spouse for one's child will come is very important. A third determinant is any *continuous marriage arrangement.* This refers to a set pattern for mate selection, which is carried on from generation to generation. For instance, cousin marriages are preferred in many societies.

The final criteria for mate choice are *sororate and levirate* arrangements, which refer to second marriages and tend to be based on brideprice obligations. These terms are more fully explained later in the [reading]. Stephens also notes nineteen societies (including, for example, some large ones such as China and Renaissance Europe) that have practiced child betrothals or child marriages. This means that the marriage is arranged before puberty and can even be worked out before the child is born.

In addition to marriage by capture, the Yanomamö also practice variety within arranged marriages. The ideal match is between cross-cousins, and the majority of unions fall into this category. Most betrothals are made before the girl is three years of age. Men initiate these arrangements at about the time they become hunters, which is shortly after they turn fifteen. Another acceptable form of mate selection is sister exchange. Two unrelated single males wish to acquire wives and have sisters who are not promised to anyone, so they simply trade sisters (Peters, 1987).

Some societies have provided an "out" for couples who have strong personal preferences that go against the arrangement of their families. This is to permit elopement. Stephens (1963) gives this account of the Iban of Borneo:

When a young woman is in love with a man who is not acceptable to her parents, there is an old custom called *nunghop bui,* which permits him to carry her off to his own village. She will meet him by arrangement at the waterside, and step into his boat with a paddle in her hand, and both will pull away as fast as they can. If pursued he will stop every now and then to deposit some article of value on the bank, such as a gun, a jar, or a favor for the acceptance of her family, and when he has exhausted his resources he will leave his own sword. When the pursuers observe this they cease to follow, knowing he is cleared out. As soon as he reaches his own village he tidies up the house and spreads the mats, and when his pursuers arrive he gives them food to eat and toddy to drink, and sends them home satisfied. In the meanwhile he is left in possession of his wife. (p. 200)

Following is a detailed look at some of the specific mechanisms of arranged marriages.

Brideprice. Throughout much of human history, marriage has been seen as chiefly an economic transaction. As an old German saying goes, "It is not man that marries maid, but field marries field, vineyard marries vineyard, cattle marry cattle" (Tober, 1984: 12). The purpose of a brideprice is to compensate the family of the bride for the loss of her services. It is extremely common and is indicative of the value of women in those societies. Stephens (1963) reports that Murdock's World Ethnographic Sample yields the following breakdown on marriage payments:

Brideprice—260 societies
Bride service—75 societies
Dowry—24 societies
Gift or woman exchange—31 societies
No marriage payment—152 societies

This means that in 62 percent of the world's societies, a man must pay in order to marry a woman. The price is usually paid in animals, shell money, or other valuable commodities and often exceeds one's annual income. Some cultures prefer payment in service, often many years of labor to the bride's parents, or at least permit it for suitors who cannot afford to pay in goods. One famous example from the Old Testament is that of Jacob, who labored seven years for each of Laban's two daughters, Leah and Rachel.

Dowry. The dowry appears to be an inducement for a man to marry a particular woman and therefore relieve her family of the financial burden of caring for her. Although relatively rare, it is a sign of a culture that places a low value on women. Actually, the key purpose of a dowry is probably to stabilize a marriage, because it is not given to the husband but is something that the bride brings with her into the marriage. For example, in Cyprus before the time of English influence, the expected dowry was often a house. If the husband divorced his wife or mistreated her and she left him, the dowry went with her. Like modern-day wedding gifts, or the bride's trousseau, it was an investment in the marriage and intended to reduce the chances of a breakup (Balswick, 1975).

The dowry has been around for a long time. The Babylonian code of Hammurabi (1955 B.C.E.) clearly stated that the wife's property stayed with her if her husband divorced her and passed on to her children when she died. Ancient Greece and Rome also considered the dowry to be essential in any honorable marriage (Fielding, 1942).

Recent research in the southern Indian state of Kerala (Billig, 1992) differentiates between the traditional dowry and an actual "groomprice." Groomprice is money paid by the bride's family directly to the husband to use as he sees fit. In the 1950s and 1960s, rapid population growth resulted in more younger women looking for husbands a few (average of seven) years older than themselves. This surplus of potential brides increased the value of husbands. Popular revulsion for the groomprice has resulted in a decrease in the age difference (now five years), women lowering their social status expectations for their husband or increasing their own education, and a government outlawing of the practice.

Sororate and Levirate. These terms refer to marriage practices designed to control remarriages after the death of the first spouse. In cultures that practice the sororate, a sister replaces a deceased wife. Assume that a man has paid a good brideprice for his wife but some time later she becomes ill and dies. He has lost his wife and the brideprice. Therefore, to make good on the original bargain, the parents who received the brideprice provide the man with a new wife. This new wife is an unmarried sister or other close relative of the first wife. Here we see how marriage is often more of an economic transaction than it is a personal relationship.

Much more widely practiced has been the levirate. Under this system, it is the husband who dies, and his wife must be married to a brother of the deceased man. There are various reasons for this practice. One is that the wife belonged to her husband as part of his property and as such would be inherited along with the other possessions by a near relative. Another is that it is presumed that women need someone to take care of them, and brothers-in-law (which is the meaning of the Latin word *levir*) should assume that responsibility. It has been reported that the levirate has been practiced by the New Caledonians, the Mongols, the Afghans, the Abyssinians, the Hebrews, and the Hindus, as well as certain Native American and African tribes (Fielding, 1942).

The chief reason that the Hindus and Hebrews practiced the levirate was religious and had to do with the importance of having a son in the family.

Hindu men needed a son to perform certain sacrifices, so if a man died before having one, a boy born to his former wife and brother would carry out those ceremonies in his name (Fielding, 1942).

For the Hebrews, it was also important that every man have a son, so that his name would not die out. There was a ritualized penalty for men who refused to marry their brother's widow and rear a son in his name:

> And if the man like not to take his brother's wife, then let his brother's wife go up to the gate unto the elders, and say, My husband's brother refuseth to raise up unto his brother a name in Israel, he will not perform the duty of my husband's brother. Then the elders of his city shall call him, and speak unto him: and if he stand to it, and say, I like not to take her; Then shall his brother's wife come in to him in the presence of the elders, and loose his shoe from his foot, and spit in his face, and shall answer and say, So shall it be done unto that man that will not build up his brother's house. (Deuteronomy 25:7–9).

The punishment for refusing to practice the levirate used to be more severe than the above-quoted ritual. In Genesis, chapter 38, we read of Judah's son Onan and how he was killed by the Lord for refusing to impregnate his dead older brother's wife. The book of Ruth in the Old Testament is also an excellent example of how the levirate worked. It is an account of how Naomi has no more sons for her daughter-in-law Ruth to marry, so she arranges for another male relative, Boaz, to take on the responsibility.

Matchmaking. There are various ways in which two young people can be brought together. Typically, the parents of both boys and girls will work out the details among themselves and then announce it to their children. The initial go-between in Turkey has been the boy's mother, who would inspect possibilities at the public baths and then give reports to her son (Tober, 1984). The popular musical *Fiddler on the Roof* is about father-arranged marriages. Often, hired go-betweens, or matchmakers, assist in making the arrangement. They might act as intermediaries between the families or suggest potential spouses.

Checking for astrological or other religious signs and requirements could also be part of their job.

In the 1800s, bachelor pioneers in the American West would sometimes find a wife by ordering one from a mail-order catalog. Even today, many Asian families publish matrimonial want ads in search of a respectable spouse for their child (Tober, 1984). I recently found the following in the classified section of a Philippine newspaper:

Foreigner: video match a decent friendship marriage consultant office introducing a beautiful single educated Filipina view friendship to marriage.

Ladies: Australian European businessmen newly arrive in town sincerely willing to meet decent Filipina view friendship to marriage. Ambassador Hotel suite 216.

Computer dating services in the United States, Japan, and elsewhere manifest the continued utility of professional matchmaking, even in societies in which the individuals involved make the final decisions themselves. There are also magazines designed for singles that include matrimonial or relationship want ads.

There are immigrants to Western societies who are not comfortable with love-based unions and prefer to have their marriages arranged by their parents or through a mediator. It is estimated, for instance, that up to 90 percent of the marriages in the East Indian community in Edmonton, Alberta, are to some degree arranged (Jimenez, 1992). Some ethnic Indians return to the Indian subcontinent to find a spouse, whereas others allow their parents to find a match locally for them. Some place ads in newspapers such as *India Today* or *India Abroad,* which focus on desired background characteristics such as education, religion, and age. In deference to Western customs, the young people can veto any match that does not appeal to them, and a dowry is rarely accepted.

Free-Choice Mate Selection

…[L]ove gradually became the principal criterion for marriage in the Western world after the Renaissance. The shift from kinship and economic motives to personal ones in mate selection led to the conclusion that the individuals themselves, rather than their parents or others, were best qualified to make the decision. In societies in which the basic family unit is nuclear, both romantic love and free mate choice are more common. This is because extended kin groups are not important enough to see marriage as needing to be group controlled.

Even though free choice is the mate selection method of the modern United States, one should not conclude that it is the most common approach in the world. In a survey of forty societies, Stephens (1963) found only five in which completely free mate choice is permitted. An additional six allowed the young people to choose their spouse, but subject to parental approval. Twelve other cultures had a mix of arranged marriages and free-choice (usually subject to approval) unions, and the final sixteen allowed only arranged marriages.

Moreover, even free choice does not mean that one can marry anyone. All societies have marital regulations. The rule of *exogamy* declares that a person must marry outside his/her group. Typically, this means that certain relatives are unavailable as marriage partners. Exogamous rules are generally the same as the incest taboos of the society, which prohibit sexual intercourse between close blood relatives. Others go beyond that, however. In classical China, two people with the same surname could not marry even if there was no kinship relation (Hutter, 1981).

The rule of *endogamy* declares that a person must marry within his/her group. This rule applies social pressure to marry someone who is similar to oneself in important ways, including religion, race, or ethnic group; social class; and age. These factors have been found to be related to marital compatibility and are precisely the kinds of things considered by parents in arranged marriages. One reason why the divorce rate seems to be higher in free-choice societies may be that many couples ignore endogamy issues and allow romantic love to be practically the sole consideration in mate selection. There is a tendency for marriages to be fairly homogamous, however, even in free-mate-choice societies.

A final factor is *propinquity* (geographical nearness). It is, of course, impossible to marry someone who lives so far away from you that you never meet. At another level, however, this principle refers to a human tendency to be friends with people with whom it is convenient to interact. Let us say that you leave your hometown to attend college elsewhere. You left a boyfriend or girlfriend back at home and you also meet someone new at college. All other things being equal, which one will you marry? Generally, it will be the one at school simply because it is easier.

Some Examples. Free mate choice is on the rise in China today. However, it is very different from the courtship pattern in North America. Young people gather information about each other first and check for mutual suitability before going public with their relationship. In fact, dating follows, rather than precedes, the decision to marry. Typically, the couple knows each other for well over two years before marrying. This cautious approach is paying off, as the quality of these marriages seems to be higher than that of arranged unions (Liao & Heaton, 1992).

The Igbo are a people living in present-day Nigeria (Okonjo, 1992). About 55 percent of the Igbo have their marriages arranged, while the remaining 45 percent are in free-choice unions. Most of the latter are younger, indicating a move from arranged to free choice, which we see occurring throughout much of the world today. Regardless of type, premarital chastity is very highly valued among the Igbo.

As the Ibgo move to free mate choice based on love, their various arranged practices are falling into disfavor. Customs that are quickly disappearing include woman-to-woman marriage. In this situation, an older childless woman pays the brideprice to marry a younger female, usually a cousin. A male mate is chosen for the "wife" to have

children with, but they belong to the older female spouse, who has the legal role of "husband."

Another way of securing an heir is *father-to-daughter* marriage. If a man has no sons, he may prohibit a daughter from marrying. She has children from a male mate (not the father) but her sons are considered her father's. Women whose husbands turn out to be impotent are allowed to have a lover from whom to have children, who are considered to be the legal husband's. Other arranged practices seldom practiced anymore are the levirate and child marriages.

CRITICAL THINKING QUESTIONS

1. What four major issues influence mate choice in societies where marriages are arranged? What societal functions do the specific mechanisms of arranged marriages (such as brideprice, dowry, sororate, levirate, and matchmaking) fulfill?
2. Does marriage by free choice mean that a person can really marry *anyone?* What factors (or rules) considerably narrow the field of eligible mates in societies with free-choice mate selection?
3. What are the advantages and disadvantages of marrying for love (in free-choice societies) rather than economic or political considerations (in societies with arranged marriages)? Would marriages in North America be less likely to end in divorce if marriages were arranged?

REFERENCES

Balswick, J. 1975. The function of the dowry system in a rapidly modernizing society: The case of Cyprus. *International Journal of Sociology and the Family*, 5(2): 158–67.

Billig, M. 1992. The marriage squeeze and the rise of groom-price in India's Kerala state. *Journal of Comparative Family Studies*, 23(2): 197–216.

Fielding, W. 1942. *Strange customs of courtship and marriage.* New York: New Home Library.

The Holy Bible. King James Version.

Hutter, M. 1981. *The changing family: Comparative perspectives.* New York: Wiley.

Jimenez, M. 1992. Many Indo-Canadians follow age-old custom. *Edmonton Journal*, (July 26): B3.

Liao, C., and T. Heaton. 1992. Divorce trends and differentials in China. *Journal of Comparative Family Studies*, 23(3): 413–29.

Okonjo, K. 1992. Aspects of continuity and change in mate selection among the Igbo west of the river Niger. *Journal of Comparative Family Studies*, 23(3): 339–60.

Peters, J. 1987. Yanomamö mate selection and marriage. *Journal of Comparative Family Studies*, 18(1): 79–98.

Stephens, W. 1963. *The family in cross-cultural perspective.* New York: Holt, Rinehart & Winston.

Tober, B. 1984. *The bride: A celebration.* New York: Harry N. Abrams.

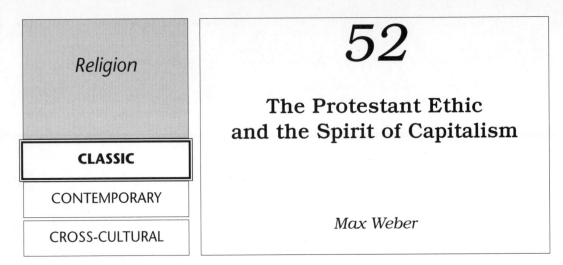

52

The Protestant Ethic and the Spirit of Capitalism

Max Weber

In perhaps his most well known treatise, Max Weber argues that a major factor in the development of the capitalist economic system was the distinctive world view of early, ascetic Protestantism, especially Calvinism and Puritanism. In this excerpt from his classic analysis, Weber explains that religious ideas about work and materials initially fostered capitalism's growth, but ultimately capitalism was able to stand on its own without religious supports.

A product of modern European civilization, studying any problem of universal history, is bound to ask himself to what combination of circumstances the fact should be attributed that in Western civilization, and in Western civilization only, cultural phenomena have appeared which (as we like to think) lie in a line of development having *universal* significance and value.... All over the world there have been merchants, wholesale and retail, local and engaged in foreign trade....

But in modern times the Occident has developed, in addition to this, a very different form of capitalism which has appeared nowhere else: the rational capitalistic organization of (formally) free labour. Only suggestions of

it are found elsewhere. Even the organization of unfree labour reached a considerable degree of rationality only on plantations and to a very limited extent in the *Ergasteria* of antiquity. In the manors, manorial workshops, and domestic industries on estates with serf labour it was probably somewhat less developed. Even real domestic industries with free labour have definitely been proved to have existed in only a few isolated cases outside the Occident....

Rational industrial organization, attuned to a regular market, and neither to political nor irrationally speculative opportunities for profit, is not, however, the only peculiarity of Western capitalism. The modern rational organization of the capitalistic enterprise would not have been possible without two other important factors in its development: the separation of business

Source: From *The Protestant Ethic and the Spirit of Capitalism* by Max Weber, copyright © 1988, Prentice-Hall, Inc. Reprinted by permission.

from the household, which completely dominates modern economic life, and closely connected with it, rational book-keeping....

Hence in a universal history of culture the central problem for us is not, in the last analysis, even from a purely economic view-point, the development of capitalistic activity as such, differing in different cultures only in form: the adventurer type, or capitalism in trade, war, politics, or administration as sources of gain. It is rather the origin of this sober bourgeois capitalism with its rational organization of free labour. Or in terms of cultural history, the problem is that of the origin of the Western bourgeois class and of its peculiarities, a problem which is certainly closely connected with that of the origin of the capitalistic organization of labour, but is not quite the same thing. For the bourgeois as a class existed prior to the development of the peculiar modern form of capitalism, though, it is true, only in the Western hemisphere.

Now the peculiar modern Western form of capitalism has been, at first sight, strongly influenced by the development of technical possibilities. Its rationality is today essentially dependent on the calculability of the most important technical factors. But this means fundamentally that it is dependent on the peculiarities of modern science, especially the natural sciences based on mathematics and exact and rational experiment. On the other hand, the development of these sciences and of the technique resting upon them now receives important stimulation from these capitalistic interests in its practical economic application. It is true that the origin of Western science cannot be attributed to such interests. Calculation, even with decimals, and algebra have been carried on in India, where the decimal system was invented. But it was only made use of by developing capitalism in the West, while in India it led to no modern arithmetic or book-keeping. Neither was the origin of mathematics and mechanics determined by capitalistic interests. But the *technical* utilization of scientific knowledge, so important for the living conditions of the mass of people,

was certainly encouraged by economic considerations, which were extremely favourable to it in the Occident. But this encouragement was derived from the peculiarities of the social structure of the Occident. We must hence ask, from *what* parts of that structure was it derived, since not all of them have been of equal importance?

Among those of undoubted importance are the rational structures of law and of administration. For modern rational capitalism has need, not only of the technical means of production, but of a calculable legal system and of administration in terms of formal rules. Without it adventurous and speculative trading capitalism and all sorts of politically determined capitalisms are possible, but no rational enterprise under individual initiative, with fixed capital and certainty of calculations. Such a legal system and such administration have been available for economic activity in a comparative state of legal and formalistic perfection only in the Occident. We must hence inquire where that law came from. Among other circumstances, capitalistic interests have in turn undoubtedly also helped, but by no means alone nor even principally, to prepare the way for the predominance in law and administration of a class of jurists specially trained in rational law. But these interests did not themselves create that law. Quite different forces were at work in this development. And why did not the capitalistic interests do the same in China or India? Why did not the scientific, the artistic, the political, or the economic development there enter upon that path of rationalization which is peculiar to the Occident?

For in all the above cases it is a question of the specific and peculiar rationalism of Western culture.... It is hence our first concern to work out and to explain genetically the special peculiarity of Occidental rationalism, and within this field that of the modern Occidental form. Every such attempt at explanation must, recognizing the fundamental importance of the economic factor, above all take account of the economic conditions. But at the same time the opposite correlation must not be left out of consideration. For though the development of economic rationalism is partly dependent on rational technique and law, it is at the same time determined by the ability and disposition of men to adopt certain types of practical rational conduct. When these types have been obstructed by spiritual obstacles, the development of rational economic conduct has also met serious inner resistance. The magical and religious forces, and the ethical ideas of duty based upon them, have in the past always been among the most important formative influences on conduct. In the studies collected here we shall be concerned with these forces.

Two older essays have been placed at the beginning which attempt, at one important point, to approach the side of the problem which is generally most difficult to grasp: the influence of certain religious ideas on the development of an economic spirit, or the *ethos* of an economic system. In this case we are dealing with the connection of the spirit of modern economic life with the rational ethics of ascetic Protestantism. Thus we treat here only one side of the causal chain....

...[T]hat side of English Puritanism which was derived from Calvinism gives the most consistent religious basis for the idea of the calling.... For the saints' everlasting rest is in the next world; on earth man must, to be certain of his state of grace, "do the works of him who sent him, as long as it is yet day." Not leisure and enjoyment, but only activity serves to increase the glory of God according to the definite manifestations of His will.

Waste of time is thus the first and in principle the deadliest of sins. The span of human life is infinitely short and precious to make sure of one's own election. Loss of time through sociability, idle talk, luxury, even more sleep than is necessary for health, six to at most eight hours, is worthy of absolute moral condemnation. It does not yet hold, with Franklin, that time is money, but the proposition is true in a certain spiritual sense. It is infinitely valuable because every hour lost is lost to labour for the glory of God. Thus inactive contemplation is also valueless, or even directly reprehensible if it is at the expense of one's daily work....

[T]he same prescription is given for all sexual temptation as is used against religious doubts and a sense of moral unworthiness: "Work hard in your calling." But the most important thing was that even beyond that labour came to be considered in itself the end of life, ordained as such by God. St. Paul's "He who will not work shall not eat" holds unconditionally for everyone. Unwillingness to work is symptomatic of the lack of grace.

Here the difference from the mediæval viewpoint becomes quite evident. Thomas Aquinas also gave an interpretation of that statement of St. Paul. But for him labour is only necessary *naturali ratione* for the maintenance of individual and community. Where this end is achieved, the precept ceases to have any meaning. Moreover, it holds only for the race, not for every individual. It does not apply to anyone who can live without labour on his possessions, and of course contemplation, as a spiritual form of action in the Kingdom of God, takes precedence over the commandment in its literal sense. Moreover, for the popular theology of the time, the highest form of monastic productivity lay in the increase of the *Thesaurus eccleslæ* through prayer and chant.

...For everyone without exception God's Providence has prepared a calling, which he should profess and in which he should labour. And this calling is not, as it was for the Lutheran, a fate to which he must submit and which he must make the best of, but God's commandment to the individual to work for the divine glory. This seemingly subtle difference had far-reaching psychological consequences, and became connected with a further development of the providential interpretation of the economic order which had begun in scholasticism.

It is true that the usefulness of a calling, and thus its favour in the sight of God, is measured primarily in moral terms, and thus in terms of the importance of the goods produced in it for the community. But a further, and, above all, in practice the most important, criterion is found in private profitableness. For if that God, whose hand the Puritan sees in all the occurrences of life, shows one of His elect a chance of profit, he must do it with a purpose. Hence the faithful Christian must follow the call by taking advantage of the opportunity. "If God show you a way in which you may lawfully get more than in another way (without wrong to your soul or to any other), if you refuse this, and choose the less gainful way, you cross one of the ends of your calling, and you refuse to be God's steward, and to accept His gifts and use them for Him when He requireth it: you may labour to be rich for God, though not for the flesh and sin."…

The superior indulgence of the *seigneur* and the parvenu ostentation of the *nouveau riche* are equally detestable to asceticism. But, on the other hand, it has the highest ethical appreciation of the sober, middle-class, self-made man. "God blesseth His trade" is a stock remark about those good men who had successfully followed the divine hints. The whole power of the God of the Old Testament, who rewards His people for their obedience in this life, necessarily exercised a similar influence on the Puritan who…compared his own state of grace with that of the heroes of the Bible.…

Although we cannot here enter upon a discussion of the influence of Puritanism in all…directions, we should call attention to the fact that the toleration of pleasure in cultural goods, which contributed to purely aesthetic or athletic enjoyment, certainly always ran up against one characteristic limitation: They must not cost anything. Man is only a trustee of the goods which have come to him through God's grace. He must, like the servant in the parable, give an account of every penny entrusted to him, and it is at least hazardous to spend any of it for a purpose which does not serve the glory of God but only one's own enjoyment. What person, who keeps his eyes open, has not met representatives of this viewpoint even in the present? The idea of a man's duty to his possessions, to which he subordinates himself as an obedient steward, or even as an acquisitive machine, bears with chilling weight on his life. The greater the possessions the heavier, if the ascetic attitude toward life stands the

test, the feeling of responsibility for them, for holding them undiminished for the glory of God and increasing them by restless effort. The origin of this type of life also extends in certain roots, like so many aspects of the spirit of capitalism, back into the Middle Ages. But it was in the ethic of ascetic Protestantism that it first found a consistent ethical foundation. Its significance for the development of capitalism is obvious.

This worldly Protestant asceticism, as we may recapitulate up to this point, acted powerfully against the spontaneous enjoyment of possessions; it restricted consumption, especially of luxuries. On the other hand, it had the psychological effect of freeing the acquisition of goods from the inhibitions of traditionalistic ethics. It broke the bonds of the impulse of acquisition in that it not only legalized it, but (in the sense discussed) looked upon it as directly willed by God.…

As far as the influence of the Puritan outlook extended, under all circumstances—and this is, of course, much more important than the mere encouragement of capital accumulation—it favoured the development of a rational bourgeois economic life; it was the most important, and above all the only consistent influence in the development of that life. It stood at the cradle of the modern economic man.

To be sure, these Puritanical ideals tended to give way under excessive pressure from the temptations of wealth, as the Puritans themselves knew very well. With great regularity we find the most genuine adherents of Puritanism among the classes which were rising from a lowly status, the small bourgeois and farmers while the *beati possidentes,* even among Quakers, are often found tending to repudiate the old ideals. It was the same fate which again and again befell the predecessor of this worldly asceticism, the monastic asceticism of the Middle Ages. In the latter case, when rational economic activity had worked out its full effects by strict regulation of conduct and limitation of consumption, the wealth accumulated either succumbed directly to the nobility, as in the time before the Reformation, or monastic discipline threatened to break down, and one of the numerous reformations became necessary.

In fact the whole history of monasticism is in a certain sense the history of a continual struggle with the problem of the secularizing influence of wealth. The same is true on a grand scale of the worldly asceticism of Puritanism. The great revival of Methodism, which preceded the expansion of English industry toward the end of the eighteenth century, may well be compared with such a monastic reform. We may hence quote here a passage from John Wesley himself which might well serve as a motto for everything which has been said above. For it shows that the leaders of these ascetic movements understood the seemingly paradoxical relationships which we have here analysed perfectly well, and in the same sense that we have given them. He wrote:

I fear, wherever riches have increased, the essence of religion has decreased in the same proportion. Therefore I do not see how it is possible, in the nature of things, for any revival of true religion to continue long. For religion must necessarily produce both industry and frugality, and these cannot but produce riches. But as riches increase, so will pride, anger, and love of the world in all its branches. How then is it possible that Methodism, that is, a religion of the heart, though it flourishes now as a green bay tree, should continue in this state? For the Methodists in every place grow diligent and frugal; consequently they increase in goods. Hence they proportionately increase in pride, in anger, in the desire of the flesh, the desire of the eyes, and the pride of life. So, although the form of religion remains, the spirit is swiftly vanishing away. Is there no way to prevent this—this continual decay of pure religion? We ought not to prevent people from being diligent and frugal; *we must exhort all Christians to gain all they can, and to save all they can; that is, in effect, to grow rich.*

As Wesley here says, the full economic effect of those great religious movements, whose significance for economic development lay above all in their ascetic educative influence, generally came only after the peak of the purely religious enthusiasm was past. Then the intensity of the search for the Kingdom of God commenced gradually to pass over into sober economic virtue; the religious roots died out slowly, giving way to utilitarian worldliness. Then, as Dowden puts it, as in *Robinson Crusoe,* the isolated economic man who carries on missionary activities on the side takes the place of the lonely spiritual search for the Kingdom of Heaven of Bunyan's pilgrim, hurrying through the market-place of Vanity....

A specifically bourgeois economic ethic had grown up. With the consciousness of standing in the fullness of God's grace and being visibly blessed by Him, the bourgeois business man, as long as he remained within the bounds of formal correctness, as long as his moral conduct was spotless and the use to which he put his wealth was not objectionable, could follow his pecuniary interests as he would and feel that he was fulfilling a duty in doing so. The power of religious asceticism provided him in addition with sober, conscientious, and unusually industrious workmen, who clung to their work as to a life purpose willed by God.

Finally, it gave him the comforting assurance that the unequal distribution of the goods of this world was a special dispensation of Divine Providence, which in these differences, as in particular grace, pursued secret ends unknown to men....

One of the fundamental elements of the spirit of modern capitalism, and not only of that but of all modern culture: Rational conduct on the basis of the idea of the calling, was born—that is what this discussion has sought to demonstrate—from the spirit of Christian asceticism. One has only to re-read the passage from Franklin, quoted at the beginning of this essay, in order to see that the essential elements of the attitude which was there called the spirit of capitalism are the same as what we have just shown to be the content of the Puritan worldly asceticism, only without the religious basis, which by Franklin's time had died away....

Since asceticism undertook to remodel the world and to work out its ideals in the world, material goods have gained an increasing and finally an inexorable power over the lives of men as at no previous period in history. Today the spirit of religious asceticism—whether finally, who knows?—has escaped from the cage. But victorious capitalism, since it rests on mechanical foundations, needs its support no longer. The rosy blush of its laughing heir, the Enlightenment, seems also to be irretrievably fading, and the idea of duty in one's calling prowls about in our lives like the ghost of dead religious beliefs. Where the fulfilment of the calling cannot directly be related to the highest spiritual and cultural values, or when, on the other hand, it need not be felt simply as economic compulsion, the individual generally abandons the attempt to justify it at all. In the field of its highest development, in the United States, the pursuit of wealth, stripped of its religious and ethical meaning, tends to become associated with purely mundane passions, which often actually give it the character of sport.

No one knows who will live in this cage in the future, or whether at the end of this tremendous development entirely new prophets will arise, or there will be a great rebirth of old ideas and ideals, or, if neither, mechanized petrification, embellished with a sort of convulsive self-importance. For of the last stage of this cultural development, it might well be truly said: "Specialists without spirit, sensualists without heart; this nullity imagines that it has attained a level of civilization never before achieved."

But this brings us to the world of judgments of value and of faith, with which this purely historical discussion need not be burdened....

Here we have only attempted to trace the fact and the direction of its influence to their motives in one, though a very important point. But it would also further be necessary to investigate how Protestant Asceticism was in turn influenced in its development and its character by the totality of social conditions, especially economic. The modern man is in general, even with the best will, unable to give religious ideas a significance for culture and national character which they deserve. But it is, of course, not my aim to substitute for a one-sided materialistic an equally one-sided spiritualistic causal interpretation of culture and of history. Each is equally possible, but each, if it does not serve as the preparation, but as the conclusion of an investigation, accomplishes equally little in the interest of historical truth.

CRITICAL THINKING QUESTIONS

1. What are the distinctive characteristics of the religious orientation that Weber called the "Protestant ethic"? In what ways did those characteristics promote the development of the capitalist economic system?
2. In what respects do early Calvinists with a "calling" differ from today's "workaholics"?
3. In what sense does Weber's analysis differ from the materialist orientation of Karl Marx (Reading 43), who suggested that productive forces shape the world of ideas?

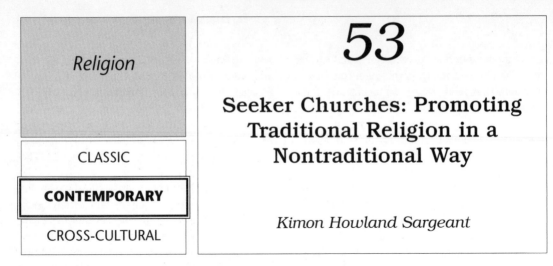

Religion

CLASSIC

CONTEMPORARY

CROSS-CULTURAL

53

Seeker Churches: Promoting Traditional Religion in a Nontraditional Way

Kimon Howland Sargeant

Seeker churches are different in style and form—but not in message—from conventional religious organizations. These new religious organizations are attracting an increasing number of people, especially among baby boomers.

Spirituality is booming in America, as any review of bestseller lists or even public television specials will show. Spiritual seekers are no longer found only among the rare free spirits but represent a growing proportion of the population, especially among members of the baby-boom generation. One reason for this is that the increase of religious pluralism in our society since changes in the immigration laws in 1965 has expanded the cafeteria of religious choices greatly. As a result, the religious landscape of America is not the same as it was a generation ago.

In this dynamic environment, evangelical churches are finding creative ways to attract seekers to churches with a conservative theology by packaging that theology in an innovative, contemporary form. Of course, religious dynamism and vitality are not new in American life; they have characterized American religion from…eighteenth-century Great Awakening to contemporary figures such as Billy Graham and…innovative evangelical churches.… What is new, according to

many observers of the American religious scene, is a very different cultural environment in which these religious innovators must operate. Put simply, consumerism has become a predominant characteristic of American religion.

Consider Mill Pond Fellowship. Pastor John Nelson was raised in a Free Methodist church and now is head pastor of Mill Pond Fellowship, a rapidly growing Free Methodist church in the suburbs of a city in the Pacific Northwest. While Nelson has remained faithful to the denomination of his youth, his church is drastically different from the one in which he was raised. Although certain aspects of the Free Methodist tradition—in particular an emphasis on small groups—play an important role at Mill Pond Fellowship, Nelson finds that, in general, the traditional Free Methodist church is unsuitable in today's religious environment. "The church I grew up in," asserts Nelson, "was small, legalistic, and dogmatic." When he decided in the late 1980s to start a church, Nelson's vision was to design a service that would appeal to those who were not attending church. His goal was "to throw out tradition [and] stay tuned to the unconvinced." Mill Pond Fellowship was therefore intentionally designed to be radically different in style and form—but not in message—from the church of Nelson's youth. The result is an unconventional, and very popular, format. The church features contemporary music, a live band, dramas, and an informal and theatrical style that attracts people who might not otherwise attend. At a communion service, for example, Mill Pond's band played the Rod Stewart song "Have I Told You that I Love You"; on Easter, it played the Eagles' song "Desperado." Such informal and contemporary services have met with an enthusiastic response. In 1989, seven families founded the church. By 1999, over one thousand people attended each weekend. Despite its Free Methodist affiliation, Mill Pond Fellowship has more in common with the large, primarily nondenominational churches that are emerging across the country than with the small, denominational, neighborhood church of Nelson's youth.

Mill Pond Fellowship is an example of an influential trend within evangelical Protestantism: the emergence of the seeker church. A seeker church is one that tailors its programs and services to attract people who are not church attenders. The most prominent seeker church in the United States is Willow Creek Community Church, the self-proclaimed "largest church in America," which attracts more than fifteen thousand people from suburban Chicago to its services every weekend. This "modern American cathedral"—so described by ABC News anchor Peter Jennings—features an attractive winding drive around a picturesque lake, and a forty-five-hundred-seat theater offering a concert-quality "seeker service" complete with live band, professional lighting and sound, dramatic presentations, and topical messages on practical concerns. Large, contemporary churches such as Willow Creek represent one of the most influential movements within American Protestantism. They also offer the hope to many pastors that churches that revise their traditional outreach strategies can grow dramatically.

Across the country, hundreds and even thousands of pastors are flocking to seminars to learn more about the seeker church approach to ministry, which has led prominent seeker churches to boast impressive growth rates that inspire awe among pastors and breed confidence among evangelicals regarding the church's mission to American society. In fact, many pastors believe that the seeker model holds great promise for reinvigorating American church life. What is not promising, say seeker church leaders, is the use of old forms to reach a new generation of seekers. Yale philosopher Nicholas Wolterstorff provides an example of the old forms that seeker church leaders reject in his recollections of growing up in the Dutch Reformed Church:

> We "dressed up" on the Lord's Day, dressed up *for* the Lord's Day, and entered church well in advance of the beginning of the service to collect ourselves in silence, silence so intense it could be touched.... We faced forward, looking at the Communion table front center, and behind that the raised pulpit. Before I understood a word of what was said, I was inducted by [the church's] architecture into the tradition. Every service included psalms, always sung, often to the Genevan tunes. There was no fear of repetition. The view that only the fresh and innovative is meaningful had not invaded this transplant of the Dutch Reformed tradition in Bigelow, Minnesota. Through repetition, elements of the liturgy and of Scripture sank their roots so deep into consciousness that nothing thereafter, short of senility, could remove them. During the liturgy as a whole, but especially in the sermon and most of all in the Lord's Supper, I was confronted by the speech and actions of an awesome, majestic God.

It is this kind of repetition, the hallmark of the traditional Protestant (and Catholic) service—this cycle of liturgy, and silence, and chant; this encounter with symbolic action and architecture—that pastors such as John Nelson want to "throw out."

THROWING OUT TRADITION

Innovative, customer-sensitive church programming is blossoming in evangelical churches across America. Saddleback Valley Community Church, for example, has grown to more than nine thousand attenders in the fifteen years since it was founded in Orange County, California; the church only recently completed its first building. Weekly services were held for many years in a large tent located on land the church had purchased. When it first sought to attract attenders, Saddleback mailed invitations to local residents, informing them. "We're a group of happy, friendly people who have discovered the joy of the Christian lifestyle." Saddleback's services are lively, upbeat, and contemporary—remarkably similar in feel to the worship style at Willow Creek. Saddleback's messages focus on applying Christianity to daily life; the church even provides fill-in-the-blank outlines to help attenders follow the sermon. Saddleback calls itself a "purpose-driven church" and it now sponsors seminars at the church and across the country that teach other pastors the principles that are the basis for its success. Senior Pastor Rick Warren confidently instructs seminar participants that "when the church is balanced around the five New Testament principles (worship, ministry, evangelism, fellowship, and discipleship), then growth is automatic." He also adds that the more pastors "target [their] community, the more effective [they] will be. Along with Bill Hybels, Warren is one of the most influential—and in-demand—seeker church pastors in the country. Warren was prominently featured as a speaker at Willow Creek's 1997 "Leadership Summit" conference.

Another innovative church is Houston's twenty-two-thousand-member Second Baptist, known as "Exciting Second," which was profiled on National Public Radio. Second Baptist Senior Pastor Dr. H. Edwin Young has instructed his staff to find ways to make the church more "user-friendly" by studying the strategies of theme parks like Disney World. Young is not apologetic about his unabashed borrowing from successful secular models. "I take what is worldly," says Dr. Young, "and baptize it." Exciting Second's marketing efforts are clearly paying off: the church has an annual budget of over sixteen million dollars. It sponsors sixty-four softball teams and forty-eight basketball teams and fields eighty-four teams in other sports such as volleyball, soccer, and flag football. The locus for all this excitement is the church's Family Life Center, which includes six bowling lanes, two basketball courts, an indoor jogging track, racquetball courts, and weight and aerobics rooms, as well as a music wing for its orchestra and five-hundred-member choir. Despite some criticisms of its marketing-based approach to outreach, Second Baptist is unapologetic. "People think because we're a church, maybe we shouldn't market," says Gary Moore, Second Baptist's music minister. "But any organization, secular or otherwise, if [it's] going to grow, [it's] got to get people to buy into the product."

In Michigan, Kensington Community Church advertised its services by mailing out glossy advertising flyers, which featured a picture of the senior pastor in hunting paraphernalia. The caption read: "Is a guy who shoots ducks worthy of your time on Sunday?" This quirky ad campaign garnered local media attention, and within two years Kensington Community Church had more than thirteen hundred people attending its weekend seeker services. CrossWinds Church in northern California has grown phenomenally as well. By incorporating the musical style of the area's most popular radio station into a seeker-friendly format, CrossWinds has attracted more than fifteen hundred attenders to a refurbished old warehouse, the site of its weekend seeker service.

The extraordinary success of these new churches has even inspired other, more traditional churches to modify their basic format. First Baptist Church of Van Nuys, California, changed its name to Shepherd of the Hills Church, dropping the word "Baptist" from its official title. Why? "People just don't like denominational tags anymore. All they want to know is, 'What's in it for me?'" says the Reverend Jess Moody. A new six-million-dollar building features beamed ceilings, a stained-glass "hayloft" over the entrance, and a giant stone fireplace equipped for cooking breakfasts. Meanwhile, the Reverend Moody has renovated his teaching style, banishing all references to hellfire and damnation from his preaching. Also missing are many of the standard terms of Christian theology. "If we use the words redemption or conversion," Moody says, "they think we're talking about bonds." Moody sells a special version of the Bible called "Kwikscan," which highlights essential passages in boldface and requires no more than thirty half-hour sittings to read from Genesis to Revelation.

Community Church of Joy in suburban Phoenix beckons to passersby with its immense front sign that reads "Welcome to Joy." The church features electric guitars instead of organs and offers worship services to fit a variety of tastes: a Saturday night country music service; a traditional Sunday morning service with a large choir; and a contemporary service with upbeat popstyle music. What the Community Church of Joy does not proclaim too loudly is its religious heritage. As one attender admitted, "We probably came here for a year before we knew it was Lutheran." Like the Community Church of Joy, the Discovery Church in Orlando, Florida, also wanted to become more inviting to seekers. To this end, it not only changed its name but also dropped its affiliation with the Southern Baptist Convention.

Innovation that pays attention to what attracts today's religious customer—and where that customer shops—is becoming more commonplace. In Minneapolis, the three-thousand-member Wooddale Church of Eden Prairie has taken church to the consumer by initiating a special service in the rotunda between Bloomingdale's and Sears at the Mall of America, the largest mall in the world. Other seeker congregations attempt to draw in the crowds by emphasizing just how different they are from traditional churches. For example, at Shiloh Crossing Community Church

("A Celebrating United Methodist Church for Contemporary People") outside Indianapolis, visitors are given ten reasons to "check out" the service. This list includes:

Great upbeat music;

Casual dress (no ties, please!);

Professional multimedia and video presentations;

Practical encouraging messages that relate to life in the real world; and

You'll get a lift for your week.

Another church offers reasons why you would *not* want to attend a typical church service. At Daybreak Community Church in Michigan, for example, one seeker service featured a David Letterman–style "Top Ten List of Things to Do During a Boring Sermon." The inventory included picking a scab, learning a foreign language, and, at the top, "mining for nose noogies." The implicit message of this irreverent skit was that the pastors of Daybreak would never deliver a boring sermon.

Other churches are likewise aware of the dangers of dull preaching and the benefits of humor. Heartland Community Church in Kansas, for example, once dedicated a service to the "Real World Series," during which a local baseball announcer teamed up with the pastor to do the "play-by-play" for the Team of Faith, starring Enoch as pitcher and Abraham behind the plate. Discovery United Methodist Church in Richmond, Virginia, promises its visitors that they will experience "the most refreshing hour of [their] week." For younger visitors, Discovery has also developed an extensive collection of live animals, which regularly appear in church. The Sunday before Thanksgiving, for example, "Tom Turkey" was the guest of honor.

NEW METHODS FOR A NEW MILLENNIUM

What these and hundreds of other churches across the country have in common is that they are all committed to using innovative methods, frequently drawn from marketing principles, to reach those who currently do not attend church. This broad movement, unlike previous movements within Protestantism that were associated with a particular theology (such as neo-Orthodoxy or fundamentalism or the Social Gospel), is not defined by doctrine or denominational affiliation. Instead, the seeker church movement is distinguished by its emphasis on a particular methodology. The "tradition" that seeker church pastors want to throw out is not the belief in the authority of the Bible or the divinity of Christ, but the form of the church in which they were raised.

Although traditional in their theology, many seeker church pastors are discovering that new methods often succeed in attracting to church people who otherwise might not come to a traditional church. These methods include an emphasis on contemporary music and on practical messages; providing excellent child care; featuring a wide variety of choice in small groups and other ministries; creating an informal atmosphere; and deemphasizing denominational identity. Pastors are not inventing these new approaches on their own. They receive training from the many conferences, books, and resource materials available today. These resources are overwhelmingly concerned with methods and programs that have proven successful in attracting baby boomers to church. Thus, when pastors flock to conferences at Willow Creek or Saddleback, they are interested primarily in methodology, not theology. They are looking for practical marketing suggestions, not theological justifications.

What do churches such as Willow Creek, Saddleback, and Mill Pond Fellowship have in common? In addition to their respective commitments to helping the church reach people more effectively, they share certain assumptions about the role of the church in society, such as: a commitment to Christian renewal through the local church (often a megachurch) rather than through politics, the culture, the denomination, or even parachurch organizations; a commitment to evangelism as the primary mission of the church; and finally, a commitment to "using the insights and tools of the behavioral sciences to aid effective evangelism."

This movement to revamp the church's form and methods is both diffuse and diverse. Numerous large churches, consultants, marketing experts, denominational leaders, parachurch organizations, and representatives from specific churches (especially Willow Creek) all participate. While there is not *one* single model that the various proponents of the "new paradigm" church recommend, many church growth analogies draw from the marketplace where large, specialized institutions compete to meet customers' needs. Thus, seeker church experts often proclaim the shopping mall, Disney, and other customer-sensitive companies as models for the twenty-first-century church.

In order to offer the services that attract seekers, many church growth consultants advise pastors to build big churches. One such consultant, Lyle Schaller, claims that the rise of megachurches (generally defined as churches with more than two thousand attenders) is one of the "most significant changes taking place in American Protestantism in the second half of the twentieth century." Schaller estimates that "between 1950 and 1990, the number of Protestant congregations averaging more than eight hundred at worship has at least tripled and perhaps quintupled."

Some seeker church leaders emphasize the importance of having a distinct seeker service, while others claim that a clear vision for the church and how it intends to assimilate newcomers is essential. Almost all stress the importance of using contemporary music and other forms of modern communication technology. Additionally, all seeker churches and their leaders share one common understanding—the church in American society today is facing a crisis so fundamental that, unless it radically alters its approach to those outside its doors, it will become increasingly irrelevant. The proper response to this crisis, say seeker church leaders, is to initiate a "paradigm shift" in the church's philosophy of ministry.

Congregations, many pastors claim, must abandon traditional methods and aggressively recast themselves in ways that are more inviting to today's religious seekers. Simply tinkering with the traditional methods will not do. The new millennium requires new forms of church.

CRITICAL THINKING QUESTIONS

1. What specific differences set off seeker churches from conventional churches? What factors are common to both?
2. In what ways do seeker churches try to "market" themselves to people by meeting their individual needs?
3. On the whole, do you favour the development of seeker churches? Why or why not?

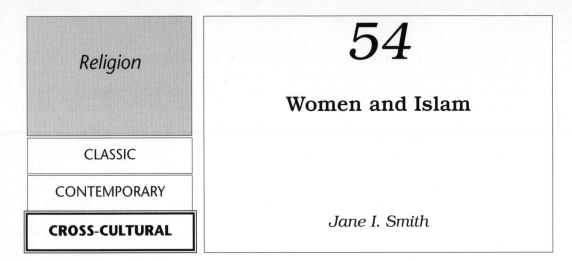

54

Women and Islam

Religion

CLASSIC

CONTEMPORARY

CROSS-CULTURAL

Jane I. Smith

Many Westerners have a vague notion that women in Iran, Saudi Arabia, and other Islamic societies are relentlessly controlled by men. Although this stereotype has some truth, a more realistic account of the relationship between Islam and the sexes must begin with a basic understanding of this unfamiliar religion. In this article, Jane Smith provides an overview of Islamic tenets, explores some of the variations that divide the vast Islamic world, and assesses the relative social standing of the sexes—as Muslims themselves understand it.

To attempt to talk about women in Islam is of course to venture into an area fraught with the perils of overgeneralization, oversimplification, and the almost unavoidable limitations of a Western bias. The first problem is simply one of raw numbers. There are perhaps close to half a billion Muslim women inhabiting all major areas of the world today. Is it possible to say anything that holds true for all of them, let alone for their sisters over the past fourteen centuries of Islam?

Then one must consider all the various elements that comprise the picture of Islamic womanhood. Many of these elements are directly related to the religion of Islam itself, such as past and present legal realities, roles permitted and enforced as a result of Muslim images of women, and the variety of Islamic and hetero-Islamic rites and practices in which

Islamic women have traditionally participated. Other elements contributing to the full picture of women in Islam—such as education, political rights, professional employment opportunities, and the like—have less to do with the religion per se but are still influenced by it.

The Holy Qur'ān (sometimes transliterated as "Koran") still forms the basis of prevailing family law in most areas of the Muslim world. It has always been and still is considered to be the last in a series of divine revelations from God given in the seventh century C.E. to humanity through the vehicle of his final prophet Muhammad. The Qur'ān is therefore the literal and unmitigated word of God, collected and ordered by the young Muslim community but untainted with the thoughts and interpretations of any persons, including Muhammad himself. It is obvious, then, why the regulations formulated by the Qur'ān in regard to women have been adhered to with strictness and why changes in Muslim family law are coming about only very slowly in the Islamic world.

Source: Reprinted by permission of the State University of New York Press, from *Women in World Religions* by Arvind Sharma and Katherine K. Young (eds.), © State University of New York. All rights reserved.

The circumstances of women in pre-Islamic Arabia are subject to a variety of interpretations. On the one hand, certain women—soothsayers, priestesses, queens, and even singular individuals—did play powerful roles in society. On the other hand, whatever the earlier realities for women in terms of marriage, divorce, and inheritance of property, it is clear that the Qur'ān did introduce very significant changes that were advantageous for women. Contemporary Muslims are fond of pointing out, quite correctly, that Islam brought legal advantages for women quite unknown in corresponding areas of the Western Christian world. What, then, does the Qur'ān say about women?

The earliest messages of the Qur'ān, and the twin themes that run through all the chapters, are of the realities of the oneness of God and the inevitability of the day of judgment. All persons, men and women, are called upon to testify to those realities.... Religiously speaking, then, men and women are fully equal in the eyes of God according to the Qur'ān.

Before looking at the specifics of the legal injunctions for women, it is necessary to consider two verses that have caused a great deal of consternation to Westerners. One is 2:228, which says literally that men are a step above women, and the other is 4:34, clarifying that men are the protectors of women (or are in charge of women) because God has given preference to one over the other and because men provide support for women. Perhaps because these verses have been so troublesome for non-Muslims (especially feminists), they have been subject to an enormous amount of explanation and interpretation by contemporary Muslim apologists eager to present a defense of their religion. These writers, men and women, affirm that it is precisely because men are invested with the responsibility of taking care of women, financially and otherwise, that they are given authority over the females of their families. And that, affirm many Muslim women today, is exactly the way it should be. We will return to

this perspective later, particularly in light of what a desire for liberation means—and does not mean—for many Muslim women....

According to the Qur'ān, a man may marry up to four wives, so long as he is able to provide for each equally. He may marry a Muslim woman or a member of the Jewish or Christian faith, or a slave woman. A Muslim woman, however, may marry only one husband, and he must be a Muslim. Contemporary Muslim apologists are quick to point out that these restrictions are for the benefit of women, ensuring that they will not be left unprotected. In Islam, marriage is not a sacrament but a legal contract, and according to the Qur'ān a woman has clearly defined legal rights in negotiating this contract. She can dictate the terms and can receive the dowry herself. This dowry (*mahr*) she is permitted to keep and maintain as a source of personal pride and comfort.

Polygamy (or more strictly polygyny, plurality of wives) is practiced by only a small percentage of the contemporary Muslim population, and a man with more than two wives is extremely rare. Many countries are now taking steps to modify the circumstances in which a husband may take more than one wife, although only in two countries, Turkey and Tunisia, are multiple marriages actually illegal. Other countries have made such moves as requiring the husband to have the permission of the court (as in Iraq and Syria) or to get the permission of the first wife (as in Egypt), or permitting the wife to write into her marriage contract that she will not allow a cowife (as in Morocco and Lebanon). It seems reasonable to expect that other countries will make changes and modifications. It is interesting to note that while for some finances have dictated monogamy—most husbands have simply not been able to afford more than one wife—changing economic realities may again dictate that a man contemplate the possibility of having several wives to work and supply income for the family.

Muslim women traditionally have been married at an extremely young age, sometimes even before puberty. This practice is related, of course, to the historical fact that fathers and other male relatives generally have chosen the grooms themselves, despite the guarantee of the Qur'ān that marriage is a contract into which male and female enter equally. While it is true that technically a girl cannot be forced into a marriage she does not want, pressures from family and the youth of the bride often have made this prerogative difficult to exercise. Today, the right of a male member of the family to contract an engagement for a girl against her wishes has been legally revoked in most places, although it is still a common practice, especially in rural areas....

In the contemporary Islamic world, divorce rates vary considerably from one country to the next. Muslim apologists insist that divorce is not nearly as common in Islamic countries as it is, for example, in the United States. This statement is generally true, although in some countries, such as Morocco, the rate is high and continues to grow. Often what is really only the breaking of the engagement contract is included in divorce statistics, skewing the measure. Many countries are now considering serious changes in divorce procedures. The simultaneous triple repudiation generally has been declared illegal, and in many countries divorce initiated by either party, the man or the woman, must take place in the court of law. Other countries add special stipulations generally favorable to the woman. It remains true, however, that men can divorce for less cause than women, and often divorces hung up in courts with male judges can prove enormously difficult for women to gain.

In accordance with Islamic law, custody of the children traditionally has gone to the father at some time between the age of seven and nine for boys and between seven and puberty for girls, depending on the legal school. This practice too is slowly changing, and in most areas women who have been divorced by their husbands are allowed to keep their sons until puberty and their daughters until they are of an age to be married.

It is considered one of the great innovations of the Qur'ān over earlier practices that women are permitted to inherit and own property. Non-Muslims have generally found great difficulty with the Qur'ānic stipulation that a woman is allowed to inherit property but that the inheritance should be only half that of a male. According to the Islamic understanding, however, the rationale is precisely that which applies to the verse saying that men are in charge of women. Because women are permitted to keep and maintain their own property without responsibility for taking care of their families financially, it is only reasonable that the male, who must spend his own earning and inheritance for the maintenance of women, should receive twice as much....

According to the Qur'ān, women should not expose themselves to public view with lack of modesty. It does not say that they should be covered specifically from head to toe, nor that they should wear face veils or masks or other of the paraphernalia that has adorned many Islamic women through the ages. The Qur'ān also suggests that the wives of the Prophet Muhammad, when speaking to other men, should do so from behind a partition, again for purposes of propriety. It has been open to question whether this statement is meant to apply to all women. In the early Islamic community, these verses were exaggerated and their underlying ideas elaborated and defined in ways that led fairly quickly to a seclusion of women which seems quite at odds with what the Qur'ān intended or the Prophet wanted. When the community in Medina was established, women participated fully with men in all activities of worship and prayer. Soon they became segregated, however, to the point where an often-quoted *hadīth* (no doubt spurious) attributed to Muhammad has him saying that women pray better at home than in the mosque, and best of all in their own closets. Today a number of contemporary Muslim writers are urging a return to the practices of the young Muslim community, with women no longer segregated from the mosque or relegated to certain rear or side portions as they generally have been, but participating fully in worship with men....

What is popularly known as "veiling" is part of the general phenomenon of the segregation of women and yet is also distinctly apart from it. The two are increasingly seen as separate by contemporary Islamic women seeking to affirm a new identity in relation to their religion. Veils traditionally have taken a number of forms: a veil covering the face from just below the eyes down; a *chador* or *burka* covering the entire body, including the face, often with a woven screen in front through which women can see but not be seen; and a full face mask with small slits through the eyes, still worn in some areas of the Arabian Gulf. These costumes, so seemingly oppressive to Western eyes, at least have allowed women to observe without being observed, thus affording their wearers a degree of anonymity that on some occasions has proven useful.

The general movement toward unveiling had its ostensible beginning in the mid-1920s, when the Egyptian feminist Huda Sha'rawi cast off her veil after arriving in Egypt from an international meeting of women. She was followed literally and symbolically by masses of women in the succeeding years, and Egyptian women as well as those in other Middle Eastern countries made great strides in adopting Western dress. At the present time in the history of Islam, however, one finds a quite different phenomenon. Partly in reaction against Western liberation and Western ideals in general, women in many parts of the Islamic world are self-consciously adopting forms of dress by which they can identify with Islam rather than with what they now see as the imperialist West. Islamic dress, generally chosen by Muslim women themselves rather than forced upon them by males, signals for many an identification with a way of life that they are increasingly convinced represents a more viable alternative than that offered by the West....

We see, then, that while legal circumstances for women have undergone some significant changes in the past half-century, the dictates of the Qur'ān continue to be enormously influential in the molding of new laws as well as in the personal choices of Muslim men and women....

I have stressed here the insistence of the Qur'ān on the religious and spiritual equality of men and women. And aside from some unfortunate *hadīth* with very weak chains of authority suggesting that the majority of women will be in the Fire on the Day of Judgment because of their mental and physical inferiority, religious literature in general, when talking about human responsibility and concomitant judgment, makes women full partners with men under the divine command to live lives of integrity and righteousness....

Of course, women do participate in many of the activities and duties considered incumbent on all good Muslims, but generally these practices have a somewhat different function for them than for men. Prayer for women, as we have said, is usually in the home rather than in the mosque, and does not necessarily follow the pattern of the regularized five times a day. Participation in the fast itself is normally the same as for the men (except when women are pregnant, nursing, or menstruating), but the particular joys of preparing the fast-breaking meals are for the women alone. While the husband determines the amount of money or goods to be distributed for almsgiving, another responsibility of all Muslims, it is often the wife who takes charge of the actual distribution.

The last duty incumbent on Muslims after the testimony to the oneness of God and prophethood of his apostle Muhammad, the prayer, the fast, and paying the almstax is the pilgrimage once in a lifetime to the holy city of Mecca. Women do participate in this journey, and as transportation becomes easier and the care provided for pilgrims in Saudi Arabia becomes more regularized with modernization, increasing numbers of females join the throngs which gather to circumambulate the Xaaba at Mecca each year....

Saints in Islam are both male and female. One is normally recognized as a saint not by any process of canonization but because of some miraculous deed(s) performed or through a dream communication after death with a living person requesting that a shrine be erected over his or her tomb. Often a woman is favored with these dreams and after the construction of the shrine she becomes the carekeeper of the tomb, a position of some honor and responsibility....

While women in the Islamic world have been segregated and secluded, and historically have been considered second-class citizens by the vast majority of males in the community, they have not been totally without power. They have been able to maintain a degree of control over their own lives and over the men with whom they live through many of the religious practices described above. The fact that they alone have the ability to bear children, the influence they continue to play in the lives of their sons, and the power they have over their sons' wives are subtle indications that there are certain checks and balances on the obvious authority invested by the Qur'ān in men. From sexuality to control of the network of communications in the family to manipulation of such external agencies as spirits and supernatural beings, women have had at their control a variety of means to exert their will over the men in their families and over their own circumstances. The subtle means of control available to women throughout the world have of course been exploited: withholding sexual favors (a questionable but often-quoted *hadīth* says that if a woman refuses to sleep with her husband, the angels will curse her until the morning), doing small things to undermine a husband's honor such as embarrassing him in front of guests, indulging in various forms of gossip and social control, and the like....

Until fairly recently, education for women in the Muslim world has been minimal. Girls were given the rudiments of an Islamic education, mainly a little instruction in the Qur'ān and the traditions so as to be able to recite their prayers properly. Beyond that their training was not academic but domestic. In the late nineteenth and early twentieth century, Islamic leaders awoke with a start to the reality that Muslims were significantly behind the West in a variety of ways, including technology and the education necessary to understand and develop it. Many of these leaders recognized that if Islamic nations were to compete successfully in the contemporary world, it had to be with the aid of a well-educated and responsible female sector. Thus, this century has seen a number of educational advances for women, and in some countries, such as Egypt, Iraq, and Kuwait, women constitute very significant numbers of the university population. Nonetheless, illiteracy in many Muslim nations continues to be high, and the gap between male and female literacy rates is even increasing in some areas. In Saudi Arabia, where at present the economic resources are certainly available, large numbers of Saudi girls are receiving a full education, though separated from boys, and are taught either by men through television transmission or by women.

In education as in most areas of life, the male understanding of women as encouraged by certain parts of the Islamic tradition continues to play an important role. The Qur'ān does state, along with the stipulation that women can inherit only half of what men inherit, that the witness (in the court of law) of one man is equal to that of two women. This unfortunately has been interpreted by some in the history of Islam to mean that women are intellectually inferior to men, unstable in their judgment, and too easily swayed by emotion. Such perspectives are certainly not shared by all but nonetheless have been influential (and in some places are increasingly so today) in making it difficult for a woman to have access to the same kinds of educational opportunities that are available to men. Certain subjects are deemed "appropriate" for a woman to study, particularly those geared to make her the best and most productive wife, mother, and female participant in the family structure.

The prevalent view, confirmed by the Qur'ān, is that women should be modest and should neither expose themselves to men nor be too much in public places, where they will be subject to men's observation or forced to interact with males not in their immediate families. This view obviously has contributed to the difficulties of receiving a full education and of securing employment outside the home. More employment opportunities are open to women today than in the past, however, and in many countries women hold high-level positions in business, government, civil service, education, and other sectors. Statistics differ greatly across the Islamic world and are difficult to assess because they often fail to take into account the rural woman who may work full-time in the fields or other occupation outside the house but does not earn an independent salary....

Saudi Arabia presents an interesting case study of the confrontation of Islamic ideas with contemporary reality. Women are greatly inhibited in the labor arena; because of conservative religious attitudes they must be veiled and covered, are not permitted to drive or even ride in a taxi with a strange man, and in general are unable to participate on the social and professional level with males. However, in a country in which production is both necessary and economically possible and which suffers from a lack of manpower, the use of women in the work force or increased importation of foreign labor seem the only two (both undesirable) alternatives. Thus more Saudi women are working, and because of their right to inherit, are accumulating very substantial amounts of money. It is interesting to note the rapid rate of construction of new banks exclusively for women in places like Jiddah and Riyadh.

The aforementioned Qur'ān verse about the witness of two women being equal to that of one man and the supporting literature attesting to female intellectual, physical (and in fact sometimes moral) inferiority have made it difficult for Muslim women to achieve equal political rights. In most Arab countries (except Saudi Arabia and certain of the Gulf States), as well as in most other parts of the Islamic world, women have now been given the vote. Centuries of passivity in the political realm, however, have made it difficult for women to take advantage of the opportunities now available to them. In some countries, such as Egypt, women are playing major political roles,

but generally women politicians find little support from men or even from other women for their aspirations. This is not to underestimate the strong current in Islamic thinking which encourages the full participation of women in politics, as well as in the educational and professional fields.

Like an intricate and complex geometric pattern on a Persian rug or a frieze decorating a mosque, the practices, roles, opportunities, prescriptions, hopes, and frustrations of Islamic women are woven together in a whole. The colors are sometimes bold and striking, at other times muted and subtle. Some contemporary Muslim women are progressive and aggressive, no longer content to fit the traditionally prescribed patterns. Others are passive and accepting, not yet able to discern what new possibilities may be open to them, let alone whether or not they might want to take advantage of such opportunities. Some are Westernized as their mothers and grandmothers were and have every intention of staying that way, while others are increasingly clear in their feelings that the West does not have the answers and that Islam, particularly the Islam of the Qur'ān and the community of the Prophet Muhammad, is God's chosen way for humankind. For the latter, their dress, their relationships with their husbands and families, and their verbal assent to Islamic priorities reflect this conviction that the time has come to cease a fruitless preoccupation with things Western and to reaffirm their identity as Muslim women.

It is difficult for Western feminists to grasp exactly what the Muslim woman may mean by "liberation." For many Islamic women, the fruits of liberation in the West are too many broken marriages, women left without the security of men who will provide for them, deteriorating relations between men and women, and sexual license that appears as rank immorality. They see the Islamic system as affirmed by the Qur'ān as one in which male authority over them ensures their care and protection and provides a structure in which the family is solid, children are inculcated with lasting values, and the balance of responsibility between man and woman is one in which absolute equality is less highly prized than cooperation and complementarity.

The new Islamic woman, then, is morally and religiously conservative and affirms the absolute value of the true Islamic system for human relationships. She is intolerant of the kind of Islam in which women are subjugated and relegated to roles insignificant to the full functioning of society, and she wants to take full advantage of educational and professional opportunities. She may agree, however, that certain fields of education are more appropriate for women than others, and that certain professions are more natural to males than to females. She participates as a contributor to and decisionmaker for the family, yet recognizes that in any complex relationship final authority must rest with one person. And she is content to delegate that authority to her husband, father, or other male relative in return for the solidarity of the family structure and the support and protection that it gives her and her children.

That not all, or even most, Muslim women subscribe to this point of view is clear. And yet, at the time of this writing, it seems equally clear that, if Western observers are to understand women in the contemporary Islamic world, they must appreciate a point of view that is more and more prevalent. The West is increasingly identified with imperialism, and solutions viable for women in the Islamic community are necessarily different from the kinds of solutions that many Western women seem to have chosen for themselves. For the Muslim the words of the Qur'ān are divine, and the prescriptions for the roles and rights of females, like the other messages of the holy book, are seen as part of God's divinely ordered plan for all humanity. Change will come slowly, and whatever kinds of liberation ultimately prevail will be cloaked in a garb that is—in one or another of its various aspects—essentially Islamic.

CRITICAL THINKING QUESTIONS

1. In what formal ways does Islam confer on men authority over women?
2. In what formal and informal ways does Islam give power to women to affect their own lives and the lives of men?
3. From a Muslim perspective, what are some of the problems with Western living and, particularly, Western feminism?

55

Education and Inequality

Samuel Bowles and Herbert Gintis

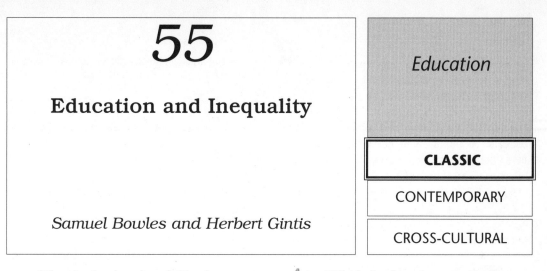

Education

CLASSIC

CONTEMPORARY

CROSS-CULTURAL

Education has long been held to be a means to realizing U.S. ideals of equal opportunity. As Lester Ward notes at the beginning of this selection, the promise of education is to allow "natural" abilities to win out over the "artificial" inequalities of class, race, and sex. Samuel Bowles and Herbert Gintis claim that this has happened very little in the United States. Rather, they argue, schooling has more to do with maintaining existing social hierarchy.

Universal education is the power, which is destined to overthrow every species of hierarchy. It is destined to remove all artificial inequality and leave the natural inequalities to find their true level. With the artificial inequalities of caste, rank, title, blood, birth, race, color, sex, etc., will fall nearly all the oppression, abuse, prejudice, enmity, and injustice, that humanity is now subject to.
—*Lester Frank Ward,* Education, 1872

A review of educational history hardly supports the optimistic pronouncements of liberal educational theory. The politics of education are better understood in terms of the need for social control in an unequal and rapidly changing economic order. The

Source: From *Schooling in Capitalist America: Educational Reform and the Contradictions of Economic Life* by Samuel Bowles and Herbert Gintis. Copyright © 1976 by Basic Books, Inc. Reprinted with permission of Basic Books, Inc., a division of HarperCollins Publishers, Inc.

founders of the modern U.S. school system understood that the capitalist economy produces great extremes of wealth and poverty, of social elevation and degradation. Horace Mann and other school reformers of the antebellum period knew well the seamy side of the burgeoning industrial and urban centers. "Here," wrote Henry Barnard, the first state superintendent of education in both Connecticut and Rhode Island, and later to become the first U.S. Commissioner of Education, "the wealth, enterprise and professional talent of the state are concentrated...but here also are poverty, ignorance, profligacy and irreligion, and a classification of society as broad and deep as ever divided the plebeian and patrician of ancient Rome."[1] They lived in a world in which, to use de Tocqueville's words, "...small aristocratic societies...are formed by some manufacturers in the midst of the immense democracy of our age [in which]...some men are opulent and a multitude…are wretchedly poor."[2] The rapid rise of the factory system, particularly in New England, was celebrated by the early school reformers; yet, the alarming transition from a relatively simple rural society to a highly stratified industrial economy could not be ignored. They shared the fears that de Tocqueville had expressed following his visit to the United States in 1831:

When a workman is unceasingly and exclusively engaged in the fabrication of one thing, he ultimately does his work with singular dexterity; but at the same time he loses the general faculty of applying his mind to the direction of the work…. [While] the science of manufacture lowers the class of workmen, it raises the class of masters…. [If] ever a permanent inequality of conditions…again penetrates into the world, it may be predicted that this is the gate by which they will enter.[3]

While deeply committed to the emerging industrial order, the farsighted school reformers of the mid-nineteenth century understood the explosive potential of the glaring inequalities of factory life. Deploring the widening of social divisions and fearing increasing unrest, Mann, Barnard, and others proposed educational expansion and reform. In his Fifth Report as Secretary of the Massachusetts Board of Education, Horace Mann wrote:

Education, then beyond all other devices of human origin, is the great equalizer of the conditions of men—the balance wheel of the social machinery…. It does better than to disarm the poor of their hostility toward the rich; it prevents being poor.[4]

Mann and his followers appeared to be at least as interested in disarming the poor as in preventing poverty. They saw in the spread of universal and free education a means of alleviating social distress without redistributing wealth and power or altering the broad outlines of the economic system. Education, it seems, had almost magical powers:

The main idea set forth in the creeds of some political reformers, or revolutionizers, is, that some people are poor because others are rich. This idea supposed a fixed amount of property in the community…and the problem presented for solution is, how to transfer a portion of this property from those who are supposed to have too much to those who feel and know that they have too little. At this point, both their theory and their expectation of reform stop. But the beneficent power of education would not be exhausted, even though it should peaceably abolish all the miseries that spring from the coexistence, side by side, of enormous wealth and squalid want. It has a higher function. Beyond the power of diffusing old wealth, it has the prerogative of creating new.[5]

The early educators viewed the poor as the foreign element that they were. Mill hands were recruited throughout New England, often disrupting the small towns in which textile and other rapidly growing industries had located. Following the Irish potato famine of the 1840s, thousands of Irish workers settled in the cities and towns of the northeastern United States. Schooling was seen as a means of integrating this "uncouth and dangerous" element into the social fabric of American life. The inferiority of the foreigner was taken for granted. The editors of the influential *Massachusetts Teacher,* a leader in the educational reform movement, writing in 1851, saw "…the increasing influx of foreigners…" as a moral and social problem:

Will it, like the muddy Missouri, as it pours its waters into the clear Mississippi and contaminates the whole united mass, spread ignorance and vice, crime and disease, through our native population?

If…we can by any means purify this foreign people, enlighten their ignorance and bring them up to our level, we shall perform a work of true and perfect charity, blessing the giver and receiver in equal measure….

With the old not much can be done; but with their children, the great remedy is *education*. The rising generation must be taught as our own children are taught. We say *must be* because in many cases this can only be accomplished by coercion.[6]

Since the mid-nineteenth century the dual objectives of educational reformers—equality of opportunity and social control—have been intermingled, the merger of these two threads sometimes so nearly complete that it becomes impossible to distinguish between the two. Schooling has been at once something done for the poor and to the poor.

The basic assumptions which underlay this commingling help explain the educational reform movement's social legacy. First, educational reformers did not question the fundamental economic institutions of capitalism: Capitalist ownership and control of the means of production and dependent wage labor were taken for granted. In fact, education was to help preserve and extend the capitalist order. The function of the school system was to accommodate workers to its most rapid possible development. Second, it was assumed that people (often classes of people or "races") are differentially equipped by nature or social origins to occupy the varied economic and social levels in the class structure. By providing equal opportunity, the school system was to elevate the masses, guiding them sensibly and fairly to the manifold political, social, and economic roles of adult life.

Jefferson's educational thought strikingly illustrates this perspective. In 1779, he proposed a two-track educational system which would prepare individuals for adulthood in one of the two classes of society: the "laboring and the learned."[7] Even children of the laboring class would qualify for leadership. Scholarships would allow "…those persons whom nature hath endowed with genius and virtue…" to "…be rendered by liberal education worthy to receive and able to guard the sacred deposit of the rights and liberties of their fellow citizens."[8] Such a system, Jefferson asserted, would succeed in "…raking a few geniuses from the rubbish."[9] Jefferson's two-tiered educational plan presents in stark relief the outlines and motivation for the stratified structure of U.S. education which has endured up to the present. At the top, there is the highly selective aristocratic tradition, the elite university training future leaders. At the base is mass education for all, dedicated to uplift and control. The two traditions have always coexisted although their meeting point has drifted upward over the years, as mass education has spread upward from elementary school through high school, and now up to the post-high-school level.

Though schooling was consciously molded to reflect the class structure, education was seen as a means of enhancing wealth and morality, which would work to the advantage of all. Horace Mann, in his 1842 report to the State Board of Education, reproduced this comment by a Massachusetts industrialist:

The great majority always have been and probably always will be comparatively poor, while a few will possess the greatest share of this world's goods. And it is a wise provision of Providence which connects so intimately, and as I think so indissolubly, the greatest good of the many with the highest interests in the few.[10]

Much of the content of education over the past century and a half can only be construed as an unvarnished attempt to persuade the "many" to make the best of the inevitable.

The unequal contest between social control and social justice is evident in the total functioning of U.S. education. The system as it stands today provides eloquent testimony to the ability of the well-to-do to perpetuate in the name of equality of opportunity an arrangement which consistently yields to themselves disproportional advantages, while thwarting the aspirations and needs of the working people of the United States. However grating this judgment may sound to the ears of the undaunted optimist, it is by no means excessive in light of the massive statistical data on inequality in the United States. Let us look at the contemporary evidence.

We may begin with the basic issue of inequalities in the years of schooling. As can be seen in [Figure 55.1], the number of years of schooling attained by an individual is strongly associated with parental socioeconomic status. This figure presents the estimated distribution of years of schooling attained by individuals of varying socioeconomic backgrounds. If we define socioeconomic background by a weighted sum of income, occupation, and educational level of the parents, a child from the ninetieth percentile may expect, on the average, five more years of schooling than a child in the tenth percentile.[11]

FIGURE 55.1 Educational Attainments Are Strongly Dependent on Social Background Even for People of Similar Childhood IQs

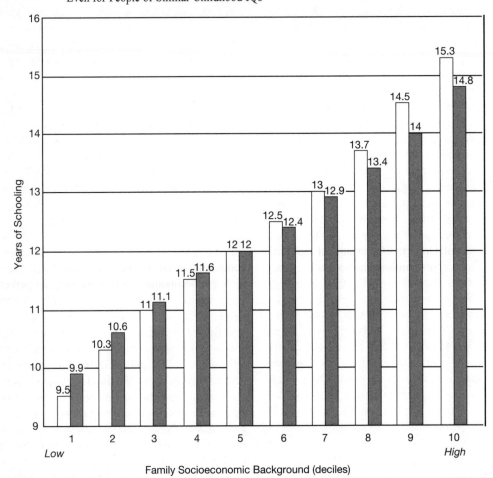

Notes: For each socioeconomic group, the left-hand bar indicates the estimated average number of years of schooling attained by all men from that group. The right-hand bar indicates the estimated average number of years of schooling attained by men with IQ scores equal to the average for the entire sample. The sample refers to "non-Negro" men of "nonfarm" backgrounds, aged 35–44 years in 1962.

Source: Samuel Bowles and Valerie Nelson, "The 'Inheritance of IQ' and the Intergenerational Transmission of Economic Inequality," *The Review of Economics and Statistics,* vol. LVI, no. 1 (Feb. 1974).

...We have chosen a sample of white males because the most complete statistics are available for this group. Moreover, if inequality for white males can be documented, the proposition is merely strengthened when sexual and racial differences are taken into account.

Additional census data dramatize one aspect of educational inequalities: the relationship between family income and college attendance. Even among those who had graduated from high school in the early 1960s, children of families earning less than $3,000 per year were over six times as likely *not* to attend college as were the children of families earning over $15,000.[12] Moreover, children from less well-off families are *both* less likely to have graduated from high school and more likely to attend inexpensive, two-year community colleges rather than a four-year B.A. program if they do make it to college.[13]

Not surprisingly, the results of schooling differ greatly for children of different social backgrounds. Most easily measured, but of limited importance, are differences in scholastic achievement. If we measure the output of schooling by scores on nationally standardized achievement tests, children whose parents were themselves highly educated outperform the children of parents with less education by a wide margin. Data collected for the U.S. Office of Education Survey of Educational Opportunity reveal, for example, that among white high-school seniors, those whose parents were in the top education decile were, on the average, well over three grade levels in measured scholastic achievement ahead of those whose parents were in the bottom decile.[14]

Given these differences in scholastic achievement, inequalities in years of schooling among individuals of different social backgrounds are to be expected. Thus one might be tempted to argue that the close dependence of years of schooling attained on background displayed in the left-hand bars of [Figure 55.1] is simply a reflection of unequal intellectual abilities, or that inequalities in college attendance are the consequences of differing levels of scholastic achievement in high school and do not reflect any additional social class inequalities peculiar to the process of college admission.

This view, so comforting to the admissions personnel in our elite universities, is unsupported by the data, some of which is presented in [the figure]. The right-hand bars of [the figure] indicate that even among children with identical IQ test scores at ages six and eight, those with rich, well-educated, high-status parents could expect a much higher level of schooling than those with less-favored origins. Indeed, the closeness of the left-hand and right-hand bars in [the figure] shows that only a small portion of the observed social class differences in educational attainment is related to IQ differences across social classes.[15] The dependence of education attained on background is almost as strong for individuals with the same IQ as for all individuals. Thus, while [the figure] indicates that an individual in the ninetieth percentile in social class background is likely to receive five more years of education than an individual in the tenth percentile, it also indicates that he is likely to receive 4.25 more years schooling than an individual from the tenth percentile with the same IQ. Similar results are obtained when we look specifically at access to college education for students with the same measured IQ. Project Talent data indicates that for "high ability" students (top 25 percent as measured by a composite of tests of "general aptitude"), those of high socioeconomic background (top 25 percent as measured by a composite of family income, parents' education, and occupation) are nearly twice as likely to attend college than students of low socioeconomic background (bottom 25 percent). For "low ability" students (bottom 25 percent), those of high-social background are more than four times as likely to attend college as are their low-social background counterparts.[16]

Inequality in years of schooling is, of course, only symptomatic of broader inequalities in the educational system. Not only do less well-off children go to school for fewer years, they are treated with less attention (or more precisely, less benevolent attention) when they are there. These broader inequalities are not easily measured. Some show up in statistics on the different levels of expenditure for the education of children of different socioeconomic backgrounds. Taking account of the inequality in financial resources for each year in school and the inequality in years of schooling obtained, Jencks estimated that a child whose parents were in the top fifth of the income distribution receives roughly twice the educational resources in dollar terms as does a child whose parents are in the bottom fifth.[17]

The social class inequalities in our school system, then, are too evident to be denied. Defenders of the educational system are forced back on the assertion that things are getting better; the inequalities of the past were far worse. And, indeed, there can be no doubt that some of the inequalities of the past have been mitigated. Yet new inequalities have apparently developed to take their place, for the available historical evidence lends little support to the idea that our schools are on the road to equality of educational opportunity. For example, data from a recent U.S. Census survey reported in Spady indicate that graduation from college has become no less dependent on one's social background. This is true despite the fact that high-school graduation is becoming increasingly equal across social classes.[18] Additional data confirm this impression. The statistical association (coefficient of correlation) between parents' social status and years of education attained by individuals who completed their schooling three or four decades ago is virtually identical to the same correlation for individuals who terminated their schooling in recent years.[19] On balance, the available data suggest that the number of years of school attained by a child depends upon family background as much in the recent period as it did fifty years ago.

Thus, we have empirical reasons for doubting the egalitarian impact of schooling.... We conclude that U.S. education is highly unequal, the chances of attaining much or little schooling being substantially dependent on one's race and parents' economic level. Moreover, where there is a discernible trend toward a more equal educational system—as in the narrowing of the black education deficit, for example—the impact on the structure of economic opportunity is minimal at best.

CRITICAL THINKING QUESTIONS

1. Does Bowles and Gintis's description of the American education system apply to the Canadian system? How are the two systems similar? How are they different?

2. In what respects, according to Bowles and Gintis, has schooling supported the capitalist economic system? How has such support shaped the content of the educational system?

3. What are Bowles and Gintis's conclusions about the relationship between schooling and natural ability? between schooling and social background?

NOTES

1. H. Barnard, *Papers for the Teacher: 2nd Series* (New York: F. C. Brownell, 1866), pp. 293–310.
2. A. de Tocqueville, as quoted in Jeremy Brecher, *Strike!* (San Francisco: Straight Arrow Books, 1972), pp. xi, xii.
3. Ibid., p. 172.
4. Horace Mann as quoted in Michael Katz, ed., *School Reform Past and Present* (Boston: Little, Brown, 1971), p. 141.
5. Ibid., p. 145.
6. *The Massachusetts Teacher* (Oct., 1851), quoted in Katz, pp. 169–70.
7. D. Tyack, *Turning Points in American Educational History* (Waltham, Mass.: Blaisdell, 1967), p. 89.
8. Ibid., p. 10.
9. Ibid., p. 89.
10. Mann, quoted in Katz, p. 147.
11. This calculation is based on data reported in full in Samuel Bowles and Valerie Nelson, "The 'Inheritance of IQ' and the Intergenerational Transmission of Economic Inequality," *The Review of Economics and Statistics,* 56, 1 (Feb., 1974). It refers to non-Negro males from nonfarm backgrounds, aged 35–44 years. The zero-order correlation coefficient between socioeconomic background and years of schooling was estimated at 0.646. The estimated standard deviation of years of schooling was 3.02. The results for other age groups are similar.
12. These figures refer to individuals who were high-school seniors in October 1965, and who subsequently graduated from high school. College attendance refers to both two- and four-year institutions. Family income is for the twelve months preceding October 1965. Data is drawn from U.S. Bureau of the Census, *Current Population Reports,* Series P-60, No. 183 (May, 1969).
13. For further evidence, see ibid.; and Jerome Karabel, "Community Colleges and Social Stratification," *Harvard Educational Review,* 424, 42 (Nov., 1972).
14. Calculation based on data in James S. Coleman et al., *Equality of Educational Opportunity* (Washington, D.C.: U.S. Government Printing Office, 1966), and the authors.
15. The data relating to IQ are from a 1966 survey of veterans by the National Opinion Research Center; and from N. Bayley and E. S. Schaefer, "Correlations of Maternal and

Child Behaviors with the Development of Mental Ability: Data from the Berkeley Growth Study," *Monographs of Social Research in Child Development,* 29, 6 (1964).

16. Based on a large sample of U.S. high-school students as reported in John C. Flannagan and William W. Cooley, *Project Talent, One Year Follow-up Study,* Cooperative Research Project, No. 2333 (Pittsburgh: University of Pittsburgh, School of Education, 1966).

17. C. Jencks et al., *Inequality: A Reassessment of the Effects of Family and Schooling in America* (New York: Basic Books, 1972), p. 48.

18. W. L. Spady, "Educational Mobility and Access: Growth and Paradoxes," in *American Journal of Sociology,* 73, 3 (Nov. 1967); and Peter Blau and Otis D. Duncan, *The American Occupational Structure* (New York: John Wiley, 1967). More recent data support the evidence of no trend toward equality. See U.S. Bureau of Census, op. cit.

19. Ibid., Blau and Duncan.

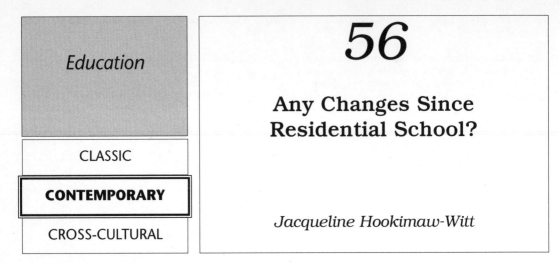

56

Any Changes Since Residential School?

Education

CLASSIC

CONTEMPORARY

CROSS-CULTURAL

Jacqueline Hookimaw-Witt

Hookimaw-Witt reviews the residential school experience of Native children and explores how the education system is partly responsible for the destruction of their culture and loss of self-esteem.

The social situation Native people find themselves in on reserves is often blamed on a lack of education. The thought behind this suggestion is that "education" itself is neutral and automatically leads to a rise of the standard of living. I discuss that the situation we Native people are in is partly due to that very "education," which, as a continuation of residential schools, is still breaking down our cultures and societies. Education for Native people can be successful only when it has grown within the culture of the people.

In this article I wish to discuss the legacy of the residential school in a different light. As well as physical and emotional abuse suffered by the Native children who were placed in these schools, there was also an onslaught on our culture and identity through the content taught in school and the way it was taught. I would even

say that "education" is partly responsible for the destruction of our cultures and the loss of self-esteem and thus has contributed directly to the problems in our community today. The content and methods of teaching have not changed in modern schools that now "help" us to "catch up." I therefore try to examine how education itself not only has not helped to prevent the social problems we have today, but has actually created them, and that when we do not change the basis of education for Native people, the process started by residential schools will still continue.

The basis for the following analysis of the problem can easily be summarized in the quote that refers to a researcher in the Arctic who was approached by an Elder:

An Elder approached me and asked what I was doing in the community. I explained that I was conducting research on dominant influences on Aboriginal student decision making, which might lead to reducing the Native student drop-out rate. He had an enigmatic response to my answer as he asked what the community would lose this time. I asked him to elaborate on his response and he said, every time the white

Source: Jacqueline Hookimaw-Witt. 1998. Any changes since residential school? *Canadian Journal of Native Education*, 22(2): 159–70. Abridged with the permission of the Canadian Journal of Native Education, University of Alberta and University of British Columbia.

man comes and offers us something, the Aboriginal people lose something. He said that at first the white man offered us Christianity, but he took our Native spirituality. Then he offered us his stores, his food, his goods, but we lost our traditional way of life and traditional diets. Then he offered us education, but we lost our language and culture. Now when I see a white man doing something for our good, I worry about what we will lose. (Common & Frost, 1994: 306)

Two major factors can be extracted from this statement. First, the help offered to so-called underdeveloped people never comes without a price. There is no real development in a scenario like this. It is, rather, that our own development is stopped and we have to adjust to something alien that is offered to us. The price is always that instead of developing our ways and adjusting them to the new environment, we have to given them up. Second, education per se is not neutral. Educational institutes have to follow curricula, and these curricula are used for "legitimation. Social groups are given legitimacy…through which social and cultural ideologies are built, recreated and maintained" (Apple & Weis, 1983: 516).

It is self-evident that the social groups and cultural ideologies Apple and Weis (1983) are referring to are not based in the culture of the Native people, but in the culture of those who suggest this kind of education. What the people who "help" us usually ignore is that we did not grow up completely uneducated, that we do not need a new education system. The only need is an adjustment of the existing system to new realities, if there are any. The content to be taught in school would not necessarily qualify to fall under the categories of new "realities," because the determination of content to be taught is usually based on a political decision.

Referring to the content, Apple (1990) rephrases the question of "*what* knowledge is most worth into *whose* knowledge is most worth" (p. viii), expressing that curricula are not neutral and that the knowledge taught in schools is not neutral when he reminds that it should hardly have to be said, but perhaps is worth remembering, that

education is not a neutral activity. It is profoundly political" (Apple, 1995: ix).

The political nature of education is explained above where it is stated that curricula are used for legitimation of social groups (Apple & Weis, 1983). Non-Native people must remember that the social groups and cultural ideologies are theirs, not ours, and when they suggest *their* education as means of healing our past wounds, they are suggesting that we give up our identity, which reopens the wounds rather than healing them.

Why the education offered to Native people is ultimately destroying Native cultures is also explained by Apple (1995):

Our formal institutions of education—because they cannot escape their history and their social conditions in which they are situated—are intimately linked with the social conditions in which they are situated—are intimately linked with the social divisions of paid and unpaid labour in this society. (p. ix)

It should be understood that these conditions are not the original conditions in Native societies, and that it is western society that is duplicated by the education that is offered to us. This underlines my statement that our societies are destroyed by the education system that is offered to us. The destruction of culture is also mentioned by Apple (1995) when he says that

the curriculum itself is always a choice from a wider universe of knowledge and values. Thus schooling is deeply implicated in cultural politics, with some groups having the power to declare their knowledge, values, and histories (i.e., "official knowledge"), while others are marginalized. (p. ix)

This power is taken away from us, because it is not the Native people themselves who decide on the content of teaching. The content is already decided on in the curricula the schools must follow when they are to be recognized.

The effect of these school politics can immediately be seen in the high dropout rates of Native students. The immediate analysis for school dropout is again based on the economic conditions in western society, as most of the dropouts are found among the economically poor people of this society (for me mainstream society). Apple (1989) therefore concludes that

it would not be an overstatement to say that our kind of economy, with its growing inequalities, its structuring of what are more and more alienating, deskilled, and meaningless jobs, its emphasis on profit no matter what the social cost—"naturally" *produces* the conditions that lead to dropping out. The phenomenon of the dropout is not an odd aberration that randomly arises in our school system. It is structurally generated, created out of the real and unequal relations of economic, political, and cultural resources and power that organize this society. Solutions to it will require that we no longer hide ourselves from this reality. The first step is looking at our economy honestly and recognizing how the class, race, and gender relations that structure it operate. (p. 220)

Looking into our communities, this analysis based on economic conditions seems to fit the case of Native youths dropping out of school. After all, the few jobs available in our communities are hardly a motivation for the youths to put an effort into their education. However, Apple (1989) also mentions cultural resources, and I will use this as a bridge to what I think is the real problem in Native education: lack of exposure to our own culture.

One explanation for the failure of Native youths in the school system has been that Native youths simply could not compete with the other youths in school because of their "cultural deprivation," meaning that our culture is so inferior to mainstream culture that we simply cannot succeed in a necessary education as long as we hold onto our culture. This led to the evaluation of a consultant for our community who was writing a proposal for the establishment of a solvent abuse treatment center. Although he emphasized the importance of including Native content in the curriculum, he stated that "Native culture and spirituality alone are not enough" (Kells, 1995) to survive in the modern world.

This observation was based on his misinterpretation of the educational goal the National Indian Brotherhood set for Native people in 1973, namely, to reinforce Indian identity *and* to provide the training necessary for making a good living in modern society (National Indian Brotherhood, 1972). Kells (1995) interpreted this as "parallel teaching," concluding that education based on Native culture is not sufficient for survival in the so-called modern world. This is not what the National Indian Brotherhood (1972) intended to suggest. In their paper, they established the basis for Native education, stating that

unless the child learns the forces that shape him: the history of his people, their values and customs, their language, he will never really know himself or his potential as a human being.... The lessons he learns at school, his whole school experience should reinforce and contribute to the image he has of himself as an Indian. (p. 9)

I interpret the reference to the whole school experience as an indication of the importance of basing the school curriculum entirely in Native culture, no matter what content is taught. This means that "western" skills to be learned are still learned on the basis of the Native perspective, which would also include Native learning and teaching styles. The basis for education is here defined as being the culture of the Native people, from where they draw their identity. Only when this is understood by Native children can they develop their potential as human beings. The learning of skills for survival in the *other*, western reality are learned from a Native basis. The Native child, like any other child, needs a reference point to her or his own cultural environment when he or she wants to understand the meanings of the skills taught to him or her. Western skills and values are learned by comparing the *other* cultural reality with one's own. A parallel teaching that does not provide this point of reference, that in fact suggests that certain skills do not exist in our culture (rather than pointing out that they are different), will therefore fail....

The Royal Commission on Aboriginal People (Government of Canada, 1996) confirms my understanding of the NIB's educational goal that although we do have to include knowledge of the *other* culture in our curriculum, it still has to be based in our own culture: "Education must develop children and youth as Aboriginal citizens, linguistically and culturally competent to assume responsibilities in their nations.... Youth that emerge from school must be grounded in a strong positive Aboriginal identity" (p. 5). Their recommendation is, therefore, to establish "a curriculum that instills a proud Aboriginal identity and competence as an Aboriginal person" (p. 5). This Aboriginal identity and competence as an Aboriginal person can be reached only when the curriculum is based on the culture from which the youths draw their identity. A parallel teaching as suggested by Kells (1995) lacks this basis.

I would interpret the cultural deprivation that was so often quoted as the major factor of school dropout by people from different cultures (Ogbu, 1989) as Native people being deprived of the security of their own culture (by being forced into an alien education system), and not as the lack of survival skills their own culture would offer.

Ogbu (1989) analyzes the reasons for school dropout on the basis of cultural differences. He counts Native people with those *involuntary minorities* who were "brought into" the country's society by "slavery, conquest or colonization" (p. 187). Native people can definitely be identified in this group, as they were colonized in their own country. The lack of motivation of children from involuntary minorities to succeed in the education system is explained as the children from this group having come "to realize or believe that it requires more than education, and more than individual effort and hard work, to overcome the barriers. Consequently, they develop a folk theory of getting ahead which differs from white Americans" (p. 188).

Although this statement might explain school dropout based on different behaviour by the youths of involuntary minorities, Ogbu's (1989) conclusion of the development of a folk theory cannot be applied to Native youth. The means of coping with difficulties in school and the different

behaviour of Native youths cannot be identified as folk theory but as the culture in which the Native youths were raised. Although it may be true that the Native youths realized that getting on in society required more than education, they did not develop their attitude toward western education on this basis. Ogbu does not consider our culture here. We had our culture long before the Europeans came to this country. Referring to our own interpretations of life, there also needs to be a definition of getting ahead, because a good life in Native culture always includes spirituality and is not merely based on economic aspirations. Dropping out of school by Native youths may certainly not be based only on the realization that the capitalist vision of life is only a dream, but also on the lack of Native culture and spirituality within the educational system.

However, Ogbu's (1989) conclusion that the problem of dropping out of school has to be analyzed on the cultural basis of the minorities can be used as explanation why the alien school system cannot be used to solve the problems of Native people:

At the moment, the definition and explanation of the school adjustment and academic performance problems of the minorities are based on a white middle-class cultural model, not the cultural model of the minorities which influence the latter's school orientations and behaviors. However, such definitions and explanations are incomplete until they incorporate the minorities' own notion of schooling which influences their school behavior. And until such an incorporation is made, social policies or remedial problems based on the definitions such as those embedded in the drop-out literature are not likely to be particularly effective. (p. 201)

This would explain why the school system offered to us Native people cannot be successful. It is not based on our own cultural values and traditions....

All the Elders I interviewed agreed that the education presently offered to our children is part of the problem in our communities. They all emphasized that education would have to be based on our own culture and that the other content, that of western culture, can be included, rather than the reverse of just including some Native cultural teaching in an altogether non-Native educational system. The importance is the foundation on which the education system is based.

This realization led to the suggestion of Indian control of Indian education. I frequently found during my time in universities that even this concept would have to be defined. Many Native people do not realize any more that mere control of the education system that was forced on us will not change the success rate of education in Native communities. Haig-Brown (1995) warns that "though it is generally asserted that Native control of Native education would be a positive move, educators, researchers, and writers only cursorily articulate the assumptions behind this belief and rarely debate their validity" (p. 21).

The way I read this statement is that Native control of Native education is only valuable for Native people when the whole education system changes and is based on Native culture. The control of an altogether alien—and for Native cultures destructive—education system cannot keep at bay the damage that this system is causing our cultures....

Having established the importance of a cultural basis for our education system, I now try to explain why a Native cultural basis for our education system was not popular in the past, why nowadays many non-Native people might still view our cultures as inferior, and coupled with this thought, that we therefore need the help of an alien education system.

I heard much about racism and anti-racism while I attended universities. The anti-racism groups, although probably well-meaning, usually thought that they were opening a path for minorities to be accepted into *society*, basing this belief on the wrong assumption that there is actually only one society, and that the other groups are marginal or minority groups. They would certainly be shocked by the thoughts that go through my mind whenever they present their ideology. In my opinion, this assumption is as

racist as the one that we as Native people are inferior to other people due to the color of our skin. The wrong assumption is that all minority groups strive toward being accepted into *society*. For me that would mean assimilation. Why would Native people want to be assimilated? The only reason for wanting to be assimilated into an alien society would be an acknowledgement that the other society is superior to ours. This would mean that our culture is inferior as well, and this view feeds directly into the attitude expressed in the help we supposedly receive from the education system that is forced on us.

The concept on which I base the following explanations is that of *cultural difference*, which is explained by Bhabha (1988):

The revision of history of critical theory rests on the notion of cultural difference, not cultural diversity. Cultural diversity is an epistemological object—culture as an object of empirical knowledge—whereas cultural difference is the process of the enunciation of culture as knowledgeable, authoritative, adequate to the construction of systems of cultural identification. (p. 206)

The suffix *able* in knowledge*able* is interpreted by Witt (1998) as the ability of each culture to enable the people to survive; the ability to create one's own programs without having to borrow from other cultures. This would certainly include that Native people can develop their own education system.

However, this *ability* is unfortunately not attributed to our culture. The way our culture is interpreted can, in my opinion, be traced to the unfortunate hierarchy of cultures exemplified in the work of Habermas (1979), who identifies four distinct stages of cultural evolution: *Neolithic societies*, *archaic civilizations*, *developed civilizations*, and the *modern age*. These stages are characterized by different principles of organization determining the kinds of institutions possible, the extent to which productive capacities will be utilized, and the capacity of societies to adapt to complex circumstances. The identification of stages of evolution necessarily also contains that notion that there is ultimately only one stage into which all cultures would develop. In fact this would defuse cultural difference altogether, because the differences would only be between stages of development, not between whole different cultures. Thus our Native cultures would ultimately develop the same way as any other culture, and the ultimate highest stage would be identified as the western culture of today. I consider an analysis like this racist and ethnocentric, as it is based on the opinion that one particular culture is superior to all others....

As in the quote by Bhabha (1988) above, the emphasis today should be on cultural difference rather than on analysis of which culture is inferior and which is superior. Western people should not fool themselves into believing they are acting as good Samaritans. The fact that other cultures are destroyed has not changed, only the methods have changed or, as Minh-Ha (1989) puts it, "tactics have changed since the colonial times, and indigenous cultures are no longer (overtly) destroyed" (p. 265). The emphasis is on the term *overtly*, because cultures are still destroyed by actions like "removal-relocation-reeducation-redefinition, the humiliation of having to falsify your own reality, your own voice" (p. 265).

The humiliation of having to falsify one's own reality lies in the suggestion that our problems can be solved by leaving our own culture behind, which would be the ultimate goal of education based on western cultural values. That the different cultures are not expressions of different developments but expressions of different realities can be concluded from the following: "Culture is the only facet of the human condition and of life in which knowledge of the human reality and the human interest in self-perfection and fulfillment merge into one. Culture is...the natural enemy of alienation. It constantly questions the self-appointed wisdom, serenity and authority of the Real" (Bauman, 1973: 176).

This tells me two things. One, *the Real* is different in any given culture, meaning that my reality is different from that of non-Native

people; second, I will not accept any self-appointed wisdom from westerners just because they claim that this is the truth because it has been researched on a "scientific" basis. This so-called science is culture as well....

As mentioned above, reality can be challenged, and it can be explained by culture. The challenge does not, however, work only one way. As much as non-Natives can challenge my reality, I can challenge their reality. As a Native woman I consider myself as much *human* as anyone from a different culture, and thus claim the right to define my own reality. This reality is, of course, also formed by the environment that surrounds the people who developed that particular culture. Culture can also be seen as means of survival in a particular environment, and "if culture is looked at as a system, it must be accepted that each is a workable means of adaptation to a given environment" (Arsenberg & Niehoff, 1971: 67)....

I conclude with the following. The negative social and economical situation Native people find themselves in today cannot be referred to as *cultural deprivation*, nor can it be improved by education that is based on a different, supposedly *superior* or *more developed* culture. The idea that this kind of education is the solution to problems in Native communities is based on an attitude toward Native culture that is, unfortunately, still widely prevalent among non-Native people. The attitude is detectable in the...statement that "these people need education" and in a statement made during a presentation in one of my university courses that "these people do not know anything about science," which referred to a classroom situation with immigrant children. Statements like this show either ignorance about educational concepts from other cultures, or feelings of superiority of the speaker, or both. This attitude is probably based on the evaluation of different cultures as exemplified in Habermas' (1979) model of cultural development. However, this model cannot be applied to all the cultures of the world, because it would distort differences in cultures and would state that all human development will ultimately be the same. This would make Native people underdeveloped white people. The attitude of the residential schools, which destroyed much of Native cultures in Canada, does not differ at all from the attitude exhibited in Habermas' model. If, as it is agreed, the residential school system was detrimental to our people, then logically any educational system that is based on the same assumptions—those of the inferiority of Native cultures—would have the same detrimental effects. Although it is true that people need education, the basis of that education will have to be defined. Education cannot be seen as neutral. It is geared to replicate society. The question is, which society? Eager educators must get used to the idea that there is no single society, but many societies, and that people who are called minorities or marginal still have the right to determine their own fate.

CRITICAL THINKING QUESTIONS

1. Discuss the assertion that education is never socially or politically neutral. How can the original decision to implement the residential school system be seen as the result of social and political motivations?
2. Review Hookimaw-Witt's discussion of *cultural deprivation*. What does this concept mean? In your opinion, can it be used to explain the social and economic position of Native peoples today? If so, how? If not, why not?
3. Residential schools have been closed for some time. What, if any, improvements can you see in how Native children are educated today?

REFERENCES

Apple, M. W. 1989. American realities: Poverty, economy and education. In *Dropouts from school: Issues, dilemmas, and solutions*, eds. L. Weis, E. Farrar, and H. G. Petrie, 205–20. Albany, N.Y.: SUNY Press.

Apple, M. W. 1990. *Ideology and curriculum,* 2nd ed. New York: Routledge.

Apple, M. W. 1995. Preface. In *Taking control: Power and contradiction in First Nations adult education*, ed. C. Haig-Brown, ix. Vancouver, B.C.: University of British Columbia Press.

Apple, M. W., and L. Weis. 1983. *Ideology and practice in schooling*. Philadelphia: Temple University Press.

Arsenberg, C. M, and A. H. Niehoff. 1971. *Introducing social change: A manual for community development*. Chicago, Ill.: Aldine.

Bauman, Z. 1973. *Culture as praxis*. Boston, Mass.: Routledge & Kegan Paul.

Bhabha, H. 1988. Cultural diversity and cultural difference. In *The post-colonial studies reader,* eds. B. Ashcroft, G. Griffiths, and H. Tiffin, 206–09. New York: Routledge.

Common, R., and L. Frost. 1994. *Teaching wigwams: A modern version of Native education*. Muncey, Ont.: Anishinabe Kendaasiwin.

Government of Canada. 1996. *Report of the Royal Commission on Aboriginal People*. Ottawa: Canadian Communication Group.

Habermas, J. 1979. *Communication and the evolution of society*. Boston: Beacon.

Haig-Brown, C. 1995. *Taking control: Power and contradiction in First Nations adult education*. Vancouver, B.C.: University of British Columbia Press.

Hookimaw-Witt, J. 1998. *Keenabonanoh Keemoshominook Kaeshe Peemishishik Odaskiwakh [We stand on the graves of our ancestors]: Native interpretations of Treaty #9 with Attawapiskat Elders*. Unpublished master's thesis, Trent University.

Kells & Associates. 1995. *The Jules Mattinas healing lodge and treatment center in Attawapiskat*. Proposal to Nishnawbe Aski Health Planning Group. Ottawa: Author.

National Indian Brotherhood. 1973. *Indian control of Indian education*. Ottawa: Assembly of First Nations.

Ogbu, J. U. 1989. The individual in collective adaptation: A framework for focusing on academic underperformance and dropping out among involuntary minorities. In *Dropouts from school: Issues, dilemmas, and solutions*, eds. L. Weis, E. Farrar, and H.G. Petrie, 181–204. Albany, N.Y.: SUNY Press.

Witt, N. W. 1998. *Opening the healing path: The cultural basis for a solvent abusers' treatment program for the Attawapiskat First Nation*. Unpublished doctoral dissertation, OISE/UT.

57

Academic Achievement in Southeast Asian Refugee Families

Nathan Caplan, Marcella H. Choy, and John K. Whitmore

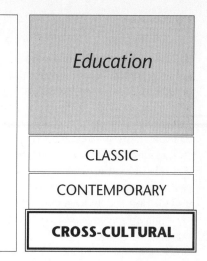

Education

CLASSIC

CONTEMPORARY

CROSS-CULTURAL

Many analysts believe that the U.S. educational system is in crisis, but are schools to blame for the modest achievement of some children? In this selection, the authors argue that socialization has a greater impact on academic performance than the quality of our schools does. Even though most Southeast Asian boat people are poor, have had limited exposure to Western culture, know virtually no English, and live in low-income metropolitan areas, their children are excelling in the U.S. school system.

The scholastic success of Asian children is well recognized. Their stunning performance—particularly in the realm of science and mathematics—has prompted American educators to visit Japanese and Taiwanese schools in an effort to unearth the foundations of these achievements. Experts recommend that American schools adopt aspects of their Asian counterparts, such as a longer school year or more rigorous tasks, in order to raise the scholastic level of U.S. students.

Yet there is no need to go abroad to understand why these children do so well. The achievement of Asian-American students indicates that much may be learned about the origins of their triumph within the American school system itself. More specifically, during the late 1970s and early 1980s,

Source: "Indochinese Refugee Families and Academic Achievement," by Nathan Caplan, Marcella H. Choy, and John K. Whitmore, in *Scientific American,* February, 1992, pp. 36–42. Copyright © 1992 by Scientific American, Inc. All rights reserved. Reprinted with permission.

devastating political and economic circumstances forced many Vietnamese, Lao and Chinese-Vietnamese families to seek a new life in the United States. This resettlement of boat people from Indochina offered a rare opportunity to examine the academic achievement of their children.

These young refugees had lost months, even years of formal schooling while living in relocation camps. Like their parents, they suffered disruption and trauma as they escaped from Southeast Asia. Despite their hardships and with little knowledge of English, the children quickly adapted to their new schools and began to excel.

In researching the economic and scholastic accomplishments of 1,400 refugee households in the early 1980s, our group at the University of Michigan studied the forces that shaped the performance of these children. Some of the standard explanations for educational excellence—parental encouragement and dedication to learning—applied to the young students, but other theories proved inadequate.

Although some of our findings are culturally specific, others point overwhelmingly to the pivotal role of the family in the children's academic success. Because this characteristic extends beyond culture, it has implications for educators, social scientists and policymakers as well as for the refugees themselves. It is clear that the U.S. educational system can work—if the requisite familial and social supports are provided for the students outside school.

Our study encompassed many features of resettlement. We gathered survey and other data on 6,750 persons in five urban areas—Orange County, Calif., Seattle, Houston, Chicago, and Boston—and obtained information about their background and home life as well as economic and demographic facts. We discovered that with regard to educational and social status, the refugees proved to be more ordinary than their predecessors who fled Vietnam in 1975 during the fall of Saigon. These newer displaced persons had had limited exposure to Western culture and knew virtually no English when they arrived. Often they came with nothing more than the clothes they wore.

From this larger group, we chose a random sample of 200 nuclear families and their 536 school-age children. Twenty-seven percent of the families had four or more children. At the time of the study, these young refugees had been in the United States for an average of three and a half years. We collected information on parents and their children during interviews conducted in their native tongues; we also gained access to school transcripts and other related documents.

All the children attended schools in low-income, metropolitan areas—environs not known for outstanding academic records. The refugees were fairly evenly distributed throughout the school levels: Grades one through eleven each contained about 8 percent of the children in the study; kindergarten and twelfth grade each contained about 5 percent. We converted the students' letter grades into a numerical grade point average (GPA): An A became a four; a D became a one. After calculations, we found that the children's mean GPA was 3.05, or a B average. Twenty-seven percent had an overall GPA in the A range, 52 percent in the B range and 17 percent in the C range. Only 4 percent had a GPA below a C grade.

Even more striking than the overall GPAs were the students' math scores. Almost half of the children earned As in math; another third earned Bs. Thus, four out of five students received either As or Bs. It is not surprising that they would do better in this subject. Their minds could most easily grasp disciplines in which English was not so crucial: math, physics, chemistry and science. As expected, their grades in the liberal arts were lower: In areas where extensive language skills were required, such as English, history or social studies, the combined GPA was 2.64.

To place our local findings in a national context, we turned to standardized achievement test scores, in particular, the California Achievement Test (CAT) results. In this arena as well, we found that the performance of the newly arrived students was exceptional. Their mean overall score on the CAT was in the 54th percentile; that is, they outperformed 54 percent of those taking the test—placing them just above the national average. Interestingly, their scores tended to cluster toward the middle ranges: They showed a more restricted scope of individual differences.

The national tests also reflected an above-average ability in math when the Indochinese children were compared with children taking the exam at equivalent levels. Half of the children studied obtained scores in the top quartile. Even more spectacularly, 27 percent of them scored in the 10th decile—better than 90 percent of the students across the country and almost three times higher than the national norm. The CAT math scores confirmed that the GPAs of these children were not products of local bias but of true mathematical competence.

Again, the lowest scores were found in the language and reading tests. In this case, the mean score was slightly below the national average. For reasons discussed earlier, this finding was expected. It remains remarkable, however, that the students' scores are so close to the national average in language skills.

The GPA and CAT scores show that the refugee children did very well, particularly in light of their background. A history marked by significant physical and emotional trauma as well as a lack of formal education would not seem to predispose them to an easy transition into U.S. schools. Yet even though they had not forgotten their difficult experiences, the children were able to focus on the present and to work toward the future. In so doing, they made striking scholastic progress. Moreover, their achievements held true for the majority, not for just a few whiz kids.

Clearly, these accomplishments are fueled by influences powerful enough to override the impact of a host of geographic and demographic factors. Using various statistical approaches, we sought to understand the forces responsible for this performance. In the process, a unique finding caught our attention, namely, a positive relation between the number of siblings and the children's GPA.

Family size has long been regarded as one of the most reliable predictors of poor achievement. Virtually all studies on the topic show an inverse relation: The greater the number of children in the family, the lower the mean GPA and other measures associated with scholastic performance. Typically, these reports document a 15 percent decline in GPA and other achievement-related scores with the addition of each child to the family. The interpretation of this finding has been subject to disagreement, but there is no conflict about its relation to achievement.

For the Indochinese students, this apparent disadvantage was somehow neutralized or turned into an advantage. We took this finding to be an important clue in elucidating the role of the family in academic performance. We assumed that distinctive family characteristics would explain how these achievements took place so early in resettlement as well as how these children and their parents managed to overcome such adversities as poor English skills, poverty and the often disruptive environment of urban schools.

Because they were newcomers in a strange land, it was reasonable to expect that at least some of the reasons for the children's success rested on their cultural background. While not ignoring the structural forces present here in the United States—among them the opportunity for education and advancement—we believed that the values and traditions permeating the lives of these children in Southeast Asia would guide their lives in this country.

Knowledge of one's culture does not occur in a vacuum; it is transmitted through the family. Children often acquire a sense of their heritage as a result of deliberate and concentrated parental effort in the context of family life. This inculcation of values from one generation to another is a universal feature of the conservation of culture.

We sought to determine which values were important to the parents, how well those values had been transmitted to the children and what role values played in promoting their educational achievement. In our interviews we included twenty-six questions about values that were derived from a search of Asian literature and from social science research. Respondents were asked to rate the perceived importance of these values.

We found that parents and children rated the perceived values in a similar fashion, providing empirical testimony that these parents had served their stewardship well. For the most part, the perspectives and values embedded in the cultural heritage of the Indochinese had been carried with them to the United States. We also determined that cultural values played an important role in the educational achievement of the children. Conserved values constituted a source of motivation and direction as the families dealt with contemporary problems set in a country vastly different from their homeland. The values formed a set of cultural givens with deep roots in the Confucian and Buddhist traditions of East and Southeast Asia.

The family is the central institution in these traditions, within which and through which achievement and knowledge are accomplished.

We used factor analyses and other statistical procedures to determine value groupings and their relation to achievement. These analyses showed that parents and children honor mutual, collective obligation to one another and to their relatives. They strive to attain respect, co-operation and harmony within the family.

Nowhere is the family's commitment to accomplishment and education more evident than in time spent on homework. During high school, Indochinese students spend an average of three hours and ten minutes per day; in junior high, an average of two-and-a-half hours; and in grade school, an average of two hours and five minutes. Research in the United States shows that American students study about one-and-a-half hours per day at the junior and senior high school levels.

Among the refugee families, then, homework clearly dominates household activities during weeknights. Although the parents' lack of education and facility with English often prevents them from engaging in the content of the exercise, they set standards and goals for the evening and facilitate their children's studies by assuming responsibility for chores and other practical considerations.

After dinner, the table is cleared, and homework begins. The older children, both male and female, help their younger siblings. Indeed, they seem to learn as much from teaching as from being taught. It is reasonable to suppose that a great amount of learning goes on at these times—in terms of skills, habits, attitudes and expectations as well as the content of a subject. The younger children, in particular, are taught not only subject matter but how to learn. Such sibling involvement demonstrates how a large family can encourage and enhance academic success. The familial setting appears to make the children feel at home in school and, consequently, perform well there.

Parental engagement included reading regularly to young children—an activity routinely correlated to academic performance. Almost one half (45 percent) of the parents reported reading aloud. In those families, the children's mean GPA was 3.14 as opposed to 2.97 in households where the parents did not read aloud. (This difference, and all others to follow in which GPAs are compared, is statistically reliable.) It is important to note that the effects of being read to held up statistically whether the children were read to in English or in their native language.

This finding suggests that parental English literacy skills may not play a vital role in determining school performance. Rather, other aspects of the experience—emotional ties between parent and child, cultural validation and wisdom shared in stories read in the child's native language, or value placed on reading and learning—extend to schoolwork. Reading at home obscures the boundary between home and school. In this context, learning is perceived as normal, valuable and fun.

Egalitarianism and role sharing were also found to be associated with high academic performance. In fact, relative equality between the sexes was one of the strongest predictors of GPA. In those homes where the respondents disagreed that a "wife should always do as her husband wishes," the children earned average GPAs of 3.16. But children from homes whose parents agreed with the statement had an average GPA of 2.64. In households where the husband helped with the dishes and laundry, the mean GPA was 3.21; when husbands did not participate in the chores, the mean GPA was 2.79.

This sense of equality was not confined to the parents—it extended to the children, especially in terms of sex-role expectations and school performance. GPAs were higher in households where parents expected both boys and girls to help with chores. Families rejecting the idea that a college education is more important for boys than for girls had children whose average GPA was 3.14; children from families exhibiting a pro-male bias had a mean GPA of 2.83.

Beyond the support and guidance provided by the family, culturally based attributions proved to be important to refugees in their view of scholastic motivation. The "love of learning" category was rated most often by both parents and students as the factor accounting for their academic success. There appeared to be two parts to this sentiment. First, the children experienced intrinsic gratification when they correctly worked a problem through to completion. The pleasure of intellectual growth, based on new knowledge and ideas and combined with increased competence and mastery, was considered highly satisfying. Second, refugee children felt a sense of accomplishment on seeing their younger siblings learn from their own efforts at teaching. Both learning and imparting knowledge were perceived as pleasurable experiences rather than as drudgery.

The gratification accompanying accomplishment was, in turn, founded on a sense of the importance of effort as opposed to ability. The refugees did not trust fate or luck as the determinant of educational outcome; they believed in their potential to master the factors that could influence their destiny. And their culture encompasses a practical approach to accomplishment: setting realistic goals. Without the setting of priorities and standards for work, goals would remain elusive. But anyone endorsing the values of working in a disciplined manner and taking a long-term view could establish priorities and pursue them.

Belief in one's own ability to effect change or attain goals has long been held to be a critical component of achievement and motivation—and our findings support this conclusion. Parents were asked a series of questions relating to their perceived ability to control external events influencing their lives. Those who had a clear sense of personal efficacy had children who attained higher GPAs.

We had some difficulty, however, interpreting the perception of efficacy as an idea generated solely by the individual. Despite a vast social science literature asserting the contrary, we believe that these refugees' sense of control over their lives could be traced to family identity. It seemed to us that the sense of familial efficacy proved critical, as opposed to the more Western concept of personal efficacy.

Other cultural values show us that the refugee family is firmly linked not only to its past and traditions but to the realities of the present and to future possibilities. This aptitude for integrating the past, present and future appears to have imparted a sense of continuity and direction to the lives of these people.

Education was central to this integration and to reestablishment in the United States. It was and still is the main avenue for refugees in American society to succeed and survive. In contrast, education in Indochina was a restricted privilege. The future of the refugee children, and of their families, is thus inextricably linked to schools and to their own children's performances within them. The emphasis on education as the key to social acceptance and economic success helps us understand why academic achievement is reinforced by such strong parental commitment.

Outside school, the same sense of drive and achievement can be seen in the parents. Having a job and being able to provide for the family is integral to family pride. Shame is felt by Asian families on welfare. Reflecting the same determination and energy that their children manifest in school, Indochinese parents have found employment and climbed out of economic dependency and poverty with dispatch.

Two of the twenty-six values included as a measure of cultural adaptation entailed integration and the acceptance of certain American ways of life: the importance of "seeking fun and excitement" and of "material possessions." These ideas are of particular concern because they address the future of refugee families and mark the potential power and consequence of American life on the refugees and subsequent generations. Not surprisingly, when our subjects were asked to indicate which values best characterized their nonrefugee neighbors, these two items were most frequently cited.

More interesting, however, was our finding that these same two values were correlated with a lower GPA. We found that parents who attributed greater importance to fun and excitement had children who achieved lower GPAs: 2.90 as opposed to 3.14. The results for material possessions were similar: GPAs were 2.66 versus 3.19.

It is not clear why these negative associations exist. Do they reflect less strict parents or families who have integrated so quickly that cultural stability has been lost? We believe it is the latter explanation. Refugees who held that "the past is as important as the future" had children whose GPAs averaged 3.14. Children of those who did not rate the preservation of the past as highly had an average GPA of 2.66. This item was one of the most powerful independent predictors of academic performance. Our findings run contrary to expectations. Rather than adopting American ways and assimilating into the melting pot, the most successful Indochinese families appear to retain their own traditions and values. By this statement we are in no way devaluing the American system. The openness and opportunity it offers have enabled the Indochinese to succeed in the United States even while maintaining their own cultural traditions.

Although different in origins, both traditional Indochinese and middle-class American values emphasize education, achievement, hard work, autonomy, perseverance and pride. The difference between the two value systems is one of orientation to achievement. American mores encourage independence and individual achievement, whereas Indochinese values foster interdependence and a family-based orientation to achievement. And in view of the position of these refugees in society during the early phase of re-settlement in this country, this approach appears to have worked well as the best long-term investment. It appears to be the reason why these children are highly responsive to American schools.

The lack of emphasis on fun and excitement also does not indicate misery on the part of these refugee children. Despite evidence that the suicide rate is growing among some Asian-American children, we found that those in our sample were well adjusted. Our interviews revealed no damaging manipulation of their lives by their parents; moreover, their love of learning sustained their academic pursuits.

The Indochinese values that encourage academic rigor and excellence are not culturally unique: earlier studies of other groups have found similar results. The children of Jewish immigrants from Eastern Europe, for example, excelled in the U.S. school system. In 1961 Judith R. Kramer of Brooklyn College and Seymour Leventman of the University of Pennsylvania reported that nearly 90 percent of the third generation attended college, despite the fact that the first generation had little or no education when they arrived in the United States. Their emphasis on family and culture was held to be instrumental in this success.

In 1948 William Caudill and George DeVos of the University of California at Berkeley found that Japanese students overcame prejudice in U.S. schools immediately after World War II and thrived academically. Their success was attributed to cultural values and to parental involvement. More recently, a study by Reginald Clark of the Claremont Graduate School documented the outstanding achievement of low-income African-American students in Chicago whose parents supported the school and teachers and structured their children's learning environment at home.

These findings, as well as our own, have significance for the current national debate on education. It is clear that the American school system—despite widespread criticism—has retained its capacity to teach, as it has shown with these refugees. We believe that the view of our schools as failing to educate stems from the unrealistic demand that the educational system deal with urgent social service needs. Citizens and politicians expect teachers and schools to keep children off the streets and away from drugs, deal with teenage pregnancy, prevent violence in the schools, promote safe sex and perform myriad other tasks and responsibilities in addition to teaching traditional academic subjects.

As the social needs of our students have moved into the classroom, they have consumed the scarce resources allocated to education and have compromised the schools' academic function. The primary role of teachers has become that of parent by proxy; they are expected to transform the attitude and behavior of children, many of whom come to school ill prepared to learn.

If we are to deal effectively with the crisis in American education, we must start with an accurate definition of the problem. We must separate teaching and its academic purpose from in-school social services. Only then can we assess the true ability of schools to accomplish these two, sometimes opposing, functions—or we can identify and delegate these nonacademic concerns to other institutions.

Throughout this article we have examined the role of the family in the academic performance of Indochinese refugees. We firmly believe that for American schools to succeed, parents and families must become more committed to the education of their children. They must instill a respect for education and create within the home an environment conducive to learning. They must also participate in the process so that their children feel comfortable learning and go to school willing and prepared to study.

Yet we cannot expect the family to provide such support alone. Schools must reach out to families and engage them meaningfully in the education of their children. This involvement must go beyond annual teacher-parent meetings and must include,

among other things, the identification of cultural elements that promote achievement.

Similarly, we cannot adopt the complete perspective of an Indochinese or any other culture. It would be ludicrous to impose cultural beliefs and practices on American children, especially on those whose progress in this country has been fraught with blocked access.

We can, however, work to ensure that families believe in the value of an education and, like the refugees, have rational expectations of future rewards for their efforts. Moreover, we can integrate components of the refugees' experience regarding the family's role in education. It is possible to identify culturally compatible values, behaviors and strategies for success that might enhance scholastic achievement. It is in this regard that the example of the Indochinese refugees—as well as the Japanese and Jewish immigrants before them—can shape our priorities and our policies.

CRITICAL THINKING QUESTIONS

1. How do Indochinese children compare with their U.S. counterparts on such measures of academic performance as grade-point average (GPA), mathematics scores, and the California Achievement Test (CAT)?
2. Do you feel that the findings for American refugees would be similar to those for Canadian refugees?
3. From a sociological point of view, what factors do you feel influence the integration of immigrant students at your own university or college?

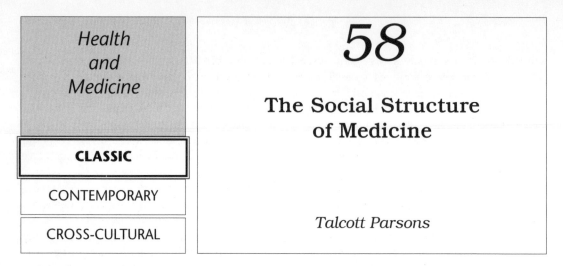

58

The Social Structure
of Medicine

Talcott Parsons

Talcott Parsons, one of the most influential U.S. sociologists during the twentieth century, contributed greatly to the development of structural-functional analysis. In this selection, he examines the significance of health and illness within a social system, with particular attention to the social roles of physicians and patients.

A little reflection will show immediately that the problem of health is intimately involved in the functional prerequisites of the social system.... Certainly by almost any definition health is included in the functional needs of the individual member of the society so that from the point of view of functioning of the social system, too low a general level of health, too high an incidence of illness, is dysfunctional. This is in the first instance because illness incapacitates for the effective performance of social roles. It could of course be that this incidence was completely uncontrollable by social action, an independently given condition of social life. But insofar as it is controllable, through rational action or otherwise, it is clear that there is a functional interest of the society in its control, broadly in the minimization of illness. As one special aspect of this, attention may be called to premature death. From a variety of points of view, the birth and rearing of a child constitute a "cost" to the society, through pregnancy, child care, socialization, formal training, and many other channels. Premature death, before the individual has had the opportunity to play out his full quota of social roles, means that only a partial "return" for this cost has been received.

All this would be true were illness purely a "natural phenomenon" in the sense that, like the vagaries of the weather, it was not, to our knowledge, reciprocally involved in the motivated interactions of human beings. In this case illness

Source: From *The Social System* by Talcott Parsons. Copyright © 1951, copyright renewed 1979 by Talcott Parsons. Reprinted with the permission of The Free Press, a Division of Simon & Schuster.

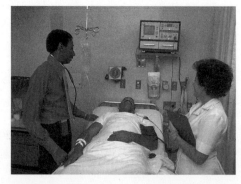

would be something which merely "happened to" people, which involved consequences which had to be dealt with and conditions which might or might not be controllable but was in no way an expression of motivated behavior.

This is in fact the case for a very important part of illness, but it has become increasingly clear, by no means for all. In a variety of ways motivational factors accessible to analysis in action terms are involved in the etiology of many illnesses, and conversely, though without exact correspondence, many conditions are open to therapeutic influence through motivational channels. To take the simplest kind of case, differential exposure, to injuries or to infection, is certainly motivated, and the role of unconscious wishes to be injured or to fall ill in such cases has been clearly demonstrated. Then there is the whole range of "psychosomatic" illness about which knowledge has been rapidly accumulating in recent years. Finally, there is the field of "mental disease," the symptoms of which occur mainly on the behavioral level....

Summing up, we may say that illness is a state of disturbance in the "normal" functioning of the total human individual, including both the state of the organism as a biological system and of his personal and social adjustments. It is thus partly biologically and partly socially defined....

Medical practice...is a "mechanism" in the social system for coping with the illnesses of its members. It involves a set of institutionalized roles.... The immediately relevant social structures consist in the patterning of the role of the medical practitioner himself and, though to common sense it may seem superfluous to analyze it, that of the "sick person" himself....

The role of the medical practitioner belongs to the general class of "professional" roles, a subclass of the larger group of occupational roles. Caring for the sick is thus not an incidental activity of other roles though, for example, mothers do a good deal of it—but has become functionally specialized as a full-time "job." This, of course, is by no means true of all societies. As an occupational role it is

institutionalized about the technical content of the function which is given a high degree of primacy relative to other status-determinants. It is thus inevitable both that incumbency of the role should be achieved and that performance criteria by standards of technical competence should be prominent. Selection for it and the context of its performance are to a high degree segregated from other bases of social status and solidarities.... Unlike the role of the businessman, however, it is collectivity-oriented not self-oriented.

The importance of this patterning is, in one context, strongly emphasized by its relation to the cultural tradition. One basis for the division of labor is the specialization of technical competence. The role of physician is far along the continuum of increasingly high levels of technical competence required for performance. Because of the complexity and subtlety of the knowledge and skill required and the consequent length and intensity of training, it is difficult to see how the functions could, under modern conditions, be ascribed to people occupying a prior status as one of their activities in that status, following the pattern by which, to a degree, responsibility for the health of her children is ascribed to the mother-status. There is an intrinsic connection between achieved statuses and the requirements of high technical competence....

High technical competence also implies specificity of function. Such intensive devotion to expertness in matters of health and disease precludes comparable expertness in other fields. The physician is not, by virtue of his modern role, a generalized "wise man" or sage—though there is considerable folklore to that effect—but a specialist whose superiority to his fellows is confined to the specific sphere of his technical training and experience. For example one does not expect the physician as such to have better judgment about foreign policy or tax legislation than any other comparably intelligent and well-educated citizen. There are of course elaborate subdivisions of specialization within the profession.... The physician is [also] expected to treat an objective problem in objective, scientifically justifiable terms. For example, whether he likes or dislikes the particular patient as a person is supposed to be irrelevant, as indeed it is to most purely objective problems of how to handle a particular disease.

...The "ideology" of the profession lays great emphasis on the obligation of the physician to put the "welfare of the patient" above his personal interests, and regards "commercialism" as the most serious and insidious evil with which it has to contend. The line, therefore, is drawn primarily vis-à-vis "business." The "profit motive" is supposed to be drastically excluded from the medical world. This attitude is, of course, shared with the other professions, but it is perhaps more pronounced in the medical case than in any single one except perhaps the clergy....

An increasing proportion of medical practice is now taking place in the context of organization. To a large extent this is necessitated by the technological development of medicine itself, above all the need for technical facilities beyond the reach of the individual practitioner, and the fact that treating the same case often involves the complex co-operation of several different kinds of physicians as well as of auxiliary personnel. This greatly alters the relation of the physician to the rest of the instrumental complex. He tends to be relieved of much responsibility and hence necessarily of freedom, in relation to his patients other than in his technical role. Even if a hospital executive is a physician himself he is not in the usual sense engaged in the "practice of medicine" in performing his functions any more than the president of the Miners' Union is engaged in mining coal.

As was noted, for common sense there may be some question of whether "being sick" constitutes a social role at all—isn't it simply a state of fact, a "condition"? Things are not quite so simple as this. The test is the existence of a set of institutionalized expectations and the corresponding sentiments and sanctions.

There seem to be four aspects of the institutionalized expectation system relative to the sick role. First is the exemption from normal social role responsibilities, which of course is relative to the nature and severity of the illness. This exemption requires legitimation by and to the various actors involved and the physician often serves as a court of appeal as well as a direct legitimatizing agent. It is noteworthy that like all institutionalized patterns the legitimation of being sick enough to avoid obligations can not only be a right of the sick person but an obligation upon him. People are often resistant to admitting they are sick and it is not uncommon for others to tell them that they *ought* to stay in bed. The word generally has a moral connotation. It goes almost without saying that this legitimation has the social function of protection against "malingering."

The second closely related aspect is the institutionalized definition that the sick person cannot be expected by "pulling himself together" to get well by an act of decision or will. In this sense also he is exempted from responsibility—he is in a condition that must "be taken care of." His "condition" must be changed, not merely his "attitude." Of course the process of recovery may be spontaneous but while the illness lasts he can't "help it." This element in the definition of the state of illness is obviously crucial as a bridge to the acceptance of "help."

The third element is the definition of the state of being ill as itself undesirable with its obligation to want to "get well." The first two elements of legitimation of the sick role thus are conditional in a highly important sense. It is a relative legitimation so long as he is in this unfortunate state which both he and alter hope he can get out of as expeditiously as possible.

Finally, the fourth closely related element is the obligation—in proportion to the severity of the condition, of course—to seek *technically competent* help, namely, in the most usual case, that of a physician and to *cooperate* with him in the process of trying to get well. It is here, of course, that the role of the sick person as patient becomes articulated with that of the physician in a complementary role structure.

It is evident from the above that the role of motivational factors in illness immensely broadens the scope and increases the importance of the institutionalized role aspect of being sick. For then the problem of social control becomes much more than one of ascertaining facts and drawing lines. The privileges and exemptions of the sick role may become objects of a "secondary gain" which the patient is positively motivated, usually unconsciously, to secure or to retain. The problem, therefore, of the balance of motivations to recover becomes of first importance. In general motivational balances of great functional significance to the social system are institutionally controlled, and it should, therefore, not be surprising that this is no exception.

A few further points may be made about the specific patterning of the sick role and its relation to social structure. It is, in the first place, a "contingent" role into which anyone, regardless of his status in other respects, may come. It is, furthermore, in the type case temporary. One may say that it is in a certain sense a "negatively achieved" role, through failure to "keep well," though, of course, positive motivations also operate, which by that very token must be motivations to deviance....

The orientation of the sick role vis-à-vis the physician is also defined as collectively-oriented. It is true that the patient has a very obvious self-interest in getting well in most cases, though this point may not always be so simple. But once he has called in a physician the attitude is clearly marked, that he has assumed the obligation to cooperate with that physician in what is regarded as a common task. The obverse of the physician's obligation to be guided by the welfare of the patient is the latter's obligation to "do his part" to the best of his ability. This point is clearly brought out, for example, in the attitudes of the profession toward what is called "shopping around." By that is meant the practice of a patient "checking" the advice of one physician against that of another without telling physician A that he intends to consult physician B, or if he comes back to A that he has done so or who B is. The medical view is that if the patient is not satisfied with the advice his physician gives him he may properly do one of two things, first he may request a consultation, even naming the physician he wishes called in, but in that case it is physician A not the patient who must call B in, the patient may not see B independently, and above all not without A's knowledge. The other proper recourse is to terminate the relation with A and become "B's patient." The notable fact here is that a pattern of behavior on the part not only of the physician but also of the patient, is expected which is in sharp contrast to perfectly legitimate behavior in a commercial relationship. If he is buying a car there is no objection to the customer going to a number of dealers before making up his mind, and there is no obligation for him to inform any one dealer what others he is consulting, to say nothing of approaching the Chevrolet dealer only through the Ford dealer.

The doctor-patient relationship is thus focused on these pattern elements. The patient has a need for technical services because he doesn't—nor do his lay associates, family members, etc.— "know" what is the matter or what to do about it, nor does he control the necessary facilities. The physician is a technical expert who by special training and experience, and by an institutionally validated status, is qualified to "help" the patient in a situation institutionally defined as legitimate in a relative sense but as needing help....

CRITICAL THINKING QUESTIONS

1. Does Parsons understand illness as a biological condition, that is, "something that happens to people"? What are the social elements in health and illness?

2. According to Parsons, what are the distinctive characteristics of the social role of the physician?

3. What are the major elements of "the sick role"? In what respects does Parsons view the social roles of physicians and patients as complementary? Can you see ways in which they may be in conflict?

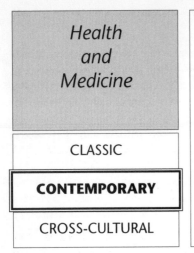

Health
and
Medicine

CLASSIC

CONTEMPORARY

CROSS-CULTURAL

59

"Even If I Don't Know What I'm Doing I Can Make It Look Like I Know What I'm Doing": Becoming a Doctor in the 1990s

Brenda L. Beagan

Beagan's article investigates how medical students are trained at Canadian universities. Her analysis provides revealing insight into how medical students incorporate new professional identities as they move through their studies.

For most medical students, a remarkable and important transformation occurs from the time they enter medical school to the time they leave.... They become immersed in the culture, environment and lifestyle of the school. They slowly lose their initial identity and become redefined by the new situation. Medical students have to look for something to hang on to. And that something is provided: their new identity as 'doctor.'

— Shapiro (1987: 27)

When students enter medical school they are lay people with some science background. When they leave four years later they have become physicians; they have acquired specialized

Source: Brenda L. Beagan. 2001. "Even if I don't know what I'm doing I can make it look like I know what I'm doing": Becoming a doctor in the 1990s. *The Canadian Review of Sociology and Anthropology,* 38(3), 275–92. Reprinted by permission of the Canadian Sociology and Anthropology Association.

knowledge and taken on a new identity of medical professional. What happens in those four years? What processes of socialization go into the making of a doctor?

Most of what we know about how students come to identify as future-physicians derives from research conducted when students were almost exclusively male, white, middle- or upper-class, young and single—for example, the classics *Boys in White* (Becker, Geer, Strauss, & Hughes, 1961) and *Student Physician* (Morton, Reader, & Kendall, 1957). When women and students of colour were present in this research it was in token numbers. Even when women and non-traditional students were present, as in Sinclair's (1997) recent ethnography, their impact on processes of professional identity formation and the potentially distinct impact of professional socialization on these students have been largely unanalysed. What does becoming a doctor look like in a medical school of the late 1990s, where many students are female, are of diverse racial and cultural backgrounds, are working-class, gay and/or parents?

This study draws on survey and interview data from students and faculty at one Canadian medical school to examine the processes of professional identity formation and how they are experienced by diverse undergraduate medical students in the late 1990s. As the results will show, the processes are remarkably unchanged from the processes documented 40 years ago.

RESEARCH METHODS AND PARTICIPANTS

The research employed three complementary research strategies: A survey of a third-year class (123 students) at one medical school, interviews with 25 students from that class, and interviews with 23 faculty members from the same school.[1] Third-year students were chosen because in a traditional medical curriculum the third year is a key point for students, an important transition as they move out of the classroom to spend the majority of their time working with patients— patients who may or may not call them "doctor," treat them as doctors, and reflect them back to themselves as doctors (cf. Coombs, 1978; Haas & Shaffir, 1987)....

Survey respondents also identified faculty members who they believed were "especially interested in medical education." Twenty-three faculty interviews were conducted. All interviews took 60–90 minutes following a semi-structured interview guide, and were tape-recorded and transcribed. The interview transcripts were coded inductively using broad categories such as "pressures toward conformity," and "conflicts experienced," and using codes such as "language of medicine" derived from the literature. Initial broad codes were later subdivided into narrower codes.

...[T]he students who completed the survey were evenly divided by gender and were heterogeneous in "race"/ethnicity, as well as in self-identified social class background.[2] Twenty students (28%) self-identified as members of "minority groups," all identifying racial or cultural groups.

The students interviewed were slightly less heterogeneous in "race"/ethnicity and first language, and were somewhat more likely to be in committed relationships. The purposive sample of faculty members and administrators was predominately male, English-speaking and of European origin— reflective of the school's faculty more generally.

FIRST EXPERIENCES BECOME COMMONPLACE

When identifying how they came to think of themselves as medical students, participants described a process whereby what feels artificial and unnatural initially comes to feel natural simply through repetition. For many students, a series of "first times" were transformative moments.

Denise:[3] I think there are sort of seminal experiences. The first cut in anatomy, the first time you see a patient die, first time you see a treatment that was really aggressive and didn't work.... First few procedures that I conducted myself, first time I realized that I really did have somebody's life in my hands.... It seems like a whole lot of first times. The first time you take a history, the first time you actually hear the murmur. There are a lot of "Ah-ha!" sort of experiences.

Part of the novelty is the experience of being entitled—even required—to violate conventional social norms, touching patients' bodies, inquiring about bodily functions, probing emotional states: "You have to master a sense that you're invading somebody, and to feel like it's all right to do that, to invade their personal space...."

CONSTRUCTING A PROFESSIONAL APPEARANCE

Students are quite explicitly socialized to adopt a professional appearance: "When people started to relax the dress code a letter was sent to everybody's mailbox, commenting that we were not to show up in jeans, and a tie is appropriate for men." Most students, however, do not require such reminders; they have internalized the requisite standards.

Dressing neatly and appropriately is important to convey respect to patients, other medical staff, and the profession. It probably also helps in patients taking students seriously (survey comment).

Asked whether or not they ever worry about their appearance or dress at the hospital, 41% of the survey respondents said they do not, while 59% said they do.

There were no statistically significant differences by gender, class background or "minority" status, yet gendered patterns emerged when students detailed their concerns in an open-ended question. Most of the men satisfied their concerns about professional appearance with a shave and a collared shirt, perhaps adding a tie: "I do make sure that I am dressed appropriately when I see patients i.e. well-groomed, collared shirt (but no tie)." Women, on the other hand, struggled with the complex messages conveyed by their clothing, trying to look well-dressed yet not convey sexual messages. For women, "dressed up" normally means feminine while a professional image is intended to convey competence. Striking a balance at the intersection can be difficult: "Is it professional enough? Competent looking?... I do not want to appear 'sexy' on the job." As one student noted, while both men and women sometimes violate standards of professional dress, men's violations tend to involve being too informal; women's may involve dressing too provocatively, thereby sexualizing a doctor-patient encounter.

CHANGES IN LANGUAGE, THINKING AND COMMUNICATION SKILLS

Acquiring a huge vocabulary of new words and old words with new meanings—what one student called "medical-ese"—is one of the central tasks facing medical students, and one of the major bases for examining them (Sinclair, 1997). Students were well aware of adopting the formal language of medicine.

Dawna: All of a sudden all I can think of is this lingo that people won't understand. My brother told me the other day, "Sometimes I just don't understand what you are talking about anymore." I don't realize it! I'll use technical terms that I didn't think that other people wouldn't know.

The language of medicine is the basis for constructing a new social reality. Even as it allows communication, language constructs "zones of meaning that are linguistically circumscribed" (Berger & Luckmann, 1966: 39). Medical language encapsulates and constructs a worldview wherein reducing a person to body parts, tissues, organs and systems becomes normal, natural, "the only reasonable way to think" (Good & Good, 1993: 98–9). Students described this as learning to pare away "extraneous" information about a patient's life to focus on what is clinically relevant.

Becky: I see how it happens.... The first day of medicine we're just people. We relate by asking everything about a person, just like you'd have a conversation with anybody. And then that sort of changes and you become focussed on the disease...because right now there's just too much. It's overwhelming I'm hoping that as I learn more and become more comfortable with what I know and I can apply it without having to consciously go through every step in my mind, that I'll be able to focus on the *person* again.

In part through the language of medicine students learn a scientific gaze that reduces patients to bodies, allowing them to concentrate on what is medically important—disease, procedures, and techniques (Haas & Shaffir, 1987).

Not surprisingly, students may simultaneously lose the communication abilities they had upon entering medical school.

Dr. W.: Their ability to talk to people becomes corrupted by the educational process. They learn the language of medicine but they give up some of the knowledge that they brought in.... The knowledge of how to listen to somebody, how to be humble, how to hear somebody else's words.... It gets overtaken by the agenda of medical interviewing.

Another faculty member noted that students' communication skills improved significantly during their first term of first year, but "by the end of fourth year they were worse than they had been before medical school."

LEARNING THE HIERARCHY

Key to becoming a medical student is learning to negotiate the complex hierarchy within medicine, with students positioned at the bottom. A few faculty saw this hierarchy as a fine and important tradition facilitating students' learning.

Dr. U.: You're always taught by the person above you. Third-year medical students taught by the fourth-year student.... Fourth-year student depends on the resident to go over his stuff. Resident depends on maybe the senior or the chief resident or the staff person. So they all get this hierarchy which is wonderful for learning because the attendings can't deal with everybody.

Students, and most faculty, were far less accepting of this traditional hierarchy—particularly of students' place in it.

Both faculty and students pointed out the compliance the hierarchical structure inculcates in students, discouraging them from questioning those above them.

Dr. G.: If they don't appear compliant and so on they will get evaluated poorly. And if you get evaluated poorly then you might not get a good residency position. There's that sort of thing over their shoulders all of the time…the fear.

For students being a "good medical student" means not challenging clinicians.

Valerie: If I ever saw something blatantly sexist or racist or wrong I hope that I would say something. But you get so caught up in basically clamming up, shutting up, and just taking it.... Is it going to ruin my career, am I going to end up known as the fink, am I going to not get the [residency] spot that I want because I told?

Though virtually every student described seeing things on the wards that they disagreed with, as long as there was no direct harm to a patient they stayed silent and simply filed away the incident in their collection of "things not to do when I am a doctor."

Other researchers have noted that medical students develop an approach geared to getting along with faculty, pleasing them whatever their demands (Becker et al., 1961: 281; Bloom, 1973: 20; Sinclair, 1997: 29). Some students, however, had *internalized* the norm of not criticizing clinicians, adopting an unspoken "code of silence" not just to appease faculty, but as part of being a good physician. In particular, one should never critique a colleague in front of patients.

Mark: As students we all critique the professors and our attendings.... But I don't think we'd ever do that in front of a patient. It's never been told to us not to. But most of us wouldn't do that. Even if a patient describes something their doctor has prescribed to them or a treatment they've recommended which you know is totally wrong, maybe even harmful, I think most of us, unless it was really harmful, would tend to ignore it and just accept, "This is the doctor and his patient. What happens between them is okay."

These students had developed a sense of alliance with other members of the profession rather than with lay people and patients—a key to professional socialization. Several faculty referred to good medical students as "good team players' (cf. Sinclair, 1997), invoking a notion of belonging.

Dr. M.: That sense of belonging, I think, is a sense of belonging to the profession.... You're part of the process of health care.... I mean, you haven't a lot of the responsibility, but at least you're connected with the team.

For some students, too, the desire to present a united front for patients was expressed as being a good team player: "You have to go along with some things…in front of the patient. For teams it wouldn't be good to have the ranks arguing amongst themselves about the best approach for patient care." To remain good team players, many students, residents and physicians learn to say nothing even when they see colleagues and superiors violating the ethics and standards of the profession; such violations are disregarded as matters of personal style (Light, 1988).

RELATIONSHIP TO PATIENTS

As students are learning their place in the hierarchy within medicine, they are simultaneously learning an appropriate relationship to patients. Within the medical hierarchy students feel powerless at the bottom. Yet in relation to patients even students hold a certain amount of power. In the interviews there were widely diverging views on the degree of professional authority physicians and student-physicians should display.

Some faculty drew a very clear connection between professionalism and the "emotional distancing" Fox documented in medicine in 1957, describing students developing a "hard shell" as a "way of dealing with feelings" to prevent over-identifying with patients. Emotional involvement and over-identification are seen as dangerous; students must strike a balance between empathy and objectivity, learning to overcome or master their emotions (Conrad, 1988; Haas & Shaffir, 1987): "I only become of use if I can create some distance so that I can function."

> Dr. E.: Within the professional job that you have to do, one can be very nice to patients but there's a distancing that says you're not their friend, you're their doctor.

In contrast, several faculty members rejected the "emotional distancing" approach to medicine in favour of one based in egalitarian connection.

> Dr. V.: I reject that way of dealing with it.... When I'm seeing a patient I have to try to get into understanding what's bothering them. And in fact it's a harder job, I mean I need to understand well enough so I can help them to understand. 'Cause the process of healing is self-understanding.

These faculty members talked about recognizing and levelling power or sharing power. They saw professional distancing as the loss of humanitarianism, the adoption of a position of superiority, aloofness, emphasizing that clinicians need to know their patients as something more than a diagnosis. Women were slightly over-represented among those expressing the egalitarian perspective, but several male clinicians also advocated this position.

PLAYING A ROLE GRADUALLY BECOMES REAL

Along with emotional distancing, Fox (1957) identified "training for uncertainty" as key to medical socialization, including the uncertainty arising from not knowing everything, and not knowing enough. Alongside gathering the knowledge and experience that gradually reduces feelings of uncertainty, students also grow to simply tolerate high levels of uncertainty. At the same time they face routine expectations of certainty—from patients who expect them "to know it all" and faculty who often expect them to know far more than they do and who evaluate the students' competence (Haas & Shaffir, 1987). Students quickly learn it is risky to display lack of certainty; impression management becomes a central feature of clinical learning (Conrad, 1988). Haas and Shaffir (1987: 110) conclude that the process of professionalization involves *above all* the successful adoption of a cloak of competence such that audiences are convinced of the legitimacy of claims to competence.

Robert Coombs argues that medical professional socialization is partly a matter of *playing* the role of doctor, complete with the props of white coat, stethoscope, name tag, and clipboard (1978: 222). The symbols mark medical students off as distinct from lay people and other hospital staff, differentiating between We and They. Students spoke of "taking on a role" that initially made them feel like "total frauds," "impostors."

> Erin: It was really role-playing. You were doing all these examinations on these patients which were not going to go into their charts, were not going to ever be read by anybody who was treating the people so it really was just practice. Just play-acting.

They affirmed the importance of the props to successful accomplishment of their role play—even as it enhanced the feeling of artifice: "During third year when we got to put the little white coat on and carry some instruments around the hospital, have a name tag...it definitely felt like role-playing."

Despite feeling fraudulent, the role play allows students to meet a crucial objective: demonstrating to faculty, clinical instructors, nurses and patients that they know something. They quickly learn to at least look competent.

Nancy: Even if I don't know what I'm doing I can make it *look* like I know what I'm doing.... It was my acting in high school.... I get the trust of the patient....

RESPONSES FROM OTHERS

The more students are treated by others as if they really were doctors the more they feel like doctors (cf. Coombs, 1978). In particular, the response from other hospital personnel and patients can help confirm the student's emerging medical professional identity.

Rina: The more the staff treats you as someone who actually belongs there, that definitely adds to your feeling like you do belong there.... It's like, "Wow! This nurse is paging me and wants to know *my* opinion on why this patient has no urine output?!"

For many students patients were the single most important source of confirmation for their emerging identity as physicians. With doctors and nurses, students feel they can easily be caught out for what they don't know; with patients they feel fairly certain they can pull off a convincing performance, and they often realize they *do* know more than the average person.

One response from others that has tremendous impact is simply being called doctor by others (Konner, 1987; Shapiro, 1987). Survey results show 68% (*n* = 48) of students had been called doctor at least occasionally by people other than family or friends. All but two fully recalled the first time they were called doctor and how they felt about it. *Not* being called doctor—especially when your peers *are*—can be equally significant. In previous accounts, being white and being male have greatly improved a medical student's chances of being taken for a doctor (Dickstein, 1993; Gamble, 1990; Kirk, 1994; Lenhart, 1993).

In this study, although social class background, minority status and first language made no difference, significantly more men than women were *regularly* called doctor and significantly more women had *never* been called doctor.[4]

These data suggest a lingering societal assumption that the doctor is a man. According to the interviews, women medical students and physicians are still often mistaken for nurses. Two of the male students suggested the dominant assumption that a doctor is a man facilitates their establishing rapport with patients and may ease their relationships with those above them in the medical hierarchy: "I've often felt because I fit like a stereotypical white male, that patients might see me as a bit more trustworthy. A bit more what they'd like to see. Who they want to see." Goffman notes that the part of a social performance intended to impress others, which he calls the "front," and which includes clothing, gender, appearance and manner, is predetermined: "When an actor takes on an established social role, usually he finds that a particular front has already been established for it" (1959: 27). In this case it appears that the role doctor, or medical student, still carries an attached assumption of maleness.

SECONDARY SOCIALIZATION: SUBSUMING THE FORMER SELF?

The fact that roles carry with them established expectations heightens the potential for clashes with the identity characteristics of new incumbents. Education processes, inevitably processes of secondary socialization, must always contend with individuals' already formed and persistent selves, selves established through primary socialization. As Berger and Luckmann (1966: 129) note, "Whatever new contents are now to be internalized must somehow be superimposed upon this already present reality."

In his study of how medical students put together identities as spouses, parents, and so on with their developing identities as physicians,

Broadhead (1983) stresses the need for individuals to "articulate" their various identities to one another, sorting out convergences and divergences of attitudes, assumptions, activities and perspectives that accompany different subject positions.

In this research, most students indicated that medicine had largely taken over the rest of their lives, diminishing their performance of other responsibilities. While 55% of survey respondents thought they were doing a good job of being a medical student, many thought they were doing a poor to very poor job of being a spouse (26%) or family member (37%); 46% gave themselves failing grades as friends. Fewer than a quarter of respondents thought they were doing a good job of being an informed citizen (18%) or member of their religion, if they had one (17%).

What emerged from most interviews and from the survey was a picture of medical school dominating all other aspects of daily life. Overwhelmingly, students talked about sacrifice.

Lew: You just sacrifice so much. I don't know about people who don't have children, but I value my family more than anything, and, and I cannot—I didn't know you had to sacrifice that much.

Many students had given things up, at least temporarily: musical instruments, art, writing, sports activities, volunteer activities. Some students spoke of putting themselves on hold, taking on new medical-student identities by subsuming former identities.

This sacrifice of self-identity can be quite serious. Several faculty and students suggested students from non-Western, non-Caucasian cultural backgrounds need to assimilate: "Students from other cultures leave behind a lot of their culture in order to succeed. There's a trade-off." Similarly, faculty and students suggested gay and lesbian students frequently become more "closeted" as they proceed through undergraduate training. One clinician said of a lesbian fourth-year student, "Now all of a sudden her hair's cut very business-like and the clothes are different.... She's fitting into medicine. Medicine isn't becoming a

component of her, she's becoming a component of the machine." Some faculty suggested women in medicine may need to relinquish their identity as women in order to fit in as physicians.

Dr. Q.: The women who are in those positions are white men. You just have to look at the way they dress. They're wearing power suits often with ties, you know, they're really trying to fit the image. [One of the women here] recently retired and in the elevator in the hospital they talked about her as one of the boys. So that's the perception of the men is that this is not a woman, this is one of the boys.

Women, they argued, become more-or-less men during medical training, "almost hyper-masculine in their interactions," "much more like men in terms of thought processes and interactions with people."

In addition to letting go of gender identity, sexual identity and cultural identity, some students described losing connections to their families and old friends after entering medical school. Often this was due to time constraints and diverging interests, but for some there was also a growing social distance as they moved into a new social status and education level. Lance was disconnecting from his working-class family:

Lance: My family actually were very unsupportive [when I got into medicine]. They didn't even know what I was doing. And there's still this huge gap between them and myself because they don't want to understand what's going on in my world, and their world seems quite simple, simplistic to me.... I see that gap getting larger over time.

Relationships with family, friends from outside of medicine, and anyone else who cannot relate to what students are doing every day are put "on the back burner." Intimate relationships are frequent casualties of medical school.

Thus some students do not or cannot integrate their medical student identities with their former sense of self; rather they let go of parts of themselves, bury them, abandon them, or put them aside, at least for a while. Another option for students who experience incongruities between their medical-student identities and other aspects of themselves is to segregate their lives. Because human beings have the ability to reflect on our own actions, it becomes possible to experience a segment of the self as distinct, to "detach a part of the self and its concomitant reality as relevant only to the role-specific situation in question" (Berger & Luckmann, 1966: 131). In this research 31% of survey respondents felt they are one person at school and another with friends and family. Perhaps as a consequence, many students maintain quite separate groups of friends, within medicine and outside medicine. Indeed, some faculty stressed the importance of maintaining strong outside connections to make it through medical school without losing part of yourself.[5]

DIFFERENCE AS A BASIS FOR RESISTANCE

Elsewhere I have argued that intentional and unintentional homogenizing influences in medical education neutralize the impact of social differences students bring into medicine (Beagan, 2000). Students come to believe that the social class, "race," ethnicity, gender and sexual orientation of a physician is not—and should not be relevant during physician-patient interactions. Nonetheless, at the same time those social differences can provide a basis for critique of and resistance to aspects of medical professional socialization. A study of medical residents found that those most able to resist socialization pressures minimized contact and interaction with others in medicine; maintained outside relationships that supported an alternative orientation to the program; and entered their programs with a "relatively strong and well-defined orientation" (Shapiro & Jones, 1979: 243). Complete resocialization requires "an intense concentration of all significant interaction within the [new social] group" (Berger & Luckmann, 1966: 145); it is also facilitated by minimal contradictions between the previous social world and the new world.

In this research, age played a clear role in students' ability to resist some aspects of professional socialization. Older students usually had careers before medicine, which helped put medical school in a different perspective. Often medicine was one of a range of possible things they could be doing with their lives—important, but not worth sacrificing for: "There are other things that are more important to me than this, so if at any point this conflicted too much with those things, I would give it up." One student suggested that being older entering medicine meant she had her goals and self-identity more clearly established. Most older students were in committed relationships with non-medical partners and had clear priorities about maintaining non-medical activities and connections, rather than abandoning them under the onslaught of medical school demands.

> Robin: I resolved that I wouldn't let my close friends go by the wayside.... My partner is important to me, and I wouldn't always make him take a back seat to what I was doing.... It was like an ultimatum. If this program won't allow me to do those things, which I thought were reasonable things, then I just wasn't willing to do it.

These outside commitments helped them minimize interactions with their new social group.

The strongest basis for resisting professional socialization, however, came from having a working-class or impoverished family background. Most of the working-class students said they are not seen as particularly praiseworthy within their families—if anything they are somewhat suspect. They expressed a sustained anti-elitism that keeps them from fully identifying with other medical professionals. Janis, for example, insisted that she is not "one of Them," that she came from the other side of the tracks and still belongs there, that she could never fit in at medical school, could never be "a proper med student." She feels very uncomfortable with social functions at school and sees herself as utterly different from her classmates and preceptors: "Let's just say I don't share Dr. Smith's interest in yachting in the Caribbean, you know what I mean? (laughing)."

Lance, who spent his summers working on fishing boats to pay for medical school, described most of his classmates as "the pampered elite." He resists the required dress code because it epitomizes elitism.

Lance: A lot of people, the first thing they did when we started seeing patients was throw on a nice pair of shoes and grab the tie and button up. I've never worn a tie. And I never will.... To me, it symbolizes everything that sets the doctor and the patient apart. It's like...'I'm somewhat better than everyone else'.... It gets in the way of good communication. I think you want a level of respect there, but you don't want that B.S. that goes with it.

Although the number of working class students was small, the data showed quite clearly that they tended to be among the least compliant with the processes of secondary socialization encountered in medical school.

Lance: I think I'm very much different from my classmates...more outspoken, definitely.... Other people tend to say the right thing because they're a little afraid of the consequences. I don't care.... It comes from my background, you know, fishing. I've seen these tough, hard guys, think they're pretty something, but they're puking their guts out being seasick. It kind of reduces to the common denominator.

CONCLUSION

What is perhaps most remarkable about these findings is how little has changed since the publication *of Boys in White* (Becker et al., 1961) and *Student Physician* (Merton et al., 1957), despite the passage of 40 years and the influx of a very different student population. The basic processes of socializing new members into the profession of medicine remain remarkably similar, as students encounter new social norms, a new language, new thought processes, and a new world view that will eventually enable them to become full-fledged members of "the team" taking the expected role in the medical hierarchy.

Yet, with the differences in the 1990s student population, there are also some important differences in experiences. The role of medical student continues to carry with it certain expectations of its occupant. At a time when medical students were almost exclusively white, heterosexually identified, upper- or middle-class men, the identity may have "fit" more easily than it does for students who are women, who are from minority racial groups, who identify as gay or lesbian or working-class. If role-playing competence and being reflected back to yourself as "doctor" are as central to medical socialization as Haas and Shaffir (1987) suggest, what does it mean that women students are less likely than their male peers to be called doctor? This research has indicated the presence of a lingering societal assumption that Doctor = Man. Women students struggle to construct a professional appearance that male students find a straightforward accomplishment. Women search for ways to be in relationship with their patients that are unmarked by gender. Despite the fact that they make up half of all medical students in Canada, women's experiences of medical school remain different. In this research, almost half (6 of 14) of the women students interviewed indicated that they do not identify themselves as medical students in casual social settings outside school lest they be seen as putting on airs; none of the male students indicated this. It remains for future research to determine whether gender differences in the "fit" of the physician role make a difference to medical practice.

Interestingly, it is commonly assumed that the source of change in medical education will be the next generation of physicians—in other words, the current crop of medical students and residents (cf. Sinclair, 1997: 323–24). Over and over again I heard the refrain, "Surely the new generation of doctors will do things differently." This was the response to the hierarchy that stifles questioning or dissent through fear; to the inhumane hours expected of student interns and residents; to the need to show deference to superiors; to the need to pretend competence and confidence; to the need to sacrifice family, friends and outside interests to succeed in medicine. Yet, there have been many new generations of doctors in the past 40 years…with remarkably little change. Why should we expect change now? Students, residents and junior physicians have very little power in the hierarchy to bring about change. Moreover, if they have been well socialized, why would we expect them to facilitate change? As one physician suggested, those who fit in well in medical school, who thrive on the competition and succeed, those are the students who return as physicians to join the faculty of the medical school. The ones who did not fit in, the ones who hated medical school, the ones who barely made it through—they are unlikely to be involved enough in medical education to bring about change.

Medical training has not always been good for patients (see Beagan, 2000). Nor has it been particularly good for medical students in many ways. Yet efforts at change on a structural level seem to have made little overall difference. In fact medical schools have a history of revision and reform without change (Bloom, 1988). Sinclair suggests moves toward entire new educational processes, such as the move to problem-based learning in medical schools throughout North America, simply "realign existing elements in the traditional training" (1997: 325). Furthermore, additions of new and very different components of the curriculum— such as classes on social and cultural aspects of health and illness, communication courses, and courses critiquing the social relations of the medical profession—are often seriously undermined in clinical teaching (Sinclair, 1997). Again, further empirical research should investigate the impact of such curriculum changes on professional socialization.

Finally, this research shows that the same sources of differentiation that mark some students as not quite fitting in also serve as sources of resistance against medical socialization. Older students, gay students who refuse to be closeted, and students who come from poverty or from working-class backgrounds,

may be more likely than others to "do medical student" differently. Whether that translates into "doing doctor" differently is a matter for further empirical research. Future research needs to examine how these "different" students, these resisting students, experience residency and professional practice, whether and how they remain in medical practice.

CRITICAL THINKING QUESTIONS

1. One new experience for medical students is learning *medical-ese*. Have you faced a similar process during your postsecondary education? Explain.
2. Why do you think that the traditional hierarchy in medical schools (i.e., faculty at the top, students at the bottom) is seen by many as a good thing?
3. Discuss the process of playing the role of doctor. Does this process help us understand the training of young medical students? If so how? If not, why?
4. Which groups of students were most likely to resist professional socialization? Why would this be the case?

NOTES

1. In order to gain access to the research site, it was agreed that the medical school would remain unnamed. The school in question was in a large Canadian city with a racially and ethnically diverse population. It followed a traditional undergraduate curriculum.
2. At this medical school classes have been 40%–50% female for about 15 years (Association of Canadian Medical Colleges, 1996: 16); the class studied here was 48% female. Using subjective assessment of club photos, over the past 15 years about 30% of each class would be considered "visible minority" students, mainly of Asian and South Asian heritage.
3. All names are pseudonyms.
4. Never been called doctor, 14% of women, 0% of men; occasionally or regularly, 57% of women, 78% of men (Cramer's V = 0.32).
5. All of the gay/lesbian faculty and students described themselves as leading highly segregated lives during medical school.

REFERENCES

Association of Canadian Medical Colleges. 1996. *Canadian medical education statistics,* Vol. 18.

———. 2000. Neutralizing differences: Producing neutral doctors for (almost) neutral patients. *Social Science & Medicine,* 51(8): 1253–65.

Beagan, B. L. Forthcoming. Micro inequities and everyday inequalities: "Race," gender, sexuality and class in medical school. *Canadian Journal of Sociology.*

Becker, H. S., B. Geer, A. L. Strauss, and E. C. Hughes. 1961. *Boys in white: Student culture in medical school.* Chicago: University of Chicago Press.

Berger, P. L., and T. Luckmann. 1966. *The social construction of reality: A treatise in the sociology of knowledge.* New York: Doubleday and Co.

Bloom, S. W. 1973. *Power and dissent in the medical school.* New York: The Free Press.

———. 1988. Structure and ideology in medical education: An analysis of resistance to change. *Journal of Health and Social Behavior,* 29: 294–306.

Broadhead, R. 1983. *The private lives and professional identities of medical students.* New Brunswick, N.J.: Transaction.

Conrad, E. 1988. Learning to doctor: Reflections on recent accounts of the medical school years. *Journal of Health and Social Behavior,* 29: 323–32.

Cooley, C. H. 1964. *Human nature and the social order.* New York: Schocken.

Coombs, R. H. 1978. *Mastering medicine.* New York: Free Press.

Dickstein, L. J. 1993. Gender bias in medical education: Twenty vignettes and recommended responses. *Journal of the American Medical Women's Association,* 48(5): 152–62.

Fox, R. C. 1957. Training for uncertainty. In *The student-physician: Introduction studies in the sociology of medical education,* eds. R. K. Merton, G. G. Reader, and E. L. Kendall, 207–44. Cambridge, Mass.: Harvard University Press.

Gamble, V. N. 1990. On becoming a physician: A dream not deferred. In *The black women's health book: Speaking for ourselves,* ed. E. C. White, 52–64. Seattle: Seal Press.

Goffman, E. 1959. *The presentation of self in everyday life.* New York: Doubleday.

Good, B. J., and M. J. DelVecchio Good. 1993. "Learning medicine." The constructing of medical knowledge at Harvard medical school. In *Knowledge, power, and practice: The anthropology of medicine and everyday life,* eds. S. Lindbaum, and M. Lock, 81–107. Berkeley: University of California Press.

Haas, J., and W. Shaffir. 1987. *Becoming doctors: The adoption of a cloak of competence.* Greenwich, Conn.: JAI Press.

Hojat, M., J. S. Gonnella, and G. Xu. 1995. Gender comparisons of young physicians' perceptions of medical education, professional life, and practice: A follow-up study of Jefferson college graduates. *Academic Medicine,* 70: 305–12.

Hostler, S. L., and R. P. Gressard. 1993. Perceptions of the gender fairness of the medical education environment. *Journal of the American Medical Women's Association,* 48: 51–4.

Kirk, J. 1994. A feminist analysis of women in medical schools. In *Health, illness, and health care in Canada,* 2nd ed., eds. B. S. Bolaria, and H. D. Dickenson, 158–82. Toronto: Harcourt Brace.

Konner, M. 1987. *Becoming a doctor: A journey of initiation in medical school.* New York: Viking.

Lenhart, S. 1993. Gender discrimination: A health and career development problem for women physicians. *Journal of the American Medical Women's* Association, 48(5): 155–59.

Light, D. W. 1988. Toward a new sociology of medical education. *Journal of Health and Social Behavior,* 29: 307–22.

Mead, G. H. 1934. *Mind, self, and society: From the standpoint of a social behaviorist.* Chicago: University of Chicago Press.

Merton, R. K., G. G. Reader, and P. L. Kendall 1957. *The student physician: Introductory studies in the sociology of medical education.* Cambridge, Mass.: Harvard University Press.

Shapiro, E. C., and A. B. Jones. 1979. Women physicians and the exercise of power and authority in health care. In *Becoming a physician: Development of values and attitudes in medicine,* eds. E. Shapiro, and L. Lowenstein, 237–45. Cambridge: Bellinger.

Shapiro, M. 1987. *Getting doctored: Critical reflections on becoming a physician.* Toronto: Between the Lines.

Sinclair, S. 1997. *Making doctors: An institutional apprenticeship.* New York: Berg.

60

Female Genital Mutilation

Efua Dorkenoo and Scilla Elworthy

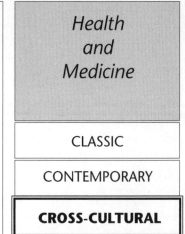

Health
and
Medicine

CLASSIC

CONTEMPORARY

CROSS-CULTURAL

Women's organizations around the world focus on a variety of women's health-related issues and problems, including domestic violence, rape, sexual harassment, and poverty. In this selection, Efua Dorkenoo and Scilla Elworthy examine the complex cultural issues surrounding female genital mutilation, a practice that has received international attention since the early 1990s.

THE FACTS

…[F]emale genital mutilation covers four types of operation:

1. *Circumcision,* or cutting of the prepuce or hood of the clitoris, known in Muslim countries as Sunna (tradition). This, the mildest type, affects only a small proportion of the millions of women concerned. It is the only type of mutilation that can correctly be called circumcision, though there has been a tendency to group all kinds of mutilations under the misleading term "female circumcision."

2. *Excision,* meaning the cutting of the clitoris and of all or part of the labia minora.

3. *Infibulation,* the cutting of the clitoris, labia minora and at least part of the labia majora. The two sides of the vulva are then pinned together by silk or catgut sutures, or with thorns, thus obliterating the vaginal introitus except for a very small opening, preserved by the insertion of a tiny piece of wood

or a reed for the passage of urine or menstrual blood. These operations are done with special knives, with razor blades or pieces of glass. The girl's legs are then bound together from hip to ankle and she is kept immobile for up to forty days to permit the formation of scar tissue.

4. *Intermediate,* meaning the removal of the clitoris and some parts of the labia minora or the whole of it. Various degrees are done according to the demands of the girl's relatives.…

Most frequently these operations are performed by an old woman of the village or by a traditional birth attendant and only rarely by qualified nurses or doctors. The age at which the mutilations are carried out varies from area to area, and according to whether legislation against the practice is foreseen or not. It varies from a few days old (for example, the Jewish Falashas in Ethiopia, and the nomads of the Sudan) to about seven years (as in Egypt and many countries of Central Africa) or—more rarely—adolescence, as among the Ibo of Nigeria. Most experts are agreed that the age of mutilation is becoming younger, and has less and less to do with initiation into adulthood.[1]

Source: From "Female Genital Mutilation," by Efua Dorkenoo and Scilla Elworthy, in *Female Genital Mutilation: Proposals for Change,* an MRG Report, 92/3. Reprinted with permission.

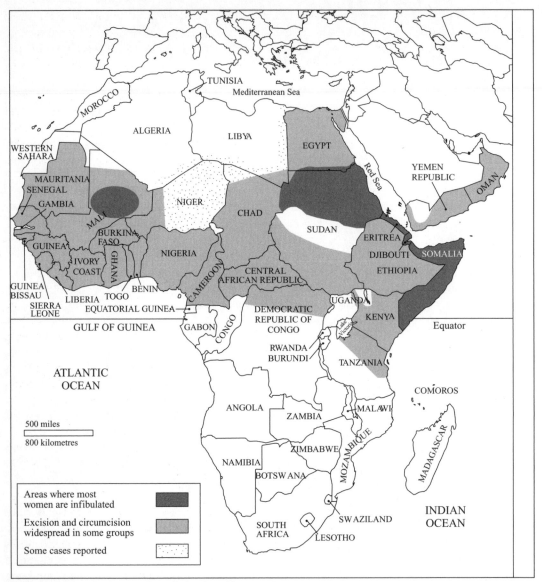

FIGURE 60.1　Female genital mutilation in Africa

Physical Consequences

Health risks and complications depend on the gravity of the mutilation, hygienic conditions, the skill and eyesight of the operator, and the struggles of the child. Whether immediate or long term, they are grave.[2] Death from bleeding is not uncommon, while long-term complications include chronic infections of the uterus and vagina, painful menstruation, severe pain during intercourse, sterility and complications during childbirth. Though evidence has yet to be collected, it is also likely that bleeding or open wounds increase the likelihood of HIV transmission and AIDS.

There is great difficulty in obtaining accurate research on the sexual experiences of mutilated women, because the majority are reluctant to speak on the subject and are generally ambivalent on questions of sexual enjoyment.[3] However, in all types of mutilation, even the "mildest" clitoridectomy, a part of a woman's body containing nerves of vital importance to sexual pleasure is amputated.

Psychological Consequences

Even less research has been done to date on the psychological consequences of these traditions. However, many personal accounts and research findings contain repeated references to anxiety prior to the operation, terror at the moment of being seized by an aunt or village matron, unbearable pain, and the subsequent sense of humiliation and of being betrayed by parents, especially the mother. On the other hand, there are references to special clothes and good food associated with the event, to the pride felt in being like everyone else, in being "made clean," in having suffered without screaming.

To be different clearly produces anxiety and mental conflict. An unexcised, non-infibulated girl is despised and made the target of ridicule, and no one in her community will marry her. Thus what is clearly understood to be her life's work, namely marriage and child-bearing, is denied her. So, in tight-knit village societies where mutilation is the rule, it will be the exceptional girl who will suffer psychologically, unless she has another very strong identity which she has lost.[4]

There is no doubt that genital mutilation would have overwhelming psychological effects on an unmotivated girl, unsupported by her family, village, peers and community. To those from other cultures unfamiliar with the force of this particular community identity, the very concept of amputation of the genitals carries a shock value which does not exist for most women in the areas concerned. For them, not to amputate would be shocking.

These observations concern social-psychological factors rather than the central question, namely, what effects do these traumatic operations have on little girls at the moment of operation and as they grow up? The fact is that we simply don't know. We do not know what it means to a girl or woman when her central organ of sensory pleasure is cut off, when her life-giving canal is stitched up amid blood and fear and secrecy, while she is forcibly held down and told that if she screams she will cause the death of her mother or bring shame on the family.

THE PRACTICE

The Area Covered

The countries where one or more forms of female genital mutilation are practised number more than twenty in Africa, from the Atlantic to the Red Sea, the Indian Ocean and the eastern Mediterranean. Outside Africa, excision is also practised in Oman, South Yemen and in the United Arab Emirates (UAE). Circumcision is practised by the Muslim populations of Indonesia and Malaysia and by Bohra Muslims in India, Pakistan and East Africa.[5]

On the map of Africa, an uninterrupted belt is formed across the centre of the continent, which then expands up the length of the Nile. This belt, with the exception of the Egyptian buckle, corresponds strikingly with the pattern of countries that have the highest child mortality rates (more than 30 percent for children from one to four years of age).[6] These levels reflect deficiencies of medical care, of clean drinking water, of sanitary infrastructure and of adequate nutrition in most of the countries.

The gravity of the mutilations varies from country to country. Infibulation is reported to affect nearly all the female population of Somalia, Djibouti and the Sudan (except the non-Muslim population of southern Sudan), southern Egypt, the Red Sea coast of Ethiopia, northern Kenya, northern Nigeria and some parts of Mali. The most recent estimate of women mutilated is 74 million.[7]

Ethnic groups closely situated geographically are by no means affected in the same way: For example, in Kenya, the Kikuyu practise excision and the Luo do not; in Nigeria, the Yoruba, the Ibo and the Hausa do, but not the Nupes or the Fulanis; in Senegal, the Woloff have no practice of mutilation. There are many other examples.

As the subject of female genital mutilation began to be eligible at least for discussion, reports of genital operations on non-consenting females have appeared from many unexpected parts of the world. During the 1980s, women in Sweden were shocked by accounts of mutilations performed in Swedish hospitals on daughters of immigrants. In France, women from Mali and Senegal have been reported to bring an *exciseuse* to France once a year to operate on their daughters in their apartments.[8] In July 1982 a Malian infant died of an excision performed by a professional circumciser, who then fled to Mali. In the same year, reports appeared in the British press that excision for non-medical reasons had been performed in a London private clinic.

Legislation

In Africa. Formal legislation forbidding genital mutilation, or more precisely infibulation, exists in the Sudan. A law first enacted in 1946 allows for a term of imprisonment up to five years and/or a fine. However, it is not an offence (under Article 284 of the Sudan Penal Code for 1974) "merely to remove the free and projecting part of the clitoris."

Many references have been made to legislation in Egypt, but after researching the available materials, all that has been traced is a resolution signed by the Minister of Health in 1959, recommending only partial clitoridectomy for those who want an operation, to be performed only by doctors.[9]

In late 1978, largely due to the efforts of the Somali Women's Democratic Organization (SWDO), Somalia set up a commission to abolish infibulation. In 1988 at a seminar held in Mogadishu, it was recommended that SWDO should propose a bill to the competent authorities to eradicate all forms of female genital mutilation.

In September 1982, President Arap Moi took steps to ban the practices in Kenya, following reports of the deaths of fourteen children after excision. A traditional practitioner found to be carrying out this operation can be arrested under the Chiefs Act and brought before the law.

Official declarations against female genital mutilation were made by the late Captain Thomas Sankara and Abdou Diouf, the heads of state in Burkina Faso and Senegal respectively.

In Western Countries. A law prohibiting female excision, whether consent has been given or not, came into force in Sweden in July 1982, carrying a two-year sentence. In Norway, in 1985, all hospitals were alerted to the practice. Belgium has incorporated a ban on the practice. Several states in the U.S.A. have incorporated female genital mutilation into their criminal code.

In the U.K., specific legislation prohibiting female circumcision came into force at the end of 1985. A person found guilty of an offence is liable to up to five years' imprisonment or to a fine. Female genital mutilation has been incorporated into child protection procedures at local authority levels. As yet no person has been committed in the English courts for female circumcision but since 1989 there have been at least seven local authority legal interventions which prevented parents from sexually mutilating their daughters or wards.

France does not have specific legislation on female sexual mutilation but under Article 312–3 of the French Penal Code, female genital mutilation can be considered as a criminal offence. Under this code, anybody who exercises violence or seriously assaults a child less than fifteen years old can be punished with imprisonment from ten to twenty years, if the act of violence results in a mutilation, amputation of a limb, the loss of an eye or other parts of the body or has unintentionally caused the death of the child.

In 1989, a mother who had paid a traditional woman exciser to excise her week-old daughter, in 1984, was convicted and given a three-year suspended jail sentence. In 1991 a traditional exciser was jailed for five years in France.

Contemporary Practices

Opinions are very divided as to whether the practice is disappearing because of legislation or social and economic changes. Esther Ogunmodede, for instance, believes that in Nigeria, Africa's most populous country, the tradition is disappearing but extremely slowly, with millions of excisions still taking place. She reports that in areas where the operations are done on girls of marriageable age, they are "running away from home to avoid the razor." This confirms Fran Hosken's assertion that operations are being done at earlier and earlier ages, in order that the children should be "too young to resist." Fran Hosken does not think that the custom is dying out, and she indisputably has the best published range of information concerning all the countries where the practice is known.

An interesting development took place in Ethiopia during the years of civil warfare which only ended in 1991. When the Eritrean People's Liberation Front (EPLF) occupied large areas from January 1977 to December 1978, among many other reforms they categorically and successfully forbade genital mutilation and forced marriage. In fact, the reason given for the large numbers of young women in the EPLF army was that they were running away from home in other parts of Ethiopia to avoid forced marriage and the knife.[10] Although it appears the practice continues in remote areas, because the consciousness of Eritrean women has changed dramatically during the war years, it is easier to persuade men and women to let go of this practice.

Since 1983, the number of educational programmes initiated to raise public awareness of the health risk associated with female genital mutilation at local, national and international levels have increased. The media have played a major role in bringing this issue from the domestic to the public domain. As a result of these efforts it can be said that the taboo surrounding even public mention of the practice has at last been broken. There is an increase in public awareness of the harmful effects of female genital mutilation.

It has been noted that female genital mutilation is becoming unpopular amongst the urban elite in some African countries. In Sierra Leone, for example, Koso-Thomas claims that urban men are willing to marry uncircumcised women, in particular when the marriage is not pre-arranged.[11]

In general, among urban educated women, reasons often cited against female genital mutilation include the pointlessness of mutilation, health risks and reduction of sexual sensitivity. The last reason points to a changing attitude towards women's fundamental human rights amongst urban Africans.

In the main, the practice continues to be widespread among large sectors and groups within Africa. Those in favour of the practice are noted in the 1986 UN study to be a passive majority who refer back to traditional society, without necessarily sharing that society's values.[12] In some cases, the practice appears to be spreading to population groups who traditionally never practised female genital mutilation, as observed with city women in Wau, Sudan, who regard it as fashionable, and among converted Muslim women in southern Sudan who marry northern Sudanese men.[13] Furthermore, even in areas where some groups are turning against the practice, the absolute numbers affected may be increasing. Rapid population growth in Africa means greater numbers of female children are born, who in turn are exposed to the risk of mutilation.

THE ISSUES

Female genital mutilation is a complex issue, for it involves deep-seated cultural practices which affect millions of people. However, it can be divided into (at least) four distinct issues.

Rights of Women

Female genital mutilation is an extreme example of the general subjugation of women, sufficiently extreme and horrifying to make women and men question the basis of what is done to women, what women have accepted and why, in the name of society and tradition.

The burning of Indian widows and the binding of the feet of Chinese girl children are other striking examples, sharp enough and strange enough to throw a spotlight on other less obvious ways in which women the world over submit to oppression. It is important to remember that all these practices are, or were, preserved under centuries of tradition, and that foot-binding was only definitively stopped by a massive social and political revolution (replacing the many traditions which it swept away by offering an entirely new social system, revolutionary in many aspects: land ownership, class system, education, sex equality, etc.) which had been preceded by years of patient work by reformers.

Thus, to be successful, campaigns on female genital mutilation should consider carefully not only eliminating but also replacing the custom. (The example of Eritrea, previously quoted, is illuminating here.) Furthermore, such success may be predicated on long-term changes in attitudes and ideologies by both men and women.

A major international expression of the goal of equal rights for women was taken in December 1979, when the U.N. General Assembly adopted the Convention on the Elimination of All Forms of Discrimination Against Women. This came into force in September 1981. The comprehensive convention calls for equal rights for women, regardless of their marital status, in all fields: political, economic, social, cultural and civil. Article 5(a) obliges states' parties to take:

> All appropriate measures to modify the social and cultural patterns of conduct of men and women, with a view to achieving the elimination of prejudices and customary and all other practices which are based on the idea of the inferiority or superiority of either of the sexes or on stereotyped roles for men and women.

To succeed in abolishing such practices will demand fundamental attitudinal shifts in the way that society perceives the human rights of women. The starting point for change should be educational programmes that assist women to recognize their fundamental human rights. This is where UNESCO, the U.N. Centre for Human Rights and international agencies could help by supporting awareness-building programmes.

Rights of Children

An adult is free to submit her or himself to a ritual or tradition, but a child, having no formed judgement, does not consent but simply undergoes the operation (which in this case is irrevocable) while she is totally vulnerable. The descriptions available of the reactions of children—panic and shock from extreme pain, biting through the tongue, convulsions, necessity for six adults to hold down an eight-year-old, and death—indicate a practice comparable to torture.

Many countries signatory to Article 5 of the Universal Declaration of Human Rights (which provides that no one shall be subjected to torture, or to cruel, inhuman or degrading treatment) violate that clause. Those violations are discussed and sometimes condemned by various U.N. commissions. Female genital mutilation, however, is a question of torture inflicted not on adults but on girl children, and the reasons given are not concerned with either political conviction or military necessity but are solely in the name of tradition.

The Declaration of the Rights of Children, adopted in 1959 by the General Assembly, asserts that children should have the possibility to develop physically in a healthy and normal way in conditions of liberty and dignity. They should have adequate medical attention, and be protected from all forms of cruelty.

It is the opinion of Renée Bridel, of the Fédération Internationale des Femmes de Carrières Juridiques, that "One cannot but consider Member

States which tolerate these practices as infringing their obligations as assumed under the terms of the Charter [of the U.N.].[14]

In September 1990, the United Nations Convention on the Rights of the Child went into force. It became part of international human rights law. Under Article 24(3) it states that: "States Parties shall take all effective and appropriate measures with a view to abolishing traditional practices prejudicial to the health of children." This crucial article should not merely remain a paper provision, to be given lip service by those entrusted to implement it. Members of the U.N. should work at translating its provisions into specific implementation programmes at grassroots level. Much could be learned (by African states in particular) from countries with established child protection systems.

The Right to Good Health

No reputable medical practitioner insists that mutilation is good for the physical or mental health of girls and women, and a growing number offer research indicating its grave permanent damage to health and underlining the risks of death. Medical facts, carefully explained, may be the way to discourage the practice, since these facts are almost always the contrary of what is believed, and can be shown and demonstrated.

Those U.N. agencies and government departments specifically entrusted with the health needs of women and children must realize that it is their responsibility to support positive and specific preventative programmes against female genital mutilation, for while the practice continues the quality of life and health will inevitably suffer. However, this approach, if presented out of context, ignores the force of societal pressures which drive women to perform these operations, regardless of risk, in order to guarantee marriage for their daughters, and to conform to severe codes of female behaviour laid down by male-dominated societies.

The Right to Development

The practice of female genital mutilation must be seen in the context of underdevelopment,[15] and the realities of life for the most vulnerable and exploited sectors—women and children. International political and economic forces have frequently prevented development programmes from meeting the basic needs of rural populations. With no access to education or resources, and with no effective power base, the rural and urban poor cling to traditions as a survival mechanism in time of socio-economic change.

In societies where marriage for a woman is her only means of survival, and where some form of excision is a prerequisite for marriage, persuading her to relinquish the practice for herself or for her children is an extraordinarily difficult task. Female (and some male) African analysts of development strategies are today constantly urging that the overall deteriorating conditions in which poor women live be made a major focus for change, for unless development affects their lives for the better, traditional practices are unlikely to change.

DIRECTIONS FOR THE FUTURE

The mutilation of female genitals has been practised in many areas for centuries. The greatest determination, combined with sensitivity and understanding of local conditions, will be needed if it is to be abolished. In every country and region where operations are carried out, the situation is different, as is the political will, whether at local or national levels. In Western countries the way forward is relatively clear. In Africa the problem is more profound and the economic and political conditions vastly more difficult, while international agencies have hardly begun to explore their potential role.

What all three have in common is that, to date, nearly all programmes have been individual or *ad hoc* efforts, with little integration into other structures, with minimal evaluation or monitoring, and lacking in long-term goals and strategies. To achieve real change will require more resources, more detailed planning, and more real, sustained commitment from governments and international organizations.

CRITICAL THINKING QUESTIONS

1. What are the four types of female genital mutilation? How widespread are these practices?
2. What do Dorkenoo and Elworthy mean when they describe female genital mutilation as a "complex" issue? Do they feel that this practice can be abolished or not?
3. Many Western countries have denounced female genital mutilation as barbaric. But what about comparable practices in Canada and other Western nations? Even though they are voluntary, are silicone breast transplants, facelifts, or liposuction more "civilized" in making women's bodies more acceptable to men?

NOTES

1. Fran Hosken, *The Hosken Report—Genital and Sexual Mutilation of Females* (third enlarged/revised edition, Autumn, 1982, published by Women's International Network News, 187 Grant St, Lexington, Mass. 02173, USA). This is the most detailed and comprehensive collection of information available.

2. The consequences of sexual mutilations on the health of women have been studied by Dr. Ahmed Abu-el-Futuh Shandall, Lecturer in the Department of Obstetrics and Gynaecology at the University of Khartoum, in a paper entitled, "Circumcision and Infibulation of Females" (*Sudanese Medical Journal,* Vol. 5, No. 4, 1967); and by Dr. J.A. Verzin, in an article entitled "The Sequelae of Female Circumcision," (*Tropical Doctor,* October, 1975). A bibliography on the subject has been prepared by Dr. R. Cook for the World Health Organization.

3. Readers interested to read more about research on the sexual experience of circumcised women may want to read Hanny Lightfoot-Klein, *Prisoners of Ritual: An Odyssey into Female Genital Mutilation in Africa* (New York, The Haworth Press, 1989).

4. These feelings of rejection are clearly articulated by Kenyan girls in "The Silence over Female Circumcision in Kenya," in *Viva,* August, 1978.

5. Q.R. Ghadially, "Ali for 'Izzat': The Practice of Female Circumcision among Bohra Muslims," *Manushi,* No. 66, New Delhi, India, 1991.

6. See map of Childhood Mortality in the World, 1977 (Health Sector Policy Paper, World Bank, Washington, D.C., 1980).

7. See Hosken for details and estimates of ethnic groups involved.

8. *F Magazine,* No. 4, March, 1979 and No. 31, October, 1980.

9. Marie Assaad, *Female Circumcision in Egypt—Current Research and Social Implications* (American University in Cairo, 1979), p. 12.

10. "Social Transformation of Eritrean Society," paper presented to the People's Tribunal, Milan, 24–26 May 1980, by Mary Dines of Rights and Justice.

11. Koso-Thomas, *The Circumcision of Women: A Strategy for Elimination* (London, Zed Books, 1987).

12. UN Commission on Human Rights, Report of the Working Group on Traditional Practices Affecting Women and Children, 1986.

13. Ellen Ismail et al., *Women of the Sudan* (Bendestorf, Germany, EIS, 1990).

14. *L'enfant mutilé* by Renée Bridel, delegate of the FIFCJ to the UN, Geneva, 1978. See also Raqiya Haji Dualeh Abdalla, *Sisters in Affliction* (London, Zed Press, 1982) and Asma El Dareer, *Woman Why Do You Weep?* (London, Zed Press, 1982).

15. Belkis Woldes Giorgis, *Female Circumcision in Africa,* ST/ECA/ATRCW 81/02.

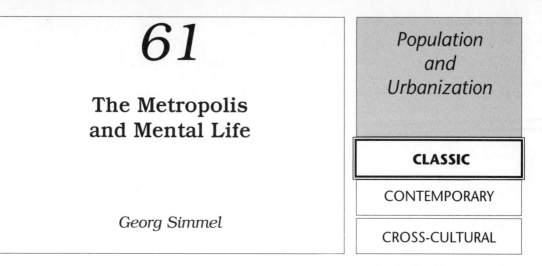

61

The Metropolis and Mental Life

Georg Simmel

Population and Urbanization

CLASSIC

CONTEMPORARY

CROSS-CULTURAL

In this, one of his best-known essays, Simmel examines what might be called the "spiritual condition" of the modern world. His focus is the city, in which forces of modernity—including anonymity, a detached sophistication, and a preoccupation with commercial matters—are most clearly evident. Note that Simmel finds reason both to praise this new world and to warn of its ability to destroy our humanity.

The deepest problems of modern life derive from the claim of the individual to preserve the autonomy and individuality of his existence in the face of overwhelming social forces, of historical heritage, of external culture, and of the technique of life. The fight with nature which primitive man has to wage for his *bodily* existence attains in this modern form its latest transformation. The eighteenth century called upon man to free himself of all the historical bonds in the state and in religion, in morals and in economics. Man's nature,

Source: Reprinted and abridged with the permission of The Free Press, a Division of Simon & Schuster from *The Sociology of Georg Simmel,* translated and edited by Kurt H. Wolff. Copyright © 1950, copyright renewed 1978 by The Free Press.

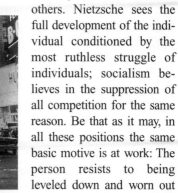

originally good and common to all, should develop unhampered. In addition to more liberty, the nineteenth century demanded the functional specialization of man and his work; this specialization makes one individual incomparable to another, and each of them indispensable to the highest possible extent. However, this specialization makes each man the more directly dependent upon the supplementary activities of all others. Nietzsche sees the full development of the individual conditioned by the most ruthless struggle of individuals; socialism believes in the suppression of all competition for the same reason. Be that as it may, in all these positions the same basic motive is at work: The person resists to being leveled down and worn out by a social-technological mechanism. An inquiry into the inner meaning of specifically modern life and its products, into the soul of the cultural body, so to speak, must seek to solve the equation which structures like the metropolis set up between the individual and the superindividual contents of life. Such an inquiry must answer the question of how the personality accommodates itself in the adjustments to external forces. This will be my task today.

The psychological basis of the metropolitan type of individuality consists in the *intensification of nervous stimulation* which results from the swift and uninterrupted change of outer and inner stimuli. Man is a differentiating creature. His mind is stimulated by the difference between a momentary impression and the one which preceded it. Lasting impressions, impressions which differ only slightly from one another, impressions which take a regular and habitual course and show regular and habitual contrasts—all these use up, so to speak, less consciousness than does the rapid crowding of changing images, the sharp discontinuity in the grasp of a single glance, and the unexpectedness of onrushing impressions. These are the psychological conditions which the metropolis creates. With each crossing of the street, with the tempo and multiplicity of economic, occupational and social life, the city sets up a deep contrast with small town and rural life with reference to the sensory foundations of psychic life. The metropolis exacts from man as a discriminating creature a different amount of consciousness than does rural life. Here the rhythm of life and sensory mental imagery flows more slowly, more habitually, and more evenly. Precisely in this connection the sophisticated character of metropolitan psychic life becomes understandable—as over against small town life, which rests more upon deeply felt and emotional relationships. These latter are rooted in the more unconscious layers of the psyche and grow most readily in the steady rhythm of uninterrupted habituations. The intellect, however, has its locus in the transparent, conscious, higher layers of the psyche; it is

the most adaptable of our inner forces. In order to accommodate to change and to the contrast of phenomena, the intellect does not require any shocks and inner upheavals; it is only through such upheavals that the more conservative mind could accommodate to the metropolitan rhythm of events. Thus the metropolitan type of man—which, of course, exists in a thousand individual variants—develops an organ protecting him against the threatening currents and discrepancies of his external environment which would uproot him. He reacts with his head instead of his heart. In this an increased awareness assumes the psychic prerogative. Metropolitan life, thus, underlies a heightened awareness and a predominance of intelligence in metropolitan man. The reaction to metropolitan phenomena is shifted to that organ which is least sensitive and quite remote from the depth of the personality. Intellectuality is thus seen to preserve subjective life against the overwhelming power of metropolitan life, and intellectuality branches out in many directions and is integrated with numerous discrete phenomena.

The metropolis has always been the seat of the money economy. Here the multiplicity and concentration of economic exchange gives an importance to the means of exchange which the scantiness of rural commerce would not have allowed. Money economy and the dominance of the intellect are intrinsically connected. They share a matter-of-fact attitude in dealing with men and with things; and, in this attitude, a formal justice is often coupled with an inconsiderate hardness. The intellectually sophisticated person is indifferent to all genuine individuality, because relationships and reactions result from it which cannot be exhausted with logical operations. In the same manner, the individuality of phenomena is not commensurate with the pecuniary principle. Money is concerned only with what is common to all: It asks for the exchange value, it reduces all quality and individuality to the question: How much? All intimate emotional relations between persons are founded in their individuality, whereas in rational relations man is reckoned with like a number, like an element which is in itself indifferent. Only the objective measurable achievement is of interest. Thus metropolitan man reckons with his merchants and customers, his domestic servants and often even with persons with whom he is obliged to have social intercourse. These features of intellectuality contrast with the nature of the small circle in which the inevitable knowledge of individuality as inevitably produces a warmer tone of behavior, a behavior which is beyond a mere objective balancing of service and return. In the sphere of the economic psychology of the small group it is of importance that under primitive conditions production serves the customer who orders the goods, so that the producer and the consumer are acquainted. The modern metropolis, however, is supplied almost entirely by production for the market, that is, for entirely unknown purchasers who never personally enter the producer's actual field of vision. Through this anonymity the interests of each party acquire an unmerciful matter-of-factness; and the intellectually calculating economic egoisms of both parties need not fear any deflection because of the imponderables of personal relationships. The money economy dominates the metropolis; it has displaced the last survivals of domestic production and the direct barter of goods; it minimizes, from day to day, the amount of work ordered by customers. The matter-of-fact attitude is obviously so intimately interrelated with the money economy, which is dominant in the metropolis, that nobody can say whether the intellectualistic mentality first promoted the money economy or whether the latter determined the former. The metropolitan way of life is certainly the most fertile soil for this reciprocity, a point which I shall document merely by citing the dictum of the most eminent English constitutional historian: Throughout the whole course of English history, London has never acted as England's heart but often as England's intellect and always as her moneybag!

In certain seemingly insignificant traits, which lie upon the surface of life, the same psychic currents characteristically unite. Modern mind has become more and more calculating. The calculative exactness of practical life which the money economy has brought about corresponds to the ideal of natural science: to transform the world into an arithmetic problem, to fix every part of the world by mathematical formulas. Only money economy has filled the days of so many people with weighing, calculating, with numerical determinations, with a reduction of qualitative values to quantitative ones. Through the calculative nature of money a new precision, a certainty in the definition of identities and differences, an unambiguousness in agreements and arrangements has been brought about in the relations of life-elements—just as externally this precision has been effected by the universal diffusion of pocket watches. However, the conditions of metropolitan life are at once cause and effect of this trait. The relationships and affairs of the typical metropolitan usually are so varied and complex that without the strictest punctuality in promises and services the whole structure would break down into an inextricable chaos. Above all, this necessity is brought about by the aggregation of so many people with such differentiated interests, who must integrate their relations and activities into a highly complex organism. If all clocks and watches in Berlin would suddenly go wrong in different ways, even if only by one hour, all economic life and communication of the city would be disrupted for a long time. In addition an apparently mere external factor, long distances, would make all waiting and broken appointments result in an ill-afforded waste of time. Thus, the technique of metropolitan life is unimaginable without the most punctual integration of all activities and mutual relations into a stable and impersonal time schedule. Here again the general conclusions of this entire task of reflection become obvious, namely, that from each point on the surface of existence—however closely attached to the surface alone—one may drop a sounding into the depth of the psyche so that all the most banal externalities of life finally are connected with the ultimate decisions concerning the meaning and style of life. Punctuality, calculability, exactness are forced upon life by the complexity and extension of metropolitan existence and are not only most intimately connected with its money economy and intellectualistic character. These traits must also color the contents of life and favor the exclusion of those irrational, instinctive, sovereign traits and impulses which aim at determining the mode of life from within, instead of receiving the general and precisely schematized form of life from without....

The same factors which have thus coalesced into the exactness and minute precision of the form of life have coalesced into a structure of the highest impersonality; on the other hand, they have promoted a highly personal subjectivity. There is perhaps no psychic phenomenon which has been so unconditionally reserved to the metropolis as has the blasé attitude. The blasé attitude results first from the rapidly changing and closely compressed contrasting stimulations of the nerves. From this, the enhancement of metropolitan intellectuality, also, seems originally to stem. Therefore, stupid people who are not intellectually alive in the first place usually are not exactly blasé. A life in boundless pursuit of pleasure makes one blasé because it agitates the nerves to their strongest reactivity for such a long time that they finally cease to react at all. In the same way, through the rapidity and contradictoriness of their changes, more harmless impressions force such violent responses, tearing the nerves so brutally hither and thither that their last reserves of strength are spent; and if one remains in the same milieu they have no time to gather new strength. An incapacity thus emerges to react to new sensations with the appropriate energy. This constitutes that blasé attitude which, in fact, every metropolitan child shows when compared with children of quieter and less changeable milieus.

This physiological source of the metropolitan blasé attitude is joined by another source which flows from the money economy. The essence of the blasé attitude consists in the blunting of discrimination. This does not mean that the objects are not perceived, as is the case with the half-wit, but rather that the meaning and differing values of things, and thereby the things themselves, are experienced as insubstantial. They appear to the blasé person in an evenly flat and gray tone; no one object deserves preference over any other. This mood is the faithful subjective reflection of the completely internalized money economy. By being the equivalent to all the manifold things in one and the same way, money becomes the most frightful leveler. For money expresses all qualitative differences of things in terms of "how much?" Money, with all its colorlessness and indifference, becomes the common denominator of all values; irreparably it hollows out the core of things, their individuality, their specific value, and their incomparability. All things float with equal specific gravity in the constantly moving stream of money. All things lie on the same level and differ from one another only in the size of the area which they cover. In the individual case this coloration, or rather discoloration, of things through their money equivalence may be unnoticeably minute. However, through the relations of the rich to the objects to be had for money, perhaps even through the total character which the mentality of the contemporary public everywhere imparts to these objects, the exclusively pecuniary evaluation of objects has become quite considerable. The large cities, the main seats of the money exchange, bring the purchasability of things to the fore much more impressively than do smaller localities. That is why cities are also the genuine locale of the blasé attitude. In the blasé attitude the concentration of men and things stimulate the nervous system of the individual to its highest achievement so that it attains its peak. Through the mere quantitative intensification of the same conditioning factors this achievement is transformed into its opposite and appears in the peculiar adjustment of the blasé attitude. In this phenomenon the nerves find in the refusal to react to their stimulation the last possibility of accommodating to the contents and forms of metropolitan life. The self-preservation of certain personalities is brought at the price of devaluating the whole objective world, a devaluation which in the end unavoidably drags one's own personality down into a feeling of the same worthlessness.

Whereas the subject of this form of existence has to come to terms with it entirely for himself, his self-preservation in the face of the large city demands from him a no less negative behavior of a social nature. This mental attitude of metropolitans toward one another we may designate, from a formal point of view, as reserve. If so many inner reactions were responses to the continuous external contacts with innumerable people as are those in the small town, where one knows almost everybody one meets and where one has a positive relation to almost everyone, one would be completely atomized internally and come to an unimaginable psychic state. Partly this psychological fact, partly the right to distrust which men have in the face of the touch-and-go elements of metropolitan life, necessitates our reserve. As a result of this reserve we frequently do not even know by sight those who have been our neighbors for years. And it is this reserve which in the eyes of the small-town people makes us appear to be cold and heartless. Indeed, if I do not deceive myself, the inner aspect of this outer reserve is not only indifference but, more often than we are aware, it is a slight aversion, a mutual strangeness and repulsion, which will break into hatred and fight at the moment of a closer contact, however caused. The whole inner organization of such an extensive communicative life rests upon an extremely varied hierarchy of sympathies, indifferences, and aversions of the briefest as well as of the most permanent nature. The sphere of indifference in this hierarchy is not as large as might appear on the surface. Our psychic activity still responds to almost every impression of somebody else with a somewhat distinct feeling. The unconscious, fluid, and changing character of this impression seems to result in a state of indifference. Actually this indifference would be just as unnatural as the diffusion of indiscriminate mutual suggestion would be unbearable. From both these typical dangers of the metropolis, indifference and indiscriminate suggestibility, antipathy protects us. A latent antipathy and the preparatory stage of practical antagonism affect the distances and aversions without which this mode of life could not at all be led. The extent and the mixture of this style of life, the rhythm of its emergence and disappearance, the forms in which it is satisfied—all these, with the unifying motives in the narrower sense, form the inseparable whole of the metropolitan style of life. What appears in the metropolitan style of life directly as dissociation is in reality only one of its elemental forms of socialization.

This reserve with its overtone of hidden aversion appears in turn as the form or the cloak of a more general mental phenomenon of the metropolis: It grants to the individual a kind and an amount of personal freedom which has no analogy whatsoever under other conditions. The metropolis goes back to one of the large developmental tendencies of social life as such, to one of the few tendencies for which an approximately universal formula can be discovered. The earliest phase of social formations found in historical as well as in contemporary social structures is this: a relatively small circle firmly closed against neighboring, strange, or in some way antagonistic circles. However, this circle is closely coherent and allows its individual members only a narrow field for the development of unique qualities and free, self-responsible movements. Political and kinship groups, parties and religious associations begin in this way. The self-preservation of very young associations requires the establishment of strict boundaries and a centripetal unity. Therefore they cannot allow the individual freedom and unique inner and outer development. From this stage social development proceeds at once in two different, yet corresponding, directions. To the extent to which the group grows—numerically, spatially, in significance and in content of life—to the same degree the group's direct, inner unity loosens, and the rigidity of the original demarcation against others is softened through mutual relations and connections. At the same time, the individual gains freedom of movement, far beyond the first jealous delimitation. The individual also gains a specific individuality to which the division of labor in the enlarged group gives both occasion and necessity....

It is not only the immediate size of the area and the number of persons which, because of the universal historical correlation between the enlargement of the circle and the personal inner and outer freedom, has made the metropolis the locale of freedom. It is rather in transcending this visible expanse that any given city becomes the seat of cosmopolitanism. The horizon of the city expands in a manner comparable to the way in which wealth develops; a certain amount of property increases in a quasi-automatical way in ever more rapid progression. As soon as a certain limit has been passed, the economic, personal, and intellectual relations of the citizenry, the sphere of intellectual predominance of the city over its hinterland, grow as in geometrical progression. Every gain in dynamic extension becomes a step, not for an equal, but for a new and larger extension. From every thread spinning out of the city, ever new threads grow as if by themselves, just as within the city the unearned increment of ground rent, through the mere increase in communication, brings the owner automatically increasing profits. At this point, the quantitative aspect of life is transformed directly into qualitative traits of character. The sphere of life of the small town is, in the main, self-contained and autarchic. For it is the decisive nature of the metropolis that its inner life overflows by waves into a far-flung national or international area....

The most profound reason, however, why the metropolis conduces to the urge for the most individual personal existence—no matter whether justified and successful—appears to me to be the following: The development of modern culture is characterized by the preponderance of what one may call the "objective spirit" over the "subjective spirit." This is to say, in language as well as in law, in the technique of production as well as in art, in science as well as in the objects of the domestic environment, there is embodied a sum of spirit. The individual in his intellectual development follows the growth of this spirit very imperfectly and at an ever increasing distance. If, for instance, we view the immense culture which for the last hundred years has been embodied in things and in knowledge, in institutions and in comforts, and if we compare all this with the cultural progress of the individual during the same period—at least in high status groups—a frightful disproportion in growth between the two becomes evident. Indeed, at some points we notice a retrogression in the culture of the individual with reference to spirituality, delicacy, and idealism. This discrepancy results essentially from the growing division of labor. For the division of labor demands from the individual an ever more one-sided accomplishment, and the greatest advance in a one-sided pursuit only too frequently means dearth to the personality of the individual. In any case, he can cope less and less with the overgrowth of objective culture. The individual is reduced to a negligible quantity, perhaps less in his consciousness than in his practice and in the totality of his obscure emotional states that are derived from this practice. The individual has become a mere cog in an enormous organization of things and powers which tear from his hands all progress, spirituality, and value in order to transform them from their subjective form into the form of a purely objective life. It needs merely to be pointed out that the metropolis is the genuine arena of this culture which outgrows all personal life. Here in buildings and educational institutions, in the wonders and comforts of space-conquering technology, in the formations of community life, and in the visible institutions of the state, is offered such an overwhelming fullness of crystallized and impersonalized spirit that the personality, so to speak, cannot maintain itself under its impact. On the one hand, life is made infinitely easy for the personality in that stimulations, interests, uses of time, and consciousness are offered to it from all sides. They carry the person as if in a stream, and one needs hardly to swim for oneself. On the other hand, however, life is composed more and more of these impersonal contents and offerings which tend to displace the genuine personal colorations and incomparabilities. This results in the individual's summoning the utmost in uniqueness and particularization, in order to preserve his most personal core. He has to exaggerate this personal element in order to remain audible even to himself....

CRITICAL THINKING QUESTIONS

1. In what respects does the metropolis symbolize modern society?
2. What does Simmel mean by suggesting that in modern cities, people experience an "intensification of nervous stimulation"? How do we react "with our heads instead of with our hearts"?
3. What does Simmel see as the achievements of modern urban life? What does he think has been lost in the process?

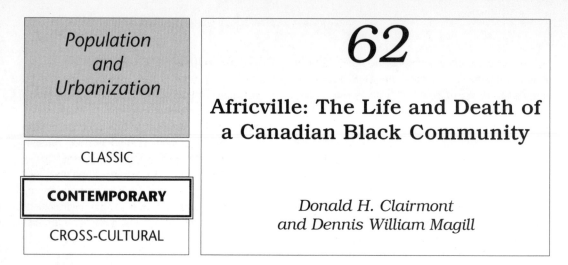

Population
and
Urbanization

62

Africville: The Life and Death of a Canadian Black Community

CLASSIC

CONTEMPORARY

CROSS-CULTURAL

*Donald H. Clairmont
and Dennis William Magill*

Clairmont and Magill review the effects of an urban redevelopment program that relocated 80 black families in Halifax during the 1960s. The program was intended to promote humanitarian motives but the experience of Africville demonstrates the many problems associated with forced relocation programs.

To seek social change, without due recognition of the manifest and latent functions performed by the social organization undergoing change, is to indulge in social ritual rather than social engineering.[1]

— *Robert K. Merton*

Halifax, the foundation city of English-speaking Canada, experienced much change during its first two hundred years of existence. Yet the facelift and redevelopment it has undergone since the late 1950s have effected a change as dramatic as the 1917 explosion that levelled much of the city. Stimulated by the Stephenson Report of 1957,[2] urban renewal and redevelopment have resulted in the relocation of thousands of people, the demolition of hundreds of buildings, and the

construction of impressive business and governmental complexes. The Africville relocation was part of the larger redevelopment pattern; Africville residents constituted some eight to ten percent of the people affected by approved urban renewal schemes in the city of Halifax during the relocation years.

Africville was a black community within the city of Halifax, inhabited by approximately four hundred people, comprising eighty families, many of whom were descended from settlers who had moved there over a century ago. Tucked away in a corner of the city, relatively invisible, and thought of as a "shack town," Africville was a depressed community both in physical and in socioeconomic terms. Its dwellings were located beside the city dump, and railroad tracks cut across the one dirt road leading into the area. Sewerage, lighting, and other public services were conspicuously absent. The people had little education, very low incomes, and many were underemployed. Property claims were in chaos. Only a handful of families could establish legal title;

Source: From Donald H. Clairmont and Dennis W. Magill. 1999. *Africville: The Life and Death of a Canadian Black Community*, Third Edition (pp. 1–19). Toronto: Canadian Scholars' Press. Reprinted by permission of Canadian Scholars' Press Inc.

others claimed squatter rights; and still others rented. Africville, long a black mark against society, had been designated for future industrial and harbour development. Many observers reported that despite these liabilities there was a strong sense of community and that some residents expressed satisfaction with living in Africville.

In 1964 the small black ghetto of Africville began to be phased out of existence. By that time most residents of Halifax, black and white, had come to think of Africville as "the slum by the dump." Most Haligonians, including some Africville residents, did not regard the community as viable and recognized a need for planned social change. The relocation plan announced by the city of Halifax, which purported to be more than simply a real estate operation, appeared to be a response to this need. The plan emphasized humanitarian concern, included employment and education programs, and referred to the creation of new opportunities for the people of Africville. To the general public, the proposed relocation was a progressive step.

In addition to official pronouncements, there were other indications that the Africville program would be more humane and progressive than the typical North American urban relocation. Halifax city council had adopted recommendations contained in a report submitted by a noted Canadian welfare specialist experienced in urban renewal. There was much preliminary discussion of the relocation by city officials among themselves, with Africville residents, and with a "caretaker" group of black and white professionals associated with the Halifax Human Rights Advisory Committee. Relocation plans were not *ad hoc* and haphazard. City officials were required to articulate their policies well and in detail; many implications and alternatives were considered.

There were also indications in the relocation decision-making structure that the Africville program might realize its official rhetoric. A social worker was appointed by the city to take front-line responsibility for the varied aspects of the relocation and to act as liaison between the city administration and the relocatees. The social worker, who was on loan from the Nova Scotia Department of Public Welfare, had a measure of autonomy vis-à-vis the city and an independent contingency fund to meet day-to-day emergencies and opportunities with a minimum of bureaucratic delay. In negotiating the real estate aspects of relocation, the social worker brought proposed agreements before a special advisory committee consisting of aldermen and several members of the Halifax Human Rights Advisory Committee.

In terms of its rationale, public rhetoric, and organizational structure, the Africville relocation seemed worthy of study. The plan was *liberal-oriented* (that is, aimed at ending segregation and providing improved opportunities for the disadvantaged), *welfare-oriented* (that is, it hoped to coordinate employment, educational, and rehabilitative programs with the rehousing of people), and run by experts (that is, the planning, execution, and advise were provided by professionals). An examination of the Africville relocation could be expected to yield greater fundamental insight into planned social change than would a study of typical relocation programs that were accomplished by administrative fiat and stressed primarily the physical removal of persons. It seemed important to study and evaluate the Africville relocation both in its particularity and against the background of general relocation issues.

There were additional reasons for studying the Africville relocation. First, Africville was part of a trend in the 1960s for governmental initiative in relocation programs, and there was reason to expect that other tentative relocations in Nova Scotia and elsewhere would be patterned after the Africville experience. Second, Africville had attracted national and even international notice, and there was broad public interest in the relocation. Third, accounts of pre-relocation social conditions and attitudes were available. Two surveys had been conducted[3] and other material was available in city records. Finally, in 1968 the Africville relocation had already been acclaimed locally as a success. One city alderman noted:

The social significance of the Africville program is already beginning to show positive results as far as individual families are concerned. The children are performing more satisfactorily in school and they seem to take more of an interest in their new surroundings. This report is not intended to indicate that the program has been 100 percent successful; however I believe it can be said that it has been at least 75 percent, judging by the comments of the relocated families.[4]

Private communication with city officials and relocation officials in the United States and Canada brought forth praise for the organization and rhetoric of the Africville relocation.

Was the Africville relocation a success? If so, from whose perspective? To what extent? What accounted for the success or lack of it? It is hoped that answers to these and related questions will contribute to an appreciation of the Africville relocation and of relocation generally.

THE RELOCATION PHENOMENON

Relocation must be seen in the context of a general North American mobility pattern, and certain distinctive features should be noted. The most important distinction is that relocation is part of planned social change carried out, or at least approved, by public agency. The initiation of relocation, as seen by the relocatees, is usually involuntary and an immediate function of the political process. Our present concern is with relocation as it pertains to private residences, involves neighbourhoods or communities, and is a function of comprehensive programs of social change. This kind of relocation accounts for but a small measure of the mobility noted in Canada and the United States, but it was significant because it was distinctive. It was noted earlier that the Africville relocation was itself part of a much larger redevelopment project in the city of Halifax. In terms of the sweep of lifestyle change, even such large urban projects have been dwarfed by post–Second World War Canadian relocation projects in the Arctic and in Newfoundland. In 1953, Newfoundland, with 6000 miles of coastline and

approximately 1150 settlements, undertook a program to move people from the small outposts to larger viable communities which could be serviced efficiently. Between 1965 and 1970 over 3250 households were moved.[5]

As many low-income Americans and Canadians can testify, urban renewal is a prime example of forced relocation. Urban renewal legislation began in the 1940s in both countries. By 1968 approximately forty-five Canadian urban redevelopments had been initiated at a cost of 270 million dollars for 1500 cleared acres.[6] While the scope of urban renewal in Canada was quite small in the light of American experience, the Canadian program was significant enough that one can complain that there were too few Canadian studies looking into the politics, issues, and human consequences of renewal programs. To overcome this lack of knowledge and to place the Africville relocation in perspective, more comprehensive themes will be discussed in this [selection].

From a political-administrative perspective there are four relocation models: the traditional, development, liberal-welfare, and political. The Africville project is the best Canadian example of the liberal-welfare type of relocation.... [T]hese models vary along six dimensions: (1) ideological premises; (2) formulation of policy; (3) implementation of policy; (4) intended beneficiaries; (5) central actors and organizational units; and (6) key problems. These models are ideal types to which actual relocation programs correspond to a greater or lesser degree.

THE DEVELOPMENT MODEL

The development model was the most prevalent political-administrative approach to relocation in North America. This type of relocation was usually justified in terms of supposed benefits for the system as a whole, whether the system is society, the city, etc. It was usually initiated by order of political authorities and administered by bureaucrats; it was not anticipated that relocatees would benefit other than indirectly. The underlying ideology of the development model was system-oriented and neo-capitalist; an accurate statement of its premise in urban renewal has been offered by Wallace: "[it considers] renewal, as a public activity, to be intervention in a market and competitive system and to be justified by the need to make up for imperfections in the market mechanism that impede the adjustment process, to eliminate conditions which are economic or social liabilities."[7] In the context of contemporary urban renewal, the development model incorporated the usual city-design approach, focusing on questions of beautification, zoning, and structure,[8] and was usually intended to increase the city tax base and achieve civic pride or attract industry.

The development model can be illustrated by past urban renewal programs in Toronto. Ignoring relocatees as viable interest groups the programs operated implicitly on the basis of certain ideological premises: to correct imperfections in the social system (removal of so-called slums) and overall system development (economic growth), or both. As is the case in many Canadian cities, Toronto's past development policy was closely linked to the businesses and commercial-property industry which provided homes, apartment buildings, shopping centres, and industrial complexes. Thus the elimination of "blight areas" and construction of highrise apartment and office buildings generated an important source of urban revenue. Referring to this policy of "dollar planning," Fraser observed:

As long as Toronto, [in 1972] like all other municipalities in Canada has to depend upon property taxes as its sole source of income, the overwhelming power of development interests in determining the direction and quality of Toronto's growth will remain unchallenged.

...[T]he key to a municipality's prosperity remains its rate of growth; Toronto planners have been consistently ignored by city councils that have been over the years almost exclusively uninterested in any discussions about the quality of that development.[9]

A non-urban example of the development model of relocation has been described by John Matthiasson, in his study of the forced relocation of a band of Cree Indians in Northern Manitoba. The Cree were relocated to make way for a gigantic power project; they were not involved in the project planning and despite their displeasure "they accepted in a fatalistic manner the announcement of the relocation. They believed that the decision had been made by higher authorities, and that they had neither the right nor power to question it."[10]

The development model of relocation had its limitations. In particular, its econocentric and "undemocratic" features were criticized. The assumption that relocatees benefit indirectly from relocation was challenged, as was the premise that the system as a whole somehow redistributed fairly the benefits accruing from forcing people to move and facilitating the development of private industry. Some critics argued that if one included social-psychological factors in one's conception of costs, the relocatees could be seen as subsidizing the rest of the system. The criticism had some effect, and the liberal-welfare model became increasingly common.[11] One official explained:

In the fifteen years since [urban renewal's] inception, we have seen a progressive broadening of the concept and a strengthening of tools. We have seen, increasingly, both the need for, and realization of, rapprochement between physical and social planning, between renewal and social action. But the fully effective liaison of the two approaches has almost everywhere been frustrated by the absence of the tools to deal as effectively with the problems of human beings as with the problems of physical decay and blight.[12]

Another writer has observed,

social welfare can no longer be treated as the responsibility of private and more or less bountiful ladies and gentlemen or as the less respected branch of the social welfare community and the city government. Tied as it is to the concerns as dear to the heart of the country as economic prosperity it merits a place in the inner sanctum, particularly of planning commissions.[13]

THE LIBERAL-WELFARE MODEL

The "rediscovery" of poverty,[14] the war on poverty, the increasing pressure "from below" upon the development model, and the broadening definition of urban renewal led to the widespread emergence of the liberal-welfare-oriented approach. The liberal-welfare model, like the development model, emphasized expertise and technical knowledge in its operation and administration, and invariably was initiated by public authority. The principal difference is that the liberal-welfare model purported to benefit the relocatees primarily and directly. Under this model, welfare officials often saw themselves as "caretakers" for the relocatees; one relocation official has said, "the department of relocation is the tenants' advocate."[15] The liberal-welfare model of relocation was characterized by a host of social welfare programs supplemental to housing policies and was regarded as an opportunity for a multifaceted attack on poverty and other problems. It was this liberal-welfare model and its assumptions that shaped the rhetoric underlying the 1963–64 decision to relocate Africville.

Ideologically, the liberal-welfare model was much like the development model in that it tended to operate with a consensus model of society and posited a basic congruency between the interests of relocatees and those of society as a whole, it was "undemocratic" in the same sense as the development model; the low-status relocatees were accorded little attention, either as participants in the implicit political process or as contributions to specific policies or plans of action. There was an effort, however, to persuade rather than to ignore the relocatees. Criticism of the liberal-welfare model of relocation was related primarily to the ideological level. Some writers noted that liberal welfarism had become part of the establishment of contemporary North American society.[16] Its proponents were presumed to be handmaidens of strong vested interests, reconciling the disadvantaged and patching up the symptoms of social malaise. Critics pointed out that the special programs associated with the liberal-welfare model of relocation tended to be short-term and unsuccessful. The welfare rhetoric often diverted attention from the gains and benefits accruing to the middle-income and elite groups in society. The critics attacked the liberal-welfare model on the premise that the social problems to which it is ostensibly directed could be solved only through profound structural change effecting a redistribution of resources, and by providing relocatees with the consciousness and resources to restructure their own lives.

The liberal-welfare model is best illustrated by the Africville relocation.... The community of Africville was defined as a social problem, and relocation was regarded as an intervention strategy designed to help solve the "social and economic problems of Africville residents." The central actors in the formation and implementation of relocation policy were politicians, bureaucrats, experts, and middle-class caretakers; there was no meaningful *collective* participation by Africville residents. The relocatees were to be major beneficiaries through compensation, welfare payments, and rehabilitative retraining programs. The major problem with the relocation was that, although rooted in liberal-welfare rhetoric, it failed to achieve its manifest goals.

THE POLITICAL MODEL

The liberal-welfare model of relocation was revised and developed both as a response to criticism at the ideological level and in reaction to its lack of operational success. There was a growing interest in citizen participation in all phases of relocation; in the firmer acceptance, structurally and culturally, of the advocacy function of relocation officials; in the coordination of relocation services; and in the provision of resources. It is difficult to assess how far this interest has been translated into fact. There appeared to be a shift in the 1970s, at least conceptually, to the political model of relocation and a frank recognition that relocation usually entailed a conflict of interest, for example, between the relocatees and the city. There was an attempt to structure the conflict by providing relocatees with resources to develop a parallel structure to that of the government. Although society and the relocatee were considered to benefit equally, this political perspective assumed that relocatees benefited both directly and indirectly; directly in terms of, say, housing and other welfare services, and indirectly by participating in the basic decision-making and the determination of their life situation. The political model of relocation was based on the premise that social problems were political problems and emphasized solutions through political action; relocation was approached primarily as a situation in which problems were solved not by the application of expertise but by the resolution of conflicting interests.

Beyond the considerable costs (the dollar cost is less hidden than in the other relocation model) and administrative difficulties entailed, there were other grounds for criticism of the political model. There was a tendency to overemphasize the solidarity and common interests of relocatees, to exaggerate the multiplying effects of political participation in relocation,[17] and to raise serious questions about how far government could proceed or would proceed in fostering extra-parliamentary political action.

Citizen participation, a core element in the political model, was institutionalized in the United States by the community action programs of the 1964 Economic Opportunity Act. Numerous books and articles, far too many to cite, have discussed the reasons, operations, and failures of "maximum feasible participation" of the poor in the war on poverty.[18] Citizen participation was also part of the United States model city programs, which required that local residents be involved in the planning process and implementation of changes in their neighbourhoods. Contrasted with the United States, Canada has relatively few examples of related social-animation projects. The rise of "mili-

tant" citizen groups was a phenomenon which developed later in Canada. The public outcry against the community work of the Company of Young Canadians and the subsequent governmental intervention to close this organization may be an indication of the limits of this perspective. The only Canadian publication illustrating the political model of a relocation is Fraser's study of Toronto's Trefann Court. Trefann Court residents successfully fought off a development-type relocation project; subsequently, the conflict arising from different interests was recognized as an integral part of the city's social organization. Despite internal community conflict between homeowners and tenants, a number of community residents, leaning heavily on outside: "resource people," developed a cohesive organization and set up a working committee (a parallel structure) to establish a conceptual scheme for community change in conjunction with the existing city bureaucracy. The Trefann Court case also pointed to a key problem in the political model, that of assessing the representativeness of any one group of citizens to speak, argue, or vote for an entire community. With the establishment of "parallel structures," many citizens grow frustrated with the tedious detail involved in committee work. In Fraser's words:

> The fact that the Working Committee operated under formal rules of order, dominated by minutes, reports, rules of procedure and legislative decorum widened the gap between the committee and the community. As debates became more lengthy, detailed and technical, the meetings became harder to follow for the ordinary Trefann resident who might drop in.[19]

THE TRADITIONAL MODEL

Finally, there is the traditional model of relocation in North American society. This is a limiting type of relocation carried out under governmental auspices, for it is a form of planned social change characterized by self-help and self-direction. It is the neighbourhood or community leaders, often indigenous minority-group leaders working through indigenous social organizations, who plan and carry out the relocation, generally with official support and some resource commitment by government agencies. The traditional model entails a largely laissez-faire strategy whereby the relocatees benefit directly and technical expertise is used to advise rather than to direct. Criticism of this approach contends that, without political action, neither the available resources nor the generation of initiative can be effective in the case of low-status groups.

There are numerous examples of the traditional model of relocation. Group settlement and resettlement in various parts of Canada have been common. The relocation of Beechville, a black community on the outskirts of Halifax, is an example within the Halifax metropolitan area. Community leaders, anticipating a government attempt to relocate the residents, organized themselves into a co-operative housing association, received funds from Central Mortgage and Housing Corporation, and reorganized their community partly on their own terms. The scope available for traditional relocation models lessens as society becomes more technocratic and centralized.

CONCEPTUAL FRAMEWORK

...[O]ur emphasis will be on the liberal-welfare model of planned social change and its implementation during the Africville relocation. During the analysis we focus on questions of power and exchange among the various participants of the relocation. Thus, from the perspective of power and exchange,[20] we can examine the power resources and relationships among the individual persons and groups involved in the relocation, the historical evolution of these social facts, the goals held by the different parties, and the strategies and tactics employed in establishing the terms of the relocation "contract." We can also analyse the role of outsiders, experts, and community "leaders" and focus on questions

such as the mobilization of advocacy, relocation resistances and alternatives, and the relation of rhetoric to action. It is vital in the Africville case to have a larger historical view, observing the historical exchange patterns between the city and the Africville people and tracing the implications of these patterns in making Africville "ripe for relocation" and in influencing the relocation decision-making and mechanics.

An aspect of this perspective concerns the context of negotiations and the bargaining strategies developed by the parties involved. Accordingly, attention was devoted to probing the relocatees' knowledge about the relocation; their strategies (use of lawyers, co-operation with fellow relocatees, and development of special arguments in dealing with city officials), and their perceptions of the city's goals, strategies, and resources. The relocation social worker completed a questionnaire concerning each relocated family which paid considerable attention to his negotiations with relocatees and his perception of their goals, strategies, and resources. This perspective included the concepts of rewards, costs, profits, and distributive justice. It would appear, for instance, that relocatees would have been satisfied with the relocation if rewards exceeded costs and if they thought that the city and other relocatees would not "get a better deal." Information concerning rewards, costs, sense of distributive justice, and satisfaction was obtained through the questionnaires, the interviews, and the case studies.

Despite problems in measuring each relocatee's perception of the relative profit accruing to himself or herself, other relocatees, and the city of Halifax, and problems occasioned by differences between long-term and short-term effects, this power and exchange approach is significant for the relocation literature which often appears to keep aloof from the "blood and guts" of relocation transaction. Equally important, by placing the Africville relocation within a typology of relocation models, it is possible to explore the domain consensus (that is, the basic terms of reference held in common and prerequisite to any exchange) associated with the liberal-welfare approach, and especially how such *domain* consensus (for example, "disadvantaged communities or people have few intrinsically valuable resources and need to be guided by sympathetic experts") develops and how it sets the limits and context of bargaining and reciprocity.

RESEARCH STRATEGIES

The methods employed in this study were varied: questionnaires, in-depth interviews, historical documents, newspapers, case studies, and "bull sessions" with relocatees. A useful baseline source of data was the survey of Halifax blacks, including Africville [residents], conducted in 1959 by the Institute of Public Affairs, Dalhousie University. The original questionnaires were available for re-analysis, an important consideration since many of the data were not published and the published material contained several significant inaccuracies.[21] The 1959 survey questionnaire provided basic demographic data as well as information concerning mobility aspirations, employment, education, and social life.

The collection of data for this study began in 1968. The researchers arranged for two students from the Maritime School of Social Work to prepare twenty case studies.[22] A review of the students' case studies and field notes, guided by the perspective developed by the researchers, aided the drafting of a questionnaire. In 1968 current addresses of the relocatees were also traced and brief acquaintance interviews were conducted.

The most intensive data collection period was June to December 1969. One of the researchers (D.W.M.) conducted in-depth, tape-recorded interviews with individual people associated with the relocation decision-making and implementation: politicians, city officials, middle-class caretakers, the relocation social worker, consultants, and Africville relocatees involved in the decision-making. During these interviews an open-ended interview guide[23] was used to explore knowledge of Africville and awareness of pre-1964 relocation attempts and also the actual relocation decision-

making and mechanics. Each of the approximately two-hour interviews was transcribed and analysed for patterns. Many quotations used in this book are taken from these tape-recorded interviews.

Concurrently, the other researcher (D.H.C.), with two assistants, was meeting informally with the relocatees, individually and in "bull sessions." On the basis of these experiences and the case studies, we all drafted and pre-tested an extensive questionnaire. From September to December, 1969, the questionnaire was employed by interviewers hired and trained by the researchers. The lengthy questionnaire[24] asked about the relocatee's background characteristics: life in Africville, personal knowledge of relocation decision-making processes, relocation strategies, negotiations, costs, rewards, and post-relocation conditions. The questionnaire was given to all household heads and spouses who had lived in Africville and had received a relocation settlement of any kind. Approximately 140 persons were interviewed, several in places as far distant as Winnipeg and Toronto.

In June, 1969, the relocation social worker spent eight days answering a questionnaire[25] on the relocatees' background characteristics, his relocation bargaining with each relocatee, and his perception of the latter's rewards, costs, and strategies. Such data enabled us to analyse more precisely the relationships among parties to the relocation, for similar data from the relocatees and their perception of the relocation social worker were obtained from the relocatee questionnaire.

Two other research tactics were employed at the same time as the interviews were conducted. One of our assistants was conducting in-depth, tape-recorded interviews with black leaders in the Halifax area concerning their assessment of Africville and the implications of relocation. Another assistant was gathering historical data and interviewing selected Africville relocatees concerning the historical development of the community. Important sources of historical data were the minutes of Halifax City Council (read from 1852 to 1969), reports of the Board of

Halifax School Commissioners, the Nova Scotia Public Archives, files in the Registry of Deeds, the Halifax *Mail-Star* library, and the minutes of the Halifax Human Rights Advisory Committee. In all phases of research, the Africville files in the Social Planning Department, City of Halifax were of especial value.

PHASES OF THE AFRICVILLE STUDY

The Africville Relocation Report, in addition to being an examination of relocation and planned social change and a contribution to the sparse literature on blacks in Nova Scotia, represents a fusion of research and action. The researchers did not begin the study until virtually all the Africville people had been relocated, and the research strategy resulted in the study being more than an evaluation.[26] The process of obtaining collective as well as individual responses, and of establishing a meaningful exchange with relocatees, fostered collective action from former Africville residents. Some local government officials objected to what they have referred to as the researchers' "activist" bias. The researchers maintain, however, that exchanges had to be worked out with the subjects of research as well as with the funding agencies. The liberal ethic posits informed voluntary consent as fundamental to adult social interaction; informed voluntary consent requires, in turn, meaningful exchange among the participants.

The study began in October, 1968 with a meeting of relocated Africville people. This was the first time since relocation that former residents of Africville had met collectively. This stormy meeting, called by the researchers, was a public airing of relocatee grievances and led to relocatee support of the proposed study. Subsequent talk of forming committees to press grievances with the city of Halifax was an important result of the meeting. The researchers encouraged this tendency, for the expressed grievances appeared legitimate, and the researchers considered that it would be both possible and important to tap a collective or group dimension in the relocation process as well as to study the usual social-psychological considerations.

Later in the same week, at a meeting that the researchers had arranged with city officials, relocation caretakers, and civic leaders, the researchers related the expressed grievances of the relocatees and urged remedial action. General support for the proposed study was obtained at this second meeting, and the pending reconsideration of relocation by the city's newly created Social Planning Department was crystallized.

During the winter and spring of 1969, as the present study was being planned in detail, the action-stimulus of the researchers' early efforts was bearing fruit. Social Planning Department officials were meeting with the relocatees and, as it were, planning the second phase (not initially called for) of the Africville relocation. With provincial and municipal grants totalling seventy thousand dollars, the Seaview Credit Union was organized to assist relocatees experiencing financial crises; in addition, plans were formulated to meet housing and employment needs, and special consideration was to be given to former Africville residents whose needs could be met within the city's existing welfare system. A relocatee was hired to manage the credit union and to assist with other anticipated programs.

During the main data-gathering period, the summer of 1969, and in line with a decision to obtain collective as well as individual responses, the researchers met with informed groups of Africville relocatees to discuss current and future remedial action, it became apparent that the so-called second phase of the relocation would be inadequate to meet the people's needs. There was little identification with the credit union and it was floundering, for many relocatees who became members were either unable or unwilling to repay loans. Other anticipated programs and action promised by the city were delayed or forgotten due to bureaucratic entanglements and to lack of organization and pressure on the part of the relocatees.

The relocatees still had legitimate grievances related to unkept promises made at the time of relocation and later. With the formation of the Africville Action Committee, a third phase of the relocation began in the fall of 1969 and winter of 1970. The task of this new committee, developed from group discussions held between the researchers and relocatees, was to effect governmental redress through organized pressure. Several position papers were developed by the Africville Action Committee and negotiations were reopened with the city of Halifax. Although numerous meetings of relocatees were held during the first half of 1970, problems within the Africville Action Committee and the absence of resource people until the fall of 1970 hindered progress. With the committee stumbling along, and the credit union and other city-sponsored projects either ineffectual or nonexistent, the relocation process appeared to have petered out. The action committee was reactivated when one of the authors (D.H.C.) returned to Halifax permanently in the fall of 1970 and groups of relocatees were subsequently reinvolved in reading and criticizing a draft of the present study and in evaluating the relocation and the remedial action taken. Since the fall of 1970, the Africville Action Committee was active. Widespread support for its claims was obtained from community organizations, subcommittees were established to deal with questions of employment, housing, and financial compensation; and city council authorized the establishment of a city negotiating team to meet with representatives of the action committee.

In 1974, at the time of publication of the first edition of this book, the Africville Action Committee, to all intents and purposes, had ceased to function. Although it could claim some credit for a special employment training program through which a number of unemployed Africville relocatees had found jobs, the action committee fell far short of its goals.

The city's lack of a positive imaginative response and the internal organizational problems of the action committee hindered other proposals. What remained in 1974 was a reorganized credit union, a modest base for further redress and group action. However, by 1999 the Seaview Credit Union was no longer in existence; it had collapsed over two decades ago. However, the community is not dead.... Africville still thrives in the hearts and minds of many of the relocatees. In addition, Africville still has rich symbolic value for fostering black consciousness in Nova Scotia.

POSTSCRIPT

Throughout the study, we consciously and deliberately attempted to achieve a viable fusion of research and social responsibility. The research focussed on the collective responses of the group as well as on individual responses. At each stage in the study (conception, data gathering, data analysis, and preparation for publication) the collective and individual inputs that gave the study an action potential were obtained from relocatees. Drafts of appropriate chapters were sent for critical comment to officials and others involved in the relocation. The study became a stimulus to action because the normal researcher-subject exchanges could be worked out in concrete, actual terms. This was preferable to the usual research situation where, in effecting exchanges with the people being studied, the researcher typically makes vague references to the possible benefit of the study and does little or nothing to follow up implied promises of action.[27] But of course, our research strategy has its weakness too. It is difficult to feel satisfied that the kind of exchange relations that we established had productive consequences. Despite our involvement (in the early 1970s) with petitions, committee work, and attempts at rational problem solving, little redress of the inadequacies of the relocation program was achieved and the manifest goals of the liberal-welfare rhetoric of the relocation remain, in large measure, unrealized.

CRITICAL THINKING QUESTIONS

1. Review the key characteristics of the *development* and *liberal-welfare* relocation models. What are the strengths and weaknesses of each?
2. Have there been any relocation or revitalization programs in your community? If so, which relocation model appears to have provided the justification for the move? Are the people who were relocated still in the community today?
3. In your opinion, can we effectively revitalize our communities without forcing people to move? How?

NOTES

1. *Social Theory and Social Structure* (Glencoe, Ill.: The Free Press, 1949), p. 80.
2. Gordon Stephenson, *A Redevelopment Study of Halifax, Nova Scotia* (Halifax, N.S.: City of Halifax, 1957).
3. *The Condition of the Negroes of Halifax City, Nova Scotia* (Halifax: Institute of Public Affairs, Dalhousie University, 1962); and G. Brand, *Interdepartmental Committee on Human Rights: Survey Reports* (Halifax, N.S.: Nova Scotia Department of Welfare, Social Development Division, 1963).
4. Minutes of the Halifax City Council, Halifax, N.S., September 14, 1967.
5. The Government of Newfoundland initiated the program in 1953. In 1965 a joint federal-provincial program was initiated under a resettlement act. In 1970 the program was placed under the direction of the Federal Department of Regional Economic Expansion. For an overview of the resettlement program, see Noel Iverson and D. Ralph Matthews, *Communities In Decline: An Examination of Household Resettlement in Newfoundland,* Newfoundland Social and Economic Studies, No. 6, (St. John's, Nfld.: Memorial University of Newfoundland, Institute of Social and Economic Research, 1968). For a critical assessment of studies of the resettlement program, see Jim Lotz, "Resettlement and Social Change in Newfoundland," The *Canadian Review of Sociology and Anthropology 8* (February, 1971): 48–59.
6. See Table 4, "Completed Redevelopment Projects" in *Urban Renewal* (Toronto: Centre for Urban and Community Studies, University of Toronto, 1968). Reprinted from *University of Toronto Law Journal,* 18. No. 3 (1968): 243.
7. David A. Wallace, "The Conceptualizing of Urban Renewal," *Urban Renewal* (Toronto: Centre for Urban and Community Studies, University of Toronto, 1968), 251.

8. An example of such a project is one reported by Thurz in southwest Washington, D.C. Little was done for the relocatees, but the relocation was widely acclaimed for its futuristic redevelopment design. For a critique of this approach, see Daniel Thurz, *Where Are They Now?* Washington, D.C.: Health and Welfare Council of the National Capital Area, 1966). See also, Jane Jacobs, *The Death and Life of Great American Cities* (New York: Random House, 1961).
9. Graham Fraser, *Fighting Back: Urban Renewal in Trefann Court* (Toronto: Hakkert, 1972), p. 55.
10. John Matthiasson, "Forced Relocation: An Evaluative Case Study," paper presented at the annual meeting of the Canadian Sociology and Anthropology Association, Winnipeg, 1970.
11. In recent years some minor progressive modifications have been introduced with reference to the development model; these deal with advance notice and public hearings, relocation compensation, and the availability of housing stock. See, Robert P. Groberg, *Centralized Relocation* (Washington, D.C.: National Association of Housing and Redevelopment Officials, 1969).
12. William L. Slayton, "Poverty and Urban Renewal," quoted in Hans B. C. Spiegel, "Human Considerations in Urban Renewal," *Urban Renewal,* op. cit., 311.
13. Elizabeth Wood, "Social Welfare Planning," quoted in Spiegel, op. cit., 315.
14. For a discussion of this, see Kenneth Craig, "Sociologists and Motivating Strategies," M.A. thesis, University of Guelph, Department of Sociology, 1971.
15. Groberg, op. cit., p. 172.
16. See Alvin W. Gouldner, *The Coming Crisis of Western Sociology* (New York: Basic Books, 1970), pp. 500–02.
17. Relocation is a short-term consideration, for most services brought to bear on relocatee problems rarely extend beyond rehousing. A more general critique of the multiplying effect of citizens' involvement in relocation is given by S. M. Miller and Frank Riessman, *Social Class and Social Policy* (New York: Basic Books Inc., 1968).
18. The historical antecedents and reasons for the legislation are discussed in Daniel Moynihan, *Maximum Feasible Misunderstanding* (New York: Free Press, 1970). For an alternative interpretation, see Francis Fox Piven and Richard A. Cloward, *Regulating the Poor: The Functions of Public Welfare* (New York: Random Vintage Books, 1972), pp. 248–84. The operation of the program is discussed by Ralph M. Kramer, *Participation of the Poor: Comparative Community Case Studies* in *the War on Poverty* (Englewood Cliffs, N.J.: Prentice Hall, 1969).
19. Fraser, op. cit., p. 262.
20. For a discussion of this theoretical perspective, see Peter M. Blau, *Exchange and Power in Social* Life (New York: Wiley, 1964); and George Caspar Homans, *Social Behavior: Its Elementary Forms* (New York: Harcourt, Brace and World, 1961).
21. *The Condition of the Negroes of Halifax City,* Nova Scotia, op. cit.

22. Sarah M. Beaton, "Effects of Relocation: A Study of Ten Families Relocated from Africville, Halifax, Nova Scotia," Master of Social Work Thesis, Maritime School of Social Work, Halifax, N.S., 1969; and Bernard MacDougall, "Urban Relocation of Africville Residents," Master of Social Work Thesis, Maritime School of Social Work, Halifax, N.S., 1969.

23. The interview guide is published in Donald H. Clairmont and Dennis W. Magill, *Africville Relocation Report* (Halifax, N.S.: Institute of Public Affairs, Dalhousie University, 1971), pp. A131–A135.

24. Ibid., pp. A97–A128.

25. Ibid., pp. A83–A96.

26. Some relocation studies have been carried out as part of the relocation decision-making, see William H. Key, *When People Are Forced to Move* (Topeka, Kansas: Menninger Foundation, 1967), mimeographed, others have been concurrent with the relocating of people, see Herbert J. Gans, *The Urban Villagers: Group and Class* in *The Life of Italian Americans* (New York: The Free Press, 1962). The present study is unique in that it fostered collective action carried out after the relocation.

27. See Craig, op. cit.

Population and Urbanization	**63**
	Let's *Reduce* Global Population!
CLASSIC	
CONTEMPORARY	
CROSS-CULTURAL	*J. Kenneth Smail*

A familiar concern is holding the line on world population increase. But, some people are asking, has population growth already gone too far? In this selection, Ken Smail argues that the long-term "carrying capacity" of the planet may only be half the number of people we have now. And the time left to begin reducing population is running out fast.

The main point of this essay is simply stated. Within the next half-century, it is essential for the human species to have in place a flexible voluntary, equitable, and internationally coordinated plan to dramatically reduce world population by at least two-thirds. This process of voluntary consensus building—local, national, and global—must begin now.

The mathematical inevitability that human numbers will continue their dramatic increase over the next two generations (to perhaps 9 billion or more by the year 2050), the high probability that this numerical increase will worsen the problems that already plague humanity (economic, political, environmental, social, moral, etc.), and the growing realization that the Earth may only be able to support a global human

population in the 2 to 3 billion range at an "adequate to comfortable" standard of living, only reinforce this sense of urgency.

There are, however, hopeful signs. In recent years, we have finally begun to come to terms with the fact that the consequences of the twentieth century's rapid and seemingly uncontrolled population growth will soon place us—if it has not done so already—in the greatest crisis our species has yet encountered.

TEN INESCAPABLE REALITIES

In order better to appreciate the scope and ramifications of this still partly hidden crisis, I shall briefly call attention to ten essential and inescapable realities that must be fully understood and soon confronted.

First, during the present century world population will have grown from somewhere around 1.6 billion in 1900 to slightly more than 6 billion by the year 2000, an almost fourfold increase in but 100 years. This is an unprecedented numerical

Source: This is a revised version of an essay published as a pamphlet by Negative Population Growth (Smail, 1995) and then—after revision and expansion—as a journal article in *Population and Environment* (Smail, 1997) and *Politics and the Life Sciences* (Smail, 1997). Reprinted with permission of the author (e-mail address: Smail@kenyon.edu).

expansion. Throughout human history, world population growth measured over similar 100-year intervals has been virtually nonexistent or, at most, modestly incremental; it has only become markedly exponential within the last few hundred years. To illustrate this on a more easily comprehensible scale, based on the recent rate of increase of nearly 90 million per year, human population growth during the 1990s alone amounted to nearly 1 billion, an astonishing 20 increase in but little more than a single decade. Just by itself, this increase is equivalent to the total global population in the year 1800 and is approximately triple the estimated world population (ca. 300 million) at the height of the Roman Empire. It is a chastening thought that even moderate demographic projections suggest that this billion-per-decade rate of increase will continue well into the century, and that the current global total of 6 billion (late 1999 estimate) could easily reach 9 to 10 billion by mid-twenty-first century.

Second, even if a fully effective program of zero population growth (ZPG) were implemented immediately, by limiting human fertility to what demographers term the *replacement rate* (roughly 2.1 children per female), global population would nevertheless continue its rapid rate of expansion. In fact, demographers estimate that it would take at least two to three generations (fifty to seventy-five years) at ZPG fertility levels just to reach a point of population stability, unfortunately at numbers considerably higher than at present. This powerful *population momentum* results from the fact that an unusually high proportion (nearly one-third) of the current world population is under the age of fifteen and has not yet reproduced. Even more broad-based population profiles may be found throughout the developing world, where the under-fifteen age cohort often exceeds 40 percent and where birth rates have remained high even as mortality rates have fallen. While there are some recent indications that fertility rates are beginning to decline, the current composite for the less-developed world—excluding China—is still nearly double (ca. 3.8) that needed for ZPG.

Third, in addition to fertility levels, it is essential to understand that population growth is also significantly affected by changes in mortality rates. In fact, demographic transition theory suggests that the earlier stages of rapid population expansion are typically fueled more by significant reductions in death rates (i.e., decreased childhood mortality and/or enhanced adult longevity) than by changes in birth rates. Nor does recent empirical data suggest that average human life expectancy has reached anywhere near its theoretical upper limit, in either the developing or developed worlds. Consequently, unless there appears a deadly pandemic, a devastating world war or a massive breakdown in public health (or a combination of all three), it is obvious that ongoing global gains in human longevity will continue to make a major contribution to world population expansion over the next half-century, regardless of whatever progress might be made in reducing fertility.

Fourth, all previous examples of significant human population expansion—and subsequent (occasionally rapid) decline—have been primarily local or, at most, regional phenomena. At the present time, given the current global rate of increase of some 220,000 people per day (more than 9,000 per hour), it is ludicrous to speak of significant empty spaces left on Earth to colonize, certainly when compared with but a century ago. And it is ridiculous to suggest that "off Earth" (extraterrestrial) migration will somehow be sufficient to siphon away excess human population, in either the near or more distant future.

Fifth, given the data and observations presented thus far, it becomes increasingly apparent that the time span available for implementing an effective program of population "control" may be quite limited, with a window of opportunity—even in the more optimistic scenarios—that may not extend much beyond the middle of the next century. As mentioned previously, most middle-of-the-road demographic projections for the year 2050 two generations from now—are in the 8 to 9 billion range. Several observations might help to bring these demographic estimates and the above-mentioned "limited" time span into somewhat better perspective:

- the year 2050 is closer to the present than the year 1950
- an infant born in 2000 will be only 50 years old in the year 2050
- a young person entering the job market in the early twenty-first century will have reached retirement age in the year 2050

These observations also make it quite clear that *those already born*—ourselves, our children, and our grandchildren—will have to confront the overwhelming impact of an additional 3–4 billion people.

Sixth, the Earth's long-term carrying capacity, in terms of resources, is indeed finite, despite the continuing use of economic models predicated on seemingly unlimited growth, and notwithstanding the high probability of continued scientific/technological progress. Some further terminological clarification may be useful. "Long-term" is most reasonably defined on the order of several hundred years, at least; it emphatically does not mean the five to fifteen year horizon typical of much economic forecasting or political prognostication. Over this much longer time span, it thus becomes much more appropriate—perhaps even essential to civilizational survival—to define a sustainable human population size in terms of optimums rather than maximums. Further, *what "could" be supported in the short term is not necessary what "should" be humanity's goal over the longer term.*

As far as resources are concerned, whether these be characterized as renewable or nonrenewable, it is becoming increasingly apparent that the era of inexpensive energy (derived from fossil fuels), adequate food supplies (whether plant or animal), readily available or easily extractable raw materials (from wood to minerals), plentiful fresh water, and readily accessible "open space" is rapidly coming to a close, almost certainly within the next half-century. And finally, the consequences of future scientific/technological advances—whether in terms of energy production, technological efficiency, agricultural productivity, or creation of alternative materials—are much more likely to be incremental than revolutionary, notwithstanding frequent and grandiose claims for the latter.

Seventh, rhetoric about "sustainable growth" is at best a continuing exercise in economic self-deception and at worst a politically pernicious oxymoron. Almost certainly, working toward some sort of *steady-state sustainability* is much more realistic scientifically, (probably) more attainable economically, and (perhaps) more prudent politically. Assertions that the Earth might be able to support a population of 10, 15, or even 20 billion people for an indefinite period of time at a standard of living superior to the present are not only cruelly misleading but almost certainly false. Rather, extrapolations from the work of a growing number of ecologists, demographers, and numerous others suggest the distinct possibility that *the Earth's true carrying capacity—defined simply as humans in long-term adaptive balance with their ecological setting, resource base, and each other—may already have been exceeded by a factor of two or more.*

To the best of my knowledge, no evidence contradicts this sobering—perhaps even frightening—assessment. Consequently, since at some point in the not-too-distant future the negative consequences and ecological damage stemming from the mutually reinforcing effects of excessive human reproduction and overconsumption of resources could well become irreversible, and because there is only one Earth with which to experiment, it is undoubtedly better for our species to err on the side of prudence, exercising wherever possible a cautious and careful stewardship.

Eighth, only about 20 percent of the current world population (ca. 1.2 billion people) could be said to have a *generally adequate* standard of living, defined here as a level of affluence roughly approximating that of the so-called "developed" world (Western Europe, Japan, and North America). The other 80 percent (ca. 4.8 billion), incorporating most of the inhabitants of what have been termed the "developing nations," live in conditions ranging from mild deprivation to severe deficiency. Despite well-intentioned efforts to the contrary, there is little evidence that this imbalance is going to decrease in any significant way, and a strong likelihood that it may get worse, particularly in view of the fact that more than 90 percent of all future population expansion is projected to occur in these less-developed regions of the world. In fact, there is growing concern that when this burgeoning population growth in the developing world is combined with excessive or wasteful per capita energy and resource consumption in much of the developed world, widespread environmental deterioration (systemic breakdown?) in a number of the Earth's more heavily stressed ecosystems will become increasingly likely. This is especially worrisome in regions already beset by short-sighted or counterproductive economic policies, chronic political instability, and growing social unrest, particularly when one considers that nearly all nations in the less-developed world currently have an understandable desire—not surprisingly expressed as a fundamental right—to increase their standard of living (per capita energy and resource consumption) to something approximating "first world" levels.

Ninth, to follow up on the point just made, the total impact of human numbers on the global environment is often described as the product of three basic multipliers: (1) population size; (2) per capita energy and resource consumption (affluence); and (3) technological efficiency in the production, utilization, and conservation of such energy and resources. This relationship is usually expressed by some variant of the now well-known I = PAT equation: Impact = Population × Affluence × Technology. This simple formula enables one to demonstrate much more clearly the quantitative scope of humanity's dilemma over the next fifty to seventy-five years, particularly if the following projections are anywhere near accurate:

- human population could well *double* by the end of the twenty-first century, from our current 6 billion to perhaps 12 billion or more
- global energy and resource consumption could easily *quadruple* or more during the same period, particularly if (as just indicated in item 8) the less-developed nations are successful in their current efforts to significantly improve their citizens' standard of living to something approaching developed-world norms
- new technologies applied to current energy and resource inefficiencies might be successful in reducing per capita waste or effluence *by half,* or even *two-thirds,* in both the developed and developing worlds

Given these reasonable estimates, the conclusion seems inescapable that the human species' total impact on the Earth's already stressed ecosystem could easily *triple to quadruple* by the middle of the twenty-first century. This impact could be even greater if current (and future) efforts at energy and resource conservation turn out to be less successful than hoped for, or if (as seems likely) the mathematical relationship between these several multipliers is something more than simply linear. It is therefore very important to keep a close watch—for harbingers of future trends and/or problems—on current events in the growing group of nations now experiencing rapid economic development and modernization, with particular attention being given to ongoing changes in India and China, two states whose combined size represents nearly half the population of the less-developed world.

Tenth, and finally, there are two additional considerations—matters not usually factored into the I = PAT equation—that must also be taken into account in any attempt to coordinate appropriate responses to the rapidly increasing global environmental impact described in points 6 through 9. First, given current and likely ongoing scientific uncertainties about environmental limits and ecosystem resilience, not to mention the potential dangers of irreversible damage if such limits are stretched too far (i.e., a permanently reduced carrying capacity), it is extremely important to design into any future planning an adequate safety factor (or sufficient margin for error). In other words, any attempt at "guided social engineering" on the massive scale that will clearly be necessary over the next century will require at least as much attention to safety margins, internal coordination, and systems redundancy as may be found in other major engineering accomplishments—from designing airplanes to building the Channel Tunnel to landing astronauts on the moon.

In addition, such planning must consider yet another seemingly intractable problem. Because the human species not only shares the Earth—but has also co-evolved—with literally millions of other life forms, the closely related issues of wilderness conservation and biodiversity preservation must also be taken fully into account, on several different levels (pragmatic, aesthetic, and moral). In simplest terms, it has now become a matter of critical importance to ask some very basic questions about what proportion of the Earth's surface the human species has the right to exploit or transform—or, conversely, how much of the Earth's surface should be reserved for the protection and preservation of all other life forms. As many have argued, often in eloquent terms, our species will likely be more successful in confronting and resolving these questions—not to mention the other complex problems that are now crowding in upon us—*if we can collectively come to regard ourselves more as the Earth's long-term stewards than its absolute masters.*

To sum up, if the above "inescapable realities" are indeed valid, it is obvious that rational, equitable, and attainable population goals will have to be established in the very near future. It is also obvious that these goals will have to address—and in some fashion resolve—a powerful internal conflict: how to create and sustain an adequate standard of living for *all* the world's peoples, minimizing as much as possible the growing inequities between rich and poor, while simultaneously neither overstressing nor exceeding the Earth's longer-term carrying capacity. *I submit that these goals cannot be reached, or this conflict resolved, unless and until world population is dramatically reduced—to somewhere around 2 to 3 billion people—within the next two centuries.*

CRITICAL THINKING QUESTIONS

1. Why, according to this reading, is simply holding the line on population increase not enough?
2. What about the fact that humans share the earth with millions of other life forms? In facing up to the problem of population increase, what responsibility do we have for other species?
3. All in all, do you agree with Smail that we must find a way to reduce global population? Why or why not?

REFERENCES

Smail, J. Kenneth. 1995. Confronting the 21st century's hidden crisis: Reducing human numbers by 80%. *NPG Forum.* Teaneck, N.J.: Negative Population Growth.

———. 1997. Averting the 21st century's demographic crisis: Can human numbers be reduced by 75%? *Population and Environment*, 18 (6): 565–80.

———. Beyond population stabilization: The case for dramatically reducing global human numbers. Roundtable: World Population Policy commentary and responses. *Politics and the Life Sciences*, 16, 2 (September, 1997): 183–236.

64

Why Humanity Faces Ultimate Catastrophe

Thomas Robert Malthus

Environment and Society

| CLASSIC |
| CONTEMPORARY |
| CROSS-CULTURAL |

In this selection, from "An Essay on the Principle of Population," Thomas Robert Malthus foretells human calamity. His dire prediction is based on a single assertion: Human beings will overwhelm the earth's capacity to provide for us. Many of today's environmentalists (sometimes termed "neo-Malthusians") accept this principle and echo his early warning.

STATEMENT OF THE SUBJECT: RATIOS OF THE INCREASE OF POPULATION AND FOOD

In an inquiry concerning the improvement of society, the mode of conducting the subject which naturally presents itself is

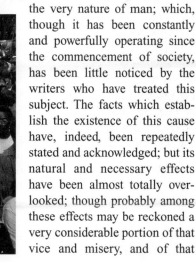

1. To investigate the causes that have hitherto impeded the progress of mankind towards happiness
2. To examine the probability of the total or partial removal of the causes in [the] future

Source: From *On the Principle of Population,* Vol. I, by T. R. Malthus (New York: E. P. Dutton & Co., Inc., 1914; orig. 1798).

To enter fully into this question, and to enumerate all the causes that have hitherto influenced human improvement, would be much beyond the power of an individual. The principal object of the present essay is to examine the effects of one great cause intimately united with the very nature of man; which, though it has been constantly and powerfully operating since the commencement of society, has been little noticed by the writers who have treated this subject. The facts which establish the existence of this cause have, indeed, been repeatedly stated and acknowledged; but its natural and necessary effects have been almost totally overlooked; though probably among these effects may be reckoned a very considerable portion of that vice and misery, and of that unequal distribution of the bounties of nature, which it has been the unceasing object of the enlightened philanthropist in all ages to correct.

The cause to which I allude is the constant tendency in all animated life to increase beyond the nourishment prepared for it.

It is observed by Dr. Franklin that there is no bound to the prolific nature of plants or animals but what is made by their crowding and interfering with each other's means of subsistence. Were the face of the earth, he says, vacant of other plants, it might be gradually sowed and overspread with one kind only, as for instance with fennel: and were it empty of other inhabitants, it might in a few ages be replenished from one nation only, as for instance with Englishmen.[1]

This is incontrovertibly true. Through the animal and vegetable kingdoms Nature has scattered the seeds of life abroad with the most profuse and liberal hand; but has been comparatively sparing in the room and the nourishment necessary to rear them. The germs of existence contained in this earth, if they could freely develop themselves, would fill millions of worlds in the course of a few thousand years. Necessity, that imperious, all pervading law of nature, restrains them within the prescribed bounds. The race of plants and the race of animals shrink under this great restrictive law; and man cannot by any efforts of reason escape from it.

In plants and irrational animals, the view of the subject is simple. They are all impelled by a powerful instinct to the increase of their species; and this instinct is interrupted by no doubts about providing for their offspring. Wherever therefore there is liberty, the power of increase is exerted; and the super-abundant effects are repressed afterwards by want of room and nourishment.

The effects of this check on man are more complicated. Impelled to the increase of his species by an equally powerful instinct, reason interrupts his career, and asks him whether he may not bring beings into the world for whom he cannot provide the means of support. If he attends to this natural suggestion, the restriction too frequently produces vice. If he hear it not, the human race will be constantly endeavouring to increase beyond the mean of subsistence. But as, by the law of our nature which makes food necessary to the life of man, population can never actually increase beyond the lowest nourishment capable of supporting it, a strong check on population, from the difficulty of acquiring food, must be constantly in operation. This difficulty must fall somewhere, and must necessarily be severely felt in some or other of the various forms of misery, or the fear of misery, by a large portion of mankind.

That population has this constant tendency to increase beyond the means of subsistence, and that it is kept to its necessary level by these causes, will sufficiently appear from a review of the different states of society in which man has existed. But, before we proceed to this review, the subject will, perhaps, be seen in a clearer light if we endeavour to ascertain what would be the natural increase of population if left to exert itself with perfect freedom; and what might be expected to be the rate of increase in the production of the earth under the most favourable circumstances of human industry.

It will be allowed that no country has hitherto been known where the manners were so pure and simple, and the means of subsistence so abundant, that no check whatever has existed to early marriages from the difficulty of providing for a family, and that no waste of the human species has been occasioned by vicious customs, by towns, by unhealthy occupations, or too severe labour. Consequently in no state that we have yet known has the power of population been left to exert itself with perfect freedom.

Whether the law of marriage be instituted, or not, the dictate of nature and virtue seems to be an early attachment to one woman; and where there were no impediments of any kind in the way of a union to which such an attachment would lead, and no causes of depopulation afterwards, the increase of the human species would be evidently much greater than any increase which has been hitherto known....

It may safely be pronounced,...that population, when unchecked, goes on doubling itself every twenty-five years, or increases in a geometrical ratio.

The rate according to which the productions of the earth may be supposed to increase, it will not be so easy to determine. Of this, however, we may be perfectly certain, that the ratio of their increase in a limited territory must be of a totally different nature from the ratio of the increase of population. A thousand millions are just as easily doubled every twenty-five years by the power of population as a thousand. But the food to support the increase from the greater number will by no means be obtained with the same facility. Man is necessarily confined in room. When acre has been added to acre till all the fertile land is occupied, the yearly increase of food must depend upon the melioration of the land already in possession. This is a fund, which, from the nature of all soils, instead of increasing, must be gradually diminishing. But population, could it be supplied with food, would go on with unexhausted vigour; and the increase of one period would furnish the power of a greater increase the next, and this without any limit....

Europe is by no means so fully peopled as it might be. In Europe there is the fairest chance that human industry may receive its best direction. The science of agriculture has been much studied in England and Scotland; and there is still a great portion of uncultivated land in these countries. Let us consider at what rate the produce of this island might be supposed to increase under circumstances the most favourable to improvement.

If it be allowed that by the best possible policy, and great encouragements to agriculture, the average produce of the island could be doubled in the first twenty-five years, it will be allowing, probably, a greater increase than could with reason be expected.

In the next twenty-five years, it is impossible to suppose that the produce could be quadrupled. It would be contrary to all our knowledge of the properties of land. The improvement of the barren parts would be a work of time and labour; and it must be evident to those who have the slightest acquaintance with agricultural subjects that, in proportion as cultivation extended, the additions that could yearly be made to the former average produce must be gradually and regularly diminishing. That we may be the better able to compare the increase of population and food, let us make a supposition, which, without pretending to accuracy, is clearly more favourable to the power of production in the earth than any experience we have had of its qualities will warrant.

Let us suppose that the yearly additions which might be made to the former average produce, instead of decreasing, which they certainly would do, were to remain the same; and that the produce of this island might be increased every twenty-five years by a quantity equal to what it at present produces. The most enthusiastic speculator cannot suppose a greater increase than this. In a few centuries it would make every acre of land in the island like a garden.

If this supposition be applied to the whole earth, and if it be allowed that the subsistence for man which the earth affords might be increased every twenty-five years by a quantity equal to what it at present produces, this will be supposing a rate of increase much greater than we can imagine that any possible exertions of mankind could make it.

It may be fairly pronounced, therefore, that, considering the present average state of the earth, the means of subsistence, under circumstances the most favourable to human industry, could not possibly be made to increase faster than in an arithmetical ratio.

The necessary effects of these two different rates of increase, when brought together, will be very striking. Let us call the population of this island eleven millions; and suppose the present produce equal to the easy support of such a number. In the first twenty-five years the population would be twenty-two millions, and the food being also doubled, the means of subsistence would be equal to this increase. In the next twenty-five years, the population would be forty-four millions, and the means of subsistence only equal to the support of thirty-three millions. In the next period the population would be eighty-eight millions, and the means of subsistence just equal to the support of half that number. And, at the conclusion of the first century, the population would be a hundred and seventy-six millions, and the means of subsistence only equal to the support of fifty-five millions, leaving a population of a hundred and twenty-one millions totally unprovided for.

Taking the whole earth, instead of this island, emigration would of course be excluded; and, supposing the present population equal to a thousand millions, the human species would increase as the numbers, 1, 2, 4, 8, 16, 32, 64, 128, 256, and subsistence as 1, 2, 3, 4, 5, 6, 7, 8, 9. In two centuries the population would be to the means of subsistence as 256 to 9; in three centuries as 4096 to 13, and in two thousand years the difference would be almost incalculable....

CRITICAL THINKING QUESTIONS

1. According to Malthus, at what rate does human population increase? At what rate can the earth's food supplies be increased?
2. Malthus published his essay in 1798; in the two centuries since then, has his dire prediction come to pass? Why or why not?
3. Following Malthus's thinking, what should be the cornerstone of the world's program to protect the environment? Do you agree with his position or not?

NOTE

1. Franklin's Miscell, p. 9.

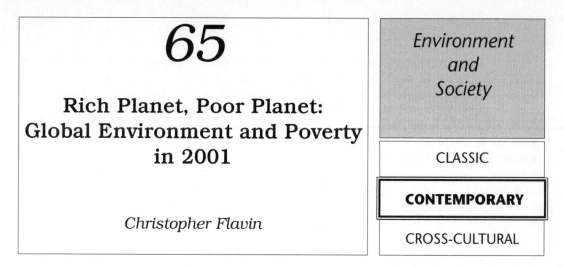

65

Rich Planet, Poor Planet: Global Environment and Poverty in 2001

Christopher Flavin

Environment
and
Society

CLASSIC

CONTEMPORARY

CROSS-CULTURAL

For decades, analysts have pointed to a steady decline in the earth's natural environment. This troubling trend, they explain, is not simply a technical problem but has much to do with the way societies operate. Moreover, environmental problems are closely linked to another pressing issue—global poverty.

A visit to Brazil's tropical state of Bahia provides contrasting views of the state of the world at the dawn of the new millennium. Bahia's capital, Salvador, has a population of over 3 million and a thoroughly modern veneer. Its downtown is full of large office buildings and busy construction cranes, and its highways are crammed with sport utility vehicles. The state is also rich in natural resources: the wealth provided by gold and sugarcane made Salvador the obvious location for colonial Brazil's leading port and capital for two centuries.[1]

Once a backwater—slavery was not outlawed until the end of the nineteenth century, one of the last regions to ban this practice—Bahia's economy is now booming. The state has a prospering manufacturing sector and has become popular with many leading multinationals, including

automobile companies that have put some of their most advanced factories there. The information economy is in a particularly competitive frenzy. Brazilian Internet service providers are connecting customers for free, and cell phones appear to be almost as common as they are in many European cities.

Scratch the surface, however, and another Bahia is still there. The large favelas that ring Salvador's outskirts are crowded with thousands of poor people who lack more than cell phones and computers: Toilets, running water, and schoolbooks are among the basic services and products that are unavailable to many of Bahia's poor. Similar gaps can be seen in the low hills that run south of Salvador along Bahia's rugged coast: The collapse of many of the country's rich cacao farms due to a devastating pathogen called witches'-broom and a sharp decline in world chocolate prices have left thousands of farm workers jobless and unable to provide for their families.

Source: From Lester R. Brown et al. *State of the World 2001* of the Worldwatch Institute, New York: Norton's 2001.

Bahia's environmental condition is just as uneven. Considered by ecologists to be one of the world's biological "hot spots," the Atlantic Rain Forest covers more than 2,000 kilometers of Brazil's subtropical coast. In 1993, biologists working in an area south of Salvador identified a world record 450 tree species in a single hectare. (A hectare of forest in the northeastern United States typically contains ten species.) In the last decade, Bahia's political and business leaders have come to recognize the extraordinary richness of their biological heritage—wildlands are being protected, ecological research facilities are being set up, and ecotourist resorts are mushrooming. A sign at the airport even warns travelers that removing endemic species from the country is a felony.[2]

And yet, signs of destruction are everywhere: Cattle ranches sprawl where the world's richest forests once stood; 93 percent of the Atlantic forest is already gone, and much of the remainder is fragmented into tiny plots. Pressure on these last bits of forest is enormous—both from powerful landowners and corporations eager to sell forest and agricultural products in the global marketplace, and from poor families desperately seeking a living.[3]

This picture of Bahia in the year 2000 is replicated at scores of locations around the globe. It is the picture of a world undergoing extraordinarily rapid change amid huge and widening disparities. Unprecedented economic prosperity, the emergence of democratic institutions in many countries, and the near instantaneous flow of information and ideas throughout a newly interconnected world allow us to address challenges that have been neglected for decades: meeting the material needs of all 6 billion members of the human race and restoring a sustainable balance between humanity and Earth's ecological systems.

This moment is historic, perhaps even evolutionary, in character. Tragically, it is not being seized. Despite a surge in economic growth in recent years and significant gains in health and education levels in many developing nations, the number of people who survive on less than $1 of income per day—the poverty threshold used by the World Bank—was 1.2 billion in 1998, almost unchanged since 1990. In some parts of the world, including sub-Saharan Africa, South Asia, and the former Soviet Union, the number living in poverty is substantially higher than the figures recorded a decade ago.[4]

The struggle to restore the planet's ecological health presents a similar picture: a number of small battles have been won, but the war itself is still being lost. Double-digit rates of growth in renewable energy markets, plus a two-year decline in global carbon emissions, for example, have failed to slow the rate of global climate change. Indeed, recent evidence, from the rapid melting of glaciers and the declining health of heat-sensitive coral reefs, suggests that climate change is accelerating. The same pattern can be seen in the increased commitment to protection of wild areas and biological diversity: new laws are being passed, consumers are demanding ecofriendly wood products, and ecotourist resorts are sprouting almost as quickly as dotcom companies. But foresters and biologists report that this host of encouraging developments has not reversed the massive loss of forests or the greatest extinction crisis the world has seen in 65 million years.[5]

Long considered distinct issues, consigned to separate government agencies, ecological and social problems are in fact tightly interconnected and mutually reinforcing. The burden of dirty air and water and of decimated natural resources invariably falls on the disadvantaged. And the poor, in turn, are often compelled to tear down the last nearby tree or pollute the local stream in order to survive. Solving one problem without addressing the other is simply not feasible. In fact, poverty and environmental decline are both embedded deeply in today's economic systems. Neither is a peripheral problem that can be considered in isolation. What is needed is what Eduardo Athayde, General Director of Bahia's Atlantic Forest Open University, calls "econology," a synthesis of ecology, sociology, and economics that can be used as the basis for creating an economy that is both socially and ecologically sustainable—the central challenge facing humanity as the new millennium begins.[6]

The challenge is made larger by the fact that it must be met simultaneously at national and global levels, requiring not only cooperation but partnership between North and South. Responsibility for the current health of the planet and its human inhabitants is shared unequally between rich and poor countries, but if these problems are to be resolved, the two groups of nations will need to bring their respective strengths and capabilities to bear. This will require a new form of globalization—one that goes beyond trade links and capital flows to strengthened political and social ties between governments and civil society.

A select group of large industrial and developing countries—a collection that can be called the E-9, given that they are key environmental as well as economic players—could have a central role in closing the North–South gap. Together, this group of countries accounts for 57 percent of the world's population and 80 percent of total economic output. (See Table 65.1.) This [reading] uses data on these nine diverse countries and areas to illuminate key economic, social, and ecological trends. But this grouping has more than just analytical value. As argued at the end of the [reading], E-9 cooperation could be a key to achieving accelerated economic and environmental progress in the new century.[7]

A TALE OF TWO WORLDS

Halfway through the year 2000, two stories from the Philippines made headlines around the world. In June, a computer virus dubbed the "love bug" appeared almost simultaneously on every continent, crashing the computer systems of scores of multinational corporations and government offices, ranging from the U.S. Pentagon to the British Parliament. The estimated total cost of the resulting disruptions: $10 billion. Computer

Table 65.1   The E-9: A Population and Economic Profile

Country Grouping	Population, 2000	Gross National Product, 1998
	(million)	*(billion dollars)*
China	1,265	924
India	1,002	427
European Union[1]	375	8,312
United States	276	7,903
Indonesia	212	131
Brazil	170	768
Russia	145	332
Japan	127	4,089
South Africa	43	137

[1] Data for European Union do not include Luxembourg.

Source: World Bank, *World Development Indicators 2000* (Washington, D.C.: 2000), 10–12; Population Reference Bureau, "2000 World Population Data Sheet," wall chart (Washington, D.C.: June 2000).

security experts and FBI agents quickly traced the diabolical love bug to a small Manila technical college and a 24-year-old student named Onel de Guzman. For computer experts, this may have been an indication of the vulnerability of the global Internet, but in the Philippines it quickly became a source of national pride. People took the love bug debacle as an encouraging sign that their developing nation was leapfrogging into the top ranks of the global economy's hottest sector.[8]

Across town, a Manila neighborhood called the Promised Land was hit by a different kind of news a month later: more than 200 people were killed in a massive landslide and subsequent fire. Although this tragedy was precipitated by Typhoon Kai-Tak, it was anything but a natural disaster. The Promised Land, it turns out, is a combination garbage dump/shantytown that is home to 50,000 people, most of whom make their living by scavenging the food and materials discarded by Manila's growing middle class. When two days of heavy rain loosened the mountain of garbage, it came crashing down on hundreds of homes as well as the dump's electrical lines, starting a massive fire. Scores of

Promised Land residents were buried, others were burned alive, and still more were poisoned by toxic chemicals released by the fire.[9]

Economic successes and social failures are now found side by side, not just in the Philippines, but around the world in this supposed time of plenty. The annual output of the world economy has grown from $31 trillion in 1990 to $42 trillion in 2000; by comparison, the total output of the world economy in 1950 was just $6.3 trillion. And in 2000, the growth of the world economy surged to a 4.7-percent annual rate, the highest in the last decade. This increase in economic activity has allowed billions of people to buy new refrigerators, televisions, and computers, and has created millions of jobs. Global telephone connections grew from 520 million in 1990 to 844 million in 1998 (an increase of 62 percent), and mobile phone subscribers went from 11 million to 319 million in that time (up 2,800 percent). The number of "host" computers, a measure of the Internet's expansion, grew from 376,000 in 1990 to 72,398,000 in 1999—an increase of 19,100 percent.[10]

The economic boom of the last decade has not been confined to the rich countries of the North. Much of the growth is occurring in the developing nations of Asia and Latin America, where economic reforms, lowered trade barriers, and a surge in foreign capital have fueled investment and consumption. Between 1990 and 1998, Brazil's economy grew 30 percent, India's expanded 60 percent, and China's mushroomed by a remarkable 130 percent. China now has the world's third largest economy (second if measured in terms of purchasing power parity), and a booming middle class who work in offices, eat fast food, watch color television, and surf the Internet. China alone now has 420 million radios, 344 million television sets, 24 million mobile phones, and 15 million computers.[11]

Still, the global economy remains tarnished by vast disparities. (See Table 65.2.) Gross national product (GNP) per person ranges from $32,350 in Japan to $4,630 in Brazil, $2,260 in Russia, and just $440 in India. Even when measured in purchasing power terms, GNP per person among

Table 65.2   Economic Trends in E-9 Nations

Country	GNP per Person, 1998	Purchasing Power per Person, 1998	Population Earning Below $2 per Day, 1993–99[1]	Share of Income or Consumption	
				Lowest 20 percent, 1993–98[1]	Highest 10 percent, 1993–98[1]
	(dollars)		*(percent)*	*(percent)*	
Japan	32,350	23,592	—	10.6	21.7
United States	29,240	29,240	—	5.2	30.5
Germany[2]	26,570	22,026	—	8.2	23.7
Brazil	4,630	6,460	17.4	2.5	47.6
South Africa	3,310	8,296	35.8	2.9	45.9
Russia	2,260	6,180	25.1	4.4	38.7
China	750	3,051	53.7	5.9	30.4
Indonesia	640	2,407	66.1	8.0	30.3
India	440	2,060	86.2	8.1	33.5

[1] Data are from a single year within the time frame.

[2] Comparable data for European Union not available; Germany is most populous EU member.

Source: World Bank, *World Development Indicators 2000* (Washington, D.C.: 2000), 10–12, 62–64, 66–68.

these countries varies by a factor of 10. Per capita income has increased 3 percent annually in forty countries since 1990, but more than eighty nations have per capita incomes that are lower than they were a decade ago. Within countries, the disparities are even more striking. In the United States, the top 10 percent of the population has six times the income of the lowest 20 percent; in Brazil, the ratio is 19 to 1. More than 10 percent of the people living in "rich" countries are still below the poverty line, and in many, inequality has grown over the last two decades.[12]

The boom in global consumption over the past decade has been accompanied by improvements in living standards in many countries and declines in others. The U.N. Development Programme estimates that the share of the world's population suffering from what it calls "low human development" fell from 20 percent in 1975 to 10 percent in 1997. Still, World Bank figures show that 2.8 billion people, nearly half the world's population, survive on an income of less than $2 per day, while a fifth of humanity, 1.2 billion people, live on less than $1 per day. An estimated 291 million sub-Saharan Africans— 46 percent of the region's population—now live on less than $1 a day, while in South Asia, the figure is 522 million. This is a staggering number of people to enter the new century without the income needed to purchase basic necessities such as food, clean water, and health care.[13]

Worldwide, some 1.1 billion people are currently estimated to be malnourished. Most of these are poor people in rural areas who have insufficient land to grow the food they need and not enough income to buy it from others. Many of these people live in countries with food surpluses, but while well-off farmers sell their products to middle-class consumers in distant nations; the proceeds have no benefit for millions of starving children. In some African countries, such as Kenya, Zambia, and Zimbabwe, as much as 40 percent of the population is malnourished.[14]

Roughly 1.2 billion people do not have access to clean water. In China, the portion that fall in this category is 10 percent (125 million people), in India it is 19 percent, and in South Africa, 30 percent. Toilets are even rarer in many countries: 33 percent of Brazil's population does not have one, nor does 49 percent of Indonesia's or 84 percent of India's.[15]

Polluted water is a major contributor to one of the largest disparities today's world faces: the health gap. Although infant mortality rates have dropped 25 to 50 percent in many countries in the past decade, they still stand at 43 per thousand live births in China and 70 per thousand in India. (See Table 65.3.) Much of the wide difference in this number around the world results from undernutrition and common infectious diseases that remain rampant in many poor countries. More intractable diseases such as cholera and tuberculosis are also becoming epidemic in many areas.

More alarming still is the fact that AIDS, which has been brought under control in some rich countries, is spreading rapidly in many developing nations. The crisis is particularly acute in southern Africa, which a decade ago had relatively low rates of infection. By 2000, HIV infection rates had reached a stunning 20 percent in South Africa, 25 percent in Zimbabwe, and 36 percent in Botswana. Decades of rising life expectancy are being reversed in a matter of years, as hundreds of thousands of young adults and children succumb to the disease. Health care budgets are being overwhelmed, and education undermined by the early deaths of many teachers. It is no accident that the countries most ravaged by AIDS are those with high rates of social disruption and limited government health services. In China, poor people who sell their blood in order to make ends meet are paying a high price in the form of HIV infection from contaminated needles. Ironically, in parts of Africa, it is those who are just emerging from poverty that are being hit the hardest—devastating a generation of educated young workers, a cataclysm that may forestall the growth of an economically secure middle class.[16]

Table 65.3   Health Indicators in E-9 Nations

Country	Health Expenditures per Person, 1990–98[1]	Infant Mortality 1980	Infant Mortality 1998	Tuberculosis Incidence, 1997	HIV Prevalence Among Adults, 1997
	(dollars of purchasing power)	*(per thousand live births)*		*(per 100,000)*	*(percent)*
United States	4,121	8	4	7	0.76
Germany[2]	2,364	12	5	15	0.08
Japan	1,757	13	7	29	0.01
South Africa	571	42	31	394	12.91
Brazil	503	70	33	78	0.63
Russia	404	22	17	106	0.05
China	142	90	43	113	0.06
Indonesia	73	115	70	187	0.82
India	38	67	51	285	0.05

[1] Data are from the most recent year available.

[2] Comparable data for European Union not available; Germany is most populous EU member.

Source: World Bank, *World Development Indicators 2000* (Washington, D.C.: 2000), 90–92, 102–04, 106–08.

One of the key ingredients of economic progress is education, and on this front, the world is doing better than it was two decades ago. (See Table 65.4.) In India, the share of children in secondary school has risen from 41 percent to 60 percent; in China, it has gone from 63 [percent] to 70 percent; and in South Africa, from 62 [percent] to 95 percent. But even with these improvements, many countries are failing to invest adequately in their young people, who are unlikely to be able to participate in or benefit from today's most vibrant economic sectors, which demand not only basic literacy but often specialized training. Girls in particular are receiving inadequate education in many countries. Adult female illiteracy rates remain as high as 25 percent in China and 57 percent in India, levels that virtually guarantee a host of social and economic problems—and that make environmental threats more difficult to address.

TESTING THE LIMITS

When the Russian icebreaker *Yamal* reached the North Pole in July 2000, the scientists abroad were confronted with a strange sight: an expanse of open, calm water in place of the two or three meters of pack ice that is common to the region even at the height of summer. In the 91 years since Robert Peary and Matthew Henson reached the North Pole by dogsled in 1909, nothing like this had been reported. But human memory is the wrong scale on which to measure this development: Scientists estimate that the last time the polar region was completely icefree was 50 million years ago.[17]

The dynamic, shifting character of the Arctic ice pack suggests that the open water over the pole itself was, for now, a fleeting phenomenon. But recent scientific evidence confirms the underlying trend: Earth's frozen top is melting at an extraordinary rate. Submarine sonar measurements indicate a 40-percent decline in the average thickness of summer polar ice since the 1950s, far exceeding the rate of melting previously estimated. Based on these observations, scientists now estimate that by the middle of this century the Arctic could be ice-free in summer.[18]

Among the myriad signs of human-induced global climate change—fossil fuel combustion was recently estimated to have raised atmospheric concentrations of carbon dioxide to their highest

Table 65.4 Education in E-9 Nations

	Adult Illiteracy Rate				Share of Children in Secondary School	
	Female		Male			
Country	1980	1998	1980	1998	1980	1997
	(percent)				(percent)	
Germany[1]	—	—	—	—	82	95
Japan	—	—	—	—	93	100
United States	—	—	—	—	94	96
Russia	2	1	1	0	98	88
Brazil	27	16	23	16	46	66
South Africa	25	16	22	15	62	95
Indonesia	40	20	21	9	42	56
China	48	25	22	9	63	70
India	74	57	45	33	41	60

[1] Comparable data for European Union not available; Germany is most populous EU member.

Source: World Bank, *World Development Indicators 2000* (Washington, D.C.: 2000), 74–76, 82–84.

levels in 20 million years—this one may be the most dramatic. In late 2000, the Intergovernmental Panel on Climate Change (IPCC), the scientific body that advises government negotiators, produced its latest report. It included the strongest consensus statement yet that societies' release of carbon dioxide and other greenhouse gases "contributed substantially to the observed warming over the last fifty years." By the end of the century, the IPCC concluded, temperatures could be five degrees Celsius higher than in 1990—an increase greater than the change in temperature between the last Ice Age and today.[19]

While the shipping industry is already beginning to view the Arctic meltdown as a potential short-term opportunity—perhaps cutting the transit distance between Europe and the Far East by as much as 5,000 kilometers—the full economic and ecological consequences would be far more extensive and hard to predict. Scientists have recently learned that Arctic ice is a key part of the "engine" that drives the powerful oceanic conveyor belt—the warm Gulf Stream—that provides northern Europe with the relatively temperate and stable climate that allowed European societies to flourish. Shutting it down could change the climate of Europe more than at any time since the last Ice Age. And because the Gulf Stream is a dominant feature in the oceanic circulation system, any major change in its course would have ripple effects globally. Moreover, with less ice to reflect the sun's rays, the warming of Earth that caused the ice to melt in the first place would accelerate.[20]

Some 10,000 kilometers south of the North Pole lies a very different environment—the world's tropical oceans and their abundant coral reefs, a biologically rich ecosystem that has been described as the rainforest of the ocean (65 percent of fish species are reef dwellers). One of the richest is the Belize Barrier Reef on the Yucatan Peninsula in the Caribbean, the site of a recent diving expedition by marine biologist Jonathan Kelsey and journalist Colin Woodard. What was intended to be an exciting exploration of the region's spectacular, multihued marine life turned out to be a disturbing disappointment: "Bright white boulders dotted the seascape in all directions, a sign of severe coral distress," Woodard reported. "A centuries-old stand of elkhorn coral as big as an elephant was now dead and smothered in a thick two-year growth of brown algae.... Across the plane, the corals appeared to be dying."[21]

Around the world, from the Caribbean to the Indian Ocean and Australia's Great Barrier Reef, similar observations have been reported in the past two years. Coral polyps are temperature-sensitive, and often sicken or die when ocean surface temperatures rise even slightly. The temporary warming of ocean waters that accompanies El Niño anomalies in the Pacific is generally hard on coral reefs, but the 1998 El Niño was something different: Reports of sick coral were soon being filed by marine biologists around the world, who estimated that more than one quarter of the coral reefs were sick or dying. In some areas of the Pacific, the figure is as high as 90 percent. For many small island nations, the loss in income from fishing and tourism, as well as increased storm damage from the loss of coral reefs, may be enough to trigger the collapse of their economies.[22]

Following another serious episode of coral bleaching just a decade earlier, this recent epidemic of coral disease is another strong indication that the world is warming. But it is more than that: Coral reefs are sort of a marine version of the famous canary in a coalmine—vulnerable to many environmental stresses that now run rampant, including urban sewage, agricultural runoff, and the sedimentation that comes from deforestation. The recent decimation of coral reefs and the growing frequency of such events suggest that the world's ecological balance has been profoundly disturbed.

Whether it is Arctic ice, tropical corals, oceanic fisheries, or old-growth forests, the forces driving ecological destruction are varied, complex, and often dangerously synergistic. Population is one factor. The nearly fourfold expansion in human numbers over the past century has drastically increased demands on natural resources. The combination of population growth and deforestation, for example, has cut the number of hectares of forest per person in half since 1960—increasing pressures on remaining forests and encouraging a rapid expansion in plantation forestry. Demand for water, energy, food, and materials have all been driven up by the unprecedented expansion in human numbers. And increasingly, it is in the world's developing countries that natural systems are declining the fastest and people face the most serious environmentally related stresses. (See Table 65.5.)[23]

Table 65.5   Ecological Health of E-9 Nations

Country	Share of Land Area That is Forested, 1995[1]	Change of Average Annual Deforestation, 1990–95	Share of Mammals Threatened, 1996	Share of Flowering Plants Threatened, 1997	Share of Land Area Nationally Protected, 1996
			(percent)		
Russia	22	0	11.5	—	3.1
Brazil	16	0.5	18.0	2.4	4.2
United States	6	−0.3	8.2	4.0	13.4
China	4	0.1	19.0	1.0	6.4
Germany[2]	3	0	10.5	0.5	27.0
Indonesia	3	1	29.4	0.9	10.6
Japan	0.7	0.1	22.0	12.7	6.8
South Africa	0.2	0.2	13.4	9.5	5.4

[1] Data may refer to earlier years.

[2] Comparable data for European Union not available; Germany is most populous EU member.

Source: World Bank, *World Development Indicators 2000* (Washington, D.C.: 2000), 126–28.

Population growth alone could not have tested environmental limits this severely, however. The pressures it imposes have been magnified by rising consumption levels as each individual demands more from nature. Meat-based diets and automobile-centered transportation systems are among the highly consumptive practices first adopted by the billion or so people living in rich countries, and now proliferating quickly in many parts of the developing world. Meanwhile, government regulations and emission control technology have lagged well behind the pace of adoption in richer countries. As a consequence, the most serious air pollution is now found in cities such as Jakarta and São Paulo. (See Table 65.6.)

The combination of population growth and increased consumption is projected to cause the number of people living in water-deficit countries to jump from 505 million to over 2.4 billion in the next twenty-five years. In countries that already face severe water shortages, such as Egypt, India, and Iran, water scarcity is likely to require large-scale food imports. In northern China, the water table under Beijing fell 2.5 meters in 1999, bringing the total decline since 1965 to 59 meters. Similarly, surging demand for oil—particularly in North America and East Asia—contributed in the

year 2000 to the highest sustained oil prices the world has seen since the early 1980s. Beyond the proximate political reasons for higher oil prices, the underlying cause is clear: world oil production is nearing its eventual all-time peak, and producers are struggling to meet the combined demands of first-time car owners in China and those who are buying the large SUVs now found in nearly half of U.S. garages.[24]

While the last decade's growth in affluence contributed to many environmental problems, keeping people poor is not the answer—either morally or practically. In impoverished areas around the world, the rural poor are pushed onto marginal, often hilly lands, from which they must hunt bushmeat, harvest trees, or clear land for pasture or crops in order to survive. A 2000 study on the root causes of biodiversity loss, sponsored by the World Wide Fund for Nature (WWF), concluded that together with other forces, poverty often plays a major role.[25]

In the Philippines, for example, the country's rich array of coral reefs, forests, and mangroves—home to an estimated 40,000 species—are shrinking rapidly in area, while the remaining pockets lose much of their original diversity. According to the WWF study, rural poverty and the unequal distribution of land in the Philippines are among

Table 65.6   Air Pollution in E-9 Nations

Country	Sulfur Dioxide, 1995	Suspended Particulates, 1995	Nitrogen Dioxide, 1995
	(micrograms per cubic meter)		
Germany (Frankfurt)[1]	11	36	45
Japan (Tokyo)	18	49	68
South Africa (Cape Town)	21	—	72
United States (New York)	26	—	79
India (Mumbai)	33	240	39
Brazil (São Paulo)	43	86	83
China (Shanghai)	53	246	73
Russia (Moscow)	109	100	—
Indonesia (Jakarta)	—	271	—

[1] Comparable data for European Union not available; Germany is most populous EU member.

Source: World Bank, *World Development Indicators 2000* (Washington, D.C.: 2000), 162–64.

the major causes of biodiversity loss that must be remedied if the country's natural wealth is to be preserved for future generations. Similarly, a study in the southern Mexican state of Campeche found that much of the pressure on the Calakmul Biosphere Reserve is coming from the efforts of local indigenous people to meet their material needs. Meeting those needs sustainably is a key component of any effective program to reverse environmental decline.[26]

NORTH MEETS SOUTH

Bridging these gaps between North and South will require a combination of innovative market reforms and a common commitment by governments to fill the gaps left by the private sector. Most of the recent emphasis has been on the market, pointing to developments such as the certified forest products market and booming consumer interest in ecotourism. And even government negotiated treaties such as the Kyoto Protocol on climate change now rely on market mechanisms as primary tools for achieving their goals. Greenhouse gas trading schemes are being viewed as a way of not only trimming emissions as efficiently as possible, but also distributing the burden of addressing the problem among various countries.

Market mechanisms are often effective, and private innovation is key to solving many problems, but North–South cooperation will have to be based on something more than commercial relationships if the world's current problems are to be surmounted. Cooperation among NGOs, for example, allows innovative social programs and political techniques to be transferred rapidly from one country to another, dramatically speeding the rate of progress. The recent surge in the number of these groups in the developing world is being spurred by the support of foundations in industrial countries, as well as by the spread of democracy in many poor nations. And the Internet is proving a boon to the spread of civil society in countries where it has been weak in the past. The ability of citizens to communicate easily among themselves—and with people in distant lands with similar concerns—is rapidly transforming the political equation in many countries, and is creating more favorable conditions for addressing social and ecological problems.

Government leadership is also key: Governments need to forge strong partnerships and provide sufficient funding to invest in the public infrastructure needed to support a sustainable economy. The failure of many industrial countries to meet the financial commitments they have agreed to under various international agreements and the failure of some developing countries to carry through on political and economic reforms have left a residue of distrust that must be overcome. Although it is unlikely that foreign aid levels will ever return to the figures that were typical in the 1960s and 1970s, a steady flow of well-targeted grants is essential to sustain progress. And with private capital taking up much of the burden of industrial growth and large-scale infrastructure, government aid can be targeted at pressing needs, with multiplier effects on human progress and environmental protection: areas such as education, health care, the status of women, micro-credit, and broad Internet access. One essential step is reducing the developing-country debt burden, which has reached onerous levels in recent years.

The economic and political weakness of many developing countries has prevented them from taking the more central position on the world stage that is now logically theirs. With 80 percent of the world's population, the bulk of its natural resources, and an opportunity to learn from the historical mistakes of today's industrial countries, it seems clear that the South will increasingly dominate the twenty-first century. Today's industrial powers will likely resist this shift, but they will soon find that they cannot achieve their own goals without the cooperation of the South. The summer of 2000 saw an intriguing sign of the changing balance of power when Mexico elected its first president from outside the traditional ruling party. Vicente Fox, a charismatic modern leader, traveled to Washington and called for allowing workers to travel as freely across the Mexico–U.S. border as capital now does.[27]

The existing structure of international institutions such as the World Bank and the World Trade Organization will have to be reformed to allow developing countries to take the more central role that is now essential to solving the world's most difficult problems. With shared power will come shared responsibility—a role that seems far more achievable today than it did two decades ago, when participatory political systems were still rare in the developing world.

One new organizing principle for countries that is particularly appropriate is the E-9 group described earlier—a coalition of northern and southern countries that between them have far greater impact on global social and ecological trends than do the Group of Eight (G-8) industrial

countries. Between them, the E-9 have 60 percent of the world's population, 73 percent of the carbon emissions, and 66 percent of higher plant species. (See Table 65.7.) They have both the ability and the responsibility to lead the world in addressing the main challenges of the twenty-first century.

CRITICAL THINKING QUESTIONS

1. The article links the problems of environmental decline and poverty. Explain how they are connected.
2. What are some of the strategies suggested by the author to protect the planet's natural environment? Which strategies do you find most important? Why?
3. Overall, what do you see as the prospects for halting the decline of the planet's natural environment? Provide reasons for your position.

Table 65.7   The E-9: Leaders for the Twenty-first Century

| Country | Share of | | | | |
	World Population, 1999	PPP Gross Domestic Product, 1998	World Carbon Emissions 1999	World Forest Area, 1995	World Vascular Plant Species, 1997
	(percent)				
China	21.0	10.2	13.5	4	11.9
India	16.5	5.4	4.5	2	5.9
European Union	6.3	20.5	14.5	3	—
United States	4.6	21.3	25.5	6	6
Indonesia	3.5	1.3	.9	3	10.9
Brazil	2.8	2.9	1.5	16	20.8
Russia	2.4	2.4	4.6	22	—
Japan	2.1	8.0	6.0	0.7	2.1
South Africa	0.7	0.9	2.0	0.2	8.7
E-9 Total	**59.9**	**72.9**	**73**	**56.9**	**66.3**

Source: Worldwatch calculations based on Population Reference Bureau, "1999 World Population Data Sheet," wall chart (Washington, D.C.: June 1999); World Bank, *World Development Indicators 2000* (Washington, D.C.: 2000), 10–12; BP Amoco, *BP Amoco: Statistical Review of World Energy* (London: June 2000), 38; U.N. Food and Agriculture Organization, *State of the World's Forests 1999* (New York: 1999), 125–30; World Conservation Union–IUCN, *1997 IUCN Red List of Threatened Plants* (Cambridge, U.K.: 1998), xvii, xxvii–xxxiii.

NOTES

1. Based on author's visit to Bahia, August 2000.

2. James Brooke, "Brazilian Rain Forest Yields Most Diversity for Species of Trees," *New York Times*, 30 March 1993.

3. "Latin America and the Caribbean: Brazil," *The Nature Conservancy*, **www.tnc.org/brazil/forest.htm**, viewed 12 October 2000.

4. World Bank, *World Development Report 2000/2001* (New York: Oxford University Press, 2000), 21–3.

5. Christopher Flavin, "Wind Power Booms," and idem, "Solar Power Market Jumps," both in Lester R. Brown, Michael Renner, and Brian Halweil, *Vital Signs 2000* (New York: W.W. Norton & Company, 2000), 56–9; Seth Dunn, "Carbon Emissions Fall Again," in ibid., 66–7; Clive Wilkinson, *Status of Coral Reefs of the World, 2000: Executive Summary*, 9th International Coral Reef Symposium, 23–4 October 2000, Bali, Indonesia; National Snow and Ice Data Center, "Mountain Glacier Fluctuations: Changes in Terminus Location and Mass Balance," **www.nsidc.colorado.edu/NASA/SOTC/glacier_balance. html**, viewed 2 February 2000; Alexander Wood, "An Emerging Consensus on Biodiversity Loss," in Alex Wood, Pamela Stedman-Edwards, and Johanna Meng, eds., *The Root Causes of Biodiversity Loss* (London: Earthscan, 2000), 2.

6. Eduardo Athayde, Atlantic Forest Open University, Salvador, Bahia, Brazil, discussion with author, 10 August 2000.

7. The E-9 concept was first introduced as the E-8 in *State of the World 1997*. This chapter adds South Africa to the group and substitutes the European Union (EU) for Germany, which substantially extends its breadth of economic and ecological coverage. The sector-specific tables that follow, however, use statistics for Germany (the EU's most populous member), due to the lack of comparable data for the EU as a whole.

8. " 'Love Bug' Suspect Charged," *Associated Press*, 29 June 2000; Mark Landler, "A Filipino Linked to 'Love Bug' Talks About His License to Hack," *New York Times*, 21 October 2000.

9. Casualties from "Payatas Relocation Coordination Ordered," Manila Bulletin, **www.mb.com.ph/umain/ 2000%2D07/mn071805.asp**, viewed 10 September 2000; Typhoon Kai Tak from Roli Ng, "Garbage Slide Kills 46 in Manila's Promised Land," Planet Ark, **www.planetark.org/dailynewsstory.cfm?newsid=7412 &newsdate=11-Jul-2000**, viewed 10 September 2000; number of residents from "Manila Urges Payatas Residents to Get Out of Dumpsite," *China Daily Information*, **www.chinadaily.net/cover/storydb/2000/ 07/15/wnmanilla.715.html**, viewed 10 September 2000.

10. Growth of world economy from Angus Maddison, *Monitoring the World Economy 1820–1992* (Paris: Organisation for Economic Cooperation and Development [OECD], 1995), 227, and from Angus Maddison, *Chinese Economic Performance in the Long Run* (Paris: OECD, 1998), 159, using deflators and recent growth rates from International Monetary Fund (IMF), *World Economic Outlook* (Washington, DC: October 1999); growth estimate for 2000 from IMF, *World Economic Outlook* (advance copy) (Washington, DC: September 2000); International Telecommunications Union (ITU), *World Telecommunication Indicators '98*, Socioeconomic Timeseries Access and Retrieval System database, downloaded 24 August 1999, and ITU, *World Telecommunication Development Report 1999* (Geneva: 1999); number of host computers from Internet Software Consortium and Network Wizards, "Internet Domain Surveys," **www.isc.org/ds**, viewed 20 February 2000.

11. Growth of various economies from World Bank, *World Development Indicators 2000* (Washington, DC: 2000), 182–83; China's economy from ibid., 10–12; consumer products in China from ibid., 300, and from Population Reference Bureau, "2000 World Population Data Sheet," wall chart (Washington, DC: June 2000), with computers from Ye Di Sheng, "The Development and Market of China's Information Industry and its Investment Opportunity," **www.caspa.com/event/augdin2.htm**, viewed 10 November 2000.

12. Wealth disparities from World Bank, op. cit. note 4, 282–83; trends in per capita income from U.N. Development Programme (UNDP), *Human Development Report 1999* (New York: Oxford University Press, 1999), 2–3; income disparities from World Bank, op. cit. note 11, 66, 68; 10 percent based on UNDP, op. cit. this note, 149, 197; inequality growth from ibid., 3.

13. UNDP, op. cit. note 12, 25; number of people living on less than $1 per day from World Bank, op. cit. note 4, 3, 23.

14. Number of people malnourished is a World Watch estimate based on U.N. Administrative Committee on Coordination, Sub-Committee on Nutrition in collaboration with International Food Policy Research Institute (IFPRI), *Fourth Report on the World Nutrition Situation* (Geneva: 1999), and on Rafael Flores, research fellow, IFPRI, Washington, D.C., e-mail to Brian Halweil, Worldwatch Institute, 5 November 1999, and discussion with Gary Gardner, Worldwatch Institute, 3 February 2000; selected countries with chronic hunger from Gary Gardner and Brian Halweil, *Underfed and Overfed: The Global Epidemic of Malnutrition*, Worldwatch Paper 150 (Washington DC: Worldwatch Institute, March 2000), 17.

15. Number without access to clean water from Peter H. Gleick, *The World's Water 1998–1999* (Washington, DC: Island Press, 1998), 40; percentages by country from World Bank, op. cit. note 11, 14–6; toilets from World Bank op. cit. note 11, 94–6.

16. Joint United Nations Program on HIV/AIDS, *Report on the Global HIV/AIDS Epidemic—June 2000* (Geneva: June 2000), 124; Elizabeth Rosenthal, "In Rural China, a Steep Price of Poverty: Dying of AIDS," *New York Times*, 28 October 2000.

17. John Noble Wilford, "Ages-Old Polar Icecap Is Melting, Scientists Find," *New York Times*, 19 August 2000.

18. D. A. Rothrock, Y. Yu, and G. A. Maykut, "Thinning of the Arctic Sea-Ice Cover," *Geophysical Research Letters*, 1 December 1999, 3469; Ola M. Johannessen, Elena V. Ahalina, and Martin W. Miles, "Satellite Evidence for an Arctic Sea Ice Cover in Transformation," *Science*, 3 December 1999, 1937; Lars H. Smedsrud and Tore Furevik, "Toward an Ice-Free Arctic?" *Cicerone*, February 2000.

19. Paul N. Pearson and Martin R. Palmer, "Atmospheric Carbon Dioxide Concentrations Over the Past 60 Million Years," *Nature*, 17 August 2000, 695; Andrew C. Revkin, "A Shift in Stance on Global Warming Theory," *New York Times*, 26 October 2000.

20. Carsten Rühlemann et al., "Warming of the Tropical Atlantic Ocean and Slowdown of Thermohaline Circulation During the Last Glaciation," *Nature*, 2 December 1999, 511.

21. Percentage of fish species as reef dwellers from Norman Myers, "Synergisms: Joint Effects of Climate Change and Other Forms of Habitat Destruction," in Robert L. Peters and Thomas E. Lovejoy, eds., *Global Warming and Biological Diversity* (New Haven, Conn.: Yale University Press, 1992), 347; Colin Woodard, "Fall of the Magic Kingdom: A Reporter Goes Underwater in the Belize Barrier Reef," *Tuftonia*, summer 2000, 20.

22. Daniel Cooney, "Coral Reefs Disappearing," *Associated Press*, 23 October 2000; Wilkinson, op. cit. note 5; Ove HoeghGuldberg et al., *Pacific in Peril*, available at **www.greenpeace.org**.

23. Hectares of forest per person from Robert Engleman et al., *People in the Balance: Population and Natural Resources at the Turn of the Millennium* (Washington, DC: Population Action International, 2000), 12.

24. Number of people living in water-deficit countries from ibid., 9; Beijing water table from James Kynge, "China Approves Controversial Plan to Shift Water to Drought-Hit Beijing," *Financial Times*, 7 January 2000; oil prices from U.S. Department of Energy, *Monthly Energy Review*, September 2000; near peak production of oil from Colin J. Campbell and Jean H. Laherrere, "The End of Cheap Oil," *Scientific American*, March 1998, 78–83.

25. Pamela Stedman-Edwards, "A Framework for Analysing Biodiversity Loss," in Wood, Stedman-Edwards, and Meng, op. cit. note 5, 15–6.

26. Wood, Stedman-Edwards, and Meng, op. cit. note 5, 283, 231–54.

27. Developing-country share of population from United Nations, *World Population Prospects: The 1998 Revision* (New York: December 1998); Fox proposal from Mary Jordan, "Mexican Touts Open Borders: Visiting President-Elect Pushes N. American Convergence," *Washington Post*, 25 August 2000.

66

Supporting Indigenous Peoples

Alan Thein Durning

A particular concern of many environmentalists (and social scientists) is the steady loss of this planet's cultural diversity as thousands of small societies are pushed aside by the relentless march of economic development. This selection describes the problem and points out that protecting indigenous peoples is not just a matter of justice—the well-being of everyone in the world depends on it.

In July of 1992, an aged chief of the Lumad people in the Philippines—a man with a price on his head for his opposition to local energy development—sat at the base of the cloud-covered volcano Mount Apo and made a simple plea.

"Our Christian brothers are enjoying their life here in the plains," said eighty-six-year-old Chief Tulalang Maway, sweeping his arm toward the provincial town of Kidapawan and the agricultural lands beyond, lands his tribe long ago ceded to immigrants from afar. Turning toward the mountain—a Lumad sacred site that he has vowed to defend "to the last drop of blood"— Maway slowly finished his thought, "We only ask them to leave us our last sanctuary."

Chief Maway's words could have been spoken by almost any tribal Filipino, or, for that matter, any Native American, Australian aborigine, African pygmy, or member of one of the world's thousands of other distinct indigenous cultures. All have ancient ties to the land, water, and wildlife of their ancestral domains, and all are endangered by onrushing forces of the outside world. They have been decimated by violence and plagues. Their cultures have been eroded by missionaries and exploited by wily entrepreneurs. Their subsistence economies have been dismantled in the pursuit of national development. And their homelands have been invaded by commercial resource extractors and overrun by landless peasants.

Chief Maway's entreaty, in its essence, is the call of indigenous peoples everywhere: the plea that their lands be spared further abuse, that their birthright be returned to them. It is a petition that the world's dominant cultures have long ignored, believing the passing of native peoples and their antiquated ways was an inevitable, if lamentable, cost of progress. That view, never morally defensible, is now demonstrably untenable.

Source: "Supporting Indigenous Peoples," by Alan Thein Durning, in *State of the World 1993: A Worldwatch Institute Report on Progress Toward a Sustainable Society,* edited by Lester R. Brown et al. Copyright © 1993 by Worldwatch Institute. Reprinted by permission of W. W. Norton & Company, Inc.

Indigenous peoples are the sole guardians of vast, little-disturbed habitats in remote parts of every continent. These territories, which together encompass an area larger than Australia, provide important ecological services: They regulate hydrological cycles, maintain local and global climatic stability, and harbor a wealth of biological and genetic diversity. Indeed, indigenous homelands may provide safe haven for more endangered plant and animal species than all the world's nature reserves. Native peoples, moreover, often hold the key to these vaults of biological diversity. They possess a body of ecological knowledge—encoded in their languages, customs, and subsistence practices—that rivals the libraries of modern science.

The human rights enshrined in international law have long demanded that states shield indigenous cultures, but instead these cultures have been dismembered. A more self-interested appeal appears to be in order: Supporting indigenous survival is an objective necessity, even for those callous to the justice of the cause. As a practical matter, the world's dominant cultures cannot sustain the earth's ecological health—a requisite of human advancement—without the aid of the world's endangered cultures. Biological diversity is inextricably linked to cultural diversity.

Around the globe, indigenous peoples are fighting for their ancestral territories. They are struggling in courts and national parliaments, gaining power through new mass movements and international campaigns, and—as on the slopes of Mount Apo—defending their inheritance with their lives. The question is, Who will stand with them?

STATE OF THE NATIONS

Indigenous peoples (or "native" or "tribal" peoples) are found on every continent and in most countries. [See Table 66.1] The extreme variations in their ways of life and current circumstances defy ready definition. Indeed, many anthropologists insist that indigenous peoples are defined only by the way they define themselves: They think of themselves as members of a distinct people. Still, many indigenous cultures share a number of characteristics that help describe, if not define, them.

They are typically descendants of the original inhabitants of an area taken over by more powerful outsiders. They are distinct from their country's dominant group in language, culture, or religion. Most have a custodial concept of land and other resources, in part defining themselves in relation to the habitat from which they draw their livelihood. They commonly live in or maintain strong ties to a subsistence economy; many are, or are descendants of, hunter-gatherers, fishers, nomadic or seasonal herders, shifting forest farmers, or subsistence peasant cultivators. And their social relations are often tribal, involving collective management of natural resources, thick networks of bonds between individuals, and group decision making, often by consensus among elders.

Measured by spoken languages, the single best indicator of a distinct culture, all the world's people belong to 6,000 cultures; 4,000–5,000 of these are indigenous ones. Of the 5.5 billion humans on the planet, some 190 million to 625 million are indigenous people. (These ranges are wide because of varying definitions of "indigenous." The higher figures include ethnic nations that lack political autonomy, such as Tibetans, Kurds, and Zulus, while the lower figures count only smaller, subnational societies.) In some countries, especially those settled by Europeans in the past five centuries, indigenous populations are fairly easy to count. [See Table 66.2] By contrast, lines between indigenous peoples and ethnic minorities are difficult to draw in Asia and Africa, where cultural diversity remains greatest.

Regardless of where lines are drawn, however, human cultures are disappearing at unprecedented rates. Worldwide, the loss of cultural diversity is keeping pace with the global loss of biological diversity. Anthropologist

Table 66.1   Indigenous Peoples of the World, 1992

Region	Indigenous Peoples
Africa and Middle East	Great cultural diversity throughout continent; "indigenous" share hotly contested lands. Some 25–30 million nomadic herders or pastoralists in East Africa, Sahel, and Arabian peninsula include Bedouin, Dinka, Masai, Turkana. San (Bushmen) of Namibia and Botswana and pygmies of central African rain forest, both traditionally hunter-gatherers, have occupied present home lands for at least 20,000 years. (25–350 million indigenous people overall, depending on definitions; 2,000 languages)
Americas	Native Americans concentrated near centers of ancient civilizations: Aztec in Mexico, Mayan in Central America, and Incan in Andes of Bolivia, Ecuador, and Peru. In Latin America, most Indians farm small plots; in North America, 2 million Indians live in cities and on reservations.(42 million; 900 languages)
Arctic	Inuit (Eskimo) and other Arctic peoples of North America, Greenland, and Siberia traditionally fishers, whalers, and hunters. Sami (Lapp) of northern Scandinavia are traditionally reindeer herders. (2 million; 50 languages)
East Asia	Chinese indigenous peoples, numbering up to 82 million, mostly subsistence farmers such as Bulang of south China or former pastoralists such as ethnic Mongolians of north and west China. Ainu of Japan and aboriginal Taiwanese now largely industrial laborers. (12–84 million; 150 languages)
Oceania	Aborigines of Australia and Maoris of New Zealand, traditionally farmers, fishers, hunters, and gatherers. Many now raise livestock. Islanders of South Pacific continue to fish and harvest marine resources. (3 million; 500 languages)
South Asia	Gond, Bhil, and other adivasis, or tribal peoples, inhabit forest belt of central India. In Bangladesh, adivasis concentrated in Chittagong hills on Burmese border, several million tribal farmers and pastoralists in Afghanistan, Pakistan, Nepal, Iran, and central Asian republics of former Soviet Union. (74–91 million; 700 languages)
Southeast Asia	Tribal Hmong, Karen, and other forest-farming peoples form Asia ethnic mosaic covering up lands. Indigenous population follows distribution of forest: Laos has more forest and tribal peoples, Myanmar and Vietnam have less forest and fewer people, and Thailand and mainland Malaysia have the least. Tribal peoples are concentrated at the extreme ends of the Philippine and Indonesian archipelagos. Island of New Guinea—split politically between Indonesia and Papua New Guinea—populated by indigenous tribes. (32–55 million; 1,950 languages)

Source: Worldwatch Institute.

Jason Clay of Cultural Survival in Cambridge, Massachusetts, writes, "there have been more...extinctions of tribal peoples in this century than in any other in history." Brazil alone lost eighty-seven tribes in the first half of the century. One-third of North American languages and two-thirds of Australian languages have disappeared since 1800—the overwhelming share of them since 1900.

Cultures are dying out even faster than the peoples who belong to them. University of Alaska linguist Michael Krauss projects that half the world's languages—the storehouses of peoples' intellectual heritages—will disappear within a century. These languages, and arguably the cultures they embody, are no longer passed on to sufficient numbers of children to ensure their survival. Krauss likens such cultures to animal species doomed to extinction because their populations are below the threshold needed for adequate reproduction. Only 5 percent of all languages, moreover, enjoy the relative safety of having at least a half-million speakers.

To trace the history of indigenous peoples' subjugation is simply to recast the story of the rise of the world's dominant cultures: the spread of Han Chinese into Central and Southeast Asia, the ascent of Aryan empires on the Indian subcontinent, the southward advance of Bantu cultures across Africa, and the creation of a world economy first through European colonialism and then through industrial development. Surviving indigenous cultures are often but tattered remnants of their predecessors' societies.

Table 66.2 Estimated Populations of Indigenous Peoples, Selected Countries, 1992

Country	Population[a]	Share of National Population
	(million)	(percent)
Papua New Guinea	3.0	77
Bolivia	5.6	70
Guatemala	4.6	47
Peru	9.0	40
Ecuador	3.8	38
Myanmar	14.0	33
Laos	1.3	30
Mexico	10.9	12
New Zealand	0.4	12
Chile	1.2	9
Philippines	6.0	9
India	63.0	7
Malaysia	0.8	4
Canada	0.9	4
Australia	0.4	2
Brazil	1.5	1
Bangladesh	1.2	1
Thailand	0.5	1
United States	2.0	1
Former Soviet Union	1.4	>1

[a] Generally excludes those of mixed ancestry.

Source: Worldwatch Institute

When Christopher Columbus reached the New World in 1492, there were perhaps 54 million people in the Americas, almost as many as in Europe at the time; their numbers plummeted, however, as plagues radiated from the landfalls of the conquistadors. Five centuries later, the indigenous peoples of the Americas, numbering some 42 million, have yet to match their earlier population. Similar contractions followed the arrival of Europeans in Australia, New Zealand, and Siberia.

Worldwide, virtually no indigenous peoples remain entirely isolated from national societies. By indoctrination or brute force, nations have assimilated native groups into the cultural mainstream. As a consequence, few follow the ways of their ancestors unchanged. Just one tenth of the Penan hunter-gatherers continue to hunt in the rain forests of Malaysian Borneo. A similar share of the Sami (Lapp) reindeer-herders of northern Scandinavia accompany their herds on the Arctic ranges. Half of North American Indians and many New Zealand Maori dwell in cities.

Tragically, indigenous peoples whose cultures are besieged frequently end up on the bottom of the national economy. They are often the first sent to war for the state, as in Namibia and the Philippines, and the last to go to work: Unemployment in Canadian Indian communities averages 50 percent. They are overrepresented among migrant laborers in India, beggars in Mexico, and uranium miners in the United States. They are often drawn into the shadow economy: They grow drug crops in northern Thailand, run gambling casinos in the United States, and sell their daughters into prostitution in Taiwan. Everywhere, racism against them is rampant. India's adivasis, or tribal people, endure hardships comparable to the "untouchables," the most downtrodden caste.

Native peoples' inferior social status is sometimes codified in national law and perpetuated by institutionalized abuse. Many members of the hill tribes in Thailand are denied citizenship, and until 1988 the Brazilian constitution legally classified Indians as minors and wards of the state. In the extreme, nation-states are simply genocidal: Burmese soldiers systemically raped, murdered, and enslaved thousands of Arakanese villagers in early 1992. Guatemala has exterminated perhaps 100,000 Mayans in its three-decade counterinsurgency. Similar numbers of indigenous people have died in East Timor and Irian Jaya since 1970 at the hands of Indonesian forces intent on solidifying their power.

In much of the world, the oppression that indigenous peoples suffer has indelibly marked their own psyches, manifesting itself in depression and social disintegration. Says Tamara Gliminova of the Khant people of Siberia, "When they spit into your soul for this long, there is little left."

HOMELANDS

Indigenous peoples not yet engulfed in modern societies live mostly in what Mexican anthropologist Gonzalo Aguirre Beltran called "regions of refuge," places so rugged, desolate, or remote that they have been little disturbed by the industrial economy. They remain in these areas for tragic reasons. Peoples in more fertile lands were eradicated outright to make way for settlers and plantations, or they retreated—sometimes at gun point—into these natural havens. Whereas indigenous peoples exercised de facto control over most of the earth's ecosystems as recently as two centuries ago, the territory they now occupy is reduced to an estimated 12–19 percent of the earth's land area—depending, again, on where the line between indigenous peoples and ethnic nations is drawn. And governments recognize their ownership of but a fraction of that area.

Gaining legal protection for the remainder of their subsistence base is most indigenous peoples' highest political priority. If they lose this struggle, their cultures stand little chance of surviving. As the World Council of Indigenous Peoples, a global federation based in Canada, wrote in 1985, "Next to shooting Indigenous Peoples, the surest way to kill us is to separate us from our part of the Earth." Most native peoples are bound to their land through relationships both practical and spiritual, routine and historical. Tribal Filipino Edtami Mansayagan, attempting to communicate the pain he feels at the destruction of the rivers, valleys, meadows, and hillsides of his people's mountain domain, exclaims, "these are the living pages of our unwritten history." The question of who shall control resources in the regions of refuge is the crux of indigenous survival.

Indigenous homelands are important not only to endangered cultures; they are also of exceptional ecological value. Intact indigenous communities and little-disturbed ecosystems overlap with singular regularity, from the coastal swamps of South America to the shifting sands of the Sahara,

from the ice floes of the circumpolar north to the coral reefs of the South Pacific. When, for example, a National Geographic Society team in Washington, D.C., compiled a map of Indian lands and remaining forest cover in Central America in 1992, they confirmed the personal observation of Geodisio Castillo, a Kuna Indian from Panama: "Where there are forests there are indigenous people, and where there are indigenous people there are forests."

Because populations of both indigenous peoples and unique plant and animal species are numerically concentrated in remnant habitats in the tropics—precisely the regions of refuge that Beltran was referring to—the biosphere's most diverse habitats are usually homes to endangered cultures. The persistence of biological diversity in these regions is no accident. In the Philippines and Thailand, both representative cases, little more than a third of the land officially zoned as forest remains forest-covered; the tracts that do still stand are largely those protected by tribal people.

The relationship between cultural diversity and biological diversity stands out even in global statistics. Just nine countries together account for 60 percent of human languages. Of these nine centers of cultural diversity, six are also on the roster of biological "megadiversity" countries—nations with exceptional numbers of unique plant and animal species.... By the same token, two-thirds of all megadiversity countries also rank at the top of the cultural diversity league, with more than 100 languages spoken in each.

Everywhere, the world economy now intrudes on what is left of native lands, as it has for centuries. Writes World Bank anthropologist Shelton Davis: "The creation of a...global economy...has meant the pillage of native peoples' lands, labor and resources and their enforced acculturation and spiritual conquest. Each cycle of global economic expansion—the search for gold and spices in the sixteenth century, the fur trade and sugar estate economics of the seventeenth and eighteenth centuries, the rise of the great coffee, copra and...tropical fruit plantations in the late nineteenth and early twentieth centuries, the modern search for petroleum, strategic minerals, and tropical hardwoods—was based upon the exploitation of natural resources or primary commodities and led to the displacement of indigenous peoples and the undermining of traditional cultures."

The juggernaut of the money economy has not slowed in the late twentieth century; if anything, it has accelerated. Soaring consumer demand among the world's fortunate and burgeoning populations among the unfortunate fuel the economy's drive into native peoples' territories. Loggers, miners, commercial fishers, small farmers, plantation growers, dam builders, oil drillers—all come to seek their fortunes. Governments that equate progress with export earnings aid them, and military establishments bent on controlling far-flung territories back them.

Logging, in particular, is a menace because so many indigenous peoples dwell in woodlands. Japanese builders, for example, are devouring the ancient hardwood forests of tropical Borneo, home of the Penan and other Dayak peoples for disposable concrete molds. Most mahogany exported from Latin America is now logged illegally on Indian reserves and most nonplantation teak cut in Asia currently comes from tribal lands in the war-torn hills of Myanmar.

The consequences of mining on native lands are also ruinous. In the late eighties, for instance, tens of thousands of gold prospectors infiltrated the remote northern Brazilian haven of the Yanomami, the last large, isolated group of indigenous peoples in the Americas. The miners turned streams into sewers, contaminated the environment with the 1,000 tons of toxic mercury they used to purify gold, and precipitated an epidemic of malaria that killed more than a thousand children and elders. Just in time, the Brazilian government recognized and began defending the Yanomami homeland in early 1992, a rare and hopeful precedent in the annals of indigenous history. Still, in Brazil overall, mining concessions overlap 34 percent of Indian lands....

Other energy projects, especially large dams, also take their toll on native habitats. In the north of Canada, the provincial electric utility Hydro Quebec completed a massive project called James Bay I in 1985, inundating vast areas of Cree Indian hunting grounds and unexpectedly contaminating fisheries with naturally occurring heavy metals that had previously been locked away in the soil. The Cree and neighboring Inuit tribes have organized against the project's next gigantic phase, James Bay II. The $60-billion project would tame eleven wild rivers, altering a France-sized area to generate 27,000 megawatts of exportable power. As Matthew Coon-Come, Grand Chief of the Cree, says, "The only people who have the right to build dams on our territory are the beavers."...

Commercial producers have also taken over indigenous lands for large-scale agriculture. The Barabaig herders of Tanzania have lost more than 400 square kilometers of dry-season range to a mechanized wheat farm. Private ranchers in Botswana have enclosed grazing lands for their own use, and Australian ranchers have usurped aboriginal lands. In peninsular Malaysia, palm and rubber plantations have left the Orang Asli (Original People) with tiny fractions of their ancient tropical forests.

Less dramatic but more pervasive is the ubiquitous invasion of small farmers onto indigenous lands. Sometimes sponsored by the state but ultimately driven by population growth and maldistribution of farmland, poor settlers encroach on native lands everywhere. In Indonesia during the eighties, for example, the government shifted 2 million people from densely populated islands such as Java to 800,000 hectares of newly cleared plots in sparsely populated indigenous provinces such as Irian Jaya, Kalimantan, and Sumatra. Half the area settled was virgin forest—much of it indigenous territory....

Few states recognize indigenous peoples' rights over homelands, and where they do, those rights are often partial, qualified, or of ambiguous legal force. Countries may recognize customary rights in theory, but enforce common or statutory law against those rights whenever there is a conflict; or they may sanction indigenous rights but refuse to enforce them. Through this cloud of legal contradictions a few countries stand out as exceptional. Papua New Guinea and Ecuador acknowledge indigenous title to large shares of national territory, and Canada and Australia recognize rights over extensive areas.... Still, across all the earth's climatic and ecological zones—from the Arctic tundra to the temperate and nontropical forests to the savannahs and deserts—native peoples control slim shares of their ancestral domains....

STEWARDS

Sustainable use of local resources is simple self-preservation for people whose way of life is tied to the fertility and natural abundance of the land. Any community that knows its children and grandchildren will live exactly where it does is more apt to take a longer view than a community without attachments to local places.

Moreover, native peoples frequently aim to preserve not just a standard of living but a way of life rooted in the uniqueness of a local place. Colombian anthropologist Martin von Hildebrand notes, "The Indians often tell me that the difference between a colonist [a non-Indian settler] and an Indian is that the colonist wants to leave money for his children and that the Indians want to leave forests for their children."

Indigenous peoples' unmediated dependence on natural abundance has its parallel in their peerless ecological knowledge. Most forest-dwelling tribes display an utter mastery of botany. One typical group, the Shuar people of Ecuador's Amazonian lowlands, uses 800 species of plants for medicine, food, animal fodder, fuel, construction, fishing, and hunting supplies.

Native peoples commonly know as much about ecological processes that affect the availability of natural resources as they do about those resources' diverse uses. South Pacific islanders can predict to the day and hour the beginning of the annual spawning runs of many fish. Whaling peoples of northern Canada have proved to skeptical western marine biologists that bowhead whales migrate under pack ice. Coastal aborigines in Australia distinguish between eighty different tidal conditions.

Specialists trained in western science often fail to recognize indigenous ecological knowledge because of the cultural and religious ways in which indigenous peoples record and transmit that learning. Ways of life that developed over scores of generations could only thrive by encoding ecological sustainability into the body of practice, myth, and taboo that passes from parent to child....

What are the conditions in which traditional systems of ecological management can persist in the modern world? First, indigenous peoples must have secure rights to their subsistence base—rights that are not only recognized but enforced by the state and, ideally, backed by international law. Latin American tribes such as the Shuar of Ecuador, when threatened with losing their land, have cleared their own forests and taken up cattle ranching, because these actions prove ownership in Latin America. Had Ecuador backed up the Shuar's land rights, the ranching would have been unnecessary.

Second, for indigenous ecological stewardship to survive the onslaught of the outside world, indigenous peoples must be organized politically and the state in which they reside must allow democratic initiatives. The Khant and Mansi peoples of Siberia, just as most indigenous people in the former Soviet Union, were nominally autonomous in their customary territories under Soviet law, but political repression precluded the organized defense of that terrain until the end of the eighties. Since then, the peoples of Siberia have begun organizing themselves to turn paper rights into real local control. In neighboring China, in contrast, indigenous homelands remain pure legal fictions because the state crushes all representative organizations.

Third, indigenous communities must have access to information, support, and advice from friendly sources if they are to surmount the obstacles of the outside world. The tribal people of Papua New Guinea know much about their local environments, for example, but they know little about the impacts of large-scale logging and mining. Foreign and domestic investors have often played on this ignorance, assuring remote groups that no lasting harm would result from leasing parts of their land to resource extractors. If the forest peoples of Papua New Guinea could learn from the experience of indigenous peoples elsewhere—through supportive organizations and indigenous peoples' federations—they might be more careful.

A handful of peoples around the world have succeeded in satisfying all three of these conditions....

RISING FROM THE FRONTIER

From the smallest tribal settlements to the U.N. General Assembly, indigenous peoples' organizations are making themselves felt. Their grassroots movements have spread rapidly since 1970, gaining strength in numbers and through improvement of their political skills. They have pooled their talents in regional, national, and global federations to broaden their influence. This uprising, which like any movement has its share of internal rivalries, may eventually bring fundamental advances in the status of all endangered cultures....

In a world where almost all nations have publicly committed themselves to the goal of sustainable development and most have signed a global treaty for the protection of biological diversity, the questions of cultural survival and indigenous homelands cannot be avoided much longer. As guardians and stewards of remote and fragile ecosystems, indigenous cultures could play a crucial role in safeguarding humanity's planetary home. But they cannot do it alone. They need the support of international law and national policy, and they need the understanding and aid of the world's more numerous peoples.

Giving native peoples power over their own lives raises issues for the world's dominant culture as well—a consumerist and individualist culture born in Europe and bred in the United States. Indeed, indigenous peoples may offer more than a best-bet alternative for preserving the outlying areas where they live. They may offer living examples of cultural patterns that can help revive ancient values within everyone: devotion to future generations, ethical regard for nature, and commitment to community among people. The question may be, then, Are indigenous peoples the past, or are they the future?

CRITICAL THINKING QUESTIONS

1. How many indigenous cultures are there on this planet? What general traits do they have in common?
2. Why are the world's tribal peoples disappearing?
3. The author asserts that sustaining the world's natural environment depends on assuring the future of indigenous peoples. Why is this so?

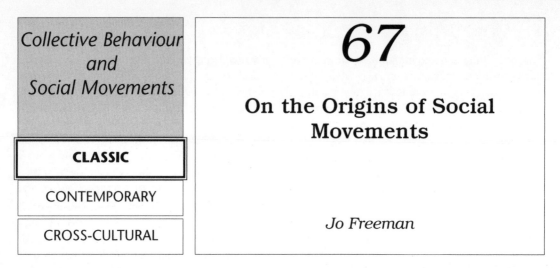

67

On the Origins of Social Movements

Collective Behaviour and Social Movements

CLASSIC

CONTEMPORARY

CROSS-CULTURAL

Jo Freeman

According to Jo Freeman, a "spark of life" sometimes transforms a group of like-minded people into a social movement. In this excerpt from her work, Freeman analyzes this process, illustrating her ideas with accounta of the civil rights movement and the women's movement in the United States.

Most movements have inconspicuous beginnings. The significant elements of their origins are usually forgotten or distorted by the time a trained observer seeks to trace them out. Perhaps this is why the theoretical literature on social movements usually concentrates on causes (Gurr, 1970; Davies, 1962; Oberschall, 1973) and motivations (Toch, 1965; Cantril, 1941; Hoffer, 1951; Adorno et al., 1950), while the "spark of life" by which the "mass is to cross the threshold of organizational life" (Lowi, 1971: 41) has received scant attention....

From where do the people come who make up the initial, organizing cadre of a movement? How do they come together, and how do they come to share a similar view of the world in circumstances that compel them to political action? In what ways does the nature of the original center affect the future development of the movement?

Before answering these questions, let us first look at data on the origins of [two] social movements prominent in the sixties and seventies: civil rights...and women's liberation. These data identify recurrent elements involved in movement formation. The ways in which these elements interact, given a sufficient level of strain, would support the following propositions:

Proposition 1. The need for a *preexisting communications network* or infrastructure within the social base of a movement is a primary prerequisite for "spontaneous" activity. Masses alone do not form

Source: From *Social Movements of the Sixties and Seventies,* ed. Jo Freeman, pp. 8–13, 17–30, copyright © 1983 by Jo Freeman. Reprinted by permission.

movements, however discontented they may be. Groups of previously unorganized individuals may spontaneously form into small local associations—usually along the lines of informal social networks—in response to a specific strain or crisis. If they are not linked in some manner, however, the protest does not become generalized but remains a local irritant or dissolves completely. If a movement is to spread rapidly, the communications network must already exist. If only the rudiments of a network exist, movement formation requires a high input of "organizing" activity.

Proposition 2. Not just any communications network will do. It must be a network that is *co-optable* to the new ideas of the incipient movement.[1] To be co-optable, it must be composed of like-minded people whose backgrounds, experiences, or location in the social structure make them receptive to the ideas of a specific new movement.

Proposition 3. Given the existence of a co-optable communications network, or at least the rudimentary development of a potential one, and a situation of strain, one or more precipitants are required. Here, two distinct patterns emerge that often overlap. In one, a *crisis* galvanizes the network into spontaneous action in a new direction. In the other, one or more persons begin *organizing* a new organization or disseminating a new idea. For spontaneous action to occur, the communications network must be well formed or the initial protest will not survive the incipient stage. If it is not well formed, organizing efforts must occur; that is, one or more persons must specifically attempt to construct a movement. To be successful, organizers must be skilled and must have a fertile field in which to work. If no communications network already exists, there must at least be emerging spontaneous groups that are acutely attuned to the issue, albeit uncoordinated. To sum up, if a co-optable communications network is already established, a crisis is all that is necessary to galvanize it. If it is

rudimentary, an organizing cadre of one or more persons is necessary. Such a cadre is superfluous if the former conditions fully exist, but it is essential if they do not.

THE CIVIL RIGHTS MOVEMENT

The civil rights movement has two origins, although one contributed significantly to the other. The first can be dated from December 7, 1955, when the arrest of Rosa Parks for occupying a "white" seat on a bus stimulated both the Montgomery Bus Boycott and the formation of the Montgomery Improvement Association. The second can be dated either from February 1, 1960, when four freshmen at A & T College in Greensboro, North Carolina, sat in at a white lunch counter, or from April 15–17, when a conference at Shaw University in Raleigh, North Carolina, resulted in the formation of the Student Non-Violent Co-ordinating Committee. To understand why there were two origins one has to understand the social structure of the southern black community, as an incipient generation gap alone is inadequate to explain it.

Within this community the two most important institutions, often the only institutions, were the church and the black college. They provided the primary networks through which most southern blacks interacted and communicated with one another on a regular basis. In turn, the colleges and churches were linked in a regional communications network. These institutions were also the source of black leadership, for being a "preacher or a teacher" were the main status positions in black society. Of the two, the church was by far the more important; it touched on more people's lives and was the largest and oldest institution in the black community. Even during slavery there had been an "invisible church." After emancipation, "organized religious life became the chief means by which a structured or organized social life came into existence among the Negro masses" (Frazier, 1963: 17). Furthermore, preachers were more economically independent of white society than were teachers.

Neither of these institutions represented all the segments of black society, but the segments they did represent eventually formed the main social base for supplying civil rights activists. The church was composed of a male leadership and a largely middle-aged, lower-class female followership. The black colleges were the homes of black intellectuals and middle-class youth, male and female.

Both origins of the civil rights movement resulted in the formation of new organizations, despite the fact that at least three seemingly potential social movement organizations already existed. The wealthiest of these was the Urban League, founded in 1910. It, however, was not only largely restricted to a small portion of the black and white bourgeoisie but, until 1961, felt itself to be "essentially a social service agency" (Clark, 1966: 245).

Founded in 1909, the National Association for the Advancement of Colored People (NAACP) pursued channels of legal change until it finally persuaded the Supreme Court to abolish educational segregation in *Brown* v. *Board of Education*. More than any other single event, this decision created the atmosphere of rising expectations that helped precipitate the movement. The NAACP suffered from its own success, however. Having organized itself primarily to support court cases and utilize other "respectable" means, it "either was not able or did not desire to modify its program in response to new demands. It believed it should continue its important work by using those techniques it had already perfected" (Blumer, 1951: 199).

The Congress of Racial Equality, like the other two organizations, was founded in the North. It began "in 1942 as the Chicago Committee of Racial Equality, which was composed primarily of students at the University of Chicago. An offshoot of the pacifist Fellowship of Reconciliation, its leaders were middle-class intellectual reformers, less prominent and more alienated from the mainstream of American

society than the founders of the NAACP. They regarded the NAACP's legalism as too gradualist and ineffective, and aimed to apply Gandhian techniques of non-violent direct action to the problem of race relations in the United States. A year later, the Chicago Committee joined with a half dozen other groups that had emerged across the country, mostly under the encouragement of the F. O. R. to form a federation known as the Congress of Racial Equality" (Rudwick & Meier, 1970: 10).

CORE's activities anticipated many of the main forms of protest of the civil rights movement, and its attitudes certainly seemed to fit CORE for the role of a major civil rights organization. But though it became quite influential, at the time the movement actually began, CORE had declined almost to the point of extinction. Its failure reflects the historical reality that organizations are less likely to create social movements than be created by them. More important, CORE was poorly situated to lead a movement of southern blacks. Northern-based and composed primarily of pacifist intellectuals, it had no roots in any of the existing structures of the black community, and in the North these structures were themselves weak. CORE could be a source of ideas, but not of coordination.

The coordination of a new movement required the creation of a new organization. But that was not apparent until after the Montgomery bus boycott began. That boycott was organized through institutions already existing in the black community of Montgomery.

Rosa Parks's refusal to give up her seat on the bus to a white man was not the first time such defiance of segregation laws had occurred. There had been talk of a boycott the previous time, but after local black leaders had a congenial meeting with the city commissioners, nothing happened—on either side (King, 1958: 37–41). When Parks, a former secretary of the local NAACP, was arrested, she immediately called E. D. Nixon, at that time the president of the local chapter. He not only bailed her out but informed a few influential women in the city, most of whom were members of the Women's Political Council. After numerous phone calls between their members, it was the WPC that actually suggested the boycott, and E. D. Nixon who initially organized it (ibid.: 44–5).

The Montgomery Improvement Association (MIA) was formed at a meeting of eighteen ministers and civic leaders the Monday after Parks's conviction and a day of successful boycotting, to provide ongoing coordination. No one then suspected that coordination would be necessary for over a year, with car pools organized to provide alternative transportation for seventeen thousand riders a day. During this time the MIA grew slowly to a staff of ten in order to handle the voluminous correspondence, as well as to provide rides and keep the movement's momentum going. The organization, and the car pools, were financed by $250,000 in donations that poured in from all over the world in response to heavy press publicity about the boycott. But the organizational framework for the boycott and the MIA was the church. Most, although not all, of the officers were ministers, and Sunday meetings with congregations continued to be the main means of communicating with members of the black community and encouraging them to continue the protest.

The boycott did not end until the federal courts ruled Alabama's bus segregation laws unconstitutional late in 1956—at the same time that state courts ruled the boycott illegal. In the meantime, black leaders throughout the South had visited Montgomery, and out of the discussions came agreement to continue antisegregation protests regularly and systematically under the aegis of a new organization, the Southern Christian Leadership Conference. The NAACP could not lead the protests because, according to an SCLC pamphlet, "during the late fifties, the NAACP had been driven out of some Southern states. Its branches were outlawed as foreign corporations and its lawyers were charged with barratry, that is, persistently inciting litigation."

On January 10, 1957, over one hundred people gathered in Atlanta at a meeting called by four ministers, including Martin Luther King. Bayard Rustin drew up the "working papers." Initially called the Southern Leadership Conference on Transportation and Nonviolent Integration, the SCLC never developed a mass base even when it changed its name. It established numerous "affiliates" but did most of its work through the churches in the communities to which it sent its fieldworkers.

The church was not just the only institution available for a movement to work through; in many ways it was ideal. It performed "the central organizing function in the Negro community" (Holloway, 1969: 22), providing both access to large masses of people on a regular basis and a natural leadership. As Wyatt Tee Walker, former executive director of SCLC, commented, "The Church today is central to the movement. If a Negro's going to have a meeting, where's he going to have it? Mostly he doesn't have a Masonic lodge, and he's not going to get the public schools. And the church is the primary means of communication" (Brink & Harris, 1964: 103). Thus the church eventually came to be the center of the voter registration drives as well as many of the other activities of the civil rights movement.

Even the young men and women of SNCC had to use the church, though they had trouble doing so because, unlike most of the officers of SCLC, they were not themselves ministers and thus did not have a "fraternal" connection. Instead they tended to draw many of their resources and people from outside the particular town in which they were working by utilizing their natural organizational base, the college.

SNCC did not begin the sit-ins, but came out of them. Once begun, the idea of the sit-in spread initially by means of the mass media. But such sit-ins almost always took place in towns where there were Negro colleges, and groups on these campuses essentially organized the sit-in activities of their communities. Nonetheless, "CORE, with its long emphasis of nonviolent direct action, played an important part, once the sit-ins began, as an educational and organizing agent" (Zinn, 1964: 23). CORE had very few staff in the South, but there were enough to at least hold classes and practice sessions in nonviolence.

It was SCLC, however, that was actually responsible for the formation of SNCC; though it might well have organized itself eventually. Ella Baker, then executive secretary of SCLC, thought something should be done to coordinate the rapidly spreading sit-ins in 1960, and many members of SCLC thought it might be appropriate to organize a youth group. With SCLC money, Baker persuaded her alma mater, Shaw University, to provide facilities to contact the groups at centers of sit-in activity. Some two hundred people showed up for the meeting, decided to have no official connection with SCLC beyond a "friendly relationship," and formed the Student Non-Violent Co-ordinating Committee (Zinn, 1964: 32–4). It had no members, and its fieldworkers numbered two hundred at their highest point, but it was from the campuses, especially the southern black colleges, that it drew its sustenance and upon which its organizational base rested....

THE WOMEN'S LIBERATION MOVEMENT[2]

Women are not well organized. Historically tied to the family and isolated from their own kind, only in the nineteenth century did women in this country have the opportunity to develop independent associations of their own. These associations took years and years of careful organizational work to build. Eventually they formed the basis for the suffrage movement of the early twentieth century. The associations took less time to die. Today the Women's Trade Union League, the General Federation of Women's Clubs, the Women's Christian Temperance Union, not to mention the powerful National Women's Suffrage Association, are all either dead or a pale shadow of their former selves.

As of 1960, not one organization of women had the potential to become a social movement organization, nor was there any form of "neutral"

structure of interaction to provide the base for such an organization. The closest exception to the former was the National Women's Party, which has remained dedicated to feminist concerns since its inception in 1916. However, the NWP has been essentially a lobbying group for the Equal Rights Amendment since 1923. From the beginning, the NWP believed that a small group of women concentrating their efforts in the right places was more effective than a mass appeal, and so was not appalled by the fact that as late as 1969 even the majority of avowed feminists in this country had never heard of the ERA or the NWP.

The one large women's organization that might have provided a base for a social movement was the 180,000-member Federation of Business and Professional Women's Clubs. Yet, while it has steadily lobbied for legislation of importance to women, as late as "1966 BPW rejected a number of suggestions that it redefine...goals and tactics and become a kind of 'NAACP for women'...out of fear of being labeled 'feminist'" (Hole & Levine, 1971: 89).

Before any social movement could develop among women, there had to be created a structure to bring potential feminist sympathizers together. To be sure, groups such as the BPW, and institutions such as the women's colleges, might be a good source of adherents for such a movement. But they were determined not to be the source of leadership.

What happened in the 1960s was the development of two new communications networks in which women played prominent roles that allowed, even forced, an awakened interest in the old feminist ideas. As a result, the movement actually has two origins, from two different strata of society, with two different styles, orientations, values, and forms of organization. The first of these will be referred to as the "older branch" of the movement, partially because it began first and partially because it was on the older side of the "generation gap" that pervaded the sixties. Its most prominent organization is the National Organization for Women (NOW), which was also the first to be formed. The style of its movement organizations tends to be traditional with elected officers, boards of directors, bylaws, and the other trappings of democratic procedure. Conversely, the "younger branch" consisted of innumerable small groups engaged in a variety of activities whose contact with one another was always tenuous (Freeman, 1975: 50).

The forces that led to NOW's formation were set in motion in 1961 when President Kennedy established the President's Commission on the Status of Women at the behest of Esther Petersen, then director of the Women's Bureau. Its 1963 report, *American Women,* and subsequent committee publications documented just how thoroughly women were denied many rights and opportunities. The most significant response to the activity of the President's commission was the establishment of some fifty state commissions to do similar research on a state level. The Presidential and State Commission activity laid the groundwork for the future movement in two significant ways: (1) It unearthed ample evidence of women's unequal status and in the process convinced many previously uninterested women that something should be done; (2) It created a climate of expectations that something would be done. The women of the Presidential and State Commissions who were exposed to these influences exchanged visits, correspondence, and staff, and met with one another at an annual commission convention. They were in a position to share and mutually reinforce their growing awareness and concern over women's issues. These commissions thus provided an embryonic communications network.

During this time, two other events of significance occurred. The first was the publication of Betty Friedan's *The Feminine Mystique* in 1963. A quick best seller, the book stimulated many women to question the *status quo* and some women to suggest to Friedan that an organization be formed to do something about it. The second event was the addition of "sex" to the 1964 Civil Rights Act.

Many thought the "sex" provision was a joke, and the Equal Employment Opportunity Commission treated it as one, refusing to enforce it seriously. But a rapidly growing feminist coterie within the EEOC argued that "sex" would be taken more seriously if there were "some sort of NAACP for women" to put pressure on the government.

On June 30, 1966, these three strands of incipient feminism came together, and NOW was tied from the knot. At that time, government officials running the Third National Conference of Commissions on the Status of Women, ironically titled "Targets for Action," forbade the presentation of a suggested resolution calling for the EEOC to treat sex discrimination with the same consideration as race discrimination. The officials said one government agency could not be allowed to pressure another, despite the fact that the state commissions were not federal agencies. The small group of women who desired such a resolution had met the night before in Friedan's hotel room to discuss the possibility of a civil rights organization for women. Not convinced of its need, they chose instead to propose the resolution. When conference officials vetoed it, they held a whispered conversation over lunch and agreed to form an action organization "to bring women into full participation in the mainstream of American society now, assuming all the privileges and responsibilities thereof in truly equal partnership with men." The name NOW was coined by Friedan who was at the conference doing research on a book. When word leaked out, twenty-eight women paid five dollars each to join before the day was over (Friedan, 1967: 4).

By the time the organizing conference was held the following October 29 through 30, over three hundred men and women had become charter members. It is impossible to do a breakdown on the composition of the charter membership, but one of the officers and board is possible. Such a breakdown accurately reflected NOW's origins. Friedan was president, two former EEOC commissioners were vice presidents, a representative of the United Auto Workers Women's Committee was secretary-treasurer, and there were seven past and present members of the State Commissions on the Status of Women on the twenty member board. One hundred twenty-six of the charter members were Wisconsin residents—and Wisconsin had the most active state Commission. Occupationally, the board and officers were primarily from the professions, labor, government, and communications fields. Of these, only those from labor had any experience in organizing, and they resigned a year later in a dispute over support of the Equal Rights Amendment. Instead of organizational experience, what the early NOW members had was experience in working with and in the media, and it was here that their early efforts were aimed.

As a result, NOW often gave the impression of being larger than it was. It was highly successful in getting in the press; much less successful in either bringing about concrete changes or forming an organization. Thus it was not until 1970, when the national press simultaneously did major stories on the women's liberation movement, that NOW's membership increased significantly.

In the meantime, unaware of and unknown to NOW, the EEOC, or the State Commissions, younger women began forming their own movement. Here, too, the groundwork had been laid some years before. The different social action projects of the sixties had attracted many women, who were quickly shunted into traditional roles and faced with the self-evident contradiction of working in a "freedom movement" but not being very free. No single "youth movement" activity or organization is responsible for forming the younger branch of the women's liberation movement, but together they created a "radical community" in which like-minded people continually interacted or were made aware of one another. This community provided the necessary network of communication and its radical ideas the framework of analysis that "explained" the dismal situation in which radical women found themselves.

Papers had been circulated on women and individual temporary women's caucuses had been held as early as 1964 (see Hayden & King, 1966). But it was not until 1967 and 1968 that the groups developed a determined, if cautious, continuity and began to consciously expand themselves. At least five groups in five different cities (Chicago, Toronto, Detroit, Seattle, and Gainesville, Florida) formed spontaneously, independently of one another. They came at an auspicious moment, for 1967 was the year in which the blacks kicked the whites out of the civil rights movement, student power was discredited by SDS, and the New Left was on the wane. Only draft resistance activities were on the increase, and this movement more than any other exemplified the social inequities of the sexes. Men could resist the draft. Women could only counsel resistance.

At this point, there were few opportunities available for political work. Some women fit well into the secondary role of draft counseling. Many didn't. For years their complaints of unfair treatment had been forestalled by movement men with the dictum that those things could wait until after the Revolution. Now these political women found time on their hands, but still the men would not listen.

A typical example was the event that precipitated the formation of the Chicago group, the first independent group in this country. At the August 1967 National Conference for New Politics convention a women's caucus met for days, but was told its resolution wasn't significant enough to merit a floor discussion. By threatening to tie up the convention with procedural motions the women succeeded in having their statement tacked to the end of the agenda. It was never discussed. The chair refused to recognize any of the many women standing by the microphone, their hands straining upwards. When he instead called on someone to speak on "the forgotten American, the American Indian," five women rushed the podium to demand an explanation. But the chairman just patted one of them on the head (literally) and told her, "Cool down, little girl. We have more important things to talk about than women's problems."

The "little girl" was Shulamith Firestone, future author of *The Dialectic of Sex,* and she didn't cool down. Instead she joined with another Chicago woman she met there who had unsuccessfully tried to organize a women's group that summer, to call a meeting of the women who had halfheartedly attended those summer meetings. Telling their stories to those women, they stimulated sufficient rage to carry the group for three months, and by that time it was a permanent institution.

Another somewhat similar event occurred in Seattle the following winter. At the University of Washington an SDS organizer was explaining to a large meeting how white college youth established rapport with the poor whites with whom they were working. "He noted that sometimes after analyzing societal ills, the men shared leisure time by 'balling a chick together.' He pointed out that such activities did much to enhance the political consciousness of the poor white youth. A woman in the audience asked, 'And what did it do for the consciousness of the chick?'" (Hole & Levine, 1971: 120). After the meeting, a handful of enraged women formed Seattle's first group.

Subsequent groups to the initial five were largely organized rather than formed spontaneously out of recent events. In particular, the Chicago group was responsible for the formation of many new groups in Chicago and in other cities. Unlike NOW, the women in the first groups had had years of experience as trained organizers. They knew how to utilize the infrastructure of the radical community, the underground press, and the free universities to disseminate women's liberation ideas. Chicago, as a center of New Left activity, had the largest number of politically conscious organizers. Many traveled widely to leftist conferences and demonstrations, and most used the opportunity to talk with other women about the new movement. In spite of public derision by radical men, or perhaps because of it, young women steadily formed new groups around the country.

ANALYSIS

From these data there appear to be four essential elements involved in movement formation: (1) the growth of a preexisting communications network that is (2) co-optable to the ideas of the new movement; (3) a series of crises that galvanize into action people involved in a co-optable network, and/or (4) subsequent organizing effort to weld the spontaneous groups together into a movement. Each of these elements needs to be examined in detail.

COMMUNICATIONS NETWORK

…The women's liberation movement…illustrates the importance of a network precisely because the conditions for a movement existed *before* a network came into being, but the movement didn't exist until afterward. Analysts of socioeconomic causes have concluded that the movement could have started anytime within a twenty-year period. Strain for women was as great in 1955 as in 1965 (Ferriss, 1971). What changed was the organizational situation. It was not until new networks emerged among women aware of inequities beyond local boundaries that a movement could grow past the point of occasional, spontaneous uprisings. The fact that two distinct movements, with two separate origins, developed from two networks unaware of each other is further evidence of the key role of preexisting communications networks as the fertile soil in which new movements can sprout.

References to the importance of a preexisting communications network appear frequently in case studies of social movements, though the theoretical writers were much slower to recognize their salience. According to Buck (1920: 43–4), the Grange established a degree of organization among American farmers in the nineteenth century that greatly facilitated the spread of future farmers' protests. Lipset has reported that in Saskatchewan, "the rapid acceptance of new ideas and movements...can be attributed mainly to the high degree of organization.... The role of the social structure of the western wheat belt in facilitating the rise of new movements has never been sufficiently appreciated by historians and sociologists. Repeated challenges and crises forced the western farmers to create many more community institutions (especially cooperatives and economic pressure groups) than are necessary in a more stable area. These groups in turn provided a structural basis for immediate action in critical situations. [Therefore] though it was a new radical party, the C. C. F. did not have to build up an organization from scratch" (1959: 206).

Similarly, Heberle (1951: 232) reports several findings that Nazism was most successful in small, well-integrated communities. As Lipset put it, these findings "sharply challenge the various interpretations of Nazism as the product of the growth of anomie and the general rootlessness of modern urban industrial society" (1959: 146).

Indirect evidence attesting to the essential role of formal and informal communications networks is found in diffusion theory, which emphasizes the importance of personal interaction rather than impersonal media communication in the spread of ideas (Rogers, 1962; Lionberger, 1960). This personal influence occurs through the organizational patterns of a community (Lionberger, 1960: 73). It does not occur through the mass media. The mass media may be a source of information, but they are not a key source of influence.

Their lesser importance in relation to preexisting communications networks was examined in one study on "The Failure of an Incipient Social Movement" (Jackson, Peterson, Bull, Monsen, & Richmond, 1960). In 1957 a potential tax protest movement in Los Angeles generated considerable interest and publicity for a little over a month but was dead within a year. According to the authors, this did not reflect a lack of public notice. They concluded that "mass communication alone is probably insufficient without a network of communication specifically linking those interested in the matter.... If a movement is to grow

rapidly, it cannot rely upon its own network of communication, but must capitalize on networks already in existence" (p. 37).

A major reason it took social scientists so long to acknowledge the importance of communications networks was because the prevailing theories of the post–World War II era emphasized increasing social dislocation and anomie. Mass society theorists, as they were called, hypothesized that significant community institutions that linked individuals to governing elites were breaking down, that society was becoming a mass of isolated individuals. These individuals were seen as increasingly irresponsible and ungovernable, prone to irrational protests because they had no mediating institutions through which to pursue grievances (Kornhauser, 1959).

In emphasizing disintegrating vertical connections, mass society theorists passed lightly over the role of horizontal ones, only occasionally acknowledging that "the combination of internal contact and external isolation facilitates the work of the mass agitator" (Kornhauser, 1959: 218). This focus changed in the early seventies. Pinard's study of the Social Credit Party of Quebec (1971) severely criticized mass society theory, arguing instead that "when strains are severe and widespread a new movement is more likely to meet its early success among the more strongly integrated citizens" (Pinard, 1971: 192).

This insight was expanded by Oberschall (1973), who created a six-cell table to predict both the occurrence and type of protest. As did the mass society theorists, Oberschall said that even when there are grievances, protest will not occur outside institutional channels by those who are connected, through their own leadership or patron/client relationships, with governing elites. Among those who are segmented from such elites, the type of protest will be determined by whether there is communal, associational, or little organization. In the latter case, discontent is expressed through riots or other short-lived violent uprisings. "It is under conditions of strong...ties and segmentation that the possibility of the rapid spread of opposition movements on a continuous basis exists" (p. 123).

The movements we have studied would confirm Oberschall's conclusions, but not as strongly as he makes them. In all these cases a preexisting communications network was a necessary but insufficient condition for movement formation. Yet the newly formed networks among student radicals, welfare recipients, and women can hardly compare with the longstanding ties provided by the southern black churches and colleges. Their ties were tenuous and may not have survived the demise of their movements.

The importance of segmentation, or lack of connection with relevant elites, is less obvious in the sixties' movements. The higher socioeconomic status of incipient feminists and Movement leaders would imply greater access to elites than is true for blacks or welfare recipients. If Oberschall were correct, these closer connections should either have permitted easier and more rapid grievance solutions or more effective social control. They did neither. Indeed, it was the group most closely connected to decision-making elites—women of the Presidential and State Commission—who were among the earliest to see the need of a protest organization. Women of the younger branch of the movement did have their grievances against the men of the New Left effectively suppressed for several years, but even they eventually rejected this kind of elite control, even when it meant rejecting the men.

Conversely, Piven and Cloward show that the establishment of closer ties between leaders of local welfare rights groups and welfare workers through advisory councils and community coordinators led to a curtailment of militance and the institutionalization of grievances (1977: 326–31). They also argue that the development of government-funded community programs effectively co-opted many local black movement leaders in the North and that federal channeling of black protest in the South into voter registration projects focused the movement there into traditional electoral politics (ibid.: 253). In short, the evidence

about the role of segmentation in movement formation is ambiguous. The effect may be varied considerably by the nature of the political system.

CO-OPTABILITY

A recurrent theme in our studies is that not just any communications network will do. It must be one that is co-optable to the ideas of the new movement. The Business and Professional Women's (BPW) clubs were a network among women, but having rejected feminism, they could not overcome the ideological barrier to new political action until after feminism became established....

On the other hand, the women on the Presidential and State Commissions and the feminist coterie of the EEOC were co-optable largely because their immersion in the facts of female status and the details of sex discrimination cases made them very conscious of the need for change. Likewise, the young women of the "radical community" lived in an atmosphere of questioning, confrontation, and change. They absorbed an ideology of "freedom" and "liberation" far more potent than any latent "antifeminism" might have been....

Exactly what makes a network co-optable is harder to elucidate. Pinard (1971: 186) noted the necessity for groups to *"possess* or *develop* an ideology or simply subjective interests congruent with that of a new movement" for them to "act as mobilizing rather than restraining agents toward that movement," but did not further explore what affected the "primary group climate." More illumination is provided by the diffusion of innovation studies that point out the necessity for new ideas to fit in with already established norms for changes to happen easily. Furthermore, a social system that has as a value "innovativeness" (as the radical community did) will more rapidly adopt ideas than one that looks upon the habitual performance of traditional practices as the ideal (as most organized women's groups did in the fifties). Usually, as Lionberger (1960: 91) points out, "people act in terms of past experience and knowledge." People who have had similar experiences are likely to share similar perceptions of a situation and to mutually reinforce those perceptions as well as their subsequent interpretation. A co-optable network, then, is one whose members have had common experiences that predispose them to be receptive to the particular new ideas of the incipient movement and who are not faced with structural or ideological barriers to action. If the new movement as an "innovation" can interpret these experiences and perceptions in ways that point out channels for social action, then participation in a social movement becomes the logical thing to do.

THE ROLE OF CRISES

As our examples have illustrated, similar perceptions must be translated into action. This is often done by a crisis. For blacks in Montgomery, this was generated by Rosa Parks's refusal to give up her seat on a bus to a white man. For women who formed the older branch of the women's movement, the impetus to organize was the refusal of the EEOC to enforce the sex provision of Title VII, precipitated by the concomitant refusal of federal officials at the conference to allow a supportive resolution. For younger women there were a series of minor crises.

While not all movements are formed by such precipitating events, they are quite common as they serve to crystallize and focus discontent. From their own experiences, directly and concretely, people feel the need for change in a situation that allows for an exchange of feelings with others, mutual validation, and a subsequent reinforcement of innovative interpretation. Perception of an immediate need for change is a major factor in predisposing people to accept new ideas (Rogers, 1962: 280). Nothing makes desire for change more acute than a crisis. Such a crisis need not be a major one; it need only embody collective discontent.

ORGANIZING EFFORTS

A crisis will only catalyze a well-formed communications network. If such networks are embryonically developed or only partially co-optable, the potentially active individuals in them must be linked together by someone.... As Jackson et al. (1960: 37) stated, "Some protest may persist where the source of trouble is constantly present. But interest ordinarily cannot be maintained unless there is a welding of spontaneous groups into some stable organization." In other words, people must be organized. Social movements do not simply occur.

The role of the organizer in movement formation is another neglected aspect of the theoretical literature. There has been great concern with leadership, but the two roles are distinct and not always performed by the same individual. In the early stages of a movement, it is the organizer much more than any leader who is important, and such an individual or cadre must often operate behind the scenes. The nature and function of these two roles was most clearly evident in the Townsend old-age movement of the thirties. Townsend was the "charismatic" leader, but the movement was organized by his partner, real estate promoter Robert Clements. Townsend himself acknowledges that without Clements's help, the movement would never have gone beyond the idea stage (Holzman, 1963).

The importance of organizers is pervasive in the sixties' movements. Dr. King may have been the public spokesperson of the Montgomery Bus Boycott who caught the eye of the media, but it was E. D. Nixon who organized it. Certainly the "organizing cadre" that young women in the radical community came to be was key to the growth of that branch of the women's liberation movement, despite the fact that no "leaders" were produced (and were actively discouraged). The existence of many leaders but no organizers in the older branch of the women's liberation movement readily explains its subsequent slow development....

The function of the organizer has been explored indirectly by other analysts. Rogers (1962) devotes many pages to the "change agent" who, while he does not necessarily weld a group together or "construct" a movement, does many of the same things for agricultural innovation that an organizer does for political change. Mass society theory makes frequent reference to the "agitator," though not in a truly informative way. Interest groups are often organized by single individuals and some of them evolve into social movements. Salisbury's study of farmers' organizations finds this a recurrent theme. He also discovered that "a considerable number of farm groups were subsidized by other, older, groups.... The Farm Bureau was organized and long sustained by subsidies, some from federal and state governments, and some by local businessmen" (Salisbury, 1959: 13).

These patterns are similar to ones we have found in the formation of social movements. Other organizations, even the government, often serve as training centers for organizers and sources of material support to aid the formation of groups and/or movements. The civil rights movement was the training ground for many an organizer of other movements.... The role of the government in the formation of the National Welfare Rights Organization was so significant that it would lead one to wonder if this association should be considered more of an interest group in the traditional sense than a movement "core" organization.

From all this it would appear that training as an organizer or at least as a proselytizer or entrepreneur of some kind is a necessary background for those individuals who act as movement innovators. Even in something as seemingly spontaneous as a social movement, the professional is more valuable than the amateur.

CRITICAL THINKING QUESTIONS

1. Why has the role of communications networks in the formation of social movements only recently received the attention of researchers?

2. How do leadership roles emerge in social movements? Are "leaders" the same as "organizers"?

3. Cite some similarities and differences between the development of the civil rights movement and the women's movement.

NOTES

1. The only use of this significant word appears rather incidentally in Turner (1964): 123.

2. Data for this section are based on my observations while a founder and participant in the younger branch of the Chicago women's liberation movement from 1967 through 1969 and editor of the first (at that time, only) national newsletter. I was able, through extensive correspondence and interviews, to keep a record of how each group around the country started, where the organizers got the idea from, who they had talked to, what conferences were held and who attended, the political affiliations (or lack of them) of the first members, and so forth. Although I was a member of Chicago NOW, information on the origins of it and the other older branch organizations comes entirely through ex post facto interviews of the principals and examination of early papers in preparation for my dissertation on the women's liberation movement. Most of my informants requested that their contribution remain confidential.

REFERENCES

Adorno, L. W., et al. 1950. *The authoritarian personality.* New York: Harper & Row.

Blumer, H. 1951. Social movements. In *New outline of the principles of sociology,* ed. A. M. Lee. New York: Barnes and Noble.

Brink, W., and L. Harris. 1964. *The Negro revolution in America.* New York: Simon & Schuster.

Buck, S. J. 1920. *The agrarian crusade.* New Haven, Conn.: Yale University Press.

Cantril, H. 1941. *The psychology of social movements.* New York: Wiley.

Clark, K. B. 1966. The civil rights movement: Momentum and organization. *Daedalus,* Winter.

Davies, J. C. 1962. Toward a theory of revolution. *American Sociological Review,* 27(1): 5–19.

Ferriss, A. L. 1971. *Indicators of trends in the status of American women.* New York: Russell Sage Foundation.

Firestone, S. 1971. *Dialectics of sex.* New York: Morrow.

Frazier, E. F. 1963. *The Negro church in America.* New York: Schocken.

Freeman, J. 1975. *The politics of women's liberation.* New York: Longman.

Friedan, B. 1963. *The feminine mystique.* New York: Dell.

———. 1967. NOW: How it began. *Women Speaking,* April.

Gurr, T. 1970. *Why men rebel.* Princeton, N.J.: Princeton University Press.

Hayden, C., and M. King. 1966. A kind of memo. *Liberation,* April.

Heberle, R. 1951. *Social movements.* New York: Appleton-Century-Crofts.

Hoffer, E. 1951. *The true believer.* New York: Harper & Row.

Hole, J., and E. Levine. 1971. *Rebirth of feminism.* New York: Quadrangle.

Holloway, H. 1969. *The politics of the Southern Negro.* New York: Random House.

Holzman, A. 1963. *The Townsend movement: A political study.* New York: Bookman.

Jackson, M., et al. 1960. The failure of an incipient social movement. *Pacific Sociological Review,* 3(1): 40.

King, M. L., Jr. 1958. *Stride toward freedom.* New York: Harper & Row.

Kornhauser, W. 1959. *The politics of mass society.* Glencoe, Ill.: Free Press.

Lionberger, H. F. 1960. *Adoption of new ideas and practices.* Ames: Iowa State University Press.

Lipset, S. M. 1959. *Agrarian socialism.* Berkeley: University of California Press.

Lowi, T. J. 1971. *The politics of discord.* New York: Basic Books.

Oberschall, A. 1973. *Social conflict and social movements.* Englewood Cliffs, N.J.: Prentice-Hall.

Pinard, M. 1971. *The rise of a third party: A study in crisis politics.* Englewood Cliffs, N.J.: Prentice-Hall.

Piven, F. F., and R. Cloward. 1977. *Poor people's movements: Why they succeed, how they fail.* New York: Pantheon.

Rogers, E. M. 1962. *Diffusion of innovations.* New York: Free Press.

Rudwick, E., and A. Meier. 1970. Organizational structure and goal succession: A comparative analysis of the NAACP and CORE, 1964–1968. *Social Science Quarterly,* 51 (June).

Salisbury, R. H. 1969. An exchange theory of interest groups. *Midwest Journal of Political Science,* 13(1), (February).

Toch, H. 1965. *The social psychology of social movements.* Indianapolis, Ind.: Bobbs-Merrill.

Zinn, H. 1964. *SNCC: The new abolitionists.* Boston: Beacon Press.

68

Collective Behaviour
and
Social Movements

Looking for Solutions in the Canadian North: Modern Treaties as a New Strategy

CLASSIC

CONTEMPORARY

CROSS-CULTURAL

*James C. Saku and Robert M. Bone**

In this article, Saku and Bone compare three Aboriginal populations in Canada's North, their experiences with various land claims, and the resulting social and economic impacts.

Modern land claim agreements (MLCAs) are having an impact on Aboriginal economic and social development. This economic impact stems from the substantial land and cash received through the surrender of land rights. The creation of an economic structure that allows the recipients to manage their land and business is another important component of modern land claim agreements. In this paper, we compare economic development of Aboriginal peoples living in three different areas of the Canadian North, namely, the Western Arctic, the Central Arctic, and Northern Quebec, over a ten year period. Even in this short-term period, we argue that those in the Western Arctic and Northern Quebec who had their agreements signed much earlier would have seen a more rapid and persistent advancement in their economic development than those in the Central Arctic (Kitikmeot and Keewatin census regions) whose claims were settled in 1993 as part of the larger Tungavik Federation of Nunavut Final Agreement. Using Principal Component Analysis (PCA) and data from the 1981, 1986 and 1991 Canadian censuses, we have undertaken a longitudinal analysis for each region. The results support our hypothesis.

* We are grateful for the thoughtful comments of the three anonymous reviewers. The encouragement and support of Dr. Barry Boots during the review process are well appreciated. Thanks to Mr. Keith Bigelow for preparing the maps and graph. This research was supported by the Social Sciences and Humanities Research Grant 803-92-0002.

Source: James C. Saku and Robert M. Bone. 2000. Looking for Solutions in the Canadian North: Modern Treaties as a New Strategy. *Canadian Geographer*, 44(3), 259–70. Reprinted by permission of the Canadian Association of Geographers.

INTRODUCTION

The economic, demographic and social conditions of Aboriginal Canadians are significantly different from those of the Canadian population as a whole

(Stabler, 1985; Stabler & How, 1990; Bone, 1992; Bone et al., 1992; Frideres, 1993; Royal Commission on Aboriginal People (RCAP), 1996). In 1991, 15 percent of Canadians earned income of $40,000 and above compared to 5 percent of Aboriginal people (Table 68.1). The poor state of economic development within Aboriginal communities is attributed to the disruption of traditional economies, the loss of control over their traditional land base and the imposition of inappropriate economic policies and practices (RCAP, 1996: 800). In 1979, the first Canada-Northwest Territory (NWT) Economic Development Agreement was announced. A host of other federal, provincial and territorial programmes, including housing, The Local Initiative Programme, Special Agricultural and Rural Development Agreement, Eskimo Loan Fund, Native Procurement Strategy, the NWT Small Business Loan Fund and job-training were initiated in the past to correct the imbalance (Chislett et al., 1987; Savoie, 1987). While some of these programmes may have yielded results (refer to Stabler & Howe, 1990), Aboriginal people are still a disadvantaged people in Canada. According to Erasmus (1989: 1) "our people have been relegated to the lowest rung on the ladder of Canadian society, suffer the worst conditions of life, the lowest incomes, the poorest education and health and can envision only the most depressing future for our children."

To improve the economic and social conditions of First Nations, Aboriginal leaders are demanding a new relationship that removes federal paternalism by giving them more control of their destiny through local economic development and self-government. Within this framework, the settlement of Comprehensive Land Claim Agreements (CLCAs) marks a new approach of improving the economic and social status of Aboriginal Canadians living in the Canadian north. These agreements involve monetary and land compensation for the surrendering of Aboriginal claims to their traditional land base. Aboriginal institutions are also created to manage the cash and land.

Table 68.1   Socio-Economic Indicators: Canada and Aboriginal, 1991

Education	Canada*	Aboriginal
% of population age 15 to 64		
Less than grade 9	11.8%	25.4%
Grades 9–13	22.8%	32.2%
High School diploma	21.3%	12.9%
University without degree	4.7%	7.9%
University with degree	12.2%	2.6%
Employment (age 15 and older)		
Employed	61.0%	43.0%
Unemployment	7.0%	14.0%
Participation rate	68.0%	57.0%
Income		
No income in 1990	9.0%	13.0%
Income of $40,000 and over	15.0%	5.0%
Average employment income	$27,880	$21,270
Employment income per person age 15+	$17,020	$9,140
Housing		
Average number of persons per dwelling	2.7	3.5
Average number of rooms per dwelling	6.1	5.8
Average number of persons per room	0.4	0.6
Houses need minor repairs	24.0%	29.0%
Houses need major repairs	8.0%	20.0%

Source: Statistics Canada, 1993(a&b) and 1994(a&b), 1991 Aboriginal People Survey.

* Canada data include Aboriginal and non-Aboriginal

This paper examines the socio-economic change in three geographic regions of the Canadian North, namely, the Western Arctic, Central Arctic and Northern Quebec. Our objective is to analyze the impacts of land allocation, cash payment and institutional structures created through the settlement of modern land claim agreements on the Aboriginal people of Northern Canada.

The central questions addressed in this paper are, what is the impact of CLCAs on Aboriginal economic and social development? Specifically, have these agreements resulted in the economic improvement of the Inuvialuit of the Western Arctic and Northern Quebec, Cree, Inuit and the Naskapi? What is the nature of the difference in the economic and social well-being between Aboriginal people whose claims were settled prior to 1991 and those that achieved a claim after that date? These issues are examined by comparing the nature of socio-economic change between regions that achieved CLCAs prior to 1991 and those that did not. While Northern Quebec and the Western Arctic represent regions that achieved CLCA, the Central Arctic (Kitikmeot and Keewatin census regions) is a region without an agreement at that time. Our hypothesis is that the resulting economic growth in the regions will lead to demographic and social transformation. By 1991, the central Arctic did not have the capital and organizational structure required to promote economic development. As such, the region continued to drift economically.

The James Bay and Northern Quebec communities were located in Census Division 98 (Territory of Northern Quebec) while the Inuvialuit region fall within Inuvik and Kitikmeot census regions (Figure 68.1). Administratively, five Inuvialuit communities including Akalvik, Inuvik, Sachs Harbour, Paulatuk and Tuktoyaktuk belong to the Inuvik census region while Holman belongs to the Kitikmeot region. Kitikmeot and Keewatin census regions are chosen to represent the Central Arctic because the population composition of the two census regions is predominately Inuit. Also, like the Inuvialuit and Northern Quebec, the population base and economic status of these communities are similar. A list of the communities, their 1991 population and labour force participation (LFP) is provided in Table 68.2.

MODERN TREATIES AS A NEW SOCIOECONOMIC DEVELOPMENT APPROACH

Aboriginal land claims in Canada are based on Aboriginal rights. The basis of these rights is linked to King George III's 1763 Royal Proclamation (Crowe, 1991; Fleras & Elliot, 1992; Frideres, 1993; Saku, 1995; RCAP, 1996). According to the Proclamation, all lands not granted to the Hudson's Bay Company or not occupied by settlers were to be reserved and held

FIGURE 68.1 Census Division of Study Regions

by the Crown on behalf of First Nations. While Canadian courts have acknowledged these rights, they have avoided a comprehensive definition of them (Usher et al., 1992). From a legal perspective, Aboriginal rights are common-law governing the Crown's assumption of sovereignty and its relations with Aboriginal people (Slattery, 1987). Judicial interpretation limits Aboriginal rights to the historical use of land and related resources for hunting and trapping rather than full ownership. In accepting Aboriginal rights to the land, the courts had looked for a proof of traditional occupancy and use of specific lands prior to European settlement.

Aboriginal people interpret Aboriginal rights to include a broad range of economic, social and political factors. These rights include full and sovereign ownership of land and resources, cultural rights, legal recognition of customary law and the right to self-government within the Canadian nation (Asch, 1988; RCAP, 1996). These rights are based on the traditional use and occupancy of land

Table 68.2   The Study Communities, 1991

	Pop.	LFP
Inuvialuit		
Aklavik	801	66.3
Holman	360	65.2
Inuvik	3206	79.6
Paulatuk	255	67.9
Sachs Harbour	125	64.3
Tuktoyaktuk	918	65.8
James Bay Inuit		
Akulivik	375	64.3
Aupaluk	135	62.5
Inukjuak	1045	46.8
Ivujivik	260	48.4
Kangiqsualjjuaq	525	50.8
Kangiqsujuaq	400	60.9
Kangirsuk	350	56.8
Kuujjarapik	605	75.3
Kuujjuaq	1105	74.3
Quaqtaq	235	62.5
Salluit	825	49.5
Tasuijaq	155	55.6
James Bay Naskapi		
Kawawachilkamach	405	51.0
James Bay Cree		
Chisasibi	2305	55.0
Eastmain	445	50.0
Nemaska	465	60.4
Waskaganish	1345	55.1
Wemindjj	920	50.8
Whapmagoostui	510	47.1
Keewatin		
Arviat	1325	51.9
Baker Lake	1190	55.3
Chesterfield Inlet	310	67.6
Coral Harbour	580	61.9
Rankin Inlet	1700	69.4
Repulse Bay	485	44.2
Kitikmeot		
Cambridge Bay	1115	70.9
Coppermine	1060	58.0
Gjoa Haven	780	58.4
Pelly Bay	410	56.5
Spence Bay	580	52.2

Source: Statistics Canada, 1994(a&b)

by Aboriginal people (Crowe, 1988; Frideres, 1993; RCAP, 1996). Comprehensive Land Claim Agreements are based on the assertion of continuing Aboriginal rights to land in those areas of Canada where treaties are not signed (Saku et al., 1998). The 1975 James Bay and Northern Quebec Agreement (JBNQA) was the first modern treaty signed in Canada. Three years later, the Northeastern Quebec Agreement (NEQA) was reached with the Naskapis. The first CLCA was achieved in 1984 when the Inuvialuit Final Agreement (IFA) was reached with the federal government. This was followed by the Gwich'in Comprehensive Land Claim Agreement (1992), the Sahtu Dene and Metis Comprehensive Land Claim Agreement (1993) and the Tungavik Federation of Nunavut Final Agreement (1993). The settlement regions are shown in Figure 68.2.

In achieving a CLCA, Aboriginal people give up claim to their traditional hunting, fishing and gathering lands in return for legal title to selected lands, cash payment, rights to manage natural resources, hunting, fishing and trapping privileges, and the formation of economic development corporations. The resulting benefits of CLCAs provide the necessary impetus for regional socio-economic change in Aboriginal communities (Smelie, 1989; Robinson et al., 1989; RCAP, 1996a; Saku et al., 1998). For example, the financial compensation associated with the Inuvialuit

FIGURE 68.2   Modern Treaties in Northern Quebec and NWT

claim was $45 million ($18,000/capita), $135 million ($29,300/capita) for the James Bay Cree, $90 million ($20,501/capita) for the Inuit of Northern Quebec and $9 million ($23,136/capita) for the Naskapi (Table 68.3).

Each agreement created an Aboriginal economic institution, such as the Inuvialuit Regional Corporation, designed to fight poverty and economic marginalization in northern Aboriginal communities (Table 68.3). The Inuvialuit, for example, are striving to achieve a more stable economy through the Inuvialuit Regional Corporation (IRC). The IRC is responsible for managing the cash benefits flowing out of the IFA with several subsidiary companies. These subsidiaries of IRC are involved in economic development projects including real estate, retail and wholesale, oil and gas exploration, environmental clean up, air, ground, and marine transportation. In 1994, the Inuvialuit Development Corporation (IDC), a subsidiary of the IRC, was awarded a $350,000 contract to service the North Warning System in the Inuvialuit Settlement Region (ISR). The terms of the contract included IDC transporting personnel and supplies to nine radar sites for corrective or preventive maintenance (Sardi, 1994: 14).

In addition to this economic venture, in July 1994, IDC won an estimated $1.5 million contract to clean up the abandoned Distant Early Warning (DEW) line sites at Horton River. About 30 Inuvialuit workers were employed by Arvik Environmental Services. Through investments and other forms of economic activities, the IDC reported a profit of $2.5 million in 1993 (Smith, 1994).

Three economic institutions, namely, the Cree Board of Compensation, Makivik Corporation (Inuit) and Naskapi Development Corporation were created when Northern Quebec agreements were achieved. Like the Inuvialuit, these are elaborate corporate institutions designed to promote economic development in Northern Quebec. The Inuit of Northern Quebec, for example, own an airline, Inuit Air and First Air, with a fleet of 20 aircraft and the James Bay Cree launched Air Creebec with an investment of $12.5 million. These transportation companies provide local and regional air services. Manufacturing and service companies were also established in Northern Quebec. The Makivik Corporation has invested in tourism promotional materials in southern markets (Braden, 1993). In 1990, Cree Regional Economic Enterprises (Creeco) obtained over $50 million of contracts from Hydro-Quebec (Frideres, 1993).

Land allocation is another important benefit of CLCAs (Table 68.3). The Inuvialuit were granted titled to 91,000 km^2 (32.38 km^2/capita). Unlike the Cree and Inuit of Quebec, the Inuvialuit were granted both surface and subsurface rights to 1,800 km^2 and subsurface rights to 78,000 km^2. Three types of land regimes were established in Northern Quebec. Type 1 include those lands that are located around the communities and are

Table 68.3   Benefits of Comprehensive Land Claims

	Economic Institution	Land Allocated per Capita (km²)	Monetary Compensation per Capita	Other Incomes ($ million)
Northern Quebec				
Inuit	Makivik Corporation	1.86	$20,501	$12.6
Cree	Cree Board of Compensation	0.83	$29,300	$140
Naskapi	Naskapi Development Corporation	1.79	$23,136	$1.26
Western Arctic				
Inuvialuit	Inuvialuit Regional Corporation	32.38	$18,000	$24.4

Source: Compiled by the authors.

administered by the Cree, Inuit or Naskapi governments. Type 2 lands are located immediately around type 1 lands. These lands are under provincial jurisdiction. However, Cree, Inuit and Naskapi have exclusive rights to hunting on these lands. Type 3 lands are designated public lands. Even though they are public lands, Cree, Inuit and Naskapi have exclusive rights to hunting specific animals on these lands.

Notwithstanding the potential economic and social spin-offs of CLCAs, there are two opposing views on the CLCAs. One school of thought, the optimists, believe the CLCAs will have a significant impact on Aboriginal societies affected by such agreements. These scholars consider CLCAs as the single most promising approach for Aboriginal people to achieve a more equitable place in the Canadian society (McAllister, 1985; Duerden, 1990; Bone, 1992; RCAP, 1996b). The former Chairman of the Inuvialuit Regional Corporation, Roger Gruben (1991), was highly optimistic when he stated that the social and economic well-being of the Inuvialuit of the Western Arctic improved significantly within the first decade of achieving their land claim agreement.

However, this view is not shared by all. The pessimists are highly sceptical about the socio-economic impact of CLCAs on northern Aboriginal communities (Kruse, 1984; Thomas, 1986). They claim that CLCAs are simply an attempt by the federal government to clarify land ownership and thereby encourage private development. The authors of the Special Committee on the Northern Economy (SCONE) report of 1989 raised serious doubts about CLCAs having significant impact on the economic well-being of Aboriginal communities. The authors believe that the massive financial gains necessary for an effective and viable Native regional economy are not present. Also, the failure of Alaskan Regional corporations to maintain sustainable economic development is often cited by pessimists about the impact of CLCAs on Native communities (Anders, 1983; Kruse, 1984; Thomas, 1986; Robinson et al.,

1989). Thomas (1986: 33) for example observed that "in many Alaskan villages, there is [*sic*] simply no viable economic opportunities available; investments in the communities have a zero chance of yielding substantial monetary returns."

CONCEPTUAL FRAMEWORK

Economic and social development is a complex subject. It is a process of societal change. Success is measured by goals aspired to by a particular society. For northern Aboriginal people, economic and social development involves both the land-based hunting economy and the wage sector industrial economy. The net result is a mixed economy. In different Aboriginal communities, the balance between the land-based and wage economies may vary. The Cree of Northern Quebec, for instance, emphasized living on the land as well as job opportunities in the wage economy. An important institutional reflection of this emphasis is the Cree Income Support Programme for Hunters and Trappers. For the Inuvialuit, the Inuvialuit Game Council (IGC) protects and enhances harvesting of game in the Inuvialuit Settlement Region. The IGC was instrumental in obtaining the International Wildlife Commission's permission to hunt for Bowhead Whales (Freeman et al., 1992).

Aboriginal people, while part of the larger Canadian society, have a distinctive history and culture. Their development aspirations are different from non-Aboriginal Canadians. However, Aboriginal peoples wish to have an adequate and secure supply of food, medical services and education. At the same time, they want to maintain some level of traditional economy. The CLCAs have sought a balance between the traditional and modern economies found in Aboriginal communities. The survival of the traditional economy depends heavily on the newly created environmental organizations found in each CLCA. For example, the Inuvialuit Game Council represents the Inuvialuit interests in environmental and wildlife matters while the Inuvialuit Regional Development Corporation looks after economic interests.

Cultural change is occurring very rapidly in Aboriginal societies in the Canadian North and may be affecting the economic aspirations and goals of Aboriginal people. Young Aboriginal Canadians are more inclined to seek education and jobs than their parents. However, we do recognize that economic development is part of cultural change and culture "directs" development. On this issue, Ovide Mercredi (1994) observed that without an economic base, the culture of Aboriginal people is either dying or dead.

In the past, scholars have used different theories to explain the complex mechanisms of economic and social development in northern Aboriginal communities. While some theories explain development within the framework of the core-periphery theory (Oppong & Ironside, 1987; Weissling, 1988; Bone, 1992; Bone et al., 1992), others appear to be locally based, that is, the bottom-up approach (Ironside, 1990).

In this paper, we have adopted the bottom-up approach because CLCAs transfer economic and political power to Aboriginal peoples, thereby allowing them to control their future much more than in the past. According to Black (1991), the bottom-up approach emphasizes community-based accountability and voluntarism. Of critical importance in community-based development is the community's support and participation (Naqvi et al., 1995). The traditional economic and political practices of northern Aboriginal peoples may predispose them to engaging in effective community-based development (McMillan, 1991). This is a basic traditional norm among Aboriginal people of northern Canada. Ironside (1990) observed that the fundamental objective of economic development in northern Aboriginal communities is one of organizing the collective resources, ingenuity and communal spirit of neighbouring small communities which are not viable individually. Similarly, Anderson (1997) noted that First Nations in Canada have adopted and are

implementing a collective approach to development in their desire to become economically self-sufficient within the market economy.

The main weakness of the bottom-up approach to development is its emphasis on a closed economy. With the globalization of the world economy, it is impossible to maintain a closed economy. Also, in northern Canada, the approach is hampered by structural problems. For example, the local population base is extremely small, making most types of economic activity unprofitable. Another structural problem is embedded in their population distribution—settlements scattered over a large area. There is, therefore, high overhead cost in terms of production and distribution. The Aboriginal economic institutions, such as the Inuvialuit Regional Corporation, have recognized that few attractive economic investments are found within their northern regions and therefore have invested heavily outside of their respective settlement areas. These same corporations, however, have competed fiercely for public contracts within their respective settlement areas.

Comprehensive Land Claim Agreements (CLCAs) exhibit the characteristics of the bottom-up approach to development. First, these agreements emphasize local control of both human and natural resources. They are also a means of bringing economically less viable small communities together to achieve economic development. These agreements recognize local initiative as an important component of regional economic growth. Also, the main objectives of these agreements involve improving the living standards of beneficiaries through provision of basic community needs. Conceptually, community development occurs as an evolutionary process over a period of time.

Within this framework, our assumption is that the monetary compensations that Aboriginal people receive through CLCAs provide a triggering mechanism for local economic growth (Figure 68.3). These funds provide much needed capital for investment by Aboriginal Regional Corporations within and outside their settlement areas. For example, the Inuvialuit Regional Development Corporation is buying businesses and investing in profitable ventures across Canada (Lamman & Hallman, 1990). They have invested in oil companies in Alberta and real estate in British Columbia. Similarly, they are investing in their local economies. This local investment and profits from southern investment should stimulate the local economy through the creation of jobs (Sardi, 1994; Schmitz & Sardi, 1994). With these economic initiatives, there will be an enlargement and diversification of the Cree, Inuit and Naskapi of Northern Quebec and Inuvialuit labour force and businesses.

As the number of skilled positions increase within the regions, a form of spread effect occurs and the labour force would become diversified. This would lead to an increase in average income, disposable income and capital accumulation could occur. New purchases and investment would boost local sales and expand the local economic base. This would provide the necessary capital and tax base and subsequent increase in the provision of social amenities and infrastructure. Within this scenario, the ultimate impact of CLCAs is a positive one (Figure 68.3). On the contrary, improper corporate or business decisions would lead to business failure and the collapse of local economy.

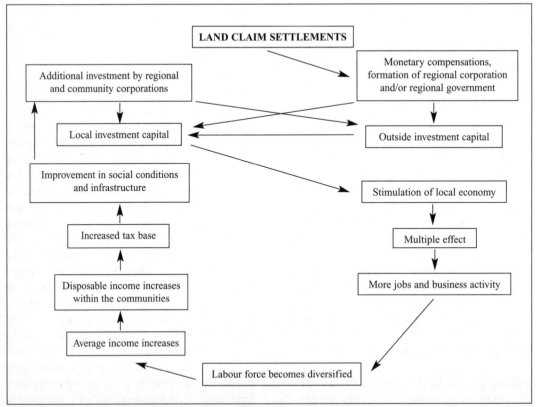

FIGURE 68.3   Positive Scenario Scores: 1981–1991

METHOD AND DATA SOURCES

The measurement of economic impact of development projects or policy initiatives is often a difficult one. Two methodological approaches, that is, before and after project analysis and comparison with regions not affected by the project or policy, have been proposed (Poister et al., 1979; Hatry et al., 1981).

The "before and after" approach is used to measure and compare the economic and social changes before and after project initiation. This approach is widely used because of its simplicity, cost-effectiveness and economic data requirements (Semple & Ironside, 1992). The second approach involves a comparison with a population/region not affected by the project. This approach is considered economically and practically reliable because a larger number of variables can be employed. A basic disadvantage of both approaches is that it is often difficult to separate non-project effects from actual project impact. The second method is employed in this study.

Several statistical techniques have been used to analyse the social and economic problems of the Canadian North (Mellor & Ironside, 1978; Bone & Green, 1984, 1986, 1987; Chislett et al., 1987; Oppong & Ironside, 1987; Stabler, 1989; Stabler & Howe, 1990; Stabler et al., 1990; Bone et al., 1992; DiFrancesco & Longeran, 1994; DiFrancesco, 1998). Based on study objectives, methodology and data availability, the type of statistical technique employed by each of these studies varies. The statistical techniques include simple descriptive analysis, regression, principal component analysis and input-output modeling.

In this study, Principal Component Analysis (PCA) is chosen because of the data limitations and the methodology employed in the study. Our study communities involve small populations scattered over large geographic areas. The populations of these communities vary from 3,206 for Inuvik and 155 for Tasuijaq (Table 68.2). Akkerman et al. (1997) have suggested that data on small populations are highly erratic. To minimise the effects of this problem requires the use of a technique such as the PCA that combines several variables into an index. "One merit of the PCA is that an increase in the number of variables that one may wish to include imposes very little costs on the analysis" (Ram, 1982, 233). More importantly, the technique weights the variables on each component by multiplying the component loading of that variable by a standardized value of the variable.

Principal Component Analysis is the statistical technique chosen to measure the longitudinal changes in the three regions. PCA is commonly used to combine several variables into a single development index (Adelma & Morris, 1967; Berry, 1961; Tata & Schulz, 1988; Davies & Murdie, 1991; Bone et al., 1992). Bone and Green (1984) advocated the use of PCA as a way of monitoring changes over time in the socio-economic status of small communities in the Canadian North. The theoretical foundation of Principal Component Analysis is extensively provided in Rummel (1970).

Censuses are the main sources of data for this longitudinal study. Twenty-three variables were selected from the 1981, 1986 and 1991 censuses of Canada (Table 68.4). These variables represent a mix of economic, demographic and social conditions of the regions. Overall, eight variables are economic, while eight are demographic and seven are social. The decision to choose these 23 variables is based on variable reoccurrence in the three censuses and inclusion of a wide variety of different aspects of socio-economic development.

A serious limitation of these data is that the variables may not fully represent the developmental aspirations and goals of northern Aboriginal people. The basic values used to determine what data are collected during census enumerations reflects those found in southern Canada's industrial society. Many census questions, therefore, emphasize the wage economy. In sharp contrast, little attention is paid to the land-based traditional economy of Aboriginal peoples.

Table 68.4   Variables Used in Principal Component
                     Analysis

Economic
Labour force participation
Percentage employed
Unemployment Rate
Percentage of household with income lower than $14,999
Percentage of labour force in primary sector
Percentage of labour force in trade industry
Average male income
Average female income

Demographic
Total population
Percentage of immigrants from other provinces
Percentage of population 15 years and over
Average number of persons per room
Percentage of husband-wife families with three or more
   children at home
Average number of persons per household
Dependency ratio
Child population ratio

Social
Average number of rooms per dwelling
Percentage of population speaking English/French
Percentage of adult population with less than Grade 9
   education
Percentage of adult population with Grade 13 education
Percentage of houses privately owned
Percentage of adult population with university degree
Percentage of people speaking Aboriginal language at home

Source: Statistics Canada, 1994a, 1994b.

Table 68.5   PCA: Eigen values, 1981, 1986
                     and 1991

	Eigen values			*Explained values*		
Components	*1981*	*1986*	*1991*	*1981*	*1986*	*1991*
1	8.5	9.1	8.9	36.9	39.7	38.8
2	2.9	2.6	3.2	12.9	11.4	13.9
3	2.1	2.2	1.6	8.9	9.3	7.1
4	1.6	1.7	1.3	6.7	7.2	5.8
5	1.3	1.3	1.3	5.5	5.5	5.7
6	1.1	1.1	1.2	4.6	4.7	5.1
% Cumulative				75.1	77.8	76.3

ANALYSIS AND RESULTS

Using PCA technique, six components were derived from the original 23 variables. The criteria used to determine the number of components retained are based on eigen values greater than 1.0 and contributing at least 4.5 percent to the total variance (Table 68.5). From our analysis, component 1 showed the highest variance in the three analyses. More significant are the similarities in total variance explained by the six components in the three tests. In 1981, the six components explained 75.1 percent of the variance, while the figures for 1986 and 1991 are 77.8 percent and 76.3 percent, respectively.

To obtain an acceptable grouping of the variables, the data were transformed into a simple structure, that is, rotated. The total of the rotation is to create component loadings which may be interpreted as the correlation between the 23 variables and the factors to which they are closely associated. In other words, variables which load strongly on the same component are highly interrelated. Our analysis revealed inconsistency among the three years in terms of component loadings. For example, in 1981, nine variables loaded strongly on component 1, in 1986 only three variables loaded strongly on component 1 while six variables loaded strongly on component 1 in 1991. On the other hand, average male income, average female income and total population loaded with component 1 in the three years.

The next step in the analysis is the creation of community component scores. These scores represent indices or measures of socio-economic conditions of each community. Regional component scores were then calculated as averages of community scores. We refer to the summation of these scores as the "development" index (Table 68.6). The scores reveal regional differences in the socio-economic development over time among the three regions (Table 68.6). The results indicate that the scores of the Invialuit and Northern Quebec communities show an upward trend over the ten year period (Figure 68.4).

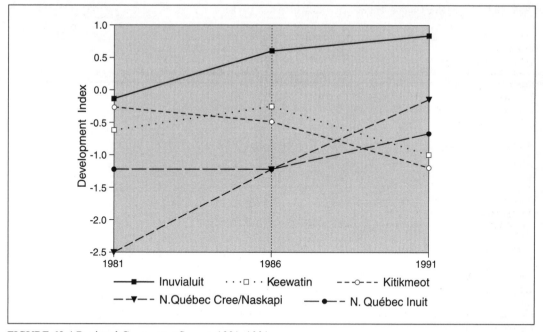

FIGURE 68.4 Regional Component Scores: 1981–1991

In 1981, the level of development of the Inuvialuit communities was –0.09. In 1986, the Inuvialuit score increased to 0.62 and in 1991, the score was 0.85. On the other hand, the Inuit of Northern Quebec scored –2.50 in 1981, –1.17 in 1986 and –0.13 in 1991. The Creed and Naskapi exhibited a similar positive trend—1981 (–1.19), 1986 (–1.17) and 1991 (–0.62).

In sharp contrast, the development index for the Keewatin and Kitikmeot regions exhibit an overall downward trend over this ten year period (Figure 68.4). While their scores increased between 1981 and 1986, they experienced a sharp decline between 1986 and 1991 (Table 68.6). The scores of the Kitikmeot region are 1981(–0.23), 1986 (–0.47) and 1991 (–1.12) while Keewatin is –0.56 (1981), –0.21 (1986) and –0.97 in 1991. There is no apparent explanation to the decline in the scores of the Keewatin and Kitikmeot regions. More

significant to our analysis is the fact that Northern Quebec communities performed much higher than the Keewatin and Kitikmeot communities in 1991.

The remarkable performance by the Cree, Inuit, and Naskapi of Northern Quebec and the Inuvialuit of the Western Arctic may be attributed to a combination of unleashing local energies and utilizing the benefits derived from modern treaties. Together, they have led to the economic and social transformations in the region. These activities may be related to the signing of the CLCA. This suggests that the Inuvialuit and the Cree, Inuit and Naskapi are taking advantage of the opportunities of the CLCAs and are investing in economic ventures within and outside the region. These investments have positive impacts on these regions in the form of higher labour force participation, average incomes and low unemployment rates.

Table 68.6   Regional Component Scores, 1981, 1986 and 1991

Components	1	2	3	4	5	6	Development Index
1981							
Central Arctic							
Keewatin	−0.02	0.39	−0.08	−0.68	−0.27	0.10	−0.56
Kitikmeot	−0.17	0.50	0.27	−0.34	−0.23	−0.26	−0.23
Western Arctic							
Inuvialuit	−0.33	0.81	−0.39	0.49	−0.55	−0.12	−0.09
Northern Quebec							
Inuit	−0.28	−0.99	0.22	−1.04	−1.00	0.59	−2.50
Cree and Naskapi	−0.57	0.73	−0.90	0.12	−0.08	−0.49	−1.19
1986							
Central Arctic							
Keewatin	0.61	0.11	0.17	−0.03	−0.65	−0.42	−0.21
Kitikmeot	0.60	−0.43	0.09	−0.39	−0.56	−0.17	−0.47
Western Arctic							
Inuvialuit	1.20	−0.60	−0.08	−0.76	0.24	0.62	0.62
Northern Quebec							
Inuit	−0.39	0.76	−1.21	−0.20	0.13	−0.26	−1.17
Cree and Naskapi	0.40	−0.24	0.16	−0.23	−0.53	−0.73	−1.17
1991							
Central Arctic							
Keewatin	−0.12	−0.25	−0.27	0.35	0.22	−0.46	−0.97
Kitikmeot	0.48	−1.02	−0.45	0.52	0.08	−0.73	−1.12
Western Arctic							
Inuvialuit	1.64	0.16	0.40	−0.24	−0.25	−0.86	0.85
Northern Quebec							
Inuit	−0.30	0.94	−0.14	−0.69	−0.01	0.07	−0.13
Cree and Naskapi	−0.47	0.16	−1.13	0.24	−0.31	0.89	−0.62

CONCLUSION

Since the 1960s, the federal, provincial and territorial governments in Canada have initiated policies designed to improve the living conditions of Native northerners. In 1979, for example, the first Canada-NWT Economic Development Agreement was signed. Despite this and other attempts, the socio-economic conditions of most Aboriginal Canadians remain at a very deplorable state. Many are still plagued with problems of low income, low levels of education, high unemployment and high dependency. Comprehensive Land Claim Agreements (CLCAs) represent a new approach at addressing the needs of Aboriginal northerners. This "bottom-up" approach involves the transfer of economic power, land ownership and the creation of institutional structures designed to improve the economic well-being of Aboriginal people. Through the institutions created after achieving the agreement Aboriginal people are given the mandate to set the strategy, undertake the planning, and control businesses and economic development in their localities.

This paper analyses the impact of these initiatives on Aboriginal socio-economic development. Our study compares the socio-economic status of Native communities which achieved an agreement prior to 1991 and those that did not over a ten year period (1981–91). The results of the analysis reveal that in the short-run, the strategy may be working for both the Inuvialuit of the Western Arctic and the Cree, Inuit and Naskapi of Northern Quebec. These regions show a persistent increase in the socio-economic development as measured by 23 variables from the Census of Canada. While the time frame of this study is rather short, our study serves as a basis for future research on CLCAs. Future research on CLCAs should include the 1996 census data of Canada. This will provide a much longer time frame for analyzing the impact of CLCAs on the regions.

CRITICAL THINKING QUESTIONS

1. According to Saku and Bone, by what key characteristics do modern treaties differ from earlier ones?
2. What are some of the social and economic impacts of modern treaties on Aboriginal populations? Which do you feel are the most important to the Aboriginal people?
3. Explain what Saku and Bone mean by a "bottom-up" approach to land claims. What do you see as the greatest social and economic benefits and costs to such an approach?

REFERENCES

Adelma, I., and C. T. Morris. 1965. Factor analysis of the interrelationship between social and political variables and per capita gross national product. *Quarterly Journal of Economics*, 79: 555–78.

Akkerman, A. R. M. Bone, and J. C. Saku. 1997. Qualitative indicators of multi-regional demographic change: potential for developing countries. In *Demographic transition: The third world scenario*, ed. A. Ahmad, D. Noin, and H. N. Sharma. New Delhi: Rawat Publications.

Anders, G. C. 1983. The role of Alaska Native corporations in the development of Alaska. *Development and Change*, 14: 555–75.

Anderson, R. B. 1997. Corporate/indigenous partnerships in economic development: The First Nations in Canada. *World Development*, 25(9): 1483–503.

Anderson, R. B, and R. M. Bone. 1995. First Nations economic development: A contingency perspective. *Canadian Geographer*, 39(1): 120–30.

Asch, M. 1988. *Home and Native homeland: Aboriginal rights and the Canadian Constitution*. Scarborough: Nelson Canada.

Berry, B. J. L. 1961. *Basic patterns of economic development. Atlas of economic development*, ed. N. Ginsburg. Chicago: University of Chicago Press.

Bone, R. M. 1992. *The geography of the Canadian North: Issues and challenges*. Toronto: Oxford University Press.

————. 1994. Population change in the provincial norths. In *Geographic perspectives on the provincial norths*, ed. M. E. Johnson, 85–109. Mississauga, Ont.: Copp Clark.

Bone, R. M., and M. B. Green. 1984. Principal component: An approach to community monitoring. *The Operational Geographer*, 4: 10–3.

————. 1986. Accessibility and development of Metis communities in Saskatchewan. *The Canadian Geographer*, 30: 66–71.

————. 1987. Frontier dualism in northern Saskatchewan. *The Operational Geographer*, 12: 21–4.

Bone, R. M., T. Johnson, and J. C. Saku. 1992. Economic growth, community development and income distribution: Northwest Territories Canada. *Ontario Geography*, 38: 1–11.

Black, J. K. 1991. *Development in theory and practice: Bridge the gap*. Oxford: Westview Press.

Braden, B. 1993. Quebec Inuit look for portable options in sparse wage economy. *News/North*, (April 1993): A16.

Chislett, K. L., M. B. Green, and R. M. Bone. 1987. Housing mismatch for Metis in northern Saskatchewan. *The Canadian Geographer*, 31: 341–46.

Coffey, W. J., and M. Polese. 1985. Local development: Conceptual bases and policy implications. *Regional Studies*, 19 (April): 85–93.

Crowe, K. 1991. Claims on the land. *Arctic Circle*, 1: 31–5.

Dacks, G. 1990. *Devolution and political development in the Canadian north*. Ottawa: Carleton University Press.

Davies, W. K. D. 1978. Alternative factorial solutions and urban social structure: A data analysis exploration of Calgary in 1971. *Canadian Geographer*, 22: 273–97.

Davies, W. K. D., and R. A. Murdie. 1991. Changes in the intraurban social dimensionality of Canadian CMAs: 1981–1986. *The Canadian Journal of Regional Science*, 14(2): 207–32.

DiFrancesco, R. J. 1998. Large projects in hinterland regions: A dynamic multiregional input-output model for assessing the economic impacts. *Geographic Analysis*, 30(1): 15–34.

DiFrancesco, R. J., and S. C. Lonergan. 1994. Examining regional sensitivity to climate change using aggregate input-output data: The case of transportation in the Northwest Territories. *Canadian Journal of Regional Science*, 17(2): 233–57.

Duerden, F. 1990. The geographer and land claims: A critical appraisal. *The Operational Geographer*, 8: 36–8.

Erasmus, G. 1989. Twenty years of disappointed hopes. In *Drum beat: Anger and renewal in Indian country*, ed. B. Richardson. Toronto: Summerhill Press.

Fleras, A., and L. J. Elliot, 1992. *The nations: Aboriginal-state relations in Canada, the United States and New Zealand*. Don Mills: Oxford University Press.

Freeman, M. M. R., E. Wein, and D. Keith. 1992. *Recovery rights: Bowhead whales and Inuvialuit subsistence in the Western Arctic*. Edmonton: Canadian Circumpolar Institute.

Frideres, J. S. 1993. *Native peoples in Canada: Contemporary conflicts*. Scarborough, Ont.: Prentice Hall Canada.

Government of Canada. 1982. *Outstanding business, A Native claims policy: Specific claims*. Ottawa: Minister of Supply and Services.

Gruben, R. 1991. *Balancing northern values and economic development*. Paper presented to the National Northern Development Conference. Yellowknife.

Hantry, H., R. Winnie, and D. Fisk. 1981. *Practical program evaluation for state and local government*. Washington: The Urban Institute Press.

Ironside, R. G. 1990. Regional development aid in the peripheral region of northern Alberta. In *A world of real places*, eds. P. J. Smith, and E. L. Jackson, 35–56. Edmonton, Alta.: Department of Geography, University of Alberta.

Kruse, J. A. 1984. Changes in the well-being of Alaska Natives since ANSCA. *Alaska Review of Social and Economic Conditions*, 21(3): 1–12.

McAllister, A. B. 1985. *Eastern Arctic study: Case study series, James Bay settlement*. Kingston: Center for Resource Studies.

McMillan, R. J. 1991. *Community development planning: The institutional impediments to state-sponsored community development in Canada's north: The case of the Northwest Territories housing corporation*. Vancouver: University of British Columbia.

Mercredi, O. 1994. A conversation with National Chief. *Mawiomi Journal*, Winter 1994.

Naqvi, K., B. Sharpe, and A. Hecht. 1995. Local attitudes and perceptions regarding development: Parry Sound, Ontario. *Canadian Journal of Regional Science*, 18(3): 283–305.

Poister, T. H., J. C. McDavid, and A. H. Magoun. 1979. *Applied program evaluation in local governments*. Lexington: D.C. Heath and Company.

Ram, R. 1982. Composite indices of physical quality of life, basic needs fulfillment and income: A principal component representation. *Journal of Development Economics*, 11: 227–48.

Robinson, R. P., M. Dickerson, J. V. Camp, W. Wuttunee, M. Pretes, and L. Binder. 1980. *Coping with the cash: A financial review of four northern land claims settlements with a view to maximizing economic opportunities from the next generation of claim settlements in the Northwest Territories*. Yellowknife: Culture and Communications.

Royal Commission on Aboriginal Peoples. 1996a. *Restructuring the relationship*, Vol. 2, Part 2. Ottawa: Minister of Supply and Services.

———. 1996b. *Perspectives and realities*, Vol. 4. Ottawa: Minister of Supply and Services.

Rummel, R. J. 1970. *Applied factor analysis*. Evanston: Northwestern University Press.

Saku, J. C. 1995. *The socio-economic impact of the Inuvialuit Final Agreement*. Ph.D. dissertation, Department of Geography, University of Saskatchewan.

Saku, J. C., R. M. Bone, and G. Duhaime. 1998. Towards an institutional understanding of comprehensive land claim agreements in Canada. *Études/Inuit/Studies*, 22(1): 109–21.

Sardi, L. 1994. Inuvialuit win $350,000 NWS helicopter contract. *Inuvik Drum*, February 17: 14.

Savoie, D. 1987. Politicians and approaches to regional development: The Canadian experience. *Canadian Journal of Regional Science*, 10: 215–29.

———. 1992. *Regional economic development: Canada's search for solutions*. Toronto: University of Toronto Press.

Schmidt, D., and L. Sardi. 1994. Inuvialuit get $1.5 million DEW line clean-up contract. *News North*, 49: A20.

Semple, H., and R. G. Ironside. 1992. The impacts of new resource industry on recipient and adjacent municipalities. *Canadian Journal of Regional Science*, 15(1): 59–80.

Slattery, B. 1987. Understanding aboriginal rights. *Canadian Bar Review*, 66: 726–83.

Smelie, J. 1989. Inuvialuit settlement generating wealth in region. *Nunatsiaq News*, September 1989: 11.

Smith, D. B. 1994. IDC turns profit for first time since 1980s. *News/North*, (May 16): A18.

Special Committee on the Northern Economy. 1989. *The Scone Report: Building our economic future*. Yellowknife: Legislative Assembly of the Northwest Territories.

Stabler, J. C. 1985. Development planning north of 60: Requirements and prospects. In *The North,* ed. M. S. Whittington, 23–51. Toronto: University of Toronto Press.

———. 1989. Dualism and development in the Northwest Territories. *Economic Development and Cultural Change*, 37(4): 805–39.

Stabler, J. C., and E. C. Howe. 1990. Native participation in northern development: The impending crisis in the NWT. *Canadian Public Policy*, 16(3): 262–83.

Stabler, J. C., G. Tolley, and E. C. Howe. 1990. Fur trappers in the Northwest Territories: An econometric analysis of the factors influencing participation. *Arctic*, 43(1): 1–8.

Statistics Canada. 1982a. *Population, occupied private dwellings, private households, census families in private households: Selected social characteristics, Quebec*. Ottawa: Minister of Supply and Services.

———. 1982b. *Population, occupied private dwellings, private households, census families in private households: Selected social characteristics, Northwest Territories*. Ottawa: Minister of Supply and Services.

———. 1983a. *Population, occupied private dwellings, private households, census families in private households: Selected social and economic characteristics, Quebec Part II*. Ottawa: Minister of Supply and Services.

———. 1983b. *Population, occupied private dwellings, private households, census families in private households: Selected social and economic characteristics, Northwest Territories*. Ottawa: Minister of Supply and Services.

———. 1987a. *Population and dwelling characteristics: Census divisions and subdivisions in Quebec—Part I*. Ottawa: Minister of Supply and Services.

———. 1987b. *Population and dwelling characteristics: Census divisions and subdivisions in Northwest Territories—Part I*. Ottawa: Minister of Supply and Services.

———. 1988a. *Population and dwelling characteristics: Census divisions and subdivisions in Quebec—Part 2, Volume II*. Catalogue no. 94-123. Ottawa: Minister of Supply and Services.

———. 1988b. *Population and dwelling characteristics: Census divisions and subdivisions in Northwest Territories—Part 2*. Catalogue no. 94-124. Ottawa: Minister of Supply and Services.

———. 1992a. *Profile of census divisions and subdivisions in Quebec—Part A, Volume II*. Catalogue no. 95-325E. Ottawa: Minister of Industry, Science and Technology.

———. 1992b. *Profile of census divisions and subdivisions in the Northwest Territories, Part A*. Catalogue no. 95-395E. Ottawa: Minister of Industry, Science and Technology.

———. 1994a. *Canada's aboriginal population by census subdivisions and census metropolitan areas*. Catalogue no. 94-326. Ottawa: Minister of Industry, Science and Technology.

———. 1994b. *Profile of census divisions and subdivisions in Quebec—Part B, Volume II*. Catalogue no. 95-326. Ottawa: Minister of Industry, Science and Technology.

———. 1994c. *Profile of census divisions and subdivisions in the Northwest Territories—Part B*. Catalogue no. 95-398. Ottawa: Minister of Industry, Science and Technology.

Tata, R. J., and R. R. Schultz. 1988. World variation in human welfare: A new index of development status. *Annals of the Association of American Geographers*, 78: 580–93.

Thomas, M. E. 1986. The Alaska native claims settlement act: Conflict and controversy. *Polar Record*, 33: 27–36.

Usher, P. J., F. J. Tough, and R. M. Galois. Reclaiming the land: Aboriginal title, treaty rights and land claims in Canada. *Applied Geography*, 12: 109–32.

Collective Behaviour
and
Social Movements

CLASSIC

CONTEMPORARY

CROSS-CULTURAL

69

Abortion Movements in Poland, Great Britain, and the United States

Janet Hadley

Perhaps one of the best-known feminist slogans during the early 1970s was that "A woman has a right to choose" whether to terminate a pregnancy. About 38 percent of the world's population lives in countries where abortion is available on request. Although abortion has been legal in the United States and most of Europe for at least twenty-five years, it remains an explosive issue in many countries and has spawned "for" and "against" social movements and collective behaviour. In this reading, Janet Hadley examines some of the controversies and campaigns of abortion rights movements in Poland, the United States, and Great Britain.

In recent years in the United States, in Poland, and in Ireland, too, national politics has at times been convulsed by the issue of abortion. In Germany the historic reunification of East and West almost foundered amid wrangling about conflicting abortion laws. How can abortion, hardly an issue comparable to the great affairs of state, such as the economy or national security, have an impact such as this?

This is an account, first, of how post-Communist Poland found itself in the grip of the abortion debate and secondly how the issue came to be such a seemingly permanent shadow on the political landscape in the United States, in the wake of the Supreme Court's 1973 landmark decision on abortion in the case of *Roe* v. *Wade*. It offers some ideas about why.

The account focuses on abortion, primarily as a method of birth control, which women have always sought out, legally when they can, illegally when they must. The controversies and campaigns recorded and the ideas offered here concentrate on women's access to affordable, safe and legal abortion—an essential part of women's reproductive freedom in a world where five hundred women die every day from the complications of unsafe abortion (World Health Organization, 1993).

The way abortion has at times dominated public debate in both Poland and the United States can hardly be exaggerated, but the contexts are very different. At times, during the 1992 American presidential election campaign, it seemed as if the fate of the United States for the next four years hung solely on the thread of the abortion issue. Economic issues, national security, even political scandals were all pushed into the background. But no one was too surprised to encounter this wild card in the United States' electoral politics. It had been thus, on and off, for around twenty years, since the 1973 Supreme

Source: Janet Hadley, "God's Bullies: Attacks on Abortion," *Feminist Review*, Vol. 48 (Fall 1994), pp. 94–113. Reprinted with permission of Taylor & Francis Ltd., Oxford, U.K.

Court judgement which had sanctioned abortion as a woman's constitutional right.

It was, however, probably a lot harder for anyone to have predicted events in Poland where, for more than four years, well before the forty-year-old Communist regime was finally sloughed off, abortion took centre stage. The renascent right in Poland selected abortion as the first block of the social welfare system for demolition. The battle over it highlights the new relationship between the Roman Catholic Church—once the main element of opposition alongside Solidarity—and the state. As the democratization of Eastern Europe got under way, abortion was one of the first laws to come under fire (Einhorn, 1993).

In some ways the abortion debate in Poland, which of all the former Soviet bloc countries has undergone by far the most draconian reversal of its abortion law, is quite straightforward: The opponents of abortion are solidly Roman Catholic and perceive their efforts as part of the task of rescuing Poland from its years of godlessness. The debate in Poland harks back to the relatively straightforward arguments which took place in Britain at the time of the passing of the Abortion Act in 1967.

In the United States, on the other hand, the issue has been linked to a much more extensive catalogue of perceived "social degeneracy." Opposition to abortion in the United States involves a curious alliance of religious and secular New Right groupings and much of the driving force has been provided, not by the Roman Catholic Church, but by evangelical Christians....

POLAND: NO PLACE TO BE A WOMAN

...What we have been witnessing in Poland since 1989, according to one observer, is the "Church's colossal efforts to replace a totalitarian state with a theocracy" (Kissling, 1992). Weekly Masses from Rome are broadcast on Polish TV these days. Scientific conferences open with High Mass, blessings and so on, and military personnel

are sent on pilgrimages. Classes in religion (i.e., Roman Catholicism) are mandatory for children in state schools. There is little doubt that the bishops of Poland, who behave more like leaders of a political party than as simple guardians of moral values, have their sights set not only on banning abortion but also divorce, provision of contraception, and other hallmarks of a secular society. One commentator wrote in 1991:

> From the very beginning until its unexpected culmination in June [1991—when a draft anti-abortion bill was rejected by parliament in the face of huge pro-choice demonstrations] the Polish controversy on abortion was a classic example of political conflict. Nobody cared any more about subtle moral or political arguments. It was clear that who wins the abortion debate will control the political situation in Poland. (Szawarski, 1991)

The irony is that not only was June 1991 far from being the "culmination," but also that nobody today could be said to have won. (Women, of course, lost.)

The final law, signed by President Lech Walesa in February 1993, was seen by opponents of abortion as a compromise. It is much weaker than they would have liked. The original anti-abortion bill, first published in 1989, promised three years' imprisonment for a woman who induced her own abortion, as well for any doctor caught performing an illegal operation. Under the new law, two years' imprisonment awaits an abortionist, but a woman inducing her own abortion will not face gaol [jail].

The new law allows abortion when a woman's life or health is in danger, after rape or incest, or if there is suspected fetal abnormality. But prenatal testing is only permissible if there is a family history of genetic disorder. There are token provisions urging local authorities to provide contraceptive services.

The Church's Power and Influence

The religious context of the abortion row in Poland goes a long way to explaining how it came to be such a passionate, extreme and dominating issue. Around 95 percent of its 39 million people consider themselves Catholic and there is a very strong family tradition of Catholicism, which during the Communist era greatly strengthened the Church as a focus of national identity and a shelter for opposition. Having a Polish Pope helps too; when John Paul II visited in 1991, he urged his fellow Poles to free themselves from a law permitting abortion, which he called a tragic inheritance of Communism.

Even when the Communist grip seemed at its most unyielding, the Church consistently harried the authorities on issues of sexual control. In a recent survey, conducted since the fall of the Communists, and reported in the *Guardian* (9/14/93), 95 percent of Polish women said they rely on personal experience for their sex education and 73 percent said they had had an unplanned pregnancy.

The only sex-education manual ever produced in Poland had to be withdrawn because of Church protest. Roman Catholic opposition to contraception has been effective—76 percent of the urban population and 87 percent of the rural population use only Church-approved 'natural' methods of fertility control (Mrugala, 1991). (Priests often determine what is sold in local pharmacies.) Poland's 1956 abortion law contained no conscience clause, but the Church's success in pressuring doctors can be judged from the fact that in some state hospitals, staff refusal made it impossible to get an abortion. As early as 1973, Church protests over the rising abortion rate and the behaviour of "callous young women" forced the government to set up a commission to consider whether the law needed amending (Okolski, 1988).

But the pressures on women to have abortions were very strong. Even for those who wanted it, contraception has never been easily available, and was of notoriously poor quality. Abortion—which was free in state hospitals after 1959, and easy to obtain—was therefore the main method of birth control. Women only had to report that they were "in a difficult life situation." "Poland's hard life finds more and more women choosing abortions," reported *The New York Times* in 1983, citing families in some cities waiting eighteen years to obtain a small apartment. Despite the Church's denunciations, there were an estimated 600,000 abortions a year, compared to just 700,000 live births.

Times may have been hard in 1983, but the economic "shock therapy" of post-Communist Poland has brought unimaginable hardship in its wake. Unemployment is now 2.8 million and will be one-fifth of the workforce in three years' time. The bishops have deplored this, by urging *women* to leave the labour market, to ease unemployment and ensure that men's wages increase. They have made no adverse comment on the virtual shutdown of state-financed child care.

The Bishops, the State, and the Medical Profession

The episcopate first floated the idea of outlawing abortion in 1988, deeming it to be a mortal threat to the "biological substance of the nation." In the spring of 1989 an Unborn Child Protection Bill was published and the Pope hurried to send his congratulations.

In 1990, however, long before the legislative battle had got into its stride, the Ministry of Health took its own initiative, saying that women wanting abortion would now need the permission of three physicians and of a psychologist, whose appointment had been approved by the local bishop, and that an abortion for social reasons must be requested in writing (*The New York Times*, 4/21/92). The psychologist's job is to dissuade women, mainly by putting the frighteners on them. Sterilization and the in-vitro fertilization programme were suspended.

As Poland created its first parliament, abortion became the bellwether for fitness to serve. Anyone supporting abortion rights was traduced as a surreptitious advocate for Communism. Throughout 1990 and 1991 the battle raged, overshadowing the upheavals of the new market economy. Huge demonstrations in favour of abortion took place in Warsaw and women's groups began to get organized to defend abortion rights. Solidarity was split on the issue. Bills were proposed and defeated in dizzying succession. Parish priests threatened to withhold sacraments from anyone who did not sign the petitions against "killing innocent children."

The anti-abortion movement targeted not only abortion but family planning provision, too, blocking the launch of an information campaign in the textile city of Lodz, where there has been an unusually high rate of congenital abnormalities among babies born to women working in the textile factories (Rich, 1991). Their activity was partly financed by pro-life organizations from the United States, such as Human Life International. This evangelical group, fired by a vision of "re-Christianized united Europe stretching from the Atlantic to the Urals," vowed to "flood Eastern Europe" with films, videos (such as *The Silent Scream* which has been shown in Polish schools), fetal models and other propaganda. In 1992, Operation Rescue blockaded a clinic in the Baltic port of Gdynia, with protesters from the United States, Canada and the U.K.

Although one smear in circulation was that "only communists and Jews favor abortion," there is little direct evidence that the antiabortion campaign was fuelled by a nationalist pro-natalism—a desire to demographically overwhelm Poland's minorities. There was, however, a definite bid to appeal to a repressive notion of proper and traditional Polish "womanhood." The term "emancipation for women" is laden with Communist overtones and has often in reality meant the notorious "double burden" or overloading of women, in Poland and Eastern Europe in general, in which they have been expected to shoulder full-time jobs as well as forty hours a week shopping, cooking, cleaning, laundry, with only the aid of very poor-quality pre-school child care and medical care (Jankowska, 1993). Against such a reality, a misty vision of womanhood may have a definite allure.

May 1992 brought another turn of the screw. A new code of medical ethics made it professionally unethical for doctors to perform abortions except in cases of rape or incest or when the woman's life was in danger. Violations would lead to suspension of the doctor's license. The code effectively ended hospital abortions and prenatal testing: Some institutions put up signs, "No Abortions."

The issue continued to rock the government, which twice postponed a final vote on abortion. By the end of 1992, the conflict was extreme enough to threaten the fragile coalition government, an improbable seven-party affair. A million people signed a petition for a referendum. Meanwhile, 61 percent of Poles said they favoured the provisions of the 1956 law.

Turning the Clock Back

Nevertheless, when the government could postpone a vote no longer, a law was finally passed early in 1993. Under the new law, only 3 percent of the abortions previously performed in Poland are now deemed legal. Two years in gaol awaits an illegal abortionist, but there is no punishment for a woman who obtains an illegal operation. Although it is the most restrictive abortion law in Europe, apart from Ireland's, pro-choice campaigners comforted themselves with the rueful thought that things could easily have been much worse.

The legislation satisfies no one. Both sides have vowed to fight on. Even before President Lech Walesa signed the new law, the 1992 doctors' code—a *de facto* ban on abortions in Poland—was having its effect. The Warsaw police morgue has begun receiving bodies of women bearing witness to botched abortions. For the last three years, cases of infanticide have steadily increased.

Deaths will be outnumbered by injuries. Romania, where abortion was illegal until the fall of Ceausescu in 1989, shows the way. Staff at a clinic for women in Bucharest, set up by Marie Stopes International, found that 80 percent of patients were suffering from past incompetent abortions.

A helpline set up in Warsaw by pro-abortion campaigners is receiving calls from men seeking advice because their wives are refusing to have sex any more. Women are phoning for help, reporting that even in circumstances which comply with the new law, they are being refused operations. In Poland's deep Catholic south, a pregnant Cracow woman, furnished with a police report confirming that she had been raped, was refused help at the hospital (Hoell, 1993).

All the desolately familiar symptoms of outlawed abortion are there: police raids on clinics, small ads appearing in the newspapers: "Gynaecologist: Interventions." The price is $350–1,000: The average monthly wage is $200. For professional women "medical tours" can be arranged—to the Ukraine, to Kaliningrad, even to Holland. (But not to the Czech Republic, which in the wake of Poland's new law, moved swiftly to outlaw abortions for foreign visitors.)

Paradoxically, the last few years have seen a burgeoning of women's organizations, formed to defend abortion and women's rights. It is an irony, comments Hanna Jankowska, "when the word 'feminist' sounds in this country like an insult" (1993). But sustaining the momentum of such organizations is uphill work. People are consumed by the effort to cope with the effects of 38 percent inflation.

There are signs that the Church may have overplayed its hand in its attempt to introduce a legislative version of "absolute morality" as part of a plan to create a theocratic Poland. There was strong public support for a referendum on abortion, which the Church opposed, and its popularity has dropped by half since Communism collapsed, according to opinion polls *(Catholic Herald*, 9/9/93). The Irish Church found itself in similar trouble after the referendum on abortion in Ireland in 1992, an event which was much reported in the Polish media.

But it is hard to draw sound parallels with Ireland: The Republic is certainly behind the times, but there are signs that slowly things are creeping forward for women in Ireland. Nothing compares with the crudeness with which the clock hands have been wrenched *back* in Poland.

In September 1993, the political coalition which fostered the anti-abortion legislation suffered a crushing defeat in national elections. The pace of reform was thought to be the main culprit, but the unpopularity of the anti-abortion law was also held to blame. Proabortion campaigners are preparing a new bill to reverse the law, scarcely before the ink is dry. In January 1994, Polish doctors amended their medical code, somewhat relaxing the abortion guidelines and increasing scope for prenatal diagnosis of fetal abnormalities.

The bishops and their allies intend to press on towards a theocratic state. They have stated: "We must reject the false and harmful belief—which unfortunately is grounded in social consciousness—that a secular state is perceived as the only and fundamental guarantee of freedom and equality of citizens" (Szawarski, 1991). If they succeed in creating a model Roman Catholic state, it will be women who suffer most directly. That is why no one in Poland, on whichever side of the abortion divide, underestimates the importance of the struggle around abortion as a stalking horse for what may yet come.

It is not possible to yoke together the national experience of abortion politics in Poland with that of the United States, only to offer them as two distinct examples of how abortion seemed at times to be the tail that wagged the dog of national politics. It has been quite remarkable to find abortion ricocheting around the political arena in Poland and other Eastern European countries. But the issue has played a crucial part in the politics of the United States for almost twenty years: in itself an astonishing phenomenon.

USA, 1973—THE SUPREME COURT LIGHTS THE FUSE

Until the historic U.S. Supreme Court judgment of 1973, in the case of *Roe* v. *Wade* (which I shall call plain *Roe*), abortion was not a major issue in the United States. In the late 1960s, when campaigners for abortion reform in California asked people to sign petitions, it took so long for people to think and talk before deciding where they stood that no more than four or five signatures could be gathered in an afternoon's work (Luker, 1984).

But the spark of *Roe* caught dry tinder at once and is still burning. Today, everyone has an opinion on abortion: After thousands of opinion polls, hours of TV debating, radio phone-ins and miles of newsprint, people know with certainty whether they are "pro-choice" or "pro-life."

In the late nineteenth century it was doctors who pressed for anti-abortion legislation in the United States, partly to strengthen the delineation of medicine as a regulated, elite profession. Making abortion illegal, unless performed by a doctor, was an effective way of cutting the ground from under the "quacks." The laws granted doctors alone the discretion to decide when a woman's life was sufficiently endangered to justify the loss of fetal life.

For almost seventy years legal abortion was a matter for medical judgement. Its prevalence and the criteria used varied enormously. Women who could not get legal abortions resorted to illegal practitioners and practices. But in the 1950s and 1960s exclusive medical control over abortion began to crumble.

Briefly, women's lives were changing as they entered the labour market in increasing numbers—for a married woman an unintended pregnancy became much more of a disaster than in the past; secondly, the improvements of medicine and obstetrics made pregnancy and childbirth much safer and made it harder for doctors to cloak a decision to perform an abortion for a wealthy patient behind the excuse that continuing the pregnancy would gravely endanger her health. Doctors' work became much more hospital-based and could be more easily scrutinized and regulated than when they worked in private consulting rooms.

Thirdly, women began to question the right of doctors and lawyers, or anyone, to decide whether or not they should have to continue an unintended pregnancy. Finally, the effects of the Thalidomide cases and the advent of effective contraception all played a part in dragging decisions and policies on abortion into the harsh public light of politics.

Some states began to permit abortion. Between 1967 and 1973, seventeen states rescinded their restrictions on abortion. Thousands of women crossed state boundaries to obtain abortions (Gold, 1990). Abortion was happening, despite its continuing prohibition under federal law.

Several decades of Supreme Court decisions—for instance, acknowledging it was no business of the state (or states) to seek to outlaw the use and purchase of contraceptives—had smoothed the path towards the *Roe* judgment, but nonetheless, when it eventually came, it was quite dramatic. The court said that a woman's right to obtain an abortion, like her right to use contraception without government interference is constitutionally protected, as part of her fundamental right to privacy. And that because the right to privacy is fundamental (rights under the American constitution are ranked, and *fundamental* trumps every other kind of right) states must show a "compelling interest" before they can intervene.

The court stressed that, of course, the decision to abort must be made together with a doctor. But it devised a sliding scale of maternal/fetal rights, practically sanctioning "abortion on demand" in the first trimester and gradually increasing the amount of protection afforded to the fetus as the weeks of pregnancy progressed.

No Room for Compromise

The significance of the Supreme Court ruling in 1973 was that it turned abortion into a constitutional issue, declaring it a fundamental right of the female citizen, and sweeping away all the various state restrictions. In doing so it called into question the deeply held beliefs of people accustomed to thinking that *theirs* was the majority opinion and set the state on a collision course with an indefatigable group of its citizens. As long as abortion had been purely a medical issue, as it is in Britain (see below) it had been much more difficult to challenge, and far less in the public domain.

The absolute divide between right-to-life/pro-life/anti-choice/anti-abortion people, and the rest is the embryo or fetus. If you believe that the embryo or later the fetus is a person, a human being in the fullest sense, the moral equivalent of a woman, everything else falls into place. The Supreme Court questioned this notion and opened the door to the years of court challenge, endless legislative pressure and single-issue pressure-group politics. For those who believe that abortion is the equivalent of homicide there can hardly be a compromise.

The impact of the *Roe* judgement was enormous. Overnight literally, the opposition mobilized.[1] Its attack has had two aims: to upset and overturn the judicial applecart and at the same time to erect as many obstacles as possible between a woman and a legal abortion. It's been a busy twenty years: *Roe* has been harried almost to extinction by state regulations, such as imposed waiting periods, demands for "informed consent," such as making the woman look at images of fetal development—at all stages, no matter how early her own pregnancy. As pro-choice campaigner Lawrence Lader said, after *Roe*, "We thought we had won. We were wrong" (*Family Planning World*, Jan/Feb, 1992).

At first, state attempts to regulate abortion after Roe received a cool response in the Supreme Court, but as the New Right has gained power and judges appointed to the court became more conservative, so the judgements have hardened against abortion rights.

Wide-ranging Success for Abortion's Opponents

The cultural and political climate today is of course very different from that surrounding *Roe* in 1973. On the day of the Supreme Court's ruling on *Roe*, newspapers reported an agreement which might bring an end to the war in Vietnam

and carried obituaries of former President Lyndon B. Johnson, whose presidency was marked domestically by the civil rights movement, Black Power and the movement against the war in Vietnam. This is not the place to rehearse the cultural "backlash" of the years since then except to highlight how wide-ranging it has been.

Susan Faludi, for instance, recounts the fate of a script for the TV show *Cagney and Lacey*. In "Choices," as the early 1980s' episode was to be called, Cagney—the single woman in the feisty female cop duo—became pregnant. CBS programming executives went beserk at the mere idea of abortion (even as an option to be rejected). They demanded numerous rewrites until in the final version, Cagney only mistakenly thinks she is pregnant. "Lacey…tells her that if she had been pregnant she should have got married. Abortion is never offered as a choice" (Faludi, 1992: 186).

The anti-abortion lobby drew comfort not only from *Cagney and Lacey* but also from the White House. As the violence against clinics increased in 1984 after Ronald Reagan's election to a second term as president, he refused to condemn the actions and their perpetrators (Blanchard & Prewitt, 1993).[2]

Opinion polls show that Americans' attitude to abortion was and generally remains "permit but discourage." It was not very hard to convert such ambivalence into support for restrictions on government funding and so on. The most significant curtailment of rights for low-income women was the Hyde Amendment of 1979 which denied Medicaid funding for abortion, except where a woman's life is in danger. There have also been severe and wide-ranging restrictions on the use of public facilities for abortion: It is illegal, for instance, to perform a private abortion in a private building standing on publicly owned land. By 1979 no federal funds could be used to provide abortion or abortion-related services (Petchesky, 1984).

Today, only half the United States' medical schools even offer the option of training in abortion procedures, and fewer and fewer young doctors are willing to perform abortions. Many gynaecologists still performing abortions are reaching retirement, and in a 1985 study, two-thirds of the gynaecologists in the United States stated that they would not terminate pregnancy. Who would choose to conduct their professional working life in a bullet-proof vest, with an armed guard at the clinic door? In 1988, 83 percent of all United States counties lacked any facilities for abortion, and those counties contain 31 percent of U.S. women aged between fifteen and forty-four (Alan Guttmacher Institute, 1993).

A shadowy world of unlicensed, unregulated abortion facilities in private doctors' offices is beginning to emerge. There are estimated to be several dozen in New York City alone, and a doctor there was recently prosecuted for a botched abortion on a twenty-one-year-old immigrant woman, who subsequently gave birth to a severely mutilated infant (*Family Planning World*, May/June, 1993).

And yet, despite all the legislative obstacles and the physical harassment, the anti-abortion movement has made no dent in the number of abortions taking place in the United States. The overall figure has hovered steadily around 1.6 million a year.

Who Opposes Abortion Rights?

The intimidation of anti-abortion activists, such as Operation Rescue, or the Lambs of Christ, and the violence and terrorism against abortion clinics is what immediately comes to mind when thinking about abortion's opponents, but it is not the only face of the opposition.

After the *Roe* judgment, the Catholic Church was the first into action, with plangent denunciation and millions of dollars poured into new anti-abortion organizations. But as the New Right in the Republican party set out deliberately to woo the anti-abortion voters, as part of its efforts to shift the party itself to the right, the anti-abortion alliance became a curious blend—from Catholics to born-again Christian evangelicals, to more secular "New Right" types. It was ultimately to prove a volatile coalition.

Abortion has been and still is the kernel of a protracted campaign against the social trends of the second half of the twentieth century, and for a reinstatement of "traditional family values." The Reagan presidency boosted the legitimacy, power and influence of "God's bullies" as they have been aptly called. Although the specific goal of the antiabortionists is to outlaw abortions, it is important to see this in a wider context of conservatism, attacks on welfare and so on.

The movement has two faces—first, the lobbyists and court challengers, as well as the image-makers, whose ideological offensive has sought to control the public perception of abortion and the women who seek it (Petchesky, 1984). In 1990 alone there were 465 abortion-related bills presented to state legislatures (McKeegan, 1992). The anti-abortion lobby has used its muscle in the ballot box with considerable effect. Single-issue voting can tip the scales when results are close and election turnouts are low. Packing state legislatures and other elected bodies has been a systematic strategy and for twenty years abortion has wracked the United States, from school boards to Congress.

Secondly, there is the face of direct action, some of it peaceful, but nevertheless extremely intimidating, some of it violent and explicitly women-hating. In 1991 in Wichita, south Kansas, there were more than 2,600 arrests as 30,000 anti-abortion protesters blockaded an abortion clinic. In the last fifteen years around a hundred clinics have been bombed or set on fire. Others have had medical equipment wrecked. Clinic staff and their families have been harassed; doctors have been shot at; in March 1993, one was even killed. Pregnant women arriving at abortion clinics have had to run a gauntlet of screaming demonstrators, some hurling plastic fetal models, some videotaping their faces and noting the numbers on their car license plates for subsequent tracing and personal harassment.

A study of men convicted of anti-abortion violence concluded that they are "clearly acting out of a desire to maintain the dependent status of women." Many also favour policies such as capital and corporal punishment (Blanchard & Prewitt, 1993). Somewhat in a grey area of legality lie the fake abortion clinics which have been set up and are listed in the Yellow Pages, which harangue women who turn up hoping to arrange an abortion, and force them to look at often gruesome pictures of fetuses.…

WHY HAS BRITAIN'S ABORTION DEBATE BEEN DIFFERENT?

It seems worth briefly comparing the struggle in the United States with that in Britain, whose political process has never been gripped by the throat as it has in the United States. Pro-choice Republican Senator Robert Packwood explained what the attentions of a single-minded group such as the U.S. anti-abortion lobby mean to his daily political life:

[The pro-lifers] are a frightening force. They are people who are with you 99 percent of the time, but if you vote against them on this issue it doesn't matter what else you stand for. (Tribe, 1992)

That's hard to imagine in Britain. Of course, there have been times when abortion has been a hot issue in the U.K., swelling MPs' mailbags and prompting heated exchanges on *Question Time,* but it has at no time been such dynamite, compelling British MPs to refer their every political step to its impact on those of their supporters who oppose abortion. Part of the reason is that Britain is relatively indifferent to religion and has no comparably powerful, organized fundamentalist or Roman Catholic population. Also, laws made in the United States Supreme Court positively invite legal challenge and counter-challenge. Laws made by Parliament are more resilient in general.

What's more, part of the reason is in the abortion law itself. It is for doctors, says Britain's 1967 Abortion Act—two doctors—to decide whether a woman needs an abortion, under the terms specified by the law. The rights of women do not remotely enter into it. Many campaigners who have defended the provisions of the 1967 Act, from no less than sixteen parliamentary attempts to curtail its scope, believe that it is the Act's reliance on doctors that has allowed it to escape relatively unscathed after twenty-five years.

When opponents of abortion in Britain have attacked the Act, its defenders have quite legitimately and cogently been able to point out that it is not *women* who make the final decision, but (respectable) professionals. (Funding cuts in the National Health Service and excessive Department of Health regulations have more stealthily debilitated abortion provision in Britain—that is another story.) Although the inherent paternalism in the framing of the Act is not only demeaning but has also led to unfair geographical differences in women's access to a sympathetic, prompt abortion service, the pragmatic, defensive value of investing the responsibility in the medical profession is worth noting.

CRITICAL THINKING QUESTIONS

1. Numerous physicians who provide abortion services have been murdered and Planned Parenthood clinics bombed in the United States. Why, in contrast, has Poland not experienced such violent attacks on the medical profession and on women who seek abortions?
2. In contrast to the United States and Poland, why has there been little debate about abortion in Great Britain?
3. Opponents of abortion in Europe and the United States often describe abortion as a breakdown of "social values" and the "traditional family." In contrast, proponents of abortion emphasize a woman's reproductive rights. According to Hadley, how do politics, religion, and economics ultimately shape policy and many women's destiny in abortion debates?

NOTES

1. Kristin Luker (Luker, 1984) describes how would-be activists phoned around frantically in the days after the court decision, trying to find an organization to join.

Many of them—women, married, housewives with small children, had never joined anything before—not even the school parent-teacher association.

2. Ronald Reagan not only refused to condemn the violence, in 1984 he wrote a bizarre call-to-arms against abortion, with help from Malcolm Muggeridge *(Abortion and the Conscience of the Nation.* Thomas Nelson, Nashville, 1984).

REFERENCES

Alan Guttmacher Institute. 1993. *Abortion in the United States: Facts in brief.* New York.

Blanchard, D., and T. J. Prewitt. 1993. *Religious violence and abortion.* University Press of Florida.

Einhorn, B. 1993. Polish backlash. *Everywoman,* April, 1993.

Faludi, S. 1992. *Backlash.* London: Vintage.

Gold, R. B. 1990. *Abortion and women's health: The turning point for America.* New York: Alan Guttmacher Institute.

Hoell, S. 1993. Strict new law drives abortion underground in Poland. *Reuters,* 14 December.

Jankowska, H. 1993. The reproductive rights campaign in Poland. *Women's Studies International Forum,* 16, 3: 291– 96.

Kissling, F. 1992. The Church's heavy hand in Poland. *Planned Parenthood in Europe* 21, 2 (May): 18–9.

Luker, K. 1984. *Abortion and the politics of motherhood.* Berkeley: University of California Press.

McKeegan, M. 1992. *Mutiny in the ranks of the right.* New York: The Free Press, Maxwell Macmillan International.

Mrugala, G. 1991. Polish family planning in crisis: The Roman Catholic influence. *Planned Parenthood in Europe* 20, 2, (September): 4–5.

Okolski, M. 1988. 'Poland' in Sachdev, P., *International handbook on abortion.* New York: Greenwood Press.

Petchesky, R. 1984. *Abortion and woman's choice.* New York, Longman.

Rich, V. 1991. Poland: Abortion and contraception. *Lancet,* 338, 875, (13 July): 108–9.

Szawarski, Z. 1991. Abortion in Poland. *British Journal of Obstetrics and Gynaecology,* 98 (December): 1202–4.

Tribe, L. 1992. *Abortion: The clash of absolutes.* New York, Norton.

World Health Organization. 1993. *Progress in human reproductive research,* No. 25. Geneva.

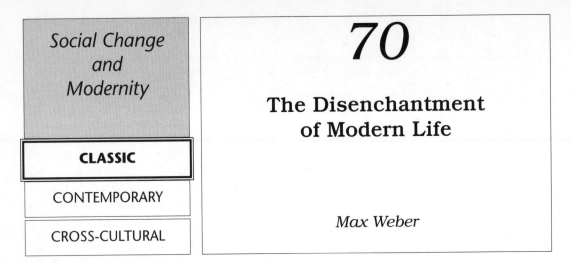

Social Change
and
Modernity

CLASSIC

CONTEMPORARY

CROSS-CULTURAL

70

The Disenchantment
of Modern Life

Max Weber

In this excerpt from the speech "Science as a Vocation," delivered at Munich University in 1918, Weber claims that the rise of science has changed our way of thinking about the world. Where, in the past, humans confronted a world of mystical forces beyond comprehension, we now assume that all things yield to human comprehension. Thus, Weber concludes, the world has become "disenchanted." Notice, however, that something is lost in the process for, unlike the churches of the past, science can provide no answer to questions of ultimate meaning in life.

Scientific progress is a fraction, the most important fraction, of the process of intellectualization which we have been undergoing for thousands of years and which nowadays is usually judged in such an extremely negative way. Let us first clarify what this intellectualist rationalization, created by science and by scientifically oriented technology, means practically.

Does it mean that we, today, for instance, everyone sitting in this hall, have a greater knowledge of the conditions of life under which we exist than has an American Indian or a Hottentot? Hardly. Unless he is a physicist, one who rides on the streetcar has no idea how the car happened to get into motion. And he does not need to know. He is satisfied that he may "count" on the behavior of the streetcar, and he orients his conduct according

to this expectation; but he knows nothing about what it takes to produce such a car so that it can move. The savage knows incomparably more about his tools. When we spend money today I bet that even if there are colleagues of political economy here in the hall, almost every one of them will hold a different answer in readiness to the question: How does it happen that one can buy something for money—sometimes more and sometimes less? The savage knows what he does in order to get his daily food and which institutions serve him in this pursuit. The increasing intellectualization and rationalization do *not,* therefore, indicate an increased and general knowledge of the conditions under which one lives.

It means something else, namely, the knowledge or belief that if one but wished one *could* learn it at any time. Hence, it means that principally there are no mysterious incalculable forces that come into play, but rather that one can, in principle, master all things by calculation. This means that the world is disenchanted. One need no longer have recourse to magical means in

Source: Excerpts from *From Max Weber: Essays in Sociology* by Max Weber, edited by H. H. Gerth & C. Wright Mills, translated by H. H. Gerth & C. Wright Mills. Translation copyright © 1946, 1958 by H. H. Gerth and C. Wright Mills. Used by permission of Oxford University Press, Inc.

order to master or implore the spirits, as did the savage, for whom such mysterious powers existed. Technical means and calculations perform the service. This above all is what intellectualization means....

Science today is a "vocation" organized in special disciplines in the service of self-clarification and knowledge of interrelated facts. It is not the gift of grace of seers and prophets dispensing sacred values and revelations, nor does it partake of the contemplation of sages and philosophers about the meaning of the universe. This, to be sure, is the inescapable condition of our historical situation. We cannot evade it so long as we remain true to ourselves. And if Tolstoi's question recurs to you: As science does not, who is to answer the question: "What shall we do, and, how shall we arrange our lives?" or, in the words used here tonight: "Which of the warring gods should we serve? Or should we serve perhaps an entirely different god, and who is he?" then one can say that only a prophet or a savior can give the answers....

To the person who cannot bear the fate of the times like a man, one must say: May he rather return silently, without the usual publicity build-up of renegades, but simply and plainly. The arms of the old churches are opened widely and compassionately for him. After all, they do not make it hard for him. One way or another he has to bring his "intellectual sacrifice"—that is inevitable. If he can really do it, we shall not rebuke him. For such an intellectual sacrifice in favor of an unconditional religious devotion is ethically quite a different matter than the evasion of the plain duty of intellectual integrity, which sets in if one lacks the courage to clarify one's own ultimate standpoint and

rather facilitates this duty by feeble relative judgments. In my eyes, such religious return stands higher than the academic prophecy, which does not clearly realize that in the lecture-rooms of the university no other virtue holds but plain intellectual integrity: Integrity, however, compels us to state that for the many who today tarry for new prophets and saviors, the situation is the same as resounds in the beautiful Edomite watchman's song of the period of exile that has been included among Isaiah's oracles:

> He calleth to me out of Seir, Watchman, what of the night? The watchman said, The morning cometh, and also the night: if ye will enquire, enquire ye: return, come.

The people to whom this was said has enquired and tarried for more than two millennia, and we are shaken when we realize its fate. From this we want to draw the lesson that nothing is gained by yearning and tarrying alone, and we shall act differently. We shall set to work and meet the "demands of the day," in human relations as well as in our vocation. This, however, is plain and simple, if each finds and obeys the demon who holds the fibers of his very life.

CRITICAL THINKING QUESTIONS

1. In what sense do members of a traditional society know more about their world than we do? In what sense do we know more?
2. What is "Tolstoi's question"? Why can science not answer it?
3. What does Weber see as the great burden of living in a modern society? In other words, what comforts of the past are less available to modern people?

71

Running Out of Control: Understanding Globalization

R. Alan Hedley

Hedley offers an introduction to globalization and its many technological, social, economic, and political ramifications. His analysis requires us to reflect on our own situation from a global perspective and from a sociological perspective.

Albert Einstein (1936) once observed that the categories are not inherent in the phenomena. In other words, concepts such as "globalization" and "information and communications technology revolution" are human constructs we have developed in order to understand better the complexities of what we believe is happening in the world. Theories are simplified models of reality, and the first step in theory construction is categorization or classification. Over the past few decades, researchers and social commentators have coined the term "globalization" in order to focus on what they believe are interrelated processes which are having tremendous impacts on our lives in the late twentieth and early twenty-first centuries. Consequently, there is no one correct definition of globalization; it has many different meanings and interpretations, depending upon who is discussing it and in what context. However, there are elements of agreement as to what globalization means.

The derivation of the term "globalization" implies that it involves worldwide processes that are relatively novel and still unfolding. These multidimensional processes are being experienced unevenly throughout the world and in different sectors of social life. *Globalization is a complex set of human forces involving the production, distribution/transmission, and consumption of technical, economic, political, and sociocultural goods and services which are administratively and technologically integrated on a worldwide basis.* This definition highlights the point that globalization comprises technological, economic, political (including military), and sociocultural dimensions. Together these interrelated dimensions make up the (human) global system which operates within the broader global ecological environment.

Source: Abridged from "Understanding Globalization" in *Running Out of Control: Dilemmas of Globalization*, by R. Alan Hedley, pp. 5–37. Bloomfield, Conn.: Kumarian Press, 2002. Reprinted with permission of the publisher.

Concerning the four dimensions of globalization,...innovations in transportation, communication, and information processing within the past three or four decades have permitted the creation of a technological infrastructure that facilitates the other dimensions of globalization. While technology may be seen as the facilitating means to modern globalization, the primary motivation has been economic—the harnessing of natural and human resources and the establishing of markets and investments worldwide by capitalist enterprise to achieve greater corporate control. In part, to counter the forces of technologically enhanced global capitalism, and to represent civic interests, governments and nongovernmental organizations have also globalized through the formation of international alliances. However, these coalitions have been insufficient to moderate the effects of another important dimension of globalization—the worldwide cultural overlay of Western values, norms, institutions, and practices. Because globalization was initiated predominately by corporations and countries in the Western world, inevitably, what is produced, transmitted, and consumed is monocultural. Thus, globalization as a multidimensional concept involves a worldwide technological infrastructure in which Western-style capitalism predominates.

Finally, if technology facilitates globalization, the ecological biosphere within which we all live represents its outside limits. Certainly during the past few decades, mounting evidence on a variety of fronts such as climate change, pollution, ozone depletion, cumulative environmental degradation, and population growth indicates we are nearing these limits. Consequently, globalization also involves a critical tension between our technological ability to modify the natural environment and the ultimate ecological constraints beyond which human existence is impossible.

In the following section, I describe the various forces instrumental in producing our globalized world.

FORCES OF GLOBALIZATION

The world has always been a large place, but in some sense it has become much smaller than it was. It measures 25,000 miles in circumference (*Britannica,* 1999). As recently as the late nineteenth century, the great science fiction writer Jules Verne wrote the then unbelievable novel, *Around the World in Eighty Days*. Today, not only can we physically circumnavigate the world in one day, we can electronically orbit the planet in just eight seconds (Phillips, 1996)—three hundred times faster than Shakespeare's magical Puck. Globalization is both feasible and viable now because of technological innovations in transportation, communication, and information processing during the latter part of the twentieth century. In fact, many experts claim that these interrelated innovations constitute the basis for a new technological revolution every bit as significant as the industrial revolution some 250 years earlier.

A major impetus for this recent revolution was World War II, itself a global phenomenon. Government-sponsored research centers produced myriad inventions and discoveries that were applied to the war effort. Some of these, most notably the work in nuclear fission, rocketry, and jet engines, contributed directly to the arsenal of the warring nations, whereas others such as materials development (plastic, superalloys, aluminum, and synthetics) made more indirect contributions. A third area of concentration involved the development of reliable, high-speed support systems, and it was in this context that the computer and telecommunications industries were created and set the stage for the information and communications technology (ICT) revolution that was to follow.

The fact that these technological innovations were organizationally sponsored highlights a second underlying force of globalization. In the years following World War II, organizations in the private, public, and civil sectors all harnessed these innovations to suit their purposes. In the private sector, corporations employed these innovations to secure competitive advantage by becoming transnational in their operations. In the public sector, governments entered into international alliances in attempts to create a stable world order out of the chaos produced by the War. And in reaction to these moves on the part of organizations in the private and public sectors, ordinary citizens—civil society—formed international nongovernmental [NGOs] organizations of their own in order to achieve what they believed were important development objectives. Consequently, technologically enhanced organizations of all types were also instrumental in ushering in the global age.

Finally, on an individual basis, people all over the world also helped to bring about globalization. They enthusiastically adopted the numerous technological innovations in transportation, communication, and information processing to reach out and touch others, both physically and electronically, all around the globe.

Following is a discussion of each of these three main forces of globalization.

Technological Forces

Transportation Notable innovations in transportation during the past fifty years include the launching of container ships for shipping raw materials and finished manufactured goods worldwide, the introduction of commercial jets, and the debut of space travel. With regard to container ships, Herman (1983: 135) states that "the impact of containerization on the shipping industry can rightly be compared to the impact which steamships had on the field when they were first introduced over a hundred years ago." A container ship has specially designed holds, hatches, and cranes which enable it to take whole truck trailers on board without loading or unloading their contents. This reduces ship time in port (from 65 [percent] to 25 percent annually), cuts stevedoring costs, and virtually eliminates pilferage. It also permits the construction of larger, faster (from fifteen [knots] to twenty-five knots), more fuel-efficient vessels which reduces total

operating expenses. For example, Herman (1983: 135) cites comparative statistics on the North Atlantic route for 1970: "fifty containerships provide a tonnage greater by approximately one-third than the one hundred and seventy vessels which operated there only one-half decade before." And given that "over 80 percent of world trade by volume is carried by ship" (Herman, 1983: 3), the inducements offered by containerization are substantial.

The idea of container ships emerged in 1951 when a shipping company "took a converted truck body as deck cargo from Miami to Puerto Rico" (Gilman, 1983: 8). Pearson and Fossey (1982: 220) report that only 106 container ships were built worldwide prior to the 1960s; however, in the 1960s, 478 were constructed, and in the following decade, 1,931 more container ships were launched.

While container ships are important for the efficient and speedy transportation of goods, jet aircraft are invaluable for transporting people and time-sensitive cargo quickly around the globe. The first commercial jet airline service was introduced in Britain in 1952 (Woytinsky & Woytinski, 1955: 500). By 1962, "the difference in speed between the fastest piston-engined transport and a jet was 240 miles an hour, a differential almost as great as all the speed increases made by commercial airplanes between 1918 and 1953" (Serling, 1982: 100). In effect, the world became smaller and more accessible. Recent figures on worldwide air traffic demonstrate this point. According to the International Civil Aviation Organization (ICAO, 2001), in 1999 world airlines carried some 1.6 billion people and 28.2 million metric tons of air cargo (see Box 71.1).

The concept of globalization received a major boost on October 4, 1957, when the Soviet Union successfully launched Sputnik I, the first-ever space satellite. About the size of a basketball and weighing 183 pounds, it took just ninety-eight minutes to orbit the planet (NASA, 2000). Subsequent space flights provided the first photographs of the Earth as a globe. No longer

BOX 71.1
FEDEX: A GLOBAL CORPORATION

At 11:45 a.m. on June 11, 2000, I shipped a paper by FedEx from my office in Victoria, Canada, to a colleague in Madras, India. From Victoria, the paper went to Vancouver (4:16 p.m.) and Memphis, Tennessee (6:14 p.m.), FedEx headquarters and central routing hub. My paper left Memphis on 06/12/00 at 2:46 a.m. bound for the European hub city of Paris (8:18 p.m.), and then on to Dubai in the Persian Gulf (2:17 p.m., 06/13/00), and Bombay, India (3:00 a.m., 06/14/00), where it had to wait for commercial customs release (11:00 a.m.). My paper arrived in Madras (9:08 a.m., 06/15/00) and was finally delivered to my Indian colleague (11:30 a.m.).

All of this information I obtained from entering my FedEx tracking number at the FedEx Web site (**www.fedex.com**). My paper was merely one of millions of shipments that FedEx handles and tracks every day.

According to a July 11, 2000, FedEx Corporation press release posted on its Web site:

FedEx Express, a $15 billion subsidiary of FedEx Corp., connects areas that generate 90% of the world's gross domestic product in 24–48 hours with door-to-door, customs cleared service and a money back guarantee. The company's unmatched air route authorities and infrastructure make it the world's largest express transportation company, providing fast, reliable and time-definite transportation of more than 3.3 million items to 210 countries each working day. FedEx employs approximately 145, 000 employees and has more than 43,000 drop-off locations, 663 aircraft and 44,500 vehicles in its integrated global network. The company maintains electronic connections with more than 2.5 million customers via FedEx Powership®, FedEx Ship®, and FedEx InternetShip®.

was it necessary only to conceptualize it in this fashion; now we could actually *see* it as a spherical whole. Space flight literally produced a new world view of planet Earth. Our world definitely became smaller.

Communication and Information Processing

While technological innovations in transportation reduced the constraints of time and space, advances in communications and information processing technology have virtually eliminated these formerly circumscribing barriers, thus accounting for the claims of a new ICT revolution.

Naisbitt (1982) discusses how developments in information and communications technology have collapsed what he calls the "information float"—the time it takes for a sender of information first to collect and process information, and then to transmit it through some communication channel to a receiver, who also must process it. Whereas the information float was a factor that could not be ignored before the 1970s, today it is trivial. Naisbitt (1982: 23) explains:

One way to think about the foreshortening of the information float is to think about when the world changed from trading goods and services to standardized currencies. Just imagine how that speeded up transactions. Now, with the use of electrons to send money around the world at the speed of light, we have almost completely collapsed the…information float. The shift from money to electronics is as basic as when we first went from barter to money.

At the very core of this transformation was the creation of the electronic microchip:

In the microchip, combining millions of components operating in billionths of seconds in a space the size of the wing of a fly, human beings built a machine that overcame all the conventional limits of mechanical time and space. Made essentially of the silicon in sand—one of the most common substances in earth—microchips find their value not in their substance but in their intellectual content: their design or software. (Gilder, 1989: 12)

Business applications of the microchip took place between 1969 and 1971 at Intel Corporation, which "developed all the key components of the personal computer—the working memory, the software memory, and the microprocessor CPU" (Gilder, 1989: 92). Thus was born the first stage of the ICT microelectronic revolution.

Another stage came into being in 1970 when scientists at Corning Glass Works announced that they had "created a medium [optical fiber] that could transport unprecedented amounts of information on laser beams for commercially viable distances" (Diebold, 1990: 132), thus providing the first revolutionary medium for what is now known as the information highway—the Internet. In parallel with this discovery, work was also proceeding on wireless and satellite connectivity (Bell Labs, 1999).

Coincident with these developments, another momentous event in the creation of the ICT revolution occurred in 1969. In order to withstand the possibility of a nuclear military attack, the U.S. Department of Defense's Advanced Research Projects Agency created a centerless network of supercomputers at major universities and research centers, such that if one computer was struck, the others could still function independently (Flower, 1997; Kahn, 1999). Called ARPNET, this electronic network was the forerunner of the Internet which was formally established in 1989. "Widespread development of LANS [local area networks], PCs [personal computers] and workstations in the 1980s, [as well as the growing use of e-mail], allowed the nascent Internet to flourish" (Leiner et al., 2000).

All of these developments, taking place at approximately the same time, together formed the foundation for a globalized world little constrained by time and space. And, given recent leading edge developments in transportation, communication, and information processing, there is every reason to expect this trajectory of innovation to continue. In fact, as a result of these innovations the distinction among these terms is becoming blurred. Consider, for example, the relatively new practice of telecommuting—the partial or complete substitution of telecommunications services for transportation to a conventional workplace. In reality, it is a creative and innovative blend of all three of these processes. According to a 2001 survey of the U.S. labor force, 28.8 million workers were transporting themselves both physically and electronically to work (International Telework Association, 2001); worldwide, the number of teleworkers is projected to rise to 137 million by 2003 (Edwards, 2001). Other creative blends of transportation, communication, and information processing include teleconferencing, teleshopping, virtual education, virtual surgery, and space satellites.

Although I have provided specific dates when these various technological innovations were recorded in history, in actual fact they took years to come to fruition. The years following World War II (particularly given the breakup of European colonial empires and the Cold War tensions between capitalism and communism) represented an era of economic reconstruction and scientific enterprise and application. However, as Table 71.1 indicates, a global ICT infrastructure is by no means in place for the vast majority of the world. Most people living in low and middle income countries (85 percent of the world's population) are on the other side of what has been termed the digital divide. Substantial proportions of people have yet even to acquire electricity or access a telephone. The World Resources Institute (2000) contends "as much as 80 percent of the world's population has never made a phone call." In addition, it estimates that there are more telephones in New York City than in all of rural Asia, and more Internet accounts in the city of London than in the continent of Africa. Although the Internet connected approximately 513 million people in 2001 (Nua Internet Surveys, 2001), that represents only 8.4 percent of the world's population. In other words, while many significant technological innovations have indeed been achieved since World War II, they have yet to be diffused globally.

Table 71.1   Transportation, Communication, and Information Indicators

Indicators	Income of Countries			
	Low	Middle	High	World
Population (millions, 1999)	2417	2667	891	5975
Percent population	40.5	44.6	15	100
Kilograms of oil equivalent consumption per capita (1997)	563	1368	5369	1692
Air passengers carried (millions, 1998)	54	292	1121	1467
Percent air passengers	3.7	19.9	76.4	100
Radios per 1000 people (1997)	157	359	1286	418
TV sets per 1000 people (1998)	76	257	661	247
Telephone main lines/1000 (1998)	23	109	567	146
Mobile telephones/1000 (1998)	2	31	265	55
Personal computers/1000 (1998)	3	23	311	71
Internet hosts/10,000 (Jan./00)	0.4	10	777	120

Source: Adapted from World Bank, 2001: 275, 293, 309, 311.

Note: According to the World Bank (2001: 271): "Economies are classified into three categories according to income…. The GNP per capita cutoff levels are as follows: low-income, $755 or less in 1999; middle-income, $756–9,265; and high income, $9,266 or more."

Organizational Forces

Transnational Corporations   A transnational corporation (TNC) is "any enterprise that undertakes foreign direct investment, owns or controls income-gathering assets in more than one country, produces goods or services outside its country of origin, or engages in international production" (Biersteker, 1978: xii). Variously termed multinational corporations or multinational enterprises, transnational corporations are formal business organizations that have spatially dispersed operations in at least two countries. One of the most transnational of all major TNCs (see Table 71.2) is Nestlé, the Swiss food giant: 84 percent of its total assets, 99 percent of its sales, and 97 percent of its workforce are foreign-based (UNCTAD, 1999: 78).

Although TNCs were in existence prior to the twentieth century (colonial trading companies such as the East India Company, Hudson Bay Company, and the Virginia Company of London were precursors of the modern TNC), it is only since the 1960s that they have become a major force on the world scene (World Bank, 1987: 45). Table 71.3 corroborates this fact by listing the foreign direct investment (FDI) stock of corporations at various intervals during the twentieth century. In 1900, only European corporations were major transnational players, but by 1930 American TNCs had begun to make their presence felt. The year 1960 is pivotal because it marks the new global era in corporate transnationalization. For each of the decades from 1960 to the present, world FDI stock has more than tripled, whereas it only doubled during the entire first half of the twentieth century.

Table 71.2   Annual Revenues of Leading Corporations and Gross National Products of Selected Countries 1998–99 (billions of US$)

Nation/Corporation	GNP/Revenues
United States (1)	$7,921.3
Japan (2)	4,089.9
Germany (3)	2,122.7
France (4)	1,466.2
United Kingdom (5)	1,263.8
General Motors (1)	176.6
Denmark (23)	176.4
Wal-Mart Stores (2)	166.8
Exxon Mobil (3)	163.9
Ford Motor (4)	162.6
DaimlerChrysler (5)	160.0
Norway (25)	152.1
Greece (31)	122.9
South Africa (32)	119.0
Mitsui (6)	118.6
Mitsubishi (7)	117.8
Toyota Motor (8)	115.7
General Electric (9)	111.6
Iran (33)	109.6
Royal Dutch/Shell Group (11)	105.4
Israel (36)	95.2
Nippon Telegraph and Telephone (13)	93.6
International Business Machines (16)	87.5
BP Amoco (17)	83.4
Volkswagen (19)	80.1
Malaysia (39)	79.8
Hitachi (23)	71.9
Chile (42)	71.3
Matsushita (24)	65.6
Philip Morris (29)	61.8
Sony (30)	60.1
Boeing (32)	58.0
New Zealand (46)	55.8
Honda Motor (34)	54.8
Nissan Motor (36)	53.7
Czech Republic (48)	51.8
Toshiba (38)	51.6
Bank of America (39)	51.4
Nestlé (41)	50.0
Hungary (51)	45.6

Sources: For annual revenues of corporations, *Fortune*, 2000: F1–F2; for GNP, World Bank, 2000: 230–31.

Notes: Gross national product (GNP) measures the total value of goods and services produced by citizens (resident and nonresident) of a particular nation. The numbers in parentheses refer to the overall rank of a nation or corporation in terms of either GNP or revenues.

The phenomenal increase in transnational corporate activity during the last four decades may be accounted for in large part by the technological innovations in transportation, communication, and information processing I have just discussed. They permitted corporations to establish profitable worldwide operations and still maintain effective and timely control. Not since before World War II and the Great Depression which preceded it had the corporate sector much opportunity to demonstrate its economic clout. It was in this mood that it eagerly embraced all technological innovations that would give it competitive advantage. Consequently the threefold increase in foreign direct investment between 1960 and 1971 by technologically enhanced, transnationalizing corporations reveals another manifestation of the new global age. Table 71.3 indicates that TNCs from just eleven countries accounted for 82 percent of all foreign direct investment in 1999. American TNCs comprised almost one-quarter of the total foreign investment, and corporations in the Triad (United States, European Union, and Japan) were responsible for nearly 80 percent of world FDI stock (UNCTAD, 2000: 300). Clearly, TNCs mainly operate out of and invest in the developed countries of the global economy.

The magnitude of foreign investment flow in the world is illustrated by the fact that worldwide sales of foreign affiliates in 1999 were $13.6 trillion. This figure is almost twice as high as world exports of goods and services valued at $6.9 trillion (UNCTAD, 2000: 4). This means that global networks of transnational corporations have replaced in importance traditional import-export practices of the past in terms of delivering goods and services to markets worldwide. In 1999, some 63,000 TNCs controlled 690,000 foreign affiliates around the globe (UNCTAD, 2000: 9). These two sets of facts underline the central and growing importance of TNCs in structuring international economic relations.

The rise of modern transnational corporations and the power they hold are reflected in Table 71.2

Table 71.3   Foreign Direct Investment Stock by Country (billions of US$)

Country	1900[a]	1930[a]	1960[a]	1971	1980	1990	1999[b]
United States	0.5	14.7	31.8	82.8	220.2	430.5	1131.5
United Kingdom	12.1	18.2	13.2	23.1	80.4	229.2	664.1
Germany	4.8	1.1	0.6	7.0	43.1	151.6	420.9
Netherlands	1.1	2.3	1.7	3.5	42.1	109.0	306.4
France	5.2	3.5	2.2	9.2	23.6	110.1	298.0
Japan	neg[c]	neg	neg	4.3	19.6	201.4	292.8
Switzerland	neg	neg	neg	6.5	21.5	66.1	199.5
Canada	neg	1.3	3.0	5.7	23.8	84.8	178.3
Italy	neg	neg	neg	NA[d]	7.3	57.3	168.4
Belgium & Luxembourg	neg	neg	neg	NA	6.0	40.6	159.5
Sweden	neg	0.5	0.5	3.3	3.7	49.5	105.0
Others	neg	neg	neg	13.5	31.9	186.2	834.9
Total[e]	23.8	41.6	53.8	159.2	523.2	1716.4	4759.3

Sources: Data for 1970–71 adapted from Buckley, 1985: 200. Data for 1980–1999 from UNCTAD, 2000: 300–5.

Notes:

a. Includes foreign portfolio (individual) investment and foreign direct (TNC) investment.

b. Estimates.

c. Negligible.

d. Not available.

e. World total, excluding Comecon countries, except for 1998.

which compares the annual revenues of some of the world's largest global companies with the gross national products (the annual total value of goods and services produced by resident and nonresident citizens of a particular country) of selected countries. For example, General Motors, the leading corporation in revenues in 1999, had the twenty-third largest economy in the world ($176.7 billion), edging out Denmark at $176.4 billion, and surpassing by far the combined national output of New Zealand, Hungary, and the Czech Republic. These statistics would appear to give some truth to the old saying that "what's good for General Motors is good for the country" (Wilson, 1952). Of the one hundred largest economies in the world, nearly half (forty-nine) are transnational corporations (*Fortune,* 2000: F1–F2; World Bank, 2000: 230–31).

Of the five hundred largest corporations in the world, more than one-quarter (128) are in the financial sector (banks, insurance, and securities) (*Fortune,* 2000: F15–F21). A major reason for this is that most of the services and products financial firms provided can be traded electronically, and consequently these organizations have taken great advantage of the new global ICT infrastructure. As the editors of *Fortune* (2000: F15) state: "Money went global long before 'globalization' became a buzzword. That's why banks have the most entries on the [Global 500] list, as well as the highest revenues and profits." Other firms well represented in the Global 500 are those instrumental in the move toward globalization: modern transportation (aerospace, airlines, and courier services), communication (telecommunications, network communications, and mass media), and information processing (computers, computer services, and electronics). Of these corporations, those in the mass media have been extremely influential in promoting a global perspective in that they transmit content as well as providing infrastructure....

Environmental Movement   The environmental movement is comprised of many grass-roots and international NGOs, as well as scientific organizations, all over the world. What makes it unique in establishing the case for globalization is the growing realization that our planet and everything on it comprise a very complex, interdependent, living whole. This means that when humans modify their environment in certain ways—such as urbanization, agriculture, forestry, mining and so forth—other consequences, both foreseen and unforeseen, are bound to follow. Approximately thirty years ago, the concept of biological diversity or biodiversity—"the total variability of life on Earth"—was coined, largely in an attempt to focus research on the extent to which human beings are contributing toward environmental degradation, and whether some of the evident trends are reversible (Heywood & Baste, 1995). It was also at this time that the concept of sustainable development originated (Fisher, 1993).

Why is biodiversity important? Aside from being important for the particular natural systems under siege and for providing needed resources such as food, water, shelter, and medicine for human survival, there is a more comprehensive set of reasons relating to globalization as a worldview.

> The sheer diversity of life is of inestimable value. It provides a foundation for the continued existence of a healthy planet and our own well-being. Many biologists now believe that ecosystems rich in diversity gain greater resilience and are therefore able to recover more readily from stresses such as drought or human-induced degradation. When ecosystems are diverse, there is a range of pathways for primary production and ecological processes such as nutrient cycling, so that if one is damaged or destroyed, an alternative pathway may be used and the ecosystem can continue functioning at its normal level. If biological diversity is greatly diminished, the functioning of ecosystems is put at risk. (Biodiversity Unit, 1993)

Contributing to the concept of Earth as an interconnected organism, the American National Aeronautics and Space Administration (NASA), in conjunction with Japan and the European Space Agency, has launched a series of satellites that have established "an international Earth-observing capability" involving "a global-scale examination of the Earth to study the interaction

of all the environmental factors—air, water, land, biota—that make up the Earth system" (NASA, 1996). NASA reports that "scientists have been observing the Earth from space for more than 30 years, making measurements of the atmosphere, the oceans, the polar regions and land masses" (NASA, 1996).

Consequently, the environmental movement has been instrumental in altering people's perceptions of the world in which they live. Instead of focusing only on the particular geographical location in which they live, human beings are now coming to realize that their actions may have consequences for the world at large and for the quality of life they and subsequent generations will enjoy.

Individual Forces

Physical Migration   As well as technological innovations and transnational organizations and alliances, individual people also comprise a globalizing force in that the human population, aided largely by improvements in transportation, has become increasingly mobile in a variety of ways.

Mass movements of people around the globe is a post-war phenomenon. During World War II, international travel was restricted, and during the Great Depression before it, the world economy rarely permitted it. With respect to emigration, the most permanent form of human migration, it is only since the war that vast numbers of people have emigrated, mostly from poor to rich countries. The major receiving countries have been the United States, Germany, Canada, and Australia (World Bank, 2000: 38), such that their populations have become increasingly diverse. The World Bank (2000: 37–40) reports that in recent years between two and three million people emigrate annually, with the consequence that now more than 130 million are living outside the countries in which they were born. To these figures must be added international refugees, and as conflicts and natural disasters have risen, so has forced migration. In

1975, the world's international refugees numbered 2.5 million, but just twenty years later, that total had multiplied almost ten times to 23 million (World Bank, 2000: 38).

Less permanent forms of migration include international guest workers (mostly to Europe and the United States), exchange students, and tourists. The demand for guest workers, mainly from North Africa, South Asia, and Mexico, is partly a function of the global economy, but increasingly it is tied to the demographic profile of the industrially developed countries. As a whole, the total fertility rate in the high income countries is below replacement level (1.7 births per woman), and the population is aging (World Bank, 2000: 243), which could lead to eventual labor shortages. To the extent that these trends continue, demand for foreign labor could increase substantially during the twenty-first century.

Study abroad and foreign exchange are also relatively recent occurrences in terms of the numbers involved and variety of programs offered. For example, at my own mid-sized university, there are currently 118 student and faculty exchange agreements with other universities in 27 different countries (UVic International, 2000). In 1998–99 in the United States, almost half a million foreign students enrolled in colleges and universities, three times more than in the mid-1970s (Open Doors, 1999a). In turn, nearly 114,000 American students studied abroad during 1997–98, a 15 percent increase over the previous year (Open Doors, 1999b). Worldwide, Switzerland has the greatest percentage (15.9 percent) of foreign students at the tertiary level, followed by Australia (12.6 percent), Austria (11.5 percent), and the United Kingdom (10.8 percent) (OECD, 2000c). Clearly, the option to complete at least part of a degree program in another country has become increasingly viable.

International tourism has also expanded enormously during the past fifty years. According to the World Tourism Organization (2000), "Between 1950 and 1999 the number of international arrivals has shown an evolution from a mere 25 million

international arrivals to the current 664 million, corresponding to an average annual growth rate of 7 percent." Not only has the number of tourists increased, so too have their destinations. In 1950, almost all of the 25 million tourists went to just fifteen countries; however, in 1999, more than seventy countries hosted at least one million international visitors. Air transport was the most common means of travel (43.7 percent), followed by road (41.4 percent), sea (7.8 percent), and rail (7.0 percent), and France, Spain, the United States, Italy, and China were the most popular destinations. (See Box 1.2 to find out who accompanies these international travelers.)

Not only is international tourism a significant force of globalization, it also contributes in a huge way to the global economy:

In 1998, international tourism and international fare receipts (receipts related to passenger transport of residents of other countries) accounted for roughly 8 percent of total export earnings on goods and services worldwide. Total international tourism receipts, including those generated by international fares, amounted to an estimated US$532 billion, surpassing all other international trade categories. (World Tourism Organization, 2000)

In other words, international tourism generates more revenue than international trade in either automotive products ($525 billion), chemicals ($503 billion), food ($443 billion), computer and office equipment ($399 billion), fuels ($344 billion), textiles and clothing ($331 billion), or telecommunications equipment ($283 billion). And considering that international tourism is on an annual growth trajectory of 7 percent, it will only become a more important contributor to the world gross domestic product.

Electronic Migration Not only are people physically traversing the globe in increasing numbers, they are also orbiting it electronically at a skyrocketing rate. The International Telecommunication Union (ITU, 2000) reports that international telephone calls in 1999 reached a new high of 100 billion minutes, climbing an average of 10 billion

BOX 71.2
MICROBES FLY THE GLOBAL SKIES

A report in my local newspaper (*Times Colonist,* 10/13/00: A1) warned of "a big year for flu" because so many people from all over the world attended the Olympics in Australia, which "had an especially prolonged flu season this year." A check at FluNet, maintained by the World Health Organization (WHO) **(http://oms2.b3e.jussie.fr/FluNet/f_recent_activity. htm)** confirmed that there had been a "regional outbreak" of influenza in Australia between September 10 and October 14, 2000.

A search at the WHO site led me to the *WHO Report on Global Surveillance of Epidemic-prone Infectious Diseases* **(www.who.int/emc-documents/surveillance/whocdscsrisr2001c.html)** which states: "In the modern world, with increased globalization, and rapid air travel, there is a need for international coordination and collaboration. Everyone has a stake in preventing epidemics." The *Report* focuses on nine infectious diseases (including influenza) all of which have "high epidemic potential."

More recently, with outbreaks of hoof and mouth and mad cow diseases in Europe, especially Britain, customs officers and disease control experts in all countries are taking special precautions to prevent the global spread of these highly infectious diseases via international travelers. These measures include prohibiting passengers from carrying any agricultural products with them, mandatory notification of any farm contact, requiring antibiotic foot baths for the shoe soles of all deplaning passengers, placing additional inspectors and dog teams at airports, and public education programs **(www.naturalhealthyliving.com/article1007.html)**.

The Centers for Disease Control and Prevention headquartered in Atlanta in the United States maintain a comprehensive "Travelers' Health" Web site **(www.cdc.gov/travel)**.

---

minutes per year since 1995. According to the ITU, "the world market for telecommunications (services and equipment) doubled between 1990 and 1999," and is being driven now by the burgeoning mobile cellular communications market. "At the end of 1999, there were more than 450 million subscribers around the world, up from just 11 million in 1990,…a compound annual growth rate of more than 50 percent per year" (ITU, 2000). The ITU estimates that mobile cellular subscribers will actually exceed conventional fixed-line users during this decade.

Also contributing to the rapid growth of electronic migration is the use of the Internet in general and for e-mail in particular. As I have already reported, Nua Internet Surveys (2001) estimated that 513 million people had accessed the Internet at least once during the three months before August 2001, and this figure is projected to rise to more than 765 million by 2005 (CommerceNet, 2000). In January 2002, the Internet Software Consortium counted more than 147 million host sites on the Internet, almost 38 million more than it enumerated twelve months earlier. Quite clearly, all forms of electronic communication are growing exponentially.

COUNTERFORCES TO GLOBALIZATION

On at least three levels, huge proportions of humanity are put at risk by the forces of globalization, and consequently, there are growing signs that many people are actively resisting the global age. On the most general level, examine how the world is divided by region. In describing various regions of the world, certain terms come to be adopted, first by official agencies such as the United Nations and national governments, and then more generally by scholars, journalists, and others interested in making sense out of international relations and development. For example, in 1980 Willy Brandt coined the terms "North" and "South" in his *Report of the Independent Commission on International Development Issues* (Brandt Report, 1980). In this report is a map of the world with a bold line dividing it into two parts—North and South.... I have used the terms "developed" and "developing" countries which are categories created by the United Nations to classify all countries in the world. This classification scheme mirrors the North–South dichotomy. These terms are often used as convenient labels to divide the world into two camps—rich and poor. The fact that the global ICT revolution is presently taking place largely in the rich, developed North is generating backlash in the poor, developing South. Many fear that it could broaden the already enormous development gap between North and South (South Commission, 1990).

Paralleling and exacerbating this development gap is a cultural gap which has widened as a result of globalization. On the one side are predominant Western cultural perspectives and values, including Christianity and the global use of English. On the other side are non-Western cultural perspectives and values, including religions other than Christianity and non-European languages. Individual countries and cultural groups within the South are voicing concerns that the forces of globalization could threaten their ethnic, religious, and linguistic heritage and ways of living (Hedley, 2000: 595–97).

Finally, within the developed countries, there is what might be termed a growing class disparity. Studies of the distribution of income and wealth over the last three decades of the twentieth century reveal increasing inequality and polarity (Morris & Western, 1999; Keister & Moller, 2000). It is claimed that global restructuring has caused at least part of this disparity. Consequently, workers and citizens who are not part of the vanguard of the global era, although they are the overwhelming majority, are increasingly disaffected by the promises of globalization.

On each of these three levels of analysis—regional, cultural, and class—it is the larger of the two categories that is at risk from the forces of globalization. Thus, from the perspective of the South, or the non-Western, or the masses, globalization is not viewed with enthusiasm, and consequently active opposition to it could result. These constitute the counterforces to globalization.

...The global technological and organizational infrastructure has been established primarily by corporations, governments, and individuals in rich developed countries for their own benefit. As I mentioned, the overwhelming majority of the world's population has yet to be connected to this infrastructure.... To date, globalization is an exclusionary force, denying active participation to particular regions, cultures, and classes. In turn, this is causing backlash. For many nations, cultures, institutions, organizations and individuals in the world, modern globalism constitutes and elitist, Northern-based, Western-focused, technologically supported form of economic and cultural imperialism. In order to turn this vicious circle into a virtuous circle, the President of the World Bank (Wolfensohn, 1997: 6) has issued a *Challenge of Inclusion* "to reduce...disparities across and within countries, to bring more people into the economic mainstream, [and] to promote equitable access to the benefits of development regardless of nationality, race, or gender." Whether this challenge becomes reality remains to be seen; however, until it does, the world as a whole cannot truly be characterized as globalized.

CRITICAL THINKING QUESTIONS

1. Review the innovations in transportation and communication discussed in this article and how they have fuelled globalization. Do you feel that these two areas will continue to influence global change? Why or why not?
2. What are the positive aspects of transnational corporations (TNCs)? What are the negative aspects?
3. Discuss why biodiversity is important when discussing globalization. Do you feel that environmental movements are becoming more or less influential? Use examples to support your position.
4. Compare and contrast physical and electronic migration. Which do you feel will be a more important source of migration over the next 50 years? Why?

REFERENCES

Bell Labs. 1999. Wireless Milestones. [Online}. Available: **http://www.lucent.com/minds/trends/trends_v4n1/ timeline.html**. Accessed 08/23/00.

Biersteker, T. J. 1978. *Distortion of development? Contending perspectives on the multinational corporation.* Cambridge, Mass.: MIT Press.

Biodiversity Unit, Commonwealth of Australia. 1993. Biodiversity Series, Paper No. 1. [Online]. Available: **http://kaos.erin.gov.au/life/general_info/op1.html**. Accessed 05/29/00.

Brandt Report. 1980. *North-South: A program for survival. Report of the Independent Commission on International Development Issues.* Cambridge, Mass.: MIT Press.

Britannica. 1999. Earth. [Online]. Available: **http://www.britannica.com/bcom/eb.arti…/ 0,5716,32267+1+31726,00.html.** Accessed 10/02/00.

Buckley, P. J. 1985. Testing theories of the multinational enterprise. In *The economic theory of the multinational enterprise,* eds. P. J. Buckley, and M. Casson. London: Macmillan.

CommerceNet. 2000. Worldwide Internet Population. [Online]. Available: **http://www.commerce.net/ research/stats/wwstats.html**. Accessed 10/05/00.

Diebold, J. 1990. *The innovators: The discoveries, inventions, and breakthroughs of our time.* New York: Truman Talley Books/Plume.

Edwards, J. 2001. Government—help or hindrance to deployment of teleworking? [Online]. Available:

http://www.cefrio.qc.ca/allocutions/presentations/ johnedwards.ppt. Accessed 01/18/02.

Einstein, A. 1936. Physics and reality. Journal of the Franklin Institute 221(3). Reprinted in *Ideas and opinions by Albert Einstein,*. ed. C. Seelig, 1954, 290–323. New York: Wings Books.

Fisher, J. 1993. *The road from Rio: Sustainable development and the non-governmental movement in the third world.* Wesport, Conn.: Praeger.

Flower, J. 1997. The future of the Internet: an overview. In *The future of the Internet,* eds. D. Bender et al., 10–7. San Diego, Calif.: Greenhaven.

Form, W. 1979. Comparative industrial sociology and the convergence hypothesis. *Annual Review of Sociology,* 5: 1–25.

Fortune. 2000. The Fortune Global 500. *Fortune,* 142(3): 227–F24.

Gilder, G. 1989. *Microcosm: The quantum revolution in economics and technology.* New York: Simon & Schuster.

Gilman, S. 1983. *The competitive dynamics of container shipping.* Aldershot, U.K.: Gower.

Hedley, R. A. 2000. Convergence in natural, social, and technical systems: A critique. *Current Science,* 79(5): 592–601.

Herman, A. 1983. *Shipping conferences.* Deventer, Neth.: Kluwer, Law and Taxation.

Heywood, V. H., and I. Baste. 1995. In *Global biodiversity assessment,* eds. V. H. Heywood, and R. T. Watson, 1–9. Cambridge: Cambridge University Press.

ICAO. 2001. Growth in air traffic projected to continue. [Online]. Available: **http://www.icao.org/icao/en/ pio200106.htm**. Accessed 06/24/01.

International Telework Association. 2001. Telework American 2001. [Online]. Available: **http://www.telecommute.org/ twa/twa2001/newsrelease.htm**. Accessed 01/18/02.

ITU. 2000. ITU Telecommunication Indicators Update. [Online]. Available: **http://www.itu.int/journal/200006/ E/html/indicat.htm**. Accessed 10/10/00.

Kahn, R. E. 1999. Evolution of the Internet. In *World communication and information report 1999–2000,* 157–64. Paris: UNESCO.

Keister, L. A., and S. Moller. 2000. Wealth inequality in the United States. *Annual Review of Sociology,* 26: 63–81.

Leiner, B. M. et al. 2000. A brief history of the Internet. [Online]. Available: **http://www.isoc.org/internet/ history/brief.shtml**. Accessed 05/11/02.

Morris, M., and B. Western. 1999. Inequality in earnings at the close of the twentieth century. *Annual Review of Sociology,* 25: 623–57.

Naisbitt, J. 1982. *Megatrends: Ten new directions transforming our lives.* New York: Warner.

NASA. 1996. The Earth Observing System: Understanding planet Earth. [Online]. Available: **http:// pao.gsfc.nasa.gov/gsfc/service/gallery/fact_sheets/ earthsci/fs-96(06)-009.htm**. Accessed 09/27/00.

NASA. 2000. Sputnik and the dawn of the space age. [Online]. Available: **http://www.hq.nasa.gov/office/pao/History/sputnik/**. Accessed 09/27/00.

Nua Internet Surveys. 2001. How many online? [Online]. Available: **http://www.nua.ie/surveys/how_many_online/index.html**. Accessed 01/18/02.

OECD. 2000c. *OECD in figures*. Paris: Author.

Open Doors. 1999a. Fast facts. [Online]. Available: **http://www.opendoorsweb.org/Press/fast_facts.htm**. Accessed 10/05/00.

———. 1999b. 113,959 U.S. students have studied abroad this year. [Online]. Available: **http://www.opendoorsweb.org/Lead%20Stories/stab1.htm**. Accessed 10/05/00.

Pearson, R., and J. Fossey. 1983. *World deep-sea container shipping: A geographical, economic and statistical analysis*. Aldershot, U.K.: Gower.

Phillips, P. 1996. *Jules Verne, around the world in eighty days*. [Online]. Available: **http://www.people.virginia.edu/~mtp0f/flips/review3.html**. Accessed 09/26/00.

Serling, R. J. 1982. *The jet age*. Alexandria, Va.: Time-Life.

South Commission. 1990. *The Challenge to the South: The report of the South Commission*. New York: Oxford University Press.

UNCTAD. 1999. *World investment report 1999*. New York: United Nations Conference on Trade and Development.

———. 2000. *World investment report 2000*. New York: United Nations Conference on Trade and Development.

UVic International. 2000. [Online]. Available: **http://www.uvic.ca/international.html**. Accessed 09/26/00.

Wilson, C. E. 1952. Statement to the Senate Armed Forces Committee. In *Familiar quotations,* ed., John Bartlett (1980), 817. Boston: Little, Brown.

Wolfensohn, J. D. 1997. *The challenge of inclusion*. Address to the board of governors of the World Bank Group, Hong Kong, China.

World Bank. 1987. *World development report 1987*. New York: Oxford University Press.

———. 2000. *World development report 1999/2000*. Oxford: Oxford University Press.

———. 2001. *World development report 2000/2001*. Oxford: Oxford University Press.

World Resources Institute. 2000. WRI conference explores new businesses to transform global digital divide into dividends. [Online]. Available: **http://www.igc.org/wri/press/dd_transform.html**. Accessed 10/17/00.

World Tourism Organization. 2000. Tourism highlights 2000. [Online]. Available: **http://www.world-tourism.org/esta/monograf/highligh/HL_MK.htm.** Accessed 10/05/00.

Woytinsky, W. S., and E. S. Woytinski. 1955. *World commerce and governments: Trends and outlook*. New York: Twentieth Century Fund.

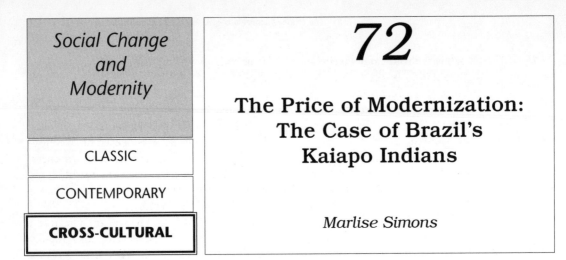

Social Change and Modernity

CLASSIC

CONTEMPORARY

CROSS-CULTURAL

72

The Price of Modernization: The Case of Brazil's Kaiapo Indians

Marlise Simons

Among the billions of poor people throughout the developing world, few have a chance for a better life. But the Kaiapo, people who live deep in Brazil's rain forest, have found a way to improve their lives. Has affluence been the blessing that the Kaiapo imagined it would be? To some, the modernization of the Kaiapo amounts to little more than the systematic destruction of their traditional way of life.

It is getting dark when Chief Kanhonk sits down in the yard outside his home, ready for a long evening of conversation. Night birds are calling from the bush that sparkles with fireflies. Whooping frogs make a racket by the river. No one seems worried by the squadron of bats sweeping low overhead.

It is that important moment of the day when Indians of the Amazon, who use no written language, meet to talk, pass on information, and tell stories. The night is when they recall ancestral customs, interpret dreams, and comment on changes in nature and other events of the day. But from a nearby home come the sounds of a powerful rival: A television set is screeching cartoons at a group of children. I understand now why, that morning, by way of saying hello, these naked children of the rain forest had shouted things like "He-Man" and "Flintstones."

Source: "The Amazon's Savvy Indians," by Marlise Simons, *The New York Times Magazine,* February 26, 1989, pp. 36–37, 48–52. Copyright © 1989 by The New York Times Company. Reprinted with permission.

Three years ago, when money from the sale of gold nuggets and mahogany trees was pouring into Gorotire, Chief Kanhonk agreed to bring in television, or the "big ghost," as it is called here. A shiny satellite dish now stands on the earthen plaza like an alien sculpture, signaling that Gorotire—a small settlement of some 800 people on the Fresco River, a tributary of the Amazon—has become one of the wealthiest Indian villages in Brazil.

Yet Chief Kanhonk appears to regret his decision. "I have been saying that people must buy useful things like knives or fishing hooks," he says darkly. "Television does not fill the stomach. It only shows our children and grandchildren white people's things."

The "big ghost" is just one of the changes that have been sweeping over Gorotire, but it seems to be worrying the elders the most. Some believe it is powerful enough to rob them of their culture. Bebtopup, the oldest medicine man in the village, explains his misgivings: "The night is the time the old people teach the young people. Television has stolen the night."

When I discuss this with Eduardo Viveiros, a Brazilian anthropologist who works with a more isolated Amazonian tribe, he seems less worried. "At least they quickly understood the consequences of watching television," he says. "Many people never discover. Now Gorotire can make a choice."

It was the issue of choice that first drew me to the Kaiapo Indians of the lower Amazon Basin. They seemed to be challenging the widely held notion that forest Indians are defenseless in face of the pressures of the competitive and predatory Western world around them. Unlike most of Brazil's 230,000 Indians, they go out into the white world to defend their interests, and it is no longer unusual to see Kaiapo men—in their stunning body paint and feathered headdresses—showing up in Congress in Brasilia, the nation's capital, or lobbying by doing a war dance outside a government office. They have even bought Western gadgets to record and film their festivals.

Once the masters of immense stretches of forest and savannas, the Kaiapo were for hundreds of years among the most skillful farmers and hunters and fiercest warriors of central Brazil. They terrified other tribes with their raids. From the seventeenth to the nineteenth centuries, they not only resisted the slaving raids of the Portuguese invaders but they also attacked white traders and gold prospectors with such a vengeance that royal orders came from Portugal to destroy the Kaiapo. The white man's wrath and his diseases killed many, yet there are still close to 3,600 Kaiapo in more than a dozen different villages near the Xingu River. They have quarreled and regrouped, but their lands, several vast reservations, are more secure than those of many other tribes.

After many years of isolation in the forest, the Kaiapo now have to deal with the growing encroachments of white society. "They are going through a great transition," says Darrell Posey, an American anthropologist who has worked in Gorotire for more than a decade. "Their survival is a miracle in itself. But I worry whether they can go on making the changes on their own terms."

Colombia, Ecuador, Peru, and Venezuela—four of nine nations in the Amazon Basin, which harbors some 800,000 Indians—each have large numbers of tropical-forest Indians. But nowhere are pressures on Indian land as great as they are in Brazil. As the Amazon is opened up, developers bring in highways, settlers, cattle ranchers, mines, and hydroelectric dams. In Brazil alone, more than ninety tribes have disappeared since the beginning of this century.

The clearing of large areas of the rain forest and the fate of the Indians are also rapidly becoming an issue of international concern. Interest in the region has risen as ecological concerns, such as ozone depletion, the greenhouse effect, and other changes in the global environment become political issues. More attention is paid to scientists who are alarmed at the destruction of the rain forest—a vital flywheel in the world's climate and the nursery of at least half of the world's plant and animal species.

This has also prompted an increasing interest in the highly structured world of the forest Indians and their ancient and intricate knowledge of nature that permits them to survive in the tropical jungle without destroying it. (The Hall of South American Peoples, which includes a life-size model of a Kaiapo warrior, recently opened at the Museum of Natural History in New York City.)

As Indians find greater support among environmentalists, they also get more organized in their fight to protect their habitat. The Kaiapo held their first international congress last week in Altamira, in central Brazil, protesting government plans to build several massive dams that would flood Indian land.

In Brazil, Indian tribes occupy 10 percent of the nation's territory, although much of their land has not been demarcated. Brazil's past military regimes elevated Indian affairs to a national-security issue, because many tribes live in large areas of border land. It is official policy to integrate Indians into the larger society, and the National Indian Foundation, with its 4900 employees, is in charge of implementing this.

In my eighteen years in Latin America, I have heard many politicians and anthropologists discuss what is usually called "the Indian problem," what to "do" about cultures that have changed little in thousands of years. One school of thought holds that the remote tribes should be kept isolated and protected until they can slowly make their own choices. Another school accepts that the Indian world is on the wane, and talks about "guiding" the Indians toward inevitable change—a process that should take several generations.

But some anthropologists and politicians, including the Brazilian government, believe in still more rapid integration. When Romeo Jucá was head of the Indian Foundation, he said that it was only right for Indians to exploit their wealth, even if it meant acculturation. "We have to be careful how fast we go," he said, "but being Indian does not mean you have to be poor."

Gerardo Reichel-Dolmatoff is one of Latin America's most respected anthropologists. He insists that the Indians are their own best guides into Western society. An Austrian-born Colombian, Reichel-Dolmatoff has worked in Colombia's forests, at the Amazon's head-waters, for almost fifty years. "We cannot choose for them," he insists. "And we cannot put them into reserves, ghettos, ashokas. They are not museum exhibits.... If Indians choose the negative aspects of our civilization, we cannot control that. If there is one basic truth in anthropology, it is that cultures change. Static cultures do not exist."

The Indians themselves are pleading for more protection and respect for their cultures. Conrad Gorinsky, son of a Guyana Indian mother and himself a chemist in London, recently said: "We don't want the Indians to change because we have them comfortably in the back of our mind like a kind of Shangri-La, something we can turn to even if we work ourselves to death in New York. But we are hounding and maligning them instead of recognizing them as the guardians of the forests, of the world's genetic banks, of our germ plasma and lifelines."

The aboriginal peoples we call Indians are as different from one another as, say, Europeans are. Even the most isolated groups remain separate fiefdoms with widely varying experiences, beliefs, and histories. The degree of contact they have with the outside world is just as varied.

I first met Kaiapo tribesmen three years ago in Belém, a large city at the mouth of the Amazon. I saw them again in Brasilia, the capital. In both places, they demonstrated their political skills and capacity to mobilize, showing up in large numbers to protest measures by the government. They seemed particularly adept at commanding the attention of the press. Their body paint, feathers, and other paraphernalia made them appear warlike, exotic, and photogenic.

Back in Gorotire, as it turns out, they are more "ordinary." Wearing feathers and beads, explains Kubei, a chief's son, is for special occasions. "It's our suit and tie." Besides the satellite dish, the Kaiapo also have their own small airplane. Their new wealth has also given them the luxury of hiring non-Indians to help plant new fields. But they remain ready to attack white intruders; some of the adult men have markings on their chests that record the number of outsiders they have killed.

Two roads fan out from the center of Gorotire. A new sand track leads east on a five-hour drive to the town of Redenção. The other road goes south and, in a sense, it leads into the past. Dipping into the forest, it becomes a path that meanders through open patches where the Kaiapo women grow corn, sweet potatoes, bananas, manioc. On the plain ahead, it joins an ancient trail system that once reached for hundreds of miles into northern and western Brazil.

One morning, Beptopup (medicine man, shaman, connoisseur of nature), the anthropologist Darrell Posey (who speaks the Kaiapo language), and I wander into the bush. Beptopup walks past the plants the way you go down a street where you know everyone. Stopping, nodding, his face lighting up with happy recognition, he sometimes goes into a song—a soft, high-pitch chant for a particular plant.

He picks leaves, each one familiar, each one useful. One serves to remove body hair. Another, he says, can prevent pregnancy. The underside of one leaf is so rough it is used to sandpaper wood and file fingernails. Beptopup collects his plants in the morning, he says, because "that is when they have the most strength."

Stopping at a shrub, we look at the large circle around its stem, where nothing grows. "This and other plants have been sent to a laboratory for analysis," says Posey. "We think this one has a natural weedkiller."

Beptopup holds up a branch of what he calls the "eye of the jaguar." "This was our flashlight," he says, showing how to set it afire and swing it gently so its strong glow will light one's path.

One afternoon, when the heat has crept into everything, the women and children come back from the fields to their village. They stop and sit in a creek to escape the swirling gnats and buzzing bees. Others sit outside their homes, going about their age-old business. One woman plucks the radiant feathers of a dead macaw. Another removes her eyebrows and eyelashes, because the Kaiapo women think they are ugly. (A nurse once told me that this custom might have a hygienic origin—to ward off parasites, for instance.) Kaiapo women also deepen their foreheads by shaving the top of their head in a triangle that reaches the crown—a fearsome sight to the unaccustomed eye.

I envy a mother who is clearly enjoying herself fingerpainting her three children. She draws black designs with genipap juice. On the face and the feet she puts red dye from the "urucu," or annatto, plant; Indians say it keeps away chiggers and ticks.

Change has come to Gorotire along the other road, the one leading east to Redenção. Recent Kaiapo history is full of "firsts," but a notable turning point came when prospectors struck gold on Gorotire land in 1980. The Kaiapo raided the camp, twenty miles from the village, but failed to drive away the trespassers. Then they made a deal.

Last fall, when I was visiting Gorotire, about 2,000 gold diggers were stripping the land to the bone farther upstream, and the River Fresco passed the village the color of mud, its water contaminated with oil and mercury. I heard no one complain about that. Gorotire gets 7 percent of the mine's profits—several pounds of gold a week.

In 1984, a lumber company completed the first road. It signed a contract with the Indian Foundation for Gorotire's mahogany (the Indians are wards of the Brazilian government). Most of the mahogany is gone now, and the government agency split the profits with the Kaiapo. Gorotire chose to spend its gold and timber profits on new water and electricity lines and rows of brick houses. Only about half of the inhabitants now live in traditional palm-frond huts.

The young Kaiapo who earn a salary as supervisors at the gold camp have bought their own gas stoves, radios, sofas, and mattresses. For the community, the four tribal chiefs ordered several boats, trucks, and a small plane that ferries people and goods among nearby Kaiapo villages.

One evening, a truck arriving from Redenção—bringing rice, sugar, bottled gas, oil for the generator—is another reminder of how fast Gorotire is adapting to a Western economy. From being a largely self-sufficient community of hunters and farmers, it is now increasingly dependent on outside goods. In Gorotire, it is clearly money, no longer disease or violence, that has become the greatest catalyst for change. Money has given the Kaiapo the means and the confidence to travel and lobby for their rights. At the same time, it is making them more vulnerable.

I have seen other villages where Indians have received large sums of money—for the passage of a railroad or a powerline, or from a mining company. Such money is usually released in installments, through banks, but its arrival has put new strains on the role of the chiefs. Money and goods have introduced a new, materialistic expression of power in societies that have been egalitarian. Among most Indians, a man's prestige has always depended not on what he acquires but on what he gives away.

In Gorotire, some of the young men complain that the chiefs are not distributing community money and goods equally, that the chiefs' relatives and favorites are getting a bigger share and more privileges.

Darrell Posey, the anthropologist, believes the greatest political change came with the road. With it, he says, "the Kaiapo chiefs lost control of which people and what goods would come in." Previously, the chiefs had been the sole distributors. They had also played the vital roles of keeping the peace and leading the ceremonies. Now, the chiefs hardly know the liturgy of the ceremonies; their main task seems to be to deal with the outside world.

The transition is also changing the role of the medicine man. Bebtopup, for example, has an arsenal of remedies for the common ailments—fevers, diarrheas, snake bites, wounds. But he and his colleagues have lost prestige because they do not know how to deal with the diseases brought to Gorotire by white men, such as the pneumonia that strikes the children and the malaria spreading from the gold miners' camp.

Anthropologists sometimes say that when outsiders visit the Indian world, they often focus on themes central not to Indians but to themselves. This might explain why I was so bothered by the garbage, the flotsam of Western civilization.

Gorotire's setting is Arcadian. It lies on a bluff overlooking the River Fresco, with views of the forests across and the mountains behind. Spring rains bring waterfalls and blossoms. But these days the village is awash with rusting cans, plastic wrappers, tapes sprung from their cassettes, discarded mattresses, and clothes. New domestic animals such as dogs, pigs, and ducks have left a carpet of droppings. And giant rats, which suddenly appeared some years ago, seem to be everywhere; some have bitten small children.

"Indians have never had garbage that was not biodegradable," says Sandra Machado, a Brazilian researching Kaiapo farming techniques here. "No one wants to take care of it."

It is a mild moonlit evening, and in the men's house many Kaiapo are watching soccer on television. The bank of the river is a quieter place to talk. "If you look beyond the garbage and the stone houses, this is still a strong and coherent indigenous culture," says Darrell Posey, speaking of the mixed feelings he has about a decade of developments in Gorotire. "Despite everything, the language is alive, the festivals and initiation rights are observed."

Posey says that the Kaiapo in Gorotire and in other villages continue with their age-old natural farming techniques, using plants to fix nitrogen in the soil, chunks of termite nests instead of chemical fertilizers, plant infusions to kill pests, the nests of ferocious ants to protect fruit trees from other ant predators.

Biologists often complain that there have been many studies of exotic rituals, paraphernalia, and kinships of Indians, but that Western science has paid scant attention to the Indians' use of animals and plants.

Like others working in the Amazon region, Posey worries about the gap between the old and the young. "The old chiefs are turning over decisions to the young because they can drive a truck or operate a video machine or go to the bank," he says. "But the young people don't see the relevance of learning the tribal knowledge and it's being lost."

"You can afford to lose one generation," he adds, "because grandparents do the teaching of their grandchildren. But you cannot afford to lose two generations."

Gorotire has a small Government school, designed to help Indians integrate into the national society. The teacher, who speaks only Portuguese, has started organizing annual Independence Day parades. On the blackboard is a list of patriotic holidays, including Independence Day and the Day of the Soldier. I ask the children later what a soldier is. "Something of white people," one of them says.

Chief Poropot agrees that everyone must learn Portuguese. "The language of the Kaiapo is very ancient and it will never end," he says. "But the women and the children need to learn Portuguese to defend themselves."

Defend themselves? "If they go to shop in Redenção, they have to talk," he says. "If they get sick, they cannot tell the doctor what they have."

Thirty miles from Gorotire, in the village of Aukre, another Kaiapo tribe is choosing a different strategy for change. Its best-known member is Paiakan, thirty-seven years old, the son of Chief Tikiri.

Calm and articulate, Paiakan has been named to "keep an eye on the whites" in the state capital of Belém. He acts as a kind of roving ambassador for the Kaiapo, even though each village is autonomous. When Kaiapo interests are threatened, he sends out warnings to the communities.

Paiakan's contacts with the outside world and the many pitfalls it holds for Indians have made him more conservative, he says, more so than in the early days, in the 1970s, when he first left home to work on the Trans-Amazonian Highway. As his father's main adviser, he has insisted that Aukre remain a traditional village.

It is built in the age-old circle of mud-and-thatch huts. There is no television, running water, pigs, or piles of garbage. Paiakan and his father have also banned logging and gold digging. This appears to have saved Aukre from the consumerism—and widespread influenza and malaria—of Gorotire.

"The lumber men have come to us with their bags of money," he says. "And we know we have a lot of gold. But we do not want to bring a lot of money in. The Indian still does not know the value of white man's objects or how to treat them." Paiakan cites clothing as an example. "The Indian wears something until it is stiff with dirt, then he throws it out."

But people now want things from the "world of the whites," he continues. "Pressure from the white society is so strong, there is no wall that can stop it." It is the task of the chief to measure the change, provide explanations, he says. "If

someone wants to get a radio or a tape recorder, the chiefs cannot stop it."

In Aukre, where two aging chiefs are still in charge of buying goods for the community, they say that they will not buy gadgets. "We explain we cannot buy this thing for you because we do not have the batteries you need and we cannot repair it," Paiakan says.

Of late, Paiakan has been invited abroad to campaign for the protection of the rain forest. He knows the problem only too well. Ranchers have moved almost to the reservation's doorstep, felled trees, and set massive forest fires. Because of deforestation, there have been unusual changes in the water level of the Fresco River.

"Our people are getting very disoriented," says Paiakan. "It would be as if people from another planet came to your cities and started to tear down your houses. The forest is our home." With all the destruction going on, he continues, "the breath of life is drifting up and away from us."

At the age of seventy-eight and retired from teaching at the University of California at Los Angeles, the anthropologist Gerardo Reichel-Dolmatoff lives in Bogotá, Colombia, and is still writing. After studying changes in the Amazon for five decades, he is not optimistic about the prospects for the Indians.

"In Colombia, I don't know of a single case where an aboriginal culture has found a strong adaptive mechanism," he says. "Physical survival is possible. But I have not seen the ancient values replaced by a workable value system. I wish I could be more positive. But in fifty years I have seen too many traditions being lost, too many tribes disappear.

"For 500 years we have witnessed the destruction of the Indians. Now we are witnessing the destruction of the habitat. I suggest more field work, and immediate field work, because soon it will be too late."

At a conference on ethnobiology last fall, Reichel-Dolmatoff urged scientists to insist on spreading the message that Western science has much to learn from Indians, from their -

well-adapted lives and deeply felt beliefs, their view that whatever man subtracts he must restore by other means.

What suggestions has he made to Indians?

"Indians have to stay in touch with their language—that is absolutely essential," he says. "It embodies their thought patterns, their values, their philosophy." Moreover, he says, talented young Indians should be given a modern academic education, but also the chance to keep in touch with their people. "They come from cultures based on extraordinary realism and imagery. They should not be forced to enter at the lowest level of our society."

One night, I ask the chiefs in Gorotire: What happens if the gold runs out? After all, most of the mahogany is already gone. Young tribesmen have wanted to invest some of the income, and the chiefs have accepted the idea. Gorotire has bought a home in Belém for Kaiapo who travel there, as well as three houses in Redenção. There is talk of buying a farm, a curious thought, perhaps, for a community that lives on 8 million acres of land. But the Kaiapo, so they say, want it so that white farmers can grow rice for them.

And there is talk of planting new mahogany trees. Soon the conversation turns to a bird that a tribesman explains is very important. It is the bird, he says, that spreads the mahogany seeds.

CRITICAL THINKING QUESTIONS

1. What have been the short-term consequences of the Kaiapo's new wealth? What are the Kaiapo's long-term prospects?
2. What arguments can be made for the continued effort by the Kaiapo to economically develop their resources? What arguments can be made against doing so?
3. In what ways are other countries involved in the changes taking place in the Amazon Basin?

PHOTO CREDITS